PERGAMON INTERNATIONAL LIBRARY
of Science, Technology, Engineering and Social Studies
*The 1000-volume original paperback library in aid of education,
industrial training and the enjoyment of leisure*
Publisher: Robert Maxwell, M.C.

Helping
People
Change
(PGPS—52)

THE PERGAMON TEXTBOOK
INSPECTION COPY SERVICE

An inspection copy of any book published in the Pergamon International Library
will gladly be sent to academic staff without obligation for their consideration for
course adoption or recommendation. Copies may be retained for a period of 60 days
from receipt and returned if not suitable. When a particular title is adopted or
recommended for adoption for class use and the recommendation results in a sale
of 12 or more copies, the inspection copy may be retained with our compliments.
The Publishers will be pleased to receive suggestions for revised editions and new
titles to be published in this important International Library.

Related Titles

Helping People Change

A Textbook of Methods
Second Edition

Edited by
Frederick H. Kanfer
Professor of Psychology
University of Illinois

Arnold P. Goldstein
Professor of Psychology
Syracuse University

Pergamon Press

New York   Oxford   Toronto   Sydney   Frankfurt   Paris

Pergamon Press Offices:

U.S.A   Pergamon Press Inc., Maxwell House, Fairview Park,
                  Elmsford, New York 10523, U.S.A.

U.K.   Pergamon Press Ltd., Headington Hill Hall,
                  Oxford OX3 0BW, England

CANADA   Pergamon of Canada Ltd., 150 Consumers Road,
                  Willowdale, Ontario M2J 1P9, Canada

AUSTRALIA   Pergamon Press (Aust) Pty. Ltd., P.O. Box 544,
                  Potts Point, NSW 2011, Australia

FRANCE   Pergamon Press SARL, 24 rue des Ecoles,
                  75240 Paris, Cedex 05, France

FEDERAL REPUBLIC   Pergamon Press GmbH, 6242 Kronberg/Taunus,
OF GERMANY   Pferdstrasse 1, Federal Republic of Germany

Library of Congress Cataloging in Publication Data

Kanfer, Frederick H   1925-
   Helping people change.

   (Pergamon general psychology series)
   Includes bibliographies and index.
   1.   Behavior modification.   I.   Goldstein, Arnold P.,
joint author.   II.   Title.
BF637.B4K35   1980   158   79-17929
ISBN 0-08-025098-X
ISBN 0-08-025097-1 pbk.

Printed in the United States of America

Contents

Preface To Second Edition

Since publication of the first edition there has been a considerable increase in the development and refinement of methods in the counseling of normal and moderately disturbed persons. New techniques and a broader research base have expanded the range of capabilities of helpers in all areas. The conceptualization and availability of methods have progressed especially rapidly in several of the areas covered in the first edition. Techniques for building and sustaining client-helper relationships have been improved and integrated more closely with behavior change methods. There has been a burgeoning of articles and methods that focus on the assessment and modification of cognitive target behaviors. Today there is an increased acceptance of the need to include both cognitive and behavioral events in the change process. Finally, there is a growing tendency in the field toward increased involvement of clients in the change process by emphasis on client responsibilities and self-management methods. As a result, revisions of the chapters vary from nearly complete rewrites for chapters in which new directions have developed since 1975 to less extensive revisions in areas in which principles and methods have remained in use without major changes.

The contributors, who are expert in their own subspecialties, revised and updated their chapters to include significant changes in trends, new research findings, and technological advances. A new chapter on biofeedback was added because of the relevance of this field for behavior change methods.

On the basis of feedback from users of the first edition, more clinical examples were added and the presentations were improved in organization and easy readability. As in the first edition, new developments were only included if there existed at least some empirical evidence in support of their utility. We believe that the book contains, in both depth and breadth, the most important psychological methods that are currently used to help people change.

In this enterprise we have enjoyed the continued effort, interest and dedication of the contributors to this edition, both old and new. We wish to express our high regard and appreciation to them. Their expertise and concern with providing and applying the best of psychological research and theory toward the increase of human happiness, satisfaction and efficiency are what has given this book both the theme and the substance.

1
Introduction
Frederick H. Kanfer and
Arnold P. Goldstein

Perhaps the most characteristic feature of our lives during the last few decades has been the rapid increase in the rate of change—in the physical environment, in our technology, and in our social, political, and moral institutions. Bombarded by mass media, by a wealth of available goods and ideas, and by the ever changing scene to which our senses are exposed, each of us finishes the day having changed for better or worse, even if ever so slightly. A conversation with a friend, an interesting movie or book, a new emotional experience, a political rally, a work of art, or a breathtaking natural scene may all make a deep impression on us and can alter our attitudes about ourselves and about the world. If an experience is sufficiently intense, it may alter our behavior to the extent that our families and friends are surprised at the change. Yet, many persons go through their daily routine given the same exposure to ideas, images, and people as others, but remain unable to change their view of themselves or others, and unable to give up self-defeating patterns of behavior even though solutions and opportunities for growth are at an arm's length. Others meet their world in rigid, fearful, or aggressive ways, finding little happiness or satisfaction, yet unable to break the vicious circles they seem to engender. It is these populations, persons who are stymied in resolving their personal and interpersonal problems, who are the focus of our attention as professional helpers.

This book is about psychological methods designed to help people change for the better, so that they can fully develop their potentials and capitalize on the opportunities available in their social environment. The helping methods we will examine share the common goal of promoting change in ways which can lead to greater personal happiness, competence, and satisfaction. Our point of view stresses that a professional or paraprofessional helper can serve as both a consul-

1

tant and an expert teacher or guide to persons whose discomforts, psychological disabilities, and social inefficiencies have been of sufficient concern to them, or to others in their environment, that the assistance of a trained outsider is deemed necessary.

People help one another in numerous ways in everyday life and, indeed, people do change as a result of such informal assistance. However, several distinct characteristics consistently differentiate the professional or paraprofessional helping relationship from friendship or other helpful interactions. Whether the helping relationship is called psychotherapy, counseling, guidance, behavior modification, or Gestalt therapy, and whether it is conducted by a physician, a psychiatrist, a psychologist, a social worker, a child care worker, a mental health technician, or a hospital nurse or aide, the same features are found in all professional or paraprofessional helping relationships: they are unilateral, systematic, formal, and time limited.

The *unilateral* aspect of the helping relationship reflects the fact that the participants agree that one person is defined as the helper and the other as the client. It is also agreed, explicitly or implicitly, that the focus of the relationship and all its activities is on solving the problems of the client. In this respect, the change process is unlike most other interpersonal interactions. The personal problems, the private affairs, the worries and the wishes of one person, the helper, are intentionally not focused upon. Treatment, therapy, or whatever the helping relationship may be called, is one-sided and concentrates exclusively on the client.

The professional or paraprofessional helping relationship is *systematic* in that the participants typically agree at the outset on the purposes and objectives of their interaction, and the helper attempts to plan and carry out procedures that move in an organized fashion toward resolution of his client's problems.

The relationship is *formal*, in that the interaction between helper and client is usually confined to specified times and places. While the interaction need not always be conducted at the same time of day and in the same office, clinic, or hospital, this usually is the case. The times and places are arranged in such a way that the helper has no other role or duty during his meetings with his client. At times, the helper may intentionally create an informal atmosphere. For example, a helping interaction can occur when a child care worker plays checkers or ping pong, or takes a walk with a child, or when an adult client is seen in his home. However, under these circumstances the child care worker's concern is not with winning the game or getting physical exercise during his walk, nor is the visit in a client's home a social occasion for mutual enjoyment. These are, instead, examples of formal treatment in an informal setting.

Helping relationships are *time limited*. The relationship terminates when the stated objectives and goals are reached. The termination is always considered as the final outcome of the relationship and can be based on mutual agreement or on either the helper's or the client's initiative.

If you consider a friendship or an interaction with a colleague or a neighbor for a moment, it will become clear that none of the features listed is common in such relationships. Social relationships are formed for mutual benefit of the participants, there is usually no fixed agenda for what is to be accomplished, the relationship is typically enjoyed for what it is rather than for what it may accomplish, and it is terminated for numerous reasons other than completion of a task.

The history of professional helpers goes back over many centuries. In each age, the predominant theory of human nature determined which professional group was considered the most competent to relieve people's discomforts and psychological problems. In societies in which theological explanations of man dominated, priests, shamans, or witch-doctors were given the task of assisting people with their personal problems or rectifying behavioral deviations. More recently, the assumption was accepted in western societies that behavioral disorders were manifestations of disturbances of the nervous system, or the biological structure of the individual. As a result, major responsibility for dealing with psychological problems was given to physicians and, in particular, psychiatrists. Indeed, early suspicions that brain damage or weak nervous system structures were the causes of many behavior disorders resulted in rigorous search for the specific roots of what was then called "mental diseases." Even Freud's comprehensive theory of human behavior was based on the assumption that the driving energy underlying human activity, psychic libido, developed by conversion from physical energy via the nervous system.

In the last three decades there has been increasing disenchantment with the view that behavioral problems represent mental illnesses associated with the organism's biological or psychic structures. Alternate models of psychological disturbances have been based on ideas derived from philosophical systems and, increasingly, from scientific psychology. Congruent with this trend, there has also been the recognition that relief of psychological problems can be offered by persons with expertise in nonmedical specialties. Further, the erosion of belief in the infallibility of the authoritative professional has hastened the development of brief training programs that permit many lay persons to participate in the treatment or behavior change process. This expansion of the helper manpower pool has helped to reduce the scarcity of assistance available, caused by the small number of highly trained professionals and the large number of persons in need of help. This greatly expanded use of paraprofessional personnel, parents, volunteer workers, and many others as helpers is a development we strongly endorse. Their success with many types of clients with a broad range of problems is already evident.

WHO IS QUALIFIED TO HELP?

Many different professions have as one of their goals the accomplishment of behavior change in their clients. Teachers, physicians, clergymen, social workers, psychologists, and probation officers are among the professionals who offer services designed to change human behavior. Even if enduring changes in the client's behavior are not the immediate focus of the professional service, they may still play a role in the total context of the services offered. Attorneys, nurses, dentists, and financial advisors are among those who can achieve their specifically stated goals more easily if they can influence their clients to change in ways ranging from minor accommodations to sweeping changes in their life patterns. For example, the more effective dentist is one who not only restores tooth damage or applies preventive treatment in the office, but who is also able to persuade his patient to alter his daily oral hygiene behaviors and, perhaps, even his eating habits sufficiently so that future damage is prevented or retarded. However, not all professionals are equally qualified to deal effectively with psychological problems. Currently, the most acceptable criteria for qualification in the helping professions has been evidence of successful completion of specified training programs. Generally, the successful completion of a study program is certified by a degree and the holder is regarded as competent to carry out a specified range of professional duties. Of course, the distinction between meeting requirements in academic courses and showing the skills needed for professional practice is not clearly made by degree-granting institutions. In fact, frequent and heated debates have centered on the type of training that qualifies persons best for helping professions.

The most widely accepted criteria of professional level competence are doctoral degrees with specialties in clinical psychology or counseling psychology, medical degrees with residency training in psychiatry, or advanced degrees in social work. However, there has been a growing recognition that the management of behavior change programs is not the province of any single discipline, nor is it necessary to expect every practitioner to be able to function in all areas within the given discipline. In fact, as treatment methods for psychological problems have moved away from their earlier foundations in religious, philosophical, or biological concepts of man, to encompass psychological, social, economic, and political components as well, there has been a parallel development that has facilitated the delivery of effective behavior change programs by persons with much shorter and less complex formal training than the mastery of four to six years of post graduate training which is required of psychologists or psychiatrists. As noted earlier, such persons can and do make significant contributions to helping people change. In part, this change in requirements is a result of the division of labor now possible because of clearer specification of the ways in which behavior change techniques can be applied. Traditional psychotherapeutic techniques were based primarily on complex and abstract personality theories, and the interpersonal relationship between helper and client was considered to be the primary instrument of change. As a result, it was necessary to train a person first, in depth, in the theories and assumptions of the therapy system. The development of treatment skills was a slow process, mainly by apprenticeship and close individual supervision. In many disciplines, e.g., in psychoanalysis, the training period might extend until the trainee was in his forties. With the realization that many components of a behavior change program can be learned rather quickly and that complete mastery of the entire field is not essential for participating in some stages of the total program, there has been the increased effort noted earlier to train persons with limited knowledge of change methods (paraprofessionals) to work under the direction of more extensively trained persons.

In a recent survey of leading writers in the field of behavior modification, Sulzer-Azaroff, Thaw, and Olsen (1974) asked respondents to indicate the type of competency expected of four levels of helpers: behavior analyst, behavior technology coordinator, behavior technologist engineer, and behavior co-technician. The expectations were quite consistent for the highest level (behavior analyst) who was seen as a person who develops programs, research, and new methods. The lowest level (behavior co-technician) was not expected to have very specific competencies; most of his skills could be obtained in on-the-job training or in relatively few college courses. The behavior technology coordinator was described generally as a skilled person, at the pre-doctoral level, who could conduct helping programs in schools, institutions, and other facilities, but who was not expected to assume research and administrative roles. The survey clearly showed that persons at different training and skill levels can collaborate successfully in the helping effort.

Supervisors must have skills in evaluating the nature and scope of a person's problems. They must understand the social, biological, and economic context of the problem. They must be skilled in making decisions that would permit them to select among available helping techniques in order to construct a therapeutic program. They must know the methods by which progress in a program can be monitored and under what conditions the helping program can be changed. Finally, they must know the limitations of both their own skills and those of their helpers and they must have knowledge of resources that can be called upon when the problem falls beyond the limits of their own competence or the resources of their agencies. In this sense, a pyramid operation can be developed with a supervisor or consultant whose role is greatest at the beginning of treatment, who can monitor progress of treatment, and who can offer to the paraprofessional any supervision and advice needed. This concept, developing a team of helpers varying in skill and competence, is also useful because it permits the delivery of psychological services to large numbers of people who previously could not have afforded expensive individual psychotherapy. Thus, qualifications for offering psychological help differ for different levels of helpers. While it is possible for a person to carry out a well planned and structured change program under supervision after only a few weeks of training, the total management of a client requires consultation or supervision by a person with thorough familiarity of psychological principles, clinical methods, and an awareness of the limitations of his and others' skills. But paraprofessionals with limited training can also make substantial contributions to successful treatment. Durlak (1979) reviewed forty-two studies comparing the effectiveness of professional and paraprofessional helpers. He found that paraprofessionals, working in narrowly defined clinical roles with specific client populations, were generally as effective as professional helpers. Their strongest effectiveness was noted in studies in which intervention was directed at such specific target responses as unassertiveness, speech anxiety, and enuresis.

A totally different qualification for a helper concerns his personal characteristics. As already indicated, and as discussed in detail in a following section on ethics, it is essential that the helper be motivated primarily by the goal of helping his client rather than furthering his own interest. In addition, the helper must be able to discern cues about the impact of his own behavior on his client. Which other particular helper characteristics are desirable has been the subject of research and theory for many years. They seem to include, at minimum, helper empathy, warmth, honesty, and expertness. These and other apparently desirable helper characteristics are examined in depth in Chapters 2 and 3.

Although the helping methods described in the following chapters have been tested and validated to some extent, it cannot be stressed too often that the methods themselves do not guarantee success. It is both the skillful *application* (i.e., the judgment of when to apply what methods to which clients) and knowledge about when to *change* a technique or an objective that is essential for successful helping programs. Most of the techniques described in the following chapters are not tied to specific client problems. Thus, they can be used in ameliorating a wide variety of personal, social, sexual, or other problems. When skillfully applied, they are likely to bring about beneficial changes in the client's behavior. But mere acquaintance with a catalog of available therapeutic techniques is insufficient preparation for competent psychological helping.

The problems and dangers of use of psychological helping techniques by persons without proper qualifications are legion. For example, operant techniques applied to continuing physical complaints may reduce the frequency of the complaints. However, such a change may also mask the inroads of a serious medical illness. Increasing assertiveness or feelings of independence in one marriage partner may indeed change the partner's behavior. However, without a thorough assessment and appreciation of the interpersonal context of the problem, an unskilled therapist may also find himself contributing to increasing problems between marriage partners, and perhaps divorce or abandonment by a partner. Treatment for homosexual behavior, even though the client wishes to change his sexual orientation, might fail simply because the client may not have a sufficiently strong repertoire of heterosexual behaviors to explore new sexual directions, or to achieve sufficient success in sexual and nonsexual activities that can take the place of his previous pleasurable experiences. The helper, therefore, must have full awareness of the range of factors that go into designing a treatment program, be aware of his own limitations, and work closely with others who can provide the necessary guidance. Premature, clumsy, or ignorant application of behavior change techniques may be wasteful and inefficient at best, and harmful at worst.

Summarizing our discussion on the necessary qualifications of the helper, it should be clear that the paraprofessional, including students, human service aides, mental health technicians, attendants, nurses, and many other persons without prolonged professional training in psychological services can make major contributions to helping people change. In fact, they are often the persons who can put a conceptual program into actual operation best. In many settings, a paraprofessional worker spends more time with a client than any professional and has, by far, more influence in his extensive contact with the client than a senior professional might have in the short time of a diagnostic or therapeutic interview. However, execution and not design is the task of the paraprofessional. Continuous self-monitoring and feedback to a consultant or supervisor are necessary to maintain the efficiency of the program and to protect the client.

WHAT IS A PSYCHOLOGICAL PROBLEM?

Psychological problems, in general terms, are difficulties in a person's relations with others, in his perception of the world about him or in his attitudes toward himself. Psychological problems can be characterized by a person's feelings of anxiety or tension, dissatisfaction with his own behavior, excessive attention to the problem area, inefficiency in reaching his desired goals, or inability to function effectively in psychological areas. Psychological problems may at times also be characterized by a situation in which the client himself has no complaint but others in his social environment are adversely affected by his behavior or judge him to be ineffective, destructive, unhappy, disruptive, or in some other way acting contrary to his best self-interest or the best interest of the social community in which he lives. Thus the major characteristics of a psychological problem are in evidence where: (1) the client suffers subjective discomfort, worry, or fears that are not easily removable by some action that he can perform without assistance; (2) the client shows a behavioral deficiency or excessively engages in some behavior that interferes with functioning described as adequate either by himself or by others; (3) the client engages in activities which are objectionable to those around him and which lead to negative consequences either for himself or for others; and (4) the client shows behavioral deviations that result in severe social sanctions by those in his immediate environment.

Psychological problems sometimes are related to problems in other areas. For example, an automobile accident may cause physical disability which in turn leads to psychological difficulties. A person who has lost his job, his marital partner, or his savings may temporarily face psychological difficulties. Socio-political climates such as discriminatory practices against a minority member, economic problems, sexual, moral, or religious demands by the environment that are inconsistent with the person's past history, all may cause psychological problems. Very frequently, transient psychological problems can be resolved not by psychological helpers but by resolution of the "source" problem. For example, concern about a medical disability or serious illness is better treated, if treatable, by medical care than by psychological help. Unhappiness over loss of a job may be more easily remedied by finding a new job than by resolving psychological problems about the loss. It is incumbent upon the psychological helper, therefore, to analyze the total problem to determine if dealing successfully with at least some aspects of it can be more effectively carried out by someone who is not a psychological helper, while those components which comprise the person's attitudes, behaviors, or interactions remain the proper domain for mental health helpers.

THE GOALS AND OBJECTIVES OF HELPING RELATIONSHIPS

A good treatment program is built with a clear conception of treatment goals, developed jointly by the helper and the client. It is possible to differentiate among five long-term treatment objectives: (1) change of a particular problem behavior, such as poor interpersonal skills; (2) insight or a clear rational and emotional understanding of one's problems; (3) change in a person's subjective emotional comfort, including changes in anxiety or tension; (4) change in one's self-perceptions, including goals, self-confidence, and sense of adequacy; and (5) change in the person's lifestyle or "personality restructuring," an objective aimed at a sweeping change in the client's way of living. The selection of any one of these goals does not eliminate the secondary achievement of other objectives. For example, while many of the techniques described in this book are oriented toward change of particular behaviors, such changes often bring with them changes in the person's insights into his own actions, modification of his attitudes toward himself, and in some cases, a rather sweeping alteration of the person's total lifestyle. At the same time, therapists who aim for improved insight and major personality changes in their clients may also achieve, during the helping process, change in social behaviors or self-reactions. Thus, treatment objectives are not mutually exclusive and the listing above is simply intended to indicate that primary emphasis can be given to a particular goal, without sacrificing the achievement of others as by-products or secondary outcomes of the change process.

Behavior Change

If the goal of a helping effort is to change a particular behavior, a thorough evaluation of the person's life circumstances is required in order to be sure not only that the target behavior is amenable to change, but also that such a change will lead to a significant improvement in the person's total life situation. A more detailed description of the steps necessary prior to beginning the change program is given below in our discussion of the diagnostic process.

Insight

Insight as a goal has been most characteristic of psychoanalysis and its variations. These helping methods are not covered in the present volume, first because the assumptions underlying psychoanalytic therapy are extensive, and thorough training of therapists in psychoanalytic methods, including personal analysis and long supervision of cases, is usually required. Secondly, the therapeutic benefits of psychoanalytic and other insight seeking methods are currently not well substantiated by empirical research and laboratory findings. They are excessively time consuming and, in our view, rarely represent the treatment of choice. The arguments in the psychological and psychiatric literature concerning the utility of insight versus behavior change, however, have sometimes been overstated. When a motivated client establishes a relationship between his current behavior problems and his past history, whether or not such a relationship is in fact accurate, the satisfaction of having achieved an explanation for his own behavior, and the new labels he can then attach to his emotional experiences, may serve as a beginning for change in his actual daily behaviors.

Emotional Relief

The reduction of anxiety has long been considered as the most critical problem in the management of neurotic disorders. * In general, when anxiety reduction or relief of chronic emotional tension is the primary objective of a helping effort, it is assumed that the client will later be able to conduct himself more effectively because: (1) he already has in his repertoire the skills necessary to deal with life situations; and (2) his use of these skills was previously inhibited by anxiety. If this is not the case (i.e., if the problem involves not only inhibition due to anxiety, but also incompetence due to skill deficiency), changes in particular skill behaviors might be set up as the next goal in the change program. If the problem is both partly emotional and partly related to particular behavior deficiencies, then both the reduction of emotional tension and behavioral skill training may be dual treatment objectives.

Change in the Client's Self-Perception

Techniques for changing a person's self-perceptions and evaluations of his own behavior are found in several chapters in this volume. In general, the application of such procedures assumes that a person's improved self-image is sufficient to

---

*The techniques for reduction of anxiety are described in Chapter 8 of this volume.

help him perform the constructive behaviors of which he is capable. For example, once a person sees himself as competent or perceives himself more realistically in relation to others, he may be able to plan and act with greater self-confidence, a greater sense of direction, and greater social effectiveness.

Lifestyle Changes

The most ambitious objective for a change program is the attempt to alter the person's total pattern of living. Frequently, this requires not only a change in the client's behavior, but also plans for changing the environment in which he lives, his circle of friends, his place of employment, and so forth. One example might be the client who is a drug addict and whose entire daily routine is subordinated to the procurement of an illegal narcotic. But every change process results in some changes of the person's daily life pattern, if it is at all successful. In some instances, the clarification of the lifestyle to which the person aspires may itself be a preparatory part of the change process. In other cases the main objective of treatment is the development of goals in a person who feels "alienated" or complains of a lack of direction and purpose. Thus, all change programs include consideration of the extent to which treatment success would alter the client's life. However, the extent to which these considerations are focal varies from minimal, as in correcting a study habit problem, to maximal, as in treating drug addiction or agoraphobia.

A PRESCRIPTIVE CAUTION

In the early years of psychotherapy research, investigators concerned with its effectiveness typically framed their research questions in global outcome terms, e.g., "Does treatment A work?" or "Is treatment A superior to treatment B?" Such questions could be answered affirmatively only in those exceptional instances in which the treatment(s) studied were sufficiently powerful to override the high degree of between-patient, within-conditions heterogeneity. Even then, the generality of such questions often provided little information either about how to improve the effectiveness of the treatment (because the treatment as a whole had been studied, with little or no concern for its separate components) or how to use the outcome information to help any *individual* patient (because only between-group effects were examined). In attempts to alleviate these weaknesses of this earlier research strategy, researchers now ask rather different and clinically more useful questions in their therapy investigations (Garfield & Bergin, 1978; Gurman & Razin, 1977).

Investigators now seek to discern "which type of patient, meeting with which type of therapist, using which type of treatment, will yield what outcome?" This is a prescriptive view of psychotherapy. It holds that most treatments cannot be classified as "good" or "bad" in any comprehensive sense. Instead, this view holds that different treatments and therapists may be appropriate for some patients but not for others. This prescriptive view of the therapy enterprise looks toward identifying optimal patient × therapist × treatment matches in designing treatment plans. Both in research and practice, a conscious and consistent effort is made to avoid the patient, therapist or treatment uniformity myths against which Kiesler (1966) has warned.

The implications of this viewpoint for the use of the present book are both clear and major. In each of the following chapters many behavior change procedures are described and explicitly or implicitly recommended for clinical use. Our prescriptive view cautions us that, although each procedure rests, at least to some extent, on supportive empirical research, almost none should be expected to lead to behavior change in all patients, or for all problems of one patient, or at all stages of the treatment process. In the next chapter, for example, the nature and value of therapist empathy is examined. The position taken is that patient perception of therapist offered empathy is a significant influence upon certain aspects of a positive therapeutic relationship and eventual patient change. Yet we must not assume this to be the case for all patients or at all times. We agree with Mitchell, Bozarth and Krauft (1977) who comment:

> . . . empathy, warmth, and genuineness might be used differentially depending on client diagnosis. Clinical wisdom suggests that high levels of empathy might overwhelm a schizophrenic client early in therapy and that, instead, empathy might best be increased slowly over time within the context of uniformly high levels of warmth. On the other hand, with a neurotic, initially high levels of warmth might best be lowered somewhat in the middle phase of therapy in order to heighten negative aspects of the "transference" and increase anxiety sufficiently so it becomes an excellent stimulus for change. (p. 490)

We and others have developed this prescriptive view of psychotherapy in detail elsewhere (Goldstein and Stein, 1976; Goldstein, 1978) for those interested in pursuing its implications further. For our present purpose, its import is to caution the helper that optimal utilization of a technique requires consideration of the joint characteristics of patient, therapist and technique.

DESIGNING A CHANGE PROGRAM

This volume is not intended to provide the helper with in-depth knowledge about diagnostic methods for analyzing the client's problem and designing a treatment program on the basis of this assessment. Nevertheless, the reader should be aware of the importance of an early analysis of the problem as the absolutely essential foundation for the application of any treatment technique. At this time there are few widely accepted principles that can guide a helper through the evaluation and assessment process. There are many books and articles that summarize available psychological tests; some also discuss the most critical features of the person's life situation that should be examined before a decision is made concerning an objective and its associated treatment technique (e.g., Goldfried and Pomeranz, 1968; Gottman and Leiblum, 1974; Kanfer and Grimm, 1977; Kanfer and Saslow, 1969; Lanyon and Goodstein, 1971; Sundberg, 1977). As a minimum requirement for deciding upon the choice of helping methods, the helper must make a thorough analysis of the context in which the problem behavior occurs, the form and severity of the problem behavior, the consequences both to the client and to his environment of the problem behavior, the resources of the client and of his environment for the promotion of change, and the effects which a change in his behavior would have on the client and others. These and other factors comprise the content of what has been called a *functional analysis* of the problem situation. The information necessary to complete such an analysis may come from interviews, from observations, from knowledge of the client's past history, from reports of other persons who know the client, or from any other source that yields reliable information. In some cases, especially when the problem behavior has some physiological components, information about the medical status and physical health of the client is absolutely necessary.

A good functional analysis reveals factors that have contributed to the problem behavior and those that currently maintain it. It also gives some information about what particular stresses and demands are placed upon the client by the environment in which he lives. For example, for a complete assessment it is not sufficient to know what a person does and what effects his actions have. It is also necessary to have an understanding of what requirements are placed upon him by his immediate circle of friends, his job situation, his community, and by persons who are important in his life. Further, a good functional analysis also yields a list of problematic behaviors that may require attention and information that would assist the helper to set priorities so that he can better decide which particular problem(s) to attack. Which items are placed high on the priority list would depend on the individual's life circumstances and his initial responses to the change program. For example, any behavior that is self-destructive or has serious social consequences would be the most central initial target. However, in some cases, several problems may have equal priority. In this instance, a decision might rest on which of these problem behaviors are more amenable to solution by the available techniques. The client's conviction that he can change, and the degree of support from other persons in his environment to assist in the change program, must also be taken into account.

Another important aspect of the assessment procedure lies in the establishment of some methods and criteria for assessing the client's progress throughout the program. For example, the operant behavior change methods described in Chapter 7 are usually applied in conjunction with quantitative records of the frequency, intensity, or duration of the behavior being changed before, during, and after the change program. With other techniques, the evaluation component is not so readily built into the treatment program. For example, relationship methods, group techniques, and attitude change methods often aim to alter more complex behavior patterns and typically do not incorporate a quantitative measurement or monitoring process into the treatment. Nevertheless, the helper should have some record of the patient's problem behaviors, complaints and expectations prior to the onset of any change program. It is only with such documentation that helper and client can decide whether the change program has been effective, and further decisions about shifting to other objectives or terminating the relationship can be made. The evaluation component of the treatment program is of importance not only for assisting the helper and client in making decisions about progress and termination. It also serves as an incentive for both client and helper by giving them some objective evidence of the progress that has been achieved, and it enables the helper to specify more clearly the areas in which the program may have failed, and the reasons for this failure.

ETHICAL CONSIDERATIONS

A helper makes a number of demands on his clients. He expects them to be frank in discussing their problems, to be involved in the change program, and to commit themselves to certain requirements of the program such as keeping appointments, paying bills, and carrying out contracted exercises or activities. Because of the very nature of the helping relationship, it is quite obvious that the client's interests must be protected to avoid damage or grief resulting from a helper's ignorance, his unscrupulousness, his self-serving manipulation of the client, or his exploitation of the client's vulnerability.

The use of the helping techniques described in this book should be restricted to situations in which a person *seeks* help from others in a formal way. Thus, the change techniques should not be applied in informal settings in which a person is unaware of the fact that attempts are being made to change his behavior; they should not be applied casually in personal relationships with friends or family members; they should not be applied when a client denies the existence of a problem even though it has been pointed out to him by others. In the latter case, more complex treatment programs would have to be used, even though the change techniques presented here may ultimately comprise part of the total treatment package.

In our discussion of professional qualifications, we pointed to the importance of the helper's training and background for the protection of the client. In this section we will consider a series of ethical considerations that a helper must abide by if he is to be helpful to the client and be accepted by the community in which he practices. On some of the matters which follow, there is debate concerning the breadth of action open to the helper. Therefore, the following items range in importance from those for which a breech of ethics may lead to expulsion from professional societies to those items which are primarily a matter of individual conscience.

Exploitation by the Helper

There is no disagreement concerning the absolute requirement that the helper must not utilize the relationship in order to gain social, sexual, or other personal advantage. The self-serving functions of a helper, however, may extend from the slight extension of a treatment program beyond its absolutely necessary limits, in order to provide a helper with financial resources, to the flagrant financial, moral, or sexual exploitation of a client. The helper has access to confidential information that may embarrass or hurt the client. Even subtle pressure implying the use of such information for self-serving purposes is equivalent to blackmail and is clearly unethical.

Deception

The purposes and goals of the interaction should be clear to the client or his guardian. The client or guardian should be informed of any hazards or potential aversive consequences which are involved in a treatment procedure and no exaggerated promises should be made about the likelihood of successful treatment outcome. It is improper to discuss the achievements or objectives of a change program with a third party, be it a marital partner, a parent, or an employer, without communicating such intentions to the client himself. Similarly, advice and guidance which would force the client into a situation over which he has no control would constitute unethical behavior. Advice to engage in illegal behaviors, or suggestions of actions that would expose the client to hazards or predictable untoward consequences are examples of deceptive helper maneuvers.

Competence and Appropriate Treatment

It is the responsibility of the helper not only to offer the highest level of service, but also to be aware of his own limitations so that he can refer the client to someone else when necessary. In addition to referrals to others in the mental health field, it is also the helper's responsibility to be certain that problems outside the area of psychological treatment be properly referred. For example, referral to a physician for medical difficulties, to an attorney for legal problems, or to a social service agency for economic assistance should be made when these problems are evident or likely. Since the helper sometimes may not be fully aware of the limitations in his own training, it is advisable for a helper to have some professional affiliation that will enable him to obtain assistance from colleagues regarding difficult cases. Persons who have paraprofessional training should discuss such problems with their supervisor under whose direction the change program is conducted.

Principle of Least Intervention

While it is obvious that almost any person might benefit from psychological counseling or a helping relationship, it is essentially the task of the helper to intervene in the client's everyday life only to the extent that the client desires a change. Once the jointly agreed upon objective is reached, the helper should either terminate the relationship or discuss in detail with the client the possibility of future change programs. Only if the client agrees to additional programs should they be undertaken. A prior problem concerns the question of whether any treatment should take place at all. In some instances, clients will seek assistance for problems that actually turn out to be common difficulties in everyday life. In such cases, for example, when a client is experiencing a grief reaction after the death of a close relative, information and reassurance may be sufficient. Similarly, parents may refer their children for assistance when, in fact, the child's behavior is not unusual for his age group. In such instances, behavior change programs would not be undertaken and it may be possible to terminate the interaction when reassurance and information are given to the client.

Some techniques of behavior change, especially those that rest heavily on the alteration of the client's social environment (discussed in Chapter 7), may involve the participation of other persons in channeling the client's behavior in a desired direction through the use of rewards and punishments. Programs in institutions such as hospitals, schools, or prisons may involve deprivation of certain privileges in order that they may be used later as rewards for appropriate behaviors. There is intense dispute concerning the appropriateness of such techniques because of their nonvolitional and manipulative aspects. As a result, special caution must be exercised to assure that the client's civil rights are not infringed upon and that the client can make the kind of choices about participating in a program that would normally be considered reasonable in the institutional setting in which they are introduced. The utilization of aversive stimuli is considered unethical when permission by the client or his guardian is not obtained. Other ethical problems associated with this method are discussed in detail in Chapter 9.

In general, the helper needs to assure himself continuously that he is maintaining the dignity of his client, that he is guarding the confidentiality of information obtained in the helping relationship, and that his therapeutic program does not have detrimental effects either on the client or on others. It is the helper's responsibility to protect the client's rights and interests so that the change program clearly contributes to the client's welfare, rather than creates new problems and conflicts for him.

WHAT IS CONTAINED IN THE FOLLOWING CHAPTERS?

The chapters in this book provide detailed descriptions of different behavior change techniques, by professionals who are expert in their respective fields. The techniques are generally appropriate for treatment of persons who show no gross social disorganization or such serious disturbances in their social or personal behavior that they require institutionalization. The techniques are, therefore, most applicable to persons who have difficulties in some areas of their lives but who can function at least marginally well in other areas. The techniques presented here are by no means exhaustive of the field of behavior change. They do constitute the most important methods that have been applied in the treatment of psychological problems. In selecting treatment approaches and techniques, we have chosen only those which are based on psychological theory that is widely accepted, and which have as their foundation at least some laboratory research and evidence of effectiveness in application. Many of the methods mentioned here are quite new or still in the exploratory stage. However, we have eliminated from presentation a large number of methods now practiced that are based only on the belief of the practitioner that they are effective but which have no other empirical evidence or theoretical rationale behind them. Anecdotal observation or limited clinical experience that has not been substantiated by research or field studies is insufficient grounds for use of a method. We have eliminated techniques which clients have reported have made them feel better, unless some independent evidence of change is also available. All of the methods that are discussed in the following chapters have been described at considerable length in the professional literature. The reader will find references at the end of each chapter that will guide him to additional reading in order to strengthen his knowledge of each technique and, consistent with the ultimate goal of this book, more fully aid the helper in helping people change.

REFERENCES

Durlak, J.A. Comparative effectiveness of paraprofessional and professional helpers. *Psychological Bulletin,* 1979, *86,* 80-92.

Garfield, S.L., and Bergin A.E. (Eds.) *Handbook of psychotherapy and behavior change: An empirical analysis* (2nd ed.). New York: John Wiley & Sons, 1978.

Goldfried, M.R., and Pomeranz, D.M. The role of assessment in behavior therapy. *Psychological Reports,* 1968, *23,* 75-87.

Goldstein, A.P. (Ed.) *Prescriptions for child mental health and education.* New York: Pergamon Press, 1978.

Goldstein, A.P., and Stein, N. *Prescriptive psychotherapies.* New York: Pergamon Press, 1976.

Gottman, J.M., and Leiblum, S.R. *How to do psychotherapy and how to evaluate it: A manual for beginners.* New York: Holt, Rinehart and Winston, 1974.

Gurman, A.S., and Razin, A.M. (Eds.) *Effective psychotherapy: A handbook of research.* New York: Pergamon Press, 1977.

Kanfer, F.H., and Grimm, L. Behavioral analysis: Selecting target behaviors in the interview. *Behavior Modification,* 1977, *1,* 7-28.

Kanfer, F.H., and Saslow, G. Behavioral diagnosis. In C. Franks (Ed.), *Behavior therapy: Appraisal and status.* New York: McGraw-Hill, 1969.

Kiesler, D.J. Some myths of psychotherapy research and the search for a paradigm. *Psychological Bulletin,* 1966, *65,* 110-136.

Lanyon, R.I., and Goodstein, L.D. *Personality assessment.* New York: Wiley, 1971.

Mitchell, K.M., Bozarth, J.D., and Krauft, C.C. A reappraisal of the therapeutic effectiveness of accurate empathy, nonpossessive warmth, and genuineness. In A.S. Gurman and A.M. Razin (Eds.), *Effective psychotherapy: A handbook of research.* New York: Pergamon Press, 1977.

Sulzer-Azaroff, B., Thaw, J., and Olsen, C. Behavioral competencies for the evaluation of behavior modifiers. Unpublished mimeo, University of Massachusetts, Mansfield Training School, 1974.

Sundberg, N.D. *Assessment of persons.* Englewood Cliffs, N.J.: Prentice Hall, 1977.

2
Relationship-Enhancement Methods
Arnold P. Goldstein

Barbara Harris is a 34-year-old woman, a wife, mother of two children, part time office receptionist and, every Tuesday at 10:00 A.M., a psychotherapy patient. Over the course of the past few years, Barbara had developed a number of concerns which more and more were interfering with her comfort and happiness. Backaches and a series of vague physical symptoms which seemed hard to cure were the apparent beginning of her change from a relatively problem-free and fully functioning person. Conflicts with her husband began around this time— about money, about sex, and about raising their children. Barbara's physical discomfort, her irritability, and her difficulty in getting along with people all increased as time passed. Eventually, these concerns and behaviors became so troublesome to Barbara and those around her that she contacted a psychotherapist recommended by her physician. She has been meeting with him for about a year now, and both feel she has made substantial progress in dealing effectively with her problems. Her physical complaints have decreased markedly, her relations with others are considerably more satisfying and, in general, Barbara seems well on her way to joining the two-thirds of all psychotherapy patients who apparently benefit from treatment.

In the same city in which Barbara lives there are four other women who have gone through similar difficulties and similar recovery from these difficulties. Yet none of them has ever met with a psychotherapist. What did they do? Pressed by the stress each was experiencing, each sought out a ''good listener'' or a ''friendly problem-solver'' with whom she felt she could share her burdens. For one, it was a friend; for the second, her minister; for the third, her family physician; and for the last, a ''paraprofessional'' helper called a ''home aide.'' All five women changed for the better, apparently in large part because of

18

whatever occurred between each and her helper. Barbara's recovery may or may not have been somewhat more complete, or somewhat more rapid but, for our present purposes, the significant fact is that all women improved.

These mini case histories are fictitious, but the facts they portray are all established. Many people do find problem relief, personal growth, and self-understanding as a result of participating in some form of psychotherapy. But many people obtain similar benefits as a result of their interactions with a wide variety of other types of helpers—friends, clergymen, bartenders, relatives, counselors, nurses, and so forth. These facts have long intrigued researchers interested in what it is that causes people to change their behavior, emotions, and attitudes. Perhaps, many of these researchers have proposed, some of the causes of such changes can be identified by determining what ingredients successful psychotherapy and successful help from others have in common. If certain procedures, circumstances, or events are clearly characteristic of successful helping of different kinds, then we have the opportunity to use them most effectively in helping others.

Dr. Jerome Frank, in his important book, *Persuasion and Healing* (1961), has made a similar point. He compared psychotherapy, ''informal'' psychotherapy (from a friend, clergyman, etc.), faith healing, religious revivalism, placebo effects in medical practice, and a host of other activities in which two people, a helper and a client, collaborate to bring about some sort of psychological change in the client. According to Frank, perhaps the major responsible ingredient in determining whether such change occurs is the quality of the helper-client relationship. The same conclusion emerges if one examines descriptions of almost all of the many different approaches to formal psychotherapy. These several approaches vary in many respects—therapist activity and directiveness, how much this focus is upon behavior versus the patient's inner world of feelings and attitudes, whether emphasis is placed upon the patient's present life or his childhood history, which aspects of his current difficulties are examined, and in a host of procedural ways. Yet, almost every approach to psychotherapy emphasizes the importance of the therapist-patient relationship for patient change. The better the relationship: (1) the more open is the patient about this feeling, (2) the more likely he is to explore these feelings deeply with the helper, and (3) the more likely he is to listen fully to and act upon advice offered him by the helper. That is, the most likely the patient is to change.

This remarkably consistent viewpoint, in the psychotherapies and in other approaches to psychological change, has also found consistent support in other fields. How well a variety of medications serve their intended purpose has been shown to be partly a result of the relationship between the drug giver and the drug receiver. Learning in school has been demonstrated to depend in part on the teacher-pupil relationship. The subject's behavior in the experimental laboratory may also be readily influenced by the experimenter-subject relationship. In brief, there now exists a wide variety of research evidence, from several different types of two-person interactions, to indicate that the quality of the helper-client relationship can serve as a powerful positive influence upon communication, openness, persuasibility and, ultimately, positive change in the client. This evidence is also useful in providing information which helps define the term "relationship." Our definition, it will be noted, places emphasis upon positive feelings and interpersonal attitudes reciprocally held by the helper and client: a positive or "therapeutic" relationship may be defined as feelings of liking, respect, and trust by a client toward the helper from whom he is seeking assistance, combined with similar feelings of liking, respect, and trust on the part of the helper toward the client.

A number of methods have been identified as ways of making the helper-client relationship a more positive one. Each of these relationship-enhancement methods has been the subject of considerable research. Each has added to both our understanding of what relationship is and helped explain the usefulness of the relationship for helping people change. These several methods, therefore, form the framework for the remainder of this chapter. We will, in turn, consider several concrete examples of each method, focusing upon how the relationship may be enhanced or improved to the benefit of client change. Figure 2.1 provides an overview of our viewpoint.

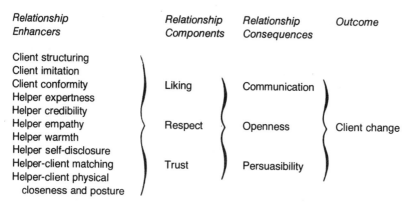

Fig. 2.1. Progression from relationship enhancement to client change.

The relationship enhancers listed above are the major means currently available for improving the quality of the helper-client interaction. This interaction or relationship may be defined in terms of the three components indicated: liking, respect, and trust. Successful enhancement of these components, in turn, has been shown to lead to greater influenceability and, subsequently, to greater client change. It should be noted that most psychotherapists and psychotherapy researchers view a positive relationship between helper and client as necessary, but not sufficient for client change. Without such a relationship, change is very unlikely. With it, the foundation exists for other more specific change procedures (such as those described in subsequent chapters) to yield their intended effects.

ATTRACTION

Laboratory research has developed several procedures for successfully increasing attraction of the experiment's subjects to their experimenter. The present writer (Goldstein, 1971) has shown that many of these attraction-increasing procedures are highly effective in enhancing the helper-client relationship, especially the client's liking of his helper. Three such procedures: structuring, imitation, and conformity pressure are presented below.

Structuring

It is perhaps fitting, in this book in which several dozen procedures for helping people change will be described, that the first procedure to be illustrated is probably one of the least complex. Structuring a client so that he will like or be attracted to his helper is, quite simply, a matter of: (1) telling him that he will like his helper ("direct" structuring), (2) briefly describing to him certain positive characteristics of his helper ("trait" structuring), or (3) clarifying what he may realistically anticipate will go on in his meetings with the helper (role expectancy structuring). Each of these three structuring procedures seeks to mold the client's expectations and feelings about his relationship with his helper. In one of the first uses of direct structuring to strengthen client attraction to the helper, new clients at a counseling center were first given certain tests which asked information about the kind of helper they would prefer to meet with—his behavior, his expectations, his goals, etc. Shortly after this testing, clients were told by the tester:

> We have carefully examined the tests you took in order to assign you to a therapist whom you would like to work with most. We usually can't match a patient and therapist the way they want most, but for you we have almost exactly the kind of therapist you described. (The tester then showed the client how well his test results describing his preferred helper apparently matched other information purportedly indicating the actual behavior, expectations and goals of the helper with whom he would be meeting.) As a matter of fact, the matching of the kind of person you wanted to work with and the kind of person Mr. _____ is, is so close that it hardly ever happens. What's even more, he has often described the kind of patient he likes to work with most as someone just like you in many respects. You two should get along extremely well. (Goldstein, 1971, p. 21.)

It should be noted that no actual matching of client preferences with helper characteristics was done here. Clients participated in the structuring procedure we have just described, and then each was assigned to a therapist whose turn it was for a new patient. Nevertheless, such structuring led the client to actually show increased liking of their helpers and increased openness about their problems. Thus, the client's belief that the helper would be a person they would like was enough to influence their actual attraction toward him.

The enhancing effect on both attraction and openness has been shown to be even stronger when trait structuring of the client is conducted. These are instances in which specific, important qualities of the helper are described to the client before they actually meet. Once again, the effect of these procedures on the actual attraction which develops is quite strong even though the helper characteristics described may in fact not be present. Which particular helper characteristics are selected to be described to the client is an important matter. In most uses of trait structuring, the two helper traits chosen have been his "warmth" and his "experience"—the first of which tells the client something important about how comfortable he is likely to feel during the helping process, the second gives him information about the likely positive outcome of this process. Both items of information, therefore, enhance client attraction to the helper. The statement which follows is an example of trait structuring of helper warmth and experience:

> The therapist has been engaged in the practice of therapy for over 20 years and has lectured and taught at some of the country's leading universities and medical schools. Questionnaires submitted to the therapist's colleagues seem to reveal that he is a rather warm person, industrious, critical, practical and determined. (Goldstein, 1971, p. 50.)

Trait structuring has also been used successfully "in reverse" to increase helper attraction toward the client. Here, qualities of the client are emphasized which lead the helper to anticipate that the client will be "a good patient." The type of problem the client supposedly has, his diagnosis, and his motivation to work hard to improve are some examples of positively structured traits of the client which have been communicated to the helper.

A great deal of psychological research has been conducted on the effects of leading a person to believe he is similar to a stranger in important attitudes, background, or values and on his liking that person when they meet. This research convincingly shows that the greater the structured similarity, the greater the attraction to the other person. This positive effect of structured similarity on attraction has also been found to operate in the helper-client relationship. It is largely for this reason that great use has been made in recent years of certain types of "paraprofessional" helpers, that is, persons who may be lacking in certain formal training or degrees but who possess beliefs, a personal background, and a lifestyle quite similar to that of the persons they are seeking to help. These similarities between paraprofessional helpers and the people they serve, like "structured similarity," enhance the quality of the therapeutic relationship.

We have seen thus far that direct structuring, and trait structuring for warmth, experience, and similarity each can have attraction-increasing effects. So, too, can the final type of structuring we wish to present—role expectancy structuring. Whereas direct and trait structuring mostly concern telling the client something about the kind of person his helper *is*, role expectancy structuring focuses on what the helper (and what the client himself) actually will *do* when they meet. If, because of misinformation or lack of information about what to expect, the client later experiences events during his meetings with the helper which surprise or confuse him, negative feelings will result. Events which confirm his expectancies will serve to increase his attraction to the helper. For example, many new psychotherapy patients come to therapy with expectations based primarily on their past experiences in what they judge to be similar relationships, such as what happens when they meet with their medical doctor. During those visits, the patient typically presented his physical problem briefly, was asked a series of questions by his physician, and then authoritatively told what to do. Now, however, when the client with such "medical expectations" starts psychotherapy, he is in for some surprises. The client describes his psychological problem, and sits back awaiting the helper's questions and eventual advice. The helper, unlike the general physician, wants the client to explore his feelings, to examine his history, to speculate about the causes for his problems. These are not the client's role expectations, and when such important expectations differ, the relationship clearly suffers. These are but a few of the several ways in which client and helper may differ in their anticipations of how each will behave. Prior structuring of such expectations has been shown to be an important contributor to increased attraction and a more lasting and fruitful helper-client relationship. This structuring may be provided by having new clients listen to a tape recording of a typical helper-client meeting. More commonly, role expectancy structuring has been accomplished by providing the client with a structuring interview (also called an "anticipatory socialization interview" or a "role induction interview") before his first meeting with his helper. The following is an excerpt from such an interview in which a helper explains to his prospective client what he can expect to occur in psychotherapy:

Now, what is therapy about? What is going on? Well, for one thing, I have been talking a great deal; in treatment your doctor won't talk very much. The reason I am talking now is that I want to explain these things to you. There is equally good reason that the doctor in treatment does not say much. Everyone expects to tell the psychiatrist about his problem and then have him give advice which will solve everything just like that. This isn't true; it just doesn't work like that . . . Before you came here you got advice from all kinds of people . . . If all of the advice you have received had helped, odds are that you wouldn't be here. Your doctor wants to help you to figure out what you really want to do—what the best solution is for you. It's his job not to give advice but to help you find out for yourself how you are going to solve your problem.

Now, what goes on in treatment itself? What is it that you talk about? What is it that you do? How does it work? Well, for one thing, you will talk about your wishes, both now and in the past. . . . You will find that with your doctor you will be able to talk about anything that comes to your mind. He won't have any preconceived notions about what is right or what is wrong for you or what the best solution would be. Talking is very important because he wants to help you get at what you really want. . . . The doctor's job is to help *you* make the decision . . . most of us are not honest with ourselves. We try to kid ourselves, and it's your doctor's job to make you aware of when you are kidding yourself. He is not going to try to tell you what he thinks but he will point out to you how two things you are saying just don't fit together.

. . . the patient . . . sometimes feels worse and discouraged at some stages of treatment. You know, you'll feel you're not getting anywhere, your doctor is a fool, and there's no point in this, and so on. These very feelings are often good indications that you are working and that it's uncomfortable. It is very important that you don't give in to these temporary feelings when they come up.

. . . say whatever comes to your mind, even if you think it is trivial or unimportant. It doesn't matter. It is still important to say it. And if you think it is going to bother your doctor, that doesn't matter either; you still say it.

So, just like the [keeping of] appointments, we make an absolute rule not to think ahead about what you'll say and therefore protect yourself from facing important things. Say whatever is on the top of your mind, no matter what. *

We may note then, in summary of our presentation thus far, that structuring can lead to increased attraction by the client toward his helper whether such structuring is a simple matter of a straightforward statement of probable liking (direct structuring), a description of certain of the helper's positive qualities or of helper-client similarity (trait structuring), or an explanation of the events and behaviors one should expect in the relationship (role expectancy structuring). Whether a given structuring statement of any of these kinds actually does increase client attraction will depend in part on matters other than the structuring itself. These statements will tend to be most effective when the person doing the structuring is perceived as trustworthy, and when the client is experiencing distress or discomfort from his problems.

Imitation

As we have just described, attempts to increase client attraction by structuring typically rely on statements about the helper presented to the client. A second approach to attraction-enhancement, i.e., to the liking component of the helper-client relationship, has relied on different procedures, those based on research concerned with imitation. Essentially, increasing attraction to the helper through imitation involves exposing the client to a person (the "model") who plays the part of a client who likes the helper and clearly says so. This approach is also called modeling or observational learning. In the typical use of imitation, an audiotape or videotape of the attracted model client is played to the real client. The content of such tapes is usually part of an actual or constructed counseling or psychotherapy session between the model and the helper. The client simply listens to or observes the tape(s) and then later meets with the helper himself. The following is an excerpt from such an attraction-imitation tape, a tape which in its entirety contained a dozen such high attraction statements by the model client:

How would I like my parents to be different? Well, I think mostly in the fact that they could've cared more, that they could have showed it, you know, been warmer and not so cold. That's

---

*From Orne, M.T. and Wender, P.H. Anticipatory socialization for psychotherapy. *American Journal of Psychiatry*, Vol. 124, 1968, pp. 1202-1212. Copyright © 1968 the American Psychiatric Association.

mainly it. . . . You know, I guess I said this before, but *even though all you've been doing the past 5 or 10 minutes is asking me questions, I still for some reason or another feel comfortable talking to you and being honest about myself. I feel that you're warm and that you care.* (Goldstein, 1973, p. 216.)

As suggested in our discussion of structuring, a change-enhancing relationship involves *both* client attraction toward the helper, and helper attraction toward the client. The more reciprocal or mutual the positive feelings, the more likely is progress toward rapid client change. For this reason, imitation has also been used to increase helper attraction to the client. The following transcript is part of a modeling tape designed for this purpose, a tape used successfully with helpers of several kinds. Each statement in italics depicts a model helper expressing attraction, liking, or positive evaluation toward a client, i.e., expressing the behaviors we were training the listening helpers to imitate.

Therapist: Since this is our first interview, I'll be asking you about a number of different areas of your life. Why don't we start off by your telling me about your family?

Patient: My family. Well, you know sometimes—sometimes I think my family could do—just as well without me. You know. Like I'm a—a useless sort of object that sort of sits around the house. When I—come home from work it's like—like there's nothing there.

Therapist: You don't feel that your family looks forward to your coming home at night?

Patient: Sometimes it—sometimes it seems that they don't even know when I'm home. Kids'll be running around and—my wife—well sometimes the way she acts it would be better if I just stayed out. Some of the things that she gets into—MMMMMMMMMMM.

Therapist: I'm not clear why your wife would act that way. *I find you a rather easy person to talk with* . . . What kind of things does your wife get into?

Patient: —I don't know. She's always yelling and screaming—wants me to do things when I come inside—always telling me I have this to do and that to do. She doesn't realize I just wanna come home and I wanna relax a little bit. Nah—I don't know how she can push me all the time—do this—do that—all the time.

Therapist: Sounds like marriage has been a lot of trouble for you.

Patient: —Yeah. Yeah—really it—it was different before. When we first got married it was—it was nice. We went out and saw different people, did . . . did some things together. Got along pretty good too. Didn't have all this that's going on now.

Therapist: From our meeting so far, *I'm finding it rather easy to get along with you too* . . . I guess things aren't going very well with your wife now.

Patient: No—my wife changed. She got—she got different. Things started—you know—she started not to care about things. We couldn't go out as much. Then—then the babies came and then—wow—feeding them and taking care of them and doing all those things. Never had any time to do the things that we used to do together.—You know, it's usually hard for me to talk about things like this, but it's easy talking to you. Like—you know when I'd come home from work—my wife—she'd be running around the house after the kids—and when I'd come in the door I'd get ignored you know. No one says hello—no one asks you how you are.

Therapist: —Somehow all this seemed to happen around the time the children came?

Patient: It—seems that way. Before we had the kids we didn't have these problems. Now it—it's just not the same.

Therapist: What about your parents, did your father—drink?

Patient: Oh, yeah. He—could down them with the best of them. My old lady will tell you that. Yeah, he really knew how to drink. Used to get into some terrible fights with my old lady though. Boy—he'd come home—have a little too much in him—she'd really let him have it.

I'd have to—pull the pillow up over my head so I wouldn't hear the noise. Couldn't get to sleep.

Therapist: Your mother was very hard on your father then.

Patient: Yeah. She really used to get mad at him. You know, for drinking and all that. She used to yell at him. Get on his back all the time. Really be nasty to him. Maybe that's one of the reasons why he's six feet under right now.

Therapist: Sort of like the same thing your wife is doing to you?

Patient: Yeah. You're right. You really hit the nail on the head. You really understand what's going on. There's a lot of things about the two that are kind of the same. I think she's trying to do the same thing to me that my mother did to my father.—Yell and fight—the yelling and carrying on. They'll both do it. Scream at you—and call you a drunk. Telling me I can't take on any responsibility. Always yelling about something. Money. Why don't you have more of it? Why can't we buy this? Why can't we buy that? I'm working—as hard as I can—and she does—she doesn't realize that. She thinks all I have to do is work—all the time. She thinks it's—it's easy for me to—to work every day.—Always pushing me. I don't like to be pushed. I get—I'll get things done. But I have to work—at my own pace, otherwise—it just doesn't matter if I work or not, if I can't work at my own pace.

Therapist: You seem to be really trying to make your marriage work. I respect people who really try like that . . . It sounds like your wife and you just—don't do things the same way.

Patient: Yeah. She's in her own world.—She doesn't care about anything that I do—or say. She doesn't care about me or anyone else. Sometimes I just feel like getting up and leaving. There's nothing there any more.

Therapist: You'd like to just go away?

Patient: Mmhmm.

Therapist: Have you ever done this?

Patient: —Not for any long time. Used to—get away for a couple of days by myself. But I always ended up coming back because I had no one else to go to.

Therapist: Well, now when you feel like that you can come see me . . . You don't like being alone.

Thus, imitation is a second established path to attraction-enhancement. Yet matters are not quite this simple. Each of us observes many people every day, but most of what we observe we do not imitate. We see expensively produced and expertly acted modeling displays of people buying things on television commercials, but much more often than not we do not imitate. People imitate others only under certain circumstances. We tend to imitate others with whom we can identify, thus to encourage imitation the taped model should be the same sex and approximate age as the viewing client whose attraction we are seeking to increase. We are especially prone to imitate behavior we see leading to rewards which we too desire. Therefore, the most successful attraction-enhancing modeling tapes are those on which the attracted model is rewarded by having his problems resolved. Further, it is not by accident that television commercials so frequently involve extensive repetition (particularly of the product's name), since imitation often increases with the repetition of the modeling display. Finally, imitation will be more likely if the viewer is encouraged to rehearse or practice what he has seen. In short, repetitive watching of a rewarded model of the viewer's age and sex, and rehearsing the observed behaviors, will all increase the amount of imitation which occurs.

Conformity Pressure

People with problems often have problems with people. Clients often seek help in the first place because of their difficulty in getting along with others, and these difficulties may be reflected in *low* attraction (dislike, suspiciousness, ambivalence) toward the helper. Under such circumstances, trying to increase attraction by telling him (structuring) or showing him (imitation) appropriate materials may not work. More powerful procedures may be required. If so, conformity pressure is one such possibility. In the typical use of conformity pressure in the research laboratory, a group of individuals meet and each member in turn is required to make a judgment aloud—about which of two lines is longer, or whether a dot of light moved, or which social or political viewpoint is more correct, or some other matter of judgment. However, unknown to one member of the group, all the other members are actually accomplices of the group leader and are told in advance to respond to his requests for their judgments in a predetermined and usually unanimous or near-unanimous manner. In at least a third of the groups arranged in this manner, the non-accomplice member conforms to the majority judgment—even when it is (to the outsider) obviously incorrect. Research conducted by the present writer in counseling settings indicates that similar use of conformity pressure can indeed serve as a powerful attraction-enhancer. After hearing a taped session between a helper and client, three members (accomplices) of a group of four ''clients'' rated aloud the helper as attractive in a variety of ways. The real client conformed to this pressure and did likewise. Of greatest interest, in other groups different real clients also rated the taped helper as highly attractive after conformity pressure from accomplices even when the taped helper being rated was (again to outside observers) highly *un*attractive in several important respects.

HELPER CHARACTERISTICS

Expertness and Status

Our definition of relationship emphasized reciprocal liking, respect, and trust. Seeking to improve the relationship by focus upon attraction-enhancement is equivalent to emphasizing the liking component of this definition. Relationship may also be enhanced by procedures relevant to the respect component. A major means for enhancing client respect for his helper concerns the helper's real or apparent expertness and status. In general, we may assume that the greater the helper's expertness, the greater is the client's respect for him.

In psychotherapy, there is much about the psychotherapist, his behavior, and his physical surroundings which testifies to his apparent expertness and authority. Haley (1963) comments in this regard:

> The context of the relationship emphasizes the therapist's position. . . . Patients are usually referred to him by people who point out what a capable authority he is and how much the patient needs help. Some therapists have a waiting list, so that the patient is impressed by standing in line to be treated, while others may imply that patients with similar symptoms were successfully treated. Furthermore, the patient must be willing to pay money even to talk to the therapist, and the therapist can either treat him or dismiss him, and so controls whether or not there is going to be a relationship. Not only the therapist's prestige is emphasized in the initial meeting, but also the patient's inadequacy is made clear. The patient . . . must emphasize his difficulties in life to a man who apparently has none. The physical settings in which most therapists function also reinforce their superior position. In many instances the therapist sits at a desk, the symbol of authority, while the patient sits in a chair, the position of the suppliant. In psychoanalytic therapy the arrangement is more extreme. The patient lies down while the therapist sits up. His chair is also placed so that he can observe the patient's reactions, but the patient cannot observe him. Finally, the initial interview in therapy usually makes quite explicit the fact that the therapist is in charge of the relationship by the rules for treatment he lays down. He suggests the frequency of interviews, implies he will be the one who decides when treatment will end, and he usually instructs the patient how to behave in the office. He may make a general statement about how the patient is to express himself there, or he may provide specific instructions as in the analytic situation where the patient is told he must lie down and say whatever comes to mind. (pp. 71-73.)*

What else is there that distinguishes the expert helper from the inexpert? In our own research, as will be seen shortly, the level of apparent helper expertness was varied by altering the external trappings surrounding the helper—his title, books, office, diploma, etc. Research reported by Schmidt and Strong (1970) shows that clients also judge expertness to a large extent from the observable behavior of their helper. According to their results, college students describe the expert and the inexpert counselor quite differently:

> *The expert* shakes the student's hand, aligning the student with himself, and greets him with his first name. He seems interested and relaxed. He has a neat appearance but is not stuffy. . . . He talks at the student's level and is not arrogant toward him. The expert assumes a comfortable but attentive sitting position. He focuses his attention on the student and carefully listens to him. He has a warm facial expression and is reactive to the student. His voice is inflective and lively, he changes his facial expressions, and uses hand gestures. He speaks fluently with confidence and sureness. The expert has prepared for the interview. He is informed as to why the student is there and is familiar with the student's test scores, grades, and background. . . . He asks direct and to-the-point questions. His questions are thought-provoking and follow an apparently logical progression. They seem spontaneous and conversational. The expert is willing to help determine if the student's decisions are right, but does not try to change the student's ideas forcefully. He lets the student do most of the talking and does not interrupt him. The expert moves quickly to the root of the problem. He points out contradictions in reasoning,

---

*From Haley, J. *Strategies of Psychotherapy*. New York: Grune and Stratton, 1963, Reprinted by permission of Grune & Stratton, Inc. and the author.

and restates the student's statements as they bear on the problem. . . . He makes recommendations and suggests possible solutions.

The *inexpert* is awkward, tense, and uneasy. He seems to be afraid of the student. He does not greet the student by name to put him at ease. . . . He is not quite sure of himself or of some of his remarks. He seems too cold, strict and dominating, and too formal in attitude and action. His gestures are stiff and overdone. . . . The inexpert slouches in his chair. He is too casual and relaxed. . . . His voice is flat and without inflection, appearing to show disinterest and boredom. . . . The inexpert comes to the interview cold. He has not cared enough about the student to acquaint himself with the student's records. The inexpert asks vague questions which are trivial and irrelevant and have no common thread or aim. His questioning is abrupt and tactless with poor transitions. He asks too many questions like a quiz session, giving the student the third degree. . . . The inexpert is slow in getting his point across and is confusing in his discussion of what the student should do. . . . The inexpert does not get to the core of the problem. . . . He just doesn't seem to be getting anywhere. (p. 117.)†

These descriptions were then used by the investigators (Strong and Schmidt, 1970) as the script outline in a study examining the effects of status on a helper's influence. Counselors taking the role of expert and inexpert were thoroughly rehearsed in the behaviors described above. The former were introduced to clients with the statement:

The person you will be talking with is Dr. _____, a psychologist who has had several years of experience interviewing students.

The inexpert helper was, contrastingly, introduced with the statement:

We had originally scheduled Dr. _____ to talk with you but unfortunately he notified us that he wouldn't be able to make it today. In his place we have Mr. _____, a student, who unfortunately has had no interviewing experience and has been given only a brief explanation of the purpose of this study. I think he should work out allright, though. (Strong and Schmidt, 1970, p. 83.)

Analysis of the helper-client interviews which were then held revealed, as predicted, greater positive change in those clients structured and in fact seen by the "expert" helper.

It thus seems that the greater the change-agent's expertness, the greater his effectiveness in altering the behavior and beliefs of his target. Laboratory research strongly supports this contention. A substantial number of investigations confirm the fact that a statement is more fully accepted and acted upon when the recipient believes it comes from an expert or high status person, than when its apparent source is a person of low or unknown expertise.

The first evidence we obtained in support of the relationship aspect of this

---

†From Schmidt, L.D. and Strong, S.R. Expert and inexpert counselors. *Journal of Counseling Psychology*, 1970, 17, 115-118. Copyright 1970 by the American Psychological Association. Reprinted by permission.

finding was obtained almost accidentally (Goldstein, 1971). We conducted a study whose purpose was to determine if client attraction to the helper would increase if the helper went out of his way to do a small favor or extend an extra courtesy to the client. The courtesy involved was offering the client coffee and a donut, not a usual event in counseling or psychotherapy. While this procedure did improve their relationship, attraction increased even more at those times when the helper made it clear that the coffee and donut he was calling for were for himself, and not for the client! We had not predicted this result, and only half-jokingly speculated that perhaps attraction increased because anyone behaving so boorishly must be an important person. That is, perhaps attraction increased here because, in the client's eyes, the helper had increased his status. We tested this notion more directly in our next investigation (Sabalis, 1969). Sabalis had four groups of clients, two of whom were seen by what appeared to be a high-status helper, two by a low-status helper. Not all persons, we predicted, are attracted to high-status persons. Authoritarian persons, those rigidly respectful of authority, seem to be highly responsive and attracted to such persons, whereas more equalitarian individuals are less drawn to experts and similar sources. Thus, in this study it was predicted that a high-status helper would increase the attraction-to-helper of high authoritarian clients, but not equalitarian clients.

The clients (of both kinds) in the high-status groups each received a postcard indicating the time of their interview. The interviewer was "Dr. Robert Sabalis." When each client arrived for his interview, the interviewer introduced himself as "Dr. Sabalis, a member of the faculty of the Psychology Department." A "Dr. Robert Sabalis" nameplate was on the interviewer's desk, and the office itself was a large, well-furnished one belonging to a faculty member. The interviewer was neatly dressed in a business suit. The session began with some test-taking by the client, which the interviewer described as tests on which he was doing research. As the client filled out the test forms, the interviewer opened a text and began to jot down notes from it, indicating to the client as he did that he was preparing an examination for one of the classes he taught.

For the low-status groups, the interviewer's name on the postcard and in his introduction upon meeting was "Bob Sabalis." He described himself to clients as a senior undergraduate psychology major who was meeting with them as a requirement for one of his own courses. His attire was consistent with the typical undergraduate's. The interview office was quite small and sparsely furnished. As the test-taking commenced, he began note-taking from a text again, but this time indicated he was preparing for an examination he had to take.

The predicted effect of status on attraction was obtained. That is, high authoritarian clients became significantly more attracted to the interviewer after the high-status, but not the low-status procedures.

As described above, Strong and Schmidt showed the positive effect of expertness by training counselors to behave either expert or inexpert. Sabalis used one interviewer, who served as both the high- and low-status helper. The positive effect on the helper-client relationship was obtained again. Streltzer and Koch

(1968) implemented expertness in yet another way. Their research concerned the effects role playing the part of lung cancer patients would have on persons needing to reduce their smoking. Participating "patients" role played a series of scenes involving meeting the doctor, the doctor giving the diagnosis, treatment plans, and advice to quit smoking immediately. Half of the "patients" enacted their role with a "doctor" who was a 21-year-old female psychology major. She used no title. The other smokers met with a 32-year-old male physician, who introduced himself as "Doctor." Both types of smokers decreased in smoking more than persons not participating in the role playing. Those role playing with the real expert, furthermore, showed by far the greatest negative change in their attitudes toward smoking.

Similar findings have been reported by other researchers. In general, it may be concluded that helper expertness and status serve to increase client respect, which in turn leads to his being more open to the helper's attempts to influence him and, subsequently, more likelihood of client change.

Credibility

The respect component of the helper-client relationship is also influenced by helper credibility. The greater the level of credibility, the greater is the client's respect for him. Johnson and Matross (1977) define helper credibility as his perceived ability to know valid information and his motivation to communicate this knowledge without bias. As Johnson (1973) observes, empirical evidence exists demonstrating that credibility is determined by several helper characteristics: (1) *expertness* as defined above, and as signified by title, institutional affiliation, and other indices of academic and professional achievement; (2) *reliability* as an information source, e.g., his dependability, predictability and consistency; (3) *motives and intentions* of the helper—the clearer it is to the client that it is his interests, and not the helper's own, toward which the helper is working, the greater his credibility, and (4) *dynamism* of the helper, his apparent confidence, forcefulness and activity level.

Empathy

We have just examined the positive effects of the helper-client relationship of the real or apparent expertness and status of the helper, as well as his perceived credibility. There are several other helper qualities of importance in this regard, and the present section will focus upon one of these—empathy. The level of empathy offered by the helper and its effects on the client has been the object of considerable research and theory. This research has consistently shown that a helper's empathy with his client's feelings strongly influences the quality of the helper-client relationship which develops and, subsequently, the degree of client change.

Truax and Carkhuff (1967) are two researchers who have been quite active in studying the effects of empathy on the helper-client relationship. They comment, as a beginning definition of "empathy":

> As we come to know some of his wants, some of his needs, some of his achievements and some of his failures, we find ourselves as therapists "living" with the patient much as we do with the central figure of a novel. . . . Just as with the character in the novel, we come to know the person from his own internal frame of reference, gaining some flavor of his moment-by-moment experience. We see events and significant people in his life as they appear to him—not as they "objectively are" but as he experiences them. As we come to know him from his personal vantage point we automatically come to value and like him. . . . We begin to perceive the events and experiences of his life "as if" they were parts of our own life. It is through this process that we come to feel warmth, respect and liking. . . . (p. 42.)

These same researchers have also developed a more detailed definition of empathy, which is quoted in full below. Described in the statement which follows is their Empathy Scale, consisting of levels of empathy which a helper may provide a client—graduated from very low (Level 1) to very high (Level 5).

EMPATHIC UNDERSTANDING IN INTERPERSONAL PROCESSES

A Scale for Measurement

Level 1
The verbal and behavioral expressions of the helper either do not attend to or detract significantly from the verbal and behavioral expressions of the client(s) in that they communicate significantly less of the client's feelings and experiences than the client has communicated himself.

Example. The helper communicates no awareness of even the most obvious, expressed surface feelings of the client. The helper may be bored or disinterested or simply operating from a preconceived frame of reference which totally excludes that of the client(s).

In summary, the helper does everything but express that he is listening, understanding, or being sensitive to even the most obvious feelings of the client in such a way as to detract significantly from the communications of the client.

Level 2
While the helper responds to the expressed feelings of the client(s), he does so in such a way that he subtracts noticeable affect from the communications of the client.

Example. The helper may communicate some awareness of obvious, surface feelings of the client, but his communications drain off a level of the affect and distort the level of meaning. The helper may communicate his own ideas of what may be going on, but these are not congruent with the expressions of the client.

In summary, the helper tends to respond to other than what the client is expressing or indicating.

Level 3

The expressions of the helper in response to the expressions of the client(s) are essentially interchangeable with those of the client in that they express essentially the same affect and meaning.

Example. The helper responds with accurate understandings of the surface feelings of the client but may not respond to or may misinterpret the deeper feelings.

In summary, the helper is responding so as to neither subtract from nor add to the expressions of the client. He does not respond accurately to how that person really feels beneath the surface feelings; but he indicates a willingness and openness to do so. Level 3 constitutes the minimal level of facilitative interpersonal functioning.

Level 4

The responses of the helper add noticeably to the expressions of the client(s) in such a way as to express feelings a level deeper than the client was able to express himself.

Example. The helper communicates his understanding of the expressions of the client at a level deeper than they were expressed and thus enables the client to experience and/or express feelings he was unable to express previously.

In summary, the helper's responses add deeper feeling and meaning to the expressions of the client.

Level 5

The helper's responses add significantly to the feeling and meaning of the expressions of the client(s) in such a way as to accurately express feelings levels below what the client himself was able to express or, in the event of ongoing, deep self-exploration on the client's part, to be fully with him in his deepest moments.

Example. The helper responds with accuracy to all of the client's deeper as well as surface feelings. He is "tuned in" on the client's wave length. The helper and the client might proceed together to explore previously unexplored areas of human existence.

In summary, the helper is responding with a full awareness of who the other person is and with a comprehensive and accurate empathic understanding of that individual's deepest feelings. (pp. 174-175.)*

A great deal of research has been done on the effects of high levels of helper empathy in counseling, guidance, and psychotherapy. Certain effects on the client regularly occur in these studies. Feeling understood, that someone has been able to truly perceive his deeper feelings, the client's liking of his helper increases. In a sense, the client also comes to trust himself more under these circumstances, for one regular result of high helper empathy is deeper and more

---

*From Truax, Charles B. and Carkhuff, Robert R. *Toward effective counseling and psychotherapy* (Chicago: Aldine Publishing Company, 1967); copyright © by Charles B. Truax and Robert R. Carkhuff. Reprinted by permission of the authors and Aldine Publishing Company.

persevering *self*-exploration by the client. In several of these studies, greater client change is a clear result. High levels of helper empathic responding may, therefore, be viewed as a necessary (but probably not sufficient) condition for client change. Carkhuff (1969) is, we feel, largely correct in his comment:

> Empathy is the key ingredient of helping. Its explicit communication, particularly during early phases of helping, is critical. Without an emphatic understanding of the helpee's world and his difficulties as he sees them there is no basis for helping. (Carkhuff, 1969, p. 173.)

A more concrete understanding of helper empathy, and its effects upon client behavior, is provided by the specific examples which follow. The first is drawn from a psychotherapy session. Note how all helper statements are at least Level 3, and often higher:

> *Helpee:* Um, I don't know whether, whether I'm right or wrong in feeling the way I do, but, uh, I find myself withdrawing from people. I don't care to go out and socialize and play their stupid little games any more. Um, I get very anxious and come home depressed and have headaches—it seems all so superficial. There was a time when I used to get along with everybody; everybody said, ''Oh, isn't she wonderful! She gets along with everybody; she's so nice and everybody likes her,'' and I used to think that was . . . that was something to be really proud of, but, oh, but, I think that only told how I, or who I was at that time, that I had no depth. I was sort of whatever the crowd wanted me to be, or the particular group I was with at the time. Um, I know it's important for my husband's business that we go out and socialize and meet people and make a good impression and join clubs and play all those stupid little games—Elks, and, you know, bowling banquets, and, uh, fishing trips and fraternity-type gatherings. Um, I . . . I just don't care to do it any more, and, um, I don't know if that means that I'm a . . . that there's something wrong with me psychologically, or, uh, or is this normal. I mean . . . uh . . . people don't really know who I am and they really don't care who one another, who the other person is. They . . . it's all at such a superficial level.
>
> *Helper:* You're darn sure of how you feel, but you really don't know what it all adds up to. Is it you? Is it the other people? What are the implications of your husband's business? You? Where is it all going?
>
> *Helpee:* Uh, huh. It's an empty life. It's, um, there's, uh, no depth to it at all. I mean, you just talk about very, very superficial things, and the first few times, it's O.K. But then after that, there's nothing to talk about. So you drink and you pretend to be happy over silly jokes and silly things that people do when they all, uh, are trying to impress one another, and they're very materialistic, and, uh, it's just not the route I want to go.
>
> *Helper:* So your feelings are so strong now that you just can't fake it any more.
>
> *Helpee:* That's right, so what do you do? People say, ''Oh, there's something wrong with you,'' then, ''You need to see a psychiatrist or something.'' because you . . . you know the thing in society is that the normal person gets along with people, and, uh, can adjust to any situation. And when you . . . when you're a little discriminating, maybe very discriminating or critical, then that means there's something wrong with you.
>
> *Helper:* While you know how strongly you feel about all these things, you're not sure you can really act in terms of them and be free.
>
> *Helpee:* I don't know if I'm strong enough. The implications are great. It may mean, uh, a break up of the marriage, uh, and it means going it alone, and that's too frightening. I don't think I have the courage. But I do feel like I'm in sort of a trap.
>
> *Helper:* You know you can't pretend, yet you're really fearful of going it alone.
>
> *Helpee:* Yes, there's nobody I can really talk to, I mean, you know, it's one thing if you have

a . . . like your husband . . . if you can share these things, if he can understand it at some level, but . . . um . . . he can't.

Helper: It's like, "If I act on how I really feel, though, it frightens the people who mean most to me. They won't understand it, and I sure can't share that with them."

Helpee: (Pause) So what do you do. (Pause) I mean . . . I . . . you know. I find myself going out and telling the people who I really feel about, about different topics and getting into controversial issues, and, uh, and that's, that's too anxiety provoking for me. I can't, because then you get into arguments and I don't want to do that either, that leads nowhere. I just get frustrated and anxious and upset and angry with myself for getting myself into the situation.

Helper: You know that doesn't set you free, you know . . .

Helpee: No, it bottles me up.

Helper: That only causes you more problems, and what you're really asking about is, how you can move toward greater freedom and greater fulfillment in your own life.

Helpee: I . . . I think I know who I am now, independent of other people, and, uh, which people aren't and . . . um . . . there's no room for that kind of person in this society.

Helper: There's no room for me out there!

Helpee: (Pause) So what do I do?

Helper: We run over and over the questions that . . . you end up with. "Where do I go from here? How do I act on this? I know how I feel, but I don't know what'll happen if I act on how I feel."

Helpee: I . . . have an idea of what'll happen.

Helper: And it's not good!

Helpee: No! It means almost starting a whole new life.

Helper: And you don't know if you can make it.

Helpee: Right, I know what I've got here, and if I don't make it all the way with the other, then I'm in trouble.

Helper: While you don't know what'll happen if you act on your feelings, you know what the alternatives are if you don't. And they're not good either. They're worse.

Helpee: I . . . I don't have much choice. (pp. 219-220.)*

A second series of examples is drawn from our own research (Goldstein, 1973), in which we sought successfully to increase helper empathy by a set of training procedures rather different from Truax and Carkhuff's. Our trainees were nurses and attendants employed in state mental hospitals. Part of our training sequence involved exposing them to a number of different examples of highly empathic responses to difficult or problematic patient behaviors and statements. These examples included:†

1. *Nurse:* Here is your medicine, Mr. _____.

   Patient: I don't want it. People here are always telling me to do this, do that, do the other thing. I'll take the medicine when *I* want to.

   Nurse: So it's not so much the medicine itself, but you feel you're bossed around all the time. You're tired of people giving you orders.

---

*From Carkhuff, R.F. *Helping and human relations*. New York: Holt, Rinehart and Winston, 1969. Reprinted by permission.

†From Goldstein, A.P. *Structured learning therapy*. New York: Academic Press, 1973. Reprinted by permission.

2. *Patient:* I can't leave the hospital, I'm still sick. What will I do when I get home?

   Nurse: You just don't feel ready to go yet, and wonder if you're up to being home.

3. *Patient:* I don't know why they keep giving me this medicine. I've taken it for weeks and I don't feel any better. I've told this to Dr. _____ twice already.

   Nurse: Not only doesn't the medicine seem to work, but the doctor doesn't seem interested in doing anything about it.

4. *Patient:* I was in the hospital before. Things were really bothering me. Finally, I just couldn't take it anymore. I left home, didn't show up at work, and somehow ended up in the hospital.

   Nurse: Things just piled up and up, from bad to worse, and you wound up here.

5. *Patient:* Sometimes I think my family could do just as well without me. It's like I almost don't exist as far as they're concerned. They almost never come to see me.

   Nurse: You'd really like them to visit, but they don't really seem to care about you.

6. *Patient:* My father and mother used to get into terrible fights. He'd come home and they'd really go at it. I'd have to pull the pillow over my head so I wouldn't hear the noise.

   Nurse: It sounds like something that would be really upsetting, especially to a child.

7. *Patient:* I'd really like to know about their school, their friends, things like that. You know, the things a father is interested in. My youngest son, he's on a football team, but he never invited me to a game. He never cared if I was there or not. I don't understand it.

   Nurse: It must hurt very deeply when he doesn't let you be a part of his life.

8. *Patient:* I don't like talking to the psychologist. He's OK but I've been asked *all* the questions many times already.

   Nurse: You're just good and tired of going through the whole procedure.

9. *Patient:* It's just not fair that I have to stay on the ward because of last weekend. My husband was nasty. He made me very nervous. It wasn't my fault. Can't I please go off the ward?

   Nurse: You feel the trouble at home was really your husband's fault, and now you're being punished for it.

10. *Patient:* I can't stand her anymore. She never shuts up, talk, talk, talk. She talks more than any other patient here. I don't want to sit near her or be near her.

    Nurse: She's really very annoying to you. You'd like to have nothing to do with her.

A similar set of high empathy examples was used to train a different type of helper, Home Aides. These are persons trained to provide psychological and physical assistance to elderly, disabled, psychiatriac outpatients, and similar persons in their own homes. Some of these examples were:

1. *Patient:* The old age home was really different from this apartment building. All my friends are still there. I don't even know anyone here.

   Home Aide: Sounds like you're lonely in your new home. Kind of like a stranger in a new place. I can see how it's pretty depressing missing all your friends.

   Patient: I sure *am* lonely. Every friend I have is still at the home. And it's so hard living all alone with three whole rooms to myself. I even get sad listening to people's voices in the other apartments.

Home Aide: You'd like to get out of your three lonely rooms and meet some of the other people in the building. You'd be happier if you made some new friends.

2. *Patient:* I don't like . . . It makes me feel silly for you to wash and feed me.

Home Aide: It makes you uncomfortable when someone takes care of you. You feel like you should be doing things on your own and you shouldn't need me.

Patient: Mm hm. I feel like a baby when someone's helping me. But I know I can't do stuff myself now 'cause I've tried.

Home Aide: You feel foolish when you have to rely on other people since you should be helping yourself. But you know that you need other people's help now for your own well being.

3. *Patient:* I think about things like falling down the stairs, or dropping my cigarette in bed, or a stranger coming to my house late at night . . . I don't really know what I'd do . . .

Home Aide: You're worried about whether you could handle an emergency all alone.

Patient: Yeah, I worry, *a lot* . . . I remember how scary it was the time I fainted and nobody was here to help me.

Home Aide: It would be nice to be able to count on somebody's help when something goes wrong and you're not sure you can take care of things all by yourself.

4. *Patient:* All I seem to do is care for these kids 25 hours a day! Which is a lot for a mother to do by herself!

Home Aide: Sounds as if you'd like more time to yourself or someone to help you. That's a lot for one person to do and you seem angry about it.

Patient: Why shouldn't I be angry! It's a lot to expect one person to change diapers, tie shoelaces, fix meals, yank the kids out of the mud, wash their filthy faces, constantly run to drag their stupid toys out of the road . . .

Home Aide: You get pretty angry when you constantly have to watch over those kids. It's like the more demands they make on you, the less time you have to do things for yourself.

5. *Patient:* My kids couldn't care less if I exist. They're only in Rochester, but somehow that's too far away to visit me.

Home Aide: You'd like them to visit, but somehow they don't seem interested enough.

Patient: Yeah, you got the idea. If they were interested in me they'd make the short trip to come see me. But they don't even call. And I'll be damned if I'll invite them one more time.

Home Aide: You're not about to beg them to visit you if they aren't interested. But you seem pretty hurt that your own children don't seem to care about you.

6. *Patient:* (Bashfully looking down). Do you think you could maybe show me how to, um, wash myself alone, instead of you helping me. The nurses helped me in the hospital when I had arthritis . . . Well . . . I still shake so much I'm afraid I'll drop the soap or fall down.

Home Aide: It's kind of embarrassing to need someone to help you wash. Even though right now it's probably safer that way, you'd really rather do it yourself.

Patient: You're not kidding. I can't tell you how I hated bathtime in the hospital. It was so embarrassing to have the nurse see me, you know, naked. But maybe it had to be that way. Like you say, it was safer. And also a lot cleaner than if I did it myself.

Home Aide: So even though you don't like people to see you naked, maybe it would make you feel more comfortable if I helped you while the arthritis is still bothering you.

7. *Patient:* This apartment's *nothing* like the old age home. There I had people to take care of me, and there was always something to do, and my room was arranged differently there . . .

   Home Aide: It's hard getting used to a brand new home which doesn't even seem like your home yet.

   Patient: But you know, I remember being afraid I wouldn't get used to the old age home, and I did. So, even if it's hard now in this new place, I guess I'll get used to it.

   Home Aide: Even though it's a little hard and scary at first, it's comforting to know you got used to a new home before and you can probably do it again.

8. *Patient:* (Annoyed) I wish you wouldn't put things away in my house any way you feel like it!

   Home Aide: I'm just barging right into your house, doing whatever I want with your things—as though I don't respect you.

   Patient: Yeah! I keep my things in certain places for certain reasons and I don't like anyone moving them without asking me.

   Home Aide: You're used to living a certain way and all of a sudden I come in and put things where *I* think they should go. I can understand that you'd be angry with me for barging in.

9. *Patient:* (Hectically) Oh! I'm really sorry about that chair! I was planning to reupholster it last week! And that lightbulb just blew out yesterday. (Heavily, shaking head in hand) Oh-h-h I'm sorry . . . This place is a rathole.

   Home Aide: It's kind of embarrassing when someone comes to your house for the first time and sees it looking like a mess.

   Patient: Well, *you'd* be embarrassed, wouldn't you? The furniture is a wreck, the walls are shabby, some of the lights don't work . . . I don't even want you see the kitchen . . . I feel terrible that you have to see everything like this!

   Home Aide: You're ashamed that everything in your house seems to be dirty or broken and you feel like apologizing for the mess.

10. *Patient:* The only reason I called Home Aides is that the doctor recommended it and he was standing right there. I really don't want you to take care of me. I don't need help.

    Home Aide: You feel that you can take care of yourself, and you resent it when I come in and start doing things for you.

    Patient: Yes, I *can* take care of myself! . . . Except, I guess I could use some help now that I don't see so good.

    Home Aide: You still feel up to taking care of things like before, but you realize it's a little harder now . . . Even so, you don't like to ask for help.

The significance of helper empathy in the helping enterprise has been emphasized in our earlier discussion, and we have now provided several examples. It will be useful to close this section with a listing of the guidelines, provided by Carkhuff (1969), for helpers wishing to become proficient in offering these levels of empathic responses to clients:

   1. The helper will find that he is most effective in communicating an empathic understanding when he concentrates with intensity upon the client's expressions, both verbal and nonverbal.

2. The helper will find that initially he is most effective in communicating empathic understanding when he concentrates upon responses that are interchangeable with those of the client (Level 3).

3. The helper will find that he is most effective in communicating empathic understanding when he formulates his responses in language that is most attuned to the client.

4. The helper will find that he is most effective in communicating empathic understanding when he responds in a feeling tone similar to that communicated by the client.

5. The helper will find that he is most effective in communicating empathic understanding when he is most responsive.

6. The helper will find that he is most effective in communicating empathic understanding when, having established an interchangeable base of communication (Level 3), he moves tentatively toward expanding and clarifying the client's experiences at higher levels (Levels 4 and 5).

7. The helper will find that he is most effective in communicating empathic understanding when he concentrates upon what is not being expressed by the client and, in a sense, seeks to fill in what is missing rather than simply dealing with what is present.

8. The helper will find that he is most effective in communicating empathic understanding when he employs the client's behavior as the best guideline to assess the effectiveness of his responses.

Warmth

As was true of empathy, warmth is appropriately considered a central ingredient of the helping relationship. Whatever specific change methods the helper uses, their likelihood of success seems in large measure to be a result of the relationship base on which he and the client are interacting. Helper warmth is a highly important aspect of this base. Without it, specific helping procedures may be technically correct but therapeutically impotent.

Helper warmth is also important in relationship terms because it appears to beget reciprocal warmth from the client. Truax and Carkhuff (1976), in fact, comment that "It is a rare human being who does not respond to warmth with warmth and to hostility with hostility. It is probably the most important principal for the beginning therapist to understand if he is to be successful in the therapeutic relationship." This contention received ample support in a research program conducted by the present writer (Goldstein, 1971). When liking of A toward B (helper or client) was increased by structuring, status-enhancement, or by other procedures, B's liking of A reciprocally increased—even though we had applied no procedures whatsoever to B directly. Several other researchers have reported the same reciprocal result. The Truax and Carkhuff definition of this helper quality, and their examples of its occurrence in counseling and psychotherapy, will help clarify the nature and significance of helper warmth.

The dimension of nonpossessive warmth or unconditional positive regard ranges from a high level, where the therapist warmly accepts the patient's experience as part of that person without imposing conditions, to a low level where the therapist evaluates a patient or his feelings, expresses dislike or disapproval, or expresses warmth in a selective and evaluative way.

Level 1. The therapist is actively offering advice or giving clear negative regard. He may be telling the patient what would be "best for him," or in other ways actively approving or disapproving of his behavior. The therapist's actions make himself the locus of evaluation; he sees himself as responsible for the patient.

Example

Patient: . . . and I don't, I don't know what sort of a job will be offered me, but—eh . . .

Therapist: It might not be the best in the world.

Patient: I'm sure it won't.

Therapist: And, uh . . .

Patient: . . . but . . .

Therapist: But if you can make up your mind to stomach some of the unpleasantness of things.

Patient: Um hm.

Therapist: . . . you have to go through—you'll get through it.

Patient: Yeah, I know I will.

Therapist: And, ah, you'll get out of here.

Patient: I certainly, uh, I just, I just know that I have to do it, so I'm going to do it but—it's awfully easy for me, Doctor, to (sighs) well, more than pull in my shell, I—I just hibernate. I just, uh, well, just don't do a darn thing.

Therapist: It's your own fault. (Severely)

Patient: Sure it is. I know it is. (Pause) But it seems like whenever I—here—here's the thing. Whenever I get to the stage where I'm making active plans for myself, they say I'm high. An . . .

Therapist: In other words they criticize you that . . .

Patient: Yeah.

Therapist: So tender little lady is gonna really crawl into her shell.

Patient: Well, I—I'll say "okay."

Therapist: If they're gonna throw, if they're gonna shoot arrows at me, I'll just crawl behind my shell and I won't come out of it. (Forcefully)

Patient: That's right. (Sadly)

Therapist: And that's worse. (Quickly)

Patient: (Pause) But why don't they let me be a little bit high? Why—right now I'm taking . . .

Therapist: (Interrupting). Because some people . . .

Patient: (Talking with him) . . . 600 milligrams of malorin, whatever that is, malorin.

Therapist: . . . because a lot of people here don't know you very well at all. And because people in general, at times, you have to allow that they could be stupid. You too. I mean you're stupid sometimes, so why can't other people . . .

Patient: So much of the time.

Therapist: Why can't other people? I mean, you're an intelligent person and are stupid. Why, why can't you allow that other intelligent people can also be stupid? When it comes to you they don't know very much.

Patient: Mmm. (Muttering)

Level 2. The therapist responds mechanically to the client, indicating little positive regard and hence little nonpossessive warmth. He may ignore the patient or his feelings, or display a lack of concern or interest. The therapist ignores the client at times when a nonpossessively warm response would be expected; he shows a complete passivity that communicates almost unconditional lack of regard.

Example

Patient: (Speaking throughout in a woebegone voice) You don't have to sit down and, and, and write like that but I thought he'd answer my letter. I thought, I didn't think he'd answer the letter, I thought he'd come up.

Therapist: Um, hm.

Patient: . . . and, and visit me; it's only 50, he hasn't been to visit me yet. It's only been about, uh, it's only about 50, 60 miles from here.

Therapist: Uh, hm.

Patient: And I kind of expected him last Sunday but he didn't . . .

Therapist: You were just sort of looking for him but he . . .

Patient: (Interrupting insistently) Well, I wasn't, I wasn't, I was looking for him, I wasn't looking for him. I had a kind of a half-the-way feeling that he wouldn't be up here. I know him pretty well and he's—walks around, you know, and thinks and thinks and thinks and—maybe it'll take him two or three weeks an' all of a sudden he—he'll walk in the house (laughs)—"Let's go see—so and so." (Nervous laughter) He's a—he's a lot like I am—we're all the same, I guess. He probably—read the letter and—probably never said very much, walked out, forgot about it (laughing nervously), then all of a sudden it dawned on 'im (nervous laughter) and, ah, that's, ah, that's about, about the size of it, as far as that goes. And, uh, uh, so as I say, I—I wouldn't be, I wasn't—too overly disappointed when he, when he didn't ah, ah, ah, ah, answer it or come to see me. He probably will yet. (Laughs) I'm an optimist, I always have been, he'll probably come and visit me some day. Maybe he'll come and let me go down there 'n live. Maybe he won't, won't make much difference (laughs) one way or another.

Therapist: Hmmm. You can sort of . . .

Patient: Yeah.

Therapist: . . . take things as they come. (Brightly)

Level 3. The therapist indicates a positive caring for the patient or client, but it is a semipossessive caring in the sense that he communicates to the client that his behavior matters to him. That is, the therapist communicates such things as "It is not all right if you act immorally," "I want you to get along at work," or "It's important to me that you get along with the ward staff." The therapist sees himself as responsible for the client.

Example

Patient: I still, you sorta hate to give up something that you know that you've made something out of, and, and, uh, in fact, it amounts to, uh, at least, uh, what you would, uh, earn working for somebody else, so . . .

Therapist: (Enthusiastically). O.K. What, well, eh, why don't—why don't we do it this way? That, uh I'll kind of give you some homework to do. (Laughs) And when you're going home these weekends, um, really talk to your wife, and, ah, think yourself about pretty specific possibilities for you, considering the location and considering what time of year it is and, what you can do and things like this, and, eh, then we can talk it out here and really do some, some working on this in earnest, and not just talk plans . . . (Patient answers "yeah" after every phrase or so)

Patient: (Interrupting). Well, I actually, I'd almost feel gettin' out right away but I, some-thin' sort of holds me back, yet the season isn't—there (*Therapist:* Uh, huh) and I don't know if it's good for me or not (*Therapist:* Uh, huh), but I, ah . . .

Therapist: O.K., but at least this next couple of months we can use in—trying at least to set something up or, or . . .

Patient: Cuz I feel that I, I don't know, I—feel I just want to do things again.

Therapist: (Um, hm). Uh, 'cuz the longer you stay away from work, I was just reading about that psychologist James here the other day, an' it seems like if once you get into things and work, you feel better (*Patient:* Sure) . . . and you don't uh, it seems like, uh the further you stay away from things, eh, you, well, eh, you sort'a think about it, put it that way. Um, hm. O.K. So, ah—in our thinking about it, though, that next few weeks, let's get closer to the doing of them. O.K.? (Warmly)

Patient: Well, yes, that's—what . . . .

Therapist: Sound okay to you?

Patient: Yes, It sounds okay to me.

Therapist: Good enough. (Amiably)

Level 4. The therapist clearly communicates a very deep interest and concern for the welfare of the patient, showing a nonevaluative and unconditional warmth in almost all areas of his functioning. Although there remains some conditionality in the more personal and private areas, the patient is given freedom to be himself and to be liked as himself. There is little evaluation of thoughts and behaviors. In deeply personal areas, however, the therapist may be conditional and communicate the idea that the client may act in any way he wishes—except that it is important to the therapist that he be more mature, or not regress in therapy, or accept and like the therapist. In all other areas, however, nonpossessive warmth is communicated. The therapist sees himself as responsible to the client.

Example

Therapist: One thing that occurs to me is I'm so glad you came. I was afraid you wouldn't come. I had everything prepared, but I was afraid you wouldn't come. (Pause)

Patient: What—would you have thought of me then? I guess maybe I shouldn't have, but I did anyway. (Rapidly)

Therapist: Is that—like saying, "Why or What?" But, partly you feel—maybe you shouldn't have come—or don't know if you shouldn't or "not should." There's something about—feeling bad that could make you—not want to come. I don't know if I got that right, but—because if you feel very bad then—then, I don't know. Is there anything in that?

Patient: Well—I've told you before, I mean, you know, two things that, when I feel bad. I mean one that always—I feel that there's a possibility, I suppose, that you know, that they might put me back in the hospital for getting that bad.

Therapist: Oh, I'd completely forgotten about that, yeah—yet, and that's one thing—But there is another?

Patient: Yeah, I already told you that, too.

Therapist: Oh, yeah, you sure did—I'd forgotten about it—and the other you've already said, too?

Patient: I'm sure I did tell it. (Pause)

Therapist: It doesn't come. All I have when I try to think of it is just the general sense that if you feel—very bad, then it's hard or unpleasant to—but I don't know—so I may have forgotten something—must have. (Pause)

Patient: You talk—you always, hear what I'm saying now, are so good at evading me, you always end up making me talk anyway.

Therapist: You're right.

Patient: You always comment on the question or something, and it just doesn't tell me.

Therapist: (Interjecting) Right, I just instinctively came back—to you when I wondered—what, I, well like saying, because—that's what I felt like saying. You mean to—you mean to say that a few minutes ago we had decided that I would talk . . .

Patient: Well, you—you mentioned it, but *(Therapist:* Right) that's as far as it got.

Therapist: You're right—and I just—was thinking of what you're asking—I'm more interested in you right now than anything else.

Level 5. At stage 5, the therapist communicates warmth without restriction. There is a deep respect for the patient's worth as a person and his rights as a free individual. At this level the patient is free to be himself even if this means that he is regressing, being defensive, or even disliking or rejecting the therapist himself. At this stage the therapist cares deeply for the patient as a person, but it does not matter to him how the patient chooses to behave. He genuinely cares for and deeply prizes the patient for his human potentials, apart from evaluations of his behavior or his thoughts. He is willing to share equally the patient's joys and aspirations or depressions and failures. The only channeling by the therapist may be the demand that the patient communicate personally relevant material.

Example

Patient: . . . . ever recovering to the extent where I could become self-supporting and live alone. I thought that I was doomed to hospitalization for the rest of my life and seeing some of the people over in, in the main building, some of those old people who are, who need a lot of attention and all that sort of thing, is the only picture I could see of my own future. Just one of *(Therapist:* Mhm) complete hopelessness, that there was any—

Therapist: (Interrupting). You didn't see any hope at all, did you?

Patient: Not, not in the least. I thought no one really cared and I didn't care myself, and I seriously—uh—thought of suicide; if there'd been any way that I could end it all completely and not become just a burden or an extra care, I would have committed suicide, I was that low. I didn't want to live. In fact, I hoped that I—I would go to sleep at night and not wake up, because I, I really felt there was nothing to live for *(Therapist:* Uh, huh [very softly]) Now I, I truly believe that this drug they are giving me helps me a lot, I think, I think it is one drug that really does me good *(Therapist:* Uh, hm).

Therapist: But you say that, that during this time you, you felt as though no one at all cared, as to what *(Patient:* That's right) . . . what happened to you.

Patient: And, not only that, but I hated myself so that I didn't, I, I felt that I didn't deserve to have anyone care for me. I hated myself so that I, I, I not only felt that no one did, but I didn't see any reason why they should.

Therapist: I guess that makes some sense to me now. I was wondering why it was that you were shutting other people off. You weren't letting anyone else care.

Patient: I didn't think I was worth caring for.

Therapist: So you didn't ev- maybe you not only thought you were—hopeless, but you wouldn't allow people . . . (Therapist statement is drowned out by patient).

Patient: (Interrupting and very loud). I closed the door on everyone. Yah, I closed the door on everyone because I thought I just wasn't worth bothering with. I didn't think it was worthwhile for you to bother with me. "Just let me alone and—and let me rot that's all I'm worth.'' I mean, that was my thought. And I, I, uh, will frankly admit that when the doctors were making the rounds on the ward, I mean the routine rounds, I tried to be where they wouldn't see me. The doctor often goes there on the ward and asks how everyone is and when she'd get about to me, I'd move to a spot that she's already covered . . .

Therapist: You really avoided people.

Patient: So that, so that she wouldn't, uh, talk with me (*Therapist:* Uh, hm) and when—the few times that I refused to see you, it was for the same reason. I didn't think I was worth bothering with, so why waste your time—let's just . . .

Therapist: Let me ask you, ask you something about that. Do you think it would have been, uh, better if I had insisted that, uh, uh, you come and talk with me?

Patient: No, I don't believe so, doctor. (They speak simultaneously).

Therapist: I wondered about that; I wasn't sure . . . (Softly).

Patient: I don't—I, I, I . . . (Truax and Carkhuff, 1967, 58-68.)

Raush and Bordin (1957) help define warmth further. Helper warmth they hold, has three components.

Commitment. The therapist demonstrates some degree of willingness to be of assistance to the patient. This assistance may vary in degree of activity and concreteness. For example, the therapist may offer help in the form of setting limits, breaking limits, or actively collaborating with the patient in the solution of an external problem, or he may offer help only by committing his time. At any given moment, the therapist occupies some point along a continuum representing degree of commitment. . . . The therapist most typically commits a specified amount of time to the patient; he commits, for the patient's use at those times, a private meeting place which will remain relatively undisturbed by extraneous factors, he commits his skills and his efforts at understanding and aiding the patient; he also commits to the patient a relationship in which the patient's needs and interests are dominant, and in which the therapist's personal demands are minimized. For the patient also there are commitments: to honor appointments, to pay fees regularly, to avoid conscious inhibitions of associations, to discuss impending decisions, and so forth.

Effort to understand. The therapist shows his effort to understand by asking questions designed to elicit the patient's view of himself and the world, by testing with the patient the impressions that he, the therapist, has gained of these views, and by indicating, by comments or other forms of action, his interest in understanding the patient's views. At the other extreme, aside from absence of the kind of behavior we have just described, the therapist tends to act as though he had a preconceived view of the patient, his actions, and his feelings. . . . Certainly, it is the therapist's efforts at understanding which produce the first major emotional tie between patient and therapist in most forms of psychotherapy . . . this effort on the part of the therapist will be a major determinant of ''rapport'' and of communication between patient and therapist. Such an effort on the part of the therapist may be communicated in many ways: by attentive and unintrusive listening, by questions indicative of interest, by sounds of encouragement, by any of the verbal or nonverbal cues which say in effect, ''I am interested in what you are saying and feeling—go on.'' But whatever the manner of communication, the effort at understanding on the part of the therapist is communication of warmth. . . . The patient's gratification and his willingness to communicate more freely under these circumstances . . . are ''natural'' responses to warmth, in the sense that both children and adults feel gratified when their serious communications are listened to seriously.

Spontaneity. The least spontaneous therapist is guarded, either consciously or unconsciously masking all of his feelings. These masked feelings may be intimately related to the underlying needs and feelings of the patient, or they may be those which occur as part of the natural interaction between any two people. Such a therapist maintains an impressive mien and is likely to be inhibited in all of his motor expressions, such as gestures. His verbal communications are marked by stereotype, formalism, and stiffness. The least spontaneous therapist may, however, seem to act impulsively. Such impulsivity will have a compelled, unnatural quality. . . . "Simply going through the motions of psychotherapy is not enough," is, and must be, emphasized by supervisors of students of the process. The therapist must be capable of expressing something of himself. . . . Observation of different therapists indicates considerable variability in the amount of effect expressed. Some therapists seem always to have a tight rein on themselves; they are or seem to be emotionless. Others seem to feel much freer to express themselves; they seem more "natural." (p. 352.) *

Similar behaviors represent warmth in yet other research. In one we read: "During a warm interview the interviewer smiled, nodded her head, and spoke warmly. During a cold interview she spoke unsmilingly, she did not nod her head; and she kept her voice drab and cold." As in much of this type of research, these investigators found that interviewees talked significantly† more to the warm interviewer. Another study with a similar result used a helper speaking in a "soft, melodic and pleasant voice" versus speaking in a "harsh, impersonal, and business-like voice" for the comparison of warm versus cold helpers. In a successful repeat study, the same researcher elaborated his definition of warmth in a manner akin to Raush and Bordin's "commitment" and "effort to understand." Specifically, in addition to the voice qualities, the warm helper "showed interest, concern, and attention," whereas his "cold" counterpart displayed "disinterest, unconcern, and nonattentiveness."

Though it is clear that helpers can be trained to reliably show the behavior described above, and these helper behaviors have been shown to affect what the client does, the reader must be cautioned against a too rigid adoption of "a warm stance." Smiling, a pleasant voice, and the like can indeed represent warmth. But if warmth at root is, as Raush and Bordin suggest, commitment, effort to understand and spontaneity, warmth can also be represented behaviorally by directiveness, assertiveness, autonomy-enhancing distancing, and even anger. To a large extent, it is the context and content of the helper-client interaction which will determine if a given instance of helper behavior is perceived by the client as warmth. Carkhuff and Berenson (1967) make a similar observation when they comment: ". . . it is not always communicated in warm, modulated tones of voice; it may be communicated, for example, in anger. In the final analysis, it is the client's experience of the expression that counts." (p. 28.)

---

*From Raush, H.L. and Bordin, E.S. Warmth in personality development and in psychotherapy. *Psychiatry*, 1957, **20**, 351-363. Reprinted by permission.

†The term "significantly" will be used throughout this book in its common statistical usage, i.e., a statistically significant result is a "real" one, one which might happen by chance only 5 times in 100.

Self-disclosure

The trust component of the helper-client relationship (see Fig. 2.1) may be positively influenced by helper self-disclosure (Jourard, 1964; Bierman, 1969; Johnson, 1972). Johnson and Matross (1977) describe a trust-enhancing, self-disclosure sequence in which: (1) the client discloses personal information about his needs, problems, history, relationships; (2) the helper responds with offering facilitative conditions, and reciprocates in self-disclosure by revealing such information as his views of the client, his reactions to the unfolding therapy situation, and information about himself.

A number of investigations have consistently shown that helper self-disclosure does function to elicit reciprocal client self-disclosure and ratings of greater helper trustworthiness (Bierman, 1969; Drag, 1968; Sermat and Smyth, 1973)*

MISCELLANEOUS METHODS

We have seen so far in this chapter that the helper-client relationship may be enhanced by direct statements to the client about the helper's likability (structuring); by the client's observation of a counterpart expressing attraction to a helper, or helper observation of a counterpart expressing attraction to a client (imitation); by a client hearing other clients rate a helper as attractive (conformity pressure); by describing the helper to the client as someone of considerable expertness, experience, and accomplishment, or by surrounding the helper with various signs and symbols of such expertness and achievement (status); by helper believability and openness about himself; helper credibility and self-disclosure; or by the facilitative conditions of helping behaviors actually offered the client by the helper (e.g., empathy and warmth). These several approaches may be considered to be the major methods of relationship-enhancement which are currently available, because of the amount and conclusiveness of research on each. However, certain other means for improving the nature of the helper-client interaction have also appeared in the professional literature. Each of these should be viewed by the reader as somewhat more tentative or speculative than those considered above, since the amount or quality of supporting research evidence for each is still rather small.

Helper-Client Matching

This approach to the helping relationship, in contrast to those considered above, typically does not seek to alter anything in the helper or client in order to enhance

---

*Simonson has shown in a number of studies that these positive effects are optimized when the content of what the helper discloses about himself is private (background, preferences, views), but not relevant to the helper's own, personal problems (Simonson and Apter, 1969; Simonson and Bahr, 1974.)

the goodness of their fit. Instead, an effort is made to (a) identify real characteristics of helpers and clients which are relevant to how well they relate, (b) measure helpers and clients on these characteristics, and (c) match helpers and clients into optimal (for client change) pairs based on these measurements. Much of the research on matching is conflicting or inconclusive, but some of it does lead to useful, if tentative, conclusions. The following are frequent characteristics of an optimal helper-client match:

1. Helper and client hold congruent expectations of the role each is to play in the relationship. They understand and agree upon their respective rights and obligations regarding what each is expected to do and not to do during their interactions.

2. Helper and client are both confident of positive results from their meetings. Each anticipates at least a reasonably high likelihood of client change.

3. Helper and client come from similar social, cultural, racial, and economic backgrounds.

4. Helper and client are similar in their use of language, conceptual complexity, extroversion-introversion, objectivity-subjectivity, flexibility, and social awareness.

5. Helper and client are complementary or reciprocal in their need to offer and receive inclusion, control, and affection. The need for inclusion relates to associating, belonging, and companionship versus isolation, detachment, and aloneness. Control is a power or influence dimension, and affection refers to emotional closeness, friendliness, and the like. Helper and client are complementary or reciprocal on these dimensions if the level of inclusion, affection, or control which one member needs to offer approximates the level of that dimension which the other member needs to receive.

Obviously, no given helper and client can be paired on all of these dimensions. However, the greater the number of them reflected in a particular pairing, the more likely it is that a favorable relationship will develop.

Proxemics

Proxemics is the study of personal space and interpersonal distance. Is there a connection between how far apart two persons sit and their posture, on the one hand, and the favorableness of their relationship on the other hand? First, it does appear that liking in an interview setting will lead to physical closeness and a particular type of posture. In an experiment by Leipold (1963), one group of college students were told, "We feel that your course grade is quite poor and that you have not tried your best. Please take a seat in the next room and Mr. Leipold will be in shortly to discuss this with you." Other groups heard neutral or positive statements about their course performance. Those receiving praise subsequently sat significantly closer to the interviewer; those who were criticized chose to sit further away.

A second study also suggests that increased liking leads to decreased physical distance. Walsh (1971) used imitation procedures to successfully increase how attracted a group of patients were to an interviewer. Before their interview, the office was arranged so that the patient's chair was physically light, on wheels and located at the other end of the room eight feet from where the interviewer would be sitting. Upon entering the room, the interviewer suggested to the patient that he "pull up the chair." Attracted patients pulled the chair significantly closer to the interviewer than did unattracted patients.

Our concern, of course, is the other way around, i.e., relationship-enhancement. Does close sitting and certain posturing *lead to* a favorable relationship? This notion was tested in one of our modeling studies. For some patients, the interviewer not only sat close by (27 inches), but also assumed a posture shown in other research to reflect liking. Specifically, he leaned forward (20°) toward the patient, maintained eye contact 90 percent of the time, and faced the patient directly (shoulder orientation of 0°). Very different distance and posture were involved in the contrasting condition. The interviewer was 81 inches from the patient, leaned backward 30°, showed eye contact 10 percent of the time, and faced partially away from the patient with a shoulder orientation of 30°. Results of this research did in part show that distance and posture can indeed influence the patient liking which develops. As was true in the case of helper-client matching, relevant proxemic research is not great. Tentatively, however, we may begin to view close distance and "interested" posture as probable relationship-enhancers.

Conversational "Do's" and "Don'ts"

A step by step relationship-building "cookbook" is neither possible nor desirable. Obviously, each helper-client pair is different enough from others that what we have provided in this chapter should be read and used as *general* suggestions only. How, when, and where a given procedure is used, and what specific form it takes, must be left to the good judgment of each helper. This same proviso applies to the material which follows. Wolberg (1976) has provided a listing of what he views as helper behaviors to include or avoid when trying to build a favorable helper-client relationship. Most of this listing, and the examples he provides, are reproduced below. His suggestions should be taken as guidelines only, and not as a recipe to be applied verbatim.

Avoid exclamations of surprise.

Patient: I never go out on a date without wanting to scream.
Unsuitable responses.
Therapist: Well, for heaven's sake!
Therapist: That's awful!
Therapist: Of all things to happen!

Suitable responses.

Therapist: I wonder why?
Therapist: Scream?
Therapist: There must be a reason for this.

Avoid expressions of overconcern.

Patient: I often feel as if I'm going to die.

Unsuitable responses.

Therapist: Well, we'll have to do something about that right away.
Therapist: Why, you poor thing!
Therapist: Goodness, that's a horrible thing to go through.

Suitable responses.

Therapist: That must be upsetting to you.
Therapist: Do you have any idea why?
Therapist: What brings on this feeling most commonly?

Avoid moralistic judgments.

Patient: I get an uncontrollable impulse to steal.

Unsuitable responses.

Therapist: This can get you into a lot of trouble.
Therapist: You're going to have to put a stop to that.
Therapist: That's bad.

Suitable responses.

Therapist: Do you have any idea of what's behind this impulse?
Therapist: How far back does this impulse go?
Therapist: How does that make you feel?

Avoid being punitive under all circumstances.

Patient: I don't think you are helping me at all.

Unsuitable responses.

Therapist: Maybe we ought to stop therapy.
Therapist: That's because you aren't cooperating.
Therapist: If you don't do better, I'll have to stop seeing you.

Suitable responses.

Therapist: Let's talk about this; what do you think is happening?
Therapist: Perhaps you feel I can't help you.
Therapist: Is there anything I am doing or fail to do that upsets you?

Avoid criticizing the patient.

Patient: I just refuse to bathe and get my hair fixed.

Unsuitable responses.

Therapist: Are you aware of how unkempt you look?
Therapist: You just don't give a darn about yourself, do you?
Therapist: That's like cutting off your nose to spite your face.

Suitable responses.

Therapist: There must be a reason why.
Therapist: Do you have any ideas about that?
Therapist: How does that make you feel?

Avoid making false promises.

Patient: Do you think I'll ever be normal?

Unsuitable responses.

Therapist: Oh, sure, there's no question about that.
Therapist: In a short while you're going to see a difference.
Therapist: I have great hopes for you.

Suitable responses.

Therapist: A good deal will depend on how well we work together.
Therapist: You seem to have some doubts about that.
Therapist: Let's talk about what you mean by normal.

Avoid threatening the patient.

Patient: I don't think I can keep our next two appointments, because I want to go to a concert on those days.

Unsuitable responses.

Therapist: You don't seem to take your therapy seriously.
Therapist: If you think more of concerts than coming here, you might as well not come at all.
Therapist: Maybe you'd better start treatments with another therapist.

Suitable responses.

Therapist: I wonder why the concerts seem more important than coming here.
Therapist: Maybe it's more pleasurable going to the concerts than coming here.
Therapist: What do you feel about coming here for therapy?

Avoid burdening the patient with your own difficulties.

Patient: You look very tired today.

Unsuitable responses.

Therapist: Yes I've been having plenty of trouble with sickness in my family.
Therapist: This sinus of mine is killing me.
Therapist: I just haven't been able to sleep lately.

Suitable responses.

Therapist: I wouldn't be surprised, since I had to stay up late last night. But that shouldn't interfere with our session.

Therapist: I've had a touch of sinus, but it's not serious and shouldn't interfere with our session.
Therapist: That comes from keeping late hours with meetings and things. But that shouldn't interfere with our session.

Avoid displays of impatience.

Patient: I feel helpless and I think I ought to end it all.

Unsuitable responses.

Therapist: You better "snap out of it" soon.
Therapist: Well, that's a nice attitude, I must say.
Therapist: Maybe we had better end treatment right now.

Suitable responses.

Therapist: I wonder what is behind this feeling.
Therapist: Perhaps there's another solution for your problems.
Therapist: You sound as if you think you're at the end of your rope.

Avoid political or religious discussions.

Patient: Are you going to vote Republican or Democratic?

Unsuitable responses.

Therapist: Republican, of course; the country needs good government.
Therapist: I'm a Democrat and would naturally vote Democratic.

Suitable responses.

Therapist: Which party do you think I will vote for?
Therapist: Have you been wondering about me?
Therapist: I wonder what you'd feel if I told you I was either Republican or Democrat. Would either make a difference to you?
Therapist: I vote for whoever I think is the best person, irrespective of party, but why do you ask?

Avoid arguing with the patient.

Patient: I refuse to budge an inch as far as my husband is concerned.

Unsuitable responses.

Therapist: It's unreasonable for you to act this way.
Therapist: Don't you think you are acting selfishly?
Therapist: How can you expect your husband to do anything for you if you don't do anything for him?

Suitable responses.

Therapist: You feel that there is no purpose in doing anything for him?
Therapist: Perhaps you're afraid to give in to him?
Therapist: How do you actually feel about your husband right now?

Avoid ridiculing the patient.

Patient: There isn't much I can't do, once I set my mind on it.

Unsuitable responses.

Therapist: You don't think much of yourself, do you?
Therapist: Maybe you exaggerate your abilities.
Therapist: It sounds like you're boasting.

Suitable responses.

Therapist: That puts kind of a strain on you.
Therapist: Have you set your mind on overcoming this emotional problem?
Therapist: You feel pretty confident once your mind is made up.

Avoid belittling the patient.

Patient: I am considered very intelligent.

Unsuitable responses.

Therapist: An opinion with which you undoubtedly concur.
Therapist: The troubles you've gotten into don't sound intelligent to me.
Therapist: Even a moron sometimes thinks he's intelligent.

Suitable responses.

Therapist: How do you feel about that?
Therapist: That's all the more reason for working hard at your therapy.
Therapist: That sounds as if you aren't sure of your intelligence.

Avoid blaming the patient for his failures.

Patient: I again forgot to bring my doctor's report with me.

Unsuitable responses.

Therapist: Don't you think that's irresponsible?
Therapist: There you go again.
Therapist: When I tell you the report is important, I mean it.

Suitable responses.

Therapist: I wonder why?
Therapist: Do you know why?
Therapist: Perhaps you don't want to bring it.

Avoid rejecting the patient.

Patient: I want you to like me better than any of your other patients.

Unsuitable responses.

Therapist: Why should I?
Therapist: I don't play favorites.
Therapist: I simply don't like a person like you.

Suitable responses.

Therapist: I wonder why you'd like to be preferred by me.
Therapist: Perhaps you'd feel more secure if I told you I liked you best.
Therapist: What do you think I feel about you?

Avoid displays of intolerance.

Patient: My wife got into another auto accident last week.

Unsuitable responses.

Therapist: Those women drivers.
Therapist: Women are sometimes tough to live with.
Therapist: The female of the species is the most deadly of the two.

Suitable responses.

Therapist: How does that make you feel?
Therapist: What do you think goes on?
Therapist: How did you react when you got this news?

Avoid dogmatic utterances.

Patient: I feel cold and detached in the presence of women.

Unsuitable responses.

Therapist: That's because you're afraid of women.
Therapist: You must want to detach yourself.
Therapist: You want to destroy women and have to protect yourself.

Suitable responses.

Therapist: That's interesting; why do you think you feel this way?
Therapist: How far back does this go?
Therapist: What feelings do you have when you are with women?

Avoid premature deep interpretations.

Patient: I've told you what bothers me. Now what do you think is behind it all?

Unsuitable responses.

Therapist: Well, you seem to be a dependent person and want to collapse on a parent figure.
Therapist: You've got an inferiority complex.
Therapist: You never resolved your Oedipus complex.

Suitable responses.

Therapist: It will be necessary to find out more about the problem before I can offer a valid opinion of it.
Therapist: We'll continue to discuss your attitudes, values and particularly your feelings, and before long we should discover what is behind your trouble.
Therapist: That's for us to work on together. If I gave you the answers, it wouldn't be of help to you.

Avoid the probing of traumatic material when there is too great resistance.

Patient: I just don't want to talk about sex.

Unsuitable responses.

Therapist: You'll get nowhere by avoiding this.
Therapist: You must force yourself to talk about unpleasant things.
Therapist: What about your sex life?

Suitable responses.

Therapist: It must be hard for you to talk about sex.

Therapist: All right, you can talk about anything else you feel is important.
Therapist: Sex is always a painful subject to talk about.

Avoid unnecessary reassurance.

Patient: I think I'm the most terrible, ugly, weak, most contemptible person in the world.

Unsuitable responses.

Therapist: That's silly. I think you're very good looking and a wonderful person in many ways.
Therapist: Take it from me, you are not.
Therapist: You are one of the nicest people I know.

Suitable responses.

Therapist: Why do you think you feel that way?
Therapist: How does it make you feel to think that of yourself?
Therapist: Do others think the same way about you?

Express open-mindedness, even toward irrational attitudes.

Patient: I think that all men are jerks.

Unsuitable responses.

Therapist: That's a prejudiced attitude to hold.
Therapist: You ought to be more tolerant.
Therapist: With such attitudes you'll get nowhere.

Suitable responses.

Therapist: What makes you feel that way?
Therapist: Your experiences with men must have been disagreeable for you to have this feeling.
Therapist: Understandably you might feel this way right now, but there may be other ways of looking at the situation that may reveal themselves later on.

Respect the right of the patient to express different values and preferences from yours.

Patient: I don't like the pictures on your walls.

Unsuitable responses.

Therapist: Well, that's just too bad.
Therapist: They are considered excellent pictures by those who know.
Therapist: Maybe your taste will improve as we go on in therapy.

Suitable responses.

Therapist: Why?
Therapist: What type of pictures do you like?
Therapist: What do you think of me for having such pictures?

Make sympathetic remarks where indicated.

Patient: My husband keeps drinking and then gets violently abusive in front of the children.

Unsuitable responses.

Therapist: Why do you continue living with him?
Therapist: Maybe you do your share in driving him to drink.
Therapist: He's a no-good scoundrel.

Suitable responses.

Therapist: This must be very upsetting to you.
Therapist: It must be very difficult to live with him under these circumstances.
Therapist: You must find it hard to go on with this kind of threat over you. (pp. 584-590.)*

PRESCRIPTIVE CONSIDERATIONS

In Chapter One we cautioned that the change methods described in this book are optimally used *prescriptively*. In this view, a given change method is or is not to be recommended as a function of specific characteristics of the client, helper and/or therapy involved. Does this caution also apply to the sacrosanct therapeutic relationship? When there exists a mass of prorelationship, individual therapy literature; a substantial case for the importance of relationship forces in group therapy; and recently, a growing body of evidence championing the potency of the relationship in the behavior therapies, do exceptions to the general rule exist? It appears that the answer may be yes. Addressing this issue elsewhere, we noted:

> There are individuals whose developmental history shows the nonreinforcement or direct punishment of affiliative behavior. This pattern can occur when parents thwart dependency responses while at the same time providing an aggressive model from whom the child can learn aggressive means of responding in interpersonal situations. . . . Fear of dependency combined with such easy access to aggression can effectively shut off possible correction by other more benevolent societal agents since they are automatically alienated at first contact. (Goldstein, Heller & Sechrest, 1966 p. 159.)

Consistent with this "low relatability potential" view, Redl and Wineman (1957) recommend that predelinquent youngsters initially be offered a somewhat impersonal and objective style of interaction by the helper. The helper in particular is warned against overwhelming the client with the type of close, warm relationship we have been encouraging throughout this chapter. What other prescriptive constraints optimally should be added vis à vis the therapeutic relationship involving other types of clients is a matter of considerable potential significance, clearly worthy of further empirical inquiry.

SUMMARY

For whom is this chapter written? Who should our helpers be? Relationship-enhancing procedures, as well as the many helper methods described in the chapters which follow, are not the private property of a chosen few who happen

---

*From Wollberg, L.R. *The technique of psychotherapy.* 2nd ed. New York: Grune and Stratton, 1967. Reprinted by permission of Grune & Stratton, Inc. and the author.

to have earned certain professional credentials. Certainly, such training can lead to skills of considerable positive consequence for client change. But, at least as important is the kind of person the helper is. We are in strong agreement with Strupp (1973), who observes:

> It seems that there is nothing esoteric or superhuman about the qualities needed by a good therapist! They are the attributes of a good parent and a decent human being who has a fair degree of understanding of himself and his interpersonal relations so that his own problems do not interfere, who is reasonably warm and empathic, not unduly hostile or destructive, and who has the talent, dedication, and compassion to work cooperatively with others. (Strupp, 1973, p. 2.)

Thus, the potential helper's personal background, degree of self-understanding, maturity, typical ways of relating, and concern for others are all as crucial to the outcome of his helping effort as is his formal training as a helper.

We have held throughout this chapter that without a favorable helper-client relationship, client change will rarely occur. With such a relationship, client change is possible, or even probable, but not inevitable. Other, more specific change measures must typically be utilized in addition. We leave to the chapters which follow the task of fully describing and illustrating these specific procedures.

REFERENCES

Bierman, R. Dimensions for interpersonal facilitation in psychotherapy and child development. *Psychological Bulletin*, 1969, 72, 338-352.

Carkhuff, R.F. *Helping and human relations.* New York: Holt, Rinehart and Winston, 1969.

Carkhuff, R.F. and Berenson, B.G. *Beyond counseling and therapy.* New York: Holt, Rinehart and Winston, 1967.

Drag, L.R. Experimenter-subject interaction: A situational determinant of differential levels of self-disclosure. Unpublished Master's thesis. University of Florida, 1968.

Frank, J.D. *Persuasion and healing.* Baltimore: Johns Hopkins Press, 1961.

Goldstein, A.P. *Psychotherapeutic attraction.* New York: Pergamon Press, 1971.

―――. *Structured learning therapy.* New York: Academic Press, 1973.

Goldstein, A.P., Heller, K. and Sechrest, L.B. *Psychotherapy and the psychology of behavior change.* New York: John Wiley, 1966.

Haley, J. *Strategies of psychotherapy.* New York: Grune and Stratton, 1963.

Johnson, D.W. *Reaching out: Interpersonal effectiveness and self-actualization.* Englewood Cliffs, N.J.: Prentice-Hall, 1972.

―――. Communication in conflict situations: A critical review of the research. *International Journal of Group Tensions*, 1973, 3, 46-67.

Johnson, D.W. and Matross, R. Interpersonal influence in psychotherapy: a social psychological view. In A.S. Gurman and A.M. Razin (Eds.) *Effective Psychotherapy*. New York: Pergamon Press, 1977. pp. 395-432.

Jourard, S.M. *The transparent self*. Toronto: Van Nostrand, 1964.

Leipold, W.E. Psychological distance in a dyadic interview. Unpublished Doctoral dissertation, University of North Dakota, 1963.

Orne, M.T. and Wender, P.H. Anticipatory socialization for psychotherapy. *American Journal of Psychiatry*, 1968, *124*, 1202-1212.

Raush, H.L. and Bordin, E.S. Warmth in personality development and in psychotherapy. *Psychiatry*, 1957, *20*, 351-363.

Redl, F. and Wineman, D. *The aggressive child*. Glencoe, Ill.: Free Press, 1957.

Sabalis, R.F. Subject authoritarianism, interviewer status, and interpersonal attraction. Unpublished Master's thesis, Syracuse University, 1969.

Schmidt, L.D. and Strong, S.R. Expert and inexpert counselors. *Journal of Counseling Psychology*, 1970, *17*, 115-118.

Sermat, V. and Smyth, M. Content analysis of verbal communication in the development of a relationship: Conditions influencing self-disclosure. *Journal of Personality and Social Psychology*, 1973, 26, 332-346.

Simonson, N. and Apter, S. Therapist disclosure in psychotherapy. Presented at Eastern Psychological Assoc., Philadelphia, April, 1969.

Simonson, N. and Bahr, S. Self-disclosure by the professional and paraprofessional therapist. *Journal of Consulting and Clinical Psychology*, 1974, 42, 359-363.

Streltzer, N.E. and Koch, G.V. Influence of emotional role-playing on smoking habits and attitudes. *Psychological Reports*, 1968, *22*, 817-820.

Strong, S.R. and Schmidt, L.D. Expertness and influence in counseling. *Journal of Counseling Psychology*, 1970, *17*, 81-87.

Strupp, H.H. On the basic ingredients of psychotherapy. *Journal of Counseling and Clinical Psychology*, 1973, *41*, 1-8.

Truax, C.B. and Carkhuff, R.R. *Toward effective counseling and psychotherapy*. Chicago: Aldine, 1967.

Walsh, W.G. The effects of conformity pressure and modeling on the attraction of hospitalized patients toward an interviewer. Unpublished Doctoral dissertation, Syracuse University, 1971.

Wolberg, L.R. *The technique of psychotherapy*, 2nd ed. New York: Grune and Stratton, 1967.

3
Attitude Modification Methods*
David W. Johnson

Attempts to influence our attitudes happen many times a day. Advertisers try to influence us to buy all sorts of goods and services, professors attempt to influence college students to study, friends try to influence each other's attitudes toward latest fads, and counselors try to influence the self-attitudes of clients. Each of us tries to change other people's attitudes and each of us is influenced by others who are trying to change our attitudes. The frequency and persuasiveness of attempts to influence our attitudes make the act of attitude acquisition and change one of the most important concerns of people interested in helping themselves and others change.

How does attitude acquisition and modification relate to helping people change? A 15-year-old girl is influenced by her friends and her boyfriend to believe that she is in love and therefore, she should engage in sexual relations. She later becomes pregnant and must decide whether to have the child or obtain an abortion. She asks her parents, her friends, her minister, her doctor, and a counselor to help her make a decision. Each of the persons from whom she has requested help will try to influence her attitudes toward abortion and childbearing.

A 23-year-old teacher begins his career in an inner-city school in which 90 percent of the students are from a lower-class background. There is a great deal of hostility toward teachers, and the students are generally uncooperative and antagonistic. After two frustrating months the teacher becomes hopelessly convinced that he is unable to teach. He goes to several fellow teachers, a couple of former college teachers, his girlfriend, his parents and two of the students, asking whether he should stay in teaching, switch schools, or quit and become an

*The author wishes to express his indebtedness to Ronald P. Matross for his help in preparing this chapter.

insurance salesman. Each of the persons he talks to will try to influence his attitudes toward teaching, his current students, his abilities as a teacher and his performance over the past two months.

A liberal student prides herself on her participation in programs aimed at reducing the discrimination against Native Americans in her community. She returns to school and finds that she has been placed with a Native American roommate. Finding that they keep different hours, have completely different friends, cannot communicate on a very intimate level, and want to study at different times, she becomes more and more hostile toward her roommate. She feels increasing guilt about mistreating a Native American as she grows more and more overtly hostile. The situation becomes unbearable because she cannot resolve the fact that she wants to campaign for Native American rights but does not want to live with her Native American roommate. She goes to friends, a counselor, and a stranger she meets in a bar for advice. Each of the persons she talks with will try to influence her attitudes toward herself, her roommate, Native Americans and civil rights.

When people ask you for help they have certain attitudes about themselves and their situations. They want to discuss their problems with you and receive guidance. Part of any helping process consists of clarifying current attitudes toward the significant people involved in their problems and toward alternative actions that can be taken to solve the problem. An integral part of many problems are attitudes that lead to self-destructive behaviors and to thought-patterns that cause depression, anxiety, anger, guilt, and resentment. You, as a helper, will want to clarify and modify such attitudes. No psychological problem can be solved, no helping process can be conducted without attempts to change attitudes.

Whenever you try to help another person, you need to know what attitudes are, why attitudes are important, and how attitudes are acquired and modified. In addition, you need to know which attitudes promote psychological health, how to establish the conditions necessary for attitude change, and the alternative procedures that exist for modifying destructive attitudes and promoting constructive ones. All of these topics will be discussed in this chapter.

WHAT ARE ATTITUDES?

Attitudes are a combination of concepts, information, and emotions that result in a predisposition to respond favorably or unfavorably toward particular people, groups, ideas, events, or objects. The affective component of attitudes consists of the evaluation, liking, or emotional response. The conceptual and informational components of attitudes consist of the frame of reference and the information the person has about the target of the attitude. When a student says, "I like my professor because she really knows what she is talking about," the student is expressing an attitude that has an emotional component (liking), a conceptual component (I, my, teacher), and an informational component (knows what she is talking about). Such an attitude does not always need to be expressed verbally. When a student leaps up and runs out of the room when a certain professor enters the room, the student is expressing an attitude toward that professor.

Attitudes can facilitate or frustrate the living of a satisfying and fulfilling life. Some attitudes, like positive self-esteem, help people function effectively in a variety of situations. Other attitudes, like fear of failure, interfere with effective functioning. *Appropriate attitudes* are attitudes that promote people's ability to carry on those transactions with their environment that result in people maintaining themselves, growing, and flourishing. *Inappropriate attitudes* are attitudes that make for a more painful and troubled life through decreasing people's abilities to maintain themselves, develop in constructive and healthy ways, and flourish as persons. Appropriate attitudes promote effective behavior and feelings of satisfaction, enjoyment, and happiness. Inappropriate attitudes promote self-defeating behavior and feelings of depression, anger, anxiety, shame, and guilt. These feelings are not only caused by attitudes; many immediate experiences can cause joy or depression. But if negative feelings become long term and habitual, it is because they are sustained by attitudes. Many people learn attitudes that sustain negative and self-destructive feelings; many people are taught attitudes that lead to self-defeating and frustrating cycles of behavior. Such attitudes are taught and may be supported by their family, peers, reference groups, society, and culture. With no opportunity for change, self-defeating attitudes affect all aspects of a person's life. People with self-destructive attitudes need help in changing to more appropriate and self-enhancing ones.

What purpose do attitudes serve? Why does a person have attitudes? In daily living a person is constantly confronted with a variety of regularly repeated situations. There probably is not a day in the life of college students that they do not see an attractive person of the opposite sex. What they consider to be attractive, what they consider an appropriate way to meet a person of the opposite sex, are attitudes that affect how they behave. Attitudes are part of the cognitive structures people learn to organize and systematize their experiences and behavior. The attitudinal component of a cognitive structure is especially useful to people in the sense that it gives them a simplified and practical guide for appropriate behavior. In daily living people are constantly confronted with a variety of regularly repeated situations. A major function of attitudes is to help people anticipate and cope with recurrent events. Because all experiences cannot be grasped in their uniqueness, people tend to group experiences into convenient categories and apply certain reactions to any experiences that fit into one of their categories. Attitudes make many reactions automatic, thus freeing people to deal with the truly unique experiences of daily life. Reliance on attitudes is part of a fundamental psychological economy that can be described as a "least-effort" principle: Whenever possible, apply past solutions to present problems or, whenever possible, apply past reactions to present experiences.

Attitudes are relatively enduring predispositions that give continuity of behavior over time. There are four important aspects of acquiring attitudes:

1. All attitudes are learned. They do not magically appear as a person matures physically. Attitudes are acquired through direct instruction, by taking on the attribute of someone a person loves or admires (identification), and by adopting social roles such as pupil-teacher, husband-wife, doctor, or mechanic.
2. All attitudes are continually open to modification and change. *Attitude change* is the acquisition, reversal, or intensification of an attitude. Once attitudes are learned, they are not written in concrete, but rather are continuously modified according to the person's experiences.
3. The learning and modification of attitudes have their origins in interaction with other people. The interaction can be direct, or indirect, through movies, advertisements, books, or television. It is, however, always within systems of human relationships that attitudes are learned and modified.
4. Acquiring and modifying attitudes is a dynamic process in which other people confront the person with expectations as to what are appropriate attitudes at the same time the person is struggling to increase his or her competence in dealing with the environment by seeking out attitudes that appear to be helpful. People are not passive learners. They seek out and select what they want to attend to, with whom they want to identify, what social roles they want to adopt, and how they want to respond to the demands of parents, professors, and peers. Others are also active, confronting people with expectations as to what are appropriate behaviors and attitudes. There are psychological forces coming from within that drive people to acquire and modify attitudes, there are external forces imposing attitudes, and the two are in a dynamic state of tension or equilibrium in which an accommodation is reached.

Changing one's attitudes is often a crucial step in changing one's way of life. A change in attitudes about one's self-worth, for example, may lead to improved social relationships, a new career, and a wide variety of other changes in behavior. The purpose of helping other people change inappropriate attitudes to appropriate ones is to promote more constructive patterns of thinking and behaving on their part. While behavior has many determinants other than attitudes, and while several years ago the relationship between attitudes and behavior was hotly debated, current evidence indicates that attitudes are an important determinant of behavior (Eagly & Himmelfarb, 1978).

MODELS FOR CHANGE

When a person approaches you for help, you need a model of psychological health and a model of the procedures you will use in helping the person. A model of psychological health indicates what the person will be like when the changes have taken place successfully. The discussion of social competencies in the next section is an example of such a model. Procedures used to help another person deal constructively with problems include: (1) clarifying what the person's problems are by asking the person to describe the problems and the patterns of thinking and behaving that lead to the problems; it is important that the person formulate his own definition of the problem rather than having you tell him what his problems are, (2) establishing the conditions for attitude change by building trust and reducing the person's defensiveness, egocentrism, and demoralization; (3) promoting changes in the person's attitudes by selecting and applying a theory (or combination of theories) of attitude change; (4) stabilizing the new attitudes by building supports that will maintain them.

PSYCHOLOGICAL HEALTH

The author once spent several months conducting group psychotherapy sessions at a home for teenage runaways who had drug abuse problems. One of those living in the home was a thirteen-year-old girl named Shirley. Shirley at that time was very young looking, intelligent, and quite appealing to other people. Yet she had repeatedly run away from home and from a mental hospital where she had been placed by her parents. She was a heavy drug user. She had attempted suicide more than once by slashing her wrists. After one such attempt, she stated, "I have nothing to live for! Every drug experience possible I have had. Every sexual experience possible I have had. There is nothing left for me to do or feel or experience!" There was no one Shirley could turn to for affection and support. She was locked into her own needs and feelings, unable to view situations from anything but an egocentric point of view. She lacked any sense of purpose and meaning in life. She viewed societal responsibilities such as school and career as arbitrary attempts to destroy her individuality. She had no sense of her interdependence with other people in her family, community, and society. Her sense of identity was fragmented and diffused, resulting in dissociation from others and a lack of any distinct impression of who or what kind of person she was.

Shirley's case is an example of the close relationship between socialization toward appropriate attitudes and psychological health. The goal of socialization is to encourage the development of productive and fulfilled individuals who contribute to the survival and improvement of their families, communities, and society. It is within such collaborative social systems that psychological health is defined. The ability to build and maintain collaborative relationships is often cited as a primary manifestation of psychological health, and several psychologists have noted that interdependent relationships are a psychological necessity for humans (see Johnson, 1979). There are literally hundreds of studies comparing the effects of cooperative, competitive, and individualistic efforts toward achieving goals; for a review of these studies see Johnson and R. Johnson

(1975, 1978). The overall results indicate that cooperation, compared with competitive and individualistic efforts, promotes positive interpersonal relationships characterized by mutual liking, positive attitudes toward each other, mutual concern, friendliness, attentiveness, feelings of obligation to each other, and a desire to earn the respect of others. In addition, cooperation promotes lower levels of personal anxiety; greater feelings of personal security; more mutual support, assistance, helping, and sharing; more frequent, effective, and accurate communication; higher levels of trust among people; more mutual influence; more prosocial behavior; more constructive management of conflicts; more positive self-esteem; greater task orientation, coordination of efforts, involvement in task, satisfaction from efforts, and achievement; and more empathy and ability to take the emotional perspective of others. These empirically demonstrated effects of cooperation are congruent with the proposition that cooperativeness is a central aspect of psychological health. Johnson and Norem-Hebeisen (1977), furthermore, have demonstrated a positive relationship between cooperativeness and psychological health. *Psychological health*, therefore, can be defined as the ability to be aware of and manage effectively one's cooperative interactions with other people.

It is within interpersonal relationships that psychological illness or health is developed. And it is within a helping relationship that inappropriate, self-destructive attitudes are changed into self-enhancing ones. In order to build and maintain the relationships so necessary for psychological health, children, adolescents, and adults need to develop a set of basic attitudes and abilities (Johnson and Matross, 1977; Johnson, 1979). The first is a generalized interpersonal trust that one can rely on the affection and support of other people. Distrustful attitudes that others are harsh and undependable have been postulated to lead to habitual affective states of depression, anxiety, fear, and apprehension and to beliefs that others are critical, rejecting, humiliating, inconsistent, unpredictable, undependable, and exploitative. The second is the ability to understand how a situation appears to another person and how that person is reacting cognitively and affectively. This competency includes all aspects of perspective-taking and is the opposite of egocentrism. Both cognitive-developmental and social psychologists have emphasized the importance of this competency for healthy social development. The third aspect of healthy psychological development is a meaningful purpose and direction in life, a sense of "where I am going." Everyone needs a purpose that is valued by others and that is similar to the goals of the significant people in one's life. Feelings of involvement, commitment, and meaning and beliefs that life is worthwhile, challenging, and has purpose depends on a sense of direction. People without direction flounder from one tentative activity to another, search for experiences to give their life meaning, refuse to assume responsibility for their choices, make little effort to achieve their goals, fail to use their competencies, and have low aspirations.

Fourth is an awareness of meaningful cooperative interdependence with other people. There is nothing more personally rewarding and satisfying than being part of a joint effort to achieve important goals. Friendships and emotional bonds are developed through cooperative interaction. In a highly technical society such as ours high levels of interdependence are the rule, not the exception. People who are unaware of their interdependence with others usually feel alienated, lonely, isolated, worthless, inferior and defeated. Their attitudes will reflect low self-esteem, an emphasis on short-term gratification, and the conviction that no one cares about them or their capabilities. Such people are often impulsive, have fragmented relationships, withdraw from relationships with other people, and are insensitive to their own and other's needs.

Finally, every person needs a strong and integrated sense of personal identity. An *identity* is a consistent set of attitudes that define "Who I am." It serves as an anchor in life. The world can change, other people can change, career and family life can change, but there is something about oneself that remains the same. During infancy, childhood, adolescence, and early adulthood, a person has several identities. Development and socialization, however, have to result in a basic unified personal identity being formulated. A diffused and ambiguous identity results in disassociation from other people and an avoidance of growth-producing experiences. People without an integrated and coherent self-identity will chronically feel anxiety, insecurity, depression, cynicism, defensiveness, unhappiness, and self-rejection. They will be unable to maintain relationships, will have transient values and interests, and will search frantically for a set of beliefs to cling to in order to superficially achieve a sense of unity.

An alarming number of young adults in our society have a basic distrust of others, are unable to view situations from perspectives other than their own, have no sense of purpose and direction, feel disconnected and estranged from the people and activities of the social systems of which they are a part, and have a diffused and ambiguous identity. They need to change inappropriate and self-destructive attitudes that prevent their building and maintaining collaborative relationships with members of their family, school, community, and career organization to more appropriate ones. In order to do so you will need to establish the conditions for attitude modification, help the person change his attitudes, and then proceed to stabilize the new, more appropriate, attitudes.

CONDITIONS FOR ATTITUDE CHANGE

Ellen, the roommate of one of your friends, has been depressed for several weeks. She is thinking about quitting school, and sometimes even talks about suicide. No one seems to know why she is so despondent. At your friend's request, you sit down with Ellen and ask her what is the matter. Ellen appears ambivalent; she wants to talk with someone about her problems but, at the same time, is afraid to do so. The first step in helping Ellen is to establish the conditions for attitude change to take place. Trust needs to be built and maintained, the defensiveness that protects her current attitudes needs to be reduced, the ego-centrism that prevents Ellen from seeing her problems from new perspectives needs to be decreased, and demoralization that decreases Ellen's motivation to solve her problems needs to be reduced. Your effectiveness as a helping person will be greatly increased if you learn to build trust and reduce the obstacles to attitude change.

Kurt Lewin, the respected social psychologist, observed that there are three ways to bring about change in a person: you can add forces for change, you can reduce forces currently preventing change, and you can redirect current forces to support change. Most individuals first try to add forces for change when they seek to alter someone's attitudes and adopt new attitudes. Adding forces for change, however, has its disadvantages. If Ellen, for example, is afraid of potential embarrassment and humiliation if she talks openly about her problems, trying to persuade her to do so will only increase her fear. Lewin notes that a more effective way to change attitudes is to reduce the forces currently prevent-ing change. Thus, you could identify Ellen's fears and try to reduce them before suggesting that she discuss them with you. The most promising strategy in helping people change their inappropriate attitudes, then, is to reduce the forces preventing such changes before advocating new and more constructive attitudes and behaviors.

Building and Maintaining Trust

If Ellen is going to openly discuss her problems and attitudes with you, if she is going to be open to your influence attempts, she must trust you. Effective communication, openness in discussing problems and being influenced, and the success of problem solving all depend on building and maintaining a high level of trust (see Johnson, 1974; Johnson and Matross, 1977). Although the attitude that one can rely on the affection and support of other people is a predisposition that varies from person to person (and tends to be unrealistically low or high in some people), within any specific helping relationship trust has to be built and main-tained. And trust constantly increases and decreases as the relationship changes and varies.

Despite the importance of trust in a helping relationship, almost no research has been done on how trust may be developed. Perhaps the only operational model specifying how a person can build and maintain trust in a helping relation-ship is as follows: (1) the client takes a risk by disclosing his problems, feelings, attitudes, ideas, and behaviors; (2) the helper responds with warmth, accurate understanding, and cooperative intentions; (3) the helper reciprocates to some extent the client's disclosures by disclosing such information as his perceptions of the client, reactions to what is taking place within the helping situation, and aspects about himself that are appropriate.

This operational model is based on the research of Johnson, 1972a; Johnson and F. Johnson, 1975; and Johnson and Noonan, 1972.

For effective helping to take place, the client must disclose relevant information concerning his attitudes and problems. Such disclosures make the client vulnerable to possible rejection, scorn, ridicule, shame, or exploitation. The client is dependent on the helper not to take advantage of the client's vulnerability. Vulnerability exists when a person has taken a risk that exposes him to potentially harmful consequences. Because of the client's vulnerability, the helper temporarily has power over the client's feelings. The helper can make the client feel bad by responding with rejection or ridicule, or the helper can make the client feel good by responding with acceptance and understanding. Trust is built when the helper does not exploit the client's vulnerability; trust is damaged when the helper uses or is seen as using his power to harm the client. When the client feels rejected, the frequency and depth of his self-disclosures will decrease (Colson, 1968; Johnson and Noonan, 1972; Taylor, Altman, and Sorrentine, 1969).

The client's choosing to self-disclose is only the initial step toward building trust in a helping relationship. The client's self-disclosures must be responded to by the helper. There is evidence that the *expression of warmth, accurate understanding*, and *cooperative intentions* increase trust in a relationship, even when there are unresolved conflicts between the two people involved (Johnson, 1971b; Johnson, McCarty, and Allen, 1974; Johnson and Noonan, 1972). In order to be an effective helper, you need to be skilled in these three behaviors.

Warmth is a feeling, and it is important to express feelings clearly and unambiguously in a helping relationship. Clearly communicating your feelings depends on your being aware of your feelings, accepting them, and being skillful in their constructive expression. Verbally, feelings are most effectively expressed by directly describing them. A description of a feeling must be a personal statement (that is, refer to "I," "me," or "my") and specify some kind of feeling by name (I like you), figure of speech (I feel close to you), or action urge (I feel like hugging you). Further examples of the verbal expression of warmth include, "I always look forward to seeing you," "I feel like you are a true friend," and "I feel warm toward you." The more clearly your words describe your feelings, the more effective the communication will be between you and the person you are helping.

In communicating feelings the verbal component will usually carry less than 35 percent of the social meaning and the nonverbal component will carry more than 65 percent (McCroskey, Larson, and Knapp, 1971). In addition to words, we communicate by our manner of dress, physique, posture, body tension, facial expressions, degree of eye contact, hand and body movements, tone of voice, continuities in speech (such as rate, duration, nonfluencies, and pauses), spatial distance, and touch. In order to communicate warmth to another person, therefore, you must be concerned with the nonverbal messages you are sending. The specific nonverbal cues used to communicate warmth are a soft tone of voice, a smiling and interested facial expression, a relaxed posture in which you are leaning forward slightly, direct eye contact, soft touches, open and welcoming gestures, and close spatial distance.

The importance of making your verbal and nonverbal messages congruent cannot be overemphasized. If you wish to express warmth, your words and your nonverbal cues must all communicate warmth. Contradictory messages can easily be interpreted by the person you are trying to help as untrustworthiness and inauthenticity. For a client to believe that your expression of feelings is genuine, the verbal and nonverbal messages must be congruent.

Expressing warmth is a skill that is developed like any other skill; it is broken down into parts and practiced until you can perform the skill naturally and easily. Readers should practice both the verbal and nonverbal messages necessary to communicate warmth until they are natural, automatic expressions of your feelings. For specific exercises and a more thorough discussion of the expression of feelings see Johnson (1972a, 1978).

Besides expressing warmth you need to be skillful in conveying to the client that you accurately understand what he is saying, how he is feeling, and the situation he is in. Accurate understanding is a nonevaluative and interested taking of the perspective or frame of reference of another person by restating the content, feelings, and meaning expressed in the other's messages. Accurate understanding has often been called role reversal as it involves taking the other's role in restating his messages. The basic rule to follow in accurate understanding is that you can reply to a person's messages only after you have first restated the content, feelings, and meaning of the other accurately and to the other's satisfaction. The general guidelines for accurate understanding are:

1. Restate the sender's expressed content, feelings, and meaning in your own words rather than mimicking or parroting his exact words.
2. Preface restated remarks with, "You feel . . .," "You mean . . .," "You think . . .," "It seems to you . . .," and so on.
3. Avoid any indication of approval or disapproval, agreement or disagreement; your statement must be nonevaluative.
4. Make your nonverbal messages congruent with your verbal restatement. Look attentive, interested, open to the other's ideas and feelings. Look like you are concentrating on what the other is trying to communicate.

For specific exercises to develop your skills in accurate understanding, see Johnson (1972a, 1978).

Communicating cooperative intentions is a third aspect of expressing acceptance. When a person asks you for help, you must express the willingness to give that help and the commitment to engage in the cooperative problem solving necessary to solve the person's problems and change the person's attitudes. Cooperative intentions indicate that you are not going to exploit the person's vulnerability and will have a nonevaluative and interested response to the disclosures and behavior of the person seeking help. In a helping relationship, mutual goals concerning constructive changes in the client's actions, feelings, and attitudes are set, and a plan for how the relationship will facilitate the accomplishment of such goals is agreed upon. Cooperative interaction is the coordination of efforts among individuals to achieve mutual goals and, therefore, all helping relationships are based on cooperative interaction and problem solving. Cooperative intentions are expressed through verbal and nonverbal messages that you want to help the other person, want to understand the person's situation, and wish to cooperate in a plan to improve the other's life. For specific exercises to build your skills in expressing cooperative intentions and in cooperative problem solving see Johnson (1972a, 1978) and Johnson and F. Johnson (1975).

After the client has risked disclosing his problems, feelings and attitudes, and after the helper has responded with warmth, accurate understanding, and cooperative intentions, there is still an important step in building and maintaining trust. The disclosures of the client must at times be reciprocated by disclosures by the helper. As a general rule, the more open and disclosing the helper is, the more open and disclosing the client will be (Bierman, 1969; Chittick and Himelstein, 1967; Drag, 1968; Jourard and Friedman, 1970; Murdoch, Chenowith, and Riseman, 1969; Taylor, 1964; Worthy, Gary, and Kahn, 1969; Sermat and Smyth, 1973). A helper is also viewed as more trustworthy and likeable when the helper discloses how he is reacting to the present situation and gives information about the past that is relevant to understanding his reaction to the present. Johnson and Noonan (1972) conducted a study in which trained confederates either reciprocated or did not reciprocate a person's disclosures; they found that the subjects trusted and liked the confederates in the reciprocation condition significantly more than did the subjects in the nonreciprocation condition.

How does a helper disclose in a way that increases trust in a relationship? Self-disclosure is revealing how you are reacting to the present situation and giving any information about the past that is relevant to understanding how you are reacting to the present; it is the sharing of information, ideas, thoughts, feelings, attitudes, and reactions relevant to the issue being discussed. Reciprocated disclosures indicate your willingness to trust the client, thus promoting the client's further trust of you. Your willingness to risk being vulnerable to a client increases the likelihood that the client will risk being vulnerable to you. If, for example, Ellen confides that she is disappointed in your efforts to help her, she is risking your rejection. You will build trust if you disclose your own feelings about the situation, such as your frustration in not being able to give her the kind of immediate relief that she expected.

Self-disclosure is based on self-awareness and self-acceptance; in order to disclose your reactions, you have to be aware of your reactions and accept them enough so that you will not defensively hide or misrepresent them. For specific exercises to develop skills in self-disclosure see Johnson (1972a, 1978).

Reduction of Egocentrism

As you and Ellen discuss her problems you may notice that her depression focuses most of her attention on herself and her sadness. Many troubled people become highly egocentric in the sense that they can view their problems and situation only from their own perspective. In order for you to influence Ellen or other clients to change their destructive and inappropriate attitudes, you must reduce their fixation on their own point of view. Egocentrism is the defensive adherence to one's own point of view and frame of reference; it is the inability or unwillingness to take the perspective of another person; it is being locked into one's personal perspective so that the world is viewed only from one's self-centered point of view and one is unaware of other perspectives and of one's own limitations in perspective. Egocentrism is closely related to closed-mindedness, which is the withdrawal (psychologically or physically) from opportunities to explore attitudes and persepctives that are discrepant from one's own and the seeking to bolster one's attitudes and perspectives by seeking out others with similar views (Rokeach, 1960). The anxiety and defensiveness generated by the fear that others are evaluating one's statements and are unwilling to consider one's point of view often promotes egocentrism (Johnson, 1971d; Rapoport, 1960; Rogers, 1965). When people are feeling defenseive they will protect themselves by stubbornly adhering to their present attitudes and refusing to communicate with others who have opposing points of view (Johnson, 1974). Defensiveness reduces the tolerance of ambiguity and one's openness to the new and unfamiliar, as well as a primitivization and stereotyping of thought processes and the reduction in ability to solve problems (Johnson and R. Johnson, 1975; Rokeach, 1960).

Clients will be influenced by the helper's messages to the extent that they attend to the messages, accurately comprehend the helper's statements, and accept the content as valid. In order for clients to change their attitudes they need to become sufficiently detached from their original viewpoint in order to see the situation from new perspectives. The basis of rational problem solving is a clear understanding of all sides of an issue and an accurate assessment of their validity and relative merits. In order to do this a client must be able to understand the perspective of other people (including the helper). A helper encourages the client's perspective-taking in order to reduce the egocentrism which prevents constructive problem solving. Perspective-taking is the opposite of egocentrism, and it is crucial for a client to view his problems, attitudes, and actions from a variety of points of view which allows him to gain insight into the destructiveness of current attitudes. Perspective-taking is the ability to understand how a situation appears to another person and how the person is reacting cognitively and affectively. It is highly related to open-mindedness, which is the willingness to attend to, comprehend, and gain insight into attitudes and viewpoints that are discrepant from one's own (Rokeach, 1960).

A helper can reduce a client's egocentrism and increase perspective-taking by the expression of warmth, accurate understanding, and cooperative intentions (Johnson, 1971b; Johnson, McCarty, and Allen, 1974), and by promoting role reversal with others. The defensiveness and closed-mindedness of a client may be reduced by his belief that he has been clearly heard, understood, and accepted as a person, and that the helper is clearly cooperatively oriented.

In your discussions with Ellen, she expresses considerable pain and bewilderment concerning the actions of her mother toward her. "Why does she criticize me so much? Why does she get so angry at me?" Ellen asks. To provide more insight into the relationship between Ellen and her mother you decide to use role reversal. Role reversal takes place when the client takes the role of another person and presents the viewpoint of that person as if he were the client (Johnson 1971a). To initiate the use of role reversal the helper identifies another person involved in the client's problems (this may be a current person, a past person, or it can even be a different personality aspect of the client). Once the different positions or roles have been identified, the helper asks the client to present the position and attitudes of the other person. In doing so the client presents the other's position and attitudes as if he were the other person. Sometimes it is helpful for the client to switch back and forth between his perspective and the perspective of another significant person; in such a case having the client switch chairs when switching viewpoints helps the process. Sometimes it is possible to have the person whose role is played observe and comment on the accuracy of the representation. Other times it is possible to have another person (such as yourself or a third person) play the role of the other and then periodically have the client and the other role player switch roles.

The use of role reversal has been found to increase a person's understanding of the content and frame of reference of another's positions (Johnson, 1966, 1967, 1968, 1971a, 1972b). The more incompatible the positions of the client and the person being role played, and the more defensive and committed the client is to his own perspective, the harder it may be to achieve insight into the perspective of others (Johnson, 1968). Many times the client, due to his defensiveness and biases, will misperceive the actions and attitudes of others. In order for successful problem solving and productive change to take place, such misunderstandings and misperceptions need to be clarified. Johnson (1966, 1967, 1968) found strong support for the notion that role reversal will clarify misunderstandings and misperceptions.

Reduction of Demoralization

People's reactions to their psychological difficulties are different from their reactions to other kinds of problems. An engineer who daily solves extremely complex technical problems can become extremely demoralized when she finds herself unable to form lasting relationships with other people. A psychologist who is adept at helping other people solve their personal difficulties can become frustrated and discouraged when he confronts a serious difficulty in his own life. When people find themselves continually unable to act, feel, and think as they believe they should, they usually become demoralized. Everyone who has personal problems that are not quickly resolved is in danger of becoming demoralized. Frank (1963) notes that to be demoralized is to be deprived of courage, to be disheartened, bewildered, confused, and disordered. Demoralized people are conscious of having failed to meet their expectations or the expectations of others, or of being unable to cope with pressing problems. They feel confused and unable to change the situation or themselves. In some cases they fear that they cannot even control their own feelings, giving rise to the fear that they may "go crazy." To various degrees, the demoralized person feels isolated, hopeless, and helpless.

Besides being intrinsically painful, demoralization blocks effective problem solving. First, it can compound the problem and make it worse. If the problem is one in which anxiety is hurting performance, worrying about the problem hurts even more. Sexual difficulties are good examples. A man who becomes impotent may find himself in a vicious circle. The longer his problem continues, the more he worries. Yet the more he worries, the worse the problem gets. All problems involving a large amount of fear or anxiety feed and grow on demoralization.

The second destructive feature of demoralization is that it keeps people from perceiving reasonable solutions. People who feel guilty, anxious, frustrated, and generally negative about themselves are in a very poor frame of mind for rationally developing and weighing alternative courses of action. Demoralized people are prone to plunge into drastic and rash solutions to their difficulties, such as running away or attempting suicide.

How do you reduce demoralization? The lasting cure is success. People who are continually able to meet their personal standards for successful living are bound to feel good about themselves. Helping clients feel successful often involves considerable attitude change which cannot be achieved without some immediate relief from demoralization. Relief is provided by helping clients reconceptualize the nature or source of their difficulties. Some explanations of the causes of problems lead people to feel better about themselves and prospects for change. Other explanations compound the distress and despair of demoralization. A short-term way to help people feel less demoralized is by shaping their explanations of their problems.

In discussing a person's problems so that they become more clearly defined, an important factor to consider is the stability of the problem implied by the explanation. People feel less demoralized when they attribute their problems to unstable causes. Explanations in terms of inappropriate attitudes, learned habits of thinking and behaving, or environmental stresses, all imply instability. Attributions of difficulties to fixed personality traits or to a malignant destiny imply stability. All too often demoralized people fear that their personality makeup has a permanent defect. Others feel that they have been singled out and fated to endure a painful existence. Neither of these attributions will lead to change and health.

A second aspect of problem explanations is whether or not the explanation implies that the individual is responsible for his problems. Virtually all theories and philosophies of helping people maintain that individuals should be responsible for changing their own difficulties. But opinion differs as to whether it is good for people to feel that they caused their problems in the first place. In some cases it may be helpful for people to believe that they caused their problems, while in other cases it may be best if people attribute their problems to external causes, such as job pressures. Phobias, sexual difficulties, depression, and any problems requiring crisis intervention may be helped by attributing them to external causes and avoiding making clients believe they are responsible for their creation (Jones et al., 1971; Skilbeck, 1973). Lecturing a guilt-ridden, suicidal individual on how he got himself into his predicament hardly seems the most effective treatment. On the other hand, if people are avoiding taking action to solve their problems, or feel generally apathetic and helpless, attributing their difficulties to their own volition may lead them to constructive action (Kirtner and Cartwright, 1958; Schroeder, 1960). Problems like smoking, losing weight, and delinquent behavior are examples of difficulties that can be helped by attributing them to personal causes.

How do you help clients define their problems in ways that reduce their demoralization? There are two basic ways. The first is to offer clients an interpretation of their difficulties that incorporates the qualities you want it to have. For fearful people you may offer a definition that attributes their problems to impersonal, unstable causes. For people who have difficulty in confronting their real problems, you may wish to consider offering an explanation that attributes their problems to a personal, unstable cause. If Ellen, for example, attributes her problems to her mother's behavior (which is beyond Ellen's control), you may wish to ignore her explanation and emphasize her unwillingness to take responsibility for her own feelings and actions. You may wish to point out to her that if she expects to change her inappropriate attitudes and her feelings, she must choose to commit herself to a program of attitude change. Such an explanation implies personal causation for problem behavior, as well as instability.

Of course, any explanation you give clients for their difficulties should make sense to you. You should never suggest an explanation that you do not find personally credible. There are enough plausible explanations for a given problem so that you need never believe that you have to lie to clients to combat their demoralization.

There is a second way to help clients define their problems in ways that reduce their demoralization. This is the method of "problem elaboration" developed by George Kelly (1955). Skilled therapists have learned that diagnostic questions can be used to reduce demoralization as well as to gain information. Kelly suggests that the following set of questions will accomplish both purposes:

1. For what problems do you wish help?
2. When were these problems first noticed?
3. Under what conditions did these problems first appear?
4. What corrective measures have been attempted?
5. What changes have come with treatment or the passing of time?
6. Under what conditions are the problems most noticeable?
7. Under what conditions are the problems least noticeable?

The formulation of these questions is designed to get clients (1) to see their problems as having a definite beginning and end; (2) to see their problems as fluid and temporary; and then (3) to interpret them as responsive to (a) treatment, (b) the passing of time, and (c) varying conditions (Kelly, 1955). Answering these questions will help clients see their problems as unstable.

People who find themselves falling short of their standards are likely to be demoralized. You can help remove this obstacle to change by offering explanations of their difficulties that reduce their fears about their problems, by providing support for the belief that their problems can be controlled, or by questioning them in a way that leads to these same insights.

Summary

You will be more effective in changing a client's inappropriate attitudes to appropriate ones if you first establish the conditions conducive to such change. This means building and maintaining a trusting relationship and reducing the egocentrism and demoralization that interfere with constructive problem-solving. After the conditions for attitude change have been established, you must select and implement a theory (or combination of theories) of attitude change. In the following sections the major theories of attitude change will be reviewed.

ATTITUDE ACQUISITION AND CHANGE

You have noticed that Ralph, one of the students in the same class as you, is immobilized in achievement situations. He has no self-confidence. He has an inferiority complex. He fears rejection. He feels humiliated whenever he fails. He thinks he's a loser. Every time he has to take a test or is involved in an achievement situation he panics out of fear that everyone will view him as dumb and despise him. Ralph even believes that no one could like him. You believe that Ralph is actually very bright, a good person, and you would like to help him acquire a more positive view of himself as a person.

You have five alternative approaches to attitude change to choose from in helping Ralph. Since attitudes are learned, it is possible to approach attitude acquisition and change with *learning* theory strategies. Yet attitudes are largely composed of meanings; how two attitudes relate to each other depends upon their meaningful content, not just upon their both being learned. Thus, there is a *cognitive* approach to attitude acquisition and change. Third, attitudes are developed only if they serve a function for the person; a person develops attitudes to cope with his world by forming relatively stable orientations toward common parts of his experience—a *functional* approach to changing and acquiring attitudes. Most attitudes are influenced by other people with whom a person interacts and identifies. These are *social influence* methods which can be used to acquire and change attitudes. Finally, the social *structure* that prescribes certain behavioral roles and the process of carrying out the roles influence the acquisition and stability of attitudes. Each of these five approaches to attitude acquisition and change will be discussed in the following sections.

LEARNING THEORY APPROACHES

Since attitudes are learned, all methods known to increase or decrease learning should be applicable to the acquisition or changing of attitudes. Attitude change may be simply a matter of new learning. There are three ways you could improve Ralph's self-attitudes using learning methods: classical conditioning, operant conditioning, and persuasion.

Classical Conditioning

From the perspective of classical conditioning, Ralph has learned his negative self-attitudes by associating achievement situations (the conditioned stimulus) with rejection, neglect, and abuse (the unconditioned stimulus). Since the response to neglect and abuse is anxiety and depression, Ralph now responds to achievement situations with anxiety, depression, and self-rejection. To condition positive self-attitudes, you utilize the unconditioned stimulus of affection, approval, and support (which result in a response of positive feelings such as satisfaction and security) and associate achievement situations with it. You study with Ralph, emphasizing support and approval, you sit by Ralph while he takes tests, emphasizing support and approval, the two of you discuss what achievement situations are like, and you emphasize support and approval. Achievement situations now become paired with receiving support and approval from friends, thus conditioning positive feelings to achievement situations. This *counter-conditioning* will change Ralph's negative self-attitudes to positive ones, given that the positive feelings of satisfaction and security are stronger than the negative feelings of anxiety and depression. (See Chapter 8 for a full examination of counter-conditioning methods.)

Another procedure from the classical conditioning approach involves *stimulus generalization*: when a particular response habitually follows a particular stimulus, elements similar to, or closely associated with this stimulus also show a tendency to elicit a similar response. This process has been suggested as an explanation for the acquisition of attitudes (Staats, 1966). For example, a girl may be consistently scolded by a stern father. Her father's behavior elicits in her feelings of fear, anxiety, and anger. Through stimulus generalization other men come to elicit these same feelings. As a result, she develops negative attitudes toward men.

Operant Conditioning

The basic principle of operant conditioning is that responses that are reinforced are more likely to be repeated than are responses that are not reinforced. (See Chapter 7 for a full examination of operant conditioning methods.) Attitudes that are reinforced are more likely to be maintained than are attitudes that are not reinforced. From the viewpoint of operant conditioning, Ralph maintains his negative self-attitudes because he receives reinforcement for doing so. The procedures for changing his self-attitudes are basically to withdraw all reinforcement for negative views of himself and begin reinforcing positive views of himself. Thus, you would identify the words and behaviors indicating a positive view of himself. Then you would reinforce Ralph every time he emitted one of these words or behaviors. Concurrently, you would ignore all expressions of negative self-attitudes. The more reinforcement Ralph receives for expressing positive self-attitudes, the more he will express them. After a point, you switch to an intermittent schedule of reinforcement, where you reinforce every third positive self-statement Ralph makes. This procedure may be summarized as follows: (1) Clearly identify the attitude you wish to strengthen and the words and behaviors that represent the attitude. (2) Every time the person makes one of the specified statements or engages in one of the specified behaviors, reward him in some way. (3) Very quickly the expression of the attitude will increase. Begin rewarding him for only every third expression of the attitude. In this way the attitude will be quickly strengthened and maintained for long periods of time.

Imagine that one of your teachers asks your help in improving her lectures. You and she identify a series of attitudes that will improve her lectures, such as the attitude that students are interested in learning and are quite fascinating people. An expression of such an attitude would be to ask students questions during class and be quite attentive when they give a reply or make a spontaneous statement about the material being covered. You enlist the aid of several students, and every time the teacher asks students questions or looks attentive you all smile and nod approval. After the teacher begins to ask lots of questions and looks very attentive, you all smile and nod every other time, then every third time, and so on. Before long the teacher not only improves her lectures, but develops positive attitudes toward students. Through operant conditioning you have significantly altered the behavior expression of her attitudes toward students, and hence the attitudes themselves.

Yale Attitude Change Program

Carl Hovland and his associates at Yale University (Hovland and Janis, 1959; Hovland, Janis, and Kelley, 1953; Rosenberg and Hovland, 1960) developed a program of research organized around the theme, "Who says what to whom with what effect?" This sentence is usually broken down into three components: the communicator, the message, and the audience. The Yale research is derived from learning theory in that it assumes that people are rational in the way they process information—they are motivated to attend to a message, learn its contents, and incorporate it into their attitudes. Through controlling the way clients perceive you, the way your messages are organized and presented, and who your clients are, you may be able to persuade clients to acquire the attitudes you wish to promote.

The Communicator. The first issue researched by the Yale psychologist was, "What personal characteristics help the communicator influence the audience?" Aristotle noted that an effective communicator must be a person of good sense, good will, and good moral character. Following Aristotle's notions, most of the research on personal characteristics of the communicator has examined credibility. The *credibility* of a communicator consists of expertise, trustworthiness, and objectivity; that is, the communicator's perceived ability to know valid information and his motivation to communicate this knowledge without bias. More specifically research has demonstrated that credibility consists of:

1. Expertness relevant to the topic under discussion;
2. Reliability as an information source; this refers to the perceived character of the communicator, such as dependability, predictability, and consistency.
3. Intentions of the communicator. It is usually important for the receiver to know whether or not the motives of the communicator are entirely selfish. Whatever effect we want our message to have upon the receiver, we should be open about it.
4. The expression of warmth and friendliness.
5. Dynamism of the communicator. A dynamic communicator is perceived to be aggressive, empathic, and forceful. A dynamic communicator tends to be perceived as more credible than does a passive one.
6. The majority opinion of other people concerning the degree of credibility of the communicator. If all our friends tell us the communicator is an expert and trustworthy, we tend to believe it.

The more you develop your skills in each of the areas above, the more credible and effective you will become. Much of what you can do to become credible requires a serious long-term effort. Credibility involves becoming genuinely knowledgeable about help-giving through study and practice, and leading the kind of life that gives you a reputation for honesty and dependability.

Fortunately, some skills contributing to credibility can be developed and practiced fairly quickly. The techniques for expressing warmth and cooperative intentions referred to earlier in this chapter are two examples. In addition you can learn to do some things to appear dynamic and competent to the person you are trying to help.

The first way to appear dynamic is to be responsive, both verbally and non-verbally. Look at the other person when you talk to him and vary your facial expression as he speaks. Avoid staring off into space or planting a "dead pan" expression on your face. As you speak, vary the tone of your voice and use mild and natural gestures. Try to get rid of things like nervous tics, recurring itches, bad breath, and anything else which might distract a listener from concentrating on what you are saying.

The second way to appear dynamic is to make your questions and comments logically coherent. Your questions should follow in a logical sequence and not ask for more than one piece of information at a time. When you make comments, you should get to your point quickly and confidently without rambling. You should take the lead in organizing and structuring the conversation. In short, you should make sense. People who need help are confused enough without your adding to their confusion.

A helper's knowledge and experience may have little impact if he is not dynamic. Schmidt and Strong (1970) found that students viewing video tapes of simulated counseling sessions considered an experienced psychologist and an advanced graduate student less responsive and coherent than beginning graduate students. Without knowing their backgrounds, the viewers rated the beginning students as more expert than the others. Being genuinely competent and trust-worthy are the most important ways to be credible, but you will be unnecessarily handicapping yourself if you do not also learn to appear warm, cooperative, and dynamic.

The Message. The ability of communicators to organize and phrase their messages skillfully determines much of their effectiveness in changing the attitudes of their audience. The nature of the arguments, their logical coherence, their emotional appeal, and the language used by the communicator are all important. The general results of the research in this area indicate that:

1. Two-sided arguments in which the side you are advocating is presented last is probably the most effective. Thus, to change Ralph's negative self-attitudes, you would briefly mention his current feelings of self-rejection and then give a detailed presentation as to why he is worthwhile, competent, and valuable.
2. Emotional appeals are useful if clients are not already anxious and distraught. If you want clients to stop "putting themselves down," for example, you may want to arouse a great deal of fear about such behaviors, provided that you recommend explicit and possible actions to take to avoid the dangers you are noting.
3. In most cases, it is helpful to state the conclusions of your arguments. If, however, you are dealing with highly intelligent clients, and you can offer convincing evidence, it is better to let them draw their own conclusions.
4. The content of the message should be phrased in the same wordings and expressions used by the client.

The Audience. There are several ways in which your audience has to be taken into account. While trying to persuade your clients:

1. Tailor your message to your intended audience—appealing to religious values may be very persuasive for some clients, but quite ineffective with clients without strong religious beliefs.
2. If your clients do not want you to influence their attitudes, it is often helpful to distract them while you are presenting your message. Clients can't argue effectively to themselves against your message when they are distracted. Giving clients something to eat while you are trying to persuade them is a common way to distract them from your message.
3. People with low self-esteem are more easily influenced than are people with high self-esteem (although some recent studies indicate that females with low self-esteems are harder to persuade than are males with low self-esteem).
4. Get clients to participate actively in the saying of the message. This can be done through having them role-play the presentation of the message. Having Ralph role-play a person with a lot of self-confidence, telling about his valuable strengths, for example, will help change Ralph's negative self-attitudes. The more emotionally involved Ralph can get in the presentation, the more effect it will have on his attitudes.
5. Try to influence clients' frame of reference or perspective by giving them the prior experiences that would lead them to perceive your message the way you want them to. If Ralph is given a series of success experiences prior to your presenting the message that he is worthwhile, for example, he will preceive the message differently than if he has had a series of prior failure experiences. Using prior experiences to create a perspective that is receptive to your message is an important persuasion procedure.

COGNITIVE THEORY APPROACHES

Ralph's self-attitudes are not discrete, separate and unrelated to each other. They are organized into a unified view of himself. One of the key aspects of attitudes is that they are organized into systems according to their content and meaning and, therefore, principles of cognitive organization need to be considered in changing someone's attitudes. Specifically, there are two principles of cognitive organization that are discussed in the attitude literature: the principle of simplicity and the principle of evaluative consistency. There is internal pressure for systems of attitudes to be simplified so that there is an overall good "gestalt" and there is internal consistency. Each of these principles are discussed below.

Simplicity

Our senses pick up a mass of stimuli that must be organized if we are to make sense out of them. In organizing our perceptions, we simplify by placing them into categories (such as boys and girls) and then organizing the categories into conceptual systems. The principle of simplicity states that people tend to organize their cognitions into a framework of maximum uniformity and regularity. Perceptions become organized into a "whole" or "gestalt" that tends to be as well organized as prevailing conditions allow. Attitudes, as one type of cognition, are organized into systems that are characterized by simplification in order to get a good "gestalt." In other words, people do not perceive things as unrelated isolates, but rather they organize things into meaningful wholes.

There are two ways in which the principle of simplicity relates to psychological problems: some attitude "gestalts" are disorganized and some are incomplete and unfinished. The lack of simple and well-organized gestalts is a malady of our times. Many people lack a solid core of appropriate attitudes to help them interpret their experiences. By helping people clarify their appropriate attitudes and unify them you can help others understand what changes need to take place in their lives. Consider the case of a young man who was threatening suicide. A series of events, including dissatisfaction with his present job, had left him demoralized and rootless. A long discussion of the young man's values and attitudes resulted in his concluding that the value of learning was one invariant factor that made life meaningful and worthwhile to him. His counselor pointed out how suicide would be shutting off all opportunities to grow and learn. With his new awareness of his attitudes the young man gave up both his thoughts of suicide and his dissatisfying job and returned to college. Thus, the way in which the principle of simplicity can be used by a helper interested in changing the attitudes of the client is through discussing the client's attitudes in ways that lead to a reorganization and a new frame of reference. Through guided discussions the client discovers better "gestalts" of a simpler way of putting several attitudes together.

Besides being disorganized, attitude "gestalts" can be incomplete or unfinished. A young lawyer once came to the author on the advice of his doctors and asked whether his ulcers were being caused by unresolved psychological tensions. After a series of sessions it became apparent that the lawyer was constantly angry about the high expectations and standards his father had for his behavior, but because of his fear of his father's disapproval he was afraid to express his anger or even admit it to himself. Consequently, he repressed all awareness of his anger most of the time. This unexpressed anger became an unfinished "gestalt" that may have contributed to his ulcers.

Evaluative Consistency

Closely related to the tendency to organize our cognitions into a framework of maximum uniformity and regularity is a tendency toward an evaluative consistency. Attitudes possess an evaluative quality. The principle of evaluative consistency holds that we tend to have similar evaluations of cognitive elements that are associated together. If we closely associate two attitudes in our thinking (attitudes toward this chapter and the author, for example), we will tend to have similar evaluations, pro or con, in regard to them (if we like the chapter we like the author). And, conversely, if we have similar evaluations of two objects, we will tend to organize them together.

There are several consistency theories of attitude change. Each theory postulates a basic "need" for consistency among attitudes or between attitudes and behavior. Most of the theories assume that the presence of inconsistency produces "psychological tension," or at least is uncomfortable, and in order to reduce this tension people "rearrange" their psychological world to produce consistency. In other words persons will try to appear rational and consistent to themselves. The most important consistency theory is Heider's (1958) and the most popular consistency theory is Festinger's (1957).

The most powerful source of inconsistency is between one's self-attitudes and one's perceived behavior or one's other attitudes. A person may believe that he is absolutely worthless and when others tell him how valuable his behavior has been there will be feelings of inconsistency, imbalance, or dissonance. A feeling of consistency will be achieved by changing one's attitudes about oneself (I really am worthwhile) or about one's behavior (I fooled them; they don't realize how worthless my behavior actually was). One way to help a person who has a low evaluation of himself is to make his behavior so apparently and clearly of value that he will have little alternative but to change his self-attitudes if he is to achieve consonance or balance. Another person may believe that he is a fair and just person, but also believe certain ethnic groups are inferior to the white majority. By highlighting these two attitudes, and emphasizing how fair and just the person is, the person will have no alternative but to change his attitudes toward the ethnic groups. The general procedure for using an evaluative consistency approach to attitude change is, therefore, to identify the self-attitudes, identify the behavior or other attitudes inconsistent with the self-attitudes, and emphasize the inconsistency while supporting the positive attitude or behavior.

In focusing consistency theory on attitude change, research has been conducted on the question of inconsistency between attitudes and behavior when the person has been "forced" into the behavior. When the attitudes are important to the person and when there is little justification for allowing oneself to be forced into the behavior, a great deal of dissonance or inconsistency is felt. Most often a person will then change his attitudes as he cannot take back his behavior. A helper may use this procedure in the following way. Suppose a person comes to you for help saying he is hopelessly a leaf in the breeze, unable to provide any direction to his life or have any impact on what happens to him. You might examine with him all the effects his behavior has had and the way in which he set a goal for his behavior and carried it through. In addition, you defeat all his attempts to deny that his behavior had no impact and emphasize the potency he has shown. The person will have no alternative but to change his self-attitudes if he wants to achieve consistency or balance or consonance. In fact, in such a situation the very fact that he came to someone for help shows a capacity for affecting the direction and effect of his behavior.

Socrates was probably the first person to use a consistency approach to attitude change. His "Socratic Method" for changing the attitudes of his students was to question them about specific cases illustrating their definitions of the concept under question, such as friendship, justice, or piety. He structured his questions in such a way as to get the students to admit exceptions to their definitions. The inconsistency between the old definition and the newly revealed specific exceptions caused the students to evolve new and more comprehensive definitions. By no coincidence, the new definitions closely resembled Socrates' own definitions, even though Socrates did not openly state his own position. The two keys to the Socratic Method were the use of questioning and the use of inductive reasoning—deriving general statements from specific cases. Socrates stood in sharp contrast to other teachers, who deduced their opinions and then lectured their students as to why these opinions should be accepted.

Matross (1974b) developed a method of changing people's attitudes toward themselves utilizing the principles of the Socratic Method. The logic of this approach is to use questioning to elicit a pattern of specific examples from the client's behavior which are inconsistent with the attitude you want to change. Confronted with concrete and specific evidence refuting unhealthy self-perception, the individual will thus be encouraged to inductively arrive at a new view of himself. The steps in this method are as follows:

1. Identify the self-perception which needs to be changed, e.g., a belief that one is incompetent and unable to achieve. Then think of actions which would be inconsistent with the target attitude. In our example, actions involving hard work, extra effort, and unusual striving are likely to have resulted from genuine achievement and would be inconsistent with a perception of incompetence.
2. Start questioning the person about specific behaviors relating to the target attitude. Start with a general lead, such as, "Let's talk about your achievement. Can you think of some examples which illustrate the ways you try to achieve?"
3. Continue the questioning, asking for exactly what you want. Initially a person may give you an example which you don't want, (e.g., "I goofed off and flunked biology"). Acknowledge such nontarget examples with the briefest of summaries, (e.g., "So biology was bad news") and move on to a question explicitly requesting a target example, "Can you think of a time when you really put out a lot of effort and came through when you had to?"

4. Ask detailed questions about the effects of the target behavior and the effects of nontarget actions the person could have taken, e.g., "What were the results of putting out that effort on the psychology paper? Did you get a better grade? Did your teacher think it was pretty good? Did you get a sense of personal satisfaction?" Summarize the answers to these questions and then ask questions about the effects of nontarget alternatives, e.g., "Suppose you hadn't researched that paper so well. Suppose you had only read a few pages and not put out much effort at all. Do you think you would have done poorly?" Give a final summary of the example, contrasting what the person did with the things he did not do, e.g., "You could have sloughed off, spent only a couple of hours in the library, and copied a lot of that paper. If you had done that, you would have gotten a low grade, disappointed your teacher and yourself. Instead you chose to push hard, studying many hours, reading several books and giving them a lot of thought. As a consequence of this effort, you got a good grade, pleased the teacher and gained self-respect."

5. Continue asking for examples of target behaviors and going through the question sequence above. When the conversation comes to a logical conclusion, offer a final summary. Take your three or four best examples of target behaviors and emphasize how these form a consistent pattern, with only a brief nonspecific acknowledgement of contrary behavior, e.g., "On the one hand there are times when you don't exert much effort and don't achieve. On the other hand there are several times when you do exert a lot of effort and do very well. For example. . . ."

The success of the Socratic Method rests on its concreteness and specificity. Rather than lecturing clients as to why they should change inappropriate attitudes, you are getting them to generate their own case for change. A person such as Ralph who is self-rejecting usually collects evidence to support his negative attitudes. By focusing his attention on examples of positive actions, you create a healthy inconsistency in his views of himself. If done well the impact of the specific examples you elicit should be enough so that you will not have to state openly the conclusion you want the client to reach. Matross (1974b) found that any additional influence attributable to an overt conclusion dissipated over time. Also, people given an overt conclusion had less confidence in their conclusions than did those who were presented only with the Socratic questions. With practice you will find that the question sequences will become quite smooth and natural.

FUNCTIONAL APPROACH

Of what use to people are their attitudes? This question epitomizes the central focus of the functional approach to attitude acquisition and change. Two major functional approaches are those of Katz (1960) and Ellis (1962). The functional approach to attitudes views humans as striving to accomplish certain goals, and analyzes attitudes in terms of the extent to which the attitudes facilitate goal accomplishment. Katz's version of the functional approach is to specify the psychological needs individuals are trying to meet by holding the attitudes they do (Katz, 1960; Katz and Stotland, 1959; Sarnoff and Katz, 1954). Katz identifies four functions of attitudes: (1) adjustive, (2) ego defensive, (3) knowledge, and (4) value-expressive.

The *adjustive function* of attitudes recognizes that people strive to maximize the rewards in their external environment and to minimize the penalties. Thus people develop favorable attitudes toward the objects which are associated with the satisfaction of their needs and unfavorable attitudes toward objects which thwart or punish them. The *ego defensive function* revolves around the notion that people protect themselves from anxiety by obliterating threatening external and internal stimuli. Thus attitudes can function like defense mechanisms to protect people from acknowledging their conflicts and deficiencies to themselves and other people. To a considerable degree, for example, prejudiced attitudes help to sustain the individual's self-concept by maintaining a sense of superiority over others. The *knowledge function* refers to the process by which people seek knowledge to give meaning to what otherwise would be an unorganized, chaotic world. People need standards or frames of reference for understanding their world and attitudes to help to supply such standards. Attitudes help people establish a degree of predictability, consistency, and stability in their perception of the world. Finally, the *value-expressive function* of attitudes involves the notion that attitudes give positive expression to an individual's central values and self-concept. Satisfactions are derived from the expression of attitudes which reflect one's cherished beliefs and self-image.

The ways in which you can use Katz's theory are as follows. When a client comes to you for help, you identify who and what are meeting his needs and who and what are thwarting his needs; your discussion should be used to build positive attitudes toward the former and negative attitudes toward the latter (adjustive function). You may also identify the ways in which the client's attitudes are protecting him from anxiety, and either increase the effectiveness of the attitudes or point out why current attitudes should be discarded for a set of more appropriate ones (ego-defensive function). You may identify the client's frame of reference and see how much predictability, consistency, and stability the frame of reference provides; you therefore attempt to strengthen the attitudes in the frame of reference or point out how they are ineffective, and try to persuade the client to discard current attitudes for a more appropriate set (knowledge function). You may identify the values and self-concept of the client and evaluate his attitudes on the basis of how well the attitudes express the client's values and promote a positive self-concept; again, you seek to either strengthen appropriate attitudes or point out the destructiveness of inappropriate attitudes, and try to persuade the client to discard the inappropriate attitudes for a more effective set (value-expressive function).

Katz's theory can also help you understand resistance to change. People may be reluctant to change an attitude that has helped them cope with the world, however inadequately. You can reduce the threat of change if you can demonstrate how a new attitude will better serve the function of the old attitude.

A second approach to the functional change of attitudes is that of Ellis (1962). Whereas Katz considers the adaptive, coping functions of attitudes, Ellis stresses the negative, self-defeating functions which attitudes can serve. He assumes that most psychological problems are rooted in certain erroneous and destructive attitudes. For instance, frustration, disappointment, and apathy can result from the attitude that everything one does must be perfect. When confronted by inevitable mistakes, people with this attitude continually criticize themselves and reindoctrinate themselves with their perfectionistic standards. The way out of this predicament is to adopt a new and more realistic set of attitudes toward performance, such as the belief that failure, while not pleasant, is not catastrophic, and that appropriate goal setting is more pleasant than demands for perfection.

To use the Ellis approach to change, you should first identify the attitudes responsible for the negative events in the client's life. You should then elaborate in considerable detail all the ways in which these attitudes serve negative and self-defeating functions. Finally, you should point out exactly how new attitudes will serve positive, self-enhancing functions. Instructions for these procedures can be found in Ellis (1962) and in Chapter 4 of the present book.

SOCIAL INFLUENCE APPROACH

The correctness of many of our attitudes cannot be checked against physical reality. There is, for example, no way to measure objectively our personal value. When physical reality cannot be used to determine the correctness of an attitude, a person is dependent upon other people as a basis of social reality. Every person is dependent upon other people for information to establish the validity of their attitudes. There are two major influences within social reality which will be discussed in this section: reference groups and reference individuals.

Reference Groups

A *reference group* is a group of persons that we use as standards to evaluate our attitudes, abilities, or current situation. People using a reference group to evaluate their attitudes assume their attitudes to be correct to the extent that most of the members of the group have similar attitudes. It is, of course, not necessary that all people they associate with agree with their attitudes, but it is important that some relevant reference group share their attitudes. There is considerable evidence that the groups to which we belong have powerful influences on our attitudes and behavior. Johnson and Neale (1970), for example, found that students involved in social action activities belong to groups which have norms favorable to social action activities and have a negative identification with groups against social action activities. Watson and Johnson (1972) summarize a great deal of research in the areas of conformity, reference groups, group norms, group decision making, and social comparison processes which demonstrates the power a group has over a person's attitudes and behavior. The implications of this research for attitude change are:

1. The attitudes of individuals are strongly influenced by the groups to which they belong and those to which they want to belong.
2. If people's attitudes conform to group standards and norms, they are reinforced; they are punished for having attitudes which deviate from group standards and norms.
3. Those individuals who are most attached to the group are the least influenced by attempts to change their attitudes.
4. The support of even one other member for a minority attitude weakens the powerful effect of the group majority upon a person's attitudes.
5. A minority of two people who are consistent in the expression of their attitudes can influence the majority of other group members.
6. Participation in group discussions and group decision making helps to overcome resistance to developing new attitudes; if a group decides to adopt new attitudes, its members will also adopt new attitudes.
7. As a person's reference groups change, so do his attitudes.

Suppose a friend comes to you and asks you to help him develop better study habits so he will not flunk out of school. You find that his friends (other than yourself) all have negative attitudes toward studying and positive attitudes toward spending every available minute in a certain bar. When the person tries to study he is teased; when he is not in the bar he is ridiculed. From a reference group standpoint there are two ways to deal with this problem: change the reference group norms or change the person's reference groups. There are two ways to change the reference group norms: conduct a group discussion in which a group decision is made to change the group norm, or influence one or two members to change their attitudes, thus forming a solid minority. Changing a person's reference groups is usually a gradual process of reducing the importance of one group while increasing the importance of another. The stabilizing effects reference groups have on attitudes points up the importance of ensuring that there will be interpersonal support for any new attitudes clients develop while you are working with them.

Another way in which reference groups can be helpful is when you are requested to help people who have never shared their attitudes with others—people who are in a state of insulated ignorance about the appropriateness and generality of their attitudes. *Insulated ignorance* is defensiveness which prevents people from sharing their attitudes with others or listening to attitude expressions of others in a sensitive area. Some individuals are so fearful of discussing their attitudes and feelings with others that they never do and therefore have distorted views of what most people believe. A person, for example, once came to the author for help in developing better sexual relationships with females. Part of his problem was that he believed that females were inherently liars, deceitful, untrustworthy, hostile toward men, uncaring, insensitive, ensnaring, and wanted only to exploit men for their bodies. He firmly believed that the vast majority of men in the United States shared his attitudes. Such ignorance of others' attitudes was insulated by his extreme defensiveness which prevented him from discussing females with any of his friends. The author encouraged the person to discuss his attitudes with others and suggested group experiences which put him in contact with men who held more favorable attitudes toward women; such experiences helped the person realize the extent to which his attitudes were unusual and should be reconsidered.

Reference Individuals

Reference individuals are individuals people use as standards to evaluate their attitudes, abilities, or current situation; such influence is often exercised through identification. *Identification* is a general process whereby one person takes on the attributes (such as attitudes) of another. Johnson and Neale (1970), for example, found that students involved in social action activities identified with persons within and outside their family who had attitudes favorable to such involvement. If the client identifies with the helper and uses the helper as a reference individual, the helper will be able to exercise a great deal of influence over the client's incorporation of more appropriate and constructive attitudes and behaviors. The helping process has been described as rectifying false identifications. Bad identifications are those which result in stunting or thwarting the individual's growth or which result in destructive and self-defeating attitudes and behavior. Good identifications are those which promote satisfying experiences and goal accomplishment. Thus you will want to encourage client identification with appropriate persons (including yourself) who have more constructive attitudes than the client now has.

How can the helper encourage a constructive identification by the client with the helper? The primary way is to establish a relationship in which the helper facilitates constructive change of the client's attitudes and expresses warmth toward the client as a person.

When a person comes to you for help he expects and hopes to receive it. You and the client become a cooperative dyad in which the goals are to alleviate the client's suffering, find constructive solutions to his problems, and improve the client's social competencies so he can better handle future crises. With specific reference to attitudes, the helper and the client cooperate to identify the current attitudes of the client, assess their impact upon his life and their current relationship to his problems, and then come to a decision about what attitudes need to be strengthened and what attitudes need to be changed or replaced. The helper then tries to facilitate these changes. The client's expectation that the helper will facilitate the accomplishment of the client's goals and the resulting cooperative problem solving produces liking for the helper (D. Johnson and Johnson, 1972; S. Johnson and Johnson, 1972; D. Johnson and Johnson, 1975). In addition, there is considerable evidence that the helper's expression of warmth toward the client will result in client liking for the helper (Johnson, 1971b, 1971d; Johnson and Noonan, 1972). Thus by cooperatively working toward constructive changes in the client's attitudes and by expressing warmth for the client as a person, the helper will facilitate the client's liking for and identification with the helper, which will give the helper more potential influence over the client's attitudes. That liking and identification are related is indicated by the finding that the expression of warmth also produces perceptions by the client that the helper is similar to the client in attitudes and values and as a person (Johnson, 1971b, 1971d; Johnson and Noonan, 1972); in order to keep such a perception valid, a client will often have to modify his attitudes to make them more congruent with those of the helper.

Once identification has been established there are a variety of ways in which the helper's behavior and actions may influence the attitudes of the client. Identification will lead to potential client incorporation and imitation of the helper's attitudes without much action on the part of the helper. Yet there are four specific helper actions which have an impact upon the attitudes of the client. Expression of accurate understanding, expression of cooperative intentions, expression of coldness and anger toward destructive attitudes, and structuring client role reversal.

. The expression of accurate understanding has been previously discussed; when it is used in a cold manner while reflecting the destructive attitudes of the client it will result in attitude change (Johnson, 1971b). The expression of cooperative intentions will promote client attitude change (Johnson, 1971b); the procedures for doing so have also been previously discussed. While the expression of warmth does produce liking, it has an interesting relationship to the expression of coldness and anger in regard to a person's attitudes.

When warmth is expressed toward people's attitudes they will believe that the helper agrees with and supports those attitudes (Johnson, 1971a, 1971b, 1971d). The expression of coldness and anger create the impression that the helper disagrees with and disapproves of those attitudes (Johnson, 1971b, 1971d). But anger and coldness can also produce disliking for the helper (Johnson, 1971b, 1971d). Thus there is a combination of warmth toward a person but coldness and anger toward destructive attitudes which a helper needs to be able to express in order for constructive attitude change to take place. The expression of coldness and anger is discussed below.

The expression of *coldness* is best achieved through nonverbal messages. A hard tone of voice, a poker face, frowning, or disinterested facial expression, a tense posture in which you are leaning away from the client, and closed, harsh gestures are all ways of expressing coldness. Verbally, coldness can be best expressed through ignoring (i.e., silence) the expression of destructive attitudes or simply saying coolly that you do not agree with the attitude and believe it to be destructive to the client's best interests.

The expression of *anger* can be expressed both verbally and nonverbally. Verbally, anger can be expressed by such statements as, "That attitude makes me angry," "That attitude turns me off," "That attitude angers me because of what it does to you," and so on. Nonverbally, anger can be expressed through cold and cutting tone of voice, a tight-lipped expression, maintaining a stiff or aggressive posture, clenching fists, and leaning back while glaring. Anger is a very delicate tool for a helper to use as Johnson (1971d) found that the expresser often underestimates the negative impact it can have on the receiver.

One of the most effective ways of influencing client attitudes is through structuring role reversal situations. In *role reversing* a person is asked to present the attitudes, thoughts, and position of another person in an involved way. Through role reversal the person increases his understanding of the content of others' positions and the perspective or frame of reference behind their position (Johnson, 1966, 1967, 1968, 1971a, 1972d). In role reversal clients are asked to enact the behavior of another person and to assume and publicly espouse a set of attitudes with which they disagree. By engaging in role reversal, clients persuade themselves to modify their attitudes. There are a number of studies which demonstrate greater modification of attitudes after active role reversal than after passive exposure to the same persuasive materials (see Johnson, 1971d). Johnson (1966, 1967, 1971a) found consistent evidence that engaging in role reversal resulted in subsequent attitude change, even when taking the position of others with whom one is negotiating a conflict.

A couple who have had a close relationship for several years requests your assistance in saving their relationship. She insists that they move to a warmer climate because of the depressions she has every winter and he insists that his job is too important and rewarding to leave. They argue constantly about this issue, each accusing the other of failing to love one enough to give in to the other's demands. A woman comes to you for help in developing more autonomy. She constantly cries about the way in which her mother treated her as a child and angrily pounds the arm of the chair as she describes the ways in which her mother has failed her. Each of these instances is an example of when you might want to use role reversal. In the first instance the couple needs to gain more understanding and attitude change about the position of the other. In the second instance the woman needs to change her attitudes about her mother, her mother's perceptions of their relationship, and her dependence upon her mother to make her life turn out well.

The procedures for the use of role reversal are as follows. First the client presents his attitudes or position. Second he presents the attitudes and position of someone else involved in the situation (such as a spouse or mother). In taking the role of the other person, the client needs to role play, as well as he can, the other person. A way in which this can be facilitated is through having another chair available to which the person moves when he is taking the role of the other. If the other person is in the room the accuracy with which the person is portraying the other's position and perspective can be determined. If the other person is not in the room the success of the role reversal depends upon the involvement the person can bring to the portrayal. To get the optimal effect it may be necessary for a person to switch back and forth between his own attitudes and perspective and the perspective and position of the other. Thus the woman in the above example may make a statement to her mother (represented by the empty chair), change seats and reply as her mother, change seats and reply as herself, and so on. This role reversal procedure can even be used when one person is ambivalent about certain of his attitudes; he can present each side of his ambivalence and argue the issue with himself while switching back and forth between chairs.

When the dramatized version of role reversal is not possible or appropriate it is possible to use modified procedures. The use of accurate understanding is a mild form of role reversal; clients can be taught to use accurate understanding in discussing their attitudes with others who have different and more constructive attitudes. The male in the couple in the example above may be asked to describe the female's position and perspective without actually dramatizing her role by pretending to be her. Such procedures will greatly enhance communication and attitude change but perhaps not as effectively as the more involved role playing.

STRUCTURE-PROCESS-ATTITUDE APPROACH

The previous four approaches to attitude acquisition and change have focused primarily on changing people in order to change their attitudes and the way in which they interact with their environment. There is another approach which focuses on changing the environment in order to change the person. By changing the types (or objective pattern) of situations in which people find themselves, the ways in which they interact with others will be changed and their attitudes will be modified. By changing jobs, marital status, schools, teachers, and so forth, the attitudes of people can also be changed. Every society includes a number of subunits of organized interaction which may be called social systems. A family, a school, a business, a baseball team, or a hospital is a social system. Within each social system, people are given roles that generally specify the expected behaviors of each member while interacting with other members. In a family there are the roles of father, mother, and children, each of which has expected behaviors as to how each should interact with the others. These role expectations are further supported by norms and values as to what is appropriate for a given role. A social system, therefore, has a certain pattern or *structure* establishing prescribed roles. In the *process* of carrying out these roles people develop corresponding outlooks, *attitudes* and feelings. A change in the system brings changes in roles, and the changed interaction alters the members' attitudes and feelings. Thus, a social system structure leads to a process of interaction among members that leads to the acquisition of attitudes. For a full discussion of this attitude acquisition and change theory see Watson and Johnson (1972).

Imagine that you are an instructor in a course Ralph is taking. Ralph is accustomed to learning within a competitive situation where students try to outperform each other to see who is best. Changing the structure of the learning situation to a cooperative one will result in different interaction patterns, which in turn will affect Ralph's self-attitudes. The cooperative learning structure establishes role expectations as to how students should behave, and in the process of carrying out the cooperative role the attitudes of the students are affected. The process of cooperating involves such actions as students: (1) facilitating each other's learning through sharing ideas and materials and helping and tutoring each other; (2) communicating ideas and feelings openly and accurately; (3) trusting each other; (4) giving support to each other; and (5) equalizing power and being open to each other's influence.

This cooperative interaction pattern creates a series of attitudes related to self-esteem. They are the attitudes that: (1) one is unconditionally liked and accepted by classmates; (2) one is supported and accepted, both academically and personally, by peers and professors; (3) one's feelings are understood by classmates; (4) one is successful in achievement situations; (5) one is psychologically safe and secure; (6) failure is only moderately anxiety arousing; and (7) one is able to take charge of one's life in solving one's problems. These attitudes create higher levels of self-esteem than results from students competing with each other or working individually (Johnson and R. Johnson, 1975, 1978). Cooperative attitudes are more strongly related to feelings of personal worth, basic self-acceptance, favorable comparison with peers, and a general sense of well-being and satisfaction with one's life.

When a person comes to you for help, it is important to look at possibilities of changes in the person's social systems or roles that will create new patterns of interaction with others, which in turn will lead to the adoption of more appropriate attitudes.

STABILIZING NEW ATTITUDES

After you have established the conditions for attitude change and have selected and implemented a theory (or combination of theories) of attitude change in your sessions with the client, it is necessary to be concerned with stabilizing the new attitudes so that they will endure during future crises and during attempts by others to change them. New attitudes may be acquired; old attitudes can be changed. Yet if people are really helped, the new attitudes have to be stabilized so that they do not change back as soon as the helping stops. There are four ways in which a helper can facilitate the stabilization of new attitudes. The first is to discuss the new attitudes so that they become integrated into the attitude systems of the person. Since attitudes are organized into systems, a change of a few attitudes will have effects on many additional attitudes, which will have to be modified and reorganized to accomodate the new attitudes. Changing people's self-attitudes, for example, may necessitate the changing or modification of their attitudes about the value of other people, the risks they should take in achievement related activities, the type of person they should ask for dates, the credibility they should ascribe to their parents' evaluations of them, and so on. Attitude change will not be permanent unless it results in new gestalts of attitude clusters.

A second way to facilitate the stabilization of new attitudes is through firmly embedding them in chains of causation with their consequences. If the new attitudes stop the old self-destructive behavior and facilitate self-enhancing behaviors the increased satisfaction, happiness, and effectiveness and the decreased pain and depression will sustain the new attitudes. Such attributions need to be clear to the client; new attitudes will not be sustained if their positive consequences are not clear.

The third method of stabilizing attitudes is through inoculation against change. Just as a person can be inoculated against physical disease a person can be, at least to some extent, inoculated against attitude change. By challenging the client's new attitudes with mild arguments against them a helper can stimulate the client to develop strong arguments supporting the new attitudes and defending them against future change attempts. Thus, by preparing the client to defend his new attitudes against opposition, the client becomes inoculated against attitude change. A helper, for example, might structure a short role playing situation in which he takes the role of one of the people who helped build the old, self-destructive attitudes in the client and challenges the new attitudes. A mild form of this can be summarized in the question, ''What will you say when x says to you, 'You do not have the ability to do y'?''

The fourth way to stabilize attitude change is by enhancing the client's feelings of being personally responsible for the change. If the client attributes beneficial change to his own efforts, he will be more likely to maintain that change than if he attributes the change to external forces such as luck, a ''magic'' technique, or a powerful helper. You can encourage personal attribution of change throughout your discussions with your clients. In the beginning of the relationship you should emphasize that the process will be a cooperative endeavor, in which the client will have to do the major work. Then, when you suggest changes, you should try to minimize the appearance of overt pressure. That is, you should not use imperative statements, commands, or very strong conclusions, unless they are the only ways to accomplish your objectives. After the client has successfully changed, you should emphasize how he *chose* to change. You can convey this attitude of personal choice by specifically pointing out all the self-defeating actions the client could have taken but did not. By taking these measures you will help the client to "own" his new and more appropriate attitudes.

ETHICS AND SOCIAL RESPONSIBILITY

There are serious ethical issues involved in deliberately attempting to influence the attitude acquisition and change of other people. Before such an attempt is made, the value and necessity of such attitude change must be weighed against the possibility of manipulating, exploiting, or brainwashing others for one's own needs and satisfactions. *Attempting to help another person carries with it a responsibility not to work against the person's best interests and needs.* It should also be noted that the only way to promote ethical standards in helping relationships is for the helpers to enforce their code of ethics on themselves and to use good judgment in what they do. As long as a helper's behavior is based on caring, respect, and regard for clients, ethical violations will be minimized. People engaging in helping activities must, therefore, develop a personal code of ethics to which they hold themselves accountable. The following points should provoke some thought as to what that personal code of ethics might include.

The first set of ethical issues in using attitude change methods to help another person revolves around the contract between the helper and the client. The nature of the contract, including number of sessions, the appropriateness and objectives of the helping activities, the ending point of the relationship, and the helper's intentions, should be clear to both the helper and the client. There must be informed consent and mutual agreement as to what is to be done before helping begins.

The second set of ethical issues involves the activities the helper engages in. What the helper does needs to be based on empirically validated knowledge. Folklore, superstition, common sense, fads and popular gimmicks, and personal experience are not an adequate base for helping other people. A thorough knowledge of the social psychology of attitude change is needed before you represent yourself as someone who can help others with attitude change problems. *To attempt to help a person when one is ignorant of how to help is both unethical and irresponsible.* A great deal of damage has been caused by people with good intentions—but no knowledge—who just wanted to help others. In addition to knowledge, helpers should have the competence, preparation, and training to apply what they know. *Knowledge is not enough; there must also be trained skills and competencies.*

A third set of ethical issues concerns the helper's conceptual basis for intervention. At any time during the helping relationship the helper should be able to explain the theory he is operating by and the way in which current activities relate to the theory. This does not mean that helpers will not use their intuition and impulses when helping others, but they should be able to reconstruct the theory behind their intuitive actions.

Fourth, the helper should be aware of his behavior styles and personal needs and deal with them productively in the performance of the helping role; the helper should be aware of the impact of personal needs and style upon the client.

Fifth, the personal information disclosed by the client should be held in strict confidence; even if you are helping a child and the parent wants to know what the child is saying, it is important to get the child's permission to reveal the child's disclosures. Any possibility of disclosed information being used in any way to damage the client must be minimized.

Sixth, ideally the helper should be able to recognize symptoms of serious psychological stress and be able to make responsible decisions when such problems arise. The helper should know where emergency services (such as the nearest hospital with psychiatric facilities) are available.

Seventh, helping sessions should be evaluated in order to provide the helper with feedback to improve his performance in the future. The helper should arrange for more experienced helpers to consult with him about the procedures being used with current clients as well as ask clients for reactions to the helping. Follow-up with clients should be possible in order to assess the long-term impact of the helping sessions on the participants.

The helping ability of most readers should improve by applying the material in this chapter with intelligence and caution. Readers interested in more specific skill building procedures are referred to Johnson (1972a, 1978) and Johnson and R. Johnson (1975). You do not have to be a skilled therapist to help a friend problem-solve an important issue or correct a set of self-defeating attitudes. But it is important to recognize the difference between being a helpful friend and conducting more formal psychotherapy. Meaningful help should be confined within the general range of your trained competencies.

REFERENCES

Bierman, R. Dimensions for interpersonal facilitation in psychotherapy and child development. *Psychological Bulletin*, 1969, *72*, 338-352.

Chittick, E.V. and Himelstein, P. The manipulation of self-disclosure. *Journal of Psychology*, 1967, *65*, 117-121.

Colson, W.N. Self-disclosure as a function of social approval. Unpublished master's thesis, Howard University, 1968.

Deutsch, M. Conditions affecting cooperation. Final Technical Report for the Office of Naval Research, Contract NONR-285, 1957.

——— Cooperation and trust: some theoretical notes. In M.R. Jones (Ed.), *Nebraska Symposium on Motivation*. Lincoln, Nebraska: University of Nebraska Press, 1962, 275-320.

Deutsch, M and Krauss, R. Studies of interpersonal bargaining. *Journal of Conflict Resolution*, 1962, *6*, 52-76.

Drag, L.R. Experimenter-subject interaction a situational determinant of differential levels of self-disclosure. Unpublished master's thesis, University of Florida, 1968.

Eagly, A and Himmelfarb, S. Attitudes and opinions. In M. Rosenzweig and L. Porter (Eds.), *Annual Review of Psychology*, Vol. 19 Palo Alto, California: Annual Reviews, 1978, 517-554.

Ellis, A. *Reason and emotion in psychotherapy*. New York: Lyle Stuart, 1962.

Festinger, L. *A theory of cognitive dissonance*. Evanston, Ill.: Row, Peterson 1957.

Frank, J.D. *Persuasion and healing. A comparative study of psychotherapy*. Revised edition. Baltimore: The Johns Hopkins University Press, 1973.

Heider, F. *The psychology of interpersonal relations*. New York: John Wiley & Sons, Inc., 1958.

Hovland, C., and Janis, I. *Personality and persuasibility*. New Haven: Yale University Press, 1959.

Hovland, C., Janis, I., and Kelley, H. *Communication and persuasion*. New Haven: Yale University Press, 1953.

Johnson, D.W. The use of role reversal in intergroup competition. Unpublished doctoral dissertation, Columbia University, 1966.

——— The use of role reversal in intergroup competition. *Journal of Personality and Social Psychology*, 1967, *7*, 135-414.

——— The effects upon cooperation of commitment to one's position and engaging in or listening to role reversal. Unpublished research report, University of Minnesota, 1968.

——— Role reversal: a summary and review of the research. *International Journal of Group Tensions*, 1971a, *1*, 318-334.

——— The effects of warmth of interaction, accuracy of understanding, and the proposal of compromises on the listener's behavior. *Journal of Counseling Psychology*, 1971b, *28*, 275-282.

——— The effectiveness of role reversal: the actor or the listener. *Psychological Reports*, 1971c, *28*, 275-282.

——— The effects of the order of expressing warmth and anger upon the actor and the listener. *Journal of Counseling Psychology*, 1971d, *18* 571-578.

——— *Reaching out: interpersonal effectiveness and self-actualization*. Englewood Cliffs, N.J.: Prentice-Hall, 1972a.

——— The effects of role reversal on seeing a conflict from the opponent's frame of reference. Unpublished Manuscript, University of Minnesota, 1972b.

——— *Contemporary social psychology*. Philadelphia: J.B. Lippincott Company, 1973.

——— Communication and the inducement of cooperative behavior in conflicts: a critical review. *Speech Monographs*, 1974, *41*, 64-78.

——— Cooperativeness and social perspective taking. *Journal of Personality and Social Psychology*, 1975, *31*, 241-244.

——— *Human relations and your career: A guide to interpersonal skills*. Englewood Cliffs, N.J.: Prentice-Hall, 1978.

——— *Educational psychology*. Englewood Cliffs, N.J.: Prentice-Hall, 1979.

Johnson, D.W. and Johnson, R.T. *Learning together and alone: cooperation, competition, and individualization*. Englewood Cliffs, N.J.: Prentice-Hall, 1975.

Johnson, D.W. and Matross, R. The interpersonal influence of the psychotherapist. In A. Gurman and A Razin (Eds.), *The effective therapist: A handbook*. Elmsford, N.Y.: Pergamon Press, 1977.

Johnson, D.W., McCarty, K., and Allen, T. Congruent and contradictory verbal and nonverbal communications of cooperativeness and competitiveness in negotiations. *Communication Research*, 1976, *3*, 275-292.

Johnson, D.W. and Neale, D. The effects of models, reference groups, and social responsibility norms upon participation in prosocial action activities. *Journal of Social Psychology*, 1970, *81*, 87-92.

Johnson, D.W. and Noonan, M.P. The effects of acceptance and reciprocation of self-disclosures on the development of trust. *Journal of Counseling Psychology*, 1972, *19*, 411-416.

Johnson, D.W. and Norem-Hebeisen, A. Attitudes toward interdependence among persons and psychological health. *Psychological Reports*, 1977, *40*, 843-850.

Johnson, D.W. and Johnson, R.T. (Eds.), Social interdependence in the classroom: Cooperation, competition, individualism. *Journal of Research and Development in Education*, 1978, *12*, Fall Issue.

Johnson, D.W. and Johnson, S. The effects of attitude similarity, expectation of goal facilitation, and actual goal facilitation on interpersonal attraction. *Journal of Experimental Social Psychology*, 1972, *8*, 197-206.

Johnson, D.W. and Johnson, F. *Joining together: group theory and group skills.* Englewood Cliffs, N.J.: Prentice-Hall, 1975.

Johnson, S and Johnson, D.W. The effects of other's actions, attitude similarity, and race on attraction towards the other. *Human Relations*, 1972, *25*, 121-130.

Jones, E.E., Kanouse, D.E., Kelley, H.H., Nisbett, R.E., Valins, S, and Weiner, B. *Attribution: Perceiving the causes of behavior.* Morristown, N.J.: General Learning Press, 1971.

Jourard, S.M. and Freidman, R. Experimenter-subject "distance" and self-disclosure. *Journal of Personality and Social Psychology*, 1970, *15*, 278-282.

Katz, D. The functional approach to the study of attitudes. *Public Opinion Quarterly*, 1960, *24*, 163-204.

Katz, D and Stotland, E.A. A preliminary statement to a theory of attitude structure and change. In S. Koch, (Ed.), *Psychology: A study of a science*. Vol. 3. New York: McGraw-Hill, 1959, 423-475.

Kelly, G.A. *The psychology of personal constructs, Vol. 2: Clinical diagnosis and psychotherapy*. New York: W.W. Norton, 1955.

Kirtner, W.L. and Cartwright, D.S. Success and failure in client-centered therapy as a function of initial in-therapy behavior. *Journal of Consulting Psychology*, 1958, *22*, 329-33.

McCroskey, J.C., Larson, C.E., and Knapp, M.L. *Introduction to interpersonal communication*. Englewood Cliffs, N.J.: Prentice-Hall, Inc., 1971.

Matross, R.P. Insight and attribution in counseling and psychotherapy. *Office for Student Affairs Research Bulletin*, University of Minnesota, 1974a.

——— Socratic methods in counseling and psychotherapy. *Office for Student Affairs Research Bulletin*, University of Minnesota, 1974b.

Murdoch, P. Chenowith, R., and Riseman, K. Eligibility and intimacy effects on self-disclosure. Paper presented at the meeting of the Society of Experimental Social Psychology, Madison, Wisconsin, 1969.

Rapoport, A. *Fights, games and debates*. Ann Arbor: The University of Michigan Press, 1960.

Rogers, R. *Client-centered therapy*. Boston: Houghton Mifflin Co., 1951.

Dealing with psychological tensions. *Journal of Applied Behavioral Science*, 1965, *1*, 6-25.

Rokeach, M. *The open and closed mind* New York: Basic Books, 1960.

Rosenberg, M., and Hovland, C. (Eds.). *Attitude organization and change*. New Haven: Yale University Press, 1960.

Sarnoff, I. and Katz, D. The motivational basis of attitude change. *Journal of Abnormal and Social Psychology*, 1954, *49*, 115-124.

Schlenker, B.R., Helm, B., and Tedeschi, J.T. The effects of personality and situational variables on behavioral trust. *Journal of Personality and Social Psychology*, 1973, *25* 419-427.

Schmidt, L.D. and Strong, S.R. "Expert" and "in-expert" counselors. *Journal of Counseling Psychology*. 1970, *17*, 115-118.

Schroeder, P. Client acceptance of responsibility and difficulty of therapy. *Journal of Consulting Psychology*, 1960, *24*, 467-471.

Sermat, V. and Smyth, M. Content analysis of verbal communication in the development of a relationship: Conditions influencing self-disclosure. *Journal of Personality and Social Psychology*, 1973, *26*, 332-346.

Skilbeck, W.M. Attribution theory and crisis intervention therapy. Paper presented at the 1973 convention of the American Psychological Association, Montreal, Quebec.

Staats, A.W. An integrated-functional approach to complex human behavior. In Kleinmuntz (Ed.) *Problem solving: Research, Method and Theory*, New York: Wiley, 1966.

Taylor, D.A. The effects of social reinforcement and self-disclosure patterns on interpersonal behavior. Unpublished manuscript, University of Delaware, 1964.

Taylor, D.A., Altman, I., and Sorrentino, R. Interpersonal exchange as a function of rewards and costs and situational factors: Expectancy confirmation-disconfirmation. *Journal of Experimental Social Psychology*, 1969, *5* 324-339.

Watson, G. and Johnson, D.W. *Social psychology: Issues and insights*. Philadelphia: Lippincott, 1972.

Worthy, M., Gary, A.L., and Kahn, G.M. Self-closure as an exchange process. *Journal of Personality and Social Psychology*, 1969, *13*, 59-63.

4
Cognitive Change Methods*
Marvin R. Goldfried and
Anita Powers Goldfried

The behavioral orientation to clinical work, as described in the late 1950s and early 1960s, reflected a marked departure from what constituted traditional practice. As originally presented, behavior therapy was typically defined as the application of learning principles to deviant behavior. Drawing upon the research and theory in learning, most of the methods that were originally used had their roots in either classical or operant conditioning. While a fair amount of research dealing with such cognitive variables as "mental set" had been carried out in the early 1900s (Hilgard and Bower, 1975), most of the literature on learning that was available to the founders of behavior therapy dealt with principles of classical and operant conditioning. According to the view at that time, most forms of maladaptive human behavior could be modified by the relatively straightforward pairing of certain stimuli or the arrangement of appropriate reinforcement contingencies.

Within the relatively short period of time that behavior therapy has been in existence, numerous advancements in theory and technique have been made. The many advancements have included a greater recognition paid to the importance of cognitive variables in understanding and changing human behavior. As behavior therapists began to deal clinically with a wide variety of human problems, it soon became evident that the client's cognitive processes played a central role in the therapeutic enterprise. In 1970, Kanfer warned his behaviorally oriented colleagues that: "Without incorporation of these [cognitive] phenomena into the behavioristic model, it is quite probable that the days of even a methodologi-

*Work on this chapter was facilitated by Grant MH24327 from the National Institute of Mental Health.

cal behaviorism are numbered'' (p. 212). Fortunately, behavior therapy responded quickly, and without necessarily denying the effectiveness of clinical procedures derived from classical and instrumental conditioning, began to acknowledge that techniques based solely on such principles were inadequate in dealing with more complex human problems.

Although the recognition of cognitive processes within the behavioral orientation to clinical work became evident in the early 1970s (Beck, 1970; Goldfried and Merbeaum, 1973; Kanfer and Phillips, 1970; A.A. Lazarus, 1971; Mahoney, 1974; Meichenbaum, 1974; Thoresen and Mahoney, 1974), the growing popularity of what has been called ''cognitive behavior therapy'' did not really begin until the mid 1970s, after which time there appeared numerous books, chapters, articles, audio-cassette tapes, a newsletter (*Cognitive-Behavior Modification Newsletter*), and a journal (*Cognitive Therapy and Research*) dealing with this newly emerging area (Beck, 1976; Beck et al., in press; Ellis and Grieger, 1977; Foreyt and Rathjen, 1978; Goldfried and Davison, 1976; Goldfried and Goldfried, 1975; Kendall and Hollon, 1979; Lange and Jakubowski, 1976; Mahoney, 1977; Mahoney and Arnkoff, 1978; Meichenbaum, 1977, 1978; Novaco, 1975; O'Leary and Turkewitz, 1978).

It should be emphasized that the cognitive change procedures that have been developed within recent years, although fitting within the general context of behavior therapy, are indeed varied. Meichenbaum, (1977) has emphasized this point, and has cautioned us to be wary of a ''uniformity myth'' that may lead us to overlook the differences among the methods that fall under this general rubric. One cognitive approach to behavior change involves the work of Beck (1976), who has developed procedures for training clients to change such illogical thought patterns as tendencies to draw arbitrary inferences from events, to exaggerate the significance of any given event, to overgeneralize from a single incident, and such ''cognitive deficiencies'' as the failure to attend to or incorporate certain life experiences. Lazarus (1971) has similarly described procedures for changing maladaptive thought processes, such as the tendency to view events dichotomously (i.e. something is either ''good'' or ''bad'') and to assume that certain social mores are logical conclusions rather than arbitrary conventions. Meichenbaum (1977), although acknowledging the existence of irrational beliefs that mediate disruptive emotions, has placed greater emphasis on training clients in the use of more adaptive coping self-statements, and has integrated the use of such cognitive skills along with relaxation procedures.

Just as clinicians and researchers have tended to differ in the content of the cognitive processes on which they focus, so have there been differences in the method of training clients in the use of cognitive change procedures. For example, Ellis (1962) has maintained that an effective way of training clients to think more realistically should involve the therapist's vigorous and repeated presentation of a more rational perspective on various problematic situations. Marvin Goldfried and his colleagues (Goldfried and Davison, 1976; Goldfried, Decenteceo and Weinberg, 1974; Goldfried and Goldfried, 1975) have attempted to incorporate many of Ellis's ideas into a social learning framework in order to encourage clients to take a more systematic and active role in monitoring and reappraising their unrealistic views. Procedures outlined by Beck (1976) and Meichenbaum (1977) have similarly used social learning principles in training clients to use cognitive methods in coping with a variety of problems, including depression (Beck, 1976; Beck et al, 1979), anxiety, anger, and pain (Meichenbaum and Turk, 1976; Novaco, 1975). Although there are differences among these several approaches (see Meichenbaum, 1977; Raimy, 1975), they all use relatively structured procedures in teaching clients more appropriate ways of cognitively appraising situations.

The plan for the remainder of this chapter is to focus on two such cognitive change methods—*systematic rational restructuring* and *problem solving*—and to describe and illustrate the use of these procedures in actual clinical practice. The section on systematic rational restructuring will deal with a procedure whereby an individual may be taught to reduce maladaptive emotional reactions by learning to label situations more accurately. Simply put, the approach involves teaching people how to "think straight." The second procedure, problem solving training, is designed to provide individuals with a general strategy for coping with the complexities of the world around them. In other words it teaches people how to "figure things out" and make wise decisions.

SYSTEMATIC RATIONAL RESTRUCTURING

Theoretical and Research Foundations

People's expectations and assumptions about the world around them can have significant implications for their emotional reactions and actual response to that world. Such "expectancies" and "assumptions" can be understood within the framework of what has generally been known experimentally as "set." It has been demonstrated in numerous experimental investigations that varying the set with which subjects approach an experimental task can greatly influence their emotional reactions to, and actual performance in that situation. Based on the findings that individuals can be taught to approach specific experimental tasks with one set or another, it may also be assumed that people learn more generalized sets which they carry with them as they approach various real-life situations. Thus, the pessimist will give up easily, if he indeed makes an effort at all, based on the belief that "things are not likely to work out anyway." The optimist will persist longer at a task on the assumption that he will eventually succeed. Further, the failure or success of one's efforts will clearly tend to reinforce these initial expectations.

In one of the earliest attempts to apply behavior principles to complex cognitive processes, Dollard and Miller (1950) described the manner in which overt language might play an important role in creating emotional arousal. They reasoned that one's emotional state frequently resulted from the way in which individuals evaluate or label stimuli, and not necessarily from the objective characteristics of the situation itself. For example, if people label a situation as "dangerous," their emotional state would be in direct response to the label "dangerous." To the extent that the situation was labeled appropriately—such as if one's car were stuck on the railroad tracks in the path of an oncoming train— the emotional arousal would be deemed as being appropriate, and even adaptive to the situation at hand. If, on the other hand, people mislabel a situation as being dangerous—as in the case of interpersonally anxious individuals who are uncomfortable even in friendly settings—then one would judge the reaction to be inappropriate or maladaptive. The important point to recognize in the second instance is that the emotional reaction is a reasonable response to the label applied to the situation; however, it is the label that is inaccurate. In such instances, it would seem appropriate that the therapeutic endeavor be directed toward the modification of the person's distorted perceptions of the world, as any such inappropriate labels are likely to mediate maladaptive emotional arousal and behavior.

The basic assumption that emotional arousal and maladaptive behavior are mediated by one's interpretations of situations has laid the groundwork for Albert Ellis's (1962) rational-emotive therapy. Ellis has observed:

> If . . . people essentially become emotionally disturbed because they unthinkingly accept certain illogical premises or irrational ideas, then there is a good reason to believe that they can be somehow persuaded or taught to think more logically and rationally and thereby to undermine their own disturbances (p. 191).

It is interesting to note that although Ellis's viewpoint was described in 1962, this orientation is most consistent with contemporary cognitive behavior therapy. It has only been in more recent years that cognitive behavior therapists have noted the relevance of Ellis's work in their own intervention approaches (Beck, 1976; Goldfried and Davison, 1976; Goldfried, Decenteceo, and Weinberg, 1974; A.A. Lazarus, 1971; Mahoney, 1974; Meichenbaum, 1977).

A contribution that has not yet made its impact in the behavioral literature involves the work of Richard S. Lazarus (1966), who has written extensively on the role that cognitive processes play in the maintenance and reduction of stress reactions. Lazarus has suggested that when confronted with a potentially stressful situation, individuals engage in a *primary appraisal*, whereby the situation is labeled potentially threatening, challenging, or benign. In the attempt to cope with such situations, there is also a *secondary appraisal*, involving a defensive distortion of the situation, a more realistic assessment, or a plan for direct action. The possible implications that such an approach has for cognitive behavior therapy has been described in detail by Roskies and Lazarus (in press).

A number of studies have been carried out to test the assumption that the way individuals label or evaluate situations affect their emotional reactions to these events (May, 1977; May and Johnson, 1973; Rimm and Litvak, 1969; Rogers and Craighead, 1977; Russell and Brandsma, 1974; Velten, 1968). Taken together, the laboratory findings indicated that the nature of individuals' self-statements do indeed have implications for their resulting emotional reactions.

An assumption central to Ellis's therapeutic approach is the idea that there are certain irrational beliefs, expectations, or assumptions with which a number of people in our culture tend to approach situations. To the extent that individuals maintain such irrational beliefs, they increase the likelihood of mislabeling situations.

According to Ellis (1962), typical irrational beliefs consist of the following:

1. The idea that it is a dire necessity for an adult human being to be loved or approved by virtually every significant other person in his community;
2. The idea that one should be thoroughly competent, adequate, and achieving in all possible respects, if one is to consider oneself worthwhile;
3. The idea that certain people are bad, wicked, or villainous and that they should be severely blamed and punished for their villainy;
4. The idea that it is awful and catastrophic when things are not the way one would very much like them to be;
5. The idea that human unhappiness is externally caused and that people have little or no ability to control their sorrows and disturbances;
6. The idea that if something is or may be dangerous or fearsome one should be terribly concerned about it and should keep dwelling on the possibility of its occurring;
7. The idea that it is easier to avoid than to face certain life difficulties and self-responsibilities;
8. The idea that one should be dependent on others and need someone stronger than oneself on whom to rely;
9. The idea that one's past history is an all-important determinant of one's present behavior and that because something once strongly affected one's life, it should indefinitely have a similar effect;
10. The idea that one should become quite upset over other people's problems and disturbances;
11. The idea that there is invariably a right, precise, and perfect solution to human problems and that it is catastrophic if this correct solution is not found.

A study by Goldfried and Sobocinski (1975) using college students found a positive relationship between the extent to which individuals held such irrational beliefs, and their scores on measures of interpersonal, public speaking, and test anxiety. It was also found that the tendency to view situations irrationally was related to the individual's susceptibility to emotional upset in situations related to such irrational expectations. Specifically, Goldfried and Sobocinski selected individuals who tended to be high or low in their irrational expectation that everyone must love and approve of them. Individuals at the two extremes were then asked to imagine themselves in a series of situations where they might interpret themselves as being rejected by others. A typical situation was as follows:

> One of your girlfriends has invited you to come to a party. Think of a person you know. You get to her house and you walk through the door. You're standing there now at the door just inside her house. Look around you and you'll see a number of people—people whom you have not met before. She says "hello," and she takes your coat. Try to see her face as vividly as you can. She takes your coat, and goes to put it away. You're standing there by yourself, and when she comes back out she walks over to some other people and starts talking to them. Try to stay in this situation, standing there by yourself, seeing your girlfriend talking to these people, and you're there alone looking around. Just notice how you feel in that situation (p. 507).

As a result of their imagining themselves in this and other similar situations, the high irrational group reported feeling more anxious and angry than did individuals who felt less of a need to be approved of by others.

Schwartz and Gottman (1976) conducted a study to demonstrate that negative self-statements are associated with unassertive behavior by comparing people who were first determined to be assertive or nonassertive. The authors found that the basic difference between these two groups was not in their knowledge of what to say in assertion-related situations, or even in their ability to demonstrate to a friend an actual assertive response in a hypothetical situation. Instead, it involved the kinds of things they thought about when they themselves were called upon to respond assertively. Specifically, Schwartz and Gottman found that highly assertive individuals tended to make positive self-statements, whereas the more unassertive people demonstrated greater concern over the possible reactions of others (e.g., "I was worried about what the other person would think of me if I refused.") A study by Alden and Safran (1978) similarly showed that subjects who held irrational beliefs described themselves as being uncomfortable and unassertive in assertion-related situations, and indeed were found to be less assertive during a role playing assessment. Thus, there appears to be growing evidence to confirm the assumption that unrealistic beliefs are associated with certain emotional reactions and problematic behaviors.

For quite some time, the efficacy of rational-emotive therapy was primarily substantiated by case studies (Ellis, 1962). In more recent years, controlled outcome studies have provided a more scientifically valid confirmation that this general approach to the modification of irrational beliefs can successfully reduce test anxiety (Goldfried, Linehan, and Smith, 1978; Meichenbaum, 1972), speech anxiety (Meichenbaum, Gilmore, and Fedoravicius, 1971; Trexler and Karst, 1972) and interpersonal anxiety (DiLoreto, 1971; Kanter and Goldfried, 1979; Linehan, Goldfried, and Goldfried, 1979). The current clinical effectiveness of this procedure has been reviewed by Ellis and Grieger (1977), Goldfried (1979a), and Meichenbaum (1977).

Therapeutic Guidelines

All of us have had the opportunity to witness how a change in attitude or thinking can reduce emotional upset and alter one's actual response to situations. This is true in our personal lives, and also within the therapeutic context, where the therapist is often successful in helping clients to sort out their concerns and fears. We also see this occur when we confide in a close friend, who can help us to place upsetting events into a different perspective. The goal of cognitive restructuring, particularly when it is presented as a coping skill (Goldfried, 1979b), is to help clients themselves develop the ability to evaluate potentially upsetting events more realistically.

There are always a variety of different ways of translating a principle of change into a therapeutic technique. This is certainly the case with cognitive restructuring, where the specific intervention procedure will vary depending upon one's particular theoretical orientation and the nature of the upsetting situations in question (Beck, 1976; Beck et al, 1979; Ellis, 1962; Goldfried and Davison, 1976; A.A. Lazarus, 1971; Meichenbaum, 1977). The similarity and differences among these varying procedures have been discussed by Meichenbaum (1977) and Raimy (1975). As yet, there are insufficient data to indicate which of our available procedures is most effective.

The approach originally described by Ellis (1962) for persuading or teaching clients to think more reasonably has involved heated debates in which the therapist's task has been to convince clients that their unreasonable beliefs are responsible for their upset and, consequently, need to be changed. Quite often, these arguments reflect disagreement between therapist and client on a variety of different issues. Goldfried and his associates (Goldfried and Davison, 1976; Goldfried, Decenteceo, and Weinberg, 1974) have attempted to place rational-emotive therapy within more of a cognitive-behavioral framework, providing clearly delineated steps that the therapist might take in training individuals to modify the emotionally arousing set with which they may be approaching various life situations. What follows is a description of the four steps used in implementing this procedure—*rational restructuring*—together with illustrative therapy transcripts.

Helping Clients Recognize that Cognitions Mediate Emotional Arousal. The therapist explains the underlying assumptions of rational restructuring, using various examples to show that what we tell ourselves can affect our feelings. It may be helpful for the therapist to indicate that we may not literally "tell ourselves" things that cause emotional upset, as these self-statements have been so well learned that they have become more or less automatic. Instead, the therapist can point out that clients are reacting as if they view the situation in a given way. At this point the therapist wants clients to understand the general significance of self-statements without applying this knowledge to their own particular problems, which is a much more complicated process. With an acceptance of the basic rationale using simple examples, the groundwork is laid for the more complicated application to the client's own problems. The illustrative transcript that follows, taken from Goldfried and Davison (1976), also includes the therapist's thinking and decision making process.

Client: My primary difficulty is that I become very uptight when I have to speak in front of a group of people. I guess it's just my own inferiority complex.

Therapist: **[I don't want to get sidetracked at this point by talking about that conceptualization of his problem. I'll just try to finesse it and make a smooth transition to something else.]** I don't know if I would call it an inferiority complex but I do believe that people can, in a sense, bring on their own upset and anxiety in certain kinds of situations. When you're in a particular situation, your anxiety is often not the result of the situation itself, but rather the way in which you *interpret* the situation—what you tell yourself about the situation. For example, look at this pen. Does this pen make you nervous?

Client: No.

Therapist: Why not?

Client: It's just an object. It's just a pen.

Therapist: It can't hurt you?

Client: No.

Therapist: If, instead, I were holding a gun or a knife, would that make you nervous?

Client: Yes.

Therapist: But a gun or a knife is also just an object. Unlike a pen, however, a gun or a knife *can* actually hurt you. It's really not the object that creates emotional upset in people, but rather what you *think* about the object. **[Hopefully, this Socratic-like dialogue will eventually bring him to the conclusion that self-statements can mediate emotional arousal.]** If you had never seen a gun or a knife, do you think you would be upset?

Client: Probably not.

Therapist: **[Now to move on to a more interpersonally relevant example, but not yet one that samples the presenting problem.]** Now this holds true for a number of other kinds of situations where emotional upset is caused by what a person tells himself about the situation. Take, for example, two people who are about to attend the same social gathering. Both of them may know exactly the same number of people at the party, but one person can be optimistic and relaxed about the situation, whereas the other one can be worried about how he will appear, and consequently very anxious. **[I'll try to get him to verbalize the basic assumption that attitude or perception is most important here.]** So, when these two people walk into the place where the party is given, are their emotional reactions at all associated with the physical arrangements at the party?

Client: No, obviously not.

Therapist: What determines their reactions, then?

Client: They obviously have different attitudes toward the party.

Therapist: Exactly, and their attitudes—the way in which they approach the situation—greatly influence their emotional reactions (pp. 163-165).

Helping Clients Recognize the Irrationality of Certain Beliefs. Before discussing the client's problems in rational terms, it is helpful to get their reaction to their various irrational beliefs. These beliefs may be stated in an even more extreme form, making it more likely for clients to disagree with them and find them untenable (e.g., "If other people do not love me or approve of everything I say or do, then this is proof that I have little worth as a person"). This is exactly what the therapist is aiming for. The therapist wants clients to distinguish between thinking that "it would be nice" if these expectations (such as perfection and universal love) were met, as opposed to the thought that they "must" or "should" be met, which will only lead to frustration. It is advisable for the therapist to play devil's advocate and let clients themselves refute the irrational beliefs, as the social psychological literature indicates that such a method can be more effective in changing attitudes (Brehm and Cohen, 1962).

It is probably unnecessary to review all eleven irrational ideas. The two that seem to be most appropriate in a large number of cases are "Everybody must love me" and "I must be perfect in everything I do." However, there is no hard and fast rule about this, and much depends on the therapist's clinical judgment and the client's particualr problems. This is an example of how this step may be implemented:

Therapist: I would like to do something with you. I'm going to describe a certain attitude or belief to you, and I'd like you to assume for a moment that I actually hold this belief. What I would like you to do is offer me as many reasons as you can why it may be irrational or unreasonable for me to hold on to such a belief. OK?

Client: All right.

Therapist: Assume that I believe the following: Everybody must approve of me, and if this doesn't happen, it means that I am a worthless person. What do you think of that?

Client: I don't think it makes much sense.

Therapist: [**We're off to a relatively good start. A certain percentage of clients—fortunately a small percentage—will initially acknowledge that the belief does not seem irrational to them. But now he has to be more specific.**] But why doesn't it make much sense?

Client: You really can't expect that people are going to do that.

Therapist: (*Naively*) Why not?

Client: It just seems unreasonable for you to expect that they would.

Therapist: [**We don't seem to be getting anywhere. I can prompt him indirectly by being a bit more extreme in my belief, hopefully making counterarguments a bit more obvious.**] I feel that every single person that I run into during the course of the day is going to have to smile and say nice things to me. And if this doesn't happen, I really feel down.

Client: But the world is simply not set up that way. There may be people who don't react to you positively because of things that are going on with themselves.

Therapist: [**That's a good reason, but it needs some elaboration.**] What other reasons could there be? I tend to think that everything is somehow caused by me.

Client: But that's ridiculous. It's possible that someone you meet may have had a bad night's sleep, or may have had an argument with their spouse and is in no mood to deal with you.

Therapist: [**I'll reinforce him by accepting this explanation, but then present another example of my irrationality.**] So you think that some of the day-to-day variations in the way people react to me can be due to things completely apart from my own adequacy?

Client: Of course.

Therapist: OK, that certainly is a possibility. But what about when someone is really disapproving of *me*? For example, a close friend may disagree with something I say. Now in that case, I usually feel that I am wrong, and I must be worthless for him to have disagreed with me.

Client: But you can't expect him to agree with everything you say.

Therapist: Why not?

Client: If you did, you would really be dishonest.

Therapist: But I feel that it is more important for me to get everyone to approve of me and like everything I say and do, than it is for me to really express the way I feel. In fact, I sometimes feel like a weather vane, shifting whichever way the wind might be blowing.

Client: But that's ridiculous! What happens to *you* as a person?

Therapist: **[He seems fairly strong on this point, so I think I'll back off a little.]** That seems to be a big problem with me; I often don't know who I am as a person. I seem to be so concerned about defining my own worth in terms of what everyone else's reactions are toward me. But how else can I think?

Client: Maybe you should consider how *you yourself* feel about certain things you do. Provided you're not really hurting anybody else, if you feel that what you are doing is right, perhaps you should be satisfied with that and realize that not everyone is going to agree.

Therapist: **[I'm satisfied that he sees the irrationality in that belief.]** That seems to make some sense. If I can only really accept it.

Client: You'll have to, because the other way is not at all reasonable.

Therapist: (Stepping out of role) OK. You seem to have a very good perspective on the rationality of that belief. Why don't we move on to another notion? (Goldfried and Davison, 1976, pp. 166-168).

The primary goal of this phase of the intervention is not only to have clients concur that certain beliefs are unrealistic, but also to begin to generate a number of specific reasons for the unreasonableness of these views. Thus, clients are likely to generate such statements as "If other people disagree with you that doesn't mean they dislike you." During the fourth step of the treatment procedure, these reasons generated by the clients themselves may be personalized by having them change "you" to "me" or "I," thereby providing them with coping self-statements. In this step, however, the entire procedure is carried out on a more objective basis, so that personal involvement does not interfere with their ability to generate believable counterarguments.

Helping Clients Understand that Unrealistic Cognitions Mediate Their Own Maladaptive Emotions. After clients agree in principle that self-statements can create emotional upset, and that certain beliefs and expectations are irrational, the therapist can begin to focus more closely on their own personal problems. Quite often, clients spontaneously acknowledge that they recognize the role played by certain unrealistic assumptions in their own particular lives. At times, however, it is necessary to explore more systematically various potentially upsetting situations in the client's current life, noting how given irrational expectations influence their emotions and behavior. The various situations reviewed during this phase can be arranged into a hierarchy and used in the fourth phase of the intervention procedure.

The client's self-statements can be analyzed from two possible sources of irrationality: (1) how likely is it that client's interpretations of particular situations are in fact realistic, and (2) what are the ultimate implications of the way in which they have labeled the situation. For example, let's look at a situation where a young woman is excessively upset because a male acquaintance she likes has declined an invitation to a party she is giving. Her readily available and upsetting interpretation might be: "He does not like me." How rational this interpretation is may be looked at from the likelihood of there being other reasonable explanations for his refusal, such as other commitments for that evening. The second source of irrationality, which is actually at a more "basic" level can take the following form: "What if this young man, in fact, really does not like you? Why should this make you so upset? Are there other things you may be implicitly telling youreslf about his not liking you?" Further questioning (e.g., "Yes, but why should that upset you?") may help the client to recognize that what she has been telling herself in situations like these stem from a previously disavowed irrational belief (e.g., everyone must love me).

Clients frequently respond to this exploration process by stating: "I agree that I'm causing my own upset. The problem is that I don't know how to change it!" This then brings us to the next phase of the procedure.

Helping Clients to Change Their Unrealistic Cognitions. Up until now the therapist has been laying the groundwork for the actual treatment. The objective has been for clients to understand how their evaluation of situations has been causing their own upset. Once this is achieved, the therapist can begin to help them to change. Simply understanding the cause of the problem will do little to alleviate it; clients must consciously and deliberately engage in doing something differently when feeling upset. This emotional reaction must now serve as a "cue" for them to stop and think: "What am I telling myself that may be unrealistic?" They must learn to "break-up" what was before an automatic reaction and replace it with a more realistic appraisal of the situation. At first, this is no easy task, but, with practice, the procedure becomes less and less tedious and deliberate, until clients eventually can totally eliminate the initial upset phase by having made the more realistic appraisal an automatic reaction.

The general procedure involves getting clients to think realistically while *in the situation* rather than through hindsight. In essence, clients learn to put things in proper perspective while the upsetting event is happening, and this involves practice in rational reevaluation. Because they must practice coping while in the problematic situation, imagination can be used as a means of controlling the training procedure. In this way the therapist can regulate the length of time clients are exposed to the situation and can control the anxiety-provoking nature of the situation. In addition, clients personalize the situation by filling in the relevant details. As with systematic desensitization, a hierarchy of least to most upsetting situations is used to enable clients to proceed systematically one step at a time. In this way clients are never faced with an overwhelming situation with which they are incapable of coping at the time. Instead, successful coping at one step determines the progression to a more difficult situation in the sequence.

In the actual procedure, the therapist describes a situation and clients imagine themselves in that situation, noting how nervous (or sad, or angry) they feel. If their emotional reaction exceeds a certain predetermined level, they stop and think as follows: "What am I telling myself that is making me upset?" They must now determine the unrealistic thought they are telling themselves. After evaluating the situation in more realistic terms, they then note the new anxiety (or depression, anger) level. In many respects, the technique is very similar to Goldfried's (1971) coping variation of systematic desensitization, except that rational reevaluation and not relaxation is the coping skill to be learned. Methods of systematic desensitization are described in detail in Chapter 8.

At the very start, the therapist can serve as a model to illustrate the rational restructuring technique. For example:

I have just arrived at a party where I know very few people. Everyone is clustered in little groups talking, and I don't feel a part of things. I feel myself becoming tense. On a scale of 0-100 percent tension, I classify my tension at about 40. I now stop what I'm doing and think: "What am I telling myself that is creating this feeling of anxiety?" Let's see, now. I'm worried that I won't handle myself well, that people won't like me—that I'll appear inadequate and foolish in their eyes. But, now why should they think that of me? I'm not behaving foolishly. Really, the very worst they can think of me is that I'm kind of quiet and that's not so bad. Actually, whatever they thought of me wouldn't change the way I really am. I'm still me. Well, I don't feel as tense about the party now—maybe I'm now at an anxiety level of about 20.

It should be recognized that the imaginal presentation of situations represents a compromise, albeit a reasonable one, based primarily on practical considerations. One may not be able to realistically bring into the consultation room emotionally arousing situations in any manner other than by imagery (e.g., situations involving intimate sexual contact). However, behavior therapists have relied so extensively on the use of imaginal presentations of problematic situations that they have often overlooked the potential for a more realistic simulation during the consultation session. Here we are referring to the utility of behavioral rehearsal, which can frequently enable clients to create a more vivid situation with which they must learn to cope. When rational restructuring is conducted in groups, the setting lends itself particularly well to the use of behavior rehearsal, particularly in instances entailing social-evaluative anxiety. For example, if the group consists of individuals experiencing interpersonal anxiety, a hierarchy of items in order of increasing anxiety can readily be constructed so that it may be simulated in interactions among the various group members. Anxiety in public speaking situations similarly lends itslef particularly well to treatment in group settings, where clients can learn to modify their anxiety-arousing expectations while presenting actual practice speeches before fellow group members. For guide lines in working with groups, the reader is referred to Chapter 13.

Despite the relatively straightforward guidelines associated with the procedure, some clients experience difficulty in following through as directed. A fair amount of clinical skill may be needed in assisting the client, as illustrated in the following transcript:

Therapist: I'm going to ask you to imagine yourself in a given situation, and to tell me how nervous you may feel. I'd then like you to think aloud about what you might be telling yourself that is creating this anxiety, and then go about trying to put your expectations into a more realistic perspective. From time to time, I will make certain comments, and I'd like you to treat these comments as if they were your own thoughts. OK?

Client: All right.

Therapist: I'd like you to close your eyes now and imagine yourself in the following situation: You are sitting on stage in the auditorium, together with the other school board members. It's a few minutes before you have to get up and give your report to the people in the audience. On a scale between 0 and 100 percent tension, tell me how nervous you feel.

Client: About 50.

Therapist: **[Now to get into his head.]** So I'm feeling fairly tense. Let me think. What might I be telling myself that's making me upset?

Client: I'm nervous about reading my report in front of all these people.

Therapist: But why does that bother me?

Client: Well, I don't know if I'm going to come across all right. . . .

Therapist: **[He seems to be having trouble. More prompting on my part may be needed than I originally anticipated.]** But why should that upset me? That upsets me because . . .

Client: . . . because I want to make a good impression.

Therapist: And if I don't . . .

Client: . . . well, I don't know. I don't want people to think that I'm incompetent. I guess I'm afraid that I'll lose the respect of the people who thought I knew what I was doing.

Therapist: **[He seems to be getting closer.]** But why should that make me so upset?

Client: I don't know. I guess it shouldn't. Maybe I'm being *overly* concerned about other people's reactions to me.

Therapist: How might I be overly concerned?

Client: I think this may be one of those situations where I have to please everybody, and there are an awful lot of people in the audience. Chances are I'm not going to get everybody's approval, and maybe that's upsetting me. I want everyone to think I'm doing a good job.

Therapist: Now let me think for a moment to see how rational that is.

Client: To begin with, I don't think it really is likely that I'm going to completely blow it. After all, I have prepared in advance, and have thought through what I want to say fairly clearly. I think I may be reacting as if I already have failed, even though it's very unlikely that I will.

Therapist: And even if I did mess up, how bad would that be?

Client: Well, I guess that really wouldn't be so terrible at all.

Therapist: **[I don't believe him for one moment. There is a definite hollow ring to his voice. He arrived at that conclusion much too quickly and presents it without much conviction.]** I say I don't think it'll upset me, but I don't really believe that.

Client: That's true. I would be upset if I failed. But actually, I really shouldn't be looking at this situation as being a failure.

Therapist: What would be a better way for me to look at the situation?

Client: Well, it's certainly not a do-or-die kind of thing. It's only a ridiculous committee report. A lot of the people in the audience know who I am and what I'm capable of doing. And even if I don't give a sterling performance, I don't think they're going to change their opinion of me on the basis of a five-minute presentation.

Therapist: But what if some of them do?

Client: Even if some of them do think differently of me, that doesn't mean that I *would* be different. I would still be me no matter what they thought. It's ridiculous of me to base my self-worth on what other people think.

Therapist: **[I think he's come around as much as he can. We can terminate this scene now.]** With this new attitude toward the situation, how do you feel in percentage of anxiety?

Client: Oh, about 25 percent.
Therapist: OK, let's talk a little about some of the thoughts you had during the situation before trying it again. (pp. 172-174).

On the basis of clinical experience, we have observed that therapists may assist clients in uncovering their unrealistic assumptions by the use of incomplete sentences. Prompting clients at various times during hierarchy presentation, the therapist can introduce such thoughts as "If people noticed that I made a mistake it would bother me because . . .," and "If I stumbled over a word during this talk I'd be upset because. . . ." In finishing these sentences, treating the thoughts as if they were their own, clients are often in a better position to recognize and subsequently reevaluate their unrealistic expectations in given situations.

Following the simulation of rational reevaluation in the consultation session—via imagery or behavior rehearsal—clients should be encouraged to utilize the same procedure in upsetting situations which occur on a day-to-day basis. Clients should be forewarned, however, that real-life situations will not occur in a hierarchical fashion, and some of the situations may be too stressful for rational reevaluation to be initially successful. Still, even if initially unsuccessful, the real-life trials will serve the purpose of giving clients a coping set. We have found it useful to provide clients with a homework sheet such as that shown in figure 4.1, which we have used in actual in-vivo homework assignments.

Date	Description of Situation	Initial Level of Upset (0 to 100)	Unrealistic Thoughts	Realistic Evaluation	Subsequent Level of Upset (0 to 100)

Fig. 4.1. Record of attempts to overcome emotional upset in daily situations.

Applications

From a theoretical point of view, rational restructuring would seem to be appropriate in the treatment of any maladaptive emotional reaction or behavior pattern that is maintained primarily by the individual's unrealistic attitudes and inappropriate labels. Among the typical problems for which the technique has been used are various forms of anxiety (e.g. test anxiety, public speaking anxiety, interpersonal anxiety), unassertiveness, depression, anger, and excessively perfectionistic standards. A review of the outcome research may be found elsewhere (Ellis and Grieger, 1977; Goldfried, 1979a; Meichenbaum, 1977).

Drawing from our experience in treating various problems with rational restructuring, we have become sensitized to particular issues that may come up in the course of treatment. For example, in utilizing rational restructuring for reduction of test anxiety, one should be aware of some typical problems likely to arise. Although test anxious individuals may tend to distort the significance of any given examination, the therapist should not fail to recognize that performance on tests can at times have a far-reaching impact on an individual's future. The central question here is just how far reaching the impact will be. Although clients may justifiably become upset because they may not have been able to get into graduate school, the amount of upset need not be equivalent to that which would be experienced if their entire life were about to come to an end. We had the occasion to see one student who was extremely anxious immediately before an examination. When asked to rate his anxiety on a scale of 1 to 10, he described his anxiety state at the level of "9." When asked how he would feel if he knew for certain he would fail the exam, he said he would be at a level of "10." The therapist then asked a series of additional questions, each reflecting a potentially more disastrous outcome (e.g., How would you feel if you failed the course? Flunked out of school? Were only able to get a poor paying job? Were unable to get any job at all?, etc.). The student's initial response to such questions was "Wait a minute. I think I'm going to have to change my use of the rating scale." What happened was that he became dramatically aware of the fact that he was being indiscriminate in his emotional reaction to the examination situation and soon realized that its importance more justifiably warranted an anxiety reaction of no more than "2."

A related potential problem using rational restructuring with text anxious students is that they may have difficulty in placing examination situations in a broader perspective. This is certainly understandable, especially if one's entire existence at any particular time consists primarily of school work. In one of our test anxiety groups, there was a married woman with a family who had recently returned to college. Although she was admittedly anxious in testing situations, she very rapidly appreciated the fact that her evaluation of such examination situations was disproportionate to its realistic import. As she put it, she still had her husband, her children, and an active social life. To the extent that one's life is dominated by school work, attempts to put exams into realistic perspective may not so readily be accomplished. Despite these potential problems, rational restructuring would certainly seem to be a method well-suited for treating test anxiety problems (see Goldfried, Linehan, and Smith, 1978).

In applying rational restructuring within a group setting, the behavior change agent should be in the position of handling the various contingencies that are likely to occur when therapy is conducted in groups. Although a group setting permits more efficient application of the procedure to larger numbers of individuals, the therapist must possess the ability to keep the group moving on course. Silent members must be drawn out, and overly talkative ones toned down. Inasmuch as the therapeutic procedures are fairly well delineated, the therapist must be able to deal with the frequently occurring problem of some group members going off on irrelevant tangents. A discussion of some of the procedures typically used in conducting groups can be found in Chapter 13.

As is the case with other therapy procedures, the specificity with which the technique may be outlined does not completely substitute for ongoing clinical judgment. This is nicely illustrated in the case of a client being treated for social-evaluative anxiety by means of rational restructuring. When asked to explain why she had missed the previous session, the client told the therapist that her children were not feeling too well, and that she felt they needed her. The therapist was about to emphasize the importance of regular attendance at the sessions, when the client went on to state: "I really didn't want to cancel. I knew you would be disappointed if I missed the session, and I felt very badly about that at first. However, after thinking things through more rationally, and realizing that I was in conflict because I was afraid of your disapproval, I decided that what I really wanted to do was to stay home and be with my children." The therapist stifled his desire to admonish the client about missing the session, and instead reinforced her for her successful attempt at rational reevaluation. The point, then, is that the procedures we have outlined should avoid being a straight jacket for therapists, but rather should serve as general guidelines within which they might function.

PROBLEM SOLVING

In taking a realistic view of the world around us, it is hard to deny the fact that we are continually confronted with situational problems with which we must cope. In what may seem to some as an overly pessimistic statement, D'Zurilla and Goldfried (1971) have argued that "our daily lives are replete with situational problems which we must solve in order to maintain an adequate level of effective functioning" (p.197). How many of us have experienced situations where we encounter car trouble just when we have to go somewhere, when the unavailability of certain library books or journals interferes with our ability to complete a written assignment, or where we have to make some decision about whether or not we should accept a given job offer. In many of these instances, the inability to arrive at an adequate solution may not only upset us, but may also have some negative consequences that will only create further problems in the future.

Theoretical and Research Foundations

In reviewing the research and theory on problem solving, D'Zurilla and Gold-fried pointed out the relevance of problem solving to the handling of real-life difficulties. Problem solving, as defined by D'Zurilla and Goldfried, consists of "a behavioral process, whether overt or cognitive in nature, which (a) makes available a variety of potentially effective response alternatives for dealing with the problematic situation and (b) increases the probability of selecting the most effective response from among these various alternatives" (p. 108). The general goal in problem solving training is not to offer individuals specific solutions to specific situations, but rather to provide a general coping skill, so that they may be in a better position to deal more effectively with a wide variety of situational problems (Goldfried, 1979b).

The problem solving process, as outlined by D'Zurilla and Goldfried, include the following five steps: (1) general orientation; (2) problem definition and formulation; (3) generation of alternatives; (4) decision making; and (5) verification. Although we are quick to acknowledge that there may exist many good problem solvers who do not utilize this exact five-step process, the essential point is that poor problem solvers can be taught to increase the effectiveness of their decision making process by following the problem solving strategy.

Before describing the problem-solving training process itself, we might briefly note the theory and research relevant to each of these several steps.

General Orientation. We are referring here to the general attitude with which one approaches the problem situation. Actually, this general orientation is composed of four subsets: (1) the recognition that the problematic situations comprise a normal aspect of living; (2) the assumption that one can actively make attempts to cope with such situations; (3) the readiness to recognize problematic situations as they occur; and (4) the set to inhibit the temptation to act impulsively.

The first two subsets relate directly to what we have discussed within the context of rational restructuring.

The ability to recognize problematic situations as they are occurring may not be as straightforward as one might imagine. There are times when we may be in problematic situations and still not realize it. Miller, Galanter, and Pribram (1960) have hypothesized that the process of problem recognition proceeds along the following lines:

> In ordinary affairs we usually muddle ahead, doing what is habitual and customary, being slightly puzzled when it sometimes fails to give the intended outcome, but not stopping to worry much about the failures because there are too many other things still to do. Then circumstances conspire against us and we find ourselves caught failing where we must succeed—where we cannot withdraw from the field, or lower our self-imposed standards, or ask for help, or throw a tantrum. Then we may begin to suspect that we face a problem (p. 171).

Thus, we frequently recognize that we are in a problematic situation only by virtue of the fact that we are upset about "something." Upon realizing this, one's task is to refocus attention from the emotional state to the situation creating the upset.

The final subset is axiomatic. If a situation is truly problematic—that is, if an effective solution is not immediately apparent—it is hard to imagine how one could even begin to engage in the actual problem solving process without first stopping to think.

Problem Definition and Formulation. In basic research on problem solving, subjects are typically presented with a relatively well-defined task for which they must arrive at some solution. In real life, problematic situations are not always clearly specified. It is therefore necessary to *define* the various aspects of the situation in relatively concrete terms. Research by Bloom and Broder (1950) has demonstrated that more effective problem solvers typically translate abstract terms into concrete examples, whereas poor problem solvers typically make no such translation. But one cannot deal directly with an array of facts. By formulating the various *issues* reflected in the details of the situation, the direction of the problem solving process becomes more clearly focused.

Generation of Alternatives. The research most relevant to this state of problem solving is based on "brainstorming" techniques (Osborn, 1963; Parnes, 1967). As a kind of focused free association, the procedure is based on two principles: (1) deferment of judgment; and (2) quantity breeds quality. The deferment of judgment principle states that if individuals can temporarily withhold any evaluation of the quality of solution, there is a greater likelihood that good ones will be included within the list. Numerous studies have been carried out on brainstorming, all of which lead to the conclusion that training in this procedure does, in fact, increase the likelihood of producing good quality solutions (D'Zurilla and Goldfried, 1971).

Decision Making. Basic research on information processing has employed utility theory in evaluating the "goodness" of any particular course of action (Becker and McClintock, 1967; Churchman, 1961; Edwards, 1961; Simon, 1955). In essence, utility theory provides one with a functional evaluation of any given alternative. In the area of business and economics, a given course of action can be evaluated in terms of its financial payoff. In using this approach for more personal or interpersonal problem situations, the utility of the alternative may be evaluated according to its likelihood of resolving the issues delineated during the problem definition and formulation phase.

Verification. Once individuals have entered the problem solving task, defined the problem and formulated the issues at hand, generated potential alternatives, and made some decision as to a particular course of action, problem solvers must verify the extent to which their alternative was a good one. This requires that they act on their decision, and then evaluate the extent to which the problem situation has been resolved.

The theoretical model most relevant to the verification stage comes from the work of Miller, Galanter and Pribram (1960), who theorized on the interrelationship between an individual's plans and actions. They suggest a "Test-Operate-Test-Exit" (TOTE) model, whereby an individual's activities (overt or covert) are guided by the extent to which the outcome of these activities matches up to a given standard. Thus, one maintains a given standard for adequacy ("Test"), and engages in relevant activities ("Operate"). The results of such activities are matched to a standard ("Test"), and if that standard is achieved, the activity is ended ("Exit"). If performace falls short of this standard, the individual continues to "Operate," until the standard has been reached.

During the verification stage, problem solvers, after having actually implemented their preferred course of action, determine for themselves whether or not the problematic situation has ever been satisfactorily resolved. If so, they "exit" from the problem solving process. If not, they return to problem solving in the hope of generating a more effective solution.

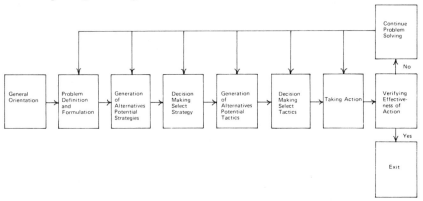

Fig. 4.2. Schematic presentation of problem solving process (from Goldfried & Davison, 1976, p. 192).

The entire problem solving procedure, as outlined schematically by Goldfried and Davison (1976), appears as figure 4.2. A distinction is made in figure 4.2 between a "strategy" and a "tactic," reflecting different levels of abstraction associated with a given course of action. A strategy refers to a more general course of action, whereas a tactic deals with those specific behaviors associated with putting this general plan into effect. In choosing the best strategy in any given instance, the decision is made with regard to the likelihood of *resolving the major issues* inherent in any given problematic situation. In selecting the appropriate tactic, the choice is made on the basis of how likely one is to *implement the strategy effectively*. Thus, if the relevant issue involved the need for more money, the strategy "Try to find additional work" would be evaluated with regard to its likelihood of resolving the issue. The tactic "Place an advertisement in the paper," on the other hand, would be evaluated on the basis of its likelihood to result in finding work.

Therapeutic Guidelines

Different people will have difficulty at different stages of the problem solving procedure. Some people will be very vague in their definition of the problem, others will not be able to think up various alternatives to a problem. Others may have a general set of helplessness—a feeling that they cannot cope with things in general. The therapist would naturally place greater emphasis on those aspects of the problem solving procedure in which the client is weakest.

The therapist introduces a "problematic situation" and the client must achieve some minimum performance at each stage of the process before going on to the next. Clients need to pass through all stages before they can be said to have "solved the problem." New and more difficult problem situations are then introduced and once again, all stages must be completed by the client. The repetition is intended so that the various stages in the problem solving sequence will become more or less automatic and so that each response in the series serves as a cue for the next response and as a reinforcer for the previous response. The entire series is reinforced by the final outcome, i.e., successful solution to the problem.

In the initial phases of training, the therapist models the problem solving procedures, verbalizing all thoughts, while the client merely observes. As the client becomes more active in the process, the therapist's role changes to that of a consultant, providing guidance in and evaluation of the real-life application.

General Orientation. At the start of the training in problem solving, the therapist explains the rationale of the treatment and in general aims for the client's understanding that problematic situations are a part of everyone's life. The therapist emphasizes that clients should learn to recognize when these situations occur, and that their response should not be made automatically or impulsively. Clients may be presented with examples of common problematic situations and/or asked to identify such situations which have occurred in their own lives. Initially, it is a good idea to have clients actually keep a record of problematic situations in which they find themselves, and to note their thoughts and emotional reactions. These thoughts and feelings (e.g., confusion, frustration, etc.) can serve as a signal for clients to look at what is happening around them—to look at the situations that are triggering these reactions. In essence the therapist wants to establish a problem-solving "set" before the actual training begins.

Problem Definition and Formulation. In the beginning, many clients will record their own problematic situations in rather vague or abstract terms, giving general descriptions of the basic nature of the problem. Consequently, they need to learn to define problems specifically and to include all related details. Not only external events, but also thoughts and feelings (internal events) are often very important in completely describing a situation. In addition, they must learn to exclude irrelevant information and to focus on those areas of information most likely to assist them in the eventual solution of the problem.

The following transcript, taken from Goldfried and Davison (1976), illustrates how a vague description of a problematic situation can be spelled out in detail:

Client: I've been depressed and upset lately.

Therapist: How long have you been feeling this way?

Client: Oh, for about the past month or so. I think a lot of it is due to the fact that my husband has started working late. I really should feel very grateful, because we really do need the money.

Therapist: In what way do you feel your upset is related to your husband's working late?

Client: Well, I've been feeling more and more lonely, nervous, and generally upset in the evenings, waiting for him to come home. I don't like being alone at night. Also, by the time my husband does get home, he's usually so exhausted that he goes right to bed.

Therapist: So your contacts with him are limited?

Client: Very much so. I really miss having the chance to sit down with him and talk about what's gone on during the day. He feels pretty much the same as I do about this. Also neither of us is very happy about the fact that our sex life has fallen off.

Therapist: And what do you feel this is due to?

Client: Sheer fatigue on his part. Our sex life has always been good up until now.

Therapist: So, one of the things that is of great concern to you involves the minimal contact—sexual and otherwise—that you've been having lately with your husband.

Client: Also, I just don't like being alone every night; I'd much prefer being with someone else. I actually do have a number of friends, and enjoy being with them.

Therapist: So it's not just missing your husband. It's also being generally lonely.

Client: I guess so. You know, I think another thing that has been bothering me about staying at home at night is the fact that we live on a dark and isolated street. I guess I am afraid that someone might find out that I'm alone every night, and try to break in.

Therapist: Do you know of any cases where this has happened?

Client: I have read about a number of robberies occurring not too far from where I live.

Therapist: Before your husband started working late, did you have any of these concerns?

Client: Not really. I think an awful lot of the difficulty is basically due to a very bad situation. I just don't know what to do about it. (pp. 194-195)

In the above example, the aim was to specify the details of the situation and to formulate the problem by identifying the major goals and issues which made it problematic. This client's goals included the desire for social interaction during the evening, more frequent communication with her husband, a greater feeling of safety in the evening, and more sexual contact. The issues in the situation involved desire for company versus being alone at night; desire for conversation versus husband's fatigue; desire to feel safe versus being alone and afraid that someone might break in; and the desire for sex versus the husband's need to get sleep.

Learning to specify goals and issues is a critical first step in the treatment program and in some instances may be sufficient to make the client immediately aware of possible solutions. When this is the case, further formal problem solving may not be necessary for that particular problem situation. However, when this is not the case, the client would then move on to the next stage in the process—learning to identify possible response alternatives.

Generation of Alternatives. In deciding how to go about solving an operationally defined problem, we noted earlier that a distinction can be made between "strategies" and "tactics." The strategy outlines a course of action stated in general terms, while the tactic gives the specifics for putting the plan into effect (i.e., *what* to do versus *how* to do it). During this stage the client is instructed to "brainstorm" possible solutions. For example:

> *Therapist:* OK. Now we seem to have a clearer picture of the kinds of things that are making life difficult for you. Let's see if you can come up with some possible solutions. Do you remember the brainstorming rules I told you about?
>
> *Client:* I think so. Let's see, I'm supposed to think of as many possibilities as I can, no matter how silly or impractical they may seem at first.
>
> *Therapist:* That's right. Just let your mind run free. Even though you come up with a possibility, it doesn't necessarily mean that you would ever really want to carry it out.
>
> *Client:* OK.
>
> *Therapist:* Also, at this particular point, I don't think you really have to worry about being too specific. Try to think of general approaches to handling the situation; later on, we can start looking at specific ways to carry out some of these approaches.
>
> *Client:* I'm not sure if I completely understand what you mean.
>
> *Therapist:* Well, for example, let's suppose that you decided that one possible solution was "I would find a babysitter." That's describing a possiblity at a very general level; it indicates *what* you would do, not *how* you would go about doing it. For example, in getting a babysitter, you could contact a relative, look in the classified section of your local newspaper, call some friends to find out if they know anyone who is available, or any one of a number of other specific ways of carrying out the general appraoch of "getting a babysitter."
>
> *Client:* I see what you mean.
>
> *Therapist:* [**Before actually getting her to start generating alternatives, I ought to review the four issues that we formulated a little bit earlier. Since they are not all that independent, I won't bother to have her brainstorm on each issue separately, but instead present them all at once.**] Fine. Now thinking at this general level, I'd like you to come up with as many possibilities as you can think of; I'll note them down as you mention them. Remember, don't make any attempt to evaluate them at this point. Although you really can be as creative, or even ridiculous, as you want in thinking of possibilities, keep in mind the four major concerns you have about your current situation: Having company at night, more communication with your husband, feeling safe in the evening, and more frequent sexual relations.
>
> *Client:* Let's see . . . I can get someone to visit me during the week. I can go out myself in the evening. I could get a stronger lock for my door, or maybe even put in a burglar alarm system. Maybe I can ask my husband to put in some bright lights outside of our house. Let's see . . .
>
> *Therapist:* [**The pause and the look on her face make me feel that she may be running into some difficulty. Maybe she's making some premature evaluations; at least all her alternatives up to now seem to be fairly sensible. Perhaps I should remind her about deferring judgment until later.**] Try not to hold back. Just include anything that comes to mind, no matter how foolish it may seem.
>
> *Client:* Well, I suppose I could always keep a gun in the house (*laughs*). Or maybe complain

to the police, and see whether or not they could have the area patrolled better. Many of the other people on the street have told me that they're also concerned about the number of robberies lately, so maybe we could all get together and sign a petition or something. I think if we all complained, it might be more effective.

Therapist: [**That sounds like a really good idea. On the other hand, she seems to be getting too specific at this point; I prefer she stay at a strategy level.**] It certainly sounds reasonable. Why don't you hold off on the specifics for a while; we can get into that a little bit later. For now, let's stay at the general level.

Client: All right. I guess I was just getting carried away. About the problem of my husband not being too interested in sex when he gets home, I guess there might be things I could do to help put him in the mood. Maybe we could have intercourse at other times, such as early in the morning or weekends. Although I probably would never do it, I could always have an affair. Maybe my husband and I could also find time to talk to each other at other times as well, like by telephoning during the day, or early in the morning. . . . I don't think I can think of anything else.

Therapist: [**She could use a little bit of prompting at this point. Perhaps I can provide her with an alternative that I thought of a few minutes ago.**] Let's keep at it a little bit more. How about the possibility of your husband looking for a better paying job?

Client: I doubt if he could find one. Oh, but I'm not supposed to think about those things, right?

Therapist: Right.

Client: Well, maybe he can work on Saturday instead of weekday nights. (pp. 196-198).

Once clients have identified most of the available response alternatives, they are ready to make some decision about the strategy or strategies to pursue. It is up to the therapist to determine when most of the potential solutions have been enumerated and it is time to move on to the next phase.

Decision Making. In this phase, clients estimate which alternatives are worth pursuing, choosing among the number of wide ranging possibilities they have freely enumerated. With each strategy, clients anticipate the likely consequences and evaluate those in terms of the major issues comprising the problematic situation. There may be some obviously unrealistic alternatives which they will want to eliminate at the outset.

In considering the likely consequences of a particular alternative, clients should keep in mind the following: (1) the personal consequences, particularly as they relate to the major issues of the situation; (2) the social consequences that the course of action would have, particularly on the significant others in their life; (3) the short-term consequences as they relate to both their own problem and the effects on others; (4) the long-term consequences that the solution will have on future personal-social functioning, and the possible prevention of a similar problematic situation in the future.

Practically speaking, we are all limited in our ability to forecast the future, and clients cannot realistically consider all possible consequences of an action. In reality, they will be examining only a limited number of ''significant'' outcomes, and the likelihood of a particular outcome occurring can only be stated in general terms such as ''highly likely,'' ''likely,'' or ''unlikely'' to occur. The judgments regarding the efficacy of the various alternatives will also be in general terms, e.g., "very good," "good," "neutral," "bad," and "very bad." However, after considering the various alternatives, clients should be able to select the one which seems likely to yield the best results. The following exchange illustrates this point:

> *Therapist:* [**Before going into detailed decision making, why don't I just get her to screen out any alternatives she obviously does not want to pursue further?**] Let's look at the alternatives you've come up with, to see if you can arrive at some decision as to which will be worth considering further. To begin with, are there any which you would want to reject out of hand?
>
> *Client:* Well, I doubt if I would really want to have an affair. As I mentioned before, my husband and I get along quite well. It's just that the situation we find ourselves in is very bad. I wouldn't want to do anything which would endanger our marriage.
>
> *Therapist:* Are there any other alternatives that might be eliminated?
>
> *Client:* I don't think so.
>
> *Therapist:* [**In having her evaluate the strategies she's come up with thus far, she should operate on the assumption that she will be able to come up with a good tactic for implementing it.**] OK. Let's look at each of these possibilities, trying to anticipate what the likely consequences would be if you *were* successful in following through with it. In trying to estimate the possible consequences, think along the lines of what the implications might be for you, as well as anyone else you care about, such as your husband, children, friends, relatives—both immediate consequences and long-term ones. (*Referring to written notes.*) Let's consider first the possibility of your going out in the evening.
>
> *Client:* All right. I think I would enjoy getting out of the house to be with some friends. I don't think it would affect my husband one way or the other, although I would have to arrange for a babysitter. That could run into money if I do it on a regular basis. If I did go out at night, I'd probably be worried about the children's safety; you know, the whole business about the robberies in the neighborhood. It would depend on whether that problem could be solved or not.
>
> *Therapist:* [**Hmm. I guess I should have seen that earlier. The issue of the robberies in the neighborhood has to be dealt with before we can go about evaluating the effectiveness of responses for dealing with the other issues.**] OK, that's a good point. Maybe it would be best to start off considering possible ways of handling that situation. Why don't we look at that for a while, and then come back to consider some of the other possibilities.
>
> *Client:* Right. Let's see. I think I mentioned something about getting together with a number of other people on the street to see if we could get the police to do something about the situation. It's hard to know exactly what the results would be. I guess a lot depends on how we carry it out. But, assuming that we handle it right, I can't see anything but good coming of it.
>
> *Therapist:* [**I don't think she's considering the time and effort involved as a potential negative consequence. I'll point that out to her and see what she says.**] How about the time and effort involved?
>
> *Client:* As far as I'm concerned, that wouldn't be much of a factor.
>
> *Therapist:* Suppose you were to evaluate this alternative then. Would you say it was very good, good, neutral, bad, or very bad?
>
> *Client:* Offhand, I would think of it as a very good possibility.
>
> *Therapist:* OK, fine. Let's go on to another possibility. (pp. 199-202).

In situations with more than one major issue, it is likely that several courses of action would be needed to resolve the problem. Also, it must be kept in mind that there are some problematic situations for which there are really no "good" solutions. Situations involving severe illness, death of a family member, or major financial crisis may have no really satisfactory solution, though the problem solving method can still enable one to carry through on the best of the available options.

After one or more strategies have been selected, clients then address themselves to the possible alternative tactics for implementing each strategy. The same guidelines are used here as was employed in generating strategies. Thus, for the strategy "Get someone to visit during weekday evenings," possible alternative tactics might involve: "Invite friends for dinner occasionally"; "Arrange to have a friend over for dinner on a regular basis"; "Ask my mother to visit me during the evening"; "Organize a rap group." After having generated a number of specific tactics, clients again go through the decision making process, so as to select the most effective way of implementing each of those strategies selected.

Although the problem solving process has been presented in a step-wise fashion, things may not always progress in such a straightforward way. Indeed, there are times when clients will generate a far more effective solution while they are in a process of evaluating alternatives. In the clinical example we have been considering thus far, this occurred as the client was in the process of making a decision about the best tactic for carrying out the strategy of "Going out more frequently during the evening."

> *Client:* If I were able to take an adult education course, I could get involved in working on ceramics and other similar activities. I've done that in the past, and I know I would enjoy it very much. This would only take up one, or at best two, nights a week. Anything more than that would involve spending too much on babysitters, which is something we can't afford at this time. But maybe there's a way to deal with that, perhaps by looking for some part-time job I could have a few nights a week. That would have a number of positive consequences: not only would I be able to get out more frequently, but I could also earn some money.
>
> *Therapist:* [Why didn't I think of that? She seems to have inadvertently hit upon an alternative that also bears directly on the origin of the entire problem situation: The reason her husband has been working late is because of their financial situation. Should I point it out to her or not? Maybe it's best to wait a bit and see if she's able to see the connection herself. It won't hurt that much to smile and offer a minimal verbal acknowledgement.] Mhm.
>
> *Client:* The more I think about it, the more I like the idea. In fact, I might be even better off if I could look for a job during the day. That would really be much better in a number of ways. If I were able to get a job, even if it were just part-time, that would mean that my husband wouldn't have to work evenings. He's only doing it for the money, and I know he dislikes the situation as much as I. A part-time job would probably be better, especially if I could find something during the time the kids are in school.
>
> *Therapist:* [I'm really glad I didn't say anything. I think that's a great idea. I hope she sees it the same way.] How does this solution compare to the others you've considered thus far?
>
> *Client:* I like it much better. It doesn't do anything about the robberies in the neighborhood, but I think that could be handled separately. The more I think of it, the more I realize that

getting a job would be the best way to approach the situation. In fact, I'm surprised I didn't think of it before. If for some reason I can't find a job, I guess I can fall back on some of the other possibilities we've discussed.

   Therapist: **[I don't think that the previous problem solving has gone to waste, in the sense that she now has some contingency plans, should she have any difficulty finding a job that would be able to pay enough to handle the financial situation. Time for her to brainstorm possible tactics for finding a job.]** That's true. Why don't we now consider some of the possible ways you might be able to locate a job. (pp. 203-204).

Verification. While much of the training in problem solving goes on at a cognitive level, the aim of it all is to have clients actually carry out in real life the behavior decided upon as the most effective course of action. In fact, all along, clients are given "homework" wherein they are encouraged to practice problem solving in real-life situations between sessions. The use of record forms to assist in the use of problem solving in real-life situations may prove to be useful (see Goldfried and Davison, 1976, pages 200-202). The therapist not only encourages the implementation of the selected behavior, but also acts as guide in helping clients verify its efficacy by observing the consequences of their actions. If consequences are produced that satisfy the client, then the problem solving sequence is complete. If the solution produces unsatisfactory consequences, then the problem solving procedure is resumed and another solution tried out.

Applications

The problem solving procedures outlined in the previous section are particularly relevant in assisting individuals who are required to cope with complex and relatively unfamiliar situational demands, for individuals whose previous learning experiences have left them ill-prepared to cope effectively, and for cases reflecting a combination of these two conditions.

   Problem solving may be found to be useful in crisis intervention, where individuals are confronted with problematic situations of the most serious sort (McGuire and Sifneos, 1970). Here we are referring to such stressful life events as divorce, separation, death of a loved one, and other major upheavals in an individual's lifestyle. The primary use of a problem solving strategy in such instances is not so much to train the person to become a better problem solver; even the most effective of individuals is likely to have difficulty under such conditions. Instead, the major purpose is to assist the person to think through more intelligently what otherwise may appear as an overwhelming situation defying any attempts at resolution. In more extreme form—although not at all atypical of the type of instance one is confronted with on telephone "hot lines" throughout the country—the individual may have reached the point where suicide seems to be the only possible resolution to the dilemma. Although we readily admit that not all of life's problematic situations have conclusive solutions, a systematic approach to problem solving can nonetheless help a person in sorting out the complexities and reaching at least partial resolutions.

   For some individuals, entering college is experienced as a life crisis, inasmuch as they are confronted with a highly complex and novel environment, and this change in lifestyle frequently results in the occurrence of numerous problem situations (Goldfried and D'Zurilla, 1969). This may be the first time individuals have had to function on a completely independent level. It would seem likely, then, that college freshman orientation sessions might include a certain amount of problem solving training, using as a training vehicle numerous hypothetical problematic situations that are likely to confront the student in the months and years to come.

Another use of problem solving has been with addictive behaviors, and has been included in a behaviorally oriented treatment program for heroin addicts (Copemann, 1973). Once the program participants became free of their drug habit, they were faced with the prospect of returning to the environment containing those very frustrations and temptations that led them to become drug users to begin with. Thus, problem solving training was used to assist ex-addicts in learning to cope more effectively with their environment without having to revert to drug use. A particularly effective approach in using problem solving to deal with relapse among alcoholics has been described by Marlatt and his associates (Chaney, O'Leary, and Marlatt, 1978; Marlatt, 1978). After conducting a situational analysis of those events that typically lead to relapse among alcoholics (e.g., social pressure, negative emotional states, etc.), Marlatt and his co-workers incorporated these high-risk situations into a programmed relapse procedure, whereby clients were taught to anticipate and problem solve more effective ways of coping with such events. The use of this programmed relapse strategy was found to significantly decrease both the duration and severity of relapse episodes one year after termination. The use of such a maintenance strategy clearly provides us with a paradigm that may be applied to a variety of other problem areas as well. Thus, Richards and Perri (1978) were successful in facilitating maintenance when problem solving training was added to a larger treatment procedure for academic underachievers.

Related to the issue of maintenance is the task of dealing with "reentry" difficulties, such as those likely to be encountered by recently discharged psychiatric patients and prisoners. Even if one assumes that they have been successfully rehabilitated and no longer manifest the problem behaviors that resulted in their original institutionalization—an assumption which may not be entirely warranted—they nonetheless may be expected to have some difficulties in coping. As observed by such writers as Goffman (1961) and Rosenhan (1973), the environment within institutions can be radically different in its demands from the way things are in the "real world." For example, in such settings there exists the tendency to discourage independent functioning. To further complicate matters, if people have been institutionalized for a long time, it is likely that they will be returning to an environment that is markedly different from that which they left. Consequently, training in problem solving represents a crucial component in assisting such individuals to cope within a noninstitutionalized setting (Coché and Flick, 1975; Levendusky, 1977).

A further use of problem solving has been in assisting children, adolescents, and families in handling various conflict situations. For example, Spivack and Shure (1974), Spivack, Platt, and Shure (1976) and Allen et al. (1976) have demonstrated that training children with behavior difficulties to use problem solving skills can improve their interpersonal functioning. In addition, training in problem solving has been applied as a method of coping with conflict situations between children and their parents (Gordon, 1970; Kifer, Lewis, Green, and Phillips, 1974; Robin et al., 1977), to assist couples in more effectively coping with their marital conflicts (Gottman et al., 1976; Jacobson and Margolin, 1979; O'Leary and Turkewitz, 1978), to help entire families to resolve their interactional difficulties (Blechman et al., 1976; Gordon, 1970), and as a technique for increasing the effectiveness of teachers (Gordon, 1975) and leaders (Almedina and Rubin, 1974; Gordon, 1977).

In most uses of problem solving, it is rare that it is employed as the only intervention method. What one frequently finds is that the inability to resolve various problematic situations is accompanied by other problem behaviors as well. For example, certain individuals may be capable of learning to apply a problem solving strategy, but may nonetheless have difficulty in carrying out the preferred course of action. This may either be due to certain inhibitions or fears of responding in a given way, or to the lack of certain responses in the individual's behavioral repertoire. In such instances, the use of supplementary behavior therapy procedures would clearly be in order. For example, people too fearful to carry out a course of action might first have their fears reduced through the use of systematic desensitization (see Chapter 8). Similarly, individuals too unassertive to carry out certain actions in a social setting would need assertion training, as described in Chapter 6.

Although we have presented general guidelines for the use of problem solving as a therapeutic procedure, the precise way in which it would be implemented will vary from instance to instance. As we have noted above, individuals will differ as to the phase of problem solving in which they may be most deficient. As a result, the exact procedures must be tailored to fit the needs of any given case. Further, the general nature of the training procedures will have to vary as a function of the ability of the client to comprehend the problem solving procedure. One clearly does not go into the same amount of detail when working with children as when one works with adults, and the training would have to be modified accordingly. For example, an innovative clinical procedure for use with children, called the "turtle technique," has been described by Schneider and Robin (1975). Children are told the story about a turtle that uses its protective shell whenever encountering problematic situations. In encountering difficult situations, including conflicts with other children, the children are taught to temporarily withdraw into their shells to calm down a bit and consider the best way to respond. When used by the child in a classroom setting, this can take the form of putting one's head on the desk for a brief period of time to engage in both relaxation and problem solving.

We want to emphasize that in providing a set of therapeutic guidelines, we would not want it to be mistaken for a cookbook. We have mentioned this point in connection with rational restructuring, but it is important enough to have it restated: Therapeutic guidelines cannot substitute for the clinical sensitivity and ingenuity of the therapist or the careful assessment needed to decide on the selection of the most appropriate intervention procedure (Goldfried and Davison, 1976).

An important point must be noted in regard to the two specific procedures described in this chapter—namely training individuals to think rationally or solve problems effectively. The goal is to teach clients a general coping strategy so that they can more effectively control their own lives. Consequently, both rational restructuring and problem solving techniques may be viewed within the broad context of coping skills training, where the ultimate objective is to provide individuals with skills for regulating their own behavior (Goldfried, 1979b). Clients frequently leave a given therapeutic session with the feeling that the therapist's support and encouragement has enabled them to put a particular problem into better perspective. The goal of systematic restructuring is to teach this technique to clients themselves, so that once they terminate treatment, they can cope with upsetting situations on their own. Problem solving techniques have been used in industry for years, particularly as a way of providing executives with the skills to manage their corporations. From a more personal standpoint, problem solving training may be used toward the goal of providing individuals with a greater capacity to manage their own lives. One can scarcely think of individuals who cannot benefit from such self-help skills.

CONCLUDING COMMENTS

As behavior therapists become more involved with cognitive factors, the question of how such variables interrelate with emotional reactions and overt behavior will need to be more clearly answered. When one sets out to teach a person to think more realistically or to solve problems more effectively, the primary goal is to have some impact on the person's emotional state and overt behavior. Although we are not certain exactly how changes in thinking influence feelings and behavior, we tend to operate on the assumption that improvement in one area facilitates change in others. As suggested by Jerome Frank:

> The emotional, cognitive, and behavior changes that psychotherapy seek to effect are obviously closely intertwined. If all goes well, each reinforces the others. A more workable assumptive world leads to behavior that is more successful and less frustrating. This reduces the patient's anxiety and fosters emotions that increase the flexibility of his new thinking and behavior. This in turn leads to a new behavior which, if successful, further strengthens the new assumptive systems. This happy state of affairs is rarely, if ever, fully achieved of course, but it affords a useful model for thinking about the methods and goals of different forms of treatment. (p. 146)

Although some of our cognitive-behavioral procedures are based on the assumption that an individual's internal dialogue or self-statements mediate emotional arousal, it is not at all uncommon to encounter clients who have difficulty in articulating those cognitions that may be causing their upset in any given situation. Nonetheless, they may readily acknowledge that they are behaving as if they are saying certain things to themselves. Perhaps our difficulties in assessing these cognitive mediators may be a function of our incorrect conceptualization of the nature of the internal dialogue. Rather than assuming that an individual is emitting one or more coherent self-statements, it might be more appropriate to view such covert events as involving *affective associations*, comprising the connotative meanings or semantic structure associated with certain events or objects (Osgood, Suci, and Tannenbaum, 1957). Indeed, one of the major characteristics of human memory is its associative nature; associations are involved both in the meaning structure assigned to concepts and in the retrieval of information (Bower, 1975). The theoretical aspects of this issue have been described at greater length elsewhere (Goldfried, 1979a).

As noted earlier in this chapter, a clinical procedure that has been found useful in the implementation of rational restructuring has involved the use of an associative task. Using incomplete sentences in assisting clients to ferret out the relevant cognitive mediators appears to help individuals to more readily recognize, and subsequently reevaluate the implicit meaning they assign to given situations in their lives. The similarity to Jung's research on the use of word associations to determine the perceived significance of certain words is particularly striking (cf. Jung, 1910). There is also a parallel to the clinical work of psychoanalysts, who have long recognized the need for gathering information on the associative meaning that individuals attribute to people and events. Some of the parallels between rational restructuring and the psychoanalytic strategy of "working through" is particularly interesting (see Horney, 1950, p. 342). In a paper entitled "The concept of irrational belief systems as primary elements of psychopathology," Bieber (1974) has independently outlined a psychoanalytically-oriented procedure having many interesting parallels with rational restructuring. As described by Bieber:

> Outside the analysis, patients become involved in various testing maneuvers related to reinforcing or relinquishing an irrational belief. In steps one and two, irrational beliefs are delineated and patients, hopefully, become convinced that their beliefs are irrational. I view these steps as the "working out" phase of therapy. These steps proceed concurrently though they may be sequential. Step three is the "working through" phase. The patient comes to identify the operations of his beliefs in his life situation and in his interpersonal transactions. If the analysis proceeds well, this phase will see the extinction of symptoms and an alteration from neurotic, or maladaptive, to appropriate behavior. (p. 98)

As behavior therapists begin to accept the role that cognitive variables play in the behavior change process, we may expect to find a growing rapprochement between the cognitive-behavioral approaches to therapy and more psychodynamically oriented techniques. Because both orientations begin from very different starting points, it is all the more significant to note points of convergence. The clinical observations of more traditional therapies, when integrated in the more systematic and operational technology of behavior therapy, should prove to be of great interest. It is also likely that the rapidly growing field of experimental cognitive psychology can have important implications for both behavioral assessment and therapeutic intervention (Bower, 1978; Goldfried, 1979a; Lang, 1977). Inasmuch as concepts from cognitive psychology are also being used by psychoanalytically oriented writers to explain various clinical phenomena (e.g., Horowitz, 1976), experimental cognitive psychology may well offer us a common language for bridging the gap between cognitive-behavioral and psychoanalytic approaches to intervention.

REFERENCES

Alden, L., and Safran, J. Irrational beliefs and nonassertive behavior. *Cognitive Therapy and Research*, 1978, *2*, 357-364.

Allen, G.J., Chinsky, J.M., Larcen, S.W., Lochman, J.E., and Selinger, H.V. *Community psychology and the schools*. Hillsdale, N.J.: Lawrence Erlbaum Associates, 1976.

Almedina, J. and Rubin, A. Environmental design. Unpublished manuscript, State University of New York at Stony Brook, 1974.

Beck, A.T. Cognitive therapy: Nature and relation to behavior therapy. *Behavior Therapy*, 1970, *1*, 184-200.

——— *Cognitive therapy and the emotional disorders*. New York: International Universities Press, 1976.

Beck, A.T., Rush, A.J., Emery, G., and Shaw, B.F. *Cognitive therapy of depression*. New York: Guilford Press, 1979.

Becker, G.M. and McClintock, C.G. Value: Behavioral decision theory. *Annual Review of Psychology*, 1957, *18*, 239-286.

Bieber, I. The concept of irrational belief systems as primary elements of psychopathology. *Journal of the American Academy of Psychoanalysis*, 1974, *2*, 91-100.

Blechman, E.A., Olson, D.H.L., Schornagel, C.Y., Halsdorf, M., and Turner, A. The family contract game: Technique and case study. *Journal of Consulting and Clinical Psychology*, 1976, *44*, 449-455.

Bloom, B.S., and Broder, L.J. *Problem-solving processes of college students*. Chicago: University of Chicago Press, 1950.

Bower, G.H. Contacts of cognitive psychology with social learning theory. *Cognitive Therapy and Research*, 1978, *2*, 123-146.

Brehm. J.W. and Cohen, A.R. *Explorations in cognitive dissonance*. New York: Wiley, 1962.

Chaney, E.F., O'Leary, M.R., and Marlatt, G.A. Skill training with alcoholics. *Journal of Consulting and Clinical Psychology*, 1978, *46*, 1092-1104.

Churchman, C.W. *Prediction and optimal decision*. Englewood Cliffs, N.J.: Prentice-Hall, 1961.

Coché, E. and Flick, A. Problem solving training groups for hospitalized psychiatric patients. *Journal of Psychology*, 1975, *91*, 19-29.

Copemann, C.D. Aversive counterconditioning and social retraining: A learning theory approach to drug rehabilitation. Unpublished doctoral dissertation, State University of New York at Stony Brook, 1973.

DiLoreto, A.O. *Comparative psychotherapy: An experimental analysis.* Chicago: Aldine-Atherton, 1971.

Dollard, J. and Miller, N.E. *Personality and psychotherapy.* New York: McGraw-Hill, 1950.

D'Zurilla, T.J. and Goldfried, M.R. Problem solving and behavior modification. *Journal of Abnormal Psychology,* 1971, *78,* 197-226.

Edwards, W. Behavioral decision theory. *Annual Review of Psychology,* 1961, *12,* 473-498.

Ellis, A. *Reason and emotion in psychotherapy.* New York: Lyle Stuart, 1962.

Ellis, A. and Grieger, R. (Eds.) *Handbook of rational-emotive therapy.* New York: Springer, 1977.

Foreyt, J.P. and Rathjen, E.D. *Cognitive-behavior therapy: Research and application.* New York: Plenum, 1978.

Frank, J.D. *Persuasion and healing.* Baltimore: Johns Hopkins Press, 1961.

Goffman, E. *Asylums.* Garden City, N.Y.: Doubleday, 1961.

Goldfried, M.R. Anxiety reduction through cognitive-behavioral intervention. In P.C. Kendall and S.D. Hollon (Eds.), *Cognitive-behavioral interventions: Theory, research, and procedures.* New York: Academic Press, 1979,.

———Psychotherapy as coping skills training. In M.J. Mahoney (Ed.), *Psychotherapy process: Current issues and future directions.* New York: Plenum, 1979b.

——— Systematic desensitization as training in self-control. *Journal of Consulting and Clinical Psychology,* 1971, *37,* 228-234.

Goldfried, M.R. and Davison, G.C. *Clinical behavior therapy.* New York: Holt, Rinehart, & Winston, 1976.

Goldfried, M.R., Decenteceo, E.T. and Weinberg, L. Systematic rational restructuring as a self-control technique. *Behavior Therapy,* 1974, *5,* 247-254.

Goldfried, M.R. and D'Zurilla, T.J. A behavioral-analytic model for assessing competence. In C.D. Spielberger, (Ed.), *Current topics in clinical and community psychology,* New York: Academic Press, 1969.

Goldfried, M.R. and Goldfried, A.P. Cognitive change methods. In F.H. Kanfer and A.P. Goldstein (Eds.), *Helping people change.* New York: Pergamon Press, 1975.

Goldfried, M.R., Linehan, M.M., and Smith, J.L. The reduction of test anxiety through rational restructuring. *Journal of Consulting and Clinical Psychology,* 1978, *46,* 32-39.

Goldfried, M.R. and Merbaum, M. (Eds.), *Behavior change through self-control.* New York: Holt, Rinehart & Winston, 1973.

Goldfried, M.R. and Sobocinski, D. The effect of irrational beliefs on emotional arousal. *Journal of Consulting and Clinical Psychology,* 1975, *43,* 504-510.

Gordon, T. *P.E.T.: Parent effectiveness training.* New York: Wyden Books, 1970.

——— *T.E.T.: Teacher effectiveness training.* New York: Wyden Books, 1975.

——— *L.E.T.: Leader effectiveness training.* New York: Wyden Books, 1977.

Gottman, J., Notarius, C., Gonso, J., and Markman, H. *A couple's guide to communication.* Champaign, Il.: Research Press, 1976.

Hilgard, E.R. and Bower, G.H. *Theories of learning* (4th ed.). Englewood Cliffs, N.J.: Prentice-Hall, 1975.

Horney, K. *Neurosis and human growth.* New York: Norton, 1950.

Horowitz, M.J. *Stress response syndrome.* New York: Jason Aronson, 1976.

Jacobson, N.S., and Margolin, G. *Marital therapy: Treatment strategies based on social learning and behavior exchange principles.* New York: Brunner/Mazel, 1979.

Jung. C.G. The association method. *American Journal of Psychology,* 1910, *21,* 219-269.

Kanfer, F.H. Self-regulation: Research and speculations. In C. Neuringer and J.L. Michael (Eds.), *Behavior modification in clinical psychology*, New York: Appleton-Century-Crofts, 1970.

Kanfer, F.H., and Phillips, J.S. *Learning foundations of behavior therapy*. New York: Wiley, 1970.

Kanter, N.J., and Goldfried, M.R. Relative effectiveness of rational restructuring and self-control desensitization in the reduction of interpersonal anxiety. *Behavior Therapy*, 1979, in press.

Kendall, P.C., and Hollon, S.D. (Eds.) *Cognitive-behavioral interventions: Theory, research, and procedures*. New York: Academic Press, 1979.

Kifer, R.E., Lewis, M.A., Green, D.R., and Phillips, E.L. Training predelinquent youths and their parents to negotiate conflict situations. *Journals of Applied Behavioral Analysis*, 1974, *7*, 357-364.

Lang, P.J. Imagery in therapy: An information processing analysis of fear. *Behavior Therapy*, 1977, *8*, 862-886.

Lange, A.J., and Jakubowski, P. *Responsible assertive behavior: Cognitive/behavioral procedures for trainers*. Champaign, Il.: Research Press, 1976.

Lazarus, A.A. *Behavior therapy and beyond*. New York: McGraw-Hill, 1971.

Lazarus, R.S. *Psychological stress and the coping process*. New York: McGraw-Hill, 1966.

Levendusky, P. Contract milieu: Self-control alternative to the token economy. Paper presented at the Association for the Advancement of Behavior Therapy, Atlanta, December, 1977.

Linehan, M., Goldfried, M.R., and Goldfried, A.P. Assertion training: Skill acquisition or cognitive restructuring. *Behavior Therapy*, 1979, in press.

Mahoney, M.J. *Cognition and behavior modification*. Cambridge, Mass.: Ballinger, 1974.

—— Reflections on the cognitive learning trend in psychotherapy. *American Psychologist*, 1977, *32*, 5-13.

Mahoney, M.J. and Arnkoff, D.B. Cognitive and self-control therapies. In S.L. Garfield and A.E. Bergin (Eds.), *Handbook of psychotherapy and behavior change*. New York: Wiley, 1978.

Marlatt, G.A. Craving for alcohol, loss of control, and relapse: A cognitive-behavioral analysis. In P.E. Nathan, G.A. Marlatt and Løberg, T. (Eds.), *Alcoholism: New directions in behavioral research and treatment*. New York: Plenum, 1978.

May. J.R. Psychophysiology of self-regulated phobic thoughts. *Behavior Therapy*, 1977, *8*, 150-159.

May, J.R. and Johnson, H.J. Physiological activity to internally elicited arousal and inhibitory thoughts. *Journal of Abnormal Psychology*, 1973, *82*, 239-245.

McGuire, M. and Sifneos, P. Problem solving in psychotherapy. *Psychiatric Quarterly*, 1970, *44*, 667-673.

Meichenbaum, D.H. Cognitive modification of test anxious college students. *Journal of Consulting and Clinical Psychology*, 1972, *39*, 370-380.

—— *Cognitive behavior modification*. Morristown, N.J.: General Learning Press, 1974.

—— *Cognitive behavior modification*. New York: Plenum, 1977.

Meichenbaum, D.H. (Ed.) *Cognitive behavior therapy* (audio-cassette series) New York: BioMonitoring Applications, 1978.

Meichenbaum, D.H., Gilmore, J.B., and Fedoravicius, A. Group insight versus group desensitization in treating speech anxiety. *Journal of Consulting and Clinical Psychology*, 1971, *36*, 410-421.

Meichenbaum, D.H. and Turk, D. The cognitive-behavioral management of anxiety, anger and pain. In P. Davidson (Ed.), *The behavioral management of anxiety, depression and pain*. New York: Brunner/Mazel, 1976.

Miller, G.A., Galanter, E., and Pribram, K.H. *Plans and the structure of behavior*. New York: Holt, Rinehart & Winston, 1960.

Novaco, R. *Anger control: The development and evaluation of an experimental treatment*. Lexington, Mass.: Lexington Brooks, 1975.

O'Leary, K.D. and Turkewitz, H. Marital therapy from a behavioral perspective. In T.J. Paolino and B.S. McCrady (Eds), *Marriage and marital therapy*. New York: Brunner/Mazel, 1978.

Osborn. A.F. *Applied imagination: Principles and procedures of creative problem-solving* (3rd ed.). New York: Scribner's, 1963.

Osgood, C.E., Suci, G.J., and Tannenbaum, P.H. *The measurement of meaning*. Urbana, Ill.: University of Illinois Press, 1957.

Parnes, S.J. *Creative behavior guidebook*. New York: Scribner's, 1967.

Raimy. V. *Misunderstandings of the self*. San Francisco: Jossey-Bass, 1975.

Richards, C.S., and Perri, M.G. Do self-control treatments last? An evaluation of behavioral problem solving and faded counselor contact as treatment maintenance strategies. *Journal of Counseling Psychology*, 1978, *25*, 376-383.

Rimm, D.C., and Litvak, S.B. Self-verbalization and emotional arousal. *Journal of Abnormal Psychology*, 1969, *32*, 565-574.

Robin, A.L., Kent, R., O'Leary, K.D., Foster, S., and Prinz, R. An approach to teaching parents and adolescents problem-solving communication skills: A preliminary report. *Behavior Therapy*, 1977, *8*, 639-643.

Rogers, T., and Craighead, W.E. Physiological responses to self-statements: The effects of statement valence and discrepancy. *Cognitive Therapy and Research*, 1977, *1*, 99-118.

Rosenhan, D.L. On being sane in insane places. *Science*, 1973, *179*, 250-258.

Roskies, E., and Lazarus, R.S. Coping theory and the teaching of coping skills. In P. Davidson (Ed.), *Behavioral medicine: Changing life styles*. New York: Brunner/Mazel, in press.

Russel, P.C. and Brandsma, J.M. A theoretical and empirical integration of the rational-emotional and classical conditioning theories. *Journal of Consulting and Clinical Psychology*, 1974, *42*, 389-397.

Schneider, M. and Robin, A.L. The turtle technique: A method for the self-control of impulsive behavior. Unpublished manuscript, State University of New York at Stony Brook, 1975.

Schwartz, R. and Gottman, J. Toward a task analysis of assertive behavior. *Journal of Consulting and Clinical Psychology*, 1976, *44*, 910-920.

Simon, H.A. A behavioral model of rational choice. *Quarterly Journal of Economics*, 1955, *69*, 99-118.

Spivack, G., Platt, J.J., and Shure, M.B. *The problem-solving approach to adjustment*. San Francisco: Jossey-Bass, 1976.

Spivack, G. and Shure, M.B. *Social adjustment of young children*. San Francisco: Jossey-Bass, 1974.

Thoresen, C.E. and Mahoney, M.J. *Behavioral self-control*. New York: Holt, Rinehart, & Winston, 1974.

Trexler, L.D. and Karst, T.O. Rational-emotive therapy, placebo, and no-treatment effects on public-speaking anxiety. *Journal of Abnormal Psychology*, 1972, *79*, 60-67.

Velten, E., Jr. A laboratory task for induction of mood states. *Behavior Research and Therapy*, 1968, *6*, 473-482.

5
Modeling Methods
Martha A. Perry and
M. Judith Furukawa

I. INTRODUCTION

Imagine the following series of events. While watching some children skate-
boarding down a steep hill, a boy sees one child fall and badly scrape her leg and
arm. He decides to go bike riding instead. Back at home, his little sister and
brother dress up in their mother's and father's clothes and play house. His older
sister, who just bought her first car, is watching her father demonstrate how to
change a tire. The children's mother is cooking a fancy French dinner using a
recipe she saw Julia Child prepare on television. The evening paper reports a
crime similar to one in a movie that was recently in town. Coming home on his
bike, the boy pauses to survey a bumpy, muddy path across a vacant lot. Seeing
several other children on bikes successfully navigate the path, the boy decides to
take this shortcut home.

What do these events have in common? In each instance, the actions or
behavior of an individual or a group influenced the behavior of another. Many
different terms have been offered to account for this process, including imitation,
copying, mimicry, identification, and modeling. In this chapter we will use the
term modeling to refer to the process of observational learning in which the
behavior of an individual or a group—the model—acts as a stimulus for similar
thoughts, attitudes, or behaviors on the part of another individual who observes
the model's performance.

In psychology, the study of imitation was almost totally neglected until the
pioneering work by Miller and Dollard (1941). These authors reviewed the

theories existing at the time and formulated their own analysis of imitation using a behavioristic framework. Over twenty years passed before the significance of imitative learning for social learning and personality development was highlighted in an important book authored by Bandura and Walters (1963). Since that time, the name of Bandura has become almost synonymous with the study of observational learning and its effects upon social behavior. The term modeling has come to replace imitation as a general term encompassing a variety of observational learning processes.

While there are a number of conflicting theories concerning the nature and operation of the modeling process, the position adopted by Bandura seems to be the most widely accepted. The interested reader may wish to refer to a recent theoretical book by Bandura (1977) which reviews these controversies and clarifies Bandura's approach to social learning. Other reviews can be found in texts by Bandura (1969, 1971a) Kanfer and Phillips (1970), and Rosenthal and Zimmerman (1978).

According to Bandura, the first stage in observational learning is *acquisition* or learning of a response. In order to learn, a person must attend to and accurately perceive the important features of a model's behavior. It is assumed that during the process of observation the observer acquires images and verbal representations (cognitions) of the model's behavior which are then coded, organized, or rehearsed to facilitate their storage in memory. It is not necessary that the observer be reinforced during the acquisition phase or engage in any overt practice for observational learning to occur.

The second phase of this process concerns *performance* of the modeled behavior by the observer. For performance to occur, the individual must be capable of initiating appropriate actions from the stored symbolic representations and must be motivated to perform. The distinction between the acquisition and performance of a modeled response is an important one, for it is often the case that a response acquired through observation is never actually performed by the observer. For example, you may have observed the behavior of a sky-diver by watching detailed films of his jumps to the extent that you have *learned* what steps are involved in this activity (acquisition phase), even though you have yet to jump out of a plane in an attempt to perform this behavior yourself.

Reinforcement and punishment may play roles both in the acquisition of modeled behavior and the performance of it. Consequences to the model may serve to selectively focus the observer's attention on the modeled behavior. Further, consequences to the model serve an informative function, notifying the observer of what results might be expected if the behavior were performed. The nature of the consequences motivate the observer to perform or not perform the modeled behavior. There are a variety of other factors which may determine whether a behavior which has been acquired through observational learning is subsequently performed by the observer. Many of these factors will be described in the discussion of the practical application of modeling principles which follows. Once the behavior is performed, consequences to the observer upon performance inform on the adequacy or appropriateness of the behavior and influence further performance.

Before beginning the discussion of how modeling methods may be applied in the clinical setting, it would be helpful to briefly review the *effects* of observational learning. Bandura (1969) outlines three major effects of modeling, each of which has an important counterpart in clinical application. The first involves both the acquisition of new skills and the performance of them. The second effect involves behaviors which have been acquired and performed and which are under some form of inhibition (either personal or social). In these cases, the desired effect of modeling may be either to disinhibit performance (to remove the restraint and increase level of performance) or to further inhibit performance. The final effect of modeling is to facilitate the performance of previously learned behaviors which though under no constraints, are not performed at all or are performed only at a low rate.

The learning of new behaviors or of newly integrated patterns of behavior is termed the *observational learning effect.* An example of this effect is when a boy learns to change a tire by watching his father demonstrate this skill. This effect lends itself to a variety of applications, such as teaching basic social skills to withdrawn or socially inept clients, training autistic or retarded children in the basic fundamentals of speech, and instructing hospitalized psychotic patients in skills needed upon their return to the community.

The second effect of modeling occurs when behaviors are under some form of inhibition or restraint for the observer. The observer has already learned how to perform the behavior prior to exposure to the model, and the effect of modeling is to either increase or decrease the rate of performance of this behavior by the observer. In these cases, observation of the consequences experienced by the model following his or her performance is of particular importance. This observation provides an expectation of what may happen to the observer when performing the same behavior. Behaviors exhibited by the model which are followed by positive consequences are likely to produce an increase in the performance of these behaviors by the observer. When this increased performance involves behaviors which were previously under inhibition, a *disinhibitory effect* is said to occur. In the case of the boy who was uncertain about riding his bike on the muddy path, the effect of observing other children successfully negotiating the path served to disinhibit his own behavior. On the other hand, if another bike rider were observed to slip and fall in the mud (a negative consequence), the boy might wish to seek a safer route home. In this latter case, an *inhibitory effect* is involved. If the boy had observed children trampling a neighbor's flowers and then being punished, this observation would have an inhibitory effect. Inhibitory effects decrease the likelihood of performance of the behavior.

Many of the clinical applications of modeling principles which have been described to date (Bandura, 1971b, Rachman, 1972) fall within the category of disinhibitory effects. Behaviors which have been inhibited by the presence of strong fears or anxiety, as in phobic disorders, have been successfully treated by having phobic individuals witness models who engage in these feared behaviors and experience positive or safe consequences. Some attention has also been paid to the use of inhibitory effects in the clinical setting. Clients who engage in unrestrained behaviors which are socially disapproved (e.g., alcoholics or delinquents who have difficulty in controlling impulsive behavior), may be able to strengthen their own inhibitions against such behaviors by observing a model experience negative consequences for performing those same actions.

The third effect of modeling is termed the *response facilitation effect*. In this case, the effect of modeling is to increase behaviors which the observer has already learned and for which there are no existing constraints or inhibitions. The effect of the model is simply to provide an information "cue" which triggers similar behavior on the part of the observer. For example, the first person to leave a party may prompt everyone else to leave as well. Assuming that almost everyone at the party has the social skills needed to excuse himself and depart, and that for few people are there inhibitions to this behavior, the effect of the first person leaving is simply to facilitate this response in others. Few clinical applications of modeling involve the response facilitation effect—except perhaps for the use of modeling in increasing the frequency of normally occurring social behaviors. In this chapter we will focus primarily upon the use of observational learning effects and disinhibitory/inhibitory effects as practical methods of changing behavior.

In Part II, which immediately follows, a review of factors which enhance modeling is presented. This section is divided into those factors which primarily facilitate acquisition of new responses and are particularly relevant to observational learning effects, and those which enhance performance of behaviors which may be either newly learned or already in the observer's repertoire. It must be noted that while this section simplifies and organizes a multitude of factors, the effects of those factors are not necessarily so well delineated. Many of the factors which foster acquisition will have some effect on performance as well. In like manner, factors affecting performance may affect acquisition. Table 5.1 is an abbreviated checklist of these factors corresponding to the text presentation. It is provided as a reference to be used in developing modeling programs after becoming familiar with the more specific content of Part II.

Part II provides a number of detailed examples of modeling as applied to specific client populations and problem areas. The use of modeling with fear-related behaviors is described in the first section. Next, a discussion of modeling in the classroom is presented. In the sections following, modeling programs are described which have been used with clinical populations, including retarded individuals, autistic children, psychotic adults, delinquents, drug addicts and alcoholics. Modelings as a training method for helping professionals and paraprofessionals is considered in the final section. Part III concludes with some comments concerning the incidental effects of modeling which are likely to occur in any setting.

Table 5.1 Factors which enhance modeling

I. Factors enhancing acquisition (learning and retention)
  A. Characteristics of the model
    1. Similarity in sex, age, race, and attitudes
    2. Prestige
    3. Competence
    4. Warmth and nurturance
    5. Reward value

  B. Characteristics of the observer
    1. Capacity to process and retain information
    2. Uncertainty
    3. Level of anxiety
    4. Other personality factors

  C. Characteristics of the modeling presentation
    1. Live or symbolic model
    2. Multiple models
    3. Slider model
    4. Graduated modeling procedures
    5. Instructions
    6. Commentary on features and rules
    7. Summarization by observer
    8. Rehearsal
    9. Minimization of distracting stimuli

II. Factors enhancing performance
  A. Factors providing incentive for performance
    1. Vicarious reinforcement (reward to model)
    2. Vicarious extinction of fear of responding (no negative consequences to model)
    3. Direct reinforcement
    4. Imitation of children

  B. Factors affecting quality of performance
    1. Rehearsal
    2. Participant modeling

  C. Transfer and generalization of performance
    1. Similarity of training setting to everyday environment
    2. Repeated practice affecting response hierarchy
    3. Incentives for performance in natural setting
    4. Learning principles governing a class of behaviors.
    5. Provision of variation in training situations.

II. FACTORS WHICH ENHANCE MODELING

Factors Enhancing Acquisition

According to Bandura, for acquisition to occur, the observer must attend to the relevant behaviors of the model, and process and retain the observations. The clinician can do much to assure that conditions facilitate this process by his choice of model and model behaviors, by attention to characteristics of the observer, and by careful structuring of the way in which the model and behaviors are presented. In the following sections, suggestions regarding these factors are presented. Table 5.1 summarizes these suggestions in a checklist that can serve as a quick guide for the helping professional who is planning a modeling program.

Characteristics of the Model. Who should play the role of the model? What characteristics of a model are most likely to produce imitative effects? A great deal of research has been conducted on these questions. Reviews by Bandura (1969) and Flanders (1968) summarize much of this research, and more recent studies expand the literature (e.g., Chartier and Ainley, 1974; Strichart, 1974). An exact answer to these questions depends on the nature of the problem to be treated, but the following guidelines may be helpful in selecting models.

A model who is similar to the observer in sex, age, race, and attitudes is more likely to be imitated than a dissimilar model. With similarity, the observer is assured that the behaviors shown are both appropriate to and attainable by someone like himself. Models who possess prestige in the eyes of the observer are generally more likely to be emulated than low prestige models. It is important, however, to avoid models whose status level is so prestigious that the observer sees their behavior as an unrealistic guide for his own behavior.

Competence in performance is another characteristic which increases the likelihood that the model's behavior will be imitated. Again, the discrepancy between the model's competence and the observer's perceived competence should not be so great that the observer rejects the model's example. He may attribute "magical powers" to the performer or may feel totally unable to match the model's superior performance. Probably the best choice of model in this regard is someone who is just one or two steps advanced from the position of the observer, or one who proceeds from a position of relative similarity to the observer to one of greater proficiency. A model who demonstrates progressively increasing ability is sometimes referred to as a "slider" model in the literature.

Warmth and nurturance on the part of the model also facilitate modeling effects. An unfamiliar model who realistically portrays warmth would be an appropriate choice as would a model who has previously developed a friendly relationship with the observer. A model who has been associated with reward to the observer is also likely to be one who captures the observer's attention.

Characteristics of the Observer. What factors relating to the observer are of importance in modeling? Bandura (1977) discusses determinants of the modeling effect which reside in the observer. Heller and Marlatt (1969), Marlatt (1972), and Rimm and Medeiros (1970) also point out relationships between characteristics of the observer and the modeling effect. Clinicians must attend to attributes of the observer and either alter the state of the observer in order to facilitate modeling or structure the situation in such a way as to best match its demands to the existing capabilities and state of the observer.

The observer's capacity to process and retain information is of primary importance to modeling. The clinician must be aware of the observer's intellectual strengths and weaknesses and alter the modeling situation accordingly. For example, the child with an attention deficit will need his attention focused through such techniques as simplification, minimization of outside distractions, use of a commentary accompanying the modeling display, etc. A mentally retarded person may need a great deal of repetition. An autistic child or schizophrenic adult may need to be taught rudimentary observation and imitation skills before more complex behaviors can be demonstrated. The clinician must also be sensitive to the effects that medications may have on a patient's intellectual processes.

Several characteristics of an observer in a particular situation affect learning. Uncertainty is such a characteristic. An observer who is unsure about the appropriateness of his behavior is more likely to attend to a model. In this case, the behavior of the model provides needed information. When an individual is faced with choosing among several behavioral alternatives and the situation itself is ambiguous, a model's behavior and its consequences can serve as a direct signpost for the observer. At a formal dinner party, for example, guests who are uncertain about the function of a finger bowl will watch the host carefully to learn its proper use. One might use this factor clinically by creating an ambiguous situation, thereby raising doubts in the client's mind about appropriate behaviors and creating a need for information. The person who then demonstrates the appropriate behaiviors for the situation will command the attention of the observer.

Anxiety is another observer characteristic which affects learning. Too much anxiety on the part of the observer may interfere with observation, processing, or retention of the model's behavior. It may be necessary to train the observer in relaxation techniques prior to model presentation and instruct him to relax during the model's actual performance. This procedure is similar to desensitization therapy where it is assumed that relaxation will counter the anxiety response. While the effectiveness of relaxation training in modeling treatment programs has yet to be fully determined, its use may prove helpful for observers who are unusually apprehensive.

Other personality factors or individual characteristics may contribute to or detract from the effectiveness of modeling. For example, research has shown that impulsive children observing reflective models are more likely to change their behavior than reflective children with impulsive models (Ridberg, Parke and Hetherington, 1971). Zigler and his associates (Turnure and Zigler, 1964; Yando and Zigler, 1971) have found that mentally retarded persons with no identifiable damage or genetic abnormality are more outer-directed than children of average intelligence. That is, they look to others for cues for how to solve problems facing them. This suggests that modeling would be an especially effective training technique for these individuals. Other characteristics of the observer such as dependency, self-esteem, perceived level of personal competence, socioeconomic status, racial status, and sex will interact to determine the effectivenss of the modeling procedure in a given situation. Specific guidelines for each situation cannot be given, but the clinician should consider the possible interaction of these characteristics with the training procedures.

Characteristics of the Modeling Presentation. How should the model be presented to the observer? What instructions or commentary can be given to enhance learning from the model? What behaviors on the part of the observer contribute to learning and retention of the modeled behaviors? A number of authors provide summaries of these considerations (Bandura, 1969; Goldstein, 1973; Goldstein, Sprafkin, and Gershaw, 1976), and many research studies have been conducted evaluating the use of the following techniques.

There are several forms of model presentation from which to choose. The first involves the use of a *live model* who performs the behavior in the presence of the observer. This approach has a number of advantages. A live model is inherently more interesting than a symbolic one to many people, focusing and sustaining their attention. In addition, a live model can alter his performance to simplify or show another way of performing the behavior. The use of live models does carry certain risks, however, in that the model's behavior cannot be exactly predicted or controlled. It would be disastrous, for example, if the model in a phobia treatment procedure began to exhibit increasing anxiety. If this were to happen, the treatment would backfire and the client would be likely to show an increase in fear—an inhibition effect instead of a disinhibition effect.

For many applications of modeling, the therapist may prefer to use a *symbolic model* consisting of representations of the model's behavior in the form of films, videotapes, audiotapes, cartoons, or even written scripts. The medium chosen for presentation of a symbolic model depends on the behavior to be changed and on other practical considerations. Research evidence (reviewed by Bandura, 1969; Thelen, Fry, Fehrenbach, and Frautschi, in press) suggests that symbolic models can be successfully used in many circumstances. Symbolic models offer several advantages over live models. The model's recorded behavior can be controlled and edited to highlight the relevant portions of the model's behavior. Modeling tapes or films can also be kept on hand for repeated use in a clinical setting and can more easily be used in a group treatment situation.

Often the modeling procedures may be improved through the use of *multiple models*, some of whom are similar to the observer and others who vary along such dimensions as age, sex, and race. Using different models enhances the presentation by showing both the generality of the behavior as well as its appropriateness for this particular observer. Multiple models will naturally show some variability in their performance of the behavior, thereby suggesting alternatives to the observer and increasing his flexibility in other situations. Not only do multiple models enhance the modeling effect for a single observer, but they are especially important for group treatment. Multiple models increase the probability that at least one of the models will be perceived as similar by each of the members of the group.

Yet another variation on model presentation is the *slider model*, which was discussed previously. In this instance, the model begins performance at a level of proficiency similar to that of the observer and gradually progresses until the behavior is modeled competently. A model who verbalizes his own initial uncertainty and subsequent problem solving or coping strategies while improving behaviorally may be extremely helpful for the observer. When the behaviors to be modeled are anxiety provoking to the observer, the use of a slider model may serve initially to reduce observer anxiety until coping behaviors can be portrayed.

Graduated modeling procedures may also be used when demonstrating complicated skills or behaviors. The skills are presented and mastered first in their component parts. Then the entire behavioral sequence is reconstructed. When teaching motor behaviors such as driving an automobile or playing a musical instrument, for example, it is advisable to break the sequence into simple components and present the basic steps individually before demonstrating the entire chain of responses. The degree to which one must simplify depends on the complexity of the skill and on the capabilities of the observer.

The use of instructions or other commentary should also be considered as part of the modeling presentation. Initial instructions which explain what the observer will see in the modeling display and tell the observer that he will be expected to reproduce the modeled behavior increase the observer's attention to the model. The instructions ''prime'' the observer to watch for particular aspects of the model's performance, thus establishing an appropriate attentional set. The importance of the behavior to be observed can be further emphasized by having the narrator point out the functional relevance of the behavior for the observer.

In cases in which the modeled behavior is particularly complicated or abstract, learning and retention may be facilitated by having either the model or a narrator comment on the important features of the modeled behavior as well as on the general principle or rule which governs the model's performance. As an example, suppose a model were demonstrating assertive behavior to a withdrawn, socially inept observer. The scene involves ordering dinner in a restaurant and discovering that the steak is too tough to eat. The model exhibits an assertive response in this situation by requesting the waitress to bring him another steak. The model can comment at this point: ''That was an example of an assertive response. I was entitled to a good steak and was willing to pay for it. I explained the difficulty in an open and friendly manner to the waitress and asked her to bring me another steak. Afterwards I felt good about myself and enjoyed my meal.'' By listening to the model highlight the essential characteristics of an assertive response, the observer is more likely to remember the behavior and is in a better position to apply this form of response in a variety of different situations. As an additional aid to retention, the observer can be asked by the therapist to summarize the main features and general rules associated with the model's behavior. Several studies (e.g., Bandura, Grusec, and Menlove, 1966) have found that observers who actively summarize the model's behavior are better able to learn and retain this information.

Retention is also aided by having the observer rehearse the modeled behavior either during the modeling presentation itself or at one or more times following the demonstration. Rehearsal may be active, that is, actual performance of the behavior, or covert, in which case the observer imagines performing the behaviors. Covert rehearsal serves as an aid for coding the modeled behavior while active rehearsal helps both in coding and in developing the necessary motor and verbal skills required to perform the behavior smoothly.

Attention should also be paid to designing the modeling situation in a way that will minimize distractions to learning. For example, when using a film or video-tape presentation, the room should be darkened and noise kept to a minimum in order to focus on the display itself. Attention to an audiotaped model can be improved by presenting it to the observer through earphones. When live models are used, particularly in a naturalistic setting, every attempt should be made to reduce the distracting influence of other individuals or environmental events.

We can see that there are many factors which can affect the processes of acquisition and retention. While not all of them may be under the control of the individual planning the modeling procedure, careful consideration of those which are will lead to more successful intervention. The goal is to produce the best possible modeling package within the constraints imposed by a particular setting. In the next section, we focus on those aspects of the modeling procedure which relate to performance.

Factors Enhancing Performance

Beyond learning a behavior and retaining cognitions about its nature and its appropriateness for a particular situation, a person must also actually produce that behavior when the right conditions present themselves. Bandura separates this performance phase of modeling from the acquisition phase discussed in the previous section. In the clinical situation, treatment is not considered successful until the modeled behavior is performed. Furthermore, it is desirable that the behavior may be one that has been learned at some earlier time, as is the case with disinhibition and facilitation, or one that has been newly acquired through modeling, as occurs with observational learning of new skills. The clinician can design modeling programs which provide incentives for performance, enhance the quality of performance, and facilitate transfer and generalization of perfor-mance. Table 5.1 summarizes the suggestions which follow.

Factors Providing Incentive for Performance. How can the therapist build *incentives* into the modeling presentation which will motivate the observer to perform these same responses? A variety of experimental studies reveal that when a model's behavior is rewarded, or even when the consequences of his actions simply are not aversive, the probability that the observer will match these behaviors is significantly increased. Observation of a model who is punished for his behavior, on the other hand, usually produces a decrease in performance of the modeled behavior.

Observation of the reinforcing consequences to the model's behavior involves the process of *vicarious reinforcement*. This procedure is to be distinguished from *direct reinforcement* in which the observer is reinforced for the performance of an imitative response. Vicarious reinforcement has two main effects. It provides the observer both with information concerning the relevant features of the model's performance and with an incentive or inducement to copy the model's behavior. As an example, suppose a model is shown engaging in a series of trial and error behaviors while attempting to solve a difficult puzzle. He discovers a response which leads to a correct solution. At this point, the model is rewarded by an onlooker who says "Good! You solved the puzzle by that last move!" By seeing the model receive social approval at that particular moment, the observer gains both information concerning the most effective response in that situation (the reinforcement identifies the correct response) and an incentive to perform the same behavior in order to receive a similar reward. In the absence of an extrinsic source of reinforcement, similar effects may be obtained by having the model reward himself for the desired behavior. An example of verbal self-reinforcement is "Wow! I solved the puzzle by myself—good for me!" The use of self-reinforcement by the model has an additional advantage in that not only is the desired behavior demonstrated but a method of self-control is shown as well.

In some situations, for example the treatment of fear-related behaviors, the fact that the model experiences no negative consequences for his behavior operates in a manner similar to vicarious reinforcement. The safe consequences contrast sharply with the unpleasant ones imagined by the fearful observer and encourage him to try the same behaviors.

Direct reinforcement to the observer for performing a modeled behavior increases the probability that the behavior, once performed, will be repeated. During practice sessions the therapist can greatly augment the effects of treatment by encouraging and rewarding the observer for successful performance. The direct experience of reinforcement is likely to be at least as effective as, if not more effective than, vicarious reinforcement. In participant modeling programs (to be explained in the next section) the model provides rewards directly to the observer as he performs along with the model. The principles of vicarious and direct reinforcement have been well documented in the modeling literature (Bandura, 1971a, Kanfer, 1965).

Some special procedures may be helpful in facilitating children's performance of modeled behaviors. Having the model first imitate the child's behaviors may increase the child's subsequent imitation of the model. While the factors relating to this effect have still to be clarified, researchers (Kaufman, Kneedler, Gamache, Hallahan, and Ball, 1977) suggest that being imitated is reinforcing to children and provides an incentive for their later imitation of the model.

Factors Affecting Quality of Performance. Given that an observer performs at least an approximation of a modeled behavior, in what ways can the therapist help to make the behavior more acceptable or of better quality? Having observed and learned about a behavior does not assure that one can perform that behavior correctly. The more complex a behavior, for example learning to play the piano, the more likely that its performance will be initially inaccurate.

Active rehearsal of a modeled behavior interspersed between repeated model-ing displays is one way to give the observer multiple opportunities to compare his performance with the standard and make modifications which improve quality. The therapist may also wish to utilize verbal prompts or "coaching" if the observer fails to respond or responds incorrectly during rehearsal. The therapist may say, for example, "Well, that was a good try, but you didn't get it exactly right that time because . . . Okay, let's try it again and see if you can do it the way I suggested." or ". . . let's watch it and look closely at those places where you didn't get it quite right."

A procedure closely related to rehearsal is *participant modeling*. Originally developed by Ritter (1968, 1969) as a treatment method for phobic disorders, this procedure involves direct interaction between the model and the observer. After demonstrating the desired behavior, the model guides the observer through the steps involved, offering physical assistance if necessary. It is easy, during the procedure, for the model to provide immediate feedback about response accuracy and to selectively reinforce more correct performance as the observer improves. The essential features of participant modeling as applied to the treatment of phobias are found in Bandura, Blanchard, and Ritter (1969).

Transfer and Generalization of Performance. Of most interest to therapists using modeling training programs is ensuring that clients will perform the trained behaviors in their daily settings—on the ward, at school, in the community. How can training be structured so as to foster transfer and generalization? Goldstein, Sprafkin, and Gershaw (1976) summarize applicable principles and demonstrate in the Structured Learning Training programs the incorporation of the principles into training.

The therapist can provide training in situations most like those that the client encounters in daily living. The people with whom the observer usually interacts can be involved in the training process. Ward staff, for example, can be asked to participate in training sessions so that the patients are able to practice with them. Or, training can take place in the actual physical setting in which the behavior should occur. The more similar the training setting is to the natural setting in which the behaviors should eventually occur, the more likely it is that observers will transfer performance of learned behaviors to that setting.

Repeated practice is a very important factor in facilitating transfer. When faced with a commonly occurring situation, the most likely behaviors to be displayed are those which are highest in an individual's response hierarchy. Although behaviors may be correctly performed in a training situation, if they have not been practiced frequently enough to make them more familiar than the old, well-established behaviors, they are unlikely to be exhibited outside of the training setting.

Just as incentives for performance are important in the training setting, so are they needed in the natural setting. Reinforcement increases the likelihood that a behavior will be transferred and will continue to be performed. Often the naturally occurring consequences for a behavior are quite different from the training consequences for the same behavior, even to the point that a desirable behavior is discontinued in the everyday setting. Children with newly-learned compliance or helping behaviors, for example, may have those behaviors inadvertently extinguished by parents or teachers who take good behavior in children for granted and therefore fail to reinforce such behaviors. Involving parents and teachers in the training process and helping them to continue providing appropriate consequences for performance of desirable behaviors helps to foster the transfer of these behaviors to the natural setting.

Many of the suggestions made for enhancing the acquisition of behaviors are also applicable for fostering generalization. Learning the rules and principles which govern a behavior rather than simply learning to copy the behavior in isolation gives the observer a way of thinking about a new situation and deciding whether a behavior from that general response category is appropriate. For example, when teaching an observer to assert himself in a restaurant when unacceptable food is served, once can also teach the principle that the person as a consumer is entitled to acceptable goods in general and can pleasantly but firmly demand his rights. Then, when the client faces a different situation in which assertion is appropriate, he will be more likely to produce behavior from the overall category of assertive responses under those circumstances as well. An observer who has simply had rote practice sending back unacceptable food is far less likely to make this generalization. A training procedure which presents general principles is therefore helpful as is dicussion of those principles with the observer and asking the observer to summarize characteristics of the overall class of behaviors.

Training for generalization can be expanded beyond cognitive training to the performance sphere as well. Rather than modeling and providing practice in one instance of a behavior, the therapist can present multiple situations which demonstrate variations of a single behavior. A client may observe and practice an assertive response in a restaurant, in a store, with a door-to-door salesman, with a man or a woman, with a submissive other or argumentative other, and so on. Such variety helps the observer to develop his own general principles and permits him to gain practice and performance feedback under a variety of conditions. The real world is likely to produce fewer surprises for the observer when training has been diverse.

It is clear that a training program which focuses only on the learning and performance of specific behaviors in the training setting is incomplete. Transfer of behaviors to the everyday setting and generalization of behaviors to new situations which may arise are just as important. In addition, clients should either be taught variations on the modeled behavior or principles governing the class of behaviors so that generalization in terms of form of response will also occur.

We now turn to specific examples of the application of modeling procedures to a variety of settings and with diverse client or patient populations.

III. APPLICATIONS OF MODELING METHODS WITH SPECIFIC POPULATIONS

Modeling in the Treatment of Fear-Related Behaviors

A common use of modeling in clinical settings has been in the treatment of behaviors which are under the inhibition of fear or anxiety, such as phobias. A successful application of modeling techniques to the treatment of snake phobia is reported in a classic study by Bandura, Blanchard, and Ritter (1969). The subjects in this study were divided into three treatment groups and one control group. The three forms of treatment were symbolic modeling, live modeling with guided participation, and a standard desensitization treatment. The following description is of the procedure for symbolic modeling:

> Subjects participated in self-administered modeling treatment in which they observed a graduated film depicting young children, adolescents, and adults engaging in progressively more threatening interactions with a snake. The colored film, which was approximately 35 minutes long, began with scenes showing the fearless models handling plastic snakes and proceeded through displays in which they touched and held a large king snake, draped it around their necks, and let it crawl freely over their bodies. (p. 178)

The participant modeling group observed a live model (the experimenter) who, after demonstrating the desired behavior, guided each subject personally through the steps involved, giving manual assistance where necessary. The essential features of the behavioral sequence in which this group participated are as follows:

> In the initial procedure, subjects observed through a one-way mirror the experimenter perform a series of threatening activities with the king snake that provided striking demonstrations that close interactions with the snake does not have harmful consequences. During this period, which lasted approximately 15 minutes, the experimenter held the snake close to his face, allowed it to crawl over his body at will, and let it loose to slither about the room. After returning the snake to its glass cage, the experimenter invited the subject to join him in the room and to be seated in one of four chairs placed at varying distances from the experimenter's chair. The experimenter then removed the snake from the cage and commenced the treatment, beginning with relatively nonthreatening performance tasks and proceeding through increasingly fear-provoking activities. This treatment was conducted without the use of relaxation techniques.
>
> At each step the experimenter himself performed fearless behavior and gradually led subjects into touching, stroking, and then holding the midsection of the snake's body with gloved and then bare hands while the experimenter held the snake securely by the head and tail. Whenever a subject was unable to perform the behavior upon demonstration alone, she was asked to place her hand on the experimenter's and to move her hand down gradually until it touched the snake's body. After subjects no longer felt any apprehension about touching the snake under these secure conditions, anxieties about contact with the snake's head area and entwining tail were extinguished. The experimenter again performed the tasks fearlessly, and then he and the subject enacted the response jointly; as subjects became less fearful the experimenter gradually reduced his participation and control over the snake until eventually subjects were able to hold

the snake to their laps without assistance, to let the snake loose in the room and to retrieve it, and to let it crawl freely over their bodies. Progress through the graded approach tasks was paced according to the subjects' apprehensiveness. The threat value of the activities for each subject determined the particular order in which they were performed. When they reported being able to perform one activity with little or no fear, they were eased into a more difficult interaction. Treatment was terminated when subjects were able to execute all the snake inter-action tasks independently. (p. 180)

The results of this study showed that both modeling groups were superior to the desensitization procedure and that participant modeling was even more success-ful than symbolic modeling. Of those in the participant modeling group, 92 percent were cured of their snake phobia as assessed by a battery of behavioral and attitudinal measures.

While snake phobia may not be a common presenting problem in clinical settings, there are many other fears which interfere sufficiently in the lives of individuals for them to need or desire help. Sometimes anxiety is generated by everyday events such as entering an elevator or driving a car. At other times, fear is related to a seldom-occurring event such as hospitalization. Melamed and Siegel (1975) investigated the use of modeling reducing the anxiety of children who were facing surgery.

Anxiety on the part of children scheduled for hospitalization and surgery is felt to create problems on several levels. Preoperative anxiety has been suggested as a significant factor in impeding recovery from surgery. Behavior problems, either transient or long term in nature, have been observed in children hospitalized for surgery. Melamed and Siegel studied 60 children between the ages of 4 and 12 who were scheduled for elective surgery (tonsilectomies, hernia or urinary-genital tract repair). Thirty of these children saw a modeling film immediately prior to hospital admission. The other thirty viewed a control film about a boy on a nature trip in the country. In the following excerpt, Melamed and Siegel de-scribe the modeling film

The experimental film, entitled *Ethan Has an Operation*, depicts a 7-year-old white male who has been hospitalized for a hernia operation. This film, which is 16 minutes in length, consists of 15 scenes showing various events that most children encounter when hospitalized for elective surgery from the time of admission to time of discharge including the child's orienta-tion to the hospital ward and medical personnel such as the surgeon and anesthesiologist; having a blood test and exposure to standard hospital equipment; separation from the mother; and scenes in the operating and recovery rooms. In addition to explanations of the hospital procedure provided by the medical staff, various scenes are narrated by the child, who de-scribes his feelings and concerns . . . at each stage of the hospital experience. Both the child's behavior and verbal remarks exemplify some anxiety and apprehension, he is able to overcome his initial fears and complete each event in a successful and nonanxious manner. (p. 514)

The investigators used multiple measures of situational and trait anxiety to study the children's response both pre- and postoperatively. Some of these in-volved observer ratings, others self-ratings, and some were physiologic mea-sures. The children were also rated on number and degree of behavior problems.

The efficacy of preoperative preparation using a modeling film was demonstrated on all measures of situational anxiety. In addition, children viewing the modeling film did not show any increase in behavior problems from the preoperative to postoperative assessment periods. This was in contrast to the children who saw the nature film (control group). These differences are of particular interest since *all* children received the usual hospital-initiated preoperative counseling and demonstration procedures. Any changes produced by the film were therefore above and beyond those produced by hospital staff efforts.

Four weeks later, the children returned to the hospital for a postsurgery examination. This provided a test of generalization of film effects since it was a similarly stressful event which was not specifically depicted in the modeling film. Group differences were maintained on all measures of situational anxiety. In addition, children who had viewed the modeling film showed a significant reduction in anxiety-related behaviors as compared to their prefilm ratings.

Melamed and her colleagues (Melamed, Hawes, Heiby, and Glick, 1975; Melamed, Weinstein, Hawes, and Katin-Borland, 1975) also demonstrated successful alleviation of children's fears of dental treatment by the use of modeling procedures. Many of the factors for enhancing both learning and performance were incorporated into these programs. They provide useful models for the development of other treatment packages for modification of fear behaviors for both children and adults.

Modification of Classroom Behaviors. The planned use of modeling in classroom settings gives schools flexible opportunities for affecting the academic and classroom behaviors of the students. What are some of the possibilities?

Typically, the teacher is the major *planned* model in the classroom demonstrating the academic skills that students are expected to perform. For example, $2 \times 2 = 4$ is written on the board; "Now, class, you do the problems on your worksheets like this one I've shown you.". or:

Johnny (reading aloud): Bob and his brother looked in the . . . uh . . . the . . .
Teacher: . . . window . . .
Johnny: . . . the window of the pet shop.

Other models are or could be available in the classroom, however, to demonstrate and elicit both academic performance and appropriate classroom behaviors. Several examples show how peers, paraprofessionals, and filmed models, could be effectively used in schools.

Csapo (1972) solicited the help of six normal primary school children to be models of appropriate classroom behavior to six emotionally disturbed classmates. Six other normal children participated in the program as behavioral observers and recorders. She reports:

I was introduced to the students as a teacher interested in children's classroom behavior and in helping the children find ways to get along better in school. I explained to the peer model that the teacher had selected him because she considered him a pupil who knew the right way to behave in the classroom. I asked the peer models to participate in an experiment designed to help the emotionally disturbed peer learn and exhibit better classroom behavior. I explained that the task of the peer model was to sit together with the emotionally disturbed peer, side by side at adjoining desks, for 15 consecutive school days, and that he would be expected to show the right kinds of behavior required by the given classroom situation. The peer model was asked to sit beside the emotionally disturbed peer all day except for 30 minutes in the afternoon.

To the emotionally disturbed children, I stated that some behaviors had been observed in the classroom which appeared to interfere with all the students' chances to learn and get along well in school. I proposed a small experiment which could help the emotionally disturbed peer learn better ways to act in the classroom. The emotionally disturbed student was told that in order to help him learn these new things, his peers had offered to help him. This fellow student would sit beside him and serve as a model. All he had to do was to look at the peer model and try to do what he was doing. If he followed this procedure for a few weeks, it was expected that he would learn and be able to exhibit the same behaviors by himself.

To let him know that he was doing things right, the peer model would give him a token whenever his behavior was appropriate. He was to record on a sheet, showing the date and a column for daily totals, each time he received a token. The number of tokens received each day would show him his progress. (pp. 20-21)

The target behaviors for each child were defined. Inappropriate behaviors to be modified included such things as speaking out of turn, thumb sucking, and poking others. Each emotionally disturbed child exhibited fewer inappropriate behaviors and more appropriate behaviors over the course of the program. In addition, it is reported anecdotally that peer models developed more positive attitudes toward their partners and that peer relationships in general improved.

What is important to note here? First, once intervention procedures are initiated, the teacher can proceed with the regular academic program for all children. She need not interrupt the entire class to attend to misbehavior. Second, not only do target students gain, but the models may show important gains as well. And third, that such young children can successfully participate in this type of program suggests that almost any mature-for-his-age child could serve as an effective peer model. Variations of this plan would permit simultaneous modeling to a number of children by one model or one-to-one peer modeling to just one child in a classroom who might need special help. Several children could be selected to model a single behavior for one child or to model different behaviors to the same child.

Sometimes, however, peer or teacher modeling is an inappropriate choice for treatment. Ross, Ross, and Evans (1971) reported the modification of behavior by modeling and guided participation of an extremely withdrawn six-year-old child. Because of the severity of the child's problem, using the teacher as a therapist was not feasible. The child needed so much attention that the teacher would have had to ignore the rest of the class to attend to him. Since the child avoided his peers, they could not serve as models for him either.

In this study, an experimenter (psychologist) and a model (undergraduate student) conducted a seven-week treatment program in the preschool. While such personnel may not be routinely available, a program could be conducted by trained paraprofessionals such as willing mothers or other volunteers. This program was designed, first, to establish generalized imitation of the model, that is, to get the child to copy or imitate any model behaviors. Second, the program used modeling to eliminate fear and avoidance behaviors and to teach social interaction, motor, and game skills.

> In the first phase, lasting four sessions, M (model) was paired with a variety of tangible and social rewards; was positive and demonstrative to S (subject) and rewarded him for imitative responses; and was immediately responsive to S's bids for attention, help, and approval. When M was absent E (experimenter) encouraged S to reproduce M's behaviors and rewarded him for imitative responses. By the end of this phase, the facilitating effect of nurturance on imitation was confirmed, S was strongly attached to M: he talked constantly about M to E, reproduced many of M's verbal and nonverbal behaviors, and waited eagerly at the door of the preschool for M to come. (p. 275)

Now that the model had become valued to the child and was imitated by him, the second phase of the program was initiated. This phase had several steps:

1. The model demonstrated social interactions with other children. These were graduated in degree of approach and interaction. If the child did not watch, as sometimes happened, a commentary by either the experimenter or the model was given.
2. Pictures, stories, and movies of children approaching and relating to other children were shown to the child and discussed with him by the model or the experimenter (symbolic modeling)
3. Reluctant peer interactions were modeled, and the model received reassurance and encouragement from the experimenter. This step was taken to create similarity between the child and the model and to show progression in social interaction.
4. The model and/or experimenter modeled appropriate social behaviors in humorous situations. The child was drawn into these sessions.
5. The model and the child together participated in a graduated series of social interactions.
6. The model demonstrated, and helped the child practice games and other preschool appropriate skills.
7. The child was tested outside of the school setting (e.g., sent into a group of strange children in a park). He received encouragement and reward from the model or the experimenter for his performance on these occasions. In addition, these situations provided material for additional role playing.

After treatment, according to the measurements used in this study, the child's behaviors were very similar to those of the socially competent children in the classroom. Thus, through the help of outside personnel, major changes can be brought about within the naturalistic school setting using models and guided participation. Note that this program made use of both live and symbolic models, guided participation, prompting, direct reinforcement and training for generalization.

Treatment approaches need not be directed at only one child at a time. Goodwin and Mahoney (1975) used modeling techniques to increase the amount of nondisruptive behavior demonstrated by three hyperactive, impulsive boys in their classrooms. These boys, who were between the ages of 6 and 11, showed a marked inability to cope with verbal aggression. The modeling procedure involved a verbal taunting game in which one child stands inside a circle two feet in diameter while other children taunt him from the perimeter of an outer circle, six feet in diameter. The three boys observed a three-minute videotape of a nine-year-old male model participating in this game. According to Goodwin and Mahoney:

> In addition to remaining ostensibly calm, looking at his taunters, and remaining in the center of the circle, the model was portrayed as coping with verbal assaults through a series of covert self-instructions. These thoughts, which were dubbed in on the tape, consisted of statements such as "I'm not going to let them bug me" and "I won't get mad." (p. 201).

One week later, the three boys saw the videotape again, but this time the thoughts and actions of the model were pointed out and discussed. After viewing the videotape, the boys were asked to recall as many of the coping responses as they could.

The boys played the taunting game before seeing the model, in between the two modeling sessions, after the second session, and subsequently at follow-up. The boys made very few coping responses before observing the model. Interestingly, their behavior remained unchanged after the first modeling session. After the second session, however, which included discussion and rehearsal of coping responses, their performances improved dramatically and were maintained at follow-up. Of more importance than their improvement in playing the taunting game was the change in the boys' classroom behavior. Prior to participation in the modeling procedure, the three boys were observed to display nondisruptive behavior 59, 64, and 54 percent of the time. At follow-up, their rates of appropriate classroom behavior had increased to 86, 91, and 91 percent, respectively.

Hosford and Sorenson (1969) also used a videotaped model in their attempt to help shy students participate more readily in classroom discussions. Because observation of filmed models is as effective in many cases as observation of live models, schools can make use of prepared film materials that apply to problems experienced by many school-aged children. Hosford and Sorenson estimated from a survey of fourth, fifth, and sixth graders that inability to participate in class discussions is a problem for about 25 percent of these children.

The authors explain their procedures:

> We began with a student, Steve, who was identified by his teachers and parents as being unable to speak up in class and who had indicated that he would like help with his problem. The counselor made a video tape recording of the interview with Steve, the "model student." Basically the counseling session consisted of verbal interchanges between Steve and the counselor in which Steve responded to cues and questions as to what he might do to begin speaking

up in class. Often the cues were such that Steve had little difficulty responding with a "good" question. Whenever he suggested, for example, "I would begin by asking a question," he was reinforced with, "That's an excellent way in which to begin." The interview was terminated after Steve had made several suggestions of things he might do. (p. 203.)

Here is an excerpt from the final eight-minute videotape:

> *Counselor:* Good, Good, Now that's one way to start, isn't it?
> *Steve:* Yeah.
> *Counselor:* You know—would you like to practice this now so that tomorrow you'll know what you're going to do?
> *Steve:* Uh huh. Okay.
> *Counselor:* Now, why don't I pretend that I'm your teacher? Now that's Mrs. Jones, isn't it?
> *Steve:* Uh huh.
> *Counselor:* Okay, class, it's time for science and we've been studying the stars. Now is there anyone in here who has read anything about the stars?
> *Steve:* I have.
> *Counselor:* Oh you have, Steve, good. What have you read about the stars that you would like to tell us?
> *Steve:* Well . . . the earth circles the sun every year.
> *Counselor:* Right! Now is the sun a star?
> *Steve:* Uh huh.
> *Counselor:* Good. Now do you think may you could try this tomorrow in Mrs. Jones' class?
> *Steve:* Uh huh. Okay. Suppose so. (pp. 203-204).

Although the critical question of whether the observers of the film actually participated more in class discussions was not asked in this study, the students indicated in a questionnaire that they learned something from watching Steve and that they would use some of the ideas they observed in the film.

Some of the advantages of planned use of modeling in school settings have been demonstrated in these examples: (1) there are many models available in a school; (2) flexibility in planning a program is maximal; (3) disruption of regular classroom procedures can be held to a minimum; and (4) programs can be planned for one child or for many, using one model or multiple models. Academic skills, appropriate classroom behaviors, and social interaction skills are the usual targets of school programs. Additional ideas for school applications of modeling can be found in Sarason and Sarason (1973).

Modeling in the Training of Mentally Retarded People

Modeling can be a valuable training aid in work with mentally retarded people. When verbal instruction fails, as it may with people who are limited in cognitive capability, helpers often automatically demonstrate a task. Does this modeling approach work with mentally retarded individuals? Laboratory studies suggest that it does, and studies in more naturalistic settings provide us with examples of possible training programs.

Survival skill training, in particular the adequate use of the telephone, was the focus of a study by Stephan, Stephano, and Talkington (1973). Retarded girls 16 to 22 years of age (mean age 19) with IQs of 55-85 (mean IQ 64.9) participated in the training. Of interest to these experimenters was the comparison of training using a live model with training through the use of videotapes.

Procedures for training programs such as this can be quite simple. In this case, some of the girls were introduced to a model (female college student) and told: "This lady is going to show you how to use the telephone. Watch closely as you will have to use the telephone in the same way as shown" (p. 65). Other girls were asked to watch a videotape on the use of the telephone. They were told: "The girl on the videotape is going to show you how to use the telephone. Watch closely as you will have to use the telephone in the same way as the girl on the videotape." (p. 65). In both cases, the model then identified six parts of the telephone, demonstrated how to make a phone call to the police, and demonstrated how to answer the phone and take a message for a person who is not at home. The girls were then asked to perform the tasks. The demonstration-test sequences were presented three times.

Findings encourage the continued development of training programs for retarded persons which incorporate the use of modeling. The two modeling groups just described performed significantly better than a control group which saw no model. The group which observed a live model, however, was not significantly different in performance from the group which watched the videotape. We suggest, therefore, that the use of a series of training videotapes could be an effective time saving method of training moderately retarded individuals to perform certain basic skills.

A group training procedure used by Perry and Cerreto (1977) also demonstrates the usefulness of videotape modeling for training retarded individuals. In this study, a broad spectrum of social skills was taught, including mealtime behaviors and social interaction skills such as meeting and conversing with people, offering to help with a task, and responding to a minor social accident. The participants were adult group home residents, most of whom were moderately retarded. The training program incorporated the following features: verbal summarization of important aspects of the modeling display, model presentation of component parts of a behavior as well as the complex reconstructed skill, rehearsal of the behavior, and feedback and reinforcement from group members and leaders. During rehearsal, behavioral sequences were practiced both exactly as they had been modeled and with variations proposed by the group members. Observations of the residents in their usual mealtime setting and in a simulated setting in interaction with a stranger indicated that the behaviors practiced in the training setting had been successfully transferred to the home environment.

We see from these two examples that modeling techniques can be effective tools in training at least one class of retarded individuals, those who are moderately retarded. What about those who have more severe deficits? Here the evidence is not so encouraging. Altman, Talkington, and Cleland (1972) found no modeling of motor skills and no following of instructions for performing motor behaviors by boys of ages 6.3 to 15.8 years and IQ of 10 to 50 (mean IQ

17.5). However, modeling combined with reinforcement has led to acquisition of generalized imitative repertoires in severely and profoundly retarded subjects who before training did not imitate (Baer, Peterson, and Sherman, 1967). One program of modeling used in treatment of institutionalized severely retarded persons is described below.

Whalen and Henker (1969, 1971) made use of both modeling and reinforcement as training procedures for a "therapeutic pyramid" program in an institution for the mentally retarded. In their program, teenagers with IQs in the 40s to high 60s were first trained in behavior modification techniques by the experimenters. Modeling was a major component of this training of assistants or tutors as shown in the following excerpts:

> During the initial session, the tutor received a brief orientation to the goals and procedures of the project. He was told he had been selected to be a "special teacher" for a younger child. He then observed an experienced behavior therapist begin to teach a trainee to imitate a particular response. Following this brief observation, the beginning tutor practiced the technique with the same trainee. The experimenter remained in the room with the dyad and closely supervised all interactions. In his supervising role, the experimenter provided the tutor with frequent verbal evaluations (feedback) regarding his performance and suggestions for improvement. In addition to verbal feedback, further demonstrations were provided when the tutor failed to understand or remember the technique and when each new phase of the program (e.g., gaining attention, extinguishing tantrums, shaping imitative speech and action) was introduced.
>
> The experimenter's use of modeling and feedback was gradually decreased as the tutor became increasingly confident and adept. The goal was to withdraw supervision progressively so that the tutor would learn to assume increasing responsibility for the training of his child. The tutors also began to teach each other, spontaneously modeling for and providing feedback to the "colleagues." (p. 332.)

When their training was completed, the tutors began to work with their charges. Again modeling and reinforcement techniques were used.

> The initial focus of training was on extinguishing tantrums and establishing eye contact. The next phase consisted of teaching the trainees to imitate simple sounds and gestures. The tutor first demonstrated the behavior he was attempting to teach the trainee. If the trainees failed to imitate, attention getting prompts were employed to elicit the desired responses. For example, in verbal imitation training the tutor would hold the reward (food) next to his mouth as he pronounced the stimulus word so that the trainee, whose attention had been focused by the reward, would see how the word was formed on the tutor's lips. When necessary, sounds were prompted by manipulating the child's mouth and lips. Analogously, the tutor prompted gestures by moving the trainee's limbs. The prompts were "faded" as rapidly as the trainee's performance allowed. . . . After the trainee performed an accurate imitative response or an adequate approximation, the tutor rewarded him with food, praise, and physical affection. (p. 333).

How successful was this program? After 25 sessions, one child "now has an imitative vocabulary of about 400 words and can understand and follow several directions, such as 'turn off the light' and 'touch your nose' " (p. 334). His tutor, "has demonstrated his ability to function relatively independently as a tutor. Moreover, he is quite adept at prompting and evaluating the performance of his fellow tutors.'' (p. 334).

From the above material, it can be seen that modeling is an important and valuable part of the training battery to be used with mentally retarded children and adults. Models and trainers may be other retarded persons, or, if available, other nonprofessional helpers can be trained as tutors. The use of modeling enhancement principles such as prompting and reinforcement maximizes the training effects. These findings are important in this field which has few effective training techniques. So many retarded individuals, particularly those in institutions, have not had the benefit of training programs due to limited staff and resources. However, if nonprofessionals can be trained as tutors and if presentation of filmed models as well as group training are effective in teaching new skills, training can be accomplished without additions of large numbers of staff and without overburdening those who are already working with the retarded. Continued development of programs using modeling alone and in combination with other training techniques is needed.

Modeling in the Training of Autistic Children

Autistic children are characterized by their lack of social responsiveness and by their general failure to imitate other people. Since much of human learning is facilitated by the use of models and imitation, this deficit is extremely limiting. In this respect, autistic children behave much like severely retarded children who demonstrate no spontaneous imitation, and training programs for imitation in autistic children are very similar to the programs described in the previous section. These programs use demonstration, prompting, and reinforcement to establish imitative behavioral repertoires.

Hingtgen, Coulter, and Churchill (1967) provide a detailed description of an intensive short-term (three-week) training program with Sonny, a six-and-one-half-year-old who spent most of his day ritualistically manipulating objects or playing with his fingers and spitting, and Becky, a five-and-one-half-year-old girl who spent her time rocking. Both children were mute. The program proceeded as follows:

> ...the child was isolated in an 8x15 room, 24 hours per day, for 21 consecutive days. Throughout this time the child received all food, water, and social contact from adults (two in the case of Sonny, six in the case of Becky) contingent upon the emission of specific behaviors. During an average of six hours of daily training sessions spread over a 12-hour period, food, water, and release from physical restraint (all paired with verbal approval) were used to reinforce three types of imitative responses (p. 37).
>
> 1. Individual and combinational uses of body parts—e.g. holding up one finger, clapping hands, touching parts of the body, various hand, tongue, and mouth positions, running, jumping, etc. . . . (p. 37).
>
> 2. Simple and complex use of objects—e.g., dropping a ball in a bucket, hooking a toy train together, buttoning, line drawing, brushing teeth, playing appropriately with toys, cutting with scissors, etc. . . . (p. 38).

3. Vocal responses—e.g., the imitation of vowel and consonant sounds with a gradual progression to words. (p. 38).

Some examples give a flavor of the procedures of the training sessions:

Imitation of vocal responses—blowing. During an 80-minute session on the third day of Sonny's isolation, he was placed on a chair sitting directly in front of and facing E-1 (the first experimenter), and was physically restrained from getting off the chair. During this session a blowing response was to be imitated in preparation for the later imitation of forcing air for the "puh" sound. Sonny had been observed making a blowing sound spontaneously during rituals, but never in imitation of an adult model. Since Sonny did blow on a harmonica in imitation of an adult during the use of objects session, E-1 started the session by blowing on a large toy harmonica, which Sonny imitated very consistently. With each imitative response, E-1 pulled the harmonica slightly away from Sonny's mouth, so that Sonny was required to blow harder to get the musical tone. Then E-1 took Sonny's hand and blew on it and asked Sonny to imitate that response. After presenting over 30 models, Sonny had not attempted to blow on his own hand, and after 15 minutes, E-1 left the room and E-2 (the second experimenter) entered. E-2 then attempted to have Sonny imitate blowing on a pinwheel, although no response was emitted during 15 minutes of continuous models. In the next 30 minutes, E-2 alternated between presenting models of blowing on the harmonica and blowing on the pinwheel. Sonny became very agitated during this period and emitted much of the avoidance behavior that was typical during the first few days of intensive training. He cried, pinched, hit, hugged, laughed, giggled, and teased in attempting to avoid making the blowing response. As his avoidance behavior increased in intensity, E-2 increased the amount of physical restraint used. Finally, Sonny made an excellent blowing response, and was rewarded by E-2 with a partial release from physical restraint and lavish praise. E-1 then entered the room again, replacing E-2, and tried to get a consistent blowing response. After ten minutes of crying and squirming by Sonny, which necessitated E-1 reinstating the physical restraint, Sonny made another excellent blowing response. E-1 rewarded Sonny by releasing the physical restraint and swinging him up in the air. During the last five minutes of this period Sonny made 33 blowing responses in imitation of E-1. Then E-2 came in for five minutes more and obtained 32 blowing responses from Sonny. No food was used as a reward during this session, and all imitative responses were rewarded by the release of physical restraint and the presentation of social reinforcers (pp. 38-39).

Imitation of use of objects—scissors. During one session in Becky's third day in the room, a pair of children's scissors were taped to the thumb and middle finger of Becky's hand. Holding scissors in her own hand, E then presented a model of opening and closing of the hand. With some help Becky was able to imitate the response. By the end of the 45-minute session Becky was beginning to make small cuts in a thick piece of paper in imitation of E. (p. 39).

Obviously the treatment of Sonny and Becky was an intensive and time-consuming one-to-one approach. Because of the degree of deficit in the functioning of an autistic child, it is perhaps inevitable that such must be the case.

Stilwell (1969) reported a case in which peer models were used to aid in the treatment of a socially isolated and self-destructive hospitalized child. The steps in setting up the training program used with Curt, an autistic boy, were clearly outlined. (1) Assessing the problem, or determining the current patterns of behavior. Curt demonstrated a behavioral chain consisting of isolated walking and crying, and when approached, gnawing on his hand. (2) Selecting behavioral goals. For Curt, the goal was to modify the first element of the chain, the isolated walking. (3) Analyzing the contingencies or determining the most effective reinforcers. M & M's as well as strong social reinforcers were used for Curt. (4) Establishing control or developing attention to the counselor. (5) Developing a sequence. (The sequence, which progresses through steps of graduated difficulty, depends on what has been determined in the previous four steps.)

Curt's sequence was designed to establish "playing on the slide." Although he had the skills to do this activity, he did not spontaneously engage in it. In a series of steps, he did perform the activity and was rewarded for it. Then the assistance of a peer model was solicited.

> *Counselor:* I will hire you to work for me, Mark. We can have a contract and shake hands and you can get paid.
> *Mark:* Silence.
> *Counselor:* I want Curt to slide down the slide. Will you help me?
> *Mark:* All right.
> *Counselor:* For every trip down the slide that Curt makes after you, I will give you one M & M. (p. 197).

After some haggling, Mark agreed to be a model, and later other children made similar contracts to help Curt.

In this case, modeling provided an important stimulus for Curt's playing on the slide. The amount of counselor time required for Curt's training, however, was not reduced. It was necessary for the counselor to continue verbal and nonverbal reinforcement of Curt's imitative behavior for, unfortunately, when the counselor was absent Curt's behavior did not continue. While Curt's peers were good models, they were not rewarding to him.

We can note in these examples that the model is made very salient to the child so that attention is assured; complex behaviors are presented in small segments first and gradually elaborated; and immediate reinforcement is given to the child for imitation. It is apparent from the work cited here and from other programs for autistic children (Lovaas, Freitag, Nelson, and Whalen, 1967) that modeling is a useful aid for teaching both verbal and nonverbal behaviors to autistic children.

Modeling in the Treatment of Psychotic Adults

The deficits of some psychotic adults resemble the deficits found in autistic children. In severely disturbed schizophrenic patients, for example, behavioral repertoires are extremely limited and may be characterized by lack of speech and social withdrawal. It is not surprising that applications of modeling to the treatment of psychotic adults are very similar to programs discussed in the previous section. One difference, however, is that in training autistic children we are usually concerned with the observational learning of new skills, since the child may not have previously learned or performed the target skills. With psychotic adults, on the other hand, the intent may be to reinstate the use of skills which were in the patient's behavioral repertoire at some time in the past.

Sherman (1965) and Wilson and Walters (1966) demonstrated the usefulness of a modeling-reinforcement combination in stimulating speech in mute or near-mute schizophrenic patients. Note how Wilson and Walters's work differs from Hingtgen, Coulter, and Churchill's training of Sonny and Becky.

Wilson and Walters examined the effects on speech output of patients receiving modeling-plus-reinforcement, modeling only, or neither modeling nor reinforcement (control). Since modeling-plus-reinforcement was the most powerful treatment, only the procedures for that condition will be presented.

Repeated sessions of watching colored slides were given to subjects individually in a testing room. During training sessions (as opposed to testing), subjects were first presented with a verbalizing model. "The experimenter, who served as model, commenced the session by taking the seat in front of the rear-projection screen and speaking rapidly and continuously in response to each slide as one of the sets was projected on the screen. The subject, whose view of the slides was obstructed by the baffle, meanwhile listened to the experimenter talk" (p. 63). Each subject, during his turn with a second set of slides, was reinforced on a fixed-ratio schedule with pennies for either specific or nonspecific verbal imitation. Prompts such as "What do you see in this picture?" and "Tell me about this one" were given to five of the 20 slides if the subject had not responded after 15 seconds of exposure to a slide. Note that this study, instead of requiring an exact match of the model's behavior, reinforced any verbalization.

Wilson and Walters were able to increase verbal behaviors in the laboratory in response to the slides. As is frequently the case with treatment procedures which occur outside of a patient's normal environment, however, ratings of verbal output on the patients' ward showed no change. Generalization of treatment effects can be achieved both by training behaviors in more than one setting (i.e., in the laboratory and on the ward) and by training behaviors appropriate to more than one setting.

Gutride, Goldstein, and Hunter (1973, 1974), in two studies with hospitalized schizophrenic patients, attempted to promote generalization by teaching the patients skills which would be useful both within the hospital and outside of it. In the first of these studies, four modeling videotapes were used for training.

> . . . the first tape contained enactments indicating how one individual (the model) can interact with another individual who approaches him. The second, how an individual (the model) can initiate interaction with a second person. The third, how an individual (the model) can initiate interaction with a group of people. Finally, continuing this progression reflecting increasing complexity of social interaction, the fourth tape depicted how an individual (the model) can resume relationships with relatives, friends and co-workers from outside the hospital. (p. 410).

These authors considered many modeling enhancement factors in the design of their videotapes, including:

> . . . portrayal of several heterogeneous models; the introduction and summarization of each tape by a high status narrator (hospital superintendent and clinic director), who sought by his

introduction to maximize observer attention and by his summary to re-emphasize the nature of the specific, concrete social interaction behaviors; portrayal of the model's characteristics as similar to that of most participating study patients (age, sex, patient status); and frequent and readily observable reward provided the model contingent upon his social interaction behavior. (p. 410).

Note in the following excerpts from the modeling tapes the attention given to the modeling enhancement variables.

Tape 1
Narrator's introduction
Hello, I'm Dr. Turner from Denver State Hospital. You are now going to see some very important movies which will show you how some patients at another hospital were able to get to know and talk to another person who came over to them. I want you to pay close attention to these movies and notice what these patients did in order to get to know the person who came over to them.

The narrator went on to give reasons (to feel better and be happier) for people to know and to talk with others. He stated four important points to be noticed about how the model would respond. He then reviewed the points made and the reasons for interacting. Finally, he directed the viewer's attention to the task.

Since we want you to feel better and since we also want you to be happier, we want you to do all these things, just like the patients in the movies. So pay close attention and learn what to do. Thank you.
Scene 1
   M (model) is seated by himself, doing nothing.
   P (patient): Hello, my name is Tom. What's your name? (extends hand)
   M: I'm Steve. (shakes his hand and looks at P)
   P: How are you today?
   M: Fine thanks, and you?

Conversation continued for a few more interchanges with M being reinforced for his friendly behaviors.

P: . . . I'm really happy to meet you. It's always nice to meet new people and to have new friends to talk to too.

Other scenes continued to model both verbal and nonverbal interaction patterns and provide reinforcement to the model for his efforts.

Scene 3
The model is seated alone, reading newspaper.
   P: Can I see a section of the newspaper?
   M: Sure, which section would you like? (looks at P)
   P: The sports page if you've finished it already. Do you read the sports page?
   M: Yes I do. I like reading about football and hockey. I've finished that section so here it is. (looks at and leans toward P)
   P: Thanks a lot. That's nice of you to share your newspaper. I also like to follow the football and hockey scores.

M: Good . . . Maybe then we can talk about our favorite teams after you read the sports news. Who do you think will go to the superbowl this year?

P: I don't know but I think it'll be Dallas again. Say, y'know, I really like talking to you about sports.

After ten scenes, the narrator returned to sum up the films just seen:

You just saw some very important movies which showed you how some patients were able to get to know and talk to another person who came over to them.

The narrator again reviewed the material stated in the introduction. Then:

Because these patients were able to get to know and talk with the person who came over to them they felt much better and they were happier. When we talk with people, we are healthier and we have more fun. We want you to feel better and be happier too, so now we want you to do all the things you saw the patients in the movies do, right here with the other people in your group. Thank you.

As is suggested in the narrator's last statement, the training did not end with the presentation of the models. The patient group then discussed and role played the scenes they had seen. They received feedback and reinforcement for their own efforts at imitation of the roles played by the model.

The second study (1974) focused on training in specific skill deficit areas. For example:

Narrator's introduction

Hello, I'm Dr. K. . . . .

This week we are starting with the absolute basics of social interaction—simple eating behavior. . . . Watch this tape carefully as it demonstrates eating behaviors that can really affect your sociability.

Scene 1

Narrator: Put your napkin on your lap.

Patient A sits down at dining hall table, takes his napkin off the table, unfolds it, puts it on his lap.

Narrator: Good

Patient A smiles.

Patient B sits down at dining hall table, takes his napkin off the table, unfolds it, puts it in his lap.

Narrator: Good

Patient B smiles

Narrator continues with patient C

Narrator: Also use your napkin during the meal when you need it.

Patients A and B perform.

Patient C, eating, takes napkin off his lap, wipes his mouth, puts napkin back in his lap.

Narrator: Very good.

Patient C smiles.

Narrator: That was good, that's how to use your napkin.

After other scenes, the narrator summed up the action:

Now that you've seen the actors demonstrate the importance of good eating posture and using your napkin, fork, and knife properly, you will have a chance to do it yourselves, and by seeing yourselves on television learn just how sociable you can look through good eating habits. Sit up straight, use your napkin, hold your knife and fork properly, and I guarantee that you will not only look good, but feel good as well. "Try it, you'll like it."

Results from these two studies are encouraging for the use of the described techniques in training hospitalized schizophrenics. Results were better for simple than for complex skills, and they were better for acute patients than for chronic patients. As in other studies, having patients use these newly practiced skills in actual hospital situations and interactions remains a problem. Training of hospital personnel to prompt and reinforce the same behaviors on the ward and in the general hospital environment might be a good supplement to the program.

The examples cited above show that procedures which incorporate modeling as a major part of training are effective in treating some of the behavioral deficits of psychotic adults. Modeling is used to elicit behaviors which have at some time been in the patients' repertoires or to teach new behavior. Attention must still be given, however, to maintenance of patient motivation to perform the behaviors outside of the treatment setting.

Modeling in the Rehabilitation of Alcoholics, Delinquents, and Addicts

In a recent evaluation of the effectiveness of a treatment program with male alcoholics (Marlatt, 1973), each patient who resumed drinking following his discharge from an alcoholism treatment hospital was interviewed concerning the exact situation and circumstances in which he took his first relapse drink. An analysis of these relapse situations reported by 48 patients revealed that over half of the sample took their first drink in one of two situations. The first type of situation, accounting for 29 percent of the relapses, was characterized by these features: the patient was frustrated in some goal-directed activity and reported experiencing anger and resentment. Rather than expressing this anger in a constructive manner, he began to drink. For example, one patient tried to call his estranged wife shortly after leaving the hospital in order to make arrangements to see his children. As soon as his wife heard his voice on the phone, she hung up on him. When asked about his feelings, at that moment, he replied, "The bitch! I could kill her for doing that!" What did he actually do? "I went down to the corner bar for a drink."

The second type of situation involved social pressure to resume drinking which the patient was unable to resist (23 percent of all relapses). In one case, the patient had just completed his first week of work on a new job. It was Friday afternoon, and his new co-workers invited him down to the corner bar for a well-deserved drink. He made a few attempts to resist but soon gave up and joined the crowd. By closing time that evening, he had consumed over thirty glasses of beer.

The inability to express anger appropriately and the inability to resist social pressure are two examples of behavioral deficits of alcoholics. Similarly, the problems of other individuals such as delinquents and addicts are often related to deficits in behavior repertoires. These individuals have not learned socially approved ways of handling everyday situations. How can modeling be used to help such individuals? One appraoch is to teach new, constructive, alternative behaviors with a program based on modeling and role-playing procedures. Such training should be done while the patient is still in treatment in order to build his behavioral repertoire before he is confronted with troublesome situations in the outside world.

Sarason (Sarason, 1968; Sarason and Ganzer, 1973) developed a program along these lines for use with institutionalized male delinquents. Some of the problem situations modeled are very similar to those encountered by alcoholics. In the following example, Tom, a newly paroled youth, is pressured to go out drinking (Sarason and Ganzer, 1971).

(George knocks on the door and Tom answers)

Tom: Hi, George how're you doing?

George: Hey, Man, we're glad to see you back. Gotta celebrate your return. We got a couple cases of beer out in the car. Come on, we're gonna have a party.

Tom: Oh, you know I got to stay clean.

George: What do you mean, you gotta stay clean? Come on, this party was planned just for you. We even got a date with Debbie lined up for you. It won't hurt just this once.

Tom: Well, you know I'm on parole. I can't go drinking . . . I might get caught and if I get caught now, I'll really get screwed.

George: Oh, Man, we won't get caught. We never get caught doing anything like that.

Tom: Well, maybe you guys have never gotten caught, but the night I got in trouble I was out drinking and ended up stealing a car. (pause) You know, I just got back.

George: Look Man, you don't have to drink. Just come to the party and have a little fun. What are we gonna tell Debbie anyway?

Tom: You know being there is the same as drinking to the fuzz. And Debbie won't have any trouble finding someone else.

George: You mean you don't want to go out with Debbie?

Tom: Not to this party. Maybe to a show sometime or something like that.

George: Boy, I sure don't understand you. You sure changed since you got back from that place. You trying to kiss us off?

Tom: No, that's not it, Man. If you want to do something else where we wouldn't get into trouble, (pause) like go to a show, the dance or something, that would be okay but . . . well . . . I know some guys who were in there for a second or third time and they don't get breaks anymore. You know what it is to be on parole.

George: Okay, look, let's just have one quick beer now out in the car, okay? For old times sake.

Tom: No, Man, I know where that leads. Then it would be just one more and then pretty soon we'll be drunk. I can't do it, Man.

George: Jeez! What is the matter with you, Man? Just one beer?

Tom: Maybe another night. My old man expects me to help him work on the boat tonight anyway. I'll be in trouble with him if I take off. Look, I'm sorry, maybe some other time, okay?

George: Okay. Can't be helped, I guess. Look, we'll be at John's place. Come on over later if you can.

Tom: Sure. See you tomorrow, anyway. (p. 139).

Other vignettes covered such topics as how to apply for a new job, how to resist social pressure from peers to engage in antisocial behaviors, and how to delay immediate gratification in order to reach more culturally accepted goals in the future. In each of the modeling groups, which consisted of four to five adolescents, two models acted out a script which demonstrated appropriate behavior in one of the problem situations. Following the modeling sequence, the observers were called upon to summarize and explain the main points made in the vignette. Each group member then rehearsed the same scene with either another group member or a model as a partner.

Sarason and his colleagues compared the effectiveness of this modeling procedure with a traditional group discussion approach. The modeling treatment package was found to be highly effective as assessed by a variety of attitudinal and behavioral adjustment measures.

Reeder and Kunce (1976) used similar modeling procedures with heroin addicts in a residential treatment program. These investigators chose to depict problem situations which residents and staff felt created the most difficulty for addicts both during and following treatment. The areas selected for modeling presentation were:

(a) accepting help from others—necessary for residential and follow-up phases of the program; (b) capitalizing on street skills—identifying skills that the addict has and helping him to apply them legitimately; (c) job interviewing—necessary in order to know the expectancies of the potential employer; (d) employer relations—important for retaining a job; (e) free-time management—necessary for maintaining drug abstinence; and (f) new life-style adjustment—enabling the addict to successfully cope with "old friends" from the drug culture. (p. 561).

Ex-addict paraprofessional staff and selected residents served as models for the videotaped presentations. In addition to demonstrating specific skills, the videotapes were designed to teach a general coping approach which could be applied to any problem situation the addict might face. A slider model was used. Initially, the model was shown to have ineffectual behavioral skills in the problem area and to be pessimistic about his ability to improve. The model would then reflect upon the problem and discuss it with a peer or staff member. Following reflection and discussion, the model would try out new problem solving abilities and behavioral skills. At the close of the vignette, the model was able to handle the situation effectively and independently.

After viewing a modeling sequence, residents engaged in a focused discussion of the presentation. Group members were encouraged to project themselves into the situation and to describe what they would do if confronted with a similar problem.

Reeder and Kunce compared this group, which viewed and discussed the videotaped modeling presentations, with a similar group which saw videotaped lectures on the same topics. Follow-up data on vocational status at 30, 90 and 180 days after release from treatment showed that subjects who participated in the modeling treatment group had substantially better outcomes than those who participated in the video-lecture treatment.

These studies suggest that modeling can be used effectively to teach new behavioral repertoires to individuals who have previously engaged in socially disapproved behaviors. Modeling, as a treatment modality, would appear to have many advantages over the more coercive forms of behavior change which are frequently (and often unsuccessfully) used with individuals demonstrating deviant and/or antisocial behavior patterns.

Modeling in the Training of Helpers

Modeling is an effective technique for behavior modification of persons of all ages (children, adolescents, adults), of many classifications (normal, delinquent, mentally retarded, psychotic), and with many different problems (fears, behavior deficits, behavior excesses). Modeling can be equally effective with professionals and nonprofessionals whose concerns are with behavior change, such as the readers of this book. Professional training has often used examples of desired behavior (symbolic modeling) and demonstrations of the behavior (behavioral modeling), but the systematic application and evaluation of these techniques is a relatively new development. We turn now to a consideration of some recent applications of modeling to the training of helping personnel.

The training of ministers to be more empathic in their responses to a counselee was the focus of studies by Perry (1975; 1970). An empathic model was presented to the ministers on an audiotape. Subjects were told that the counselor they would hear was a "minister who has been doing a great deal of therapeutic counseling in his ministry for the past four years and is highly thought of by his colleagues for the quality of his counseling" (same sex and occupation as subjects, high status, experienced). In the modeled interactions between the minister (model) and client, the client periodically rewarded the minister (as indicated by the italicized statements).

Patient: Well—I've been drinking quite a few years I guess. I think—I can't figure out the exact time.—It just happens you know, you—you don't really know when you start, when you—start drinking—there's no big change in your life. You know I—I really don't drink that much I—have a few drinks now and then—but not that many.
Therapist: You don't think that drinking's the big problem.
Patient: Probably every guy I know drinks more than I do. My wife thinks I drink a lot

though—she's—boy, you talk to her you'd think I was the biggest bum on skid row. *My wife doesn't understand me the way you do.*
   Therapist: Sounds like she nags you about drinking as well as money.
   Patient: You do—do understand . . . (p. 90.)

And later:

   Patient: . . . People just don't care anymore—they don't seem to care about anything—care about other people. But you seem to care about me. *You remind me of an uncle I had that I liked a lot. . . .* (p. 93).

And:

   Patient: . . . I'm no superman—I just—do the work I'm supposed to do. Or try to do it anyway. You seem to understand that. I wish everybody understood me the way you do. *I really like you.* But . . . (p. 96).

Subjects heard 12 scenes between the minister and his client during which the minister made a total of 44 responses to the client. At the end of each scene, the subject was requested to respond empathically to the client as he would if he were counseling. For example:

   Patient: It seems that way. Before we had the kids we didn't have these problems. Now it—it's just not the same. Now it seems like I'm either ignored or it's nag, nag, nag—all the time.
   Other voice: What would you say? (p. 88).

Subjects who heard a high empathy model, as in the examples above, gave response to the standard interview that were significantly higher in empathy than subjects who heard no model or heard a model low in empathy. When the minister subjects were asked to conduct an actual interview with an alcoholic client /actor), those who had heard the high empathy model still tended to offer higher levels of empathy than those who did not. The results for the interview, however, were not as strong as those from the immediate posttest. This is common in studies of training and therapy and suggests the need to program for generalization.
   Some authors have suggested that instructions explaining empathy and its importance in counseling, particularly when accompanied by varied examples of empathic responses and comments about what makes the responses empathic, could increase generalization. In the following study, the usual modeling procedures have been expanded in this manner. The trainee has also been given immediate feedback and reinforcement providing an opportunity for developing discriminations between empathic and nonempathic responses.
   Goldstein and Goedhart (1973) offered a two-day, 10-hour training course to nurses in a psychiatric hospital. Their training program consisted of the following:

1. A presentation and discussion of the meaning and nature of empathy and its importance for patient change, nurse skill development, and hospital climate.

2. Distribution and discussion of the Carkhuff empathy scale (Carkhuff, 1969) highlighted with concrete examples the five levels represented.

3. Discussion of such supporting topics as (a) means for identifying patient feelings, (b) means for communicating to patients that their feelings are understood, (c) empathy versus sympathy, (d) empathy versus diagnosis or evaluation, (e) empathy versus directiveness or questioning, and so forth.

Following the introductory group discussion, the modeling and role playing phases of the training were initiated:

4. Initial modeling. All 30 situations from the Hospital Training Questionnaire (developed by these authors) were enacted by the two group leaders. One served as patient and the other as nurse (model), the latter offering a level 3, 4, or 5 response on the empathy scale to each patient statement. Examples of such situation enactment include:
   (a) *Nurse:* Here is your medicine, Mr. _____ .
   Patient: I don't want it. People here are always telling me to do this, do that, do the other thing. I'll take the medicine when I want to.
   Nurse: So it's not so much the medicine itself, but you feel you're bossed around all the time. You're tired of people giving orders.
   (b) *Patient:* My husband was in his own world. He didn't care about anything I did or said. He just didn't care about me. There's nothing there anymore.
   Nurse: It sounds really kind of sad and lonely, like he has turned his back   on you and walked away.

During each situation enactment, group members were requested to refer to the empathy scale after each patient statement and silently role play their own response prior to hearing the model's.

5. Initial role playing. Using the same 30 situations, one group leader then read each patient statement aloud and asked group members, first on a volunteer basis and then in turn, to offer a response. Nonempathic responses (levels 1 and 2) by the participants were responded to by the group leader with further modeling of empathic responses (levels 3, 4, and 5) for that situation.

6. Further modeling-role playing. This sequence of empathy modeling by the group leaders and role play responding by the group members was repeated two additional times, thus providing each member the opportunity to respond to several patient statements and receive feedback thereon. Following this procedure, each member engaged in one or more extended role play sequences, in which one group leader was the patient and the member the nurse. These sequences began with one of our standard situations, but led wherever the enactors took it. Again, both the group leaders and other members provided corrective feedback when necessary, in the form of high empathy modeling. This same modeling-role playing feedback sequence was then implemented again, this time in response to new problematic situations volunteered by each group member. Finally, the two group leaders once again modeled and role played across all 30 situations. (pp. 169-170).

After training, nurses responded in a more empathic manner to situation items than before training. One month later, higher levels of empathic response were continued. As an added bonus in this study, head nurses who were participant members and observers in the original training groups became trainers for a second group. Their nurse trainees increased in empathy as well. Thus, not only were intensive modeling and role playing techniques effective in altering the nurses' verbal behavior, but these techniques were also effective in teaching trainers to produce positive changes in other trainees. In an extension and replication of the above study, Goldstein added on-the-ward feedback and training for the psychiatric hospital personnel. Results showed that the trainees used their new skills on the ward as well as in the testing situations.

Modeling of quite a different sort was used by Wallace et al. (1973) to change staff behavior in a hospital setting. This was not a training program. The intent of the investigators was to encourage the psychiatric nurses and technicians to continue offering a "social interaction" hour on the unit. Often treatment staff are initially excited by a new program such as a social interaction hour, but when the newness wears off, getting them to continue the program is difficult. In a series of treatments and reversals, this study tried to determine how staff behavior might best be maintained. The first phase involved modeling by the professional staff:

> They (clinical psychologist and research assistant) . . . modeled the target behavior by (a) appearing on the Clinical Research Unit at 1:15; (b) announcing to the patients that the social interaction hour was beginning; (c) proceeding to the dining areas; (d) setting up the various games; (e) participating with the patients in these activities. No mention was made to the staff that it was the appropriate time for the social interaction hour nor that they should participate in the activities.

This was an effective procedure. Staff participation averaged approximately 40 percent during this phase. When modeling was discontinued, however, the participation of both staff and patients declined. A memorandum to the staff failed to improve the situation (no staff attendance). However, a still later procedure did again increase staff participation in these activities: the nursing supervisor repeated the initial modeling procedure. This time participation jumped to a mean of about 67 percent. Those in charge of treatment programs such as this must be aware that their own behavior is an effective tool in establishing and maintaining staff behaviors.

Incidental Modeling in Treatment Settings

While the study described in the previous section demonstrates a planned program of modeling, it also suggests that we must concern ourselves with the modeling effects that treatment personnel, in positions of status and authority, have on the behavior of patients when neither staff nor patients are directly aware of such influences. In other words, what incidental modeling occurs in treatment settings? The following sampling of studies suggests that incidental modeling effects may be quite pervasive:

1. If the nurses and aides in the psychiatric unit model the head nurse's behaviors during the social intersection hour (Wallace et al., 1973), we would expect that they would also model them during her other seven hours on duty.
2. Emotionally disturbed children have been shown to model child care workers more than they do therapists and they model both of these more than they do a neutral person (Portnoy, 1973). Child care workers spend many hours with those children and could have a powerful influence on them.
3. Psychotherapy research suggests that therapists, without intention, may be models for their clients in a variety of areas. Rosenthal's finding (1955) that moral values of improved patients come to be more like the values of their therapists might be explained, in part, by modeling.
4. In a very different domain, Yando and Kagan (1968) found that teacher tempo (reflective or impulsive) had an effect over a school year, on the behavioral tempo of the children in the classroom.

While other explanations than modeling can be put forward as alternatives in all these studies the strong possibility that we in the helping professions are imitated by our clients, patients, and charges should lead us to examine our behaviors and to attempt to be more aware of the influences we may have on others.

SUMMARY

This chapter describes the use of modeling as a technique which can be used to modify behavior in a wide variety of clinical settings. The term modeling refers to the process by which the behavior of one individual or group, the model, acts as a stimulus for similar thoughts, attitudes, and/or behavior on the part of another individual, the observer. Some of the basic concepts which apply to modeling are discussed in Part I of the chapter. An important distinction is drawn between the acquisition phase of modeling, in which the model's behaviors are first acquired or learned by the observer, and the performance phase, in which the observer subsequently performs the behavior demonstrated by the model. Three effects of modeling on behavior are described: (1) the observation learning effect, in which observers both acquire and perform new responses; (2) the disinhibitory/inhibitory effect, in which performance of previously learned but inhibited behavior is either disinhibited (increased) or inhibited even further (decreased) and; (3) the response facilitation effect, in which the performance of an already learned behavior, which is not under existing restraint or inhibition, is increased.

A review of those factors which contribute to the successful use of modeling procedures is presented in Part II. This section is divided into a discussion of those factors which primarily facilitate acquisition of new responses and those factors which enhance performance of responses (either newly learned or previously acquired). Considered under factors enhancing acquisition are characteristics of the model, characteristics of the observer, and characteristics of the modeling presentation. Incentives for performance, factors affecting quality of performance, and transfer and generalization of performance are among the topics discussed in the second half of this section. Table 5.1 presents these factors in checklist form and is meant to serve as a guideline for those who are creating modeling programs.

Part III of the chapter describes the use of modeling methods with a variety of special populations and problem areas. This section begins with two examples of the application of modeling to fear-related behavior. At first, modeling had been used extensively in the treatment of snake phobias. More recently, this form of treatment has also been used to help alleviate fears of children facing surgery or hospitalization. Next, examples are given in which teachers, peers, and nonprofessionals act as models, teaching new behaviors to socially disturbed and withdrawn children in the classroom. Filmed models are presented as a method of facilitating classroom discussion. Modeling has also proven effective in the treatment of mentally retarded persons. Basic survival skills, such as the use of a telephone, can be taught to retarded individuals by the use of either live or videotaped models. Success has also been reported in training more intellectually competent retarded youths to serve as models for the less able. The combined use of modeling and reinforcement procedures is illustrated in the treatment of autistic children. Basic verbal and motor skills can be acquired by autistic children who observe adult or peer models and then receive rewards for their performance of the modeled behaviors.

Modeling has been used successfully in the treatment of psychotic adults as well. In contrast to the treatment of autistic children, where the aim of treatment is to develop new behaviors, the goal of modeling treatment methods with psychotic patients often is to reestablish previously learned but no longer performed responses (e.g., reinstating speech patterns in a mute patient). Other examples presented in this section show how modeling can be introduced as a method of teaching psychotic adults appropriate interpersonal behaviors to use upon their return to the community.

The training of new interpersonal skills has also been emphasized by those working with alcoholics, delinquents, and addicts. One problem common to each of these groups seems to be the inability to resist social pressure. Many other skills have received attention and have been effectively taught by modeling.

Modeling can also be used to teach counseling and therapeutic skills to the staff members in clinical settings. Examples are presented which show how the modeling of empathy can lead to a changed therapist-client interaction. In one study, a combination of methods (instructions, modeling, feedback, reinforcement, and role playing) was incorporated into a training program for nurses to increase their empathic level of responding when working with their patients. Such "package" treatment programs which combine several modification methods are likely to increase generalization of treatment effects. The chapter concludes with a brief discussion of incidental modeling effects which occur in all treatment situations. Staff members who serve as role models for their clients need to be aware of their possible impact in this regard. It is hoped that this chapter will serve as a symbolic model to the reader who plans to employ modeling methods in the treatment setting.

REFERENCES

Altman, R., Talkington, L.W., and Cleland, C.C. Relative effectiveness of modeling and verbal instructions on severe retardates' gross motor performance. *Psychological Reports*, 1972, *31*, 695-698.

Baer, D.M., Peterson, R.F., and Sherman, J.A. The development of imitation by reinforcing behavioral similarity to a model. *Journal of the Experimental Analysis of Behavior*, 1967, *10*, 405-416.

Bandura, A. *Principles of behavior modification*. New York: Holt, Rinehart and Winston, 1969.

Bandura, A. (Ed.), *Psychological modeling: Conflicting theories*. Chicago: Aldine-Atherton, 1971a.

——— Psychotherapy based upon modeling principles. In A.E. Bergin and S.L. Garfield (Eds.), *Handbook of psychotherapy and behavior change*. New York: Wiley, 1971b.

——— *Social learning theory*. Englewood Cliffs, N.J.: Prentice-Hall, 1977.

Bandura, A, and Walters, R.H. *Social learning and personality development*. New York: Holt, Rinehart and Winston, 1963.

Bandura, A., Blanchard, E.E., and Ritter, B. Relative efficacy of desensitization and modeling approaches for inducing behavioral, affective, and attitudinal changes. *Journal of Personality and Social Psychology*, 1969, *13*, 173-199.

Bandura, A., Grusec, J.E., and Menlove, F.L. Observational learning as a function of symbolization and incentive set. *Child Development*, 1966, *37*, 499-506.

Carkhuff, R.F. *Helping and human relations*. New York: Holt, Rinehart and Winston, 1969.

Chartier, G.M., and Ainley, C. Effects of model warmth on imitation learning in adult chronic psychotics. *Journal of Abnormal Psychology*, 1974, *83*, 680-682.

Csapo, M. Peer models reverse the "one bad apple spoils the barrel" theory. *Teaching Exceptional Children*, 1972, *4*, 20-24.

Flanders, J.P. A review of research on imitative behavior. *Psychological Bulletin*, 1968, *69*, 316-337.

Goldstein, A.P. *Structured learning therapy: Toward a psychotherapy for the poor*. New York: Academic Press, 1973.

Goldstein, A.P., and Goedhart, A. The use of structured learning for empathy enhancement in paraprofessional psychotherapist training. *Journal of Community Psychology*, 1973, *1*, 168-173.

Goldstein, A.P., Sprafkin, R.P., and Gershaw, J. *Skill training for community living: Applying structured learning therapy*. New York: Pergamon Press/Structured Learning Associates, 1976.

Goodwin, S.E., and Mahoney, M.J. Modification of aggression through modeling: an experimental probe. *Journal of Behavior Therapy and Experimental Psychiatry*, 1975, *6*, 200-202.

Gutride, M.E., Goldstein, A.P., and Hunter, G.F. The use of modeling and role playing to increase social interaction among asocial psychiatric patients. *Journal of Consulting and Clinical Psychology*, 1973, *40*, 408-415.

——— The use of structured learning therapy and transfer training in the treatment of chronic psychiatric inpatients. *Journal of Clinical Psychology*, July 1974, 277-279.

Heller, K., and Marlatt, G.A. Verbal conditioning, behavior therapy and behavior change: Some problems in extrapolation. In C.M. Franks (Ed.), *Behavior therapy: Appraisal and status*. New York: McGraw-Hill, 1969.

Hingtgen, J.N., Coulter, S.K., and Churchill, D.W. Intensive reinforcement of imitative behavior in mute autistic children. *Archives of General Psychiatry*, 1967, *17*, 36-43.

Hosford, R.E., and Sorenson, D.L. Participating in classroom discussions. In J.D. Krumboltz and C.E. Thoresen (Eds.), *Behavioral counseling: Cases and techniques*. New York: Holt, Rinehart and Winston, 1969.

Kanfer, F.H. Vicarious human reinforcement: A glimpse into the black box. In L. Krasner and L.P. Ullmann (Eds.), *Research in behavior modification*. New York: Holt, Rinehart and Winston, 1965.

Kanfer, F.H. and Phillips, J.S. *Learning foundations of behavior therapy*. New York: Wiley, 1970.

Kaufman, J.M., Kneedler, R.D., Gamache, R., Hallahan, D.P., and Ball, D.W. Effects of imitation and nonimitation on children's subsequent imitative behavior. *Journal of Genetic Psychology*, 1977, *130*, 285-93.

Lovaas, O.I., Freitag, L., Nelson, K., and Whalen, C. The establishment of imitation and its use for the development of complex behavior in schizophrenic children. *Behaviour Research and Therapy*, 1967, *5*, 171-181.

Marlatt, G.A. Task structure and the experimental modification of verbal behavior. *Psychological Bulletin*, 1972, *78*, 335-350.

——— A comparison of aversive conditioning procedures in the treatment of alcoholism. Paper presented at the annual meeting of the Western Psychological Association, Anaheim, California, April, 1973.

Melamed, B.G., and Siegel, L.J. Reduction of anxiety in children facing hospitalization and surgery by use of filmed modeling. *Journal of Consulting and Clinical Psychology*, 1975, *43*, 511-521.

Melamed, B.G., Hawes, R.R., Heiby, E., and Glick, J. The use of filmed modeling to reduce uncooperative behavior of children during dental treatment. *Journal of Dental Research*, 1975, *54*, 797-801.

Melamed, B.G., Weinstein, D., Hawes, R., and Katin-Borland, M. Reduction of fear-related dental management problems using filmed modeling. *Journal of the American Dental Association*, 1975, *90*, 822-826.

Miller, N.E., and Dollard, J. *Social learning and imitation*. New Haven: Yale University Press, 1941.

Perry, M.A. Didactic instructions for and modeling of empathy. Unpublished Doctoral dissertation. Syracuse University, 1970.

——— Modeling and instructions in training for counselor empathy. *Journal of Counseling Psychology*, 1975, *22*, 173-179.

Perry, M.A. and Cerreto, M.C. Structured learning training of social skills for the retarded. *Mental Retardation*, 1977, *15*, 31-34.

Portnoy, S.M. Power of child care worker and therapist figures and their effectiveness as models for emotionally disturbed children in residential treatment. *Journal of Consulting and Clinical Psychology*, 1973, *40*, 15-19.

Rachman, S. Clinical applications of observational learning, imitation, and modeling. *Behavior Therapy*, 1972, *3*, 379-397.

Reeder, C.W., and Kunce, J.T. Modeling techniques, drug-abstinence behavior, and heroin addicts: a pilot study. *Journal of Counseling Psychology*, 1976, *23*, 560-562.

Ridberg, E.H., Parke, R.D., and Hetherington, E.M. Modification of impulsive and reflective cognitive styles through observation of film-mediated models. *Developmental Psychology*, 1971, *5*, 369-77.

Rimm, D.C., and Medeiros, D.C. The role of muscle relaxation in participant modeling. *Behaviour Research and Therapy*, 1970, *8*, 127-132.

Ritter, B. The group treatment of children's snake phobias using vicarious and contact desensitization procedures. *Behaviour Research and Therapy*, 1968, *6*, 1-6.

——— Treatment of acrophobia with contact desensitization. *Behaviour Research and Therapy*, 1969, *7*, 41-45.

Rosenthal, D. Changes in some moral values following psychotherapy. *Journal of Consulting Psychology*, 1955, *19*, 431-436.

Rosenthal, T.L., and Zimmerman, B.J. *Social Learning and cognition*. San Francisco: Academic Press, 1978.

Ross, D.M., Ross, S.A., and Evans, T.A. The modification of extreme social withdrawal by modeling with guided participation. *Journal of Behavior Therapy and Experimental Psychiatry*, 1971, *2*, 273-279.

Sarason, I.G. Verbal learning, modeling, and juvenile delinquency. *American Psychologist*, 1968, *23*, 254-266.

Sarason, I.G., and Ganzer, V.J. Modeling: An approach to the rehabilitation of juvenile offenders. Final report to the Social and Rehabilitation Service of the Department of Health, Education and Welfare, June, 1971.

——— Modeling and group discussion in the rehabilitation of juvenile delinquents. *Journal of Counseling Psychology*, 1973, *20*, 422-449.

Sarason, I.G., and Sarason, B.R. *Modeling and role-playing in the schools: A manual with special reference to the disadvantaged student*. Los Angeles, California: Human Interaction Research Institute, 1973.

Sherman, J.A. Use of reinforcement and imitation to reinstate verbal behavior in mute psychotics. *Journal of Abnormal and Social Psychology*, 1965, *70*, 155-164.

Stephan, C. Stephano, S., and Talkington, L.W. Use of modeling in survival social training with educable mentally retarded. *Training School Bulletin*, 1973, *70*, 63-68.

Stilwell, W.E. Using behavioral techniques with autistic children. In J.D. Krumboltz and C.E. Thoresen (Eds.), Behavioral counseling: *Cases and techniques*. New York: Holt, Rinehart and Winston, 1969.

Strichart, S.S. Effects of competence and nurturance on imitation of nonretarded peers by retarded adolescents. *American Journal of Mental Deficiency*, 1974, *78*, 665-673.

Thelen, M.H., Fry, R.A., Fehrenbach, P.A., and Frautschi, N.M. Therapeutic videotape and film modeling: A review. *Psychological Bulletin*, in press.

Turnure, J., and Zigler, E. Outer-directedness in the problem solving of normal and retarded children. *Journal of Abnormal and Social Psychology*, 1964, *69*, 427-436.

Wallace, C.J., Davis, J.R. Liberman, R.P., and Baker, V. Modeling and staff behavior. *Journal of Consulting and Clinical Psychology*, 1973, *41*, 422-425.

Whalen, C.K., and Henker, B.A. Creating therapeutic pyramids using mentally retarded patients. *American Journal of Mental Deficiency*, 1969, *74*, 331-337.

——— Pyramid therapy in a hospital for the retarded: Methods, program evaluation, and long-term effects. *American Journal of Mental Deficiency*, 1971, *75*, 414-434.

Wilson, F.S., and Walters, R.H. Modification of speech output of near-mute schizophrenics through social learning procedures. *Behaviour Research and Therapy*, 1966, *4*, 59-67.

Yando, R.M., and Kagan, J. The effect of teacher tempo on the child. *Child Development*, 1968, *39*, 27-34.

Yando, R., and Zigler, E. Outer-directedness in the problem-solving of institutionalized and non-institutionalized normal and retarded children. *Developmental Psychology*, 1971, *4*, 277-288.

6

Simulation and Role Playing Methods

John V. Flowers and Curtis D. Booraem*

INTRODUCTION

The major difficulty in writing about simulation and role playing in psychotherapy and related helping endeavors is that almost all therapy can be viewed as
a simulation of the client's real life. To simulate means to imitate or to assume the
form of something or someone else without assuming the reality. Therapies vary
in the way they simulate real life along a number of dimensions. These dimensions include: time reference, covert or private versus overt or public behavior,
real versus exaggerated enactments, and the choice of content area. The present
chapter will deal primarily with simulations that are realistic, overt, and aimed at
extratherapeutic behavior change.

    With respect to the time reference dimension, the basic concept of transference
in psychodynamic therapy describes a process in which the client simulates
earlier important relationships in the present therapeutic situation. This simulation allows the client to work through previously unresolvable conflicts by re-
experiencing them in an environment where the therapist is present to help the
client with the earlier difficulty. Psychoanalysis is a simulation in which historical conflicts are brought into the present so that they can be dealt with in a real
relationship rather than in an imagined or remembered one. Interestingly, the
most common form of role playing in analytic therapy—psychodrama—was
originated by Moreno (1953) not primarily as a method of resolving conflicts, but

*The authors wish to express their gratitude to Dr. Albert R. Marston, Dr. Frederick H. Kanfer,
and Dr. Arnold P. Goldstein for their helpful comments during this chapter's preparation.

as a skill development program for delinquent girls living in institutions. Moreno felt that the girls with whom he was working were living in a limited social world that did not prepare them for the problems they would face outside the institution. Despite this origin, psychodrama has been more widely used to resolve presumed intrapsychic difficulties than to help clients with behavioral deficits. Since analytic therapy is in a sense a simulation, the use of psychodrama in psychoanalytic therapy is a role playing simulation within a larger simulation.

Somewhat differently, client-centered therapies (Rogers, 1951) attempt to create an atmosphere of ''unconditional positive regard'' as a simulation of what a person with greater self-esteem would have experienced in a healthier childhood. By this description one can see that the simulations involved in analytic and client-centered type therapies are not identical. The analytic use of simulation places more emphasis on the historical use of conflict, while the client-centered therapy places more emphasis on creating a present therapeutic atmosphere which fosters personal growth.

This chapter will not deal with either of these types of therapeutic simulation but rather, will deal with simulation and role playing with a distinct future orientation. In a future oriented simulation, which was Moreno's original conception of psychodrama, the client is systematically taught skills for use in the extratherapeutic or natural environment. Such simulation uses a step-by-step learning procedure that is clearly aimed at improving what the client does outside of therapy.

On another dimension, therapists vary as to whether the simulation is overt and deals with observable behavior, or whether it is covert and deals with nonobservable behavior such as thoughts or imagination. On the overt side of the dimension the therapist may choose to have the client simulate his life difficulty in terms of observable behavior, such as role playing assertive behavior. Simulation of covert behavior is accomplished by having the client imagine some stimulus event such as a feared object. This method is employed in systematic desensitization. Hypnotherapy is another example of focusing on covert phenomena. This will deal primarily with overt simulation.

Additionally, overt simulation can be accomplished in exaggerated overdramatic form, or in a manner closely identical to the real life situation. Psychodrama frequently overdramatizes interpersonal problems for the purpose of gaining insight. On the other hand, behavioral rehearsal techniques strive to create as realistic a simulation as possible. This chapter will address realistic overt simulation as opposed to exaggerated forms of simulation.

Finally, there is the content of the simulation. One can use simulation exercises as a behavior change device in business, education, psychotherapy, or, for that matter, in any area where behavior change is appropriate. By and large, this chapter will deal with the use of simulation and role playing in the therapeutic context, although business and educational uses will be briefly inspected. To summarize, we will be dealing with therapeutic, overt, realistic, systematic simulation exercises.

Why use simulations at all? Insofar as you are not dealing with the client in his actual life situation, you are automatically dealing with a simulation of his life. Even when the behavior change agent is present in the client's real life situation, the agent's presence has changed the situation into a simulation of what it would be without the agent present. The reason for the increase in the use of simulation strategies over the past few years is based on evidence that simulation exercises possess distinct therapeutic advantages. Simulation exercises are fun and highly engaging; many therapists using role playing and simulation report lower dropout rates when the exercises are being used, as contrasted to when they are not. Systematic simulation also allows the therapist to structure the behavior engaged in by the client, at least in the therapeutic setting. This structuring allows the therapist to deal effectively with two major therapeutic problems—anxiety and behavioral deficits.

Many clients become highly anxious when they are asked to change their behavior. If you ask a timid Casper Milquetoast to send back an incorrectly cooked steak in a restaurant, he will probably tremble at the thought of sending it back. In the real situation, he will most probably eat the steak, and, if he even remembers your therapeutic instruction, he will eat it in the fear that the terrifying waiter has read his mind. By using systematic simulation, the therapist can help the client to engage in behavior that is not as anxiety-provoking with more chance of success. The therapist continues to change the simulation exercises, literally working up a hierarchy of situations of increasing capacity potential as the client is ready for more difficult tasks. Technically, simulation allows the therapist to systematically design successive approximations toward the treatment objectives.

Secondly, many clients simply don't know how to change their behavior. We often presume that the behaviors that most of us execute with ease have been universally taught and learned, and that anyone not performing them must be incapable because of some intrapsychic difficulty. If the behavior involves an uncommon or complex skill, such as programming a computer, we are more willing to view someone's inability to carry it out as due to a simple lack of training in the necessary skills. If the behavior is common, such as asking another person for a date, we usually presume that any difficulty in its execution must be psychic. In fact, many people don't know and have never been taught how to start conversations. Such a person may be acutely anxious in a situation where he wishes to meet someone, but we may be premature in our presumption that it is anxiety that prevents him from starting the conversation. He actually may not know what kinds of questions to ask, or what to do with a certain type of response. Simulations have the therapeutic advantage of breaking behaviors down into discrete steps which can be easily learned. Any teacher knows that for most students you teach division by one number before you teach division by two numbers, i.e., most skills are best learned in small, easily manageable steps. Simulation allows this same model to be applied to the therapy situation. One might describe it as participatory programmed interaction. As will be pointed out later in the chapter, the fact that simulations can lead to generalized learning presents a complex phenomenon, one which may be explained on the basis of a number of important factors, of which role playing is only one.

While this chapter distinguishes role playing and simulation in the title, this distinction is made for convenience and is not meant to point out a general or essential theoretical distinction. As stated before, to simulate means to imitate, or to assume the form of something or someone else without assuming the reality. In this sense, role playing, which means to play a role not normally one's own, is a specific example of simulation and is a form of what Kanfer and Phillips (1970) have called replication therapy. When we use role playing therapeutically, we often ask the client to enact a set of behaviors different from his usual behaviors in the world, but which we as therapists presume to be performable and useful for him in the outside world. Even more specifically, we ask the client to replicate a situation in his life that has really happened or is likely to happen, and have him practice behaving differently than he would or thinks he would behave. We call it "playing" both as a propaganda device to reduce potential anxiety, and with the understanding that, at least at first, the behaviors are feigned.

Simulation is often presented lightly and called a game. The distinction between simulation and role playing is usually that simulation operates under more rules than role playing and represents less of an attempt to replicate the client's actual life situations. Instead of replicating the client's actual problems in the therapy situation, simulation usually attempts to teach the client a general problem solving repertoire. For this reason, the same simulation game is often used with many different clients. While this distinction between role playing and simulation is useful, it should not be taken too seriously. As we will find, many specific role playing exercises are used with many clients, and many simulation games are tailored to individual situations.

ROLE PLAYING

Assertion Training

Many people, clients and professionals alike, encountering assertion training for the first time, simply do not believe that it is a form of behavior therapy. It is too human, too complex, and resembles traditional therapy too much. This confusion occurs because behavior therapy is often misunderstood as being simplistic instead of specific, and mechanistic instead of systematic.

Initial Assessment. As in almost all behavior therapy, assertion training begins with an assessment of the client's need for, and the appropriateness of, this form of therapy. Sometimes, the appropriateness of assertion training is evident from the referral or from previous acquaintance with the client. However, it should not be presumed that assertion training is the treatment of choice simply because the client appears passive or reports some difficulties that might be dealt with by assertion training. If the initial interview leads the therapist to believe that assertion training may be appropriate, he may wish to give an assertion test. One of the more reliable and valid is the test designed by Rathus (1973). However, in addition to relying on general self-reports or on paper and pencil tests, the therapist should instruct the client to record for a period of several days, all interactions where he wished he had behaved differently and to specify how he wished he had behaved. In order not to concentrate solely on deficits, the client should also be encouraged to record situations in which he judged that he behaved assertively.

Recently, several tests have been developed to specifically assess sexual assertiveness. The Sexual Assertiveness Test and the Sexual Pleasant Events Schedule (Flowers, et al., 1978) provide the therapist with process and content situations that are troublesome for individual clients. These instruments were developed because of the high frequency of reported difficulties with sexual requests and refusal in assertion training groups.

Stage One— the Therapist as an Assertive Model. Given that the therapist considers assertion training appropriate, the therapy begins, as does a great deal of effective behavior therapy, with an explanation of the therapy and its rationale. The therapist should be assertive and confident about the use of assertion training in this case. The client should be told exactly what is going to happen and why, and should be told that this has worked in the past with similar cases. Two points seem to be critical in this introduction to assertion training. One is that the client be repeatedly told he has the right to ask for what he wants and the right to refuse what he doesn't. If he doesn't exercise these rights and acts like a rug, people (even good people) will walk on him. If he looks like a loser and acts like a loser, people will treat him like a loser and he will lose. Secondly, assertion should be clearly differentiated from aggression. Clients seem to understand this distinction if behavior is placed on a continuum

Passive ————————Assertive ————————— Aggressive

in which assertion is the right to ask and the right to refuse, without involving the deliberate violation of another person's rights. Aggression, on the other hand, does involve the violation of another's rights and often involves the use of a more imperative request, i.e., a demand. When one person asks, the other person can refuse, but when a demand is made, the other person is presumed not to have the right to refuse. Passive behavior is the stance that one does not have the right to ask or refuse. While the client's behavior will usually not be changed by such insight, a number of assertion trainers have found that such an introduction facilitates the actual therapy and role playing that follows.

Review Life Situation. When possible, the client should be seen in an assertion training group since many of the procedures outlined below are more difficult or actually impossible to do in individual sessions. Whether in individual sessions or in a group, the therapy begins with a thorough assessment of the individual's life situation. This may seem like a repetition of what was done to assess if assertion training is appropriate for the client, but the purpose is quite different; namely, to find out what situations to deal with in the therapy and to continually assess if the therapy is effective. It is critical that after the initial assessment, clients not only record assertion problems, but also record situations in which they behaved assertively, that they record every situation in which they wished to behave differently, and that they answer four questions: (1) what happened; (2) with whom; (3) when; and (4) where. In this regard, good record keeping is like good journalism. Just as answers to the questions "why?" are left to the editorial section of a newspaper and are not found in the story section, the client's answer to the question "why?" should not be encouraged in the client's weekly report. Therapeutically, encouraging the question "why?" and its answers may cause the client to feel defeated because he cannot provide an answer, or it may encourage him to write long essays and make the problem seem unsolvable. On a purely pragmatic level, writing about "why" may often make the client tired of record keeping. When this happens, the therapist finds himself using the therapy time to design programs to get a change in data keeping behavior rather than in assertive behavior.

One strategy that has been found useful in helping the client keep records and conceptualize assertive behavior is to break assertive behavior into requests and refusals of objects and interactions: (1) Refusing of objects is the right to refuse to give an object when one does not want to; for instance, refusing to loan one's car to a friend who is a bad driver. The caution here is that in the first blush of assertion training success, some clients begin to sense their power and say no before assessing if the answer really should be no, i.e., before looking at the consequences of the refusal. (2) Requesting an object is the right to ask for things, such as for a glass of water in a restaurant without having to buy something. (3) Refusing an interaction is the right to terminate an interaction that is aversive, such as telling a salesman that you are "not interested" and closing the door or hanging up the phone. (4) Requesting an interaction means asking for some form of relationship, and is usually the most difficult class of assertive behaviors for a nonassertive person to perform. This breakdown of categories of assertive behavior helps the client and therapist assess the client's strengths and deficits. One final recommendation for reviewing the client's life situation is always to assess both strengths and weaknesses. This is important not only for planning the session content, but also for reinforcing the client's present level of competence and for later reinforcing the client's gains.

A technique that we have found useful for therapist assessment is for the therapist to remember to check the F.AT.E.S. For each client in each situation, the therapist should determine if the lack of assertion is either a deficit or a barrier in the areas of:

> Fantasy
> Action
> Thought
> Emotion
> Sensation

Role Playing in Structured Situations. After the daily record keeping has been explained and the client has clearly understood the types of situations, the therapy should proceed with role playing of structured situations supplied by the therapist. Since the rehearsal is done in successive order, with those situations that are least difficult being practiced first, the early role play situations are supplied by the therapist and are not taken from the client's life situation. The therapist can create these standard situations before the session or can have the group or the individual help create them in the session. For example, a standard practice hierarchy would be: (1) refusing to lend $10 to an acquaintance when you don't have it; (2) refusing to lend $10 to a friend when you don't have it; (3) refusing to lend $10 to an acquaintance when you do have it; (4) refusing to lend $10 to a friend when you do have it.

It is always wise to check with each client to find if the hierarchy as constructed is in fact in increasing order of difficulty. Sometimes, to make a situation harder, the therapist may have to make the issue smaller, e.g., refusing a request for less money, or projecting the request into the future; whereas to make an item easier, the therapist can make the issue bigger, e.g., refusing a request for more money.

In a group, such role playing is done in triads, with one client being the asserter and one the recipient. At first, the therapist is the coach and keeps the interaction going by suggesting words and strategies to either party. When coaching suggestions are made, it is important that the client carry them out, or at least carry out his version of them, i.e., actively practice and not merely listen. As the group progresses, the coaching postion should be taken by other clients, since it has been demonstrated that the clients who have coached others are better in later assertive performance than clients who have not coached (Flowers and Guerra, 1974). Such standard scenes should be role played until the client is comfortable with his performance. If any scene continues to cause discomfort, an easier scene should be chosen or created. Always try to end a session with a success for the client.

The SUDS Scale. An assessment device which has been found useful in such role playing is the "Subjective Units of Discomfort Scale" (SUDS) of Wolpe and Lazarus (1966) that the client is taught to use in both the role playing and in his daily records. This scale is totally subjective, with 0 the most comfortable the client can remember ever having been and 100 being the most uncomfortable. By and large, discomfort as used in this scale's description means anxiety, although there seems to be therapeutic value in calling it discomfort instead of anxiety.

The client is given a homework assignment of constructing a hierarchy of situations no more than 10 units apart to get a feeling for the use of the scale. In a session, it is helpful to have the client report his present SUDS level and then question him strongly as to whether he is sure he is correct. Usually this mild attack will cause him to feel more discomfort and he will see the similarity between the scale and a temperature gauge which goes up and down in various situations. After the scale has been learned reasonably well, usually by the end of the second session, the client's SUDS level should be reported on every critical incident in his daily record and after each role playing situation.

Recently we have been employing biofeedback (E.M.G.) to verify the client's hierarchy in terms of SUDS level. The client's muscle tension is recorded as he imagines his own hierarchy presented by the therapist in random order. This technique helps both the client and therapist verify both the ranking and interval size of items and can be employed at various stages of treatment to assess anxiety reduction.

Role Playing Life Situations. After the client has learned how to keep life situation records, how to play roles, how to use the SUDS scale, and how to coach if in group training, the next stage of treatment can proceed with real life situations created for the role playing situations from the client's own records. The situations producing the least discomfort should be used first. Furthermore, the client in a group should be able to choose the recipient who also causes the least discomfort. Again, as the client becomes comfortable in the role, he should move to both more difficult situations and more difficult (for him) recipients. A client who is chosen as a difficult recipient should be reminded that this means that he is either like someone difficult for the client to deal with in the real world, or that he is being perceived as assertive. But being chosen for this role does not mean he is a "bad" person.

It has been demonstrated (Booraem, 1974) that the therapist sometimes terminates the role playing with too few trials, i.e., before the skill has been learned well enough, or before the client is comfortable enough to perform it in the outside world. It is important that the therapist remember that the role playing is used for practice and not for insight. The therapist, with his own relatively higher levels of assertive skill, will often become bored and may assume that the client is ready to perform the behavior in the world before the client is actually ready.

The step-by-step model that we employ in conducting role playing exercises is as follows: (Booraem and Flowers, 1977).

1. The asserter briefly describes the situation to be practiced
2. The coach asks the recipient if he or she understands enough to role play
3. The coach sets up the physical situation, e.g., standing, not facing, as in phone calls, etc.
4. The coach asks the asserter his or her goal which should be short and clear (Flowers & Goldman, 1976)
5. The coach asks the asserter what he or she will say
6. The coach instructs the recipient how to respond or start the role play. The coach should

have the recipient initially be easy and positive and only later allow more difficult requests or refusals

7. The coach asks the asserter his or her SUDS level
8. The coach instructs both players to stop after 1 line
9. The coach starts the role play
10. The coach asks the asserter what he or she *liked* about their performance
11. The coach asks the asserter his or her SUDS level
12. The coach and recipient give positive feedback
13. The coach asks the asserter what could be improved
14. If no more than 2 points of improvement have been identified (one for more disturbed clients), the coach or asserter may suggest improvements, but the asserter should never be working on more than 2 items at a time
15. The coach asks the asserter if he or she wants to role play again with the same response
16. When the asserter is comfortable with his or her performance, the coach asks if the asserter wants to make the role play more difficult and/or go on to a 2-line role play.
17. If appropriate, the coach asks the asserter if he or she is willing to report their success to the recipient and coach the next session.

Playing the Role in the World—Mini Exercises. Mini exercises are much like structured ''canned'' situations except that they are homework assignments to be attempted in the real life situation of the client. They involve such tasks as (1) going into a drycleaning store and asking for a hanger because one has locked oneself out of one's car; (2) going into a drycleaning store and asking for a hanger with no explanation; (3) going into a market, selecting one item, and asking a person with a full basket if you can go ahead in the checkout line; (4) sending back food in a restaurant; (5) interrupting and hanging up on a telephone salesman within 20 seconds.

The task should be role played in a group, should not be a regular problem in the client's life situation, and should only be assigned with the client's willing acceptance and the therapist's judgment that the client has a good chance of success. The results of such exercises should be reviewed in the next group or individual session. If the client has not succeeded, the therapist should point out that he was not ready (not that he failed) and either find an easier exercise or role play the assigned one again until both the client and the therapist think it can be accomplished.

"Playing" the Assertive Role in Life. When a client is ready to try assertive behavior in a real life situation that he has reported as difficult, the whole group should review his strategy and his goal. This is because there is evidence that nonassertive people have less clear goals than assertive people. If the goal of an assertive interaction is unclear, the client will fail more often than if the goal is clear. A rule of thumb is that is the goal cannot be stated in one sentence, it is usually two goals.

A second rule is that if the goal puts the power in the recipient's hands (Rehm and Marston, 1968), it is a poor goal. For example, if a client wishes to call another person for a date, he should judge his assertive performance on how well he does this, and not on whether the other person accepts or not. Just as the client has the right to request, the other person has the right to refuse. Assertion training uses role playing to teach the client how to request clearly, and sometimes repeatedly, with the understanding that people who don't request get very little. The success of the request is not guaranteed, only its chances are improved. In rare cases (Davison, 1969) the therapist will realize that the client's life situation is such that assertive behavior will usually be punished. In such cases, the therapist should discontinue assertion training and try to change the environment or move the client from that environment. However, the therapist should not jump to the conclusion that he has one of these rare cases simply because the client gets punished for his first assertive attempt.

The group, or the therapist in individual sessions, should also review the consequences of an assertive behavior that the client is going to attempt. For instance, while the client has the right to refuse to do what his employer tells him to do, the consequences of such a refusal may be highly unpleasant to the client. The client's daily records, which are kept throughout the therapy, should be reviewed in terms of the appropriateness of the goal and the consequences of the desired assertive behavior.

Special Issues in Group Training. If the client is in an assertion group and has outside exercises, either "mini" or real life ones, he should report the results of his attempt to the group before role playing starts. The group should not be allowed to attack failure, but should be encouraged to cheer success. A single report of success can carry over through the entire group session. Assertion training groups seem to function best when they consist of from eight to ten members and two therapists. After the group has been going for a while (three weeks), more than one triad can practice at a time, with the therapist acting as a consultant. Groups can be time limited, from six to twelve sessions, or can be open-ended with new members replacing those who graduate. Both homogeneous and heterogeneous groups have been conducted with good results. Assertion training has been used with inpatients, outpatients, delinquents, normal therapy clients, and students. The major issue in the use of assertion is not how a person is labeled, but whether or not he can behave more adaptively when he behaves more assertively. If videotape is available, it should be used. Videotape feedback allows the client to view both the verbal and nonverbal (eye contact, posture, or nervous habits) components of his assertive role playing and improves his performance more quickly than merely having the group tell him about these components. Eisler, Miller, and Hersen (1973) have demonstrated that the most important component in having someone else judge a client as assertive is his display of affect, and this display is more easily taught with videotape than without it.

A simulation that this author has recently used within the role playing situations is to have the clients who are not role playing give tokens to the active participants for the purpose of feedback. Thus, the "silent" clients give a blue token for what they consider a passive response, a red token for what they consider an aggressive response, and a white token for what they consider an assertive response. The token giving simulates verbal feedback, but has the advantage of not interrupting the role playing exercise. While this simulation within the role playing situation is still being investigated, it has already shown two distinct results. First, it keeps the silent members more involved by significantly increasing their visual contact with the participants. Secondly, there are a number of clients who enter assertion training with the idea that assertive responses are unreasonable and aggressive. Clients giving tokens see their evaluation of a response as compared with that of other "silent" members, and can more quickly rate their own assertive behavior as reasonable or unreasonable, assertive or aggressive, than do clients not using the tokens.

A modification of this token system using only two colors—one for assertive and one for passive behaviors—has also been employed for the client to rate his own behavior in the role playing situation. In comparisons between clients who evaluate themselves and those who are evaluated by the therapist, it has been found that clients who self-evaluate their role playing as assertive are more likely to engage in assertive behavior outside of the therapy session than those who are similarly evaluated by the therapist. While this simulation and a similar one for use in group therapy will be considered again in the section on simulation games, it is included here to demonstrate a technique that has both clinical and research applications for assertion training.

Other Populations. Since the initial writing of this article, researchers have attempted to apply the above model to various populations other than the traditional adult inpatient or outpatient in individual or small group treatment. We have recently conducted a study in which over 100 people were simultaneously given assertion training to test the feasibility of massed delivery of such service. The study used two professionals and four paraprofessionals to conduct the workshop. Results indicated that clients demonstrated behavior change equivalent to individual and small group projects.

In still another expansion, Flowers et al. (1978) employed the assertion training model for clients who were unassertive in the specific area of sexual communication. Employing the tests of sexual assertion and sexual activity cited above, the authors found that such training significantly improved the client's self-reported sexual happiness and fulfillment. Extending this work to the more difficult population of mentally disordered sex offenders, Flowers, Talcot, and Hartman (1977) demonstrated that a prison hospital staff could be trained to deliver sexual assertion training to incarcerated offenders and that trained clients demonstrated immediate and long-term changes such as a higher release rate and lower recidivism rate than nontrained control clients.

It has long been the authors' contention that appropriate assertive behaviors can and should be taught to children in the same manner as traditional academic skills. Just as children are taught to read and play structured games, they can be taught to be assertive in their classrooms, on the playground, and in their communities. In pursuing this belief, a longitudinal study was developed in a Southern California elementary school in which four 4th grade and four 5th grade classrooms were targeted for either academic assertion training, social assertion training, or both. Appropriate control conditions were provided (Marston et al., 1977). Results indicated that the children in the academic assertion training programs (Flowers and Marston, 1972) improved significantly in academic areas, while children in the social assertion training program improved significantly on a broader array of variables including teacher ratings, academic grades, self-esteem, and peer interaction. The effect of training was still observable one year later when compared with the control population.

While this study has broad implications, the most important personal observation was the high frequency with which children verbally punish one another. This observation led us to emphasize positive interactions and, furthermore, to begin investigation in populations in which the frequency of positive input might be less dense. Our first effort in that area was with orthopedically handicapped children enrolled in integrated normal public school classrooms. These children were physically, but not intellectually, handicapped. As such, they were often the target of criticism. They were called "cripple," "retarded," "spastic," and the like on a frequent basis. This high-frequency negative input clearly takes its toll on both the individual's academic performance and, more importantly, his social performance. Social performance involves the issues of self-esteem and/or self-worth and their concomitant behavioral manifestations. Our efforts with this group of children were designed to protect and/or develop feelings or cognitions of positive self-worth through a combined program of positive cognitive evaluation and behavioral rehearsal of positive assertive responses.

Results of this study (Cohn, Booraem, and Flowers, 1978) demonstrated significant increases in appropriate peer contact, verbal behavior, and participation in cooperative classroom behavior when rated by teachers blind to the experiment. In this study simulation procedures included behavioral rehearsal of positive and negative social interactions and positive self-evaluation. Also of interest was the finding that the younger the children, the greater the improvement.

The training procedures developed for work with children are available to parents and teachers in the book *Help Your Children Be Self Confident* (Booraem, Flowers, and Schwartz, 1978).

Another population of documented low density social reinforcement is the retarded. Employing a scaled-down social skill simulation program, Wiese et al (1979) observed that severely retarded inpatients could be taught to significantly increase the frequency of request and positive expressions with a consequent decrease in the frequency of aggressive incidents. However, this study also demonstrated a lack in generalization of these behaviors to other environments. Additional research is presently underway to determine what further treatment components are necessary for treatment generalization.

Other Role Playing

While the most extensive use of role playing has been in the area of assertion training, it should be clear that role playing can be used as a behavior change technique whenever the client can benefit by learning a new way of behaving, especially in social situations. Aside from its use in teaching assertive behavior, role playing has been used to develop appropriate social behavior in delinquents (Sarason, 1968), to teach job interview skills (Prazak, 1969), to help control overt aggressive behavior (Kaufmann and Wagner, 1972) and to change the social behavior of minimally dating males (Melnick, 1973). Each of these uses of role playing bears some resemblance to assertion training, yet each extends either what is being taught in the role playing situation, or how it is being taught.

In Sarason's use of role playing to develop appropriate social behavior in delinquents, complete scripts are preconstructed dealing with how to behave outside the institution where the youths were held. These scenes were first role played by graduate students with the youths watching. The scripts were then role played by the youths in pairs. Some of the youths also got audio or video feedback so that they could review their own performance in the scene. Some groups discussed their performance and some did not. Fifteen scenes, one per session, were used and the youths were encouraged to personalize each scene when they played it. Generally, the scenes fell into four categories: (1) coping with authority figures such as police, school principals, etc.; (2) resisting nega-tive peer pressure such as showing off or skipping school; (3) self-control, such as planning ahead or handling anger; and (4) making a good impression, such as how to join a new group or function in a job interview.

Sarason's scenes were constructed by having the graduate students meet in-formally with the youths to learn the youths' perceptions of their problem areas outside the institution. The youths were asked to spontaneously role play their difficulties and these sessions were tape recorded and edited into scripts for use. (It is important for therapists to be aware that the source for role playing scripts need not originate in the therapist's imagination. It is both easier and probably more relevant to look to his clients as Sarason did, to provide the content for role playing situations.)

Role playing can be used to teach any behavior in which the client shows deficiency. Of course, to be sure the behavior is in fact taught and can be performed appropriately, it is necessary to assess the client's behavior out of therapy. In the Sarason example, delinquents were trained in the general class of responses that might be labeled social skills. Some of the situations used closely resemble those used in assertion training; however, Sarason's use of role playing encompasses other areas of social skills. Again, there is more involved in this treatment than merely role playing. It also includes modeling, instructions, and for some groups there is feedback and a special kind of feedback that can be labeled self-observation. How much each component contributes to the change effort is still being investigated. For the practicing therapist, the key point is that role playing provides another tool for use in trying to help people change.

Another use of role playing that somewhat resembles assertion training, but is designed to change behavior in only one specific situation is that used by Prazak (1969) to teach clients job interview skills. Prazak points out that rehabilitation services have the same problems that mental health agencies have—namely, that many clients return again and again for treatment in what has been called the "revolving door." The rehabilitation service gets the clients jobs which they often promptly lose. Since the clientele has a job turnover rate twice that of the national average, Prazak decided that directly placing the clients in jobs was a losing cause. She decided instead to teach the clients the skills necessary to seek their own jobs.

The skills that this program attempts to teach are: (1) the ability to explain one's skills; (2) the ability to answer problem questions; (3) appropriate appearance and mannerisms; (4) the appearance of enthusiasm; (5) the call back techniques of how to terminate the interview.

In this, as in any role playing situation, the behaviors that the therapist wants to teach have to be clearly defined. The rule is generally that if you don't know what you want the client to be able to do, he generally won't do it. In this use of role playing, Prazak first showed the clients a videotape of a good interview. In any modeling situation such as this, the therapist should be aware that the tape or demonstration should not be too good at the beginning since there is evidence that modeling occurs more readily if the modeled behavior is not too different from what the client can actually perform, or at least imagine himself performing. Next, the clients role played mock interviews which were videotaped for feedback. Instead of confronting the clients when they fell short of the model's performance, the therapist praised them for those behaviors that were like the model's performance. The staff also used these tapes of the initial role played situations to assess the clients' strengths and weaknesses in the interview situation. It is critical that both strong and weak points be explored, since there is a widespread and destructive tendency to explore only deficits when dealing with people in need of help.

The first behavior that is necessary in the job interview is to explain one's skills. Each client explores his assets and records them in a notebook so that he can memorize them. Few clients are aware of their skills until the staff help them explore their past history in detail, including hobbies, military service, high school classes, etc.

The next behavior that is taught is how to deal with problem questions. Most people using rehabilitation services have more problems than the average interviewee, e.g., intermittant employment history, jail sentences, hospitalizations, physical problems, etc. Role playing is used to teach the client how to handle these issues in the interview. The reason that role playing is crucial is that knowledge is not sufficient to insure success; the client must practice until he is skilled enough and/or comfortable enough to perform the behaviors in the real situation. Again, the behaviors are specified:

1. Keep the answer short and end on a positive note.
2. If the problem is obvious to the employer, bring it up before the interviewer asks.

3. Never use psychiatric or medical labels and never say that you were sent to the hospital, say that you went.

The client is also taught grooming and postural skills necessary for appropriate self-presentation during the interview. Prazak takes Polaroid pictures of her clients before and after training so the clients can see graphic evidence of their improved appearance. During the role play, the clients are taught to display enthusiasm and are reinforced for its display. The clients are also taught to maintain eye contact and to shake hands firmly. They are taught to terminate the interview by asking if they can call back to learn the employer's decision.

This use of role playing demonstrates that the technique can be adapted to very specific problem areas. The reader should be aware that this particular use of role playing has not yet been accurately assessed in terms of its success. In any use of a role playing technique, especially in essentially untested ones, it is the therapist's responsibility to assess the outcome and to determine if the treatment in fact helps his clients change.

Another intriguing role playing technique is one labeled ''barb'' by Kaufmann and Wagner (1972). With the possible exception of Sarason's use of scripts with delinquents, most role playing techniques deal with ''passive'' people and are used to train the client in adaptive responses. ''Barb,'' on the other hand, is used with very aggressive people to teach them alternatives to aggressive behavior. Cues that elicit aggression can be either verbal (such as ''why didn't you clean your room?'') or physical, such as having one's pencil taken out of one's hand forcibly. To stop such situations from escalating into either a verbal or physical confrontation, the client in ''barb'' training role plays: (1) maintaining eye contact when responding; (2) maintaining an assertive, but nonaggressive posture; (3) maintaining a moderate, not loud or soft tone of voice; (4) responding verbally to avoid problems, but to try to get positive consequences (i.e., assertive verbal responses).

One of the assertive techniques that this author has found to be useful in step 4 is ''negative assertion.'' In it the client, if he is wrong, responds with words to the effect that ''I was wrong, but I am not a bad person.'' For instance, if the client is, in fact, somewhere he shouldn't be, he may be coached to role play the response ''You're right, I shouldn't be here and I'll try not to let it happen again.'' Or, ''My mistake, I'll do better next time.'' The reason that techniques like this are given titles like ''negative assertion'' is that they are easier for the client to call to mind when they are appropriate strategies with which to respond. An appendix of assertion techniques for use in ''barb'' and in assertion training in general will be found at the end of the chapter.

''The ''barb'' program was first used with delinquents on an inpatient basis, but it has been used by this author on an outpatient basis as well. A barb is any stimulus which, by the client's own admission, has led or would lead to a fight. In the first stage, the counselor explains that he is going to deliberately barb the client, but that he will clearly warn the client by saying ''this is going to be a barb.'' The counselor then coaches the client in how to respond. In a group inpatient population, the counselor increases the number of people barbing and the severity of the barbs while fading the cue that what is being said or done is a barb.

Most of the role playing literature mentioned above concerns primarily clinical applications of the technique. Two other uses, while having clear clinical applications, are primarily experimental in nature. Melnick (1973) compared six methods of changing the social behavior of minimally dating males who were uncomfortable about their behavior. Three of the groups (the control, traditional therapy, and modeling) had no role playing involvement, while three of the groups (modeling plus role playing, modeling plus role playing plus self-observation, and modeling plus role playing plus self-observation plus reinforcement) did role play interactions with females. Before and after treatment, these clients were rated in a simulated dating interaction and in a structured test in which the clients responded to ten videotape simulated situations. Melnick's results demonstrate that neither traditional therapy, nor modeling, nor modeling plus role playing alone caused significant changes. However, when self-observation via videotape feedback was added to the modeling plus role playing, the clients significantly changed their behavior in the test situations. In terms of this chapter, Melnick's findings about the modeling plus role playing group are important. The participant modeling clients were shown a model, did role play in how to interact with a female and received a minimum level of feedback (three suggestions), but did not improve in their after treatment interactions with either a live female, or in their responses to videotaped sequences. This strongly suggests that when the client is attempting to change a complex behavior, such as a social interaction, modeling, role playing and minimum feedback are not enough. In the successful uses of role playing cited above, there has been much more extensive feedback, such as an entire group helping the client, videotape feedback for self-observation, or both. While Melnick's study does not address the issue of more feedback, it clearly shows that videotape feedback increases the effects of the treatment.

Thus, role playing, insofar as it is merely the practice of a response, may not be the most effective method of changing behavior. However, while Melnick's study suggests that neither modeling nor participant modeling alone are sufficient for behavior change, this should not be taken to mean that they are not necessary for changing behavior. Freedman (1971, 1972) has demonstrated that modeling plus role playing is more effective than role playing alone. In a more cognitive domain, Flowers (1978a) demonstrated that people who initially test higher in their self-reported assertive behavior also have clearer goals than people who test lower, and that a major result of assertion training with unassertive people is increased goal clarity. If one thinks of the therapeutic process as one that involves instructions, modeling, role playing, feedback, external reinforcement, self-observation, and self-reinforcement, role playing may simply be a behavior that increases the effects of instructions and modeling, and may be an event which provides an easily instituted opportunity for various types of feedback and reinforcement. Clinically, the therapist should be aware that when he employs role playing, he is employing a technique that is almost surely made less effective without modeling and self-evaluation, and may be made less effective without clear instructions, external feedback and both external and self-reinforcement. Actually, it would be very difficult to use role playing without other components in a clinical setting. However, the key issue for the therapist is not that role playing almost always involves more than merely practicing a behavior by virtue of the situation created, but that it is a technique that should be employed with other components in as effective a way as possible.

SIMULATION GAMES

As pointed out earlier, the distinction between role playing and simulation is actually one of convenience. The simulation exercises that are presented in this chapter differ from the role playing examples in that the simulations are less specific to a single client's life problems and are predesigned to teach a set of skills to a broad range of clients. This section will concentrate on simulation exercises that a therapist or behavior change agent would use to help people change, and will focus only briefly on the extensive literature of simulations designed for business and academic uses. Simulation exercises are often called simulation games. While they have been shown to have high motivational value, i.e., people tend to like to play them, the actual research on the effectiveness of simulation games on behavior change is less extensive than the research in role playing. For this reason, many of the simulation games presented below are chosen on the basis of clinical rather than experimental evidence. The counselor should keep this in mind when using simulation games to help people change and should continually monitor the results to determine that the simulation is accomplishing what he has in mind.

Simulation Games in Education

While simulation games in business and business schools are usually very complex, those in education are usually less complicated. Most of the academic simulators in education involve the general area called social studies. Games in this area have been designed for all age students from kindergarten to graduate school. Behavior change agents interested in these or in the business games should review the journal titled *"Simulation and Games: An international journal of theory, design and research,"* in which such games are researched, reviewed, and annotated.

Of the many such games, one, *The Life Career Game* (Boocock, 1968), has been used by school counselors to help people change in a more therapeutic sense. This game is designed to show students how to plan the daily activities of a fictitious person to maximize that person's life satisfaction over an 8-year period. Scoring is based on probability data from national statistics and does not require the use of a computer. Teams of students take the fictitious person through life with future options based on past decisions. Thus, a team cannot get their person a job requiring a college education without planning a daily high school schedule which will qualify the person for college. If the character is presented in such a way to make college questionable, and if the team makes the decisions to get the fictitious character through college, the character will ultimately lose satisfaction points when his college education gets him a job he will not like. There are decisions to be made in terms of education, employment, marriage and family, and there are unexpected event cards such as being laid off, being promoted, being drafted, having an unexpected child, etc., which add reality to the game. At various times the team stops and discusses the life they are planning. In the original study, Boocock found that the game taught career information, especially to females. While this game has not been experimentally demonstrated to be effective in helping students with their own decisions, Varenhorst (1969) cites clinical examples of students helped with their own life by virtue of having played the game. She uses the game as an adjunct to career counseling.

In this author's experience, the major problem with complex games such as this is that counselors and teachers who read of them will seldom order them. Of those who do order them, few will use them. Of the few who use them, most will not use them to completion or follow-up. Since professionals who help people change are busy people, simpler simulation games that do not require purchase or complicated scoring systems seem more useful, or at least more likely to be used.

The Honesty Game (Flowers, 1972) is an example of a simple game that can be applied in a classroom without extensive commitment of time or money. This game is designed to be used with a student or students who cheat extensively in class. The behavior change agent selects the subject areas in which the game is to be used and informs the student that for four days a week, the student will grade his own work. The student is told that the purpose of these scores is to tell the student what he does and does not know, i.e., what to study. These scores are entered by the student on a personal chart with a special pen. On the fifth day, the teacher gives the student a closely supervised test over the same material and enters the score on the chart with a different colored pen. The student's weekly grade is based on the match of the student's self-evaluations and the teacher assessed score. If the student's score on the teacher proctored test is below his weekly average, he loses one grade for every 10 points of difference. Thus, if the student got four 100 scores when he evaluated his daily work, and got 80 on the test, he would receive a C. On the other hand, if his self-evaluation average was 75 for four days and he received 80 on the closely monitored test, he would receive an A.

Since the game itself offers an opportunity for cheating, the author originally included rules to prevent a student from deliberately lowering his self-evaluation scores so that the proctored tests could not fall below his average self-evaluation. First the teacher was told to assign a minimum below which the weekly work would have to be done again. Thus, a student could not evaluate his own work at 40 for his four days and receive a 70 on the monitored test and thereby get an automatic A. Interestingly, this rule has never had to be applied. Apparently a cheating student finds it difficult to lower his self-evaluation, even if it would appear to offer the desired payoff.

This game can be used for one or more students and can be modified to fit almost any classroom schedule; for instance, the self-evaluation can be done every other day and the test given every two weeks. In the original use, the game was applied for six weeks with the student's cheating ceasing not only in the subject areas involved in the game, but in all other subject areas as well, even after the game was discontinued. In that case, and in subsequent uses of the game, the students' grades in the classroom actually increased after the game was discontinued.

This game demonstrates a principle common to simulation games: If the behavior change agent can clearly define what is to be changed, the design of the simulation game becomes much easier. In this case, the definition of the desired behavior is not that the child be ''honest.'' Such a definition does little to help us change the behavior. The desired behavior is that the child's self-evaluation of his performance when cheating is possible, closely match an external evaluation when cheating is not possible. Obviously, if the student changes answers on his work after seeing the correct ones, his self-recorded score will not match the score from a test in which answers are not changed. However, there is another issue which may be even more important. If the child changes answers to get a better score, he is not using the test as a feedback device to tell him what he needs to study, i.e., he has been taught that the purpose of evaluation is absolute scores, not feedback. It seems to this author that this is actually more maladaptive in an educational sense than the case of a child taking credit for a performance which he did not achieve. Simulation games are very useful in behavior change areas such as this in that they can present the player with rules that do more than specify the behaviors and the rewards: simulation games can specify the tactics or process the player should use and reward him for a strategy as well as for a specific behavior.

Take for example the common classroom problem that some children ask more questions of the teacher than other children, and that some of these high frequency question-asking students ask many questions that are unwarranted. An example of an unwarranted question would be a student asking what page to turn to immediately after the teacher had said to turn to page 21; or a student asking where the paper is when the paper has been in the same place throughout the year and the whole class has been repeatedly told where it is. The behavior change desired is not that these students stop asking questions, or, to put it more prosaically, to ''shut up.'' Such students have legitimate needs for real assistance and for the teacher's attention. The behavior change that is desired is that the students refrain from asking unwarranted questions but continue to ask warranted ones. While such a discrimination would be difficult to teach per se, simulation game rules can be designed to make warranted questions more reinforcing than unwarranted questions, i.e., to teach the student a question-asking behavior. To design such a game (Flowers, 1974), we have only to look at how people in general are directed to limit their responses to those defined as valuable. When someone on a limited budget shops at a market, the buying is shaped by need and resources. The budget in a classroom is determined by the fact that the teacher does not have infinite resources, i.e., time to interact continually with each individual student. To make this budget clear to the consumer—in this case, the child—he, too, must be put on a budget.

In this simulation, the purpose is to make questions and interactions with the teacher valuable so that they will be wisely used. Each student asking a high frequency of unwarranted questions is given five certificates each morning, each of which is good for one question. Each question requires the expenditure of one certificate, and after five have been spent, no more questions will be answered by the teacher. This simulation is presented to the students as a game, and the teacher is told to play it as a game, dramatically holding out her hand for a certificate before answering a question, and dramatically turning away holding her lips together with her fingers when the student is out of certificates. This game has elements of response cost and extinction in its playing. Each response costs a certificate, and after the certificates are spent, the student is ignored. By the end of the game period, usually three to four weeks, the students who previously asked well above 10 questions a day had "saved" at the end of the day and came up to show the teacher their "savings" or to spend them at that time on interpersonal or problem solving situations such as: "I'm getting teased because I have a boy friend, what can I do about it?"

Experimental results from this game clearly demonstrate that the students involved learn to ask warranted questions as they play it. This is not surprising. An unwarranted question from the student gets the teacher's attention, while a warranted question gets both attention and information that the student needs—a double payoff. Teachers who use the game maintain that warranted questions actually get more attention than unwarranted ones, making for a triple payoff. Not only do the behavior changes continue after the game has been discontinued, but other students in the classroom also begin to ask more warranted questions, probably because the teacher is now more available to the less assertive students. This last finding brings up a critical point for behavior change agents who use simulation games in a classroom. The classroom is a closed ecology in which a change in any one part will probably cause changes in other nontreated parts. In this game, decreasing the frequency and increasing the percentage of warranted questions by the high frequency question-askers also increased the frequency of warranted questions by the previously quiet children. Both changes were desired; however, it would be possible for a simulation to change the treated subjects for the better, while changing some other part of the system for the worse. In any ecological system such as a classroom or a family, the results of the simulation should not only be assessed insofar as the target subjects are concerned; the entire system should be measured for change even if only one part is being treated.

With the exception of the *Life Career Game*, the simulation games above are quite simple and easy to implement. An example of a more complicated game that can still be used in a regular classroom to help people change is the *Self-Confidence Game* (Flowers and Marston, 1972; Flowers, 1972). This game is designed to change the self-confident behavior of upper elementary junior high school students in the classroom. Again, as with all simulation games, the behavior to be changed must be clearly defined. On the basis of a suggestion by Marston (1968), self-confidence in a classroom can be simply defined as a student raising his hand to answer a question posed to a group of students in the classroom. School personnel are well aware that many students get through early school years by being "good, quiet" students. This generally means they don't move their bodies or mouths much. While such behavior may indeed keep a classroom in control, it is highly questionable if such behavior is adaptive in terms of later educational and vocational performance. In college, there are many students who will not go to a professor for help with a subject, to become involved in research in which they are interested, or to legitimately bargain how to make up incomplete work, etc. In business there are even books and courses that sell "confidence" as a major element of vocational success.

Unlike the honesty game or the questions game, the *Self-Confidence Game* requires that classroom time be spent solely in the performance of the game. The game is played as follows:

Instructions for the Self-Confidence Game

1. Have questions made up by the students on any and all classroom subjects. The questions should be from material to which all students have been exposed. The question, answer, and the name of the originating student should be put on similar size cards (3 × 5 inches are good) and filed in a question box. The teacher or advanced students should exclude inappropriate questions. Generally, the students should be allowed five minutes, twice a week, to make up new questions so that recent material and new questions are in use. This assignment should be voluntary and no student should ever be forced to make up questions or to perform in the game against his will.

2. Randomly compose teams of three students each. This can be done by drawing names from a hat.

3. The game, as explained below, should be played from two to three times a week for 20 to 30 minutes each time. Randomly select which teams will play with the understanding that all teams will play at least three times and no more than four in this phase. If a team member is absent when a team is drawn to play, either replace him with an alternate member or draw another team to play.

4. Besides the six players, three from each team, the following students are involved in running the game:

(a) Moderator
(b) Blackboard scorer
(c) Hand-raising judge
(d) Score keepers (2)
(e) Timer

5. The two teams sit in front of the class and the moderator reads a question from the question box to the two competing teams. The first person on either team who raises his hand gets the first opportunity to answer the question. This is judged by the hand-raising judge whose decision is final. The moderator announces whether the answer is right or wrong. If it is right, the blackboard scorer scores a point for that team. The scorers keep track of who answers each question and whether the answer is right or wrong. If the question is answered incorrectly, the first person on the other team to raise his hand gets the next and final opportunity to answer the question. The timer calls time if 20 seconds elapse between a question and either the first or second attempt to answer it. The timer does not interrupt an answer in progress. If time is called, the next question is read. If a question is answered correctly, the next question is read.

6. At the end of the game the scorers turn in their score cards to the teacher.

7. The questions in the box should be shuffled prior to each game. In the game, the moderator should not use a question made up by one of the game playing students.

Phase one of the game simply consists of the players playing at least three times. This is a "baseline" phase and students who answer less than ten percent of the questions asked are considered low in self-confidence in the game. Research has demonstrated that such students are rated low in general self-confidence by the teacher and by other students prior to the game.

Phase two consists of what has been called forced response, and its purpose is similar to that of junior varsity teams in athletics. All students who answered less than ten percent of the questions posed in phase one are randomly placed on teams with other such students. All students who answered more than ten percent of the questions in phase one are likewise placed on teams together. In phase two, the low self-confident teams only play the other low self-confident teams, and the high self-confident teams only play the other high self-confident teams. Just as junior varsity athletics give the lesser athlete a chance to play without having to compete with the better athlete, this gives the low self-confident child a chance to raise his hand to answer questions without the competition from the quicker students.

Phase three is the same as phase one with the teams being composed totally at random and with students playing against all students. The results of this phase determine if the treatment in phase two is effective in increasing the child's hand-raising in the regular competition of the classroom.

Results from the extensive use of this simulator demonstrate the motivational properties of such games. In over 5000 team trials, no student has ever willingly missed a trial. However, the behavior change agent should not confuse the motivational properties of simulation games, which have been cited often, with the more important result of behavior change. A simulator could be highly motivating and not change anything. About half the students in an elementary school classroom will answer less than ten percent of the questions in phase one, with over 80 percent of these students answering less than five percent. The distribution tends to be bimodal, since about 70 percent of the high self-confident students will answer more than 20 percent of the questions posed in phase one. After the treatment phase, the previously low self-confident students will answer two to three times the number of questions they answered in phase one, and will answer significantly more of those correctly. In terms of generalization, these same students will answer significantly more questions in the open class situation where the teacher asks a question of the whole class than before treatment. Beyond this question-answer response, these previously low self-confident students will demonstrate a significant increase in their grades, will volunteer more often for public speaking assignments in the class, and will volunteer more often to be class officers.

Again, the behavior change agent should be aware that he is dealing with an entire ecology in the classroom, and should be aware that this ecology includes the teacher. If the teacher attempts to create a quiet nonquestioning student population, the game may be inappropriate for the classroom. Twice in this author's experience, the game has been instituted in classrooms where the teacher did not like the results and wished to discontinue the game. In both cases, the phase two treatment was already well in progress and the students strongly questioned why the game should be discontinued. In both cases, the students, especially the ones low in self-confidence, were successful in continuing the game. While this may demonstrate that the results of this simulation game generalize to other classroom interactions, it should be remembered that this change in the students' behavior made the rest of the year difficult for the teachers involved. Both teachers had been informed of the purpose of the game and both had said they approved of increased self-confidence in the nonconfident children; however, debriefing clearly showed that neither teacher understood that self-confidence needed to be more than an abstract concept. It is not enough that the behavior change agent explain the simulation to be used in general terms. The changes that the simulation attempts to accomplish should be explained in terms of likely behavior changes to the involved parties before the simulation is used. So far, about 20 percent of the teachers who have used this simulation don't like its results, about 20 percent like it but discontinue it after the experimenter is gone, and about 60 percent continue it on their own.

A recent revised version of the game appears to be even more compelling in terms of continued use after the experimenters have left the scene. We have recently been using the game with bilingual classes for the purpose of increasing confidence in both the English and Spanish language. In this version of the game, half the cards are written in Spanish and half are written in English with key words in every question given in both languages. For phase two, two sets of low self-confident students are identified—those less confident in English, and those less confident in Spanish. Teams of these students play each other separately in the first part of phase two and play together in a second part of phase two. During phase two the number of trials is increased to ten or more and the cross language cues in each question are faded, forcing the students to depend more and more on the language in which they are weakest. Despite the fact that this version of the game requires much more teacher time and energy, namely, to systematically change the question cards by crossing out more and more of the cross language cues, to date the teachers have all continued the game's use in the second year.

Thus, there are really two issues involved in the use of simulation games in education. One is whether or not the simulation changes behavior in the desired manner; the second is whether the simulation is continued. Many simulation games instituted by outsiders fail, not because they don't achieve the behavior change, but because they are no longer used when the outsider's involvement ends. The more the outside behavior change agent can involve the indigenous professional as a behavior change agent in the simulation, in its application, assessment, and revision, the greater the chance that the indigenous professional will continue as the behavior change agent after the outsider is gone. If the simulation games are presented as reasearch, there is a decreased probability that they will be used again. Sadly, many indigenous professionals are used to research being done in their environment, the results subsequently published, without its ever being explained to them. Often their only involvement is to supply subject populations; and they have little or no understanding of how the research might be useful to them. Since this series of events is a common experience, if the change agent presents himself as an outsider bouncing in and collecting data for a Ph.D. or his personal use, and bouncing out, the simulation game will meet the same fate that other relevant research now meets.

Those who wish to help people change can use existing simulators. Behavior change agents can also design their own simulations for their specific needs. To construct a game, the behavior change agent must clearly specify the change and make game rules that encourage the behavior in question. Often the behavior change agent can look to the natural environment of athletics, business, or life in general, to see how natural rules shape behavior and construct the game accordingly. Results from one game will help the designer improve that game and others. For instance, results from the self-confidence game indicate that low self-confident students who only watched high self-confident students play together in the treatment phase do not model the question-asking behavior. However, low self-confident students being forced to respond more during the treatment phase did model the question-asking behavior. This result recalls a point made earlier, namely, that the model should not be too different from the modeler if the modeler's behavior is to be changed. While such a result is not unexpected, it suggests a way to improve the game effectiveness, i.e., to have low self-confident students run the game when other low self-confident students are playing it in the treatment phase. Thus, the issue of assessment bears not only on the utility of the simulator but on its continued improvement as well. As in the acquisition of any skill, once the behavior change agent has designed and tried one simulation game, he will find that the next one is easier to construct and usually better. Since the hardest step is the first one, you may wish to try successive approximation by using an existing simulation game, then revise it to make it better for your needs, before designing a complete simulation game for yourself.

Simulation in Psychotherapy

While role playing has been investigated and used extensively in psychotherapy, other forms of simulation have been used less frequently. One reason for this involves the individual nature of psychotherapy. While role playing can be tailored to an individual's unique problem, simulation games tend to be more general and are used when the same behavior change is desired from a group of people. For this reason, simulation games tend to be used more frequently in group therapy and by therapists who deal with a group of persons who have similar problems.

One form of well-known simulation that has been extensively employed with groups other than traditional psychotherapy or training groups is the ward wide token economy (see Chapter 7). While many readers may not initially perceive a token economy as a simulation game, the work of Winkler (1971) demonstrates token economy (see Chapter 7). The token economy program attempts to roughly simulate the more subtle (often meaning more delayed) payoff system that operates for prosocial behavior in the outside world. In the token economy program, as in many simulation games, what we essentially have is an attempt to adjust the psychoeconomy of the individual, i.e., what behaviors are paid off or what behaviors the individual has in her repertoire to use to get payoff. The most successful simulation games are probably those which simulate both the behavior and the payoff expected in the outside world. However most psychotherapeutic simulation games foster the expected behavior and merely hope for the payoff, both in and out of the group.

An example of the use of such a simulation for a group of people who are presumed to have similar problems is the fight training exercises of Bach and Bernhard (1971). In this form of therapy the clients are trained to fight with each other, first verbally, and then physically, with a foam rubber bat called a bataca. Some of the simulation exercises are more like role playing than simulation games in that the participants, especially if they are couples, fight about real life problems. Other exercises, such as trying to break into a circle of people whose arms are interlocked to prevent entry, is more like a simulation game in that the rules are specified for all the participants.

Handbooks of such exercises are available (Pfieffer and Jones, 1970; Morris and Cinnamon, 1974). While most of the games in these books are more applicable to educational settings such as management or teacher training, a number of the games are directly applicable to therapy groups, especially during the warm-up phase; others could be easily adapted to therapeutic use.

These books list over 150 games ranging from very simple games to highly complex games with scoring sheets. Included are verbal techniques such as "active listening" wherein a group participant makes a declaratory statement and the responder acknowledges the message by saying, "You feel (somehow) about (something)." The sender simply says yes or no and the responder then makes a declaratory statement to which the first sender responds. This is continued until the pair agrees that they understand each other. These books also include non-verbal techniques such as having a group member express his feelings toward another group member in pantomime without use of words. While still untested, such exercises may prove useful and testable in terms of helping people change.

One possible explanation for the lack of extensive research in the use of simulation games as a therapeutic tool (as opposed to other therapy interventions) is that the behavior to be changed is often not clearly defined. When the behavior to be changed is not clearly specified, it is difficult to know whether the simulation has worked or not. For example, if a client tries to break into a circle of people with arms locked, the counselor using this simulation exercise usually does not specify what change he wants in the client's behavior after the exercise. When the client changes are specified, they are usually changes that the therapist defines in terms of the therapy session itself, and not in terms of desired changes in the client's daily living.

However, there is nothing in the nature of simulation games that prevents clear definitions of the behavior to be changed. Of course clear specification of the behavior to be changed still does not guarantee that the simulation game actually helps actualize that change, but at least a clearly defined change is a therapeutic goal that can be assessed.

One area of therapy where simulation games seems particularly useful is that of marital and family therapy. Defining simulation broadly, one can classify the work of Stuart (1969) and Azrin, Naster and Jones (1973) as therapeutic interventions that attempt to transform marital relationships into a reciprocal fair trade or "win-win" games. More specifically, Blechman (1974) has developed the family contract game which is designed to increase family problem solving within the context of a programmed game board. Programmed instruction guides the players through four interaction units in which they: (1) select a problem behavior as the target for their contract; (2) agree upon a pleasing replacement behavior; (3) determine reinforcers and a method of recording the behaviors involved; and (4) write a contract that agrees to the foregoing details. Subsequent research (Blechman, Olson and Hellman, 1976) has demonstrated that the family contract game has effective stimulus control over family problem solving behavior. In six single subject studies, the game contributed to increments in on-task problem solving behavior and increments in off-task antagonistic behavior.

In the game the board is divided into 14 squares. Each square tells a player (identified by color) to: 1) perform an action (e.g., draw a problem card); 2) make a statement (e.g. tell another player what to do more of and when to do it); 3) ask a question (e.g., ask another player if he agrees to the reward you have specified for doing what you ask). These squares guide the players through the steps specified above to come to a contract.

When the players agree about the current interaction and what should be done about it, the board tells them to award themselves play money and to draw humorous bonus cards. When they cannot agree, the board tells them to begin the unresolved problem again, to pay play money fines and to draw humorous risk cards. The players have 15 minutes to resolve the problem in order to win extra play money. The time left is publicly displayed so that the players will be encouraged to stay on task and avoid irrelevant behavior that will penalize them.

The players alternate the roles of problem-raiser, contract-writer and target (the person requested to change). When the game is played by more than two persons, players form partnerships and alternate the requester and requestee roles.

This game specifies who is to do what to whom, in what amount of time and for what purpose. In this case the purpose is a contract for behavior change that the participants both agree to as fair. Fairness is defined in terms of both the behavior change specified and the reward for that change. The game alternates the roles so that each participant gets to ask for what they want and also is asked for what the other wants. The guidance and the timer are used so that the contract can be attained with minimum antagonism and irrelevant behavior. Since the game is clearly defined in terms of both process and outcome, research is possible, and in this case the results are promising.

Another simulation game that the author (Flowers, 1978b) has found useful in marital and family therapy is a communication game. Many couples or families coming into therapy demonstrate a communication pattern that reveals that they disagree with each other even before the issue under discussion is made clear. Often one or more parties are phrasing their response before the other person has stopped talking; hence they do not listen to the last part of the other person's message. In such cases the communication of one or more of the parties often becomes faster—more words per minute are spoken and disagreement increases. The communication game is structured to discourage early disagreements, to decrease the number of words per minute in the debate, and to create longer pauses between the time one person finishes speaking and the start of the next communication. The couple, or a parent and older child set up the game board as shown in Fig. 6.1.

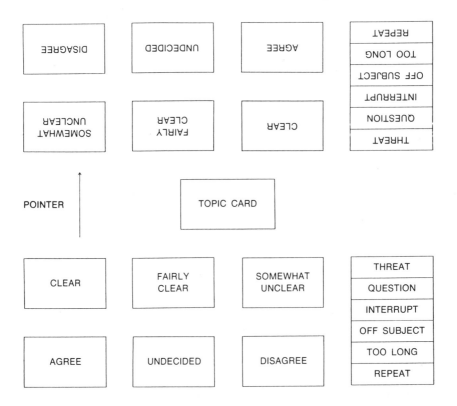

Fig. 6.1. Communication game board.

The discussion card is a 3 × 5 card on which the issue to be discussed is written. The pointer is rotated to the first speaker who says what he wishes. The therapist hands him a penalty token if he says more than two or three sentences and explains that long messages are hard to respond to because they contain too much information. The therapist assures the client that he will get another chance to talk. When the first speaker has finished the message, he places a chip assessing whether his own communication is absolutely clear, fairly clear, or somewhat unclear, and he rotates the pointer to the other party. Before starting to speak, the second player indicates with a chip whether he assesses the message to be absolutely clear, fairly clear, or somewhat unclear and indicates whether he agrees, is uncertain, or disagrees. The therapist gives a penalty token if there is an agreement or disagreement with any message that is not rated clear by both the sender and receiver. The therapist also coaches the clients as to when to place a chip in the six penalty squares. The I square indicates that a speaker has been interrupted without turning the pointer. If true, the therapist gives the interrupter a penalty chip. The T square means the listener perceived an implied or open threat. When this square is used, the pointer is turned back to the speaker without reply. The therapist asks if the speaker meant a threat. If he did, he gets a penalty chip, if he did not, he does not get a chip, but he is asked to try to communicate his message so that the other party will not perceive a threat. The Q square means the listener perceived a rhetorical question, i.e., a question that did not ask for information. The rules for the use of this square are the same as for the T square. The S square means the listener thinks the speaker has strayed from the subject. The rules for this square are the same as for the T square except that any speaker can ask for a subject change and if the other party agrees, the topic card is rewritten. The R square is used by the listener when he thinks his last message was misunderstood. A chip in this square asks for a repeat of the last message sent by the person putting the chip in the square. Penalty chips are not given with this square. The L square is used when the listener perceives a message that is too long or one that has two parts, one of which he may agree with, and one of which he may disagree with. If the therapist has sensed this, he should have already given a penalty token. In theory, there is a winner in that one person can get fewer penalty tokens than the other player. However, in actual use, this does not seem to matter, and this therapist never emphasizes this competitive aspect of the game.

After the parties learn the game, usually in two to four sessions, they take it home and use it about four times a week. During the week, each player writes out one problem to which he would like a solution. He must also write one discussion card that does not require agreement. Each player takes alternate turns at specifying what is discussed. When either player says "finish," that game is over. In week two (at home), the player must call one "time out" of 30 minutes, then return to the game before he or she can call "finish."

Within the therapy session the game quickly equalizes the amount of time each party talks. Within the therapy the game also quickly stops agreement or disagreement when the message is not rated clear by both parties. The agreement on the clarity ratings usually starts at 40 to 60 percent and rises to 90 percent agreement by session three.

Client data recorded at home indicate that the game increases the amount of time the parties talk to each other, equalizes the talk time (even when the game is no longer played), and reduces the number of unresolved disagreements. Clients also report a slowdown in the rate of communication (especially in disagreements), and an increase of laughter during disagreements when the game is not in use; but these latter results have not yet been experimentally verified.

When using this game with older children and parents, the author has found it helpful to teach the game by having children play with parents other than their own, and parents with children who are not theirs. After the game is learned, the therapy sessions are realigned to have the children and their parents try it with the aid of the therapist's coaching before taking it home. This simulation game obviously attempts to institute many changes in behavior, not all of which have been demonstrated in experiments. The counselor using the game in cases where outcomes not yet tested are required or expected, should carefully assess the results of the use of this simulation game. One advantage of simulations such as this is that they can be used after counseling is terminated. The author has been told by previous clients that after discontinuing use of the game for up to four months, they would get it out during particularly stressful problem situations and use it to resolve the problem.

Group Therapy as a Simulation Game

For many therapists, group therapy is a simulation of interactions that the client should attempt to carry out in the extratherapeutic environment. While group therapy obviously can focus on the content of the clients' problems, it can also be used as a laboratory in which clients are encouraged to experiment with new ways of interacting. From the point of view of this chapter, the difficulty with such a simulation is that the specific behavior change being taught is usually only vaguely defined.

In an attempt to specify more clearly the communication process that a therapy group might help the client to change, this author and others (Flowers et al., 1974; Flowers and Booraem, 1976; Flowers, 1978c; Flowers, 1979) have devised a simulation game used within group therapy that aims to specify clearly and help change communication behavior. Much like the token simulation described in the section on assertion training, the clients or therapists hand out a blue token with positive verbal evaluation and a red token with negative verbal evaluation for any behavior occurring in the group session. Each group member, including the therapists, are provided with 20 blue and 20 red 2 × 2 inch tokens made of constuction paper. Each token set is assigned a different number so that who gave exactly what to whom can be determined after the group session terminates. Each group member is also provided an empty container into which they place every token that they receive during the course of the group session. While groups of any theoretical orientation can be conducted in this manner, our groups are conducted with a behavioral orientation (Flowers, 1979). Group members are informed that all messages delivered or received are either positive, negative or neutral and that the purpose of the token is to clarify positive and negative messages by visible means. It should be clear to the reader that enhancing the visibility of positive and negative messages concomitantly enhances the power of these messages as change agents. Receiving a positive or negative statement accompanied by a hand delivered tangible token makes ignoring, dismissing or denying the message very difficult. This procedure also enhances the therapist's ability to shape a variety of behaviors by systematically reinforcing approximations of a predetermined goal. This practice differs from the use of tokens described in the assertion training section in that in assertion training, the tokens can be used without interrupting the group process. In the present use of tokens, the token must accompany a verbal evaluation. Clinically, this simulation seems to allow the quick identification of verbal statements with a discrepant affect and content such as handing a blue (positive) token and saying, "Damn it, you're right" with negative nonverbal cues. The ease of identifying ambiguous evaluations is probably increased because of the added source of feedback (i.e., the color of the token given). Experimentally, when this simulation game was used in a therapy group, there was a significant increase in the frequency of both positive and negative verbal evaluations and a significant increase in the proportion of patient to patient (as opposed to therapist to patient, or patient to therapist) interactions. Furthermore, the clients in such a token group engaged in significantly more desirable behaviors outside of therapy, such as getting a job, engaging in social interactions, and going back to school, than similar clients from a traditional therapy control group.

In another study (Flowers, Booraem, and Seacat, 1974), the same simulation was used to help train group therapists. In this study, it was first demonstrated that the count of tokens given and received during the therapy session accurately reflected the number of positive and negative statements rated from an audio tape. Thus, a count of the tokens used in a therapy group gives the trainer an objective measure of the behaviors in which each participant engaged. Each participant can therefore be classified as high, medium, or low in terms of the frequency of evaluations in which he was involved. Each participant could be classified along the dimension of giving versus getting evaluations. In terms of the evaluations that each participant got or gave, he could be classified along the positive-negative dimension. By asking each trainee to rate the behavior of every other participant prior to counting the tokens, their subjective "sensitivity" as to who did what to whom could be matched to an objective count. Experimentally, it has been demonstrated that this procedure increased the trainee's sensitivity, even in later groups that did not use tokens. It has also been shown that trainees who were independently rated higher in terms of therapeutic ability, changed their behavior more from session to session than trainees who were rated lower.

This last finding suggests an intriguing use of the token data, namely, to see if a client can change his token giving and receiving behavior in different therapy sessions and in different situations. Such a change of behavior might be considered one sign of behavioral flexibility. Pilot data by this author indicates that a number of clients have something like a standard role, or set of behaviors, session after session regardless of what happens during the session. Thus, a client who is high in interactions, who tends to give more than he receives, and tends to give a high proportion of negative evaluations in a session, may continue that behavior in the group session after session. One obvious question is whether or not such an in-group behavior reflects the client's behavior out of group, and whether change in this in-group behavior would produce similar change out of group.

Recently, employing an individualized client outcome assessment technique (Flowers, Booream, and Hartman, 1977; Flowers and Kidder, 1978) have found that clients who change such roles more during group therapy sessions demonstrate more improvement in their outside lives (as rated by external raters) than clients who adopt fixed roles in therapy sessions.

Interestingly, the tokens have also proved useful in group therapy in a totally different area—that of group cohesion (Yalom, 1975; Krumboltz and Potter, 1973) To date (Flowers, 1979) we have identified eight components of group cohesion that systematically covary either in session to session or group to group. In a high cohesion session or group these are: 1) increased eye contact with the speaker; 2) increased percentage of client-to-client interactions; 3) decreased number of members to whom negative messages are repeatedly focused or by whom they are repeatedly delivered; 4) increased percentage of negative messages delivered by the entire group; 5) increased frequency of self-disclosure; 6) client changes in patterns of activity from session to session; 7) increased self-reported session satisfaction; and 8) increased number of group members rated as trusted by other group members. The token procedures allows the therapist to quantify variables 2, 3, 4 and 6 above by merely counting the results after each group session. While this may appear to be a side issue, recent research (Flowers, Booreaem, and Hartman, in press) has indicated that clients improve more on problems discussed in higher cohesion sessions than they do on problems discussed in lower cohesion sessions. Thus this simulation game's ability to quantify cohesion is a significant additional advantage in terms of the assessment of the impact of the intervention.

A final way in which the token simulation games have been used in group therapy is still totally experimental, but is included here as a technique that the counselor may wish to test for himself. The rules can be changed so that the client has to self-administer evaluations in the group session, rather than to receive them from others. The frequency of such self-administered evaluations can be changed by having alternate sessions where tokens can be administered when any other group member thinks the client should have self-administered an evaluation but did not. Preliminary data (Cohn, Mann, Flowers, and Booream, 1977) indicates that an increase in positive self-administered tokens relates to increases in daily mood ratings and to increases in the reinforcement ratings of pleasant events in which the client engages out of group. However, it should be remembered that such training can potentially also increase the frequency of negative self-administered tokens and the counselor should proceed with caution and with continual assessment to determine exactly what is being changed, and whether or not this change is helping the client. The possibilities are intriguing; however, the possibilities are only just that until the counselor finds that such simulations work for him, that is, that they are helpful for his clients. (For a more detailed review of this simulation group therapy, see Flowers, 1979.)

Future Trends in Simulation

The counselor who is interested in the use of simulation and role playing should be aware that there are two other complete bodies of literature which bear upon the issues discussed in this chapter. There is a large body of literature in the use of games, such as *Prisoner's Dilemma*, as assessment devices (see Harris, 1971 for a review). *Prisoner's Dilemma* generally involves a game structured after the anecdote in which two collaborators in crime are questioned separately by the police. The police explain to each prisoner (who must choose in isolation from the partner) that if neither confesses they will both receive a one year sentence for a minor crime in which they were both caught. If both confess, they will receive the standard sentence of five years each for the major crime of which they are both suspected. If one of them turns "state's evidence" while the other holds out, the person who confesses will get off with a reprimand from the judge, while the holdout will get the maximum sentence of 20 years. In this type of game, confessing is called "noncooperative" behavior, while holding out is called "cooperative." For the individual, noncooperative behavior has the greatest advantage for, if he confesses when the partner does not, he only receives a reprimand instead of a year prison sentence, whereas if he confesses and the partner also confesses, he gets a 5 versus a 20 year sentence. However, for the team, cooperative behavior is best, since each only gets a one year sentence if both partners hold to their innocence.

This game, and others of similar design, have generally been used to explore differing rates of cooperative and noncooperative behavior with respect to differing populations and situations, such as male versus female participants, or normals versus hospitalized patients. However, the game could also be used to teach people how to respond to different situations of gain and loss and different partners. Such games can be used by the counselor to provide simulations that may have some effectiveness in helping produce behavior change.

Another related literature area is that of microteaching (see McAleese and Unwin, 1973 for an annotated bibliography) in which simulation games and role playing are used to teach teachers and counselors.

The process of microteaching usually involves an abbreviated (five to ten minute) teaching or counseling session. This microsession is often preceded by a videotape presentation of a desired behavior or set of behaviors, and is followed by immediate feedback, usually using videotape, concerning the trainee's performance. The behavior change desired depends on the trainer. Wagner (1973), for example, has used microteaching to increase the percentage of student, as opposed to teacher, talk time in lessons given by student teachers. In the area of counseling, Ivey (1971) has used the microteaching technique to increase counseling students' rates of attending, reflecting the client's feelings, and summarizing the client's feelings. This miniaturized practice and feedback prior to the trainee's actual exposure to a live classroom or counseling session provides a training method that reduces risk for clients or students, and potential anxiety for the trainee. This literature, while not precisely relevant for the present chapter, can provide the counselor with valuable material.

Additionally, the reader should be aware of recent articles in the area of academic simulation games that attempt to: 1) compare what is learned through the simulation process to what is learned in the traditional classroom (Pierfy,

1977); 2) develop a general evaluation model for simulation games (Dukes and Waller, 1976); and 3) specify which students will benefit from simulation games experiences.

Like any therapy intervention, simulations are only a tool—one of many. The question the behavior change agent should ask is which tool is best for which job. Insofar as simulations help people change their behavior so that their lives are more satisfying, these simulations have a future in therapy. But if simulations are used merely as novel ways to spend time, they will be relegated to the class of other games and become recreation, whether called therapy or not. The necessity now is for more outcome data and a more thorough evaluation of the variables to measure the permanence or transience of behavior change through simulation therapy.

APPENDIX

Assertion Techniques

The reader should be aware that these techniques involve standard types of interaction that the client should use only in appropriate situations. The interactions are not novel but require practice for use in stressful situations. The therapeutic issue in the acquisition of these skills is not insight but practice; however, considerable discrimination is required in learning when to use them.

Broken Record. The Broken Record technique involves having the client ignore any extraneous issues brought up by the other person and return to his original point. The standard phrase taught is "but the point is . . ."

Disarming Anger. The Disarming Anger technique involves having the client ignore the content of the angry message and focus his attention and conversation on the fact that the other person is angry. The client must openly promise to take up the content as soon as the other person calms down, but must politely refuse to address the content until the other person has cooled off. The client must attempt to maintain eye contact and must use a moderate, not loud or soft tone of voice.

Content-Process Shift. The Content-Process-Shift involves shifting the focus of the conversation from the content to some process observed in the speaker such as an emotion he is "displaying" or something like the speed of the client's speech. Disarming anger is a specific example of process-content shift, but also involves a clear promise to shift back to the content after the anger has subsided.

Negative assertion. Negative Assertion is only used when the client has, in fact, made a mistake. Negative assertion involves a clear admission of the mistake, but also clearly separates the fact that an error has been made from any implication that the client is a bad person or incompetent, etc. It can involve direct confrontation such as, "Are you saying because I forgot to deliver the one paper, which I did forget, that I am not a good paperboy?," or can involve, "I did do it, damn, I'm usually better than that."

Shelter. This assertion technique is used primarily with severely disturbed clients. It involves having the client respond with only yes, no, or straight facts (such as his name) in stressful situations. The client counts to five slowly, and if not asked another question he leaves the interaction.

Clipping. Clipping is a technique that is used when a criticism is delivered that the asserter thinks is true, but not really a criticism. For instance, having the other person say, "This report looks like it was written by four different people," when in fact it was. The asserter says yes or no as appropriate and then remains silent.

Free Information. Free information is a technique designed to train an individual in how to start and maintain verbal interactions and in how to move the conversation to areas of content where maximum contact is made.

The first step in free information involves asking open, as opposed to closed, questions. A closed question can be answered "yes" or "no" or can be answered by a single piece of information. Questions involving "where," "when," and "who" are usually closed.

An open question is a question that seeks additional information, i.e., information beyond the specific content of the question. Questions stressing "what," "how," and especially, "why" are usually open.

If free information is given, the second step involves following up that information where your level of expertise is greatest or asking further questions in the area where the other person's expertise seems to be greatest.

Since free information is information not specifically asked for by the question, it can usually be presumed that such information is in a high interest for the speaker. The asserter's task is to find and follow up free information about which he can converse or interrogate.

The third, and critical step, is to offer free information about oneself. If the recipient follows up any of the asserter's free information, the conversation has truly become communication, and no further systematized steps are necessary for deepening social contact.

REFERENCES

Azrin, N.H., Naster, B.J. and Jones, R. Reciprocity counseling: A rapid learning based procedure for marital counseling. *Behavior Research and Therapy*, 1973, 11, 365-382.

Bach, G., and Bernhard, Y. *Aggression lab*. Dubuque, Iowa: Kendall/Hunt, 1971.

Blechman, E.A. The family contract game: A tool to teach interpersonal problem solving. *Family Coordinator*, 1974, 23, 268-281.

Blechman, E.A., Olson, D.H.L. and Hellman, I.D. Stimulus control over family problem solving behavior: The family contract game. *Behavior Therapy*, 1976, 7, 686-692.

Boocock, S.S. An experimental study of the learning effects of two games with simulated environments. In S.S. Boocock and E.O. Schilds (Eds.), *Simulation games in learning*. Beverly Hills, Calif.: Sage, 1968, pp. 107-133.

Booraem, C.D. Differential effectiveness of external versus self reinforcement in the acquisition of assertive responses. Unpublished doctoral dissertation, University of Southern California, 1974.

Booraem, C.D., and Flowers, J.V. A procedural model for the training of assertive behavior. In J.M. Whiteley and J.V. Flowers (Eds.), *Approaches to assertion training*. Monterey, Calif.: Brooks/Cole, 1977.

Booraem, C.D. Flowers, J.V., and Schwartz, B. *Help your children be self confident*. Englewood Cliffs, N.J.: Prentice-Hall, 1978.

Casey, G.A. Behavioral rehearsal: Principles and procedures. *Psychotherapy: Theory, Research and Practice*, 1973, *10*(4), 331-333.

Cohn, N.B., Booraem, C.D., and Flowers,J.V. Assertion training with orthopedically handicapped children. Paper presented at the Western Psychological Association, San Francisco, California, 1978.

Cohn, N.B., Mann, R.J., Booraem, C.D., and Flowers, J.V. A comparison of methods designed to increase self-reinforcement in group therapy. Paper presented at the Western Psychological Association, Seattle, Washington, 1977.

Davidson, G.C. Self-control through "imaginal aversive contingency" and "one downsmanship": Enabling the powerless to accommodate unreasonableness. In J.D. Krumboltz and C.E. Thorsen (Eds.), *Behavioral counseling: Cases and techniques*. New York: Holt, Rinehart & Winston, 1969, pp. 319-328.

Dukes, R.L. and Waller, S.J. Toward a general evaluation model for simulation games: GEM. *Simulation and Games*, 1976, 7, 75-96.

Eisler, R.M., Miller, P.M., and Hersen, M. Components of assertive behavior. *Journal of Clinical Psychology*, 1973, *29*(3), 295-299.

Flowers, J.V. Modification of low self-confidence in elementary group children by reinforcement and modeling. Unpublished doctoral dissertation, University of Southern California, 1972.

———— Behavior modification of cheating in an elementary school student: A brief note. *Behavior Therapy*, 1972, *3*, 311-312.

———— A behavior modification technique to reduce the frequency of unwarranted questions by target students in an elementary school classroom. *Behavior Therapy*, 1974, *5*, 665-667.

———— Goal clarity as a component of assertive behavior and as a result of assertion training. *Journal of Clinical Psychology*, 1978a, *34*(3), 744-747.

———— A simulation game to systematically improve marriage communication. *Journal of Clinical Psychology*, 1978b, *4*(4), 51-57.

———— The effect of therapist support and encounter on the percentage of client-client interactions in group therapy. *Journal of Community Psychology*, 1978c, *6*, 69-73.

———— Behavioral analysis of group therapy and a model for behavioral group therapy. In

D. Upper and S.M. Ross (Eds.), *Behavioral Group Therapy: An Annual Review*. Vol. 1. Champaign, Ill.: Research Press, 1979.

Flowers, J.V., and Booraem, C.D. The use of tokens to monitor process and facilitate outcome in group psychotherapy. *International Journal of Group Psychotherapy*, 1976, *26*(2), 191-201.

Flowers, J.V., Booraem, C.D., Brown, T.R., and Harris, D.E. An investigation of a technique for facilitating patient to patient interactions in group therapy. *Journal of Community Psychology*, 1974, *2*(1), 39-42.

Flowers, J.V., Booraem, C.D., and Hartman, K.A. The effects of cohesion and disclosure on group therapy outcome. Paper presented at the Western Psychological Association, Seattle, Washington, 1977.

Flowers, J.V., Booraem, C.D., Miller, C.V., and Yeargen, L. A sexual function and dysfunction workshop, content, assessment, and results. Symposium presented at the meeting of the Western Psychological Association, San Francisco, California, April, 1978.

Flowers, J.V., Booraem, C.D., and Seacat, G.F. The effect of positive and negative feedback on group members' sensitivity to the roles of other members in group therapy. *Psychotherapy: Theory, Research and Practice*, 1974, *4*, 346-350.

Flowers, J.V., and Goldman, R.D. Assertion training for mental health paraprofessionals. *Journal of Counseling Psychology*, 1976, *23*(2), 147-150.

Flowers, J.V., and Guerra, J. The use of client-coaching in assertion training with large groups. *Journal of Community Mental Health*, 1974, *10*, 414-417.

Flowers, J.V., and Kidder, S.W. The relationship between role flexibility and client outcome in group therapy. Paper presented at the Western Psychological Association, San Francisco, California, 1978.

Flowers, J.V., and Marston, A.R. Modification of low self confidence in elementary school children. *Journal of Education Research*, 1972, *66*(1), 30-34.

Flowers, J.V., Talcot, C.A., and Hartman, K.A. Assertion training with mentally disordered sex offenders. Symposium presented at the meeting of the Western Psychological Association, Seattle, Washington, 1977.

Freedman, P.H. The effects of modeling and role playing on assertive behavior. In R.D. Rubin, H. Fensterheim, A.A. Lazarus, and C.M. Franks (Eds.), *Advances in behavior therapy 1969*. New York: Academic Press, 1971, pp. 149-169.

Freedman, P.H. The effects of modeling, role playing and participation on behavior change. In B.A. Maher (Ed.), *Progress in experimental personality research*. Vol. 6. New York: Academic Press, 1972, pp. 42-81.

Harris, R.J. Experimental games as tools for personality research. In P. McReynolds (Ed.), *Advances in Psychological assessment*. Vol. II. Palo Alto, Calif.: Science and Behavior Books, 1971, pp. 236-259.

Ivey, A.E. *Microcounseling: Innovations in interview training*. Springfield, Ill.: Thomas, 1971.

Kanfer, F.H., and Phillips, J.S. *Learning foundations of behavior therapy*. New York: Wiley, 1970.

Kaufmann, L.M., and Wagner, B.R. Barb: A systematic treatment technology for temper control disorders. *Behavior Therapy*, 1972, *3*, 84-90.

Krumboltz, J.D. and Potter, B. Behavioral techniques for developing trust, cohesiveness and goal accomplishment. *Educational Technology*, 1973, 13, 26-30.

Lazarus, A.A. Behavioral rehearsal vs. non-directive therapy vs. advice in effecting behavior change. *Behavior Research and Therapy*, 1966, *4*, 209-212.

Marston, A.R. Dealing with low self-confidence. *Educational Research*, 1968, *10*, 134-138.

Marston, A.R., Rotheram, M.J., Booraem, C.D., Kenny, B., and Armstrong, M. Assertion training with children and adolescents. Paper presented at the Western Psychological Association, Seattle, Washington, 1977.

McAleese, W.R., and Unwin, D. A bibliography of microteaching. *Programmed Learning and Educational Technology*, 1973, *10*(10), 40-54.

McFall, R.M., and Lillesand, D.B. Behavioral rehearsal with modeling and coaching in assertion training. *Journal of Abnormal Psychology*, 1971, *77*, 313-323.

McFall, R.M., and Marston, A.R. An experimental investigation of behavior rehearsal in assertive training. *Journal of Abnormal Psychology*, 1970, *76*, 295-303.

Melnick, J. A comparison of replication techniques in the modification of minimal dating behavior. *Journal of Abnormal Psychology*, 1973, *81*(1), 51-59.

Moreno, J.L. *Who shall survive?* Beacon, N.Y.: Beacon House, 1953.

Morris, K.T. and Cinnamon, K.M. *A handbook of verbal group exercises*, Springfield, Ill.: Charles Thomas Publishers, 1974.

Perls, F.S., Hefferline, R.F., and Goodman, P. *Gestalt therapy*. New York: Julian Press, 1951.

Pfeiffer, J.W., and Jones, J.E. *A handbook of structured experiences for human relations training*. Iowa City, Iowa: University Associates Press, 1970. 4 vols.

Pierfy, D.A. Comparitive simulation game research. *Simulation and Games*, 1977, 8, 255-267.

Prazak, J.A. Learning job-seeking interview skills. In J.D. Krumboltz and C.E. Thorsen (Eds.), *Behavioral counseling: Cases and techniques*. New York: Holt, Rinehart & Winston, 1969, pp. 414-428.

Rathus, S.A. An experimental investigation of assertive training in a group setting. *Journal of Behavior Therapy and Experimental Psychiatry*, 1972, *3*, 81-86.

———— A thirty-item schedule for assessing assertive behavior. *Behavior Therapy*, 1973, *4*, 398-406.

Rehm, L.P., and Marston, A.R. Reduction of social anxiety through modifications of self-reinforcement: An instigation therapy technique. *Journal of Consulting and Clinical Psychology*, 1968, *32*, 565-574.

Rogers, C.R. *Client centered therapy*. New York: Houghton Mifflin, 1951.

Sarason, I.G. Verbal learning, modeling and juvenile delinquency. *American Psychologist*, 1968, *23*, 254-266.

Stuart, R.B. Operant-interpersonal treatment for marital discord. *Journal of Consulting and Clinical Psychology*, 1969, 33, 675-682.

Truax, C.B., and Mitchell, N. Research on certain therapist interpersonal skills in relation to process and outcome. In A.E. Bergin and S.L. Garfield (Eds.), *Handbook of psychotherapy and behavior change*. New York: Wiley, 1971, pp. 299-344.

Uretsky, M. The management game: An experiment in reality. *Simulation and Games*, 1973, *4*(2), 221-240.

Varenhorst, B.B. Learning the consequences of life's decisions. In J.D. Krumboltz and C.E. Thorsen (Eds.), *Behavioral counseling: Cases and techniques*. New York: Holt, Rinehart & Winston, 1969, pp. 306-318.

Wagner, A.C. Changing teaching behavior: A comparison of microteaching and cognitive discrimination training. *Journal of Educational Psychology*, 1973, *64*(3), 299-305.

Wiese, C.R., Janssen, L., Booraem, C.D., and Flowers, J.V. Social skills training with the developmentally disabled: An issue of assertion. Paper presented at the Western Psychological Association, San Diego, California, 1979.

Winkler, R.C. The relevance of economic theory and technology to token reinforcement systems. *Behavior Research and Therapy*, 1971, *9*, 81-88.

Wolpe, J., and Lazarus, A.A. *Behavior therapy techniques*. New York: Pergamon Press, 1966.

Yalom, I.D. *The theory and practice of group psychotherapy*. New York: Basic Books, 1975.

7
Operant Methods*
Paul Karoly

INTRODUCTION

The operant approach is, perhaps, the most proliferated, yet ideologically unified, branch of contemporary behavioral psychology. It is a "self-examining,
self-evaluating, discovery-oriented research procedure for studying behavior"
(Baer, Wolf and Risley, 1968, p. 91). The Skinnerian perspective, which rests
essentially on a natural science model, hinges upon the assumption that beneficial changes in client behavior can be most efficiently achieved through the direct
manipulation of observable stimulus-response relationships. In addition to offering a functional orientation to the causes and treatment of abnormal behavior, the
operant domain boasts a growing collection of specific behavior change techniques as well as a set of definite guidelines for the design and evaluation of
behavior change methodologies (Bijou and Baer, 1978; Kazdin, 1978).

The purpose of this chapter is to familiarize readers with the basic assumptions
underlying operant psychology and to explain and illustrate its basic applications
to such diverse matters as therapy, education, classroom management, interpersonal communication and environmental enrichment.

Beginnings

The operant approach is based upon the assumption that a great many complex
human activities are learned. A useful working definition of learning is:

---

*The author would like to thank R.J. Senter and Frederick J. Sautter for their advice in the
preparation of this chapter.

the process by which an activity orginates or is changed through reacting to an encountered situation, provided that the characteristics of the change in activity cannot be explained on the basis of native response tendencies, maturation, or temporary states of the organism (e.g., fatigue, drugs, etc). (Hilgard and Bower, 1966, p. 2.)

This general definition illustrates the learning-oriented psychologist's concern with: (1) the person-environment relationship; (2) the questions of how behavior originates and how it changes as a result of the person-environment interaction; (3) the necessity for specifying "reactions" as observable behaviors; (4) the necessity for representing measurable aspects of situations; and (5) the necessity of a reliable system for detecting change (Levy, 1970).

The behavioral psychologist may be characterized by objectivity in the definition of behavior (dealing typically with small, observable units), practicality in the choice of behavior to be changed (focusing on target behaviors that can be easily recorded; measuring behaviors in terms of their short- or long-term benefits to the client), and responsivity to the flow of information in the system (modifying or correcting interventions to insure maximum learning and development of the client). Unlike the traditional psychotherapist who searches "inside the head" of his client, the behavior psychologist's domain of investigation includes both the person and his social and physical surroundings.

Historically, one can trace the study of learning (the organism-environment relationship) to the work of the Russian reflexologist Ivan Pavlov, and to the American investigator Edward L. Thorndike, both working at around the turn of the century. Pavlov's classical conditioning view placed heavy emphasis on how new or neutral stimuli (usually external events) come to elicit innate responses by virtue of their having been temporally paired with eliciting stimuli (events which automatically lead to innate responding). Pavlov, studying the digestive system of dogs, noticed that while the presence of food (the eliciting stimulus) in the animal's mouth could reliably predict the flow of saliva (the innate response), the sight of the experimenter who brought the food (who was paired with the food) soon came to elicit salivation. Learning had occurred (following the above definition). In his laboratory, Pavlov and his co-workers set out to verify, quantify, and systematize their "casual" observations, giving a major impetus to the study of animal and human learning. Today, several widely used behavior change techniques can be termed derivatives of the Pavlovian experimental perspective (e.g., systematic desensitization and aversive conditioning.

The operations and measurements of the typical Pavlovian experiment can be distinguished from those associated with the instrumental conditioning, and operant conditioning paradigms developed in America by E.L. Thorndike (1898) and B.F. Skinner (1938), respectively.

Thorndike's experiments with dogs and cats, for example, differed in at least one basic way from those of Pavlov; namely, Thorndike's animals were active in their engagement of the environment. Thorndike placed his experimental subjects in an enclosed "puzzle box" from which they were required to escape by the manipulation of the correct lever or pulley in order to obtain a bit of food reward. Through the process of trial-and-error, Thorndike's subjects eventually "learned" (i.e., their behavior changed as a result of a situational encounter). Since the animal's behaviors were instrumental in affecting escape from the box and in obtaining food, the paradigm was labelled instrumental conditioning. Thorndike viewed the animal as learning through "selecting and connecting." That is, the animal in the puzzle box selected a response from the variety of responses available, tried it out, and continued to sample response options until the "solution" (escape from the box) was discovered. The animal would eventually connect the correct response to a particular puzzle box arrangement (stimulus). Learning came to be understood as obeying several basic laws of stimulus-response connectionism, the most important of which was articulated as the *law of effect*. Simply put, the law states that behavior is controlled by its consequences. Specifically, behavior that is followed by a satisfying state of affairs is *stamped in* (strengthened), and behavior followed by an annoying state of affairs is *stamped out* (weakened). Annoyers and satisfiers correspond to the more familiar terms punishment and reward.

Skinner (1937) referred to the Pavlovian model built upon the pairing of two stimuli as Type S conditioning, and to the Thorndikean operation of having a reward contingent upon the emission of a response as Type R conditioning. Skinner is credited with ushering in a science and technology built upon Type R or, as it is now called, operant conditioning. This position and the experimental elaborations upon it form the nucleus of the present chapter.

The Operant and the Contingency

At the center of Skinner's (1938) research program are operants; behaviors freely emitted which operate upon the environment and which are, in turn, controlled by their environmental consequences (i.e., their future probability of occurrence is either increased or decreased by the events that follow their emission). Operants are learned behaviors, and can be distinguished from respondents in that a respondent is a behavior under the control of prior eliciting stimuli and is a part of the individual's biological equipment (present at birth or as a result of maturation). The knee jerk reflex is an example of a respondent. Although the term free operant is often used to fully describe the absence of constraints on the organism's responding, most contexts actually include limiting features that set natural boundaries on the quality and quantity of behaviors emitted. Even the pigeon in the familiar Skinner box could not peck on the response key and gain a food pellet if that key were withdrawn or absent. Similarly, the youngster whose tantrum behavior may be considered an operant (rewarded by parental attention) can only throw his toys about the room when those toys are available to him. These examples simply underscore the interdependence of the individual and his context—a recognition that is central to the Skinnerian perspective.

Bijou and Baer (1978) point out that an operant investigator selects stimulus-response episodes (behaviors and their eliciting and maintaining conditions) in accordance with the time frame dictated by his experimental purpose. The study of pigeons in operant chambers is appropriate to a good many questions. However, in order to explain a complex sequence of real world events, the operant researcher will readily widen the analytic lens. It is important to note that the experimental analysis of behavior according to Skinnerian principles does not, by definition, limit its focus to discrete activities in contrived and/or controlled settings. A basic assumption is that the person and the external world exist in a continuous, reciprocal, and interdependent relationship. Where to start an analysis is always an arbitrary decision. A response can also be a stimulus; and, indeed, in social interactions each participant successively plays many roles.

A key concept in operant analysis is the contingency relationship between an operant and the environmental events which follow it. The term contingency refers to the nature of the relationship between a response and the subsequent environmental events. To exist in a contingent relationship, event B, in fact, follows event A—but need not do so. In contrast, event B is in a dependent (not contingent) relationship if B must, by its very nature, follow A. For example, the relationship between walking in the rain (A) and getting wet (B) represents a dependency. However, the relationship between a student raising his hand in a classroom and the teacher calling upon that student is typically a contingent one. That is, the teacher selectively recognizes the child; he isn't forced to do so. Hand raising can be considered an operant under the control of contingent environmental events (including, not only the teacher's response, but the reactions of the other students, and the internal responses of the hand-raiser himself).

Schedules of Reinforcement and Punishment

Having set the stage for a learning based understanding of how behavior originates and is changed, it is now time to introduce the leading players. As we shall see later in this chapter, the majority of the therapeutic uses of operant conditioning have been aimed at some combination of the following objectives: (1) the development or establishment of a behavior (e.g., reading in a nonreading child; social interaction in a withdrawn adult); (2) the acceleration or strengthening of a behavior (e.g., cooperative play in a group of nursery school children; the exchange of approving statements in a married couple); or (3) the elimination or weakening of a response (e.g., reduction in the amount of alcohol ingested by a chronic drinker; elimination of self-injurious behavior in developmentally-handicapped children). The operations of *reinforcement, extinction,* and *punishment* represent specialized response-environment relationships which may produce changes in the probability of emission of operant behavior. In other words, these factors are generally responsible for learning—in humans as well as lower animals. Before discussing how these basic procedures may be employed to modify problem behavior, let us examine each in more detail.

A reinforcer is a stimulus which, when presented contingent upon the emission of an operant response, will tend to maintain or increase the probability of that response in the future. Reinforcement is a term that refers to the operations involved in using reinforcers to maintain or increase the likelihood of a particular response. Skinner (1938) has distinguished between two kinds of reinforcing stimuli: positive reinforcers and negative reinforcers. A positive reinforcer is a stimulus which produces a reinforcing effect (response maintenance or acceleration) when presented, while a negative reinforcer is a stimulus which strengthens a response (increases its probability or rate of emission) when contingently removed. Upon first encounter, the term negative reinforcement seems a bit odd since the word reinforcement connotes response strengthening, while *negative* suggests weakening. What must be remembered however is that the process of reinforcement always defines a response-strengthening operation; the adjectives positive and negative refer to the response-contingent delivery and withdrawal of stimuli. If a stimulus is reinforcing when removed, it must possess unpleasant or aversive qualities. Negative reinforcers range from malodorous substances, "dirty looks," and verbal attacks, to minor physical discomforts, pain, and severe psychological or physiological shock. Good examples of negative reinforcement in everyday life are difficult to find. Perhaps the best illustration is the behavior of coming in out of the rain (assuming that getting wet is aversive).

Thousands of experiments have been conducted over the years to identify factors that influence the effectiveness of reinforcement operations. We can state with a large degree of confidence that, in general, reinforcers exert their greatest effect on response acquisition and strengthening when they are delivered contingently, consistently, and with minimal delay. The number of times a response is reinforced and the quantity of reinforcers per response are related to the strength of the behavior in a negatively accelerated function. That is, small increases in number or magnitude of reinforcers will result in large increases in response strength (rate, speed, probability of occurrence), until the response reaches a plateau (also called an *asymptotic level*), after which the net addition to response strength declines (Deese and Hulse, 1967).

Reinforcers can also be categorized as either *primary* or *conditioned*. A primary reinforcer is a stimulus whose reinforcing properties do not derive from a history of prior conditioning. Primary reinforcers can be viewed as "biological givens." Food, water, air, etc. are examples of potential primary reinforcing stimuli. A neutral stimulus (one that does not serve a reinforcing function prior to conditioning) can be closely associated in time with a primary reinforcer and eventually acquire the power to increase or maintain responding. A neutral stimulus with reinforcing properties acquired in this Pavlovian fashion (i.e., through previous pairing with a primary reinforcer) is called a conditioned reinforcer. The term *generalized reinforcer* is used to describe conditioned reinforcers that have been paired with more than one primary reinforcer. Much of human behavior is established and maintained through the action of generalized reinforcers such as affection, attention, praise, and money (not necessarily in that order).

A behavior can be contingently reinforced every time it occurs and common sense might tell us that such a practice would maximize learning. Yet further thought will surely prompt us to reconsider on the grounds that very few important human (or animal) activities are or can be reliably reinforced after every occurrence. Skinner and his colleagues (e.g., Ferster and Skinner, 1957) have pioneered the study of reinforcement schedules, the specification of contingencies in terms of responses emitted (ratio schedules) and in terms of elapsed time (interval schedules). In his *Primer of Operant Conditioning*, Reynolds (1968) explains that:

> Schedules of reinforcement have regular, and profound effects on the organism's rate of responding. The importance of schedules of reinforcement cannot be overestimated. No description, account, or explanation of any operant behavior of any organism is complete unless the schedule of reinforcement is specified (p. 60).

Four simple schedules of intermittent (in contrast to continuous) reinforcement are the *fixed interval, fixed ratio, variable interval,* and *variable ratio* types. In a fixed interval schedule (FI), a reinforcer is presented after the first response emitted in a constant (fixed) interval of time. The timing interval begins from the moment the last reinforcer is delivered. When a laboratory animal is exposed to an FI schedule, its rate of responding eventually forms a recurring pattern: responding is slow at first (as though the animal were pausing), but suddenly speeds up as the time for potential delivery of the reinforcer draws near. A crude human analogy may be found in the work habits of people at dull, repetitive jobs as quitting time approaches. A fixed-ration (FR) schedule, wherein reinforcement is made contingent upon a fixed number of responses, tends to produce high, stable rates of responding. An everyday example is the piece-work system used in some industries. The more a worker produces, the more he earns. In the variable interval schedule (VI), reinforcement is made available sometimes after long intervals, and sometimes after shorter ones, in a continuously varied pattern. Generally, individuals work faster on VI schedules when the average intervals are shorter. Finally in variable ration (VR) schedules, the number of responses necessary for a reward to occur varies form reward to reward, in an irregular but repeating fashion. The VR schedule produces very high and almost constant rates of responding. The best example of behavioral persistence established by a VR schedule is that of the gambler working at a slot machine. When teaching people new forms of behavior, we often desire that they show persistently high rates of responding. Consequently, we employ the most powerful schedules at our disposal (usually variable schedules). The reader is referred to Reynolds (1968), Rachlin (1970), and Williams (1973) for further details on the operation of reinforcement schedules, the nature of reinforcement, and the influence of training conditions (delay, number of reinforcements, etc.) on response acquisition and maintenance.

Thus far we have considered only reinforcement operations. However, applied behavioral psychologists are also interested in procedures that weaken or eliminate the tendency to respond (when responding is dangerous, inappropriate, or excessive). Punishment refers to a class of operations resulting in the decline, deceleration, suppression (a temporary reduction), or termination of the behavior upon which they are contingent. An operant may be weakened in any of three ways: (1) by making a negative reinforcer (aversive or noxious stimulus) contingent upon it; (2) by causing a positive reinforcer to be lost or removed contingent upon its emission; or (3) by presenting a neutral stimulus contingently and consistently after each instance of it.

The first method is termed punishment, or sometimes *positive punishment* (positive because the event is added; punishment because the result is response reduction). The second type of procedure involves the manipulation of positive reinforcers for the purpose of reducing the frequency of responding. There exist several ways of producing a punishing outcome without having to apply aversive stimuli. *Time-out* is the name given to the practice of cutting off any access to any and all pleasant events that may be available in a given setting for a limited period of time, contingent upon the emission of a to-be-changed behavior. Sending a disobedient or disruptive child to his room is an oft-cited example of the use of time-out in everyday life. In most cases, however, the example is a poor one—bordering on the ridiculous, in fact, depending upon the opulence of the child's room! A related operation is the loss of previously held items of value (such as money earned or points won) contingent upon a response. Such a procedure, called *response cost*, is involved in a parent's taking back part of a child's allowance when the youngster misbehaves. Finally, the complete withdrawal or discontinuation of the positive events that had previously followed a behavior is called *extinction*. This procedure is equivalent to presenting neutral events where positive outcomes used to occur. Everyday examples of extinction are common. Parents will ignore a whining child whose cries formerly elicited attention. A jealous lover will ignore the amorous advances of the wayward partner. Or a therapist might ignore the promises of a client to "go on the wagon, once and for all," and pay attention only to "documented" signs of progress.

Later in this chapter, the therapeutic uses and potential misuses of punishment procedures will be addressed. For now, the reader is advised to remember two basic facts about behavior modification via the control of reinforcement contingencies: (1) consequences can either be added or taken away; and (2) both pleasant and unpleasant consequences can be used for the purpose of increasing behavior and for the purpose of decreasing behavior. Therefore:

• Positive reinforcement	= *adding* a pleasant consequence resulting in *increased* responding.
• Negative reinforcement	= *taking away* an unpleasant consequence, resulting in *increased* responding.
• (Positive) Punishment	= *adding* an unpleasant consequence resulting in *decreased responding*.
• Extinction, Response Cost, Time-Out (Negative Punishment)	= *removing* a pleasant consequence, resulting in *decreased* responding.

When the reader is clear on the above definitions, he will have succeeded where many professionals and textbook writers appear to have failed. Here's a simple memory aid. If asked the definition of negative reinforcement, for example, think of negative as taking away consequences and reinforcement as increased responding. Negative reinforcement involves taking something away resulting in behavioral increase. Common sense will tell you that what must be removed is something unpleasant.

Discrimination

An all too common misunderstanding with regard to the application of operant methods is the equating of operant psychology with an exclusive emphasis upon the manipulation of response-contingent events in the control of behavior. In fact, the stimulus events which precede the operant response may also serve a number of vital functions.

It is necessary to remember that in the Skinnerian framework, stimuli do not act as automatic goads to action, as do eliciting (unconditioned) stimuli in the Pavlovian model. Preceding stimuli can, however, serve as cues or signals that reward, punishment, or extinction is likely to occur in their presence. Stimuli that promise a probable time or place for either positive or negative contingency relationships are said to offer a *discriminative function*. When a person performs a response consistently in the presence of *discriminative stimuli* the response is called a *discriminated operant*. The process of learning to perform in the context of certain classes of stimuli is called *discrimination* (Bijou and Baer, 1978).

It should be obvious that discrimination is central to adjustment. According to Keller and Schoenfeld (1950) the "process of discrimination gives our behavior its specificity, variety, and flexibility." Since few, if any, forms of behavior are correct in all situations, it is imperative that individuals learn to respond in accordance with "go" and "no go" signals, presented either successively (successive discrimination) or at the same time (simultaneous discrimination). For example, children must learn to approach the appropriate restroom when they feel the urge to void, but to suppress the urge until they discover if the door is open or if a toilet is available.

The operant approach to discrimination is most practical when discriminatory failure is noted. The operant psychologist takes the position that biologically intact organisms are capable of sensing the difference between stimuli, but must be explicitly taught, in some instances, that certain cues predict reinforcer availability, others predict punishment, while still others have indeterminate predictive value in specific circumstances. The individual learns to respond to the best predictor of reinforcement (Schwartz, 1978).

Generalization

Not only do discriminative stimuli exert powerful influences over responding, but stimuli that are similar to the original predictor of reward/punishment serve a like function. This spread of influence across similar cues is called *stimulus generalization*. Stimulus generalization can account for considerable savings in an individual's time and energy. Among the important contributions of operant psychology is the recognition of the need for insuring that appropriate generalization learning occurs—e.g., that children understand their language (and can respond to it) irrespective of the speaker, or that adult clients can generalize their newly found skills from the context of treatment to home and work environments.

Stimulus Control and Setting Events

The essence of discrimination and generalization is behavior control—by very specific cues, in the first case, and by a variety of cues, in the second. In many clinical problems, as we shall see, the most efficient way to influence behavior is through the manipulation of antecedent cuing stimuli. Control of antecedent stimuli for purposes of establishing discriminated or generalized responding is called *stimulus control*.

Including the discriminative stimulus in a formula, along with the operant response and the contingent reward/punishment, yields the basic road map of operant psychology—the "Three-term contingency":

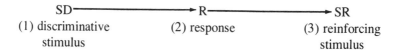

SD	R	SR
(1) discriminative stimulus	(2) response	(3) reinforcing stimulus

Of course, the cue could signal an upcoming punishing stimulus; the relationship is still the same.

Since the environment is not limited to specific preceding cues or signals, there are actually four terms in the behavioral formula. A *setting event* is the larger context (of time and space) in which a stimulus-response interactional sequence occurs (Bijou and Baer, 1978). Previous deprivation or satiation of reinforcers is a frequently cited setting event that influences the effectiveness of operant conditioning.

METHODS OF BEHAVIOR CHANGE

Although many techniques exist for the alteration of behavior, our focus rests exclusively with those that derive from the operant experimental perspective. Presentation of behavior influence methods has been segmented into four sections to mirror the four interdependent functions of operant intervention: (1) the establishment of effective behavior; (2) the acceleration of desirable activities; (3) the elimination of maladaptive responding; and (4) the maintenance of therapeutic gain. Virtually all progammatic efforts to help people change will include all four elements. Why? Beginning with the propositions that both adaptive and maladaptive behavior must be learned, and that the proper study of behavior is the study of relationships, the behavioral practitioner never deals with problem behavior in isolation. Every intervention is (or should be) a three-pronged attack: first, increasing (or establishing) desirable responses; second, eliminating the undesirable behaviors that compete with the acquisition or use of acceptable responses, and finally, arranging for the stimulus control or eventual generalization of the newly-acquired habits. It is understood, of course, that successful intervention will be followed by programs to insure maintenance. The three-pronged attack is suggested, therefore, regardless of the apparent singularity of the target (e.g., "All I want to do is get Johnny to stop soiling his pants"; "If Mary would only start paying attention in class . . ."). While some of the techniques will be illustrated individually, the reader should keep in mind the complementary nature of operant procedures.

Building Behavioral Capabilities

Shaping (Differentiation Plus Extinction). Rationale: If a response must occur to be reinforced (strengthened), how can new behaviors be acquired? A procedure known as *response differentiation* provides the answer. Simply put, the behavioral psychologist relies on already existing forms of behavior to establish new forms. Every action or movement, verbal or motoric, varies along qualitative and quantitative dimensions. A verbal utterance varies in pitch and loudness; a movement in direction, form, force, or duration. We can produce a new behavior by picking one level of variant of an existing response and reinforcing it, while we withdraw all reward from other levels. Soon, new variations will appear. If we apply the procedure of response differentiation progressively and gradually, we may move the behavior in a planned direction. Each new form is an approximation of the desired terminal behavior. This selective reward and extinction process is called *successive approximation* or *shaping* (see Millenson, 1967, Chapter 8 for a more detailed analysis). While the early laboratory demonstrations of shaping were interesting and amusing (Skinner taught pigeons to play ping pong, for example), the procedure can be used to program academic (reading), social (approaching, speaking, cooperating), and complex motor behaviors in normal and biologically deficient children and adults. Shaping is typically used to establish single behaviors. When the goal is the establishment of behavior sequences (e.g., getting dressed; toileting, etc.) shaping is used in conjunction with *chaining* (see below).

Illustration: Lovaas (1977) and his colleagues have long employed shaping procedures to help establish vocal repertoires in severely disturbed, mute children. Nonverbal children will, on occasion, emit vowel-like sounds; the therapist will seek to reinforce sound emission in order to provide enough raw material for a program of shaping sounds into words, and words into sentences. The therapist might wait for a sound, or manually close the child's lips, letting the natural release of air produce a vocalization. Immediately upon hearing the sound, the therapist reinforces the child with a valued reward—like food. Children may also be rewarded for visually fixating on the adult's mouth. After a period of reliable response emission (e.g., one sound every five seconds) and visual fixation on the adult's mouth (at least 50 percent of the time), the therapist might shift the criterion a bit and only reinforce a sound if it occurs within five seconds of the adult's verbal cue, such as the word "baby." No reward would be administered if a sound occurred six seconds after the cue word (extinction). After reliably bringing verbalization under discriminative control, the therapist could next try to elicit imitation on the part of the child. That is, the adult would say "m," prompt such a response from the child (e.g., by holding the child's lips and then releasing), and only reinforce correct matching. If matching were to become a reliable phenomenon, then the therapist's next step would be to differentially reward the consecutive emission of two sounds. New pairs of sounds would be introduced after the therapist was sure that the child had mastered the previous discriminations (i.e., emitting ten consecutive correct imitations of the adult's utterances).

Recommendations: The steps in behavior shaping are as follows:

1. Begin by observing the individual whose behavioral repertoire is considered deficient. What responses occur at high frequency? Identify the antecedent and consequent (reinforcing) environmental stimuli associated with these high frequency behaviors. Note the variability in topography (form, force, or duration) of the available responses.
2. Based upon the observational data, decide whether a desired terminal response can be differentiated out of existing behaviors and if so, what a first approximation to the end goal should be.
3. Establish the criterion for the first approximation. As Blackwood (1971) points out: "In setting the criterion, we are dividing the responses into two classes; responses most like those we want and responses least like those we want. Notice here that the criterion must be set low or all responding will be extinguished." (Chapter 7, p. 6).
4. Arrange the setting for maximum likelihood of response emission. If the desired response involves other people or particular stimuli, arrange to have them present during shaping.
5. Differentially reinforce (with the most powerful reinforcers at your disposal—food, praise, physical affection, etc.) variants of ongoing behavior that may be crude first approximations of the desired response. Withdraw reinforcement from variants that are incompatible with the desired end goal. For example in shaping her son to pay attention to her demonstrations of proper dressing behavior, a mother will talk to her child affectionately when he looks in her direction, but will be silent when the child turns away, closes his eyes, screams, etc.
6. Observe the shift in the direction of the goal behavior and shift the criterion accordingly. If repeated reinforcement fails to reliably establish a response,

the criterion may need to be lowered. When a behavior is established at a high, stable rate with little fluctuation (e.g., a child's verbalization of "da" occurs to the cue "Say da," 95 percent of the time), the criterion may be shifted in the direction of the desired response (reinforce only two consecutive "da" responses; reinfoirce two consecutive "da" responses separated by a maximum of two seconds of silence; then one second, etc.).

7. Use verbal or gestural cues or instructions at all stages of the process, even though the cues do not at first reliably elicit the behavior being shaped. At the outset of the shaping procedure the child's behavior will determine what cues the shaper will use (Step 1). That is, if the child spontaneously says "goo," the shaper will reinforce the sound and then attempt to establish stimulus control by instructing the child, "Say goo," and rewarding compliance.

Chaining. Rationale: Complex human behaviors are composed of chains of simpler responses. The response units of a behavior chain are joined by stimuli that act as cues (discriminative stimuli) and as reinforcers. For example, the chain of actions that is initiated by the ring of one's alarm clock and that terminates (for the sake of this example) in the eating of one's breakfast is a sequence of operations upon the environment, with reinforcing consequences that likewise set the occasion for (cue) subsequent operations—culminating in the satisfying state of hunger reduction. The overt responses, (referred to as members of the chain just described, are numerous (sitting up in bed, putting on slippers, walking to bathroom, washing, brushing teeth, walking to kitchen, sitting down at table, etc.) as are the environmental connectors (links) that tie the chain members together (the slippers that cue walking and make walking more comfortable, the toothpaste tube which cues brushing and whose release of toothpaste reinforces its squeezing, etc.).

The technology of establishing (teaching) adaptive behavior chains with individuals—adults as well as children—whose performance is judged deficient is built upon the principles of shaping, stimulus control, and reinforcement. Precision and common sense in the use of these basic behavioral procedures can produce long, intricate, and socially-relevant chains of behavior, the smooth flow of which belies their premeditated origin (see Findley, 1962, for a discussion of the complex topic of branching chains).

Illustration: The purpose of therapeutic chaining is to take already existing responses (members) and tie them together by imposing conditioned reinforcement value upon the various links. First the teacher or therapist decides on the order in which the sequence of behaviors is to occur. For example, Watson (1973) and his colleagues, in their psychoeducational approach to child treatment, might establish dressing behavior by connecting the following members: putting on underpants, putting on pants, putting on a shirt, putting on socks, and putting on shoes. Next, these members are connected by reinforcing the last behavior in the sequence first. By consistently rewarding the putting on of shoes, it is assumed that the discriminative stimuli controlling the "shoe member" of the chain will come to serve as reinforcers for the "sock member," and so on in a backward direction toward the first response.

To build chains of responses, one need not always work backwards in the manner just described. Shaping can often be employed to establish chains of responses, especially when initial members of the chain can be elicited easily via simple cues, like instructions (Kazdin, 1975). Note, therefore, the important difference between *chaining* (a specific response building process) and *chains* (specific patterns of responding).

Recommendations: The basic rules for teaching behavior chains are:

1. Divide the desired behavior sequence into component units. Size of units should be determined by the demands of the individual case.
2. Determine which members of the to-be-continued chain already exist and which will need to be individually shaped.
3. Shape the chain members which are at low strength (low probability of emission) or at zero strength.
4. Begin the chaining procedure by strengthening the final member. Do so in a distraction-free environment.
5. Bring the final member under reliable stimulus control. The accomplishment of this and the preceding step is aided by the use of strong reinforcers (determined by observing the client and asking him what he likes), consistently, immediately, and frequently given, contingent upon emission of the desired response. Social reinforcers should also be used (e.g., smiles, praise, etc.).
6. Add the next-to-last member of the behavior already acquired. Add each remaining member working backwards to the first response in the chain. For example, a three-member chain can be diagrammed as follows:

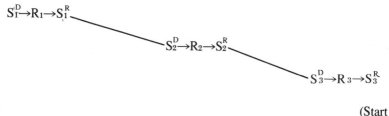

$$S_1^D \rightarrow R_1 \rightarrow S_1^R$$
$$S_2^D \rightarrow R_2 \rightarrow S_2^R$$
$$S_3^D \rightarrow R_3 \rightarrow S_3^R$$

(Start here)

Let us assume that we are dealing with the last three members of a toothbrushing chain, (R_3) is brushing reinforced by (S_3) the delightful-tasting toothpaste. The cue for brushing (S_3) is the toothbrush in hand. Holding the toothbrush will eventually take on reinforcing power. When holding the toothbrush reliably predicts brushing, we can expect toothbrush holding (S_3) to reinforce (S_3 is also S_2) toothbrush lifting

(R_2). The cue for toothbrush lifting (S_2) may be the sight of the toothbrush. Eventually seeing the toothbrush will reinforce (S_1^R) the first response in our mini-chain (R_1) which is switching on the light in the bathroom.

7. When an error occurs during performance of a chained sequence, correct the error as soon as possible and require the performer to go back as far as possible in the chain and start over.

8. When errors occur in a learned sequence it may be necessary to punish them. One may need to punish errors that occur early in the chain, since disruption of the initial behaviors undercuts acquisition and may have adverse effects on the learner's motivation.

9. In teaching chained sequences (such as proper dressing, toileting, bathing, eating behavior, etc.) it is often helpful and necessary to physically guide the performer through the sequence. The teacher may also demonstrate (model) appropriate behavior.

10. Fading and prompting techniques may also be useful in establishing effective chains (see below).

Fading and Prompting. Rationale: Thus far, we have concentrated largely on behavior building by the manipulation of consequences. We are now ready to consider, more specifically, methods of placing newly established responses under discriminative stimulus control.

Adequate adjustment to an ever-changing environment calls for quick and accurate tuning in to the cues (stimuli) that signal the expected forms of behavior. Examples are: stop at the red light; take off your hat in church (or put it on in synagogue); stand when the national anthem is played; talk softly in the library. And there are the subtler social signals which dictate how we approach, converse with and relate to members of the opposite sex, to persons older or younger than ourselves, to authorities, to strangers, to friends, and to enemies. Maladaptive behavior is often the result of responding to an inappropriate stimulus (i.e., the form of the behavior is correct, but it is emitted at the wrong time or place) or a failure to respond to the appropriate cue. If we can bring the responses of others or of ourselves under the influence of verbal or nonverbal signals—hints, cues, prompts, directions, advice, requests, or instructions—we can often achieve more efficient management, and set the stage for generalization (extension) and maintenance of change.

Prompts are behavioral interventions which direct the learner's attention to the to-be-learned task and its requirements. In shaping dressing behavior, for example, the teacher may physically guide the child through a series of movements and administer reinforcement at appropriate intervals. In shaping speech behavior, the teacher may utter the required sound first, and direct the learner to repeat it. A close approximation of the sound will then be rewarded. *Fading* refers to the gradual elimination of aspects of the cuing stimulus, so that the learner is responding to the minimal cues that exist in the natural environment.

Fading refers also to the gradual removal of cues that are artificially established for purposes of aiding acquisition (writing numbers on the keys of a piano, then, literally "fading them out"). In combination, prompting and fading procedures are used to develop discriminative control of behavior.

Illustrations: An important aspect of adjustment among elderly residents of nursing homes is active participation in recreational opportunities. McClannahan and Risley (1975) conducted a study in a proprietary, skilled-care nursing facility to determine the effects of prompts upon the residents' participation in a lounge area. Trained observers noted the residents' typical activities prior to intervention. On the average weekday, 54 percent of the residents were to be found in their own rooms, 16 percent in the lounge area, 10 percent in the dining hall, and the remainder relatively unoccupied. At any given time, most residents were sitting (63 percent), or lying down (23 percent). A full 87 percent were not engaged in any social interaction. The experimental procedure involved the setting up of a "manipulative area" in the lounge, and alternating days when items such as puzzles and games were made available. On days when the equipment was available, the activity leader would seek out any resident who did not request a piece of equipment, place recreational material in his hands, and briefly request that he use it appropriately. The results indicated that prompting increased participation in lounge activities from 20 to 74 percent. The authors concluded that "prompting of initial participation is an essential component of recreation programs for the institutionalized elderly" (p. 267).

Barlow and Agras (1973) used a fading procedure to alter the stimulus control of sexual arousal in three homosexual men. The clients sought treatment voluntarily for a problem which the investigators considered to be an example of inappropriate stimulus control. Each subject was seated before a screen on which slides of nude men and /or nude females could be shown. A device that measured expansion of the penis in response to the slides was worn by the subject. Degree of arousal was measured as a percentage of full erection. Prior to the fading treatment, each homosexual subject showed a marked penile response to slides of male nudes and relatively little response to the females slides. The fading procedure operated as follows: An attractive male slide and "the least unattractive" female slide were placed in two synchronized slide projectors. The slide projectors displayed the images superimposed over each other including the genital area. The projector controls were rigged so that increasing the brightness of one image resulted in a simultaneous decrease in the brightness of the other. The subjects began by viewing a 0 percent female, 100 percent male image. If they showed at least 75 percent of full erection during the two-minute presentation, the next step (in a 16-step process) was initiated (six percent female, 94 percent male). This stepwise process continued until the subject was making the criterion response (75 percent of full erection) to the 100 percent female, 0 percent male presentation. Stimulus control was successfully altered in all three subjects (responding in the presence of the female slide alone took 16, 29, and 105 trials for the three clients, respectively). Two of the three subjects were able to successfully approach females and engage in heterosexual intercourse subsequent to treatment. Obviously the alteration of arousal cues is not sufficient to change behavior. Barlow and Agras pointed out that "an additional important step in the treatment of sexual deviation is to teach the client the necessary social behavior needed to implement newly acquired arousal and thus insure the presence of positive environmental contingencies." (p. 365).

Recommendations:

1. Use fading and prompting in combination with reinforcement for desired behavior or successive approximation procedures.
2. Use prompts that are as close as possible to those which the learner will encounter in the real life situation for which he is being groomed.
3. Prompts must be distinctive to snare the attention of young, active learners or elderly clients with sensory impairments.
4. Gradually fade out the use of artificial prompts (i.e., those not found in the natural environment).
5. Establish a criterion for fading (as in Barlow and Agras' example) when the objective is the switching of control from one stimulus to another. The reader is referred to the section on Stimulus Control below for further examples and recommendations relevant to the topics of fading and prompting.

Increasing the Likelihood of Desirable Behavior

Positive Reinforcement. Rationale: We have seen how the systematic application of response-contingent positive reinforcement can aid in the development of new behaviors. With response strengthening or maintenance as the objective, positive reinforcement again plays a major, if not a starring, role. Whether the target be simple motor acts or higher level responses such as attitudes or opinions, the contingent application of reinforcing outcomes is likely to affect the desired acceleration in rate. Positive contingency control may well be the most versatile tool in the realm of behavior change.

Illustrations: The varied role of positive reinforcements in the formation, maintenance and change of married relationships is illustrated in the work of Azrin, Naster, and Jones (1973). These authors suggest that the expectation of reinforcement from marriage (sex, companionship, financial gain, social approval, etc.) is a key factor in its initiation, but that, in a marriage, new sources of positive and negative reinforcers are created and existing sources are rearranged. "The nature and degree of the positive and negative reinforcers for each marital partner will, therefore, be in a constant state of flux. As such, no fixed contract or agreement prior to or during marriage can assure maximum happiness and minimal annoyance in the future." (p. 367). Generally, the absence of reciprocity in reinforcer exchange is a major source of marital discord. Specifically, reinforcers received by each spouse may be too infrequent, too restricted, and bought at too great a price, such as the loss of new sources of satisfaction and of personal independence. Reciprocity counseling is designed to maximize the success of marital exchange by focusing on the presence of reinforcers in the current, problematic situation, by discovering new sources of mutual satisfaction within marriage, and by establishing a contract system that ensures "reciprocity as a general relation." As the authors state: "The overall feeling induced in a partner should be that the spouse is continuously striving to please him (her) and he (she) in turn will strive equally to please the spouse . . ." (p. 368). Azrin and his colleagues use a "package" approach in that they concentrate their training in nine marital problem areas, involving broad response classes and rather indirect measures of personal satisfaction. Yet the procedures are theory-derived, systematic, internally consistent, and apparently quite effective.

The application of reward techniques in classrooms and other remediation-training-rehabilitative settings has been growing in popularity and sophistication since Dr. Arthur Staats' demonstrations in the late fifties of the efficacy of token reinforcers in the treatment of reading problems of children. Ward and Baker (1968), for example, taught first grade teachers how to switch their payoffs in order to correct the disruptive classroom behavior of selected children. Following a five-week baseline phase during which eight categories of behavior were observed by trained college undergraduates, a seven-week treatment phase was introduced. Teachers ignored (extinguished) deviant behaviors such as crying, screaming, running, and thumb sucking, and reinforced with attention and praise (conditioned reinforcers) task relevant "productive" behaviors. Teachers were taught to follow the rule of giving reinforcers contingently, consistently, and immediately. The use of this rather restricted intervention with minimal training of teachers resulted in an almost 20 percent decline in deviant behavior.

Kohlenberg and Phillips (1973) employed a reinforcement procedure in an urban park setting to increase the rate of litter depositing. Their experiment was conducted eight hours per day over an eight-week period. During the baseline period, observers stationed near the target trash receptacle made recordings of each litter deposit made by park patrons. Prior to intervention, the particular area chosen was unusually littered (despite the fact that there were 12 trash receptacles within a 50-foot radius). During the reinforcement period, some patrons who deposited litter in the receptacle received a coupon redeemable for a soft drink at a nearby concession stand (litter depositing was reinforced on a variable ratio schedule). The results were dramatic. Total deposits during the first baseline period was 723. During the first reinforcement phase, the total was 4,577.

Recommendations:
1. Identify reinforcers by observing their functional effects on behavior rather than assuming that what is a reward for one individual will serve the same function for another.
2. Identify activity reinforcers after systematic observation of the individual across and within a variety of natural settings.
3. Deliver reinforcers immediately, contingently, and consistently to maximize response strengthening.

4. Reinforce behavior often while bringing it to optimal frequency, then thin out reinforcement to maximize loss of potency due to repeated presentation of a single reinforcing stimulus or event.
6. Use social reinforcement (the verbal and nonverbal behavior of people) whenever feasible to permit the developing behavior to be maintained across settings. If necessary develop social reinforcer effectiveness by fading the use of primary reinforcers.

Negative Reinforcement. Rationale: If an individual is subjected to aversive (unpleasant or painful) stimulation, any action which results in the withdrawal of that stimulation is reinforced. In nature, learning to escape or avoid harm or fear of harm is strengthened by a process of negative reinforcement. The reader will note that, in terms of operations and effects, negative reinforcement is the mirrored reverse of punishment—noxious stimuli are terminated (rather than presented) for the purpose of increasing (rather than decreasing) response frequency. Negative reinforcement is most often used for strengthening adaptive avoidance responses (e.g., learning to give up smoking, drinking, or fattening foods). It should be clear, however, that the use of negative reinforcement in a controlled setting (the animal laboratory or a therapist's office) constitutes an aversive approach to behavior change, with many of the potential drawbacks associated with punishment procedures (see the present discussion of punishment and also Chapter 9 in this volume).

Illustration: Penick et al. (1971) employed a "symbolic" aversive stimulus in a negative self-reinforcement program for weight control. The behaviors to be accelerated were associated with dieting. While weight reduction can be thought of as resulting in the positive consequence of looking and feeling better, the subjects also arranged for a negatively reinforcing event to occur contingent upon weight loss. The dieter stored large pieces of pork fat in his refrigerator equal in amount to the excess weight to be lost. The investigators simply instructed their subjects to remove the bags of fat contingent upon proportional weight loss. This technique, in combination with others, seemed very effective. Of course the nature of the aversive stimulus, the delay of removal, its "self-mediation," and the absence of any warning stimulus made the weight control program quite unlike most of the laboratory-derived techniques currently in use. However, negative reinforcement is sometimes effective for the treatment of such problems as drug addiction, alcoholism, smoking, and obesity for which the acquisition of avoidance responses seems clinically desirable and is an expressed goal of the client. In general, escape or avoidance conditioning (as the sole intervention method) has not produced unequivocally positive outcomes.

Recommendations:
1. When using negative reinforcement to teach avoidance, provide an incompatible, alternate approach response. In treating an alcoholic, for example, one might arrange for shock during alcohol consumption to be terminated by a response which causes some other beverage to be delivered.

2. The termination of the aversive stimulus should be contingent, immediate, and consistent.
3. Remember that in avoidance conditioning two events are connected—the aversive stimulus, and the cue to the onset of the aversive stimulus (called the *conditioned aversive stimulus* or CAS). The individual who learns to avoid or remove himself from a situation containing the CAS also causes the association of the CAS and the aversive event to be weakened. Thus, avoidance may also start to weaken. As conditioning proceeds, it is advisable to pair the CAS and the aversive stimulus on an intermittent basis with decreasing frequency.
4. The time between escape or avoidance trials must not be too brief. The aversive stimulus should be off long enough to make the relief enjoyable.
5. If, over time, the individual is not making reliable avoidance or escape responses, bring the training to a halt and determine if unknown contingencies outside of therapy are interfering with the program or if the aversive consequences are, indeed, functionally aversive.

Stimulus Control. Rationale: Systematically observing the variations in individual behavior across situations will reveal that certain stimuli reliably predict responding more than others. By controlling the antecedant conditions that set the occasion for reinforced behavior, one can produce an increase in the likelihood of response emission. Four classes of antecedent events can be identified: (1) discriminative stimuli that have been linked to response-contingent reinforcement in the past; (2) verbal cues or "rules," the adherence to which have previously resulted in reinforcement; (3) facilitating stimuli, the provision of which makes responding easier (e.g., new clothes facilitate social interaction); and (4) motivational operations that heighten the effectiveness of reinforcement (such as prior deprivation).

In many therapeutic situations, it is easier, cheaper, or faster to program antecedent stimuli for appropriate responding than to try to identify and alter the contingencies. And, as we have already seen, not all clinical problems require behavior acceleration or deceleration, but rather responding in the right place and at the right time (stimulus control development).

Illustrations: Schutte and Hopkins (1970) developed adult verbal control in a kindergarten classroom by training the teacher in the differential use of contingent attention (reinforcement). A list of ten instructions was drawn up (e.g., "Pick up the toys," "Come and get a pencil and paper,") and presented to a group of five girls between 4.8 and 6 years old. The teacher, equipped with stopwatch and score sheet recorded whether her instructions were followed within 15 seconds. The teacher waited two minutes between instructions. During the first baseline the children had a mean daily instruction-following rate of 60 percent. However, when the teacher made a natural verbal response contingent on compliance to instructions (such as "That's nice," or "Thank you for doing what I asked"), the children followed the instructions 78 percent of the time.

Removal of the contingencies led to a decline to 68.7 percent; and a second reinforcement phase produced instruction following between 80 and 90 percent (average = 83.7 percent). These results were accomplished in just 20 daily sessions of 20 minutes each.

Despite the general usefulness of establishing stimulus control (or the *discriminative function*) by teacher instructions, such a procedure tends to tie the child's behavior to a rather narrow set of cues. Children under the control of one teacher's verbal cues tend not to evidence transfer of behaviors to other school personnel. Indeed, appropriate classroom behavior is likely to decline when the teacher is absent or momentarily out of sight, to the extent that teacher presence per se has come to serve as a discriminative stimulus for academic behavior. Marholin and Steinman (1977), therefore, developed a procedure designed to (1) partially abolish the control exerted by a teacher's presence on children's behavior; and (2) to establish the stimulus control potential of the academic materials themselves. These authors simply arranged for teachers to leave the classroom at scheduled times, and then set up a contingency whereby successful completion of academic work could earn rewards. They found that fifth and sixth grade children in a typical public school classroom could be taught to respond with appropriate academic and social behaviors in the absence of external monitoring.

We might also ask if stimulus control procedures can work in more complex settings with adults, involving more resistant problems—such as obesity. As one component in their successful behavioral program for weight control, Stuart and his colleagues (Stuart and Davis, 1972) teach their clients to strengthen the antecedents of appropriate eating. For example, dieters are urged to provide themselves an assortment of acceptable (prescribed) foods and monitor their cumulative consumption on handy pocket record sheets. In essence, the dieter restricts or programs his environment to maximize success. Fussy eaters can pick and choose—but only from among appropriate food stimuli. Since eating is often cued by the physical characteristics (size, texture, color, etc.) of food, the dieter is also taught to employ low-calorie garnishments and embellishments such as parsley and paprika.

Another method of stimulus control, usually employed in conjunction with provision of cues for appropriate behavior, is the weakening of cues for inappropriate behavior. This simultaneous strengthening-weakening tactic employing antecedent stimuli parallels the tandem application of positive reinforcement and extinction in contingency management. In the case of Stuart's dieters, the stimulus control program included such suggestions as eating in only one room, not engaging in any other behaviors while eating (such as talking or watching television), and clearing one's plate directly into the garbage. These elimination steps were designed to narrow or reduce the range of cues precipitating overeating.

Recommendations:

1. To use stimulus control effectively, identify by observation (not deduction)

the functional links between antecedent cues and behaviors not to be accelerated.

2. Identify the cues for inappropriate behavior.
3. Remove cues for inappropriate behavior.
4. Make cues for appropriate responding more conspicuous. If certain individuals serve as S$_D$ for the appropriate behavior of others, then arrange to have the facilitating persons occupy a more central place in the environment.
5. Do not overwork stimulus control. Remember, each nonreinforced presentation of a stimulus will weaken its power to evoke responding.
6. If an arbitrary cue has been established as a discriminative stimulus, gradually fade in natural antecedents in order to foster generalization to the posttreatment environment.
7. Train the individual to take over the cue control of his own behavior (see Chapters 10 and 11).

Reducing the Likelihood of Excessive Behavior

Response-Contingent Aversive Stimulation. Rationale: Aside from legal and ethical considerations physical punishment as a method of behavior influence is an aversive topic for psychologists because of technical complexities. Reese (1966) succinctly points out that punishment is a complex process:

> It can affect emotional respondent behavior . . . it can affect operants other than the one punished; and its effects on the punished operant itself are a function of several variables, including the subjects' motivation, the severity of the aversive stimulus, the schedule on which punishment is delivered, and many more. (p. 31).

Punishment procedures involving painful or otherwise unpleasant stimulation can be effective when properly applied to behaviors that (1) involve immediate physical danger to the actor or to others in his environment, or that (2) cannot be prevented through the control of antecedent cues or reinforcing consequences. When using punishment, one should be prepared to deal with the client's frequent efforts to avoid or escape the "treatment," and, in so doing, to engage in behaviors that are more detrimental than those that are supposedly being treated. Undesirable outcomes are also likely to occur when punishment is used as a last resort. Indeed, any procedure that is instituted by an individual or a system—a hospital, school, or prison—"when all else has failed" has a good chance of being misapplied. Anger, frustration, resentment, desperation, and/or overcommitment can all too easily undermine the goal of therapeutic behavior change.

Illustration: Aversive procedures have been frequently used for the suppression of alcohol consumption, with reported success rates varying between 30 percent and 70 percent (Doleys et al., 1977). It is usually presumed that the pairing of electrical shock and drinking serves to impart conditioned aversive properties to the act of alcohol consumption. In a semi-naturalistic setting (the

Alcohol Behavior Research Laboratory at Rutgers University), Wilson, Leaf and Nathan (1975) examined several methods of deconditioning excessive alcohol indulgence in chronic, nonpsychotic male alcoholics. These investigators found that an escape-conditioning procedure was not effective in promoting abstinence. The participants were shocked when sipping alcohol, and could turn off the shock by spitting it out. This escape contingency was used in conjunction with positive suggestions about its potency. But during posttraining the drinking patterns of the men who experienced this procedure did not show appreciable changes compared to pretraining levels. The use of aversive response-contingent shocks (positive punishment) was then tried, and proved to be quite effective with eight other alcoholics (seven of whom were "failures" from Alcoholics Anonymous programs). Wilson, Leaf and Nathan also discovered that the participants could be trained to self-administer shocks, and that the punishment contingency, rather than mere expectancy effects, was responsible for effectively suppressing alcohol consumption subsequent to treatment.

Recommendations: Where positive control and nonphysical forms of punishment are ineffective in changing behavior, the use of response-contingent aversive stimulation (RCAS) is best carried out in keeping with the following guidelines:

1. Use RCAS in conjunction with positive reinforcement of appropriate behavior.
2. Deliver RCAS as soon as possible after a misbehavior.
3. The duration of RCAS need not be very long (with moderate electric shocks, a duration of 0.1 second has proven effective).
4. Deliver RCAS on a continuous schedule until the response is suppressed or eliminated.
5. The materials used to deliver RCAS should be checked often for safety and reliability (see Butterfield, 1975).
6. Different individuals should be involved in the delivery of RCAS. If possible and necessary, persons with whom the client will have contact outside of therapy should be involved in the delivery of RCAS.
7. Be on guard for negative side effects.
8. Avoid extended periods of RCAS.
9. The individual who delivers RCAS should do so only if he is in agreement with the clinical decision that dictates its use.
10. Effective and acceptable alternatives to shock and intense auditory stimulation should be sought. For example, shaking, pinching, hand-slapping, and even tickling can suppress behavior in youngsters for whom shock would appear to caretakers as unduly harsh or untenable.
11. Use fading techniques to bring punished responses under discriminative control.

Extinction. Rationale: Many deviant or maladaptive behaviors are strengthened by the reinforcing effects of attention. Parents and teachers turn to look at, stare down, speak to, or scream at children who are acting in a disorderly or inappropriate fashion in an effort to eliminate the behavior. When these tactics produce the opposite effect, namely, an increase in disruptive behavior, caretakers and educators tend to lapse into mentalistic explanations: "Billy is unmanageable because he has his father's temper," "Jackie is high strung and temperamental," "Karen cannot be treated owing to an inadequately-formed superego." One of the most compelling arguments for the operant approach to the alleviation of problem behavior is in the demonstrated effect of extinction—the mere withdrawal of reinforcement from high probability responding. One of the early accounts of successful behavior modification using operant principles was Williams' (1959) study of tantrum elimination through extinction. Since that time, extinction combined with reinforcement of incompatible, desirable behavior has been employed in literally thousands of cases—in classrooms, hospitals, nursery schools, and homes.

Extinction by itself does not produce immediate and consistent response reduction as is often the case in the application of aversive stimulation. In fact, when extinction is first introduced, the frequency of a response may increase. The clinician using extinction procedures is, therefore, advised to prepare himself, the client, and/or the nonprofessionals working on a behavior problem for the initial extinction-induced worsening of the target response. However, extinction will produce a gradual reduction in responding over time. The rate at which a behavior is extinguished has been shown to be a function of the reinforcement schedule under which it was acquired or maintained. Generally speaking, extinction takes longer when the response was acquired under an intermittent or irregular schedule of reinforcement (recall our slot-machine example). Resistance to extinction is a characteristic of a behavior which is troublesome only when the goal is the elimination of excessive responding. On the other hand, when establishing newly-acquired, desirable behaviors, the clinician will try to make them resistant to extinction.

Illustration: Ayllon and Michael (1959) provided one of the first demonstrations of the efficacy of extinction in the treatment of hospitalized psychotic patients. Prior to the enactment of behavioral interventions, the ward nurses conducted systematic observations of patient behavior. Data were collected on the frequency of problem behavior, on the kind and frequency of naturally occurring reinforcement, and (a step often neglected by untutored behavior modifiers) on the frequency of incompatible behavior that could be used to displace the deviant responding. The results indicated that much of the undesirable patient behavior was being maintained by the contingent social approval and attention of the nursing staff. Subsequently, the nurses, who served as the behavioral engineers or change agents, were instructed in the use of extinction (being asked, for example, to "ignore the behavior and act deaf and blind whenever it occurs").

The goal for Helen, a patient described as delusional , was the extinction of her "psychotic talk." More than 90 percent of Helen's conversation focused on her illegitimate child and the men who were after her. After the nurses were instructed to use extinction plus reinforcement of other conversational topics, the sick talk dropped steadily—to a low of less than 25 percent relative frequency on the tenth week (the delusional talk had persisted for three years previously). When the psychotic talk appeared again at higher frequency, it was discovered that Helen was obtaining "bootleg" reinforcement from individuals unfamiliar with the extinction program. The power of extinction was, nonetheless, clearly demonstrated. The reader is referred to Ayllon and Azrin (1968) for further illustrations of the use of extinction with hospitalized patients, to O'Leary and O'Leary (1977) for examples of classroom applications, and to Harris and Ersner-Hershfield (1978) for a discussion of extinction with severely disturbed and retarded populations.

Recommendations:

1. Use extinction of inappropriate responding in conjunction with positive reinforcement for incompatible or appropriate behavior.
2. Extinction is effective only if the behavioral engineer has correctly identified the reinforcing stimulus to be withheld. Difficulties and failures in the use of extinction can be minimized by careful and reliable observation of the problem situation, with an eye toward identifying all possible reinforcers contingent upon undesirable behavior, and by interviewing the target person to ascertain (e.g., through the use of a reinforcer survey) the current effective reinforcers in his life.
3. Extinction works best if all those who are potential reinforcers of inappropriate behavior work toward withholding the payoff. Thus teachers may need to work with parents, hospital personnel will need to be coordinated, and, in general, every available resource person will need to become involved in the extinction program. Failing this, the deviant response will be intermittently reinforced, making it resistant to extinction.
4. Prepare those involved with the client, especially program implementers, for the initial increase in the frequency of the undesirable response when extinction begins.
5. Extinction, as the exclusive change method, is inappropriate when the behavior must be stopped at once because it is physically harmful to the client or to others (as in the self-mutilation of children, assaultive behavior, or fire-setting); when the frustrating effects produced by reward removal cue other behaviors which are dangerous and potentially uncontrollable (i.e., behaviors for which the cues and reinforcement contingencies are unknown or unmanageable); and when the withholding of rewards for inappropriate behavior also requires the withholding of rewards for desirable responses.

Differential Reinforcement of Other (or Incompatible) Behaviors.

Rationale: It is a rare case in which a clinician would simply desire to extinguish or decelerate a troublesome behavior without, at the same time, wishing to establish another, more adaptive, response. In many instances, it is also advisable to maintain the absolute amount of reward available to an individual. In such cases, the therapist may select a DRO (differential reinforcement of other behavior) procedure (Gelfand and Hartmann, 1975). The objective is "out with the old, and in with the new"—or, in operant language, "extinguish the target, DRO the alternative"!

The term DRO has not been used consistently in the operant literature. The "other" behavior being reinforced may or may not be incompatible with the target. For example, a teacher can reinforce *any* behavior, other than talking out of turn, if it occurs within a specified time period. Or, the teacher can reinforce silence. The first procedure may be called *omission training*, while the latter is termed DRI (differential reinforcement of incompatible behavior). In general, DRO, DRI, or omission training procedures work best in conjunction with other methods (such as extinction and prompting). Corte, Wolf, and Locke (1971) compared the relative effects of aversive stimulation (shock), omission training, and extinction in the treatment of self-injurious behaviors in retarded children. The results were mixed.

Illustration: Goetz and Baer (1973) provided three preschool girls with contingent social reinforcement for the production of divergent forms in a block-building task. These investigators reasoned that children's block play is a potential contributor to their emergent concepts of form, space, mathematics, and visual esthetics. The investigators sought to engender creative block building by systematically reinforcing the children for any block arrangement other than one they may have previously constructed within play sessions. The DRO procedures were shown to be effective in stimulating form diversity among the preschoolers. This study also illustrates the manner in which typically vague, but socially significant concepts (such as creativity) can be operationalized within an experimental analysis framework.

Recommendations:

1. Use DRO schedules in concert with other nonaversive change methods, such as extinction and verbal prompting.
2. When the target (undesirable) behavior occurs at high rates, it may be necessary to prompt the "other" or incompatible response.
3. Employ brief time intervals for initial reinforcement of the desirable response, to permit the learner to earn sufficient reward for its emission.
4. Be sure to avoid reinforcing "other" behaviors which themselves are apt to become problematic to the client in the long run.
5. Use DRO schedules consistently to eliminate the undesirable behavior in as many contexts in which it is likely to occur.
6. Avoid sole use of DRO procedures if the response-to-be-eliminated is lifethreatening and must be rapidly suppressed.
7. Try to select an incompatible response for DRI contingencies which is already in the client's skill repertoire and which is likely to be maintained in the natural environment (see Sulzer-Azaroff and Mayer, 1977 for further discussion of DRO and related methods).

Response Cost. Rationale: Response cost (RC) represents a form of punishment in which previously acquired primary reinforcers (such as food) or conditioned reinforcers are forfeited contingent upon an undesirable response. RC has been used in institutional settings to suppress the maladaptive behavior of psychiatric patients and retarded individuals, and in outpatient settings wherein clients negotiate therapeutic contracts that include RC contingencies (or the threat of RC). In most applied settings RC is combined with positive reinforcement for appropriate responding. Occasionally, other punishment techniques, such as time-out or aversive stimulation, are used in conjunction with RC and positive control. In a review of research findings, it was tentatively concluded that RC does not evoke the undesirable side effects attributed to punishment, nor do RC-suppressed behaviors return when the RC contingency is removed (Kazdin, 1972).

Illustrations: A twenty-year old, hospitalized woman who had been labeled an anxiety-depressive, hysterical, and borderline psychotic was treated in a Behavior Modification Unit by response cost and positive reinforcement methods (Reisinger, 1972). The patient's depressed behavior (low rate of smiling; high rate of unprovoked crying) was the target of a change program implemented by aides trained in the use of behavior modification procedures. A baseline (non-intervention) period, where target responses were observed three times per day for a maximum of two hours per observation, showed smiling to be at zero frequency and crying—inarticulate sounds accompanied by tears . . . from five to 30 minutes duration—at approximately 29 episodes per week. After baseline, the patient was informed of two new contingencies: that crying would result in loss of tokens (poker chips redeemable for privileges), while smiling would result in receipt of tokens. Thereafter, the aide either presented a token to the patient if she was observed to engage in a smile ("a slight opening of the lips, an upward turn of the corners of the mouth, and an increase in the protrusion of the skin covering the cheek bones"), or when she cried he would approach and simply say "You will be fined one token for crying." Over a seven-week period, the rates for crying and smiling were practically reversed (27 smiles and two crying episodes in the final week of the treatment phase). A three-week extinction and three-week reversal phase brought crying up and smiling down (thus demonstrating the power of the contingencies). The RC contingency was then reinstated along with social (praise) and token reinforcement. Finally, the RC contingency was dropped and crying was simply ignored. The token reinforcement for smiling was discontinued but social praise was continued. A 14-month follow-up after discharge showed the patient functioning well in the community for the first time in six years.

Boudin (1972) reported the use of a response cost contract in the outpatient treatment of amphetamine abuse. His patient, a female graduate student, had been using amphetamines for three years prior to treatment. She had resorted to lying and stealing in order to obtain drugs, and was panic-stricken at the thought that she had become an addict. Although the treatment plan involved many elements including stimulus control, verbal encouragement, and aversive techniques, it also included a "stiff" response cost arrangement wherein the client established a joint bank account with her therapist which included all of her capital ($500). The client signed ten $50 checks, which needed only the therapists' signature to be valid. It was agreed that each drug use or suspected drug use would result in the loss of one check. The RC contingency was used only once during the three month contract violation. The client (who was black) was told that valid checks would be sent to the Ku Klux Klan.

Recommendations:

1. Use response-cost (RC) procedures in conjunction with positive reinforcement for appropriate and incompatible behaviors.
2. Before establishing an RC system, determine if the reinforcers potentially lost are indeed valued. They must be genuine "reinforcers" in the sense that individuals will work to earn them and will spend them on items not otherwise available.
3. Arrange the overall earnings-cost program so that items lost or forfeited cannot be easily or rapidly replaced.
4. Arrange the overall earnings-cost program in such a manner that "fines" are realistic (neither bankrupting the individual in a single trial, nor making so little dent in his savings that the loss goes unnoticed).
5. Institute the fine as soon as possible after a misbehavior.
6. For individuals who have not earned them, it may be necessary to supply reinforcers noncontingently at first. RC procedures can then be applied.
7. If RC is paired with verbal criticism, it is possible to fade out the punishment contingency and bring disruptive behavior under the verbal control of change agents (therapists, teachers, parents, aides, etc.).
8. With highly motivated clients, it is conceivable that imagined rather than actual reinforcer loss can be used as a punishment procedure (Kazdin, 1972; Weiner, 1965).

Time-Out. Rationale: Behavior reduction can be accomplished through the withdrawal of opportunities to obtain positive reinforcers. Time-out (from reinforcement), although an unpleasant outcome (Leitenberg, 1965), does not evoke the fear and avoidant tendencies that often undermine the effects of aversive control programs. Time-out has proven useful in the management of high frequency disruptive (aggressive, assaultive, destructive) or self-defeating behaviors that appear to be cued and reinforced by the actions of observers and co-performers. When it is not feasible to identify and remove all the reinforcers for deviant behavior, the person emitting the inappropriate responses may be excluded from the problem-enhancing setting. Thus, time-out is useful in classrooms and in institutional settings where it is sometimes simpler to deal with disruptive individuals than with the entire group. If an inappropriate behavior is evidenced across diverse situations, time-out contingencies must be consistently used by controlling agents in each setting (Chapman, 1962).

Illustrations: Tyler and Brown (1967) reported the successful application of a time-out program with a group of institutionalized delinquent boys, aged 13-15, whose disruptive behavior in their cottage recreation room was of serious concern to staff. After deciding on target behaviors (throwing or hitting with a pool cue, fighting around the pool table, breaking the rules of the game, and others), the investigators initiated a procedure wherein misbehavior resulted in isolation in a time-out room for 15 minutes. "There were no warnings, no discussions, no arguments, and no second chances. When an S misbehaved, he was simply taken in a very matter-of-fact way to the time-out room. Staff might explain to the point of saying 'You fouled up,' but no more" (p. 2). The 4 × 8 ft. isolation room was constructed in one corner of the cottage, permitting rapid removal and return of each youngster. Misbehaviors declined under the time-out contingency, increased during reinstatement of the original conditions, and declined once again with reintroduction of time-out.

In recent years, however, the time-out procedure has often been misrepresented and misapplied. Noting that some institutions have used the time-out concept to justify inhumane practices (such as isolation and extreme deprivation), or have permitted time-out to occasion escape from a demanding learning situation, Foxx and Shapiro (1978) developed a nonexclusionary time-out procedure. Their procedure worked as follows: all students in a classroom would wear a ribbon that signified that they were eligible for teacher-dispensed reinforcement. Whenever misbehavior was noted in a child, that child would have his ribbon removed for a specified period. No reward would be administered to any child without a ribbon. Thus, students could remain in the classroom, but in a time-out condition.

Among the potential advantages of such a procedure are its ease and rapidity of implementation, the potential for monitoring the target child during time-out, and the fact that the individual in time-out would see what he was missing by way of reward and social participation. The procedure also obviates the necessity for a special time-out room or time-out area. The major disadvantage is the potential for the individual in time-out to disrupt the environment by continued misbehavior, and to elicit attention (reinforcement) from others for so doing.

Foxx and Shapiro (1978) experimentally evaluated the effectiveness of the "time-out ribbon" procedure (actually the ribbon is a time-in signal) with a group of five severely retarded children in a special education classroom. The procedure proved to be quite powerful in controlling the misbehavior levels in the class. Misbehavior occurred 42 percent of the time prior to treatment, fell to 32 percent during a differential reinforcement period, and to an average of six percent during the time-out plus reinforcement phase.

Recommendations:

1. Use time-out (TO) in conjunction with positive reinforcement of desirable and incompatible behaviors.
2. Arrange the time-out area to be free of attractive or distracting activities. It should be small, but well ventilated. Arrange the area in which appropriate behavior is desired in as attractive a manner as possible (with reinforcing activities and objects immediately available for appropriate behavior). Absence of effects for TO are often attributable to the relatively low magnitude of payoff for correct responding.

3. The majority of successful programs with children employ TO durations of between five and 20 minutes. Long durations are undesirable because the individual is removed from opportunities to learn more adaptive responses. One should experiment with short durations of TO first and, if need be, work up to longer durations. Starting out with long durations and subsequently shortening them is not recommended (White, Nielsen, and Johnson, 1972).
4. In keeping with the TO duration requirements, the distance and travel time to the TO area should be short.
5. If possible, monitor the individual's behavior while in TO. The child who can make a "game" out of TO, will not benefit from it.
6. Try not to reinforce any behaviors (either with positive attention or with a display of anger or disappointment) while going to or returning from the TO area.
7. Use verbal and/or nonverbal signals before initiating a TO. The chain of behaviors leading up to the TO signal should include a "stop cue" which, if noticed, may come to suppress the disruptive behavior at lower magnitudes.
8. Never use TO if the situation from which the individual is being removed is primarily an unpleasant one. The individuals will simply turn TO into an escape or avoidance opportunity, and the behavior upon which TO is contingent will increase in frequency.

Overcorrection. Rationale: Overcorrection, developed by Foxx and Azrin (1972), is a form of punishment that may be of particular value when misbehaviors occur as high rates, when there are few appropriate alternative behaviors available to reinforce, and/or when there are few effective reinforcers to remove contingent upon inappropriate responding. Thus, when ignoring (extinction), DRO, response cost, or time-out measures cannot be applied, overcorrection may fill the need for a mild, educational, response-reduction procedure.

Overcorrection involves two fundamental components: restitution and positive practice. Restitution requires that, if misbehavior has led to environmental disruption, the actor responsible must repair or restore the behavior setting to a state better than it was before the disruption. If an individual has angrily hit and insulted another person in a group, the restitution would call for an apology to the injured party as well as to everyone else who was present at the time of the misbehavior. Positive practice requires repeated practice of adaptive, prosocial behaviors. Thus, the aggressor in the previous example might be required to practice complimenting or praising his associates in the group for appropriate reasons. The therapist may often be required to guide the client through the restitution and positive practice elements. Such guidance may be both educational and aversive (Harris and Ersner-Hershfield, 1978; Sulzer-Azaroff and Mayer, 1977).

Illustration: Rollings, Baumeister, and Baumeister (1977) treated the body-rocking behaviors of a profoundly retarded 35-year-old man using therapist guidance and the positive practice form of overcorrection. Commands such as "Sit back" or "Look at me" were employed in order to cue the patient to engage in responses incompatible with body-rocking. While the overcorrection procedure successfully reduced the target behavior after only seven training sessions, the investigators also noted that: (1) suppression of the target was associated with a marked increase in head-nodding behavior, (2) self-hitting behaviors became more severe during overcorrection, (3) generalization effects were not found, (4) no signs of maintenance were obtained, and (5) the patient's appropriate behaviors were tied to the nearness of the trainer (i.e., special tests revealed that the rocking increased as the therapist moved from one, to five, to ten feet away from the patient).

Recommendations:

1. Overcorrection procedures should be applied as quickly as possible after a misbehavior.
2. Be sure that the restitution and positive practice focus upon actions that are clearly beneficial to the client, rather than upon behaviors that are physically taxing or painful (or that can be interpreted as punitive).
3. Use overcorrection only with patients capable of cooperating and of understanding its educative function.
4. Minimize reinforcement available during the restitution period.
5. Use overcorrection in concert with reinforcement for appropriate behaviors.
6. Be on the lookout for changes in other inappropriate nontargeted behaviors during and subsequent to overcorrection periods.
7. Keep the overcorrection intervals as brief as possible, i.e., no longer than is needed to restore the environment. Briefer intervals mean more time for practice and increased access to reward for appropriate behavior.
8. To maximize generalization, the overcorrection procedures should be instituted in a variety of settings and by a variety of intervention agents.

Satiation and Restraint. Rationale and Illustrations: A response that is continuously emitted and reinforced over a brief time span may show a temporary decline in frequency. The individual may tire of responding, and the reinforcer will lose its power to motivate and to inform. Indeed, the requirement of continued performance may turn a once pleasant activity into an aversive one. Perhaps the most well known clinical example of satiation is provided in Ayllon's (1963) famous towel hoarding case. A hospital patient who collected towels in her room (averaging about 20) was, after a baseline period, presented with free towels on a noncontingent basis (reaching 60 a day by the third treatment week). The patient started removing the towels after she had upwards of 625 of them in her room. Following satiation treatment the patient permanently gave up towel hoarding.

Although a classic, Ayllon's is not a pure case of satiation treatment since the reinforcer was delivered noncontingently. The satiation approach to the treatment of habitual cigarette smoking, however, requires that smokers engage in the response continuously (on command) and experience the outcome until the process becomes intolerable. Schmahl, Lichtenstein, and Harris (1972) have reported that stimulus satiation combined with having to inhale either warm smoky air or mentholated air rapidly reduced smoking behavior to zero, with approximately 60 percent of the subjects still abstaining after six months.

Response reduction can also be accomplished via physical restraint. In severe or extreme cases involving dangerous or life-threatening behavior, the individual may need to be confined and physically restricted. This is a practical method which only temporarily reduces disruptive responding. However, the risks are so great that the theoretically low long-range efficiency is not important.

Recently, Favell, McGimsey, and Jones (1978) noted, in attempts to use restraint as a nonaversive punishment for self-injurious behaviors, that some clients seemed to enjoy being physically bound. These investigators successfully reduced self-injury in several retarded persons by making physical restraint contingent upon increasing periods of no self-injury. Thus, restraint, for these individuals, functioned as a positive reinforcer. This experiment nicely illustrates the importance of a functional analysis prior to the implementation of any behavior change procedure.

Maintaining Behavioral Progress

The *adaptational-learning* model outlined in this chapter is built upon the proposition that human adjustment is a fluid process, that shifts in what is considered the appropriate direction or form of behavior represent the challenge and excitement as well as the stress and upheaval of modern life. As therapists or change agents we want our interventions to have durable effects in the face of ever-changing environmental demands. Yet, we do not want to produce an improved behavior which, in time, may itself be in need of alteration. Let's briefly examine the problems of *persistence* and *obsolescence* of learning.

Persistence of Treatment Effects. The paradox of operant technology is that its power to affect change may be bought at the expense of generalization or persistence of treatment gains. Evidence is now accumulating which suggests that changes brought about in hospitals, clinics, residential facilities, or in the therapist's office often fail to extend to the other relevant behavior settings in a client's life. One reason for the failure of persistence is the dissimilarity of treatment environments from the real life settings in which clients are expected to function. Obviously, when discriminative stimuli and reinforcement contingencies change, so does behavior.

However, our knowledge about stimulus control procedures, schedule effects, and the creation of conditioned reinforcers provides some possible remedies to persistence and generalization problems, as do newer developments in the area of environmental control. Data bearing on the comparative effectiveness of the various techniques for maintenance-induction are, unfortunately, not yet available.

The following is a partial listing of suggestions for the establishment of long-term learning (maintenance) and transfer (generalization):

1. Continue behavioral assessment—without reliable information about extra-therapy behavior and changes in collateral responses, programmatic alterations or improvements cannot be instituted.
2. Reinforce desired behaviors on an intermittent schedule to prevent ready discrimination of contingencies.
3. Transfer control to common stimuli and agents in the client's natural environment by including as many of these as possible within the training environment.
4. Diversify and widen the initial training through the use of extensive examples, explanations of how and why to respond, exposure to models of correct responding, and preprogrammed exercises in generalization.
5. Teach clients to monitor their own activities and to control contingencies that affect them (see the chapters by Kanfer and Meichenbaum in this volume; also Stokes, Fowler and Baer, 1978).
6. Establish conditions that permit clients to attribute success or failure to their own efforts (rather than to fate, luck, or powerful others).
7. By instructing significant individuals in the client's natural environment, attempt to reprogram the natural contingencies (e.g., the behavior of teachers, parents, peers, employers, co-workers, etc.) in therapeutic directions.

For further discussion of issues and methods of maintenance and generalization the reader is referred to Atthowe (1973), Conway and Bucher (1976), Goldstein and Kanfer (1979), Karoly and Steffen (in press), Koegel and Rincover (1977), Marholin and Siegel (1978), O'Leary, Poulos and Devine (1972), Stokes and Baer (1977), Walker and Buckley (1972), and Wildman and Wildman (1975).

Obsolescence. The requirement of building the potential for flexibility into our training involves a recognition of the nonmechanical nature of people and of programs. Although still a controversial issue, the question of what is learned in behavioral training is being answered by some in terms of learning sets, self-regulatory skills, expectancies, problem-solving abilities, and rules of the game. Obsolescence (the long-range limiting effects) of training is certainly mitigated to the extent that recognition is given to the active role of the learner in the process of behavior change.

Recent Advances

Operant methods have grown in scope and emphasis in recent years. Durable and flexible learning, and behavior enrichment through environmental design are current concerns. Training efforts extend not only to identified clients but also to parents, peers, and paraprofessionals. A growing awareness of legal and ethical issues in behavior control has helped to humanize what was often taken to be a cold and calculated Orwellian world view among operant practitioners. A few of these new directions will be briefly reviewed to give the reader a fuller appreciation of the vitality of contemporary behavioral psychology.

Environmental Design. Despite an avowedly environmentalistic philosophy, operant investigators have only recently concerned themselves with systematic design and/or alteration of the physical and material environment. Following the pioneering work of Roger Barker and his associates (Barker and Wright, 1955), Todd Risley and his colleagues at the Lawrence Day Care Program Infant and Toddler Centers in Kansas have developed an open environment model based upon the belief that "the arrangement of the physical environment should be one of the first considerations when planning a program of providing care for dependent persons" (Twardosz, Cataldo and Risley, 1974, p. 530). Among the contributions of the "living environments group" are more efficient ways of assigning staff supervisory responsibilities, the development of interior designs that facilitate adult-child and child-child interaction, and the discovery of innovative ways to use physical space to facilitate learning and reduce disruptive behavior in youngsters (see Risley, 1977). The design of a behaviorally-oriented adult therapy center has recently been described by Kanfer, Mai, Oberberger and Brengelmann (1978). In general, the thrust of ecological or community-oriented behaviorists is to supplement a person-oriented and technique-centered approach with an environment-centered view of intervention and prevention.

A second major characteristic of the ecological view is a concern for the intrapersonal and systems effects of behavioral interventions. Investigators have asked how the changes in one set of behaviors influence related responses and the larger network of interrelationships. Willems (1977) has cautioned that the proper use of behavioral technology requires an anticipation of long-range outcomes, unintended side effects, and subtle interdependencies between responses and among micro- and macroelements. For a more thorough introduction to ecological perspectives the reader is referred to Rogers-Warren and Warren (1977), Holland (1978), and Krasner (in press).

Social Problems and Social Validation. Extensions of the operant focus not only touch upon the "how" of behavioral intervention, but on the "what" and "why" as well. Among the new targets of behavioral clinicians are pollution and litter control (Kohlenberg and Phillips, 1973), energy conservation (Palmer, Lloyd and Lloyd, 1977; Seaver and Patterson, 1976), and racial integration (Hauserman, Walen and Behling, 1973).

It has recently become evident that criteria for evaluating the success of behavioral interventions have widened (Kazdin, 1978). In addition to change or demonstrations of control, exponents of behavioral technology have been called upon to establish: (1) the social significance of behavioral goals; (2) the social appropriateness of the means used to achieve these goals; and (3) the social importance of the effects of intervention (including consumer satisfaction and side effects). Judgments such as these are referred to as *social validity* (Wolf, 1978). Wolf noted that a:

> consensus seems to be developing. It seems that if we aspire to social importance then we must develop systems that allow our consumers to provide us feedback about how our applications relate to their values, to their reinforcers. . . . Our use of subjective measures . . . is an attempt to assess the dimensions of complex reinforcers in socially acceptable and practical ways (p. 213).

SUMMARY

This chapter has provided a broad overview of the applied science of operant conditioning, known as the experimental analysis of behavior. The defining characteristics of this approach include: (1) a focus on precise definition and measurement of observable behaviors; (2) the functional analysis of environmental antecedents and consequences that control maladaptive responding; (3) the use of principles derived from experimental studies of learning in the design of treatment interventions; and (4) the continuous evaluation of behavior change.

But it is not just technology that sets an operant approach apart from the traditional insight-oriented systems of psychotherapy. The techniques described here for establishing new behaviors, accelerating personally and interpersonally desirable behaviors, decelerating maladaptive modes of responding, and maintaining treatment-induced learning are all applied in the context of an objective and nonjudgmental view of human action. A behavior is not selected for change because it is unconventional, contrary to someone's view of human nature, or listed in a catalogue of symptoms. Rather, when the relationship between an individual's behavior, or pattern of behaviors, and the effective environment is reliably disruptive of that individual's pursuit of personal objectives, his abiltiy to adjust to his life circumstances, or his sense of comfort, satisfaction, or freedom *and* when the behavioral clinician is technically and ethically able to intervene, then the two will embark jointly on a venture in behavior modification. In the case of behavior modification with problem children, the negotiating client may be the parents or the teacher; but their behavior change objective must, in fact, be in the adaptive interests of the child.

REFERENCES

Atthowe, J.M. Behavior innovation and persistence. *American Psychologist*, 1973, *28*, 34-41.

Ayllon, T. Intensive treatment of psychotic behavior by stimulus satiation and food reinforcement. *Behaviour Research and Therapy*, 1963, *1*, 53-61.

Ayllon, T. and Azrin, N.H. *The token economy: A motivational system for therapy and rehabilitation*. New York: Appleton-Century-Crofts, 1968.

Ayllon, T. and Michael, J. The psychiatric nurse as a behavioral engineer. *Journal of the Experimental Analysis of Behavior*, 1959, *2*, 323-334.

Azrin, N.H., Naster, B.J., and Jones, R. Reciprocity counseling: A rapid learning-based procedure for marital counseling. *Behaviour Research and Therapy*, 1973,*11*, 365-382.

Baer, D.M., Wolf, M.M., and Risley, T.R. Some current dimensions of applied behavior analysis. *Journal of Applied Behavior Analysis*, 1968, *1*, 91-97.

Barker, R.G. and Wright, H.F. *Midwest and its children*. New York: Harper and Row, 1955.

Barlow, D.H. and Agras, W.S. Fading to increase heterosexual responsiveness in homosexuals. *Journals of Applied Behavior Analysis*, 1973, *6*, 355-366.

Bijou, S.W. and Baer, D.M. *Behavior analysis of child development*. Englewood Cliffs, New Jersey: Prentice-Hall, 1978.

Blackwood, R.O. *Operant control of behavior*. Akron, Ohio: Exordium Press, 1971.

Boudin, H.M. Contingency contracting as a therapeutic tool in the deceleration of amphetamine use. *Behavior Therapy*, 1972, *3*, 604-608.

Butterfield, W.H. Electric shock safety factors when used for the aversive conditioning of humans. *Behavior Therapy*, 1975, *6*, 98-110.

Chapman, R.W. School suspension as therapy. *Personnel and Guidance Journal*, 1962, *40*, 731-732.

Conway, J.B. and Bucher, B.D. Transfer and maintenance of behavior change in children: A review and suggestions. In E.J. Mash, L.A. Hamerlynck, and L.C. Handy (Eds.), *Behavior modification and families*. New York: Brunner/Mazel, 1976, pp. 119-159.

Corte, H.E., Wolf, M.M., and Locke, B.J. A comparison of procedures for eliminating self-injurious behavior of retarded adolescents. *Journal of Applied Behavior Analysis*, 1971, *4*, 201-213.

Deese, J., and Hulse, S.H. *The psychology of learning*. New York: McGraw-Hill, 1967.

Doleys, D.M., Ciminero, A.R., Wallach, E.S., and Davidson, R.S. Responding by alcoholics during aversive conditioning. *Behavior Modification*, 1977, *1*, 205-220.

Favell, J.E., McGimsey, J.F., and Jones, M.L. The use of physical restraints in the treatment of self-injury and as positive reinforcement. *Journal of Applied Behavior Analysis*, 1978, *11*, 225-241.

Ferster, C.B., and Skinner, B.F. *Schedules of reinforcement*. New York: Appleton-Century-Crofts, 1957.

Findley, J.D. An experimental outline for building and exploring multi-operant behavior repertoires. *Journal of the Experimental Analysis of Behavior*, 1962, *5*, 113-166.

Foxx, R.M., and Azrin, N.H. Restitution: A method of eliminating aggressive-disruptive behavior of retarded and brain-damaged patients. *Behaviour Research and Therapy*, 1972, *10*, 15-27.

Foxx, R.M., and Shapiro, S.T. The timeout ribbon; a non-exclusionary timeout procedure. *Journal of Applied Behavior Analysis*, 1978, *11*, 125-136.

Gelfand, D.M., and Hartmann, D.P. *Child behavior: Analysis and therapy*. New York: Pergamon, 1975.

Goetz, E.M. and Baer, D.M. Social control of form diversity and the emergence of new forms in children's blockbuilding. *Journal of Applied Behavior Analysis*, 1973, *6*, 209-217.

Goldstein, A.P., and Kanfer, F.H. (Eds.), *Maximizing treatment gains: Transfer-enhancement in psychotherapy*. New York: Academic Press, 1979.

Harris, S.L., and Ersner-Hershfield, R. Behavioral suppression of seriously disruptive behavior in psychotic and retarded patients: A review of punishment and its alternatives. *Psychological Bulletin*, 1978, *85*, 1352-1375.

Hauserman, N., Walen, S.R., and Behling, M. Reinforced racial integration in the first grade: A study in generalization. *Journal of Applied Behavior Analysis*, 1973, *6*, 193-200.

Hilgard, E.R., and Bower, G.H. *Theories of learning*. New York: Appleton-Century-Crofts, 1966.

Holland, J.G. Behaviorism: Part of the problem or part of the solution. *Journal of Applied Behavior Analysis*, 1978, *11*, 163-174.

Kanfer, F.H., Mai, N., Oberberger, H., and Brengelmann, J.C. Planning an institution for behavior therapy: A project report. *Behavioural Analysis and Modification*, 1978, *2*, 146-162.

Karoly, P., and Steffen, J.J. (Eds.), *Improving the Long-Term Effects of Psychotherapy*. New York: Gardner Press, 1979.

Kazdin, A.E. Response cost: The removal of conditioned reinforcers for therapeutic change. *Behavior Therapy*, 1972, *3*, 533-546.

——— *Behavior modification in applied settings*. Homewood, Illinois: Dorsey Press, 1975.

——— *History of behavior modification: Experimental foundations of contemporary research*. Baltimore, Maryland: University Park Press, 1978.

Keller, F.S., and Schoenfeld, W.N. *Principles of psychology: A systematic text in the science of behavior*. New York: Appleton-Century-Crofts, 1950.

Koegel, R.L., and Rincover, A. Research on the difference between generalization and maintenace in extra-therapy responding. *Journal of Applied Behavior Analysis*, 1977, *10*, 1-12.

Kohlenberg, R., and Phillips, T. Reinforcement and rate of litter depositing. *Journal of Applied Behavior Analysis*, 1973, *6*, 391-396.

Krasner, L. (Ed.). *Environmental design and human behavior: A handbook of theory and application*. New York: Pergamon, in press.

Leitenberg, H. Is time-out from positive reinforcement an aversive event? A review of experimental evidence. *Psychological Bulletin*, 1965, *64*, 428-441.

Levy, L.H. *Conceptions of personality*. New York: Random House, 1970.

Lovaas, O.I. *The autistic child*. New York: Irvington, 1977.

Marholin, D., and Siegel, L.J. Beyond the law of effect: Programming for the maintenance of behavior change. In D. Marholin (Ed.), *Child behavior therapy*. New York: Gardner Press, 1978.

Marholin, D., and Steinman, W.M. Stimulus control in the classroom as a function of the behavior reinforced. *Journal of Applied Behavior Analysis*, 1977, *10*, 465-478.

McClannahan, L.E., and Risley, T.R. Design of living environments for nursing-home residents: Increasing participation in recreation activities. *Journal of Applied Behavior Analysis*, 1975, *8*, 261-268.

Millenson, J.R. *Principles of behavioral analysis*. New York: Macmillan, 1967.

O'Leary, K.D., and O'Leary, S.G. (Eds.), *Classroom management: The successful use of behavior modification* (2nd Edition). New York: Pergamon Press, 1977.

O'Leary, K.D., Poulos, R.W., and Devine, V.T. Tangible reinforcers: Bonuses or bribes? *Journal of Consulting and Clinical Psychology*, 1972, *38*, 1-8.

Palmer, M.H., Lloyd, M.E., and Lloyd, K.E. An experimental analysis of electricity conservation procedures. *Journal of Applied Behavior Analysis*, 1977, *10*, 665-671.

Penick, S.B., Filion, R., Fox, S., and Stunkard, A. Behavior modification in the treatment of obesity. *Psychosomatic Medicine*, 1971, *33*, 49-55.

Rachlin, H. *Introduction to modern behaviorism*. San Francisco, California: Freeman, 1970.

Reese, E.P. *The analysis of human operant behavior*. Dubuque, Iowa: Brown, 1966.

Reisinger, J.J. The treatment of "anxiety-depression" via positive reinforcement and response cost. *Journal of Applied Behavior Analysis*, 1972, *5*, 125-130.

Reynolds, G.S. *A primer of operant conditioning*. Glenview, Illinois: Scott, Foresman, 1968.

Risley, T.R. The ecology of applied behavior and analysis. In A. Rogers-Warren and S.F. Warren (Eds.), *Ecological perspectives in behavior analysis*. Baltimore, Maryland: University Park Press, 1977, pp. 149-163.

Rogers-Warren, A., and Warren, S.F. (Eds.) *Ecological perspectives in behavior analysis*. Baltimore Maryland: University Park Press, 1977.

Rollings, J.P., Baumeister, A.A., and Baumeister, A.A. The use of overcorrection procedures to eliminate the stereotyped behaviors of retarded individuals. *Behavior Modification*, 1977, *1*, 29-46.

Schmahl, D.P., Lichtenstein, E., and Harris, D.E. Successful treatment of habitual smokers with warm, smoky air and rapid smoking. *Journal of Consulting and Clinical Psychology*, 1972, *38*, 105-111.

Schutte, R.C., and Hopkins, B.L. The effects of teacher attention on following instructions in a kindergarten class. *Journal of Applied Behavior Analysis*, 1970, *3*, 117-122.

Schwartz, B. *Psychology of learning and behavior*. New York: Norton, 1978.

Seaver, W.B., and Patterson, A.H. Decreasing fuel-oil consumption through feedback and social commendation. *Journal of Applied Behavior Analysis*, 1976, *9*, 147-152.

Skinner, B.F. Two types of conditioned reflex: A reply to Konorski and Miller. *Journal of General Psychology*, 1937, *16*, 272-279.

Skinner, B.F. *The behavior of organisms: An experimental analysis*. New York: Appleton-Century-Crofts, 1938.

Stokes, T.F., and Baer, D.M. An implicit technology of generalization. *Journal of Applied Behavior Analysis*, 1977, *10*, 349-367.

Stokes, T.F., Fowler, S.A., and Baer, D.M. Training preschool children to recruit natural communities of reinforcement. *Journal of Applied Behavior Analysis*, 1978, *11*, 285-303.

Stuart, R.B., and Davis, B. *Slim chance in a fat world*. Champaign, Illinois: Research Press, 1972.

Sulzer-Azaroff, B., and Mayer, G.R. *Applying behavior-analysis procedures with children and youth*. New York: Holt, Rinehart and Winston, 1977.

Thorndike, E.L. Animal intelligence: An experimental study of associative processes in animals. *Psychological Monographs*, 1898, *2*, (No. 2).

Twardosz, S., Cataldo, M.F., and Risley, T.R. Open environment design for infant and toddler day care. *Journal of Applied Behavior Analysis*, 1974, *7*, 529-546.

Tyler, V.O., and Brown, G.D. The use of swift, brief isolation as a group control device for institutionalized delinquents. *Behaviour Research and Therapy*, 1967, *5*, 1-9.

Walker, H.M., and Buckley, N.K. Programming generalization and maintenance of treatment effects across time and across settings. *Journal of Applied Behavior Analysis*, 1972, *5*, 209, 224.

Ward, M.H., and Baker, B.L. Reinforcement therapy in the classroom. *Journal of Applied Behavior Analysis*, 1967, *1*, 323-328.

Watson, L.S. *Child behavior modification: A manual for teachers, nurses, and parents*. New York: Pergamon Press, 1973.

Weiner, H. Real and imagined cost effects upon human fixed-interval responding. *Psychological Reports*, 1965, *17*, 659-662.

White, G.D., Nielsen, G., and Johnson, S.M. Time-out duration and the suppression of deviant behavior in children. *Journal of Applied Behavior Analysis*, 1972, *5*, 111-120.

Wildman, R.W. II, and Wildman, R.W. The generalization of behavior modification procedures: A review—with special emphasis on classroom applications. *Psychology in the Schools*, 1975, *12*, 432-448.

Willems, E.P. Steps toward an ecobehavioral technology. In A. Rogers-Warren and S.F. Warren (Eds.), *Ecological perspectives in behavior analysis*. Baltimore, Maryland: University Park Press, 1977, pp. 39-61.

Williams, C.D. The elimination of tantrum behavior by extinction procedures: A case report. *Journal of Abnormal and Social Psychology*, 1959, *59*, 269.

Williams, J.L. *Operant learning: Procedures for changing behavior*. Monterey, California: Brooks/Cole, 1973.

Wilson, G.T., Leaf, R.C., and Nathan, P.E. The aversive control of excessive alcohol consumption by chronic alcoholics in the laboratory setting. *Journal of Applied Behavior Analysis*, 1975, *8*, 13-26.

Wolf, M.M. Social validity: The case for subjective measurement, or how applied behavior analysis is finding its heart. *Journal of Applied Behavior Analysis*, 1978, *11*, 203-214.

8
Fear Reduction Methods
Richard J. Morris[1]

Much of the effort of psychotherapists is directed toward helping people overcome their fears of situations, other people, animals, and/or objects. Fear is a very strong emotion and is associated with many signs of anxiety—for example, rapid pulse rate and a pounding heart, very tense muscles, perspiring in a room of average temperature and humidity, "butterflies" in the stomach, irritability, feelings of panic, inability to concentrate, dizziness and headaches. When someone experiences fear in a situation where there is no obvious external danger, the fear is irrational and is called a *phobia*. Table 8.1 lists a number of common phobias that people experience. When a person begins to avoid a nondangerous feared situation—even though he realizes that such behavior is foolish or irrational—the fear then becomes a *phobic reaction*.

Table 8.1. Selected Phobias Which People Experience.

Technical Name	Fear
Acrophobia	Heights
Agoraphobia	Open places
Aichmophobia	Sharp and pointed objects
Aquaphobia	Going into water
Claustrophobia	Enclosed places
Menophobia	Being alone
Nyctophobia	Darkness
Ochlophobia	Crowds
Pyrophobia	Fires
Xenophobia	Strangers
Zoophobia	Animals

Phobic reactions are among the most common forms of maladaptive behaviors in people. They occur in children and adults. Some phobias, because of their high incidence, are considered "normal" in children, while others are viewed as "normal" in adults. For example, fear of dogs and other animals, the dark, ghosts, strangers, and being alone are among the more common childhood phobias; while fear of heights, public speaking, spiders and other bugs, and snakes frequently occur in adults. Some irrational fears are fleeting while others persist over a long time.

When fears become intolerable to an individual, professional help is sought. Over the past 75 years, various procedures have been used in the treatment of fears. Psychoanalysis, client-centered therapy, and other forms of verbal therapy have been utilized, as well as drugs, hypnosis and electroconvulsive shock treatment, and certain forms of brain surgery (e.g., leucotomy). In general, these methods have been found to be only moderately successful.

Some therapy procedures, however, have been found to be much more effective. These procedures are based on the learning theory positions of, for example, Skinner (1938, 1953), Pavlov (1927), Hull (1943), Mowrer (1950), and Bandura (1969, 1977; Bandura and Walters, 1963). Though the specifics of each therapy method differ, they do share certain general underlying assumptions: (1) phobias and the avoidance reactions that accompany them are learned by the individual, (2) phobias do not occur as a result of innate factors, and (3) phobias are not the result of an underlying psychic or psychological disturbance.[2] In the present chapter, we will discuss three therapy procedures that have been found to be effective in the treatment of phobic reactions and fears: *systematic desensitization*, *assertive training*, and *implosive therapy*. Variations of these methods will also be discussed. Each method will be described in detail and case examples will be presented that demonstrate their use.

SYSTEMATIC DESENSITIZATION

Systematic desensitization was developed in the early 1950s by Joseph Wolpe, a psychiatrist. The basic assumption of this technique is that a fear response (for example, a fear response to heights) is learned or conditioned and can be inhibited by substituting an activity that is antagonistic to the fear response. The response that is most typically inhibited by this treatment process is anxiety, and the response frequently substituted for the anxiety is relaxation and calmness. For example, if a person has a fear of heights and feels very anxious and uncomfortable each time he enters an office building and takes an elevator higher than the third floor, we would help him inhibit the anxiety in this situation by teaching the person to relax and feel calm. Thus we would desensitize the person or countercondition his fear of heights.

Desensitization is accomplished by exposing an individual, in small, graduated steps, to the feared situation while the person is performing the activity that is antagonistic to anxiety. The gradual exposure to the fear can take place either in the person's fantasy—where he is asked to imagine being in various fear-related situations—or it can occur in real life. Wolpe termed the principle that underlies the desensitization process *reciprocal inhibition*. He described this principle in the following way: "If a response inhibitory to anxiety can be made to occur in the presence of anxiety-evoking stimuli, it will weaken the connection between these stimuli and the anxiety responses" (p. 562).

The Initial Interview

Before initiating the desensitization procedure, or any of the other fear reduction methods discussed in this chapter, the therapist must first identify the client's fear as well as the circumstances under which the fear occurs. This is not an easy assignment. The interview must be conducted within a therapeutic atmosphere of respect for the client, sensitivity to and understanding of the client's difficulties, and genuine concern for the client's overall well-being. The therapist has to probe thoroughly into the client's life history to make sure the therapist and the client have a clear understanding of all aspects of the client's fear and of those factors that have contributed (and are contributing) to the fear. The goal of the interview, however, is not to identify the causal factor that is responsible for the client's fear. Therapists who use these fear reduction methods generally accept the premise that people's learning histories are very complex, and to assume that a time-limited retrospective account of one's past will uncover the factor or factors that caused the fear is a fruitless endeavor. The best that this interview can be expected to accomplish is to provide the therapist with a comprehensive picture of who the client is, what kind of environment the client comes from, and how the client came to be what he is today. The interview will also help the therapist support or refute various hypotheses about the client's problem, specify the goals of therapy, determine which fear reduction method is most appropriate for the client, and assess whether the treatment objectives can be accomplished within the limitations set by the client and his life situation (Kanfer and Grimm, 1977). It is therefore quite likely that the initial interview will last over a number of sessions. Though there is neither a standardized approach nor a standard set of questions used in the initial interview, most therapists explore the following topic areas with clients.

Identification of the Target Behavior. This involves not only helping the client identify what is specifically troubling him but also trying to determine the types of situations and circumstances in which the fear occurs. In addition, the therapist asks the client how long he has had the fear, whether it has gotten better or worse with the passage of time, and the types of situations in which it seems to be better or worse than "usual." It is also desirable to ask the client about his thoughts and feelings concerning the fear.

General Background Information. Here, discussion is centered around the date and place of the client's birth, number and age of siblings, where the client stands in the family birth order, and the types of interactions the client has had with siblings while growing up. Inquiry is also made into which of the children was favored in the family, as well as how the client was treated by each of the parents relative to the other children. The therapist should also discuss other aspects regarding the parents, e.g., the client's perception of each of the parents during childhood and adolescence, and how the client was punished and by whom, characteristics that were liked and /or disliked in each parent. It is also important to know the manner in which the parents interacted with each other and to determine what type of role models they provided for the client. For example, did they generally like one another; did they fight, and, if so, was it usually in front of the children; did they ever talk about divorce or separation; and did one parent try to use one or all of the children against the other parent?

For many clients, a favorite aunt, uncle, grandparent, neighbor, or friend may have been as important as, or more important than, their parents during childhood. These "significant others" should also be discussed to determine the unique contribution of such people in the client's life.

One additional aspect of the individual's background involves the fears that were experienced during childhood. The therapist should not only determine the particular childhood fears but also when they occurred, when they ended, and whether they were still present.

School and Job. For this category, inquiry should be made into the client's likes and dislikes in elementary and high school and college, the best and least-liked subjects, what the client did after school, the client's extracurricular activities, and so forth. Moreover, the therapist should discuss the client's friendships in and out of school, e.g., whether the client had any close friends and if these friendships had been maintained over the years.

The client's work experience should also be brought into this discussion—the therapist asking how far he went in school and, if appropriate, why he did not continue. Particular attention should be paid to the client's work history, his likes and dislikes about the job, ability to advance, and whether the present job is consistent with the client's own goals and desires.

Dating and Marriage. Here, the therapist explores the client's dating pattern during the teenage and adult years. In addition, the client's sexual experiences before and after marriage are discussed. Difficulties in the marriage are also discussed, as well as relationships with in-laws and children, and the environment in which the client lives. Since these are very sensitive topics for some people, they should be explored within a framework of understanding and acceptance of the client.

A summary of a suggested guide for the initial interview is presented in Table 8.2. As the reader has no doubt already determined, the information gained in the initial interview is quite extensive. Some therapists use tape recorders to record this information, while others take notes on the client's answers. Still others have asked their clients to fill out a standard background information packet that contains many of the same types of questions as those outlined in Table 8.2.

Table 8.2 Suggested Guide For The Conduct Of The Initial Interview[3]

A. *What is the problem behavior? . . . What seems to be troubling you?*
   1. How long have you had this difficulty?
   2. When does this fear or thought usually come into your mind? When does this problem seem to occur the most? In what types of situations or circumstances does the problem occur? Are there any reasons you can think of for its occurrence?
   3. Has the problem been the same all along—or has it gotten better or worse?
      (a) Is there any situation that you can associate with it getting better or worse?

B. *General Background*
   1. When born? Where?
   2. How many brothers and sisters do you have?
      (a) Where are you in the birth order?
      (b) How much older is your eldest or youngest same sex sibling?
      (c) How did (do) you get along with him (her)?
   3. Parents—are they still alive? When did each die?

C. *Father*
   1. What kind of person was (is) he—especially during your childhood?
   2. Was he interested in you? Were you interested in what he had to say?
   3. Did he ever punish you?
   4. Did he play favorites with the children? How did you feel about this?

D. *Mother*
   Same questions asked about the father

E. *Parents*
   1. Did they like each other? Did they like you?
   2. Did they behave toward you as though they liked you?
   3. Did they get along together?
      (a) Fight much? . . . Divorce threats? etc.
      (b) Did they fight in front of children or in privacy?

F. *Significant others*
   1. Were there any other adults who played an important part in your life?
   2. Describe what they were like and how they played an important role in your life.

G. *Fears during childhood*
   1. Any particular fears?
   2. When did they occur?
   3. Do you still have some of these? When did they stop?

H. *School*
   1. Like school?
   2. Best liked subjects? Worse liked subjects?
   3. Sports.—Did you participate in them or watch them?
      (a) How were you in them?
   4. Friends
      (a) Did you make any friends at school (college)?
      (b) Any close ones?
      (c) Do you maintain any of those friendships today?
      (d) Anyone at school (college) that you were afraid of? Was the person the same sex as you? Were you afraid of any teachers? Why?
      (e) How far did you go in school? Why did you stop your education?
   5. What did you do after you stopped school?

Table 8.2. Suggested Guide For The Conduct Of The Initial Interview
(Continued)

I. *Job*
1. What kind of work do you do?
2. Do you like your job? What do you like the best/least about your job?
3. Any thoughts about quitting?
4. What other types of jobs have you had? Why did you leave them?
5. If client is a housewife, ask: How do you like being a housewife?
    What do you specifically like about it?
    What don't you specifically like about it?
    Was it your choice to be a housewife?
    Would you like to be doing something else? What?

J. *Sex*
1. At what age did you begin to have any kind of sexual feelings?
    (a) If client has problem in answering, ask: Well, roughly, were you 10, 15, 20 . . . more or less?
    (b) or go to the following: Before 10? . . . Before 15? . . . Before 20? . . .
2. In what kind of situation did you have your first sexual feelings?
    For example, was it out with boys? . . . (girls?) . . . At a movie house? or what?
3. At this stage, did you date several boys (girls) or just one at a time?
    (a) Did you go to parties?
    (b) What was the pattern of your dating? . . . Always movies? . . . Dinners?
4. When did you especially become interested in anybody?
5. Was there anyone else whom you became interested in?
6. When did you become really serious? (implying steady dating, become engaged, etc.) or, have you ever become serious with anyone?
    (a) What did you like about him (her)?
7. Have you ever petted (made-out) with anyone? Did you ever masturbate? Any feelings of guilt or fear about doing (not doing) either of these?
8. Have you ever had intercourse? Have you ever wanted to? What stopped you?
9. (If married, ask: Did you ever have intercourse before you were married?)

K. *Marriage*
1. When did you meet your husband (wife)?
    (a) What did you like about him (her)?
2. When did you feel that you were ready to marry him (her)?
3. Was he (she) interested in marrying you?
4. Since (or while) you were married, did you ever become interested in other men (women)?
5. Is (was) your marriage satisfying? What about it makes it satisfying? What about it doesn't make it satisfying? In what way would you like to change your marriage?
6. If divorced and remarried, how about with your second husband (wife)? Is this marriage satisfying?
    (a) How is he (she) different from your first husband (wife)?
    (b) How soon after the divorce did you remarry?
    (c) Was he (she) married before?

L. *Sex and Marriage*
1. How is the sexual side of your marriage (dating)? How about the sexual side of your second marriage?
2. Do you have orgasms?
    (a) How often?

Table 8.2. Suggested Guide For The Conduct Of The Initial Interview (Continued)

3. Are you happy with your marriage (the person you are dating)?
   (a) Any complaints?
4. Do the two of you fight with each other? That is, are there arguments?
   (a) What do you usually fight about?
   (b) How long do they usually last?
   (c) How are your fights usually resolved?
5. Any plans for marriage (thoughts of divorce)?

M. *Children*
   1. How many children do you have? (Do you plan to have children? How many?)
   2. Do you like all of your children? Any favorites?
      (a) Are they all well?
   3. How old is each?
   4. Were they each planned?

N. *Environment*
1. Do you like where you are now living?
2. Anything that you are not satisfied with?
3. What's your religion?
   (a) Is it important to you? In what way?
   (b) How religious are you? . . . not at all, mildly, moderately, or extremely?
   (c) Do you spend a lot of time in church activities?

An excerpt from part of the first session of an initial interview with a 35-year-old woman who had been recently divorced illustrates the manner in which the interview is conducted.[4]

Therapist: . . . What is the difficulty that you are having?

Client: I can't fly in airplanes or go up in elevators . . . at least not higher than the third floor, though I am still nervous even then.

Therapist: Let's talk about the airplane difficulty first. What about flying makes you feel uncomfortable?

Client: Well, watching a plane take off is fearful, though as a child I did take lessons in flying and was not afraid. (*Pause*) It's the feeling of being suspended in air and immobile, and of being trapped and feeling that I can't get out.

Therapist: When do you remember this fear beginning?

Client: It started about 10 years ago. My husband had to fly as part of his job with his company, and I would go with him on a number of occasions. Then the fear began getting worse as I would fly more, and about five years ago I began having difficulty looking down [out the window]. Now I can't look down at all or even out the window—even if I got up enough nerve to fly in a plane.

Therapist: Can you think of any situation regarding flying that doesn't make you feel uneasy?

Client: Yes (*laughs*), if I don't think about it, it doesn't bother me.

Therapist: Let's be a little more specific. If we could rate your level of fear about airplanes on a 10 point scale, what about flying would be most anxiety provoking to you; that is, a 10 for you?

Client: Flying over the ocean.

Therapist: What would be a zero?

Client: . . . Being at the airport to pick someone up.

Therapist: What would be a five?

Client: The plane taking off.

Therapist: So, your fear is related to all aspects of you actually flying in a plane. What about seeing a plane on television, or in a movie, for example, seeing one in the air?

Client: That bothers me, too . . . especially watching a movie of a plane which was filmed from another plane, and especially when the plane banks.

Therapist: What number would this be on the rating scale?

Client: A five or six.

Therapist: Are there any reasons that you can think of, or ideas that you might have, concerning the development of your fear?

Client: Not really, except that around the time my nervousness began my husband was seeing another woman, and sometime during that period the fear developed . . . I guess I was feeling very threatened that we would break up.

Therapist: What was your relationship with your husband like during this time.

Client: Very poor . . . a lot of fighting and yelling.

Therapist: Any talk of divorce at that time?

Client: No, not really. I guess we both knew that the marriage was shaky, but that we would stay together at least until the children got older.

Therapist: And what about your fear of elevators. When did it begin?

Client: (*Pause*). I think it goes back almost 20 years ago. I remember being in a tall building in Chicago . . . don't remember why . . . and getting a feeling of fright in an express elevator. But I guess you can say I became really scared about five years ago. And, it became very bad three years ago, right after I took an express elevator to the 20th floor of the Acme building and threw-up as I came out after feeling so nervous and nauseous while going up.

Therapist: Is there anything about riding in an elevator or about elevators in general that doesn't make you feel uncomfortable?

Client: Walking past an elevator with someone and knowing that I don't have to go in.

Therapist: What about going past it, and you're by yourself?

Client: It bothers me a bit. It's at the point now where just walking by one by myself makes me feel uncomfortable.

Therapist: How much . . . using for a moment our 10 point rating scale?

Client: About one.

Therapist: What would be zero?

Client: Walking past it with someone and knowing I don't have to take it.

Therapist: What would be a 10?

Client: (*Laughs and then a pause*). Being stuck in the elevator and alone by myself.

Therapist: Any thoughts about what events contributed to this fear?

Client: None. I can't figure it out, unless it's related to my airplane fear. But I don't know how.

Therapist: Let's hold on that for a bit and talk a little more about your background. Where were you born and in what year?

Client: In Chicago . . .

At the end of the first or second session, the therapist often gives the client some questionnaires to fill out at home for the next session. They are used to help the therapist gain additional information about the client which was or could have been missed during the initial interview. In addition, it is a good idea for the therapist to ask the client to write out a paragraph or two about his fear or fears—describing each of them and any reasons why the clients feels they occur, as well as any thoughts about them. An example of this write-up is presented below:

My biggest fear is of choking to death. Also, I have a fear of choking for my children and husband. I get very nervous when my family are eating. I find myself not being able to eat when I am sitting at the same table. I also fear being sick or dying [*sic*] and leaving my family all alone. I try very hard not to let on to my family how I feel or how sick I really am, at times. I don't like people worrying about me and keep asking how I feel. I also have the fear of being alone or not wanted by anyone.

The three most commonly used questionnaires are presented in the Appendixes at the back of this chapter. They are the following:

The Fear Survey Schedule. This is a five-point rating scale that asks the client to rate the amount of fear or discomfort caused by each of the things and events listed in the questionnaire from "Not At All" to "Very Much."

The Willoughby Questionnaire. This questionnaire is also a five-point rating scale. It contains questions about how the client reacts in various situations. The client is to respond with an answer ranging from "Never," "Not At All," "No," to "Practically Always," "Entirely."

The Bernreuter Self-Sufficiency Inventory. The Bernreuter lists a number of questions regarding self-sufficiency. The client is asked to circle "Yes" if the question applies to him, "No" if it does not apply to him, or to circle the question mark ? if he is not sure whether it applies to him.

The information gained from the interview and questionnaires should provide the therapist with a thorough analysis and understanding of: (1) the client's life situation; (2) the circumstances and situations under which the client's fear occurs; and (3) the relative intensity in various situations of the feelings associated with the fear—and the degree to which the client will actively avoid the feared situation. The general assumption is that a person's fear is learned and that it can be unlearned by applying procedures based on theories of learning.

The therapist must remember, however, that in an interview the client is also assessing the therapist. The client is concerned with whether the therapist understands the nature of his problem, whether the therapist is concerned with the client's welfare, whether the client feels comfortable talking with the therapist, and so forth. The interview, therefore, should not be so mechanical and matter-of-fact that the client as a person is disregarded. The therapist should take care that the amount of detailed information gained from the interview not be obtained at the expense of the client's comfort. This is where the therapeutic relationship and rapport with the client are important. The therapist may even want to anticipate some of the client's concerns by informing the client that some of their discussions will involve detailed questioning, explaining that details will provide the therapist with a thorough understanding of the client's problem which is necessary for successful therapy (Goldfried and Davison, 1976).

Specific questions are asked and extensive discussion occurs in the interview because the goal of therapy is very specific, namely, the reduction of the person's fear. As such, it is important to learn as much about the nature of the problem and the circumstances under which it occurs as is reasonably possible. No attempt is made in therapy to reorganize the client's personality, nor is there any general goal of helping the client achieve a higher level of emotional and psychological functioning. The only goal is to reduce the client's fear or phobic reaction, using a procedure best suited for the client, to a point where he can carry on daily activities without being bothered by the fear.

If the therapist believes it is possible that the client is suffering from a physical disorder that could be causing the problem or that could interfere with treatment, the client should be referred to a physician for a thorough examination before proceeding further.

THE DESENSITIZATION PROCEDURE

After obtaining all of the relevant information about the client, the therapist then decides on the treatment procedure and discusses with the client what will take place next. If systematic desensitization is used, the therapist briefly explains the rationale behind the treatment procedure, and describes the various stages in the treatment process. For example, the therapist might say the following:

> The emotional reactions that you experience are a result of your previous experiences with people and situations; these reactions oftentimes lead to feelings of anxiety or tenseness which are really inappropriate. Since perceptions of situations occur within ourselves, it is possible to work with your reactions right here in the office by having you . . . [imagine] or visualize those situations. (Paul, 1966, p. 116.)

The therapist would then mention that a technique called systematic desensitization is going to be used with the client, and that it consists of two primary stages.

> The first stage consists of relaxation training where I am going to teach you how to become very relaxed—more relaxed than you have probably felt in a very long time. Once you have learned to relax, we will then use this relaxed state to counter the anxiety and tenseness that you feel whenever you are in the feared situation(s). We will do this by having you imagine—while you are still very relaxed—a series of progressively more tension-provoking scenes which you and I will develop . . . and which are directly related to your fear. We will thus countercondition your fear or desensitize your tenseness to the feared situation(s).
>
> This procedure has been found to be very effective in the treatment of many types of fears, and we have used it successfully in the past with people who have fears like yours. We will start the procedure by first teaching you how to become more relaxed and then asking you to practice the procedure at home.
>
> Do you have any questions?[5]

Before proceeding further, the therapist should answer any questions that the client has about the procedure or his expectations regarding treatment.

Throughout this initial period, as well as during the remainder of therapy, the therapist should make sure that he has established a good relationship with the client. The therapist should behave in a way that conveys warmth and acceptance of the client. Many writers (e.g., Goldfried and Davison, 1976; Wilson and Evans, 1977) have suggested that desensitization procedures should be conducted within a context of a sound therapist-client relationship. In fact, therapist warmth was found by Morris and Suckerman (1974a, 1974b) to be a significant factor in the outcome of systematic desensitization with snake fearful college students. (The reader is referred to Chapter 2 by Goldstein for a detailed discussion concerning methods of enhancing the therapeutic relationship.)

There are essentially three steps in the use of systematic desensitization: (1) relaxation training; (2) development of the anxiety hierarchy; and (3) systematic desensitization proper. Since therapists differ from one another in regard to some of the details of systematic desensitization, what is described here is the manner in which the present author conducts this therapy.

Relaxation Training

The therapist begins desensitization by training the client to relax. This training should take place in a quiet, softly lighted room located in a building where there is a negligible amount of outside noise (Where possible, the therapist should use the same room as the one in which the initial interview took place.) Besides comfortable office furniture, the therapist should have either a couch or recliner chair in the room so that relaxation can be facilitated by having the client lie down.

The first step in the procedure is to have the client lean back in the chair or lie down on the couch and close his eyes. The therapist then says the following:

I am going to teach you how to become very relaxed. In doing this I am going to ask you to tense up and relax opposing sets of muscles—proceeding through a series of these. That is, I am going to ask you to tense up and relax different sets of muscles so that there is a cumulative effect of relaxation over your whole body. (*Pause*) Okay, now, I would like you to . . .

The relaxation steps presented in Table 8.3 are then initiated. These steps represent a modified version of a technique developed by Jacobson (1938) for inducing deep muscular relaxation. The procedure should be presented in a very quiet, soft, and pleasant tone of voice. Each step should take about 10 seconds, with a 10-15 second pause between each step. The whole procedure should take 20-25 minutes.[6]

Table 8.3. An Introduction To The Relaxation Training Steps Of Systematic Desensitization.

Steps in Relaxation
1. Take a deep breath and hold it (for about ten seconds). Hold it. Okay, let it out.
2. Raise both of your hands about half way above the couch (or, arms of the chair), and breath normally. Now, drop your hands to the couch (or, down).

Table 8.3. An Introduction To The Relaxation Training Steps Of Systematic Desensitization (Continued)

3. Now, hold your arms out and make a tight fist. Really tight. Feel the tension in your hands. I am going to count to three and when I say "three," I want you to drop your hands. One . . . Two . . . Three.

4. Raise your arms again, and bend your fingers back the other way (toward your body). Now drop your hands and relax.

5. Raise your arms. Now drop them and relax.

6. Now, raise your arms again, but this time "flap" your hands around. Okay, relax again.

7. Raise your arms again. Now, relax.

8. Raise your arms above the couch (chair) again and tense your biceps until they shake. Breathe normally, and keep your hands loose. Relax your hands.
(Notice how you have a warm feeling of relaxation).

9. Now hold your arms out to your side and tense your biceps. Make sure that you breathe normally. Relax your arms.

10. Now arch your shoulders back. Hold it. Make sure that your arms are relaxed. Now relax.

11. Hunch your shoulders forward. Hold it, and make sure that you breathe normally and keep your arms relaxed. Okay, relax.
(Notice the feeling of relief from tensing and relaxing your muscles).

12. Now, turn your head to the right and tense your neck. Relax and bring your head back again to its natural position.

13. Turn your head to the left and tense your neck. Relax and bring your head back again to its natural position.

14. Now, bend your head back slightly toward the chair. Hold it. Okay, now bring your head back slowly to its natural position.*

15. This time bring your head down almost to your chest. Hold it. Now relax and let your head come back to its natural resting position.*

16. Now, open your mouth as much as possible. A little wider, okay, relax. (Mouth must be partly open at end).

17. Now tense your lips by closing your mouth. O.K., relax.
(Notice the feeling of relaxation).

18. Put your tongue at the roof of your mouth. Press hard. (Pause) Relax and allow your tongue to come to a comfortable position in your mouth.

19. Now put your tongue at the bottom of your mouth. Press down hard. Relax and let your tongue come to a comfortable position in your mouth.

20. Now just lie (sit) there and relax. Try not to think of anything.

21. To control self-verbalization, I want you to go through the motions of singing a high note—Not aloud! Okay, start singing to yourself. Hold that note, and now relax.

22. Now sing a medium note and make your vocal cords tense again. Relax.

23. Now sing a low note and make your vocal cords tense again. Relax.
(Your vocal apparatus should be relaxed now. Relax your mouth).

24. Now, close your eyes. Squeeze them tight and breathe naturally. Notice the tension. Now relax.
(Notice how the pain goes away when you relax).

25. Now, let your eyes relax and keep your mouth open slightly.

26. Open your eyes as much as possible. Hold it. Now, relax your eyes.

27. Now wrinkle your forehead as much as possible. Hold it. Okay, relax.

28. Now, take a deep breath and hold it. Relax.

29. Now, exhale. Breathe all the air out . . . all of it out. Relax.
(Notice the wondrous feeling of breathing again).

*The client should not be encouraged to bend his neck either all the way back or forward.

Table 8.3. An Introduction To The Relaxation Training Steps Of Systematic Desensitization (Continued)

---

30. Imagine that there are weights pulling on all your muscles making them flaccid and relaxed . . . pulling your arms and body into the couch.
31. Pull your stomach muscles together. Tighter. Okay, Relax.
32. Now extend your muscles as if you were a prize fighter. Make your stomach hard. Relax. (You are becoming more and more relaxed).
33. Now, tense your buttocks. Tighter. Hold it. Now, relax.
34. Now, search the upper part of your body and relax any part that is tense. First the facial muscles (Pause . . . 3-5 sec.) Then the vocal muscles. (Pause . . . 3-5 sec.) The neck region. (Pause . . . 3-5 sec.) Your shoulder . . . relax any part which is tense. (Pause) Now the arms and fingers. Relax these. Becoming very relaxed.
35. Maintaining this relaxation, raise both of your legs (to about a 45° angle). Now relax. (Notice that this further relaxes you).
36. Now bend your feet back so that your toes point toward your face. Relax your mouth. Bend them hard. Relax.
37. Bend your feet the other way . . . away from your body. Not far. Notice the tension. Okay, relax.
38. Relax. (Pause) Now curl your toes together—as hard as you can. Tighter. Okay, relax. (Quiet . . . silence for about 30 seconds).
39. This completes the formal relaxation procedure.
    Now explore your body from your feet up. Make sure that every muscle is relaxed. (Say slowly)—first your toes, . . . your feet, . . . your legs, . . . buttocks, . . . stomach, . . . shoulder, . . . neck, . . . eyes, . . . and finally your forehead—all should be relaxed now. (Quiet—silence for about 10 seconds).
    Just lie there and feel very relaxed, noticing the warmness of the relaxation. (Pause) I would like you to stay this way for about one more minute, and then I am going to count to five. When I reach five, I want you to open your eyes feeling very calm and refreshed. (Quiet—silence for about one minute).
    Okay, when I count to five, I want you to open your eyes feeling very calm and refreshed. One . . . feeling very calm; Two . . . very calm, very refreshed; Three . . . very refreshed; Four . . . and, Five.

Adapted in part from Jacobson (1938), Rimm (1967, personal communication), and Wolpe and Lazarus (1966).

During the first relaxation training session, it is often helpful for the therapist to practice the relaxation procedure with the client so that the client can observe (whenever necessary) how to perform a particular step. It is also advisable for the therapist to pace the presentation of each step to the client's ease of performing the steps.

It is not uncommon for clients to feel uncomfortable during the first relaxation session and not achieve a very deep relaxation level. But over a few sessions, the client will become more comfortable and will be able to reach deep relaxation more easily. The client should also be encouraged to practice the relaxation at home alone, preferably twice a day for 10-15 minutes. In order to enhance the client's practice at home some therapists record the relaxation procedure on cassette tapes and have the client play the tape while practicing each day. Others give the client an outline of the muscle groups to be relaxed. Both could be done. The most important goal is to teach the client how to relax by himself with a fair degree of ease.

In most cases relaxation training will last for about two or three sessions and will usually overlap with part of the initial interview. Throughout this training, it is a good idea to repeat such phrases as: "Breathe normally"; "Smooth, even breathing"; "Keep your _____ (Muscle Groups) relaxed". "Just let your body relax . . . and become more and more relaxed."

It is also helpful throughout relaxation training to point out to the client the changes he will be experiencing in bodily sensations. For example, the therapist might say: "Notice the warm, soft feeling of relaxation"; "Notice how your _____ (particular muscle group) now feel . . . they are warm, heavy and relaxed"; "Notice how relaxed your _____ (particular muscle group) feel in contrast to when you were tensing them"; "Notice how you are becoming more and more relaxed—feeling relaxation throughout your whole body."

For various reasons, a few clients have difficulty relaxing with this procedure. No matter how motivated they are, they just find it difficult to respond. They have learned over the years *not* to relax, to be tense, and it may take time for them to change. For example, some have difficulty closing their eyes for longer than a few seconds, or feel uneasy when they lie back in a recliner chair or on a couch while someone is watching them. A few have even reported being afraid to relax. In an attempt to deal with this problem effectively, some writers (Brady, 1966, 1972; Friedman, 1966) have recommended the use of drugs like Brevital (methahexitone sodium) to help their clients relax during relaxation training and desensitization. Others have suggested the use of hypnosis or carbon dioxide-oxygen (Wolpe and Lazarus, 1966; Wolpe, 1973), a shaping procedure (Morris, 1973), or biofeedback-assisted relaxation (Javel and Denholtz, 1975; Reeves and Maelica, 1975).

Development of the Anxiety Hierarchy

Upon completion of the initial interview and during the relaxation training phase the therapist begins planning out an anxiety hierarchy with the client for each of the identified fears. This hierarchy is based on the fear that the therapist and client have agreed upon as requiring change and which the therapist has consented to treat and the client has agreed to work on. The therapist should not impose treatment on a client for a fear which the client has not agreed is in need of being reduced.

At the end of the first relaxation training session (assuming the initial interview has now been completed), the client is given ten 3× 5 index cards and asked to come to the next session with the cards filled out—each containing a description of a situation which produces a certain level of anxiety. Specifically, the client is asked to identify on the cards those situations that are related to the fear and which produce increasingly more anxiety and tension. The client is asked to divide up the fear on a zero to 100 scale and assign an anxiety-provoking

Table 8.4. Sample—Initial Anxiety Hierarchies.

Fear of being alone

10. Being with a group of people at the lab either at night or during the day.
20. Being alone in a room with another female.
30. Thinking about the possibility of being alone in my house during the day.
40. Walking in class early in the morning when they are few people outside.
50. Actually alone in my bedroom at home and it's daylight.
60. Driving a car alone at night and feeling a man is following me.
70. Walking alone on a city street downtown at night with a girlfriend.
80. Being alone in a house with a young child for whom I am babysitting.
90. Thinking about being alone at night a few hours before I will actually be alone.
100. Sitting alone in the living room of my house at night with the doors closed.

Fear of flying in airplanes

10. Watching a movie of a plane moving up and down and banking.
20. Sitting in a private plane—on the ground with the motor idling.
30. Sitting in a private plane on the ground and the pilot begins to taxi down to the runway.
40. Sitting in a private plane on the ground, taxiing, and the pilot revs the engine.
50. Planning a trip with a friend on a commercial jet and it's three months before the trip.
60. One month before the trip on the jet.
70. Three weeks before the trip by jet.
80. Three days before the trip by jet.
90. In a private plane at take-off.
100. In a commercial jet over land.

Fear of driving in high places

10. Entering a ramp garage on ground level.
20. Going up to third level of the garage from the second level.
30. Riding with a friend in a car and approach the bridge over the Chicago River on Michigan Avenue.
40. Driving a car with a friend and begin to approach the bridge over the Chicago river.
50. Driving my car over the Chicago River bridge.
60. Driving with a friend and crossing the bridge over the Mississippi River near Moline.
70. Driving my car on the bridge over the Mississippi River near Moline.
80. Driving my car with a friend on a hilly road in Wisconsin.
90. Driving my car with a friend on a hilly road in Wisconsin going halfway up a fairly steep hill.
100. Driving my car with a friend up to the top of a fairly steep hill. We get to the top and get out of the car and look around at the valley below . . . then go into a restaurant nearby—and later drive back down the hill.

Fear of leaving the house

10. Going out the front door to my car to go to the store.
20. Getting in the car and starting it up.
30. In the car and pulling out of the driveway.
40. On the street and pulling away from my house.
50. Two blocks from my house on way to the store.
60. Arrive at the store and park.
70. Enter the store.
80. Get a shopping cart and begin looking for items on my list.
90. Have all the items and go to check-out girl.
100. Have all the items and have to wait in a long slow line to go through check-out.

situation to every tenth value (100 representing the most anxiety-provoking situation). Examples of some initial anxiety hierarchies are listed in Table 8.4.

The exact nature of a hierarchy will vary depending on the client's particular fear and perception of the various situations. For example, someone who has a fear of being criticized may describe a number of very different situations when this fear occurs—each differing in the level of fear that it arouses. Someone else may have a very specific fear, where the descriptions of the increasing anxiety-provoking situations differ on a spatio-temporal dimension. This was the case of the woman in Table 8.4 who had a fear of leaving her house. The hierarchy can also vary in terms of the number of people present in a particular situation (e.g., an elevator), the perceived attitudes of others toward the client, as well as a combination of some of these dimensions (see the fear of flying hierarchy in Table 8.4).

When the client returns with the prepared hierarchy, the therapist goes through it with him and adds intermediary items where it seems appropriate. The final hierarchy should represent a slow and smooth gradation of anxiety-provoking situations, each of which the client can easily imagine. Most hierarchies contain 20-25 items. It is not unusual, however, for those hierarchies that represent a very specific fear (e.g., driving on the highway at night) to contain fewer items, while those representing a more complex fear (e.g., fear of being alone, fear of open spaces) to contain more items. In Table 8.5, we have listed an example of a final hierarchy.

Table 8.5. Sample—Final Hierarchy.

Elevators

  *1. At my (therapist's) office and seeing the elevator as you walk down the stairs
  2. Pushing button to summon elevator at my office (on second floor)
  3. Elevator comes to second floor . . . doors open . . . and you go inside and down to first floor
  *4. In the new elevator with others at the Acme building below the fourth floor—going down
  5. You enter the elevator at my office, the doors close, and there is a slight pause before it begins going down
  6. Alone in the elevator in my office building going up from the first to the third floor
  *7. In a new elevator alone at the Acme building, going up between the first and fourth floors
  *8. In the new elevator with others at the Acme building going down between the fifteenth and fourth floors (15 story building)
  9. In the elevator at my office going down. As the elevator reaches the first floor there is a slight pause before the doors open
  *10. In a new elevator with others at the Acme building and going up between the fourth and fifteenth floors
  11. In the elevator alone at the Acme building, going up between the fourth and fifteenth floors and as you reach the twelfth floor to get out there is a momentary pause before the doors open

*Indicates original items which client developed.

Table 8.5. Sample-Final Hierarchy (Continued)

*12. You're on the fifth floor of the Marshall building (a very familiar old building to the client) and you enter the elevator alone, push the button, and it starts to go down to the first floor

13. As you are going down in the elevator you begin hearing a few noises from the elevator machinery

*14. You enter the Marshall building and walk up to the elevator, step inside, and press the button to go up to the fifth floor

*15. You enter the elevator alone at the Ajax building (30 floors) and you take it up to the 10th floor

16. . . . to the 15th floor

17. . . . to the 20th floor

*18. You enter the elevator alone at the Thomas building (50 floors) and you take it to the 20th floor

19. . . . to the 30th floor

20. You are in the elevator alone in my office building and press the button to go up to the fifth floor and it doesn't stop until the seventh floor

21. You are in the elevator alone at the Marshall building, going down to the first floor, and it stops between the second and first floors. You press the first floor button again and the elevator goes to the first floor

*22. You are in an elevator alone in the Thomas building going up to the 45th floor and it gets stuck between the 20th and 21st floors—and then starts up a while later after you pressed the alarm button

---

The therapist should also determine what the client considers a relaxing scene, one which would be zero on the hierarchy. This is often called the "control scene." The scene should be unrelated to the client's fears and totally satisfying and comforting. Some common "zero-level" scenes are the folowing:

"Walking through the forest on a nice sunny day with my wife (husband)."
"Lying on the beach by the ocean on a sunny, warm day."
"Lying in bed and reading an interesting novel."
"Sitting in a lounge chair in my backyard on a beautiful spring day—watching the clouds go by."
"Lying on the couch and watching a good movie on T.V."

Hierarchy development usually occupies at least part of the two or three sessions, though less time may be spent with those cases which involve a single phobia.

Systematic Desensitization Proper

Desensitization proper usually begins about three or four sessions after the completion of the initial interview. By this time the client has had the opportunity to practice relaxation at home as well as in the therapist's office, and has been able to construct the anxiety hierarchy. If the client has developed a number of hierarchies, the therapist should first work on the one which is most distressing and troublesome to the client. If time allows, the therapist can also work on other hierarchies during the hour, but probably should not go beyond exposing the client to more than three different hierarchies in a given session.

The first desensitization session starts with having the client spend about three to five minutes relaxing himself on the couch or in the recliner chair. During this time, the therapist suggests to the client that he is becoming increasingly more relaxed and is achieving a deeper and deeper level of relaxation. The therapist might add the following comments during this phase:

> Your whole body is becoming heavier . . . all your muscles are relaxing more and more. Your arms are becoming very relaxed. (Pause) Your shoulders. (Pause) and your eyes . . . very relaxed. Your forehead . . . very relaxed . . . noticing that as you become more relaxed you're feeling more and more calm (Pause) Very relaxed . . . relaxing any part of your face which feels the least bit tense. (Pause) Now, back down to your neck . . . your shoulders . . . your chest . . . your buttocks . . . your thighs . . . your legs . . . your feet . . . very, very relaxed. (Pause) Feeling very at ease and very comfortable.

The client is also asked by the therapist to indicate, by raising his right index finger, when he has achieved a very relaxing and comfortable state.

After the client signals, the therapist asks the client to visualize a number of scenes from the hierarchy that the two of them developed over the past few sessions. The therapist asks the client to imagine each scene as clearly and as vividly as possible—"As if you are really there"—while still maintaining a very relaxed state. If the client feels the least bit of anxiety or tension when he imagines a particular scene, he is told to signal immediately with the right finger.

At this point, the therapist asks the client to indicate with his index finger if he is still feeling very calm and relaxed. If the client signals, the therapist presents the control scene. If the client does not signal, the therapist reviews with the client the earlier relaxation sequence until he no longer indicates feeling tense.

The control scene is presented for approximately 15 seconds. The therapist then proceeds with the desensitization procedure. An example of a desensitization session with a test phobic individual is presented below.

> . . . Now stop imagining that scene and give all your attention once again to relaxing . . . Now imagine that you are home studying in the evening. It is the 20th of May, exactly a month before your examination. (Pause of 5 seconds) Now stop imagining the scene . . . (Pause of 10-15 seconds). Now imagine the same scene again—a month before your examination . . . (Pause of 5-10 seconds). Stop imagining the scene and just think of your muscles. Let go, and enjoy your state of calm. (Pause of 15 seconds). Now imagine again that you are studying at home a month before your examination . . . (Pause of 5-10 seconds). Stop the scene and think of nothing but your own body . . . (Pause of 15 seconds). (Wolpe, 1969, p. 126.)[7]

Each hierarchy scene is presented three to four times with a maximum exposure time of five seconds for the first presentation, and a gradual increase up to ten seconds for subsequent presentations. The hierarchy items are presented first in ascending order, starting with the lowest feared item first, with relaxation periods between each scene varying from ten to 15 seconds. In most cases, three to four different scenes are presented per session. This means that a particular desensitization session will last between 15 and 20 minutes. The remainder of the hour can be devoted to discussing issues related to the client's fear (e.g., what occurred during the week regarding the fear), to the desensitization of another fear hierarchy, or to working on some other problem with the client.

After the last scene is presented for a particular session, and if the decision is to go onto another hierarchy, the therapist usually asks the client to relax for a short period of time. The therapist then starts the ending phase of the session by saying the following:

> . . . Just relax . . . feeling very comfortable and at ease. I would like you to stay this way until I count to five. When I reach five, I want you to open your eyes feeling very calm and refreshed. (Pause) One . . . feeling very calm; two . . . very calm, very refreshed; three . . . very refreshed; four . . .; and, five.

The same general format is followed for all subsequent desensitization sessions. The scenes should not be presented in a rapid manner; rather, they should be presented in a conversational manner which conveys both understanding and concern for the client. In order to keep track of which scenes the client passes, how many times a scene has been passed, and where on the hierarchy each session started and stopped, it is advisable to follow a procedure on each hierarchy card like the one outlined in Table 8.6.

Table 8.6. Suggested Notational System

2/4/74 STOPPED	‖Ø 15 ‖‖	25
	You are approaching the supermarket. As you come closer you notice that it is nearly empty and walk inside to shop.	
	No noticeable discomfort	

10/14/73 STARTED	‖Ø 25 ‖‖	40
	At the Tango Bar and you leave your table for five minutes with your drink on it, and come back and start drinking from your glass again.	
	Moving around in chair at first	

The date on each card refers to when the scene was presented. The words "stopped" and started" indicate whether the session stopped or started with the scene. The "hash marks" help the therapist recall how often the scene was presented—one mark per presentation. The circle through the mark indicates that the client signaled anxiety, and that the scene was stopped and followed by a relaxation period of the number of seconds indicated next to the circle. Comments are also made at the bottom of the card about the client's observed comfort level while imagining the scene.

The therapist should present each scene until the client has three consecutive successes. If, however, the client has two consecutive failures (indications of anxiety), the therapist should go back to the previous successfully passed scene and work back up again. If failure persists, the previously successful scene should be presented again so that the client ends the session with a positive experience. The ending phase of the procedure should then begin. The problems associated with the difficult scene should be discussed with the client and modifications made either in the scene or in other aspects of the desensitization procedure.

Even if a client does not signal anxiety, it is often helpful during the conduct of desensitization (especially during the first few sessions) to determine if the client was disturbed by a particular scene, whether the client was able to fully imagine the scene, and if the client continues to feel very relaxed. To do this, the therapist asks between scene presentations, "If you were not the least bit disturbed by that scene ("If you were able to imagine that scene very clearly . . .," or "If you continue to feel very relaxed . . .") do nothing; otherwise raise your right index finger." If the client raises his finger, the therapist then takes appropriate action which might entail going through additional relaxation enhancing suggestions or presenting either the problematic scene or the control scene again and suggesting that the client imagine it in detail. If, after reintroducing a particular scene, the client indicates again that he was disturbed by it or could not vividly imagine it the session is stopped, using the ending phase described above. The therapist then explores in detail the difficulty the client is having, and makes any modifications necessary in the hierarchy or relaxation procedure.

A second useful procedure involves assessing the client's overall level of relaxation before, during, and after a particular desensitization session. This usually takes place after desensitization has been completed for the day. The client is asked to rate his relaxation level on a ten-point scale—where zero is "extremely" relaxed and ten is "not at all" relaxed. This approach not only gives the therapist information regarding the client's relative change in relaxation level from pre-to posttreatment across sessions, but also provides feedback to the client regarding his own progress.

Additional Considerations

Throughout desensitization proper, the client should be watched for signs of fatigue. In this regard, it may be helpful to ask the client whether he feels too many scenes (or hierarchies) are being presented at each session. It is also advisable to be sensitive to any discomfort the client is showing during either relaxation training or desensitization proper. Some of the ways clients express discomfort while lying on the couch or sitting back in a recliner are the following: moving their bodies around as if to find a comfortable position; rapid movement of their eyelids; excessive yawning; or, unsolicited verbalizations while their eyes are closed.

Occasionally, as in the following example, discomfort can be unrelated to the client's fear.

Mrs. Farber was well into her fifth desensitization session, progressing slowly, but steadily up her hierarchy concerned with a fear of being alone in her house. She fluttered her eyelids sporadically, but did not indicate any anxiety to the scenes being presented. During subsequent relaxation enhancing instructions, she began crossing her legs and shifting her body around. Just as the therapist was about to inquire about her relaxation level, she opened her eyes, sat up in the recliner chair and said, "You'll have to excuse me, I had a lot to drink today and must go to the washroom. I forgot to go before I came here."

At other times, as in the next example, deep relaxation may set the occasion for very tense clients to begin thinking about their problem.

Mr. Martin had difficulty learning how to relax. Several sessions passed with him unable to achieve a relaxation level lower than four on the ten point rating scale. In the fourth session, a relaxation enhancing technique was used. He became very relaxed, more relaxed than on previous occasions, and seemed to be pleased with his success. Within a few minutes, he began moving his head from one side to the other and tears began falling down his cheeks. He then started crying and said that this was the first time he has ever "let . . . [himself] really think about" the difficulties he has had with his impotence "and all the turmoil it has caused in my life."

Similar events can also contribute to a client's repeated failure of an item in a session. In the following example, the particular hierarchy item did not produce the signaled anxiety; rather, the anxiety was triggered by a telephone call that day from an old friend of the client.

Mrs. Carol was progressing steadily through her hierarchy concerned with a fear of leaving her home by herself . . . and driving more than a mile from the house. During her ninth session, an item was presented concerned with driving by herself nine miles to the therapist's office. As soon as the item was presented, she signaled anxiety and repeated this action until the session was stopped. Upon inquiring about her repeated signaling, she began crying and said she had received a telephone call that day from an old college friend with whom she was very close but had not seen for 10 years. The friend had an unexpected three hour layover at the airport, and decided to call Mrs. Carol and ask her to come out to see her (a distance of 20 miles). Mrs. Carol wanted to go very, very much but was afraid to take a chance and declined, but did talk to her friend for a long time. She felt terrible and angry at herself for having such a "stupid problem."

Another reason for repeated failure of a hierarchy item may be the psychological distance between the last passed item and the next failed one. Two examples of this situation are the following:

Client A.

Item passed. Flying in the plane after leveling off at 30,000 feet and not hearing any change in the sound of the engines. (#60 on the hierarchy)

Item failed. Feeling the tilt of the plane as it is banking, and not hearing any change in the sound of the engines. (#65 on the hierarchy)

Client B.

Item passed. Planning a trip on an airplane with a close friend to the Bahama Islands, and it's nine months before the trip (#20 on the hierarchy)

Item failed. Reviewing plans of airplane trip to the Bahamas with close friend, and it's one month before the trip. (#25 on the hierarchy)

In example A, the client and therapist decided on an intermediary scene that described a change in the noise of the airplane engines which the client could hear just before she felt the plane banking. A temporal dimension, on the other hand, was inserted between the two scenes in example B. Specifically, three additional scenes were developed: . . . six months before the planned trip; . . . four months before; . . . two months before. . . . In both cases these additions to the respective hierarchies facilitated successful passage of the heretofore failed items.

Just as some clients signal repeated difficulty with one or more hierarchy scenes, others never signal anxiety about particular scenes. In some cases, this is good because it suggests that the hierarchy represents a smooth, even, gradation of the client's fear. In other cases, this means that the client feels reluctant to signal that anxiety is indeed being experienced. To reduce the possibility of the client not signaling anxiety when, in fact, he should, it is a good idea for the therapist to mention at various times throughout the session: "Remember to signal whenever you feel the slightest amount of anxiety." The therapist should also make every effort neither to convey dissatisfaction with a client's signaling of anxiety nor satisfaction that a client did not signal anxiety at all during a particular session. In both instances, the client may begin to feel that the therapist does not really want any signaling of anxiety.

It is also important for the therapist to end each desensitization session with a positive experience for the client (i.e., ending on a hierarchy item which was passed successfully). Moreover, the therapist should leave sufficient time at the end of the session (as well as before the session begins) to discuss any issues or concerns that the client has or discuss how things went during the week.

Most desensitization sessions last from 30 minutes to one hour, depending on the number of different hierarchies presented. Some researchers, however, have reported successfully treating a phobia by conducting a massed desensitization session which lasted 90 minutes (Wolpin and Pearsall, 1965) while others (Richardson and Suinn, 1973) have reported success after a three hour massed session. The spacing of most desensitization sessions varies from once to twice a week, though Wolpe (1973) reports that some clients have received two or more sessions per day.

Finally, during the initial stages of desensitization, the client is encouraged to avoid the temptation of entering the actual feared situation. Since this may be an unrealistic request for some clients, they are asked to try to avoid entering the feared situation at "full throttle." As desensitization progresses, however, they are encouraged to enter aspects of the feared situation which correspond to lower hierarchy items which have been passed successfully and for which the client now feels little, if any, tension or anxiety.

Variations of Systematic Desensitization

Various alternatives to desensitization have been proposed by researchers. In *in vivo desensitization* (Sherman, 1972), the client is exposed to the items on the hierarchy in the real situation rather than through imagination. Relaxation training is not used as the counterconditioned response to the situation. Instead, those feelings of comfort, security, and trust that the client has developed for the therapist (which have emerged from the therapeutic relationship) are used as the counterconditioning agent. The therapist goes into the real-life situation with the client and urges him to gradually go through each item on the hierarchy. An example of this procedure is the following:

> Mr. Kay is a very successful salesman in a large metropolitan area, and often must attend business meetings in high rise office buildings in the downtown area. But, he is extremely afraid of elevators. Lately, his fear has become so intense that he has avoided attending meetings which occur on a level higher than the fourth floor. *In vivo* desensitization entailed having Mr. Kay and the therapist approach various elevators throughout the city, ride up and down in them, and purposely get stuck in them—following a hierarchy sequence developed earlier with the therapist. Mr. Kay was also encouraged to go up elevators, etc. on his own while the therapist waited for him at various floors.

A similar technique called *contact desensitization* (Ritter, 1968, 1969a, b) is used with both children and adults. This technique also involves a graded hierarchy, but adds to it a modeling, touch, information/feedback and practice component in addition to the therapist's interpersonal relationship with the client. The procedure is outlined in the next example:

> In the application of this method to the elimination of snake phobia, at each step the experimenter himself performed fearless behavior and gradually led subjects into touching, stroking, and then holding the snake's body with first gloves and then bare hands while he held the snake securely by the head and tail. If a subject was unable to touch the snake after ample demonstration, she was asked to place her hand on the experimenter's and to move her hand down gradually until it touched the snake's body. After subjects no longer felt any apprehension about touching the snake under these secure conditions, anxieties about contact with the snake's head area and entwining tail were extinguished. The experimenter again performed the tasks fearlessly and then he and the subject performed the responses jointly; as subjects became less fearful the experimenter gradually reduced his participation and control over the snake until subjects were able to hold the snake in their laps without assistance, to let the snake loose in the room and retrieve it, and to let it crawl freely over their bodies. Progress through the graded approach tasks was paced according to the subjects' apprehensiveness. When they reported being able to perform one activity with little or no fear, they were eased into a more difficult interaction. (p. 185.)[8]

A third variation is very similar to desensitization proper, but involves the use of a tape recorder. It is called *automated desensitization*. In this procedure, the client goes through the desensitization process by listening to a series of tape recorded scene presentations prepared by the therapist with the client's assistance. Developed by Lang (Wolpe, 1969) and later used by Migler and Wolpe (1967), this procedure allows the client to pace himself in the desensitization process and to become desensitized at home. This method has been found to be as effective as live desensitization. A variation of this automated procedure is called *self-directed desensitization* (Baker, Cohen, and Saunders, 1973; Rosen, Glasgow, and Barrera, 1976; Rosen, 1976). In this procedure, clients use instructional materials typically provided them by the therapist and conduct the treatment at their own pace. In some cases the therapist continues to function as a consultant, while at other times the therapist sees the client only once for the initial structuring of treatment. The major difference between this procedure and automated desensitization is that the latter uses equipment to mechanically present treatment, whereas in self-directed desensitization the client develops and presents the treatment package to himself. An interesting fading procedure which makes use of both automated and self-directed methods of fear reduction has been discussed by Öst (1978a). He reports that this procedure is as effective as live desensitization (Öst, 1978b).

The last variation to be discussed is *self-control desensitization* (Goldfried, 1971; Meichenbaum, 1974). In this approach the desensitization procedure is construed as training the client in coping skills, i.e., desensitization treatment is viewed as teaching the client to cope with anxiety. Clients are told, for example, to apply relaxation training whenever they become aware of an increase in their feelings of anxiety and tension. They are also encouraged, during the desensitization proper phase, to continue imagining a scene which produces anxiety and to "relax away" the anxiety and/or to imagine themselves becoming fearful and then seeing themselves coping with the anxiety and tenseness that they feel. This variation is based on the view that clients will not always be in a position where they can readily leave a fearful and anxiety arousing situation—that they must learn to cope with the situation on their own. Rehearsal for this possibility, therefore, should take place in therapy. In this regard, it is not important for the anxiety hierarchy to be theme-oriented as in standard systematic desensitization (Goldfried and Goldfried, 1977). The hierarchy need only be composed of situations arousing increasing amounts of anxiety, independent of theme. The following rationale for clients has been suggested by Goldfried (1971):

> There are various situations where, on the basis of your past experience, you have learned to react by becoming tense (anxious, nervous, fearful). What I plan to do is help you to learn how to cope with these situations more successfully, so that they do not make you as upset. This will be done by taking note of a number of those situations which upset you to varying degrees, and then having you learn to cope with the less stressful situations before moving on to the more difficult ones. Part of the treatment involves learning how to relax, so that in situations where you feel yourself getting nervous you will be better able to eliminate this tenseness. Learning to

relax is much like learning any other skill. When a person learns to drive, he initially has difficulty in coordinating everything, and often finds himself very much aware of what he is doing. With more and more practice, however, the procedures involved in driving become easier and more automatic. You may find the same thing occurring to you when you try to relax in those situations where you feel yourself starting to become tense. You will find that as you persist, however, it will become easier and easier (p. 231).

ASSERTIVE TRAINING

A second procedure for reducing fears is called *assertive training*. This method is especially useful in helping people reduce their fear of acting appropriately in social and interpersonal situations. It is utilized when the therapist believes that the client: (1) is presently unable to stand up for himself in those situations where the person feels unjustly treated; (2) cannot respond, or has difficulty responding, in his own best interests to those events which directly affect the person's life or the lives of family members; and (3) has difficulty expressing feelings of love and affection toward significant persons in his life.

Unlike the assertive individual, the unassertive person does not feel confident in social situations and interpersonal relationships, is not spontaneous in the expression of emotions and feelings, often feels tense and anxious in social situations, and typically allows others to make decisions for him. The following example describes a situation in which Mr. A. is behaving in an unassertive manner.

Mr. and Mrs. A. are at dinner in a moderately expensive restaurant. Mr. A. has ordered a rare steak, but when the steak is served, Mr. A finds it to be very well done, contrary to his order . . . Mr. A. grumbles to his wife about the "burned" meat, and observes that he won't patronize this restaurant in the future. He says nothing to the waitress, responding "Fine!" to her inquiry "Is everything alright?" His dinner and evening are highly unsatisfactory, and he feels guilty for having taken no action. Mr. A's estimate of himself, and Mrs. A.'s estimate of him are both deflated by the experience. (Alberti and Emmons, 1970, pp. 26-27).

The decision to initiate assertive training with a client is usually based on information gathered during the initial interview. In listening to the client, the therapist learns how the client interacts with people, the frequency and pattern of these interactions, and the anxiety level associated with these interactions. From questionnaires like the Willoughby Schedule (see Appendix 2), the therapist gains further information and can confirm some speculations about the client. In addition, some writers have listed behaviors that clients demonstrate in the interview which may signal assertiveness problems. For example, Walen, Hauserman, and Lavin (1977) mention the following behaviors: ". . . inappropriate facial expression, inappropriate or stiff gestures, poor eye contact, . . . inadequate voice quality or tone, . . . hesitancy, long latency or nonfluency of speech, [and] inappropriate physical distance between communicants" (p. 221, commas have been added in place of authors' numbers).

The therapist may also wish to ask a series of questions like those listed below and/or have the client fill out the Rathus Assertiveness Schedule (see Appendix 4) or similar inventories developed for college students (Galassi, et al. 1974) and other adults (Gay, Hollandsworth and Galassi, 1975). Each of these assessment procedures helps delineate those areas in which the client has difficulty being assertive.

When a person is blatantly unfair, do you usually try to say something about it to him?

Are you always very careful to avoid all trouble with other people?

Do you often avoid social contacts for fear of doing or saying the wrong thing? . . .

When a clerk in a store waits on someone who has come in after you, do you call his attention to the matter?

Do you find that there are very few people with whom you can be relaxed and have a good time? . . .

If a person keeps on teasing you, do you have difficulty expressing your annoyance or displeasure? . . .

If someone keeps kicking the back of your chair in a movie, would you ask him to stop?

If a friend keeps calling you very late each evening, would you ask him or her not to call after a certain time?

If someone starts talking to someone else right in the middle of your conversation, do you express your irritation?

In a plush restaurant, if you order a medium steak and find it too raw, would you ask the waiter to have it recooked?

If the landlord of your apartment fails to make certain necessary repairs after promising to do so, would you insist upon it?

Would you return a faulty garment you purchased a few days ago? . . . (pp. 132-133).[9]

Conducting Assertive Training

A number of writers have speculated about the basis of assertive training. For example, Wolpe and his colleagues (Wolpe and Lazarus, 1966; Wolpe, 1973) maintain that assertive training gradually counterconditions the fear and anxiety that a person associates with a particular situation. By being assertive the client develops confidence in appropriately expressing his feelings in these situations and begins to notice that assertive behavior does not lead necessarily to negative reactions from people (Salter, 1949; Wolpe, 1973). Other writers (Goldfried and Davison, 1976) view assertive training as teaching a skill to a client who, "presumably . . . [because of] faulty social learning experiences," has a specific skill deficit and/or a behavioral inhibition.

Assertive training consists of three primary components: role playing, modeling, and social reward and coaching. Role playing (or behavioral rehearsal) is used to help the client rehearse how he should act in a particular situation, e.g., what the client should say to a demanding spouse, what the client's facial expression should be like, and so forth. The client usually plays himself and the therapist plays the individual to whom the client reacts. Modeling and role-reversal are used to help the client observe how a more assertive person would behave in the same situation. In most cases, the therapist plays the client, and the client plays the person to whom the therapist reacts. Some therapists, use professional actors to play the various roles and have utilized this occasion to point out to the client what he should be doing in the same situation. Social reward and coaching from the therapist are also important. The therapist not only comments on how well the client is progressing but also makes suggestions and gives the client feedback on his behavior to facilitate further improvement in the level of assertiveness.

Assertive Training Proper

The steps in conducting training are:

1. The therapist and client work out a series of situations in which the client feels increasing difficulty being assertive. Like the anxiety hierarchy items used in systematic desensitization, these situations should be described in sufficient detail (including the use of a script in some cases) so that the client can adequately portray what goes on in real life. The events described at the lower end of the series should be such that there is a high probability the client will have no trouble being assertive and that no negative consequences will occur as a result of his assertiveness.

2. The therapist and client act out each of the scenes through role playing. The therapist then comments on the client's behavior and offers suggestions about improvement—especially concerning facial expression, posture, gait, arm movements, tone of voice, eye contact, etc. Modeling also takes place during this stage. The number of situations role played and modeled per session varies, and is based on the severity of the client's nonassertiveness as well as the client's tolerance level for practicing assertive behavior.

3. Upon completing the role playing stage and feeling confident in what the client should do in certain situations, the client and therapist then decide on alternative responses which can be made in these situations. For example, they may discuss what the client should say or do if a negative reply is given in response to an assertive statement, or what would be a more empathic and warm response instead of a mildly aggressive one. Once these alternatives are decided upon, role playing and modeling again occur until the client has also mastered these alternatives.

4. After the assertive responses have been mastered and the therapist and client agree that the client is aware of when he should be appropriately assertive, the client is encouraged to practice being assertive in the real situation. Since this is often a difficult step to take, the client should be encouraged to rehearse the behavior at home and to write down any feelings he has about performing the behavior, as well as what events, people, etc. in the particular situation produce these feelings. The client should also take notes on how he felt after the assertive behavior was performed, or

what prevented the client from being as assertive as he wanted to be. The purpose of notetaking is to help the client recall to the therapist any problems which had occurred since the last session so that they can be worked out and prevented from recurring.

5. At the next session, the client's performance during the interview since the previous session is reviewed. If the client behaved appropriately, he should be enthusiastically rewarded with praise. The client's notes should be discussed and any problems worked out. The client should also be encouraged to continue practicing the assertiveness in these situations and continue the notetaking on his performance. The therapist should then go on to the next situation where the client has had difficulty being assertive—following the above steps.

If the client had difficulty being assertive, the reasons for this difficulty (i.e., what in the situation prevented the client from being assertive) should be discussed, and appropriate retraining take place by reviewing with the client steps 1-4.

An example of assertive training is described in the following case.

Mr. P.R., aged 38 years, complained of depression and described himself as an "occupational misfit." Although highly qualified in accountancy and economics, he held only junior positions in his work. He stated that he felt frustrated and demoralized. At the time that he sought behavior therapy, he had received promotion to the position of Assistant Chief Ledger Clerk in a large organization. This slight elevation in status, utterly absurd for a man with his excellent qualifications, tended to reactivate his personal misgivings about his station in life, and led him to behavior therapy "as a last resort." During the initial interview it became clear that Mr. P.R. was grossly deficient in assertive behavior. . . . [At the next session, the] therapist stressed that Mr. P.R.'s lack of assertiveness was responsible for his occupational failures and that vocational advancement would have to follow rather than precede increased assertiveness. It was clear, however, that Mr. P.R. would use the work situation as the sole criterion for gauging his general improvement. A careful analysis showed that opportunities for advancement in his firm were extremely limited. It was obvious that Mr. P.R. would have to go elsewhere to achieve the desired elevation in occupational status, but he rationalized that he would feel less secure in an unfamiliar work milieu. Further inquiries revealed that Mr. P.R. abhorred the idea of being interviewed by prospective employers. This area was then made the focus of attention for assertive training by means of behavior rehearsal.

Mr. P.R. was told to pretend that the therapist was a prominent business executive who had advertised for an experienced accountant to take charge of one of his companies. Mr. P.R. had applied for the position and had been asked to present himself for an interview. The therapist instructed Mr. P.R. to leave the consulting room, to knock on the door and to enter when invited to do so. . . .

At the therapist's deliberately resonant "Come in!" Mr. P.R. opened the door of the consulting room and hesitantly approached the desk. The therapist interrupted the role-playing procedure to mirror the patient's timid posture, shuffling gait, downcast eyes, and overall tension. Mr. P.R. was required to sit at the desk and to play the role of the prominent business executive while the therapist reenacted Mr. P.R.'s entry into the room. The patient was asked to criticize the therapist's performance. The therapist then modeled the entry of an "assertive individual," asking the patient to note the impact of variations in posture and gait and the all-important absence or presence of eye-contact.

The "correct" entry was rehearsed several times until Mr. P.R.'s approach to the prominent executive-behind-the-desk was completely devoid of any overt signs of timidity or anxiety. He was then taught to deal with a variety of entries—being met at the door; the employer who makes himself incommunicado while studying important-looking documents; and the over-effusive one who self-consciously tries to place him at ease.

Next the content of the interview was scrutinized. Mr. P.R.'s replies to questions concerning his background, qualifications, and experience were tape-recorded. Mr. P.R. was instructed to place himself in the position of the prospective employer and asked to decide whether or not he would employ the applicant on the basis of his recorded interview. It was clear from the recording that the elimination of Mr. P.R.'s hesitant gait and posture had not generalized to his faltering speech. Above all, it was noted that Mr. P.R. tended to undersell himself. Instead of stressing his excellent qualifications, he mumbled rather incoherent and unimpressive generalities about his background and training. The therapist demonstrated more efficient verbal responses which the patient was required to imitate. In this manner, Mr. P.R. was able to rehearse adequate replies to specific questions, and to prepare an impressive-sounding discourse for use in unstructured interviews. . . . (pp. 48-50).

Additional Considerations

The client should not be forced by the therapist into being assertive. Such activity will only threaten the client and contribute further to his nonassertiveness. Assertive training, like desensitization, should take place within a therapeutic environment which facilitates learning and growth—where the therapist shows concern for the client, warmth, and understanding of his problem. In this regard, assertive training should progress slowly, with enough time allowed for the client to practice this new behavior. The therapist should therefore plan to have no more than one or two sessions per week with the client.

In addition, before initiating treatment, the therapist should explain to the client the rationale behind the use of assertive training. For example, the client could be told that the assumption made in this treatment method is that nonassertive behavior is learned. And, by teaching him to be assertive in various situations, this will countercondition the anxiety and fear he has associated with these situations so that the end result will be that he feels satisfied with acting appropriately. Alternatively, the client could be told that for various reasons in the past, he never learned to behave in an assertive manner, to dwell on reasons for this would not help the client learn to be assertive. Because the client is not presently assertive, therapy will concentrate on teaching him how to behave assertively in various situations so that the end result will be that he feels satisfied and pleased about acting appropriately.

It is important to begin assertive training with situations in which it is highly probable that no adverse consequence will occur to the client and that the client's expectancy for success will be rewarded. The client, however, should not be given a 100 percent guarantee that his efforts will not be met with negative consequences. The client should be made aware of this possibility, and told that though it is unlikely that such consequences will occur, he should be prepared to give one of the alternative responses discussed in step 3 above.

In some cases, a client will be very reluctant to act in an assertive manner—even in a situation where it is highly probable that no negative consequence will result from assertiveness. When this occurs, the therapist should consider using systematic desensitization (see pp. 249 to 272) to help the client feel more calm and relaxed in these situations. As an alternative, or as an adjunct to standard assertive training, the therapist could make use of *covert modeling* (Kazdin, 1974). Here, the client imagines himself behaving in an assertive manner. In addition, the client might be encouraged to imagine more than one person performing the assertive response and/or imagine reinforcing himself for behaving in an assertive manner (Kazdin, 1976). The therapist could also ask the client to imagine modeling alternative responses when unfavorable comments are made following the client's assertive behavior (Nietzel, Martoreno and Melnick, 1977).

As a final precautionary note, the therapist should not assume that successful assertive training in one situation, or applied to one area of the person's life (e.g., special interactions with colleagues at work) will generalize to other important areas such as interpersonal relationships with one's spouse and/or children. The experience of the present author is that generalization does not usually occur. Assertive training, therefore, should also be performed in those other areas of the person's life in which he is behaving in a nonassertive manner. The result of such training will be that the client will be able to appropriately demonstrate love, affection, warmth, and aggressive behavior.

IMPLOSIVE THERAPY

The third method which will be discussed is called *implosive therapy*. Like systematic desensitization, this procedure makes use of the imaginal presentation of anxiety-provoking material. But unlike desensitization, this procedure from the very beginning requires the client to imagine a very fearful and threatening scene for a prolonged period of time without undergoing any previous relaxation training.

The purpose of implosive therapy is to produce a frightening experience in the client of such magnitude that it will actually lessen his fear of the particular situation rather than heighten it. Developed by psychologist Thomas G. Stampfl (Stampfl, 1961; Stampfl and Levis, 1967), this method utilizes principles from both learning theory and psychodynamic theory (e.g., Freud's psychoanalytic theory). Though Stampfl maintains that fears and their associated anxiety are learned, he does not assume that such fears can be most effectively reduced by using a counterconditioning approach. Rather, he believes that a person can best unlearn a fear by using a procedure based on an *extinction model*. Here, extinction refers to the gradual reduction in the occurrence of an anxiety response, as a result of the continuous presentation of the fear producing stimulus situated in the absence of the reinforcement which perpetuates the fear. In therapy, this extinction process is accomplished by having the therapist ". . . represent, reinstate, or symbolically reproduce the stimuli (cues) to which the anxiety response has been conditioned . . .'' without presenting the concomitant reinforcement which maintains the response (Stampfl and Levis, 1967, p. 499.)[11]

The Development of the Avoidance Serial Cue Hierarchy

From information gathered during the initial interview, the therapist develops hypotheses concerning what are the important cues involved in the client's fear. Many of these cues are situational events in the client's life and can be readily identified. For example, in the case of those people who have a fear of heights, the situational events may be the sight of high-rise office and apartment buildings, winding roads in the mountains, airplanes, bridges, and so forth.

The remaining cues are formulated by the therapist, and are based on psychodynamic theory and on the therapist's knowledge of common reactions by clients with similar problems. They are derived from the client's statements in the initial interview as well as from the client's nonverbal behavior, and represent those psychodynamic areas which the therapist believes are relevant to the client's fear. These cues are usually related to themes of aggression and hostility, oral and anal activity, sexual activity, punishment, rejection, bodily injury, loss of impulse control, and guilt. For example, Stampfl and Levis (1967) describe four of the hypothesized dynamic cues in the following manner:

Aggression. Scenes presented in this area usually center around the expression of anger, hostility, and aggression by the patient toward parental, sibling, spouse, or other significant figures in his life. Various degrees of bodily injury are described including complete body mutilation and death of the victim.

Punishment. The patient is instructed to visualize himself as the recipient of the anger, hostility, and aggression of the various significant individuals in his life. The punishment inflicted in the scene is frequently a result of the patient's engaging in some forbidden act.

Sexual material. In this area a wide variety of hypothesized cues related to sex are presented. For example, primal and Oedipal scenes and scenes of castration, fellatio, and homosexuality are presented.

Loss of control. Scenes are presented where the patient is encouraged to imagine himself losing impulse control to such an extent that he acts out avoided sexual or aggressive impulses. These scenes usually are followed by scenes where the individual is directed to visualize himself hospitalized for the rest of his life in a back ward of a mental hospital as a result of his loss of impulse control. This area is tapped primarily with patients who express fear of ''becoming insane'' or concern about being hopeless and incurable. (p. 501.)[12]

Those cues which are lowest on the hierarchy are assumed to be the situations and events which the client can associate wtih his fear. The highest cues are those internal dynamic cues that the therapist believes are closely associated with the client's basic psychological problem. The particular dynamic themes emphasized in the hierarchy will depend on the client's problem and the information obtained in the initial interview.

The hierarchy scenes are developed by the therapist after the initial interview is completed. They are not developed jointly by the client and the therapist, as in systematic desensitization. Overall, the hierarchy is quite different from the one developed in systematic desensitization. For example, the Avoidance Serial Cue Hierarchy only contains items which are thought to be capable of producing a maximum level of anxiety in the client. This is not the case for the desensitization hierarchy. The latter hierarchy is developed for a different reason, namely, to proceed gradually up the hierarchy in order to minimize the possibility that the client will experience any anxiety. The Avoidance Serial Cue Hierarchy starts with items which produce anxiety in the person and proceeds from external stimuli that evoke anxiety to hypothesized internal stimuli which also produce maximum levels of anxiety.

An example of this type of hierarchy concerned with a fear of enclosed spaces is presented below:

> . . . [The client] is instructed to imagine that he is entering a closed room. He remains there and is instructed to imagine that he is slowly suffocating to death. . . [the therapist supplies many details about suffocation and then, based on information obtained in the interview, might present] scenes involving wrongdoing, with a parental figure supervising confinement to the closed space as a punishment. The parental figure might beat and scold the patient while he suffocates. Early traumatic incidents that appear to be related to the phobia may also be introduced, as represented in teasing sequences by being covered and held under blankets. If the patient appears to have been involved in a typical Oedipal situation in childhood, the therapist may suggest scenes that include sexual interaction with a mother figure followed by apprehension by a father figure, who places the patient in a closed space and castrates him . . . the cues related to bodily injury are vividly described (pp. 199-200)[13]

Implosive Therapy Proper

After the hierarchy has been planned, the therapist describes implosive therapy to the client. This usually occurs at the beginning of the third session. It involves telling the client that a number of scenes will be presented to him, and that he is to sit back in the recliner chair and make every effort to lose himself in that part of the scene which is being imagined. In addition, the client is told to "live" the scenes with genuine emotion and feeling. The goal then is ". . . to reproduce in the absence of physical pain, as good an approximation as possible, the sights, sounds, and tactual experiences originally present in the primary . . ." situation in which the fear was learned (Stampfl and Levis, 1968, p. 33).

The client is neither asked to accept the accuracy of what he is imagining nor to agree that the scenes are representative of his fear. The scenes are then described by the therapist and are elaborated on in vivid detail. The more dramatic the presentation of the scenes, the easier it is for the client to participate fully in the experience. Then, as Stampfl and Levis (1967) state,

> . . . an attempt is made by the therapist to attain a maximal level of anxiety evocation from the patient. When a high level of anxiety is achieved, the patient is held on this level until some sign of spontaneous reduction in the anxiety-inducing value of the cues appears . . . the process is repeated, and again, at the first sign of spontaneous reduction of fear, new variations are introduced to elicit an intense anxiety response. This procedure is repeated until a significant diminution in anxiety has resulted. (p. 500.)[14]

One way of determining if the scenes are producing anxiety in the client is to observe if the client is flushing, sweating, grimacing, moving his head from side to side, or increasing his motoric activity in the chair. The implosion procedure is maintained for about 30-40 minutes. After a scene has been presented a few times and upon observing that the client experiences anxiety to this scene, he is given the opportunity to present the scene to himself through imagination, and is encouraged to act out fully his participation in the scene. The therapist continues to monitor the presence of anxiety and aids the client by suggesting that he imagine the scene vividly. Sometimes during treatment the client will mention to the therapist a few additional situations or events which produce fear. These should be noted by the therapist and included in the next implosive therapy session.

The session ends after 50-60 minutes and after the client has demonstrated a diminution in his anxiety response to the implosive scene. The client is then told to practice imagining the implosive scenes at home about once a day until the next session. This practice not only extends treatment outside the therapist's office and therefore aids in the generalization of the treatment effects, but it also helps the client realize that he can effectively deal with his fears by using the implosive therapy procedure. In fact, it ". . . is hoped that at the termination of treatment the patient will be able to handle new anxiety-provoking situations without the therapist's help" (Stampfl and Levis, 1967, p. 500).

The following excerpt from a therapy session with a snake phobic woman demonstrates how implosive therapy has been used. The reader will notice that external stimuli which are associated with the fear are first introduced into the imagined scene.[15]

. . . Close your eyes again. Picture the snake out in front of you, now make yourself pick it up. Reach down, pick it up, put it in your lap, feel it wiggling around in your lap, leave your hand on it, put your hand out and feel it wiggling around. Kind of explore its body with your fingers and hand. You don't like to do it, make yourself do it. Make yourself do it. Really grab onto the snake. Squeeze it a little bit, feel it. Feel it kind of start to wind around your hand. Let it. Leave your hand there, feel it touching your hand and winding around it, curling around your wrist.

In the next excerpt, the client's level of anxiety is increased by including material in the imagined scene which is based on hypothesized internal stimuli that are contributing to the fear.

Okay, now put your finger out towards the snake and feel his head coming up. Now, it is in your lap, and it is coming up. Its head [is] towards your finger and it is starting to bite at your finger. Let it, let it bite at your finger. Put your finger out, let it bite, let it bite at your finger. Oooh, feel the pain going right up your arm and into your shoulder. You want to pull your hand away, but leave it there. Let the snake kind of gnaw at your finger. Feel it gnawing, look at the blood dripping off your finger. Feel it in your stomach and the pain going up your arm. Try to picture your bleeding finger. And the teeth of the snake are stuck right in your finger, right down to the bone. And it is crunching like on your finger there. Let it. Feel it biting, it is biting at your finger, it is biting, now it is coiling around your finger, and it is biting at your hand. Again and again and again . . .

In the next excerpt, the client's level of anxiety is further increased by involving the snake in areas which come close to the actual hypothesized fears of the clients.

Okay, feel him coiling around your hand again, touching you, slimy, now he is going up on your shoulder and he crawls there and is sitting on your chest and he is looking you right in the eye. He is big and he is black and he is ugly and he's coiled up and he is ready to strike and he is looking at you. Picture his face, look at his eyes, look at those long sharp fangs. He is staring at you, he is evil looking, he is slimy, he is ready to strike at your face. Feel him sitting there, just staring at you. Those long sharp teeth with the blood on them. He strikes out at you, [therapist slaps hands] . . . Feel him bite at your face. Feel him bite at your face, let him bite; let him bite; just relax and let him bite; let him bite at your face, let him bite; let him bite at your face; feel his fangs go right into your cheeks; and the blood is coming out on your face now. And the poison is going into your body and you are getting sick and nauseated and he is striking at your face again and again. Now he coils up on this shoulder and he is ready to strike again at your face. Feel him bite, put your head down towards him, put your head down, let him bite at your face, let him bite as much as he wants. Feel him bite, he is putting his head, his little head up by your ear and he is snapping at your ear. Feel him snap at your ear. Now he is going up by your eyes and he is starting to bite at your eyes. Feel him bite, let him bite, feel his fangs go into your eyes and he is pulling at them and tearing at them and ripping at them. Picture what your face looks like. Get that sick feeling in your stomach and now he is gnawing at your nose, and biting at your mouth. Just take a deep breath and let him do it. Now he is coiling around your neck, slimy and wet and dirty, and he is squeezing you. He is choking you, feel him choke you, feel the breath coming out of you, that sick feeling in your stomach. He snaps out at you, feel him snap at you. Now he is crawling across your face. Can you feel him? He is wet and slimy and he's touching your face, he is crawling up into your hair. Feel him up in your hair, coiled around up there . . . Feel him snap at you. Feel him snap; that sick feeling in your stomach, feel him biting you; he is gnawing at your cheeks now feel him, bluhh—and just picture how ugly you're looking and terrible, and he's enraged and he's biting and biting and biting and biting and biting and biting and biting. . . .

In commenting on this highly intensive experience, Hogan (1969) states ". . .For the most part, I do not let the S verbalize at will, because speech is often used as a defense to avoid anxiety. I am satisfied with a nod of the head or a brief comment to verify . . . [my] clinical hypothesis." (p. 178). It should be further noted that therapists do not engage in any discussion with a client during this period. After the client gives some indication of the appropriateness of the interpretation, the therapist continues with the scene and may even intensify it.

In the next excerpt, the psychodynamic interpretation of the fear is presented, emphasizing its sexual nature. Regarding this presentation, Hogan (1969) states: "I might have the snake swallowed by the S, and later it might exit from her vagina. I would have her play a male sexual role, or she might be castrated in an attempt to relive, in imagery, Freudian-related conflict" (p. 182).

Therapist: I want you to picture yourself getting ready to get into your bed and there in your bed are thousands of snakes. Can you see them there crawling around in your bed? I want you to lay down with them. Get down with them. Feel yourself moving around with the snakes and they are crawling all over you. And you are moving and turning in bed and they are touching you. Feel them crawling on you, touching you, slimy and slithering. Feel yourself turn over in your bed, and they are under you and on you and around you, and touching your face and in your hair. And they are crawling across your face. Can you feel them touch you? Describe the feeling.

　　Subject: Kind of cold.

　　Therapist: Feel, you are now cold and clammy like a snake and they are touching you with their cold, clammy, wet, slimy, drippy, cold bodies that are wiggling and touching your skin and feel them. Uhhh how can you feel them touch you? They are touching you. Can you feel them touch you? Move around so you can get greater contact. Move your body like that woman in the Sealy [mattress] ad and feel them touch you, uhh, wiggly and slimy, they are crawling on you, on your face. Uhhh!

Alternatives to Implosive Therapy

A variant of implosive therapy is called *flooding*. The major difference between this method and implosive therapy is in the type of scenes to which clients are exposed. Instead of exposing clients to horrifying scenes in which certain aversive consequences occur (e.g., eating flesh, castrating people, death, etc.), scenes are described in which the feared external stimuli are presented for an extended period of time.[16] For example, compare the last two implosive therapy excerpts with the following scene:

> While studying at your desk in the laboratory you suddenly become aware of a large rat crawling up your leg. You jump up and try to shake it off, but it runs up your side . . . across your face . . . into your hair and is caught there. In an attempt to get loose, its tail falls down onto your face and touches your lips. You try to get him off your head, but you fail . . . etc. (Adapted from Rachman, 1966, p. 3)

Thus, psychodynamic cues and/or interpretations are not used in the formulation of the scenes; rather, the therapist uses only the external cues and vividly describes the scenes in a way similar to implosive therapy. Scenes are presented for about the same period of time as in implosive therapy, and an attempt is made at also maintaining the client's anxiety arousal at a maximum level throughout the session. Some writers (Emmelkamp and Wessels, 1975; Marshall, et al., 1977) have suggested that *in vivo* flooding (real-life exposure to the feared situation is preferable to imaginal flooding procedures; however, it is readily recognized by these writers that *in vivo* exposure may be too terrifying for some clients. As an alternative, Marshall, et al. (1977) report that by adding a brief real-life exposure component to imaginal flooding immediately following each treatment session, clients may still receive maximum benefit from therapy.

Limitations of Implosive Therapy

Stampfl and Levis (1967) state that "the more accurate the hypothesized cues and the more realistically they are presented the greater the extinction effect . . . will be" (p. 499). This statement suggests that the therapist should be quite knowledgeable in psychodynamic theory, especially psychoanalytic theory. If the therapist is not, he should probably refrain from using this approach. Furthermore, some writers (Marshall et al., 1977; Redd, Porterfield, and Andersen, 1979) have suggested that imaginal exposure to horrifying situations may, under certain conditions, strengthen a client's fear. A possible substitute for this therapy is the flooding procedure, but this, too, should be used with caution. The therapist should be very familiar with identifying anxiety cues, formulating highly anxiety-provoking scenes, and capable of dealing with a client who might have a very negative experience to the anxiety-provoking scenes that are presented.

CONCLUSION

The three methods discussed in this chapter have been widely used in the reduction of fears. Major questions which remain involve ''which fear reduction method should be used, under what conditions and for which type of fear? These questions are not easily answered, but we will attempt to provide guidelines regarding the use of each method.

Without a doubt the most useful and most heavily researched fear reduction method is systematic desensitization. It has been shown in many studies to be very effective in reducing various types of fears. Its prime limitation is that it is extremely time consuming, especially when the client has a great number of fears. But even considering this limitation, it appears that systematic desensitization (with or without a coping component) is the treatment of choice for most fears. If, however, the client is a child, contact desensitization should be used.

On the other hand, if a client's fears are strictly related to social situations— where he is afraid to act in his own behalf—assertive training should be tried first. Where the client is afraid to practice assertiveness training in the real situation, the therapist should use covert modeling or desensitization to help the client relax.

Finally, because of the limitations mentioned at the end of the implosive therapy section and because implosive therapy has not been generally found to be more effective than systematic desensitization (see Morganstern, 1973), implosive therapy should not be used as the first treatment of choice.

APPENDIX 1

FEAR SURVEY SCHEDULE[17]

The items in this questionnaire refer to things and experiences that may cause fear or other unpleasant feelings. Write the number of each item in the column that describes how much you are disturbed by it nowadays.

	Not at All	A Little	A Fair Amount	Much	Very Much
1. Open wounds					
2. Dating					
3. Being alone					

APPENDIX 1 (Continued)

	Not at All	A Little	A Fair Amount	Much	Very Much
4. Being in a strange place					
5. Loud noises					
6. Dead people					
7. Speaking in public					
8. Crossing streets					
9. People who seem insane					
10. Falling					
11. Automobiles					
12. Being teased					
13. Dentists					
14. Thunder					
15. Sirens					
16. Failure					
17. Entering a room where other people are already seated					
18. High places on land					
19. Looking down from high buildings					
20. Worms					
21. Imaginary creatures					
22. Strangers					
23. Receiving injections					
24. Bats					
25. Journeys by train					
26. Journeys by bus					
27. Journeys by car					
28. Feeling angry					
29. People in authority					
30. Flying insects					
31. Seeing other people injected					
32. Sudden noises					
33. Cockroaches					
34. Crowds					
35. Large open spaces					
36. Cats					
37. One person bullying another					
38. Tough looking people					
39. Birds					
40. Sight of deep water					
41. Being watched working					
42. Dead animals					
43. Weapons					
44. Dirt					
45. Crawling insects					
46. Sight of fighting					
47. Ugly people					
48. Fire					
49. Sick people					
50. Dogs					

APPENDIX 1 (Continued)

	Not at All	A Little	A Fair Amount	Much	Very Much
51. Being criticized					
52. Walking on dark streets alone					
53. Being in an elevator					
54. Witnessing surgical operations					
55. Angry people					
56. Mice					
57. Blood					
(a) Human					
(b) Animal					
58. Parting from friends					
59. Enclosed places					
60. Prospect of a surgical operation					
61. Feeling rejected by others					
62. Airplanes					
63. Medical odors					
64. Feeling disapproved of					
65. Harmless snakes					
66. Cemeteries					
67. Being ignored					
68. Darkness					
69. Premature heart beats (Missing a beat)					
70. Nude men (a) Nude women (b)					
71. Lightning					
72. Doctors					
73. People with deformities					
75. Looking foolish					
76. Losing control					
77. Fainting					
78. Becoming nauseous					
79. Spiders (Harmless)					
80. Being in charge or responsible for making decisions					
81. Sight of knives or sharp objects					
82. Becoming mentally ill					
83. Being with a member of the opposite sex					
84. Taking written tests					
85. Being touched by others					
86. Feeling different from others					
87. A lull in conversation					
88. Laboratory rats					
89. Taking any type of test					
90. Public speaking (speaking in front of groups)					
91. Looking down from high places					

APPENDIX 2

REVISED WILLOUGHBY QUESTIONNAIRE FOR SELF ADMINISTRATION[18]

Instructions. The questions in this schedule are intended to indicate various emotional personality traits. It is not a test in any sense because there are no right and wrong answers to any of the questions. After each question you will find a row of numbers whose meaning is given below. All you have to do is to draw a ring around the number that describes you best.

0 means "No," "never," "not at all," etc.

1 means "Somewhat," "sometimes," "a little," etc

2. means "About as often as not," "an average amount," etc.

3 means "Usually," "a good deal," "rather often," etc.

4 means "Practically always," "entirely," etc.

1. Do you get anxious if you have to speak or perform in any way in front of a group of strangers?—0 1 2 3 4

2. Do you worry if you make a fool of yourself, or feel you have been made to look foolish?—0 1 2 3 4

3. Are you afraid of falling when you are on a high place from which there is no real danger of falling—for example, looking down from a balcony on the tenth floor?—0 1 2 3 4

4. Are you easily hurt by what other people do or say to you?—0 1 2 3 4

5. Do you keep in the background on social occasions?—0 1 2 3 4

6. Do you have changes of mood that you cannot explain?—0 1 2 3 4

7. Do you feel uncomfortable when you meet new people?—0 1 2 3 4

8. Do you daydream frequently, i.e. indulge in fantasies not involving concrete situations?—0 1 2 3 4

9. Do you get discouraged easily, e.g. by failure or criticism?—0 1 2 3 4

10. Do you say things in haste and then regret them?—0 1 2 3 4

11. Are you ever disturbed by the mere presence of other people?—0 1 2 3 4

12. Do you cry easily?—0 1 2 3 4

13. Does it bother you to have people watch you work when you do it well?—0 1 2 3 4

14. Does criticism hurt you badly?—0 1 2 3 4

15. Do you cross the street to avoid meeting someone?—0 1 2 3 4

16. At a reception or tea do you go out of your way to avoid meeting the important person present?—0 1 2 3 4

17. Do you often feel just miserable?—0 1 2 3 4

18. Do you hesitate to volunteer in a discussion or debate with a group of people whom you know more or less?—0 1 2 3 4

19. Do you have a sense of isolation, either when alone or among people?—0 1 2 3 4

20. Are you self-conscious before 'superiors' (teachers, employers, authorities)?—0 1 2 3 4

21. Do you lack confidence in your general ability to do things and to cope with situations?—0 1 2 3 4

22. Are you self-conscious about your appearance even when you are well-dressed and groomed?—0 1 2 3 4

23. Are you scared at the sight of blood, injuries, and destruction even though there is no danger to you?—0 1 2 3 4

24. Do you feel that other people are better than you?—0 1 2 3 4

25. Is it hard for you to make up your mind?—0 1 2 3 4

APPENDIX 3

BERNREUTER S-S SELF-SUFFICIENCY INVENTORY[19]

1. Yes No ? Would you rather work for yourself than carry out the program of a superior whom you respect?
2. Yes No ? Do you usually enjoy spending an evening alone?
3. Yes No ? Have books been more entertaining to you than companions?
4. Yes No ? Do you feel the need of wider social contacts than you have?
5. Yes No ? Are you easily discouraged when the opinions of others differ from your own?
6. Yes No ? Does admiration gratify you more than achievement?
7. Yes No ? Do you usually prefer to keep your opinions to yourself?
8. Yes No ? Do you dislike attending the movies alone?
9. Yes No ? Would you like to have a very congenial friend with whom you could plan daily activities?
10. Yes No ? Can you calm your own fears?
11. Yes No ? Do jeers humiliate you even when you know you are right?
12. Yes No ? Do you think you could become so absorbed in creative work that you would not notice the lack of intimate friends?
13. Yes No ? Are you willing to take a chance alone in a situation of doubtful outcome?
14. Yes No ? Do you find conversation more helpful in formulating your ideas than reading?
15. Yes No ? Do you like to shop alone?
16. Yes No ? Does your ambition need occasional stimulation through contacts with successful people?
17. Yes No ? Do you have difficulty in making up your mind for yourself?
18. Yes No ? Would you prefer making your own arrangements on a trip to a foreign country to going on a prearranged trip?
19. Yes No ? Are you much affected by praise, or blame, of many people?
20. Yes No ? Do you usually avoid taking advice?
21. Yes No ? Do you consider the observance of social customs and manners an essential aspect of life?
22. Yes No ? Do you want someone with you when you receive bad news?
23. Yes No ? Does it make you uncomfortable to be 'different' or unconventional?
24. Yes No ? Do you prefer to make hurried decisions alone?
25. Yes No ? If you were to start out in research work, would you prefer to be an assistant in another's project rather than an independent worker on your own?
26. Yes No ? When you are low in spirits do you try to find someone to cheer you up?
27. Yes No ? Have you preferred being alone most of the time?
28. Yes No ? Do you prefer traveling with someone who will make all the necessary arrangements to the adventure of traveling alone?
29. Yes No ? Do you usually work things out rather than get someone to show you?
30. Yes No ? Do you like especially to have attention from acquaintances when you are ill?
31. Yes No ? Do you prefer to face dangerous situations alone?
32. Yes No ? Can you usually see wherein your mistakes lie without having them pointed out to you?
33. Yes No ? Do you like to make friends when you go to new places?
34. Yes No ? Can you stick to a tiresome task for long without someone prodding or encouraging you?

APPENDIX 3 (Continued)

35. Yes No ? Do you experience periods of loneliness?
36. Yes No ? Do you like to get many views from others before making an important decision?
37. Yes No ? Would you dislike any work which might take you into isolation for a few years, such as forest ranging, etc.?
38. Yes No ? Do you prefer a play to a dance?
39. Yes No ? Do you usually try to take added responsibility upon yourself?
40. Yes No ? Do you make friends easily?
41. Yes No ? Can you be optimistic when others about you are greatly depressed?
42. Yes No ? Do you try to get your own way even if you have to fight for it?
43. Yes No ? Do you like to be with other people a great deal?
44. Yes No ? Do you get as many ideas at the time of reading as you do from a discussion of it afterwards?
45. Yes No ? In sports do you prefer to participate in individual competitions rather than in team games?
46. Yes No ? Do you usually face your troubles alone without seeking help?
47. Yes No ? Do you see more fun or humor in things when you are in a group than when you are alone?
48. Yes No ? Do you dislike finding your way about in strange places?
49. Yes No ? Can you work happily without praise or recognition?
50. Yes No ? Do you feel that marriage is essential to your happiness?
51. Yes No ? If all but a few of your friends threatened to break relations because of some habit they considered a vice in you, and in which you saw no harm, would you stop the habit to keep friends?
52. Yes No ? Do you like to have suggestions offered to you when you are working a puzzle?
53. Yes No ? Do you usually prefer to do your own planning alone rather than with others?
54. Yes No ? Do you usually find that people are more stimulating to you than anything else?
55. Yes No ? Do you prefer to be alone at times of emotional stress?
56. Yes No ? Do you like to bear responsibilities alone?
57. Yes No ? Can you usually understand a problem better by studying it out alone than by discussing it with others?
58. Yes No ? Do you find that telling others of your own personal good news is the greatest part of the enjoyment of it?
59. Yes No ? Do you generally rely on your judgment?
60. Yes No ? Do you like playing games in which you have no spectators?

APPENDIX 4

RATHUS ASSERTIVENESS SCHEDULE[20]

Directions. Indicate how characteristic or descriptive each of the following statements is of you by using the code given below.

+3 very characteristic of me, extremely descriptive
+2 rather characteristic of me, quite descriptive
+1 somewhat characteristic of me, slightly descriptive
−1 somewhat uncharacteristic of me, slightly nondescriptive
−2 rather uncharacteristic of me, quite nondescriptive
−3 very uncharacteristic of me, extremely nondescriptive

APPENDIX 4 (Continued)

_____ 1. Most people seem to be more aggressive and assertive than I am.*

_____ 2. I have hesitated to make or accept dates because of "shyness."*

_____ 3. When the food served at a restaurant is not done to my satisfaction I complain about it to the waiter or waitress.

_____ 4. I am careful to avoid hurting other people's feelings, even when I feel that I have been injured.*

_____ 5. If a salesman has gone to considerable trouble to show me merchandise which is not quite suitable, I have a difficult time saying "No."*

_____ 6. When I am asked to do something, I insist upon knowing why.

_____ 7. There are times when I look for a good vigorous argument.

_____ 8. I strive to get ahead as well as most people in my position.

_____ 9. To be honest, people often take advantage of me.*

_____10. I enjoy starting conversations with new acquaintances and strangers.

_____11. I often don't know what to say to attractive persons of the opposite sex.*

_____12. I will hesitate to make phone calls to business establishments and institutions.

_____13. I would rather apply for a job or for admission to a college by writing them letters than by going through with personal interviews.*

_____14. I find it embarrassing to return merchandise.*

_____15. If a close and respected relative were annoying me, I would smother my feelings rather than express my annoyance.

_____16. I have avoided asking questions for fear of sounding stupid.*

_____17. During an argument I am sometimes afraid that I will get so upset that I will shake all over.*

_____18. If a famed and respected lecturer makes a statement which I think is incorrect, I will have the audience hear my point of view as well.

_____19. I avoid arguing over prices with clerks and salesmen.*

_____20. When I have done something important or worthwhile, I manage to let others know about it.

_____21. I am open and frank about my feelings.

_____22. If someone has been spreading false and bad stories about me, I see him (her) as soon as possible to "have a talk" about it.

_____23. I often have a hard time saying "No."*

_____24. I tend to bottle up my emotions rather than make a scene.*

_____25. I complain about poor service in a restaurant and elsewhere.

_____26. When I am given a compliment, I sometimes just don't know what to say.*

_____27. If a couple near me in a theatre or at a lecture were conversing rather loudly, I would ask them to be quiet or to take their conversation elsewhere.

_____28. Anyone attempting to push ahead of me in a line is in for a good battle.

_____29. I am quick to express an opinion.

_____30. There are times when I just can't say anything.

*Reversed item
Total score obtained by adding numerical responses to each item, after changing the signs of reversed items.

NOTES

[1]The author wishes to express his gratitude to Vinnie Morris, George Domino, Dawn Riley, Kenneth V. Karrels and Kirby Brown for critically reading various preliminary drafts of this chapter. Appreciation is also due Barbara Troncoso for her assistance in the literature review.

[2]An alternative learning theory view on the etiology of fears has been developed by Seligman (1971, 1975). He does not completely agree with each of these assumptions. Seligman has incorporated the notion of "biological preparedness" into his theory and states that people, for example, are "prepared" to develop particular fears based on the biological and evolutionary significance of certain stimuli and situations which are tied to their struggle for survival.

[3]Adapted from Wolpe and Lazarus (1966).

[4]Throughout this chapter the case transcripts, case descriptions, and hierarchies have been changed slightly to protect the anonymity of the clients involved.

[5]Adapted from Paul, G.L. Insight vs. desensitization in psychotherapy. Stanford, Calif.: Stanford University Press, 1966.

[6]Before initiating the relaxation procedure, it is often helpful, as a precaution, to ask the client if any physical problem exists which might interfere with the tensing and relaxing of various muscles. If the client mentions a problem area, the therapist should omit this muscle grouping from the procedure or not request the client to strongly tense this set of muscles.

[7]Sections in brackets have been added by the present author.

[8]From Bandura, A. Principles of behavior modification. New York: Holt, Rinehart and Winston, 1969. Reprinted by permission.

[9]From Lazarus, A.A. Behavior therapy and beyond. New York: McGraw-Hill, 1971. Reprinted by permission.

[10]From Wolpe, J. and Lazarus, A.A. Behavior therapy techniques. New York: Pergamon Press, 1966. Reprinted by permission.

[11]In this statement, Stampfl and Levis (1967) are using the term "reinforcement" in the classical conditioning sense of the word, i.e., the procedure of following a conditioned stimulus (CS) with an unconditioned stimulus (UCS).

[12]From Stampfl, T.G. and Levis, D.J. Essentials of implosive therapy: A learning-based-psychodynamic behavioral therapy. Journal of Abnormal Psychology, 1967, 72, 496-503. Reprinted by permission.

[13]From Stampfl, T.G. Implosive Therapy: An Emphasis on Covert Stimulation. In D.J. Levis (Ed.), Learning approaches to therapeutic behavior change. Chicago: Aldine, 1970. Reprinted by permission.

[14]Reprinted by permission.

[15]The excerpts appearing on pp. 280-282 are reprinted from Hogan, R.A. Implosively oriented behavior modification: Therapy considerations. Behaviour Research and Therapy, 1969, 1, 177-184. Reprinted with permission.

[16]This distinction between flooding and implosive therapy has been questioned by Levis (1974).

[17]Adapted from Wolpe, J. The practice of behavior therapy (2nd ed.). New York: Pergamon Press, 1973, by permission.

[18]From Wolpe, J. The practice of behavior therapy (2nd ed.). New York: Pergamon Press, 1973, by permission.

[19]From Wolpe, J. The practice of behavior therapy (2nd ed.). New York: Pergamon Press, 1973, by permission.

[20]From Rathus, S.A. A 30-item schedule for assessing assertive behavior. Behavior Therapy, 4, 1973, pp. 399-400. Reprinted by permission from author and Academic Press; for research purposes only.

REFERENCES

Alberti, R.E. and Emmons, M.L. *Your perfect right*. San Luis Obispo, Calif.: Authors, 1970.

Baker, B.L., Cohen, D.C., and Saunders, J.T. Self-directed desensitization for acrophobics. *Behaviour Research and Therapy*, 1973, *11*, 79-89.

Bandura, A. *Principles of behavior modification*. New York: Holt, Rinehart and Winston, 1969.

——— *Social learning theory*. Englewood Cliffs, N.J.: Prentice-Hall, Inc., 1977.

Bandura, A. and Walters, R.H. *Social learning and personality development*. New York: Holt, Rinehart and Winston, Inc., 1963.

Brady, J.P. Brevital-relaxation treatment of frigidity. *Behaviour Research and Therapy*, 1966, *4*, 71-77.

——— Systematic desensitization. In W.S. Agras (Ed.), *Behavior modification: Principles and clinical applications*. Boston, Mass.: Little, Brown, 1972.

Emmelkamp, P.M.G. and Wessels, H. Flooding in imagination vs. Flooding in vivo: A comparison with agorophobics. *Behaviour Research and Therapy*, 1975, *13*, 7-15.

Friedman, D.E. A new technique for the systematic desensitization of phobic symptoms. *Behaviour Research and Therapy*, 1966, *4*, 139-140.

Galassi, J.P., Delo, J.S., Galassi, M.D., and Bastien, S. The college self-expression scale: A measure of assertiveness. *Behavior Therapy*, 1974, *5*, 165-171.

Gay, M.L., Hollandsworth, J.G., and Galassi, J.P. An assertiveness inventory for adults. *Journal of Counselling Psychology*, 1975, *22*, 340-344.

Goldfried, M.R. Systematic desensitization as training in self-control. *Journal of Consulting and Clinical Psychology*, 1971, *37*, 228-234.

Goldfried M.R. and Davison, G. *Clinical behavior therapy*. New York: Holt, Rinehart, and Winston, 1976.

Goldfried, M.R. and Goldfried, A.P. Importance of hierarchy content in the self-control of anxiety. *Journal of Consulting and Clinical Psychology*, 1977, *45*, 124-134.

Hogan, R.A. The implosive technique. *Behaviour Research and Therapy*, 1968, *6*, 423-431.

Hogan, R.A. and Kirchner, J.H. A preliminary report on the extinction of learned fears via short term implosive therapy. *Journal of Abnormal Psychology*, 1967, *72*, 106-111.

Hull, C.L. *Principles of behavior*. New York: Appleton-Century-Crofts, 1943.

Jacobson, E. *Progressive relaxation*. Chicago: University of Chicago Press, 1938.

Javel, A.F. and Denholtz, M.S. Audible GSR feedback and systematic desensitization: A case report. *Behavior Therapy*, 1975, *6*, 251-254.

Kanfer, F.H. and Grimm, L.G. Behavioral analysis: Selecting target behaviors in the interview. *Behavior Modification*, 1977, *1*, 7-28.

Kazdin, A.E. Effects of covert modeling, multiple models, and model reinforcement on assertive behavior. *Behavior Therapy*, 1976, *7*, 211-222.

Kazdin, A.E. Effects of covert modeling and model reinforcement on assertive behavior. *Journal of Abnormal Psychology*, 1974, *83*, 240-252.

Lazarus, A.A. *Behavior therapy and beyond*. New York: McGraw-Hill, 1971.

——— On assertive behavior: A brief note. *Behavior Therapy*, 1973, *4*, 697-699.

Levis, D.J. Implosive therapy: A critical analysis of Morganstern's review. *Psychological Bulletin*, 1974, *81*, 155-158.

Marshall, W.L., Gauthier, J., Christie, M.M., Currie, D.W. and Gordon, A. Flooding therapy effectiveness, stimulus characteristics, and the value of brief *in vivo* exposure. *Behaviour Research and Therapy*, 1977, *15*, 79-87.

Meichenbaum, D. Self-instructional methods. In F.H. Kanfer and A.P. Goldstein (Eds.), *Helping people change*. New York: Pergamon, 1974.

Migler, B. and Wolpe, J. Automated self-desensitization. A case report. *Behaviour Research and Therapy*, 1967, *5*, 133-135.

Morganstern, K.P. Implosive therapy and flooding procedures: A critical review. *Psychological Bulletin*, 1973, *79*, 318-334.

Morris, R.J. Shaping relaxation in the unrelaxed client. *Journal of Behavior Therapy and Experimental Psychiatry*, 1973, *4*, 353-343.

Morris, R.J. and Suckerman, K.R. The importance of the therapeutic relationship in systematic desensitization. *Journal of Consulting and Clinical Psychology*, 1974a, *42*, 148.

———— Automated systematic desensitization: The importance of therapist warmth. *Journal of Consulting and Clinical Psychology*, 1974b, *42*, 244-250.

Mowrer, O.H. *Learning theory and personality dynamics*. New York: Roland Press, 1950.

Nietzel, M.T., Martoreno, R.D. and Melnick, J. The effects of covert modeling with and without reply training on the development and generalization of assertive responses. *Behavior Therapy*, 1977, *8*, 183-192.

Öst, L-G. Fading—a new technique in the treatment of phobias. *Behaviour Research and Therapy*, 1978a, *16*, 213-216.

———— Fading vs. systematic desensitization in the treatment of snake and spider phobia. *Behaviour Research and Therapy*, 1978b, *16*, 379-390.

Paul, G.L. *Insight vs. desensitization in psychotherapy*. Stanford, Calif: Standford University Press, 1966.

Pavlov, I.P. *Conditioned reflexes*. London: Oxford University Press, 1927.

Rachman, S. Studies in desensitization, II: Flooding. *Behaviour Research and Therapy*, 1966, *4*, 1-6.

Rathus, S.A. A 30-item schedule for assessing assertive behavior. *Behavior Therapy*, 1973, *4*, 398-406.

Redd, W.H., Porterfield, A.L., and Andersen, B.L. *Behavior modification*. New York: Random House, 1979.

Reeves, J.L. and Maelica, W.L. Biofeedback—assisted cue-controlled relaxation for the treatment of flight phobias. *Journal of Behavior Therapy and Experimental Psychiatry*, 1975, *6*, 105-109.

Richardson, F.C. and Suinn, R.M. A comparison of traditional systematic desensitization, accelerated massed desensitization, and anxiety management training in the treatment of mathematics anxiety. *Behavior Therapy*, 1973, *4*, 212-218.

Ritter, B. The group desensitization of children's snake phobias using vicarious and contact desensitization procedures. *Behaviour Research and Therapy*, 1968, *6*, 1-6.

———— Treatment of acrophobia with contact desensitization. *Behaviour Research and Therapy*, 1969a, *7*, 41-45.

———— The use of contact desensitization, demonstration-plus-participation and demonstration-alone in the treatment of acrophobia. *Behaviour Research and Therapy*, 1969b, *7* 157-164.

Rosen, G. *Don't be afraid. A program for overcoming your fears and phobias*. Englewood Cliffs, N.J.; Prentice-Hall, 1976.

Rosen, G.M., Glasgow, R.E., and Barrera, M., Jr. A controlled study to assess the clinical efficacy of totally self-administered systematic desensitization. *Journal of Consulting and Clinical Psychology*, 1976, *44*, 208-217.

Salter, A. *Conditioned reflex therapy*. New York: Farrar, Strauss, 1949. Republished: New York: Capricorn Books, Putman, 1961.

Sherman, A.R. Real-life exposure as a primary therapeutic factor in the desensitization treatment of fear. *Journal of Abnormal Psychology*, 1972, *79*, 19-28.

Skinner, B.F. *The behavior of organisms*. New York: Appleton-Century, 1938.

——— *Science and human behavior*. New York: MacMillan, 1953.

Stampfl, T.G. Implosive therapy: A learning theory derived psychodynamic therapeutic technique. Paper presented at the University of Illinois, 1961.

——— Implosive therapy: An emphasis on covert stimulation. In D.J. Levis (Ed.) *Learning approaches to therapeutic behavior change*. Chicago: Aldine, 1970.

Stampfl, T.G. and Levis, D.J. Essentials of implosive therapy: A learning-based-psychodynamic behavioral therapy. *Journal of Abnormal Psychology*, 1967, *72*, 496-503.

——— Implosive therapy—A behavioral therapy? *Behaviour Research and Therapy*, 1968, *6*, 31-36.

Walen, S., Hauserman, N.M. and Lavin, P.J. *Clinical guide to behavior therapy*. New York: Oxford University Press, 1977.

Wilson, G.T. and Evans, I.M. The therapist-client relationship in behavior therapy. In A.S. Gurman and A.M. Razin (Eds.), *Effective psychotherapy: A handbook of research*. New York: Pergamon Press, 1977.

Wolpe, J. *Reciprocal inhibition therapy*. Stanford University Press, 1958.

——— The experimental foundations of some new psychotherapeutic methods. In A.J. Bachrach (Ed.), *Experimental foundations of clinical psychology*. New York: Basic Books, 1962.

——— *The practice of behavior therapy*. New York: Pergamon Press, 1969.

——— *The practice of behavior therapy*. (2nd ed.) New York: Pergamon Press, 1973.

Wolpe, J. and Lazarus, A.A. *Behavior therapy techniques*. New York: Pergamon Press, 1966.

Wolpin, M. and Pearsall, L. Rapid deconditioning of a fear of snakes. *Behavior Research and Therapy*, 1965, *3*, 107-111.

9

Aversion Methods

Jack Sandler

The use of aversive methods in human interactions is probably the oldest approach to dealing with problem behaviors known to mankind. Even the earliest observers of human behavior noted the essential feature underlying such efforts: that undesirable behavior can usually be terminated if a sufficiently noxious event is brought to bear on the behavior in question. Such practices have been repeated by individuals and institutions since the dawn of history and variations on this theme have also been employed by practitioners in the field of mental health.

Unfortunately, aversive methods have also created numerous problems and many authorities have expressed their concern with the use of such techniques. Recently, behavior therapists have responded to this controversy by establishing a set of guidelines delineating the appropriate use of aversive methods for treatment purposes. The thrust of this position maintains that such practices are defensible if they are used to improve a patient's condition as contrasted with the conventional use of aversive events for expedience or merely to control another person's behavior. Thus, aversive procedures may be regarded as a form of treatment if the pain and discomfort involved is small, relative to the far greater degree of pain and discomfort experienced by the individual if the problem condition were to continue. This principle is analagous to the use of aversive procedures employed by dentists and physicians in their practices. To limit the potential for inappropriate and/or abusive use of these methods, most authorities have argued that a problem condition should be treated by the lowest risk techniques first. Only after these have been ineffective should one consider the use of more extreme aversive or intrusive procedures. Finally, because many of these issues are complex and difficult to apply in any given case, practitioners should be trained and qualified in the area of aversion therapy.

In the state of Florida, these emerging guidelines have resulted in the formulation of a guide for the use of aversive procedures by a distinguished committee of professionals, scientists and legal experts (May, J.G., et al. 1976) which might serve as a model for other states and institutions concerned with such issues.

The continued attempt to establish guidelines for the use of aversive procedures has also been accompanied by a continuing search for nonphysical painful aversive methods.

GENERAL DESCRIPTION

At the practical level, a description of aversive procedures appears to be relatively straightforward and uncomplicated. For the most part, such arrangements involve an undesirable and/or maladaptive behavior on the part of the patient and the presentation of an unpleasant stimulus or event in close temporal relationship with the behavior. All forms of aversive treatment reflect these characteristics, whether commonplace and informal as in the case of the parent who spanks a child for playing with matches, or unusual and more systematic as in the case of administering shock to the fingertips of a child molester while he is handling children's clothing. The objective in each case is to reduce the future probability of occurrences of the maladaptive behavior.

However, a detailed analysis of the procedures which have been used quickly reveal the complexities which are involved in aversion therapy. Although it is not the intent of this chapter to analyze the theories underlying these efforts, the interested reader should at least be acquainted with the issues.

Briefly stated, there are two major theoretical positions which have attempted to explain the change processes. Although there are areas of overlap between the two, they start from different assumptions and more often than not are designed to generate divergent treatment practices. Most of the aversion therapy reports in the literature reflect either one or the other theoretical position, although in actual practice, the differences between the two are often blurred.

The first of these emerged out of Pavlov's well-known research on conditioned responses in dogs. In this system, a previously neutral stimulus such as a buzzer, of a flashing light, is presented in close temporal contiguity with an unconditioned stimulus, i.e., a stimulus which naturally elicits a reflex reaction. After a sufficient number of such pairings, the previously neutral stimulus also acquires the power to elicit the reflex. Thus, when an organism is exposed to an aversive stimulus, certain physiological reflexes are evoked which are typically identified as the fear response. Furthermore, under appropriate circumstances, neutral stimuli which are present on such occasions also acquire the power to evoke the same or similar response. In this fashion, the fear response is "conditioned" to these previously neutral stimuli. Although this is by necessity an oversimplification of the conditioned fear hypothesis, these observations have been invoked to suggest both the manner in which certain maladaptive responses may be *acquired* as well as the manner in which certain pathological responses may be *modified*. Thus, if an alcoholic is required to drink liquor while exposed to a painful stimulus which elicits the fear response, after a sufficient number of such experiences, the fear will become conditioned to the liquor. In the future, the sight, taste, and smell of liquor will elicit the physiological changes associated with the fear responses and the patient will be repelled by such substances. Indeed, as we shall see, procedures of this sort have been employed in a variety of problem conditions with varying degrees of success.

An alternate theory has been proposed by operant conditioners who focus their attention on the consequences of a response rather than on the events which precede a behavior. In this system (see Chapter 7 for an extensive discussion of the operant conditioning paradigm) the theory specifies that virtually all behaviors, abnormal as well as normal, are maintained or at least heavily influenced by reinforcing events. Thus, when a response produces a positively reinforcing event or avoids a negatively reinforcing event, the probability of future occurrence of that response increases. Conversely, when a response produces an aversive stimulus or is followed by no consequences, the probability of future occurrence of that response decreases. The last two arrangements are respectively defined as punishment and extinction. Again, such procedures have been employed in actual clinical practice. Thus, if a child who is a head banger (a form of self-injurious behavior often observed in disturbed and retarded children) receives shock contingent on the undesirable behavior, that is, if each head banging response produces the aversive event, after a sufficient number of such experiences, the response will decline in frequency.

It must be remembered that the above description represents the procedures and results obtained in the laboratory. In the clinical situation, there may be considerable departure from these arrangements such that an accurate anlysis of the actual procedures is precluded. Thus, Pavlovian procedures may be inadvertently combined with operant procedures, and vice versa. For example, a Pavlovian procedure may dictate the use of shock paired on every occasion with alcohol-related stimuli, independent of the patient's behavior. The actual arrangement, however, may deviate from this procedure by virtue of the patient's response, thus confounding the procedure with operant conditioning. For this reason, it would appear that many techniques ostensibly designed within the context of one of the above systems frequently may be interpreted as involving processes from the alternate system.

MAXIMIZING THE EFFECTS OF AVERSION THERAPY

Once the decision to use aversion therapy has been made, it is the therapist's responsibility to apply the chosen technique in the most efficient manner possible, i.e., his efforts should include all of the ethical and scientific safeguards which are part of any therapeutic procedure. Ideally, then, the procedure should be designed to eliminate the problem condition permanently, as quickly as possible, and without undesirable residual effects.

Although it is impossible at the present time to specify all the conditions which would aid in reaching this objective, the therapist should attempt to approach the ideal as closely as possible. Since most of the recommendations for the effective use of aversive techniques have emerged from the operant literature, the assumption here is made that most problem conditions encountered by clinicians can be regarded as the unfortunate learning of undesirable operants that create problems for the individual, or as the failure to learn those operants which enable a satisfactory adjustment in daily life.

First and foremost, at least at the beginning of treatment, the aversive event should be completely coincident with the problem behavior. That is, it should be administered in the absence of the response. This rationale stems from research which indicates that response reduction occurs most rapidly when the aversive stimulus is paired with the response whenever it occurs.

In many instances this principle can be easily applied without fear of error because of the specific characteristics of the response. A pronounced facial tic, for example, is usually easily identified (i.e., has discrete characteristics) and is of brief duration. With such a condition it is a relatively simple task to insure that the aversive event will be paired with each response and that it will never be presented under other circumstances.

A slightly more complex situation is encountered with head banging which may actually encompass a variety of responses with different topographics and durations. Thus, the head banger may involve different muscle groups from time to time; he may move the head forward, backward, or from side to side, or strike with different intensity. Furthermore, the head banging response also involves components of normal head movement which may be misinterpreted as precursors to head banging. In practice, such subtle variations may result in the delivery of inappropriate stimulation.

Even more difficulties are presented by the aversive treatment of alcoholism which involves elaborate response chains which are subject to considerable variation from time to time and place to place.

One way to resolve these problems is to circumscribe the variability of the behavior, for example, in head banging, by applying a mechanical device which enables only a forward thrust of the head, thus increasing the reliability of treatment. The disadvantage of this approach is that the treatment regime becomes somewhat artificial since it will differ from the natural circumstances under which the response occurs. This problem is dealt with in detail later on.

A second recommendation for maximizing treatment effectiveness is to continue treatment until the problem behavior is no longer evident, thus enhancing the durability of the effect. This may appear to be so obvious as to require no elaboration. The fact of the matter, however, strongly suggests that aversion therapy is frequently ineffective precisely because the clinician has failed to continue treatment beyond a limited time range. How long therapy should be maintained can only be answered empirically, i.e., it may be terminated after some reasonable length of time has elapsed (two weeks, six months) during which time the response has not occurred under nonclinical circumstances. A good criterion (and one which is unfortunately rarely employed) is the appearance of adaptive behavior under circumstances in which the problem behavior had previously occurred.

A third recommendation is to employ a stimulus or an event which is in fact aversive (in the sense that it would ordinarily be avoided) and not merely a stimulus which is alleged to be aversive on the basis of some a priori consideration. It has been shown that many ostensibly aversive stimuli may lose their noxious qualities with repeated occurrences. In fact, under special circumstances, they can even acquire reinforcing properties, thereby producing an effect which is directly opposite to the goal of aversion therapy. For example, there are numerous instances in the clinical literature referring to individuals who continually expose themselves to normally painful stimuli. Such masochistic behavior has been the subject of considerable interest in clinical psychology (Sandler, 1964). Socially offensive stimuli such as threats, ridicule, insults, and menacing gestures have become reinforcing to some subjects and even physically painful stimuli may on occasion become reinforcing. It is probably for this reason that a number of aversion therapists are turning to the use of electric shock. The advantages of shock have been described on numerous occasions and require little elaboration (Azrin and Holz, 1966). Suffice it to say that electric shock may be considered as an almost universal aversive stimulus when used appropriately. Furthermore, shock has none of the brutal characteristics associated with conventional physical punishment such as paddling, beating, or slapping.

More recently, as suggested earlier, the search for non-physical aversive events has also produced several new techniques which appear to be extensions of traditional fines and penalties. These are more fully described in the section on operant procedures.

There are, of course, many other aspects of aversion therapy procedures which will enhance their effectiveness, especially when they are combined with other techniques as described in a later section. To paraphrase Johnson (1972), the successful use of aversion therapy cannot be reduced to a concise summary of principles; the basic principles must be expanded in application to a variety of procedural details, the importance of any one of which will vary with each situation. Ignoring any of these variables will not necessarily doom any particular therapeutic endeavor; rather the probability of maximal effectiveness is increased to the extent that such factors are carefully considered in the therapeutic attempt.

PROCEDURES AND TECHNIQUES

Pavlovian Procedures

It has been suggested that the therapeutic uses of aversive methods have generally followed one of the two learning paradigms: the Pavlovian model and the operant model. In the former case the procedure generally involves pairing an attractive stimulus with an aversive stimulus that ordinarily elicits pain, nausea, muscular retraction, etc. Although many such attempts are reported in the literature, they are subject to serious methodological and conceptual criticism (Feldman, 1966; Franks, 1963; Kushner and Sandler, 1966; Rachman, 1965).

We have already mentioned the major difficulty in this connection; that is, applying the Pavlovian model to responses which have pronounced operant components. In addition, Franks has argued that some Pavlovian procedures (especially those used in the treatment of alcoholism) may actually involve backward conditioning, a tenuous form of learning, at best. Finally, a number of writers have indicated that Pavlovian effects may not be as durable as effects generated by means of operant conditioning procedures.

Perhaps the weight of these criticisms explains the increasing shift away from Pavlovian techniques in favor of operant techniques. Consequently, this review will be restricted to several representative reports.

By far, the most extensive body of literature based on Pavlovian aversive methods has been reported by investigators concerned with alcoholism. Of these, Lemere and Voegtlin (1950) present the most extensive and systematic series of observations. In their procedure, patients are administered emetine or apomorphine (unconditioned stimuli) which frequently elicit nausea and vomiting within thirty minutes. Shortly before vomiting occurs, the patient is instructed to drink a preferred alcoholic beverage. This procedure is repeated several times each day for ten days. Occasional "booster" sessions are administered after the patient is discharged. Voegtlin (1947) reports that about half of the patients treated in this fashion remain abstinent for at least two years.

The Pavlovian rationale is evident in the procedure. Ostensibly, after a sufficient number of pairings with emetine, the taste, sight, and smell of liquor should elicit nausea and vomiting. A similar rationale is offered in the treatment of alcoholism with antabuse, a drug which causes a violent physiological reaction when mixed with alcohol. Obviously, the validity of the rationale depends upon how closely these procedures approximate the Pavlovian paradigm. In fact, it would appear that such techniques may involve considerable departure from the classical conditioning procedure (Franks, 1963). Among other problems is the variation in individual responses to the drug. If a patient responds very quickly or very slowly (and this is hard to determine with certainty) the alcohol may be delivered too early or even after the patient experiences nausea.

Somewhat better control over the relevant events can be provided when the aversive event is electric shock, but even here methodological problems are still encountered. Pavlovian type procedures have also been used in a variety of therapeutic attempts designed to modify sexual deviancy. Close inspection of these procedures strongly suggests that operant processes were also involved and for this reason they are reviewed under that heading.

Operant Procedures

The second major category of aversion therapy techniques generally reflect the characteristics of the operant model. The rationale here stems from the assumption that behavior which results in unpleasant consequences will decrease in frequency. While there are important exceptions to this rule, the assumption has been well documented.

As we have seen, there are a number of conditions which must be taken into account, perhaps the most important of which is the close temporal relationship between the response and the aversive event—the contingency. For this reason, operant conditioners frequently describe such arrangements as examples of "response produced" aversive stimulation, even though the noxious event may be administered by an external agent.

This requirement can be properly implemented in the laboratory situation when the appropriate procedural controls are available. In clinical practice, however, limitations arise that frequently require some departure from the laboratory procedures. The degree of departure depends upon a variety of circumstances, the most important of which is the nature of the problem condition. For example, if therapy is designed to reduce the frequency of a writer's cramp, then the real-life circumstances in which such behavior occurs can be reasonably represented in the clinic, enabling the use of a contingency with the same or a similar response. The situation changes quite drastically, however, in the case of other problem conditions. For example, it is difficult (but not impossible) to recreate a reasonable approximation of the real-life circumstances related to alcoholism, and even greater problems are encountered with certain sexual deviations and aggressive behavior. Consequently, practitioners have devised a number of methods designed to circumvent this problem. For example, homosexuals are provided with problem-related stimuli such as pictures of same-sex nudes. They are then shocked in the presence of these stimuli. Or patients are asked to imagine a real-life scene and then shocked when they signal the imagined presence of the scene. Although such techniques are by now almost standard practice, it must be acknowledged that these procedures involve (perhaps, at best) problem-related events rather than the actual problem behaviors themselves. That is not to imply that such techniques are therefore ineffective. On the contrary, many of these efforts have resulted in profound constructive changes in behavior. The reasons for this success, however, remain to be identified since they involve processes beyond those specified by a strict response-contingency model.

This section describes several techniques which are organized from the least physically aversive to the most physically aversive. This also represents a continuum from the lowest potential for abuse to the greatest potential for abuse.

Time-Out from Positive Reinforcement. Over the last few years, increasing attention has turned to an aversive technique which has been termed time-out from positive reinforcement (TP). This procedure assumes that a decrease in response frequency can be effected if the opportunity to obtain positive reinforcement is denied the individual on the basis of some target behavior, for example, separating a child from the opportunity to receive peer reinforcement contingent on show-off behavior.

There are two major TO procedures: (1) removing the reinforcer from the individual; and (2) removing the individual from the reinforcing system. In most instances, the choice will be made on the basis of practical considerations. In the first case, the major changes involve the removal of reinforcement with little change in the individual's status. A commonplace example is turning off the TV set as a result of an argument between children over a program preference. This makes the reinforcement inaccessible for a while. Or, in the case of a clinical example, turning away from a child during a rewarding activity when the child begins to engage in a temper tantrum. Thus, the adult's potential reinforcing stimuli are temporarily removed.

In the second case, the major changes usually involve the physical removal of the individual from the potentially available reinforcers. The teacher who isolates an aggressive child from the positive effects of classroom presence exemplifies a commonplace use of TO.

TO can be applied successfully with individuals of differing ages, personal characteristics, and problem conditions. Several examples are given in a later section of this chapter. In each case, the successful use of the technique depends upon (1) identifying the positive reinforcement; and (2) ensuring that the interruption of positive reinforcement is immediately and precisely contingent on the target behavior. In other words, before considering the use of TO, the practitioner must specifically isolate the positive reinforcement and develop a procedure which ensures the response-contingent nature of the arrangement. When these rules are neglected in actual practice, the effectiveness of TO will be reduced. The teacher who removes an aggressive child from a class activity which the child dislikes is not fulfilling the requirements of TO. Moreover, if he is sent to the office and becomes the target of individual attention on the part of the guidance counselor or principal, the undesirable behavior may increase rather than decrease in frequency. Similarly, the parent who sends a misbehaving child to a room in which there is a TV, games, and toys, has not deprived the child of positive reinforcement and therefore failed to maximize TO.

Some question has also been raised regarding the duration of TO. That is, once the undesirable response-reinforcement relationship has been determined, how long should the individual remain in TO? Although there is no simple rule of thumb, the duration should be established on the basis of combining practical and behavioral criteria. If a child is placed in TO, for example, in general he should remain there until he has lost several reinforcement opportunities and the undesirable behavior has stopped. In actual practice, it is probably best to limit TO to 10 to 15 minutes (although occasionally longer durations may be required initially), and then to gradually reduce the duration, thus more clearly defining the response consequence relationship.

In some cases, the difference between TO and an extinction procedure (see Chapter 7 for a detailed discussion) may be obscure. For example, the popular current practice of turning away from a child during a temper tantrum is frequently regarded as an attempt to extinguish such behavior, but may also be regarded as Time-Out, primarily depending upon whether or not the reinforcement is completely withdrawn, as in extinction, or is merely withheld, as in TO. Obviously, in actual practice, it is difficult to distinguish between such arrangements.

In any event, the TO technique makes available to the clinician concerned with reducing the frequency of undesirable behavior an important addition to the more conventional aversive methods. When used as described above, there are many clinical problems which are amenable to such treatment.

Response Cost. A second aversive procedure which has received increasing attention has been termed response cost (Weiner, 1962). These arrangements are analogous to the conventional penalty technique in which an individual is fined for undesirable behavior. The major difference between the two is in terms of the systematic nature of response cost. Thus, driving illegally may occasionally result in a fine under the assumption that the loss in money will serve as a deterrent to such future behavior. The fact of the matter, however, is that these efforts frequently do not produce the desired outcome or are effective for only a limited duration.

Response cost, on the other hand, requires a clear explication of the relationship between each undesirable response and the appropriately assigned penalty. When these requirements are maximized, the effectiveness of response cost as a deterrent is maximized. Perhaps for this reason, the clinical application of response cost has usually involved a loss of rewards that were previously earned for appropriate behavior.

For example, hospitalized patients may be operating under a token economy in which several different dimensions of constructive behavior earn tokens exchangeable for tangible rewards or privileges. Additional rules may be involved in which behavioral infractions result in the loss of tokens. Such combined reward, response-cost arrangements are usually very effective in generating desirable changes in constructive behavior.

On the other hand, if the ratio between amount earned and amount lost results in an overall deficit, the incentive of working for reinforcement decreases and the system may break down. It is important, then, for the practitioner to continuously monitor the effects of response cost in relation to earnings and to adjust the values of each accordingly.

Feedback. Several behavior modification techniques include the monitoring of behavior for the purpose of recording the frequency of a response. The monitoring procedure may take a variety of forms which range from a patient observing his own heart rate on an oscilloscope to the mere act of making a mark on a sheet of paper as in the case of an individual recording the number of cigarettes he has smoked.

Under such circumstances, and independent of any formal treatment, the mere act of alerting the individual to the response occurrence may influence the rate of the response (see discussion of self-monitoring in Chapter 10). Such effects have been termed *feedback* since they essentially provide information not ordinarily available to the person that a particular response has occurred. With certain problem conditions, feedback may result in a decrease in the frequency of a response. Although the causes of these effects are not well understood, the changes which are produced may have implications for aversion therapy.

Subsequently, a number of investigators have suggested procedures designed to enhance the effectiveness of feedback for reducing the frequency of a response. Thus, there are several examples in the behavior modification literature which demonstrate that self-charting resulted in a reduction in the frequency of smoking, drinking, overeating, or arguing. In these cases, it would appear that merely bringing attention to the high incidence of the behavior in question was sufficient to effect a constructive change. The client who suddenly realizes he is smoking three packs per day rather than the two initially reported must make an adjustment to this new information.

In still other situations, the effectiveness of feedback can be enhanced if it is systematically presented in connection with an appropriate change in behavior. Several investigators, for example, have found that stuttering rates can be suppressed if each dysfluency was immediately followed by delayed auditory feedback (Siegel, 1970). In these cases, since delayed auditory feedback is regarded as aversive by most individuals, the procedure seems to be analogous to the punishment paradigm described in greater detail below.

There are still many questions which remain to be answered about response-feedback techniques; their major role as a treatment device would seem to be largely in terms of generating initial changes, but these changes will probably be transitory unless buttressed by other techniques.

Overcorrection. Although its present theoretical status is unclear, the overcorrection procedure developed by Azrin and his colleagues (Foxx and Azrin, 1973) reflects some of the characteristics of an aversive procedure and is therefore included in the present chapter. Used primarily with individuals for reducing self-stimulatory and disruptive behaviors, overcorrection requires that the individual first restore the environment to its natural condition immediately following the inappropriate act (correction), and then experience an appropriate penalty for having engaged in the inappropriate behavior (overcorrection). For example, if a client has broken several objects in a burst of anger, he is then required to clean up the broken materials as well as to straighten the rest of the room. If a client has bitten another individual he is required to cleanse his mouth with antiseptic as well as assist in administering to the individual who was bitten. The overcorrection routine is implemented each time the problem behavior occurs and is conducted in a firm but nonpunitive manner. The typical procedure lasts approximately thirty minutes.

Unconditioned Aversive Stimuli. By far the bulk of the operant aversion therapy literature involves the use of stimuli which are physically unpleasant or even painful. In these techniques, the noxious event occurs in a specifically response-produced or temporally correlated arrangement and is typically employed for repeated self-injurious behaviors which have been resistant to change by other techniques. A wide variety of stimuli have been employed for this purpose, most of which usually elicit the withdrawal response (for example, foul odors, uncomfortable sound, and painful stimuli such as slaps, hair pulls, and electric shock applied to an area of the limbs). Sometimes these stimuli have been paired with explicit conditioned stimuli such as shouts, reprimands, and disapproving gestures and facial expressions.

The vast majority of these efforts have employed shock, since such techniques facilitate the need for maximizing the effects of aversion therapy as described earlier. In addition, the intensity and duration of shock can be adjusted in the light of treatment requirements. For these reasons, the current review is largely restricted to shock procedures.

The usual procedure in the employment of shock involves the following sequence of events before initiating treatment:

1. An analysis of the history of the problem condition clearly documenting the ineffectiveness of less severe procedures.
2. An analysis of the problem condition in terms of how often it occurs, when it occurs, where it occurs, and any other relevant circumstances.
3. Involvement of qualified professionals familiar with shock procedures and the ethical guidelines which are obtained under such circumstances.

A number of shock delivery devices are commercially available for use in aversion therapy, the most practical of which are battery operated, portable instruments. The responsible practitioner should insure that the device incorporates appropriate safeguards as well as those features which will facilitate a successful outcome. Thus the device should be purchased from a reputable vendor with a complete description of the safety features. The electrode unit (typically attached to a limb) should be small, comfortable, and unobtrusive, thereby minimizing interference with normal routine.

The shock control unit should provide easily identified controls and offer a variety of shock intensities and durations with the lowest ranges below detectable thresholds. Prior to the use of the device with a client, the clinician should self-administer the shock, starting at the lowest level and gradually increasing the intensity up to the point of discomfort.

The initial treatment session should be conducted in accord with the information obtained from the prior analysis. For example, with a child who displays a high rate of head banging, the child should be moved to a quiet, isolated room and restraints removed. An observably safe intensity level and duration (e.g. .05 seconds) of shock is applied to the limb each time the response occurs. In addition, a high density of tangible reinforcers should be provided in the absence of the head banging response. The initial session will usually last about 30 minutes after which the child is returned to the prevailing routine. This is repeated each day until the behavior no longer occurs during the treatment session. These effects are generally observed within three to four sessions. As aversive control over the behavior is acquired, additionally relevant circumstances are generally incorporated into the procedure for the purpose of generalizing the effects over a wider range of circumstances. In the typical case, by the fourth or fifth session, merely strapping on the electrodes is sufficient to control the behavior. Once the effect has generalized over all the relevant circumstances, the electrode routine is gradually faded so that the ultimate control over the behavior falls completely under the positive contingencies and the shock procedure may be abandoned. Occasional "booster" sessions may be required if the problem condition reoccurs.

Combining Aversion Therapy with Other Techniques

This section is concerned with the manner in which the techniques described above can be used with additional procedures in order to maximize treatment effectiveness.

Although they are usually a part of any behavior change program (and as such they are also described in other chapters), the emphasis here is upon their use in conjunction with aversion therapy.

There are two reasons for including such practices. First, practically speaking, as we have seen, any attempt to apply a laboratory procedure to clinical situations usually results in some departure from the use of the technique under "pure" circumstances. Secondly, there is increasing evidence that the effects of aversion therapy can be enhanced if the practitioner systematically includes other learning techniques. That is, a more rapid and longer lasting reduction of the undesirable behavior can be achieved under such circumstances than would be true if time-out, response cost, etc. were used alone.

Including Response Alternatives. Several studies have shown that a change in target behavior can be expedited if an alternative response is available to the patient. In some cases, the therapist may explicitly encourage such new learning, and if this technique is combined with a procedure designed to eliminate an undesirable response, positive treatment results can be maximized. Although such procedures have been variously termed counterconditioning, differential reinforcement of other behavior (DRO), or reinforcement of incompatible behavior, they share the practice of concurrently manipulating more than one response dimension in a treatment program. Thus, a counterconditioning program might involve shock contingent on an undesirable response such as aggressive behavior and, at the same time, provide positive reinforcement for an adaptive alternative response, such as cooperative behavior.

While it may be assumed that some new response will emerge in every aversive procedure, the response alternative technique requires that the alternative response be identified prior to treatment. For this reason, we distinguish between those programs which formally and explicitly incorporate a response alternative and those procedures in which this process might have occurred but was not planned for. Obviously, the clinician interested in such techniques should acquire some understanding of general learning principles beyond those which are limited to aversive conditioning.

The advantages of the response alternative procedure are numerous: (1) it can be used with all of the techniques described above; (2) it enhances the treatment process, thereby reducing the number of aversive experiences required to modify behavior; (3) it enhances the durability of the effect; and (4) it offers an adaptive alternative to the individual which may generalize outside the clinic arena. The common practice of substituting mints for cigarettes reflects some of the features of the alternative response technique.

Fading. As we have seen, constructive changes which occur in one situation may not necessarily generalize to other situations. The child who is trained to cooperate in the classroom may continue to be aggressive at home or on the playground. Such limited change effects are particularly characteristic of attempts to treat certain problem conditions, such as alcoholism. It is not unusual, for example, for patients in a hospital treatment program to show a reduction in alcoholic behavior while in the hospital, only to break down soon after return to the environment in which the original drinking behavior occurred. The problem may be construed as an example of different reactions to different circumstances.

Obviously then, the most effective treatment is that which accomplishes the greatest generality of change. The fading technique offers distinct advantages in this connection (also described in conjunction with operant methods in Chapter 7).

Essentially, fading involves a gradual change in the treatment situation so that either reduction in undesirable behavior is maintained in the presence of new (and preferably more relevant) circumstances, or new circumstances are introduced in order to enhance changes in behavior. Such techniques have been used informally for many years.

A growing practice in penology, for example, involves a gradual series of discharge experiences in which a prisoner is first placed on a work-release program for limited duration while readjusting to the requirements of normal life. He may also, at first, see his parole officer several times a week. If his readjustment appears successful, he may be advanced to a half-way house and the number of parole visits reduced. In this fashion, the transition from prison life is gradually effected, under the assumption that constructive changes in behavior will be better maintained in the process.

Similarly, an improving psychiatric hospital patient is first allowed several weekend passes at home. If no problems arise, the patient is advanced to a month's "trial visit." This may subsequently be extended depending upon the patient's adjustment outside the hospital.

The difference between these practices and a fading technique involves the greater degree of detail and rigor in the latter case. An ideal fading technique would provide for a gradual exposure to the patient's real-life physical and social stimuli so that all of the natural events relevant to the problem behavior are ultimately reflected in the treatment situation.

The closer the fading technique approaches the ideal, the greater the generality of treatment effects. One growing practice in the modification of children's behavior involves first instructing parents in treatment skills and then gradually increasing their share of responsibility for treatment. Similarly, in aversion therapy, parents may be instructed in the use of a shock procedure to be applied in the home situation. In this fashion, the fading technique incorporates those individuals and those situations which will ultimately determine the durability of any constructive changes which first occurred in the treatment setting.

Schedules. Another technique which in some respects resembles fading involves changes in reinforcement schedules. It was mentioned earlier that treatment is initially most effective if the aversive event is applied to each instance of the undesirable response since this will result in the most rapid reduction of behavior. Greater durability of the desired reduction, however, can probably be achieved if the schedule of aversive events is unpredictable, e.g., every third or fourth response on an average. The frequency of aversive stimulation can be further gradually reduced if desired, although at some stage the practitioner will obviously be dealing with events which occur only infrequently. Thus, a cigarette smoker may initially receive ten shocks distributed over thirty cigarettes per day, but as the smoking rate declines to perhaps three or four cigarettes per day, adjustments in the shock schedule will also be required.

The Use of Significant Others. Where possible and appropriate, individuals who bear an important relationship to the patient may be incorporated into the treatment program. The rationale here again is similar to that underlying the use of fading—enhancing the durability of the change. Some instruction is obviously necessary, including specifically designating a time-out area, a response-cost system and even the use of response-contingent shock. Depending upon the degree of instruction and preparation, results of this technique have been most impressive. For example, self-injurious behavior in disturbed children is very effectively controlled when parents are instructed to use the treatment technique in the home environment.

Self-Control. Finally, and perhaps most important, are the techniques designed to make the patient himself responsible for change (see Chapter 10 on self-management). The rationale here scarcely requires any explanation, although this is a development representing a radical departure from some conventional treatment practices which covertly, at least, place the major responsibility for change on the therapist.

Techniques of this sort were first initiated in conjunction with problem behaviors which were difficult to analyze publicly, such as cigarette smoking, drinking, obsessions and compulsions. More recently, self-control techniques have been employed with a wider variety of problem behaviors, including aggression, family arguments and temper tantrums. Essentially, the procedure requires instructing the patient in a variety of techniques which are designed to alter one or more of the following: (a) typical undesirable reactions to particular occasions, (2) the sequence of responses which comprise the aggregate response (breaking up the chain); and (3) the consequences of the undesirable behavior. Thus, an analysis of the relevant components of an undesirable behavior may reveal that it occurs under certain identifiable circumstances; that it is comprised of several discrete responses; and that it produces certain reinforcing events. Cigarette smoking, for example, usually occurs at regular intervals and in typical stimulus situations. This would provide a picture of the frequency of the smoking behavior. The chain for one smoker may be characterized by removing the package from the shirt pocket, withdrawing a cigarette with the right hand, tapping it on a hard surface, inserting it in the mouth, lighting it, taking several deep drags, keeping it dangling from the lips, alternating between deep drags and knocking off the ashes, and smoking it down rapidly to a short butt before extinguishing the cigarette. This would provide a picture of the topography of the response. Finally, an attempt might be made to analyze the response-reinforcement relationship.

With this information, the patient can be instructed in self-control techniques which would enhance the aversion therapy effects. For example, he might be instructed to avoid some of the circumstances in which smoking occurs with high frequency. He may be instructed to change some of the components of the chain, such as holding the cigarette in the left hand, placing the cigarette in an ashtray between drags, smoking less rapidly, etc. Finally, the patient may also be instructed in the self-administration of aversive events which could range anywhere from accumulating all the butts and inhaling the stale aroma, and placing a picture of a diseased lung in the pack, to self-imposing fines, denying privileges, and delivering shock.

Kanfer and Karoly (1972) recently offered a learning theory analysis of the issues related to self-control processes. Among other things, they suggest the manner in which relevant events can be employed to enhance clinically relevant changes. They point out the necessity for increasing client motivation, for example, through a contractual negotiation between the client and therapist. Such contracts represent a statement of the client's intention or a promise of performance on his part.

There are probably additional procedures which should be considered along with those described above. In practice, there is sufficient overlap between the techniques so that the distinctions may be blurred. For the most part, the practitioner need not be concerned with the theoretical purity of the technique. What is probably more important is that as many techniques as possible should be employed in a systematic fashion, thereby optimizing the chances of a successful outcome.

SUMMARY

In brief, the information advanced in the preceding sections suggests several important steps that the therapist must take in any program using aversion methods. First, he should provide evidence that the event to be employed is indeed aversive; that it be applied on a response-contingent basis, and that it be maintained long enough to suppress the behavior for as long as possible.

Furthermore, durable changes can be imposed if an alternative (adaptive) response is available, if ordinary, real-life circumstances are represented in the treatment setting, and if self-control techniques are integrated into the treatment program.

PRACTICAL APPLICATIONS

Up to now, the discussion has focused on general principles and guidelines. Representative applications of the above from the operant aversion therapy literature will be described in the present section.

An arbitrary distinction is offered between: (1) those problem conditions which are relatively circumscribed and easily defined; and (2) problem behaviors which are more complex in their response dimensions and are less accessible to a public analysis. The term "compulsion" has been traditionally applied to many of the problem behaviors in the latter category under the assumption that there is an internal drive which compels the individual to engage in such behavior despite the maladaptive consequences. Although the behavior modification movement has called this assumption into question, there is some reason to believe that, at least in our present state of knowledge, greater success has been realized with problems in the first category. This conclusion must be qualified by the understanding that aversion therapy is a relatively young approach, and as yet, not fully tested. It must also be recognized that successful treatment is determined not only by the complexity of the problem condition but by the precision and rigor of the treatment technique.

Where possible, examples contrasting each major aversion therapy technique within a problem condition are described.

Discrete and/or Easily Defined Problem Conditions

Self-Injurious Behavior. One of the problem behaviors frequently encountered in extreme forms of pathology are various forms of self-injurious behavior (SIB). Although many other problem conditions such as smoking, alcoholism, and gambling reflect similar characteristics, the SIB label is usually reserved for those behaviors which, if left unchecked, would *shortly* threaten the biological welfare of the individual. Thus they require immediate intervention, including physical restraint. Unfortunately, most of these interventions are temporary and ineffective.

In the clinical literature, the term SIB usually implies the involvement of the voluntary motor-response system as manifested by head banging, self-mutilation, pulling one's hair out, etc. In the present review, we shall also include examples possibly involving involuntary (or autonomic) processes.

Head banging, self-biting, and similar problem behaviors. By far the most extensive application of aversion therapy with discrete problem conditions has involved the use of painful shock, contingent on head banging and self-mutilation in children. There are now a sufficient number of observations which confirm the effectiveness of such procedures, especially when compared with non-aversive techniques, in terms of rapid suppression of the behavior. Furthermore, when additional measures are incorporated in the procedure (for example, treatment administered by parents of SIB children in the home) the suppressive effects generalize, thereby enabling the emergence of other more productive responses.

Perhaps the most impressive evidence of the efficacy of aversion therapy in such cases is provided by Lovaas and Simmons (1969). In this study, three severely retarded children displaying extreme forms of SIB (requiring long periods of time in physical restraints) were exposed to response-contingent shock. In each case SIB was effectively and completely suppressed in the treatment setting after only a few shocks. The same treatment was also successfully applied by other individuals in other situations in order to maximize the generality of the effects.

Similar results have been reported by a number of other investigators. Tate and Baroff (1966) administered response shock to a blind nine-year-old boy who employed a wide assortment of SIB (head banging, face slapping, self-kicking, etc.). During 24 minutes prior to the treatment condition, 120 instances of SIB were recorded. For the next 90 minutes, a half-second shock was administered for each SIB and only five SIB responses occurred. The child was also praised for non-SIB. As the treatment progressed, the child was moved from restraints for increasing time intervals (fading). The rate of SIB continued to decline and no such responses were observed for 20 consecutive days. Interestingly enough, an increase in prosocial behavior emerged during this time.

Risley (1968) attempted to eliminate dangerous climbing behavior in a six-year-old retarded girl who was constantly injuring herself due to numerous falls. After several other techniques proved to be ineffective (DRO and TO) the use of response shock combined with verbal reprimands completely eliminated the climbing behavior in the treatment setting. After instruction, the child's mother employed the same technique in the home setting with the result that climbing behavior declined from about 20 responses to two responses per day. Once again, these changes were accompanied by a concurrent increase in constructive behavior in terms of attending and responding to social stimuli.

These efforts have been followed by a host of similar procedures with highly successful outcomes. Corte, Wolf, and Locke (1971) almost immediately and completely reduced SIB (including self-slapping, eye poking, hair pulling, and scratching the skin) in four retarded adolescents with response contingent shock, after an extinction procedure and a DRO procedure proved ineffective. Again, the treatment had to be applied outside the first treatment setting to enhance generalization.

A similar procedure was employed by Scholander (1972) for reducing a response in which a 14-year-old male continuously placed his hands around his neck. This behavior (which evidently emerged out of an epileptic condition) occurred with such high frequency that it was interfering with many ordinary activities, such as eating or dressing. The shock procedure resulted in a change from about 25 responses per day to zero in four and a half weeks, after which the shock apparatus was removed. No further responses occurred during a nine-month follow-up.

Merbaum (1973) reduced SIB (beating face with hands) in a psychotic boy from an average of about 221 responses per ten-minute period to virtually zero in a two-hour treatment period. Similar results were obtained by the child's teacher and mother who were also instructed in providing positive reinforcement for non-SIB (differential reinforcement for other behavior or DRO). These effects were maintained over a one-year follow-up period and were accompanied by improvement in a variety of behavioral dimensions.

More recently, Dieker (1976) treated two different forms of SIB in a retarded 16-year-old by means of two different aversive procedures. A shock escape-avoidance procedure (absence of response postponed shock) was employed for banging head against the wall, and a punishment procedure (response followed by shock) was administered each time the child hit her head with her fists. Both procedures successfully reduced the self-injurious behaviors, but the escape-avoidance procedures produced a longer posttreatment effect.

This survey represents only a small sample of the breadth and variety of aversion therapy with SIB. Suffice it to say that, at least in this area, aversion therapy has been highly successful, not only in rapidly reducing the frequency of undesirable behavior but also in establishing long-term constructive changes. We have also seen that some of the reservations regarding the use of shock procedures are not supported by the evidence. On the contrary, it would appear that once control over the SIB is established, the path is clear for the development of other more adaptive responses. In this connection, Lichstein and Schreibman (1976) reviewed the literature on shock procedures for SIB, in order to evaluate the validity of concerns regarding negative side effects. Their study suggests that these concerns are not supported by the data and that, in fact, the majority of side effects reported were actually positive in nature.

Despite these observations, as we have seen, it is important to acknowledge the problems involved in the use of such techniques. For this reason aversion therapists have continued to search for additional nonshock alternatives. In this connection several recent efforts have administered "soaking" contingent on self-injurious behaviors. Drabman (1978), for example, instructed a parent to pour a glass of water over the head of her 3½-year-old developmentally-delayed child, contingent on the child's temper tantrums (which involved extreme self-scratching during the tantrum episodes). In addition, the parent was instructed in delivering praise for good behavior following the technique. Follow-up results revealed continued improvement in the child's condition and a substantial recovery in the child's skin condition eight months after the training program was initiated.

Iwata and his colleagues (Dorsey, Iwata, and McSween, 1974) reported on the use of a fine mist of water applied to the face of seven retarded individuals contingent on a variety of self-injurious behaviors. The water was dispensed from a standard plant sprayer approximately one foot from the client's face and adjusted to insure a maximum misting effect, as opposed to a concentrated stream. The results of this technique revealed that all self-injurious response fell below five percent of the number of observed intervals within four 20 to 30-minute sessions. Similar efforts employed by staff working with the retarded in other facilities have replicated these findings. The advantages of such a procedure over more severe measures such as shock, are obvious.

Drabman and his associates (Drabman et al., 1978) combined a number of the techniques described earlier in a highly intriguing procedure designed to suppress inappropriate sucking and chewing. The target child in this study was a 2½-year-old retarded, blind child. The problem behavior involved an extremely high rate of finger and shirt sucking which produced open sores on the child's fingers. The investigators trained three older, higher level retarded children to serve as the mediators of the program. After demonstrating their skill in observing, recording, and physically controlling the problem behavior (each response was followed by the mediator child holding the target child's hands to the side and saying "no!"), the children implemented the treatment procedure which involved placing an ice cube in the target child's mouth for three seconds, contingent on each sucking response. This resulted in a rapid reduction in the rate of the problem behavior during the half-hour treatment sessions. In order to facilitate the generalization of these effects to other circumstances, the children were instructed to administer the "icing" procedure at varying times throughout the entire day. These beneficial effects were maintained even during sessions in which the icing procedure was not in effect.

Finally, Harris and Romanczyk (1976) used what they described as overcorrection to treat head banging and chin hitting in a moderately retarded 8-year-old boy. Following each SIB, staff members were instructed to guide the child's head through a four movement cycle (up-down, left-right pattern) repeated every five seconds for five minutes. In addition, the child's arms were also guided "to the side, in front, over his head, out to the side at the shoulder level, and back to the side."

These efforts produced a decrease in SIB from an average of 32 responses per day to two responses per day by the second week of treatment. Once successful control was accomplished in the treatment setting, a similar home program was implemented by the parents with comparable results. These effects were maintained during nine-month follow-up. In addition, substantial improvement was also observed in reading ability and sociability.

Self-induced vomiting. Perhaps as a result of the growing confidence in aversion therapy with SIB, several clinicians have attempted to use similar procedures with other serious problem conditions which have been traditionally resistant to treatment.

One potentially dangerous but fortunately rare problem behavior involves self-induced vomiting. This is a condition characterized by the absence of physiological determinants as well as resistance to drug therapy, thus suggesting the influence of psychological factors. In extreme cases such conditions may result in a severe loss of weight, retarded development, and even threaten loss of life. For these reasons, immediate intervention is required and four studies report the successful cure of excessive nonorganically determined vomiting behavior.

Luckey, Watson, and Musick (1968) employed a response contingent shock with a chronic six-year-old retarded vomiter, after standard medical treatment failed to produce any constructive changes. The child was observed throughout the day and one-second uncomfortable shock was administered whenever vomiting or its precursors occurred. By the fifth day, the treatment was reduced to two hours at each meal. Further reductions were introduced at later stages as the frequency of the behavior decreased.

Except for a minor reversal several days after the treatment was initiated, no evidence of vomiting was observed on the last nine days of treatment. Again, this marked reduction in maladaptive behavior was accompanied by improvement in a variety of prosoccial and self-care dimensions.

Lang and Melamed (1969) employed a similar procedure with a nine-month-old chronic vomiter whose life was threatened by continuation of the behavior. In this case, the vomiting act was preceded by sucking behavior and accompanied by vigorous throat movements. The aversion therapy procedure involved a one-second shock which was administered as soon as vomiting occurred and continued until the response was terminated.

The vomiting response was substantially reduced after two brief sessions and by the third session only one or two responses occurred. These changes were accompanied by a substantial weight gain and increased alertness and responsiveness to the environment.

After approximately three weeks, the child was discharged from the hospital and continued to do well one year after treatment.

Kohlenberg (1970) reported similar success in treating excessive vomiting in a 21-year-old severely retarded female. In this case, shock was administered contingent on the presence of stomach tensions which served as the precursor to the vomiting response. Similar successful efforts using shock contingent on self-induced vomiting have also been reported by Toister, et al. (1975) and Cunningham and Linscheid (1976).

Sajwaj, Libet, and Agros (1974) reported on the successful elimination of chronic rumination in a six-month-old by administering response contingent lemon juice. In this case, five to ten cc's of the juice were squirted into the child's mouth with a medical syringe as soon as vigorous tongue movements were detected during 20-minute post-feeding intervals. This procedure resulted in a dramatic reduction of the problem behavior almost immediately and by the twelfth day of treatment, regurgitation had virtually ceased. By the 33rd session, treatment was terminated. Follow-up revealed a continuing improvement in the child on a number of developmental dimensions. Again, the advantages of the lemon juice technique over electric shock requires no elaboration. For these reasons, additional efforts along these lines are currently being conducted by staff members working in training centers for the retarded in the state of Florida (Chimonides, 1978).

Seizures. As in the case of vomiting, seizures are generally considered to be the result of some physiological dysfunction. However, some investigators have argued that such conditions may also be induced or influenced by external factors. In any event, if left unchecked, the frequency and severity of seizures may constitute a serious threat to the individual. Wright (1973) suggested that at least some forms of seizure-related events may be suppressed by aversion therapy, thereby resulting in a decrease in seizure activity.

Wright worked with a five-year-old retarded boy who induced his own seizures by moving his hand back and forth before his eyes and blinking, while looking at a light source. Observation and EEG recording confirmed the correlation between these events and seizure episodes. They further revealed the occurrence of several hundred self-induced seizures per day.

The treatment technique consisted of shock delivered contingent on each hand-eye response in five one-hour sessions extending over a three-day period. All responses were suppressed by the third session. However, five months later the child was again inducing as many as 400 seizures per day by blinking. Shock was then administered contingent on the blinking response, resulting in a substantial reduction of seizures by the fourth session. A seven-month follow-up revealed a 90 percent decrease from the pretreatment frequency of hand-eye responses.

Enuresis. Several examples of aversion therapy have also been employed for the purpose of reducing nocturnal bed wetting (enuresis). Tough, Hawkins, McArthur, and Ravenswaay (1971) found that a cold bath contingent on bed wetting, plus praise for bladder control (DRO) completely eliminated the enuresis problem in a retarded eight-year-old boy but was less effective for his younger brother.

Atthowe (1972) found that a combination of aversive events could reduce enuresis in seven disabled elderly patients. Chronically enuretic patients (who otherwise participated in a token reward program) were moved to a generally aversive environment: crowded ward, lights turned on for ten minutes, four times each night, and patients escorted to the bathroom for ten minutes. These procedures were maintained for two months after which continence was rewarded (DRO), while incontinence resulted in loss of reward (response cost). By the eighth month of the program all of the patients were continent, including some who were severely neurologically disabled, an effect which was maintained almost four years after the study was initiated.

By far the largest number of successful attempts to treat enuresis have used a variety of the Mowrer alert system in which bed wetting results in a signal which arouses the individual. After a number of such experiences most children begin to wake up prior to wetting the bed and are then encouraged to urinate appropriately.

When the apparatus was first described by Mowrer (1938) he invoked a Pavlovian model in explaining the effectiveness of the technique. Thus, the distended bladder served as the conditioned stimulus (CS) which was paired with the unconditioned stimulus (UCS, the alerting stimulus). By means of Pavlovian conditioning, the CS alone would result in arousal. More recently, Jones (1960) has suggested that the technique relies upon an operant aversion therapy model.

Sneezing. Kushner (1970) has shown that excessive sneezing may also be controlled by means of aversion therapy. This case involved a 17-year-old girl who had been vigorously and rapidly sneezing (approximately one response per 40 seconds) for six months with no relief. Extensive medical examinations failed to isolate the cause of this condition and a variety of treatment techniques had not produced any substantial improvement.

During treatment, a microphone was placed around her neck which was connected to a voice key and a shock source. Each sneeze activated the voice key and automatically delivered a shock to the fingertips (response-contingent shock). Following an adjustment of the shock procedure, in which the electrodes were taped to her arm, thereby insuring better contact, the patient stopped sneezing after four hours of treatment. There was no evidence of a relapse during a thirteen-month follow-up period.

Functional ("Hysterical") Paralysis. In an unpublished study conducted at the Veteran's Administration Hospital in Miami, a modified aversion therapy program was employed for the purpose of treating functional paralysis. The patient was a middle-aged male whose presenting complaint was a loss of feeling and impaired locomotion in the lower half of the left limb, causing him to be confined to a wheelchair. Extensive neurological examination ruled out the possibility of any organic dysfunction. The aversion therapy procedure was conducted as follows: electrodes were placed on the patient's leg and on two fingertips. He was then informed that a mild shock would be administered to his leg, followed in five seconds by a stronger shock to his fingers. If he felt the leg shock he was to press a switch which he held in his hand. No further instructions were provided, although each switch response enabled the patient to avoid the shock to the fingers.

This procedure was presented for three trials in the first session, during which time no avoidance responses occurred. The second session was interrupted after the first trial because the patient became naus ited. In the third session, the patient emitted two switch-press responses and verbally indicated that feeling had returned to his leg, whereupon the electrodes were removed and the patient walked back to the ward. He was discharged several days later without complication. Although the results in this case were successful, the procedure employed represents a departure from the typical response-contingent paradigm and seems to be more similar to the anticipatory avoidance procedure described more fully in the next section.

Writer's Cramp. Two studies have appeared which report on attempts to treat various forms of writer's cramp by means of aversion therapy. This form of motor impairment is usually characterized by muscular contractions or spasms and prevents the individual from continuing in tasks which require the use of hand muscles such as writing, typing, etc. The condition is usually attributed to fatigue or emotional problems. In any event, sufferers of writer's cramp are frequently capable of performing other tasks even though such tasks may involve the operation of the same or similar hand muscles.

Liversedge and Sylvester (1955) identified 39 cases of writer's cramp as a function of either hand tremors or muscular spasms; each of these conditions was separately treated with a different apparatus. The tremor patients were required to insert a metal stylus into a series of progressively smaller holes in a metal chassis. Deviations (striking the side of the hole) resulted in shock. The contraction response was treated by delivering shock to the patient whenever excessive thumb pressure (as measured by a gauge) was applied to a pen. Normal writing was regained after three to six weeks of treatment in 24 of the patients. These improvements were maintained for up to four and a half years.

Kushner and Sandler (1966) used a similar procedure for treating a hand contraction response in a 42-year-old male teletype operator. The patient was required to operate a typewriter in the clinic and pretreatment observations revealed a high frequency of rapid, spasmodic contractions of the right hand, resulting in errors at the keyboard. The patient was then seen for 12 30-minute sessions with shock delivered contingent on each contraction response. The electrodes were removed during the next three sessions and no contractions were observed. Shortly thereafter, however, the contraction response recurred and his performance remained erratic and gradually declined through the 46th session. Consequently, the number of weekly sessions was increased. No contractions were observed by the 61st session and the patient was then switched to a teletype machine. Almost immediately, he was functioning effectively even when the electrodes were removed.

Stuttering. The behavior modification literature reveals a long and continued interest in the use of aversive techniques for improving the speech of stutterers. Numerous response-contingent events have reduced the frequency of stuttering, including delayed auditory feedback, response cost arrangements, time-out arrangements, and electric shock. Since only a brief overview of these efforts is provided in the present account, the interested reader is referred to Siegel's comprehensive review (Siegel, 1970). In each of the studies described, stuttering is defined in terms of the frequency of speech dysfluencies (repetitions, interjections, prolongations, interruptions, etc.).

Adams and Popelka (1971) employed a time-out technique with eight young adult stutterers. Essentially, the procedure imposed a nonspeaking period contingent on each dysfluency, under the assumption that the opportunity to speak was positively reinforcing. Although the dysfluency rate decreased during the TO condition, it seems apparent that the results are subject to alternative explanations.

Kazdin (1973) compared the relative effectiveness of response cost, loud response-contingent sound and feedback on the suppression of dysfluent speech in 40 retarded patients. In the response cost procedure, tokens which could be exchanged for tangible rewards were removed upon the occurrence of dysfluencies. In the second condition, a loud noise was presented contingent on each dysfluency; and in the feedback condition, each dysfluency was marked by a light being turned on. The results indicated that both response cost and aversive stimulation procedures reduced dysfluencies, but response cost was more effective during a posttest.

Delayed auditory feedback (DAF) has also been studied in this connection since such events seem to reflect aversive properties. Typically, the DAF procedure involves a brief delay of the dysfluency which is then transmitted through the client's earphones during a speech task. This requires the individual to reduce his verbal rate while simultaneously speaking and listening for dysfluencies. Goldiamond (1965) has shown that such treatment produces fluent and rapid speech. Soderberg (1968) obtained similar results with eleven student stutterers, and, in addition, observed that these effects generalized beyond the experimental condition.

Finally, Daly and Frick (1970) employed a shock procedure with 36 adult male stutterers. Stuttering expectations as well as actual stuttering responses were treated independently in some patients and simultaneously in others. The results indicated that employing shock with stuttering expectancies did not reduce the frequency of stuttering responses but the other conditions did produce a constructive change. Furthermore, these effects were maintained during a 20-minute posttest period.

Complex Problem Conditions

General Compulsions. As noted previously, there is by now an extensive literature describing attempts to deal with chronic, long-standing compulsive type problem conditions via aversion therapy. Perhaps it is natural for behavior therapists to turn in this direction, since most conventional treatment efforts in this area have not been very successful. The literature is replete with examples of treated alcoholics who have returned to heavy drinking, dieters who eat more after treatment than before, cigarette smokers who quit during treatment only to smoke again at higher rates after discharge, etc.

One of the problems encountered with some of these conditions is that they are directly promoted and reinforced in certain circumstances. Drinking and smoking are, for the most part, socially acceptable and, in fact, abstinence may even result in social disapproval. Eating, of course, is a biological necessity and the rewards are built in to the response. It is only when they occur at excessive frequency and/or under inappropriate circumstances that they represent problem behaviors. Under these circumstances, such conditions may be considered as a breakdown in discrimination. The current review is not an attempt to survey the entire range of activity, but rather a sampling of representative efforts.

Alcoholism. The history of the aversive treatment of alcoholism stretches back to the Roman era. It is only within recent years, however, that treatment techniques have achieved an advanced level of sophistication. Starting in the early and middle 1960s, behavior therapists began to employ aversive controls under carefully planned conditions. Many of the early studies clearly reflected a Pavlovian methodology but the later investigations are more congruent with operant procedures. Furthermore, they are characterized by attempts to find alternatives to shock and their objectives are to establish controlled (moderate socially appropriate) drinking rather than complete abstinence. A study by Blake (1965) is perhaps representative of the earlier aversion therapy efforts involving operant processes. In this procedure, electric shock was presented at the same time the patient complied with instructions to sip his drink. The shock was increased until the patient spat out the drink, thus terminating the shock (escape behavior). In addition, the shock was presented only 50 percent of the time in a random manner. When this treatment was combined with relaxation training, Blake found that approximately 50 percent of the 37 patients in the program remained abstinent one year after follow-up.

Continuing interest in treating hospitalized alcholics by means of such aversive procedures is also reported by other investigators. A recent example is provided by Glover and McCue (1977). In this study the drinking rates of 39 alcoholics treated with a shock escape procedure were compared to drinking rates of 46 control subjects who received conventional treatment. The aversion therapy subjects revealed a much lower incidence of alcohol consumption on follow-up than did the control subjects.

In contrast to these efforts, most recent investigations reflect an increased attempt to incorporate ''natural'' circumstances in the treatment program and involve other treatment modalities in addition to analyzing a greater variety of aversion methods in order to optimize treatment effects.

An example of such natural procedures is provided by Vogler et al. (1970). In this study, liquor was served to hospitalized alcoholic patients in a simulated bar arrangement. Each drinking response was accompanied by a shock, which was maintained until the patient spat out the drink. Although it is difficult to isolate the punishment effects (the shock for drinking) from the escape effects (the cessation of shock contingent on spitting the drink out), these investigators did include several control conditions and also provided for ''booster'' treatments after discharge. The results indicated that abstinence was engendered by the treatment.

The Vogler technique in which treatment was conducted in a naturalistic setting represents an important development and is evidently being used with increasing frequency. Wards are converted so that they reflect many of the characteristics of settings in which the drinking response actually occurs. Obviously, the effects produced under these conditions stand a better chance of generalizing to the patient's real-life situation than would seem to be true when more artificial circumstances are used.

A more clearly operant approach has been reported by Davidson (1973). Alcohol-related responses are assessed by an automated device which dispenses 2 cc. of preferred liquor per 30 responses in a half-hour period. The patient is given the opportunity to drink the liquor at each delivery interval. Once his response rate stabilizes, the patient receives a shock as he actually picks up the drink. Shock intensities are maintained until the effects at a given intensity can be reliably demonstrated and then a new and higher shock intensity is employed until the patient's response rate is completely suppressed. Once this criterion is achieved, the patient is allowed to respond to liquor in the absence of shock (the electrodes are removed). Following these observations, the patient is discharged and requested to make follow-up visits during which time measurement is continued. Over 80 percent of the patients did not respond for liquor in the follow-up visits, and information from the patient as well as other sources suggested a substantial reduction in drinking behavior in over 65 percent of the patients for at least one year after discharge.

In addition to these advancements, other recent studies offer suggestions for the use of aversive procedures with nonhospitalized alcoholics. In this connection, Wilson, Leaf, and Nathan (1975) analyzed the effects of several aversive procedures (shock escape, experimenter administered response contingent shock, and self-administered response shock) on drinking rates. All subjects were in their middle 30s to middle 50s and still living in their community despite a problem drinking history of at least five years in duration. Both of the response shock procedures (punishment) suppressed drinking rates but the escape procedure was shown to be ineffective. Unfortunately, no treatment produced any substantive long-term effects.

Wilson and Tracey (1976) compared the effectiveness of an aversive imagery technique, a shock escape procedure, and a shock punishment procedure on drinking rates in a similar group of alcoholic subjects. The aversive imagery procedure involved a symbolic representation of a typical drinking sequence followed, on half of the scenes, by suggestions of uncontrollable vomiting (symbolic punishment) and, on the other half of the scenes, by imagining relief from sickness by ceasing the imagined drinking response (symbolic escape-avoidance). The punishment procedures were equally effective in reducing drinking rates but shock escape and the aversive imagery techniques showed little or no treatment effect.

Vogler and his associates (1977) employed a multiple-component treatment package with a similar group of nonhospitalized problem drinkers. The aversive treatment component of the package involved eight to ten shocks to the fingers whenever a subject's blood alcohol concentration (BAC) level was greater than eighty percent milligram. All the various combinations of the treatment package produced a significant decrease in alcohol intake, although there were no differences between the various treatment conditions. The overall results suggest that combining aversive procedures with other treatment modalities is more effective than employing aversive procedures alone.

A different approach was initiated by Hunt and Azrin (1973) in which significant individuals in the alcoholic's social and employment environment were trained to reward abstention and to punish excessive drinking by withdrawing vocational, social and other reinforcements. Miller (1975) employed a similar procedure with 20 chronic alcoholics. In this study, staff involved with service provider agencies were instructed to offer goods and services contingent of sobriety, whereas excessive drinking (public intoxication and/or high BAC levels) resulted in a five-day suspension of goods and services. These efforts resulted in a decrease in public intoxication and alcohol consumption. No such changes were observed in a control group receiving services on a noncontingent basis. Such approaches seem to offer genuine promise for improving the treatment of what many authorities consider to be the most serious mental health problem of modern times.

Cigarette smoking. Almost from the beginning of the aversion therapy movement, therapists have revealed a strong interest in the use of aversive methods for treating cigarette smoking. By now the number of suggested techniques which incorporate some form of aversive control probably runs into the thousands. Unfortunately, this burgeoning development has not been accompanied by a comparable interest in providing evidence to support the efficacy of the various techniques. Probably everyone knows someone who has tried to stop smoking, even through various aversive means, only to have failed. Without a proper scientific analysis, it is impossible to assess the effectiveness of any given technique. In a recent issue of a major psychological journal devoted entirely to the topic of behavioral approaches to smoking, a review of a variety of modification efforts (including aversive methods) found that at least 75 percent of the individuals treated had started to smoke again after treatment was terminated (Hunt and Matarazzo, 1973). With this in mind, let us consider several of the aversion therapy studies that have been reported.

Gendreau and Dodwell (1968) applied the "increasing shock-escape response" technique to reduce the frequency of cigarette smoking. Patients received shock as soon as they complied with instructions to light up a cigarette. Shock intensity was gradually increased until the patient extinguished the cigarette. Differences in smoking rates between treated and nontreated smokers were observed both at the end of treatment and two years later.

By the late 1960s, a series of studies had reported on various techniques and equipment designed to enhance the effects of aversion therapy with smokers. Perhaps the most sophisticated of these involves a portable shock apparatus which automatically administers shock at some point during the cigarette smoking period. The assumption which seems to underlie such efforts is that if the patient complies with the instructions, he will receive response shock contingent on each smoking response and in every smoking situation. This will result in a satisfactory treatment outcome. Although the assumption is a reasonable one, appropriate controls have not been exercised and the assumption, therefore, has yet to be verified. The limitations of these procedures is that they rely completely upon the cooperation and reliability of the individual patient.

Elliot and Tighe (1968) offered an aversive alternative to the shock procedure—again with ambiguous results. Their procedure involved a modified response cost-avoidance technique in which volunteer patients posted money for a 12-week or 16-week period. The money was refunded to those patients who abstained from smoking during this time. Of 25 patients, 21 abstained for the duration of the study. Furthermore, 38 percent of the patients remained abstinent at a twelve-month follow-up. Although far from a satisfactory success index, the rate compares very favorably with the results reported by investigators using other techniques.

Two recent studies compared the relative effects of several different aversive procedures. In one of these studies (Conway, 1977) attempted to enhance the efficacy of the aversive procedure by including self-control training in the treatment program. None of the treatment conditions (including two forms of response contingent shock) produced any substantive effects during a posttreatment follow-up.

In what is perhaps the best controlled study to date in the area of cigarette smoking, Dericco, Brigham, and Garlington (1977) assessed the effectiveness of three aversive treatment programs—satiation, cognitive control and response contingent shock. The subjects were 24 volunteers ranging in age, socio-economic background, and smoking rates. In the satiation procedure, subjects were instructed to smoke continuously for 30 minutes. In the cognitive control procedure, the subjects reclined in a lounger and heard two recorded messages, one of which associated pleasant images with smoking cessation, the other of which associated negative images with continuous smoking. The subjects were also instructed to imagine the pleasant scene before smoking, and the unpleasant scene after smoking. In the contingent shock procedure, 25 painful shocks were administered to subjects' forearms at various (unpredictable) times throughout the smoking sequence. The subjects were contacted six months after the treatment was terminated in order to assess the long-term effects of the three procedures over the other two procedures. The results clearly demonstrated the superiority of the shock procedure over the other two procedures in producing long-term effects. Though the bewildering assortment of aversive treatment programs that have been applied to cigarette smoking demonstrate only limited success, the DeRicco, et al. study does suggest that if a response shock procedure is employed which involves frequent, intense and extended shock, success rates will increase.

Overeating. As with cigarette smoking, prematurely applied aversive treatment methods are now widely used for the treatment of obesity, resulting in the emergence of questionable practices and undocumented claims of effectiveness. Again, because of the lack of rigorous studies, only a few examples from the aversion therapy literature will be presented.

Perhaps the earliest example of a response-contingent shock procedure with two overweight women is described by Meyer and Crisp (1964). Temptation food (food for which the patient had most craving as distinguished from food on a prescribed diet) was displayed for increasing periods of time and the patients received shock for approach responses. The shock contingency was gradually faded while weight changes were constantly monitored. Any increase in weight resulted in a return to the treatment regime. Although the results for one patient were highly satisfactory (a weight reduction of about 75 pounds during six months which was maintained almost two years after discharge), no durable constructive change was observed in the second patient.

Although this procedure appears to have been adapted by a substantial number of behavior therapists, an alternative approach is offered by other investigators employing nonphysically painful aversive events. Ferster, Nurnberger and Levitt (1962) described a procedure which involved a variety of techniques, including emphasizing the ultimate aversive consequences of overeating. Obese women met in groups and discussed the expected outcome of their problem behavior (putting on weight, undesirable appearance, etc.). In addition they were required to monitor their own food intake and weight changes. All of the women reported weight losses although these effects were not maintained for any great length of time.

A number of investigators have also employed covert sensitization as an aversive procedure with weight problems. An example of such an approach was reported by Elliot and Denney (1975). Forty-five overweight college student volunteers were treated by one of three procedures: (1) attention placebo (control condition); (2) covert sensitization in which aversive images (e.g., feelings of nausea) were paired with identified "problem" foods; or (3) covert sensitization augmented by false physiological feedback designed to enhance the efficacy of CS by relating physiological changes to nausea and relief from nausea. No superiority in terms of maintained weight loss during follow-up was observed for either of the two aversive procedures as compared to the control situation.

Finally, response cost arrangements have also been attempted with obese persons (Mann, 1976). Such arrangements usually involve a contract in which the subject donates a number of items which are returned if the terms of the contract are satisfied or lost if the terms are not met. When such requirements are related to daily, specified reasonable changes in dieting habits, the results are quite promising (Rodriguez and Sandler, 1978).

Other compulsive conditions. Other investigations have reported the successful treatment of gambling (Barker and Miller, 1968) and shoplifting (Kellam, 1969). Although it is clear that operant aversive techniques were intimately involved in these efforts, the complexity of the procedures makes it impossible to analyze the relative contribution of each component.

"Covert" Problem Conditions

Another interesting development which has emerged over the last several years involves the use of aversion therapy in the treatment of covert problem conditions. In such cases, the patient's verbal complaint is usually regarded as the external concomitant of disturbing thoughts frequently involving sexual or aggressive ideations. Despite this commonly accepted assumption, the following review suggests that such conditions are also amenable to aversion therapy.

Kushner and Sandler (1966) used a shock procedure for treating suicidal thoughts in a 48-year-old male. These obsessions were characterized by persistent, daily ruminations focusing upon six different suicidal images. The patient was instructed to imagine a particular scene and received shock upon a signal that the image was clear. 15 to 20 such trials were presented in each session and after the 12th session, the patient reported that only one image was still present. Treatment was temporarily discontinued after three more sessions because of a death in the family, but reinstated after the patient returned. (No suicidal ruminations occurred during this time). Treatment was terminated after five more sessions and a total of 350 trials. A three-month follow-up revealed no recurrence of the former problem.

Bucher and Fabricatore (1970) employed a self-shock procedure in an attempt to reduce the frequency of hallucinations in a 47-year-old hospitalized patient diagnosed as a paranoid schizophrenic. The hallucinations were described as frequent, obscene, and critical voices which occurred from four to seven times per day and lasted for as long as 20 minutes.

The patient was supplied with a portable shock device and instructed to administer shock to himself at the onset of the hallucinations. This resulted in an apparent immediate and virtually complete cessation of hallucinatory episodes during 20 days when the shock device was abruptly removed, and the patient was unfortunately discharged without his consent. He was returned to the hospital two weeks later and the hallucinations had reappeared.

Haynes and Geddy (1973) showed that hallucinations could be suppressed by means of a time-out procedure. The patient was a 45-year-old hospitalized female diagnosed as schizophrenic. She showed a high incidence of loud and incomprehensible verbal behavior which was considered to be evidence of hallucinations. During treatment each hallucinatory episode resulted in a staff member informing the patient that she had to go to the TO room, closing the door and then opening the door ten minutes later. Two treatment periods were separated by a nontreatment interval to observe the effects of discontinuing treatment.

The results indicated that the hallucinatory behavior decreased by about one half during the two TO procedures. Even more pronounced changes were produced in a second patient displaying similar problems.

Reisinger (1972) showed that depression-related behavior could be treated by a nonphysically aversive treatment procedure. The patient in this case was a 20-year-old institutionalized female diagnosed as anxiety-depressive. Her behavior was characterized by a high frequency of crying without any apparent provocation and little or no positive emotional behavior. The treatment consisted of presenting tokens (exchangable for tangible rewards) contingent on smiling and removing tokens contingent on crying. Thus the procedure involved a DRO plus response-cost arrangement. Two treatment periods were interspersed with a reversal condition in which the contingencies were withdrawn. Appropriate changes in both response systems accompanied the various conditions. Finally, the tokens were faded and ultimately replaced by social reinforcement (praise, compliments, etc.) in order to maintain the positive changes under more natural conditions.

Sexual Deviations

An extensive variety of aversion therapy techniques have been employed for the purpose of modifying deviant sexual behavior. The work in this area has been heavily criticized on the basis of ethical and practical grounds. Once again, many of these criticisms do not appear to be warranted in the sense that a large number of previously unhappy individuals have achieved a more satisfactory level of sexual adjustment as a consequence of such treatment. Nevertheless, the concern for better controlled observations is genuine and one can only hope that this will be resolved by future research.

As was true in the case of alcoholism, many of the earlier efforts in this area were formulated in the context of the Pavlovian model although it shortly became apparent that operant processes (frequently uncontrolled) intruded into the procedures. The major value of this earlier work then, was more of a heuristic and historic nature rather than in terms of contributing any hard knowledge to theory and practice. Moreover, the initiative displayed by these investigators in attacking complex problems via previously suspect methods, thereby challenging many prevailing myths, should not pass unmentioned.

One of the first attempts to apply an operant aversion therapy procedure with sexual deviations is reported by Blakemore et al. (1963). Prior to this study most of these efforts used nausea-producing drugs in order to produce a conditioned aversion in the presence of stimuli related to the deviant practices.

The particular problem condition treated in the Blakemore study was a long-standing transvestism. A variety of such activities was reported by the patient which usually led to sexual gratification. Marital and legal circumstances served as the impetus for his seeking assistance.

The treatment was conducted in a private room of a hospital which housed a full-length mirror and an electric grid floor. The patient's favorite outfit of female clothing was placed on the chair.

The procedure involved a series of trials in which the patient was instructed to start dressing in the female clothes. At some point during a trial, he received a signal to start undressing. The signal was either a buzzer or shock to the feet. These were randomly presented and occurred at varying time intervals until all the female clothes were removed. Following a one-minute rest, the procedure was repeated for a total of five trials in each treatment session. A total of 400 trials was administered over six treatment days. No transvestite behavior was reported six months after treatment.

It is difficult to classify the Blakemore procedure because it involves mixed components of different paradigms. It seems clear that a response contingency was involved since shock occurred in connection with at least some transvestite responses, and the patient could escape shock by undressing. In any event, this study represented a transition procedure from earlier aversion therapy efforts with sexual deviations and within the next several years a host of similar efforts was reported.

Thorpe et al. (1964) applied an "aversion relief" procedure to a variety of sexual problems including homosexuality (in individuals who desired to change) and transvestism. This technique relies upon the relief experienced by an individual who has escaped a painful event. Furthermore, if an aversive stimulus, such as shock, is removed in the presence of another stimulus, the latter stimulus may acquire positive properties in the process. In the Thorpe study a series of problem behavior-related words was presented, followed by shock. At the end of the series, an opposite and "normal" series of stimulus words (e.g., female breasts) was presented which was not accompanied by shock, and therefore produced relief. Although the procedure is a complicated one, the constructive changes in the patient's sexual behavior may be at least partially attributed to the use of response-contingent shock.

Further refinement of the aversion therapy procedure with sexual problems was reported by Marks and Gelder (1967) in a study detailing the treatment of five patients with fetish and/or transvestite related behaviors. In addition to other pretreatment measures, each patient's penile reactions to problem-related stimuli was assessed by means of an instrument which measures penile volume (plethysmograph).

The procedure involved two one-hour sessions each day for two weeks. During the first stage of treatment, the patient was instructed to imagine performing the deviant behavior and shock was delivered whenever a clear image was indicated. On about the third or fourth day, the patients were asked to actually practice the problem behavior and shock was delivered on a contingent basis on 75 percent of the trials.

In general, the results showed that the clients experienced increasing difficulties in fantasizing the deviant acts, and, what is probably more important, a reduction in penile reactions to the relevant stimuli.

This procedure, then, used well-defined pre- and posttreatment measures and introduced the technique of partial and random shock which may have increased the durability of the suppression effect, as described earlier.

During approximately the same period of time, several studies employing aversion therapy exclusively with homosexuals who desired to change their sexual preferences were also reported. Again, although the procedures were complicated and therefore make analysis difficult, the results ranged from moderately to highly successful. Perhaps the most extensive of these efforts was reported by Feldman and MacCulloch (1965) and MacCulloch, Birtles, and Feldman (1971). Their procedure, termed "anticipatory avoidance" involved response-contingent shock, negative reinforcement (avoidance of shock), fading, and probably DRO. In any event, anywhere from 50 percent to 70 percent of these patients treated showed complete cessation of homosexual behavior and an increase in heterosexual behavior during therapy. Moreover, these effects were maintained for as long as 24 months.

Additional reports have also suggested that fetishism (Kushner, 1965), exhibitionism (Kushner and Sandler, 1966), and voyeurism (Bancroft, Jones, and Pullan, 1966) can all be reduced or eliminated via the shock-contingent-on-fantasy procedure.

Finally, a more clearly operant procedure was reported in the treatment of a pedophilia (child molesting) which was so serious the patient was being considered for brain surgery (Bancroft, et al., 1966). The procedure attempted to recreate the natural condtions in which the pedophilia-related behaviors occurred (as measured by the penile plethysmograph) a painful shock was administered to the arm. These were continued until there was a reduction in the response. Each trial lasted ten minutes with no shock administered in the absence of a criterion response. Six to eight trials were administered each day over a period of eight weeks for a total of 200 shock trials. In addition, on every fourth trial, the shock apparatus was disconnected and the patient saw photographs of adult women while encouraged to engage in normal sexual fantasies.

Although the investigators did not consider their results to be a complete therapeutic success, there was a marked reduction in pedophilia-related activities and an increase in normal heterosexual behavior.

In any event, the study represents the continued refinement of the aversion therapy procedures with sexual deviations. It employed a discrete response-shock contingency; the procedure was repeated often enough until a marked reduction in undesirable behavior was realized and an alternative response was incorporated. Although it is not clear which of these components contributed to the final outcome, the general procedure represents an important advancement of the aversion therapy paradigm for such problem conditions.

A number of studies was reported in the last several years which reflect the trend of greater refinement in treatment procedures and improved experimental design. In addition, several investigators employed innovative techniques which offer great promise in the use of aversive procedures with sexual problems. McConaghy (1975) reported a reduction in homosexual preferences for a group of subjects treated by means of a discrimination training procedure (picture of nude males associated with shock to the forearm) which was also accompanied by an increase in heterosexual preferences in about half of the subjects. Maletzky (1977) used covert sensitization to treat a variety of problem behaviors such as homosexuality, exhibitionism and child molesting with good results, especially when "booster" sessions were administered following the regular course of treatment.

Marshall (1974) eliminated a trouser fetish and produced an increase in heterosexual activity by means of combining punishment to fetish activity and orgasmic reconditioning to normal sex-related stimuli. Wickramasekra employed a procedure termed Aversive Behavior Rehearsal with 20 exhibitionists which has apparently produced dramatic changes in one to four sessions. The procedure requires that the subject perform his exhibitionism under controlled circumstances arranged by the therapist and based on the idiosyncratic experiences of the subject. Wickramasekera claims that the observed changes are due to aversive internal consequences produced by the procedure. Although other explanations may be considered (extinction, for example) these results are promising enough to warrant further investigation by others.

Finally, Forgione (1976) has shown how the use of mannequins in assessing child molesting may enhance the effects of aversive procedures such as discrimination training (shock associated with taboo slides, and no shock associated with socially appropriate slides) with individuals who manifest such problem behaviors.

Generalized Asocial Behaviors

The last problem condition to be considered represents a category which encompasses a wide variety of socially deviant acts from mild forms of nuisance and asocial behaviors to dangerous acts of aggression directed at objects and other people.

The literature in this area is quite extensive and only a brief overview is presented here.

There are by now a whole series of studies indicating the effectiveness of time-out for reducing a wide assortment of aggressive, asocial, negativistic behaviors. In addition, these studies have been conducted with a wide variety of people of various ages and sexes in a diversity of institutional settings. Bostow and Bailey (1969) for example, reduced severe disruptive and aggressive behaviors (loud abusive vocalizations, attacking others) in two retarded female adults by making a brief TO contingent on such responses. White, Nielsen, and Johnson (1972) extended these observations to 20 retarded children. Ramp, Ulrich, and Dulany (1971) reduced out-of-seat behaviors and inappropriate talking in a classroom situation, and Wahler (1969) demonstrated that similar techniques could be employed in the home environment through parental instruction. Tyler and Brown (1967) found that aggressive asocial behavior (throwing objects, physical assault, etc.) in 15 adolescent males could be similarly treated.

Aggressive behavior has also been effectively reduced by means of response cost. Winkler (1970) for example, suppressed episodes of violence and loud noise in chronic psychiatric patients by removing tokens contingent on such responses. Kazdin (1972) provides a review of the relevant literature in which he describes the variety of problem behaviors successfully treated by response cost (smoking, overeating, stuttering, psychotic talk); the durability of such procedures in terms of long-range effects; and several aspects of response-cost procedures which may enhance their efficacy.

As noted earlier the overcorrection procedure has also been used successfully in treating a number of disruptive and asocial behaviors. These efforts have typically been conducted in institutional settings where the appropriate procedures can be implemented.

A recent example by Azrin and Wesolowski (1974) is representative. In this case the overcorrection procedure was designed to reduce the high incidence of stealing on an entire ward of profoundly retarded adults. The overcorrection was preceded by simple correction—staff members requiring the thief to return the stolen items. After five days of correction, the overcorrection procedure was initiated. Now each theft required the return of the stolen items plus an additional item. This resulted in a 50 percent reduction in thefts on the first day and in complete elimination of the problem after the third day.

Finally, response-contingent shock has also been employed with asocial behaviors, especially where the problem conditions are highly dangerous. In this fashion, Bucher and King (1971) suppressed the rate of highly destructive acts in an 11-year-old psychotic boy in the treatment setting as well as at home where the treatment was continued by the child's parent. Royer, Flynn, and Osadca (1971) also used a shock procedure to reduce the frequency of fire setting in a severely regressed disorganized psychiatric patient. In this case, shock correlated with arson-related words had no effect on the patient's actual behavior. Subsequently, the patient was required to rehearse a series of fire setting activities with shock administered on a response-contingent basis. This procedure resulted in a marked reduction of the problem behavior and a complete absence of such acts during a four-year follow-up assessment.

SUMMARY

In a relatively short period of time, the aversion therapy literature has increased at an astounding rate. Each new review attests to the growing elaboration of techniques. What is perhaps even more impressive is that this progress has been accomplished despite the fact that few if any of these procedures have incorporated all of the techniques designed to maximize the effectiveness of treatment.

In the light of these developments, it no longer seems appropriate to dismiss such practices out of hand. On the contrary, knowledge of these procedures would seem to add an important dimension to the total range of skills which the behavior therapist can bring to bear on the problems encountered in clinical settings.

Aversion therapy is indeed a legitimate treatment modality, especially when dealing with problems which require immediate intervention. Anyone who has observed the dramatic improvement produced in a head banger, for example, is almost forced to accept this conclusion. Furthermore, in the process of expanding our knowledge, it appears that many of the traditional reservations and criticisms are being laid to rest. True, there have been excesses in the other direction, especially in the indiscriminate and unsystematic use of electric shock by unrestrained enthusiasts. But the alleged horrors that have been linked to the use of aversion therapy expressed by many critics have been greatly exaggerated—they are not a necessary outcome of such practices as long as the proper safeguards, as described in preceding sections, are exercised.

What is desperately needed is a body of controlled, clinical investigations which more closely correspond to the well-designed efforts emerging from the laboratory. Moreover, we need to devise better change measures, to extend outcome assessment, to use more realistic treatment techniques, and to make comparison studies of the relative effectiveness of different treatment methods within the same problem condition.

The behavior modification movement is proud of its alleged reliance upon scientific rigor. Perhaps in this area more than any other, the opportunities are presently available to justify this claim.

REFERENCES

Adams, M.R. and Popelka, G. The influence of "time out" on stutterers and their dysfluency. *Behavior Therapy*, 1971, *2*, 334-339.

Atthowe, J.M., Jr. Controlling nocturnal enuresis in severely disabled and chronic patients. *Behavior Therapy*, 1972, *3*, 232-239.

Azrin, N.H. and Holz, W.C. Punishment. In W.K. Honig (Ed.), *Operant behavior: Areas of research and application*. New York: Appleton-Century-Crofts, 1966.

Bancroft, J.H., Jr., Jones, H.G., and Pullan, B.R. A simple transducer for measuring penile erection, with comments on its use in the treatment of sexual disorders. *Behavior Research and Therapy*, 1966, *4*, 239-241.

Barker, J.C. and Miller, M.E. Aversion therapy for compulsive gambling. *Journal of Nervous and Mental Disorders*, 1968, *16*, 285-302.

Blake, B.G. The application of behavior therapy to the treatment of alcoholism. *Behaviour Research and Therapy*, 1965, *3*, 75-85.

Blakemore, C.B., Thorpe, J.G., Barker, J.C., Conway, C.G., and Lavin, N.I. The application of faradic aversion conditioning in a case of transvestism. *Behaviour Research and Therapy*, 1963, *1*, 29-34.

Bostow, D.E. and Bailey, J.B. Modification of severe disruptive and aggressive behavior using brief time-out and reinforcement procedures. *Journal of Applied Behavior Analysis*, 1969, *2*, 31-38.

Bucher, B. and Fabricatore, J. Use of patient-administered shock to suppress hallucinations. *Behavior Therapy*, 1970, *1*, 382-385.

Bucher, B. and King, L.W. Generalization of punishment effects in the deviant behavior of a psychotic child. *Behavior Therapy*, 1971, *2*, 68-77.

Chimonides, S. Personal communication.

Corte, H.E., Wolf, M.M., and Locke, B.J. A comparison of procedures for eliminating self-injurious behavior of retarded adolescents. *Journal of Applied Behavior Analysis*, 1971, *4*, 201-215.

Conway, J.B. Behavioral self-control of smoking through aversive conditioning and self-management. *Journal of Consulting and Clinical Psychology*, 1977, *45*, 348-357.

Cunningham, C.E., and Linscheid, T.R. Elimination of chronic infant ruminating by electric shock. *Behavior Therapy*, 1976, *7*, 231-239.

Daly, D.A. and Frick, J.V. The effects of punishing stuttering expectations and stuttering utterances: A comparative study. *Behavior Therapy*, 1970, *1*, 228-239.

Davidson, R.S. Alcoholism: Experimental analyses of etiology and modification. Personal communication, 1973.

Dericco, D.A., Brigham, T.A., and Garlington, W.K. Development and evaluation of treatment paradigms for the suppression of smoking behavior. *Journal of Applied Behavior Analysis*, 1977, *10*, 173-181.

Dieker, P.C. Remotely applied punishment versus avoidance conditioning in the treatment of self-injurious behavior. *European Journal of Behavior Analysis and Modification*, 1976, *3*, 179-185.

Dorsey, M.F., Iwata, B.A., and McSween, T.E., Treatment of self-injurious behaviors in profoundly retarded persons using a water mist. Unpublished report, 1972.

Drabman, R. Decreasing the self-injurious behavior of a 3½ year old from an economically underprivileged family through contingent soaking. *The Behavior Therapist*, 1978, *1*, 19-20.

Drabman, R.S., Ross, J.M., Lynd, R.S., and Cordua, G. Retarded children as observers, mediators, and generalization programmers using an icing procedure. *Behavior Modification*, 1978, 2 371-385.

Elliot, C.H., and Denney, D.R. Weight control through covert sensitization and false feedback. *Journal of Consulting and Clinical Psychology*, 1975, *43*, 842-850.

Elliot, R. and Tighe, T.J. Breaking the cigarette habit. *Psychological Record*, 1968, *18*, 503-513.

Feldman, M.P. Aversion therapy for sexual deviation: A critical review. *Psychological Bulletin*, 1966, *65*, 65-79.

Feldman, M.P. and MacCulloch, M.J. The application of anticipatory avoidance learning to the treatment of homosexuality. I. Theory, technique and preliminary results. *Behaviour Research and Therapy*, 1965, *2*, 165-183.

Ferster, C.B., Nurnberger, J.L., and Levitt, E.B. The control of eating. *Journal of Mathetics*, 1962, *1*, 87-109.

Forgione, A.C. The use of mannequins in the behavioral assessment of child molesters: Two case reports. *Behavior Therapy*, 1976, *7*, 678-685.

Foxx, R.M. and Azrin, N.H. The elimination of autistic self-stimulatory behavior by overcorrection. *Journal of Applied Behavior Analysis*, 1973, *6*, 1-14.

Franks, C.M. Behavior therapy: The principles of conditioning and the treatment of the alcoholic. *Quarterly Journal of Studies on Alcohol*, 1963, *24*, 511-529.

Gendreau, D.E. and Dodwell, P.C. An aversive treatment for addictive cigarette smokers. *Canadian Psychologist*, 1968, *9* 28-34.

Glover, J.H., and McCue, P.A. Electrical aversion therapy with alcoholics: A comparative follow-up study. *British Journal of Psychiatry*, 1977, *30* 279-286.

Goldiamond, I. Stuttering and fluency as manipulative operant response classes. In L. Krasner and L.P. Ullman (Eds.), *Research in behavior modification*. New York: Holt, Rinehart and Winston, 1965.

Harris, S.L., and Romanczyk, R.G. Treating self-injurious behavior of a retarded child by overcorrection. *Behavior Therapy*, 1976, *7*, 235-239.

Haynes, S.M. and Geddy, P. Suppression of psychotic hallucinations through Time-out. *Behavior Therapy*, 1973, *4*, 123-127.

Hunt, G.M., and Azrin, N.H. A community reinforcement approach to alcoholism. *Behavior Research and Therapy*, 1973, *11* 91-104.

Hunt, W.A. and Matarazzo, J.D. Three years later: Recent developments in the experimental modification of smoking behavior. *Journal of Abnormal Psychology*, 1973, *81*, 107-114.

Johnson, J.M. Punishment of human behavior. *American Psychologist*, 1972, *27*, 1033-1054.

Jones, H.G. The behavioral treatment of enuresis nocturna. In H.J. Eysenck (Ed.) *Behavior therapy and the neuroses*. Oxford: Pergamon Press, 1960.

Kanfer, F.H. and Karoly, P. Self-control: A behavioristic excursion into the lion's den. *Behavior Therapy*, 1972, *3*, 398-416.

Kazdin, A.E. Response cost. The removal of conditioned reinforcement for therapeutic change. *Behavior Therapy*, 1972, *3*, 398-416.

——— The effect of response cost and aversive stimulation in suppressing punished and non-punished speech dysfluencies. *Behavior Therapy*, 1973, *4*, 73-82.

Kellam, A.P. Shoplifting treated by aversion to a film. *Behaviour Research and Therapy*, 1969, *7*, 125-127.

Kohlenberg, R.J. The punishment of persistent vomiting: A case study. *Journal of Applied Behavior Analysis*, 1970, *3*, 241-245.

Kushner, M. and Sandler, J. Aversion therapy and the concept of punishment. *Behaviour*

In L. Ullmann and L. Krasner (Eds.), *Case studies in behavior modification*. New York: Holt, Rinehart and Winston, 1965.

Kushner, M. and Sandler, J. Aversion therapy and the concept of punishment. *Behaviour Research and Therapy*, 1966, *4*, 179-186.

Kushner, M. Faradic aversive controls in clinical practice. In C. Neuringer and J.L. Michael (Eds.), *Behavior modification in clinical psychology*. New York: Appleton-Century-Crofts, 1970.

Lang, P.J. and Melamed, P.G. Case report: Avoidance conditioning therapy of an infant with chronic ruminative vomiting. *Journal of Abnormal Psychology*, 1969, *74*, 1-8.

Lemere, F. and Voegtlin, W.L. An evaluation of aversion treatment of alcoholism. *Quarterly Journal of Studies on Alcohol*, 1950, *11* 199-204.

Lichstein, K.L., and Schreibman, L. Employing electric shock with autistic children: A review of the side effects. *Journal of Autism and Schizophrenia*, 1976, *6*, 163-173.

Liversedge, L.A. and Sylvester, J.D. Conditioning techniques in the treatment of writer's cramp. *Lancet*, 1955, *2*, 1147-1149.

Lovaas, O.I. and Simmons, J.Q. Manipulation of self-destruction in three retarded children. *Journal of Applied Behavior Analysis*, 1969, *2*, 143-157.

Luckey, R.E., Watson, C.M., and Musick, J.K. Aversive conditioning as a means of inhibiting vomiting and rumination. *American Journal of Mental Deficiency*, 1968, *73*, 139-142.

MacCulloch, M.J., Birtles, C.J., and Feldman, M.P. Anticipatory avoidance learning for the treatment of homosexuality: Recent developments and an automated aversive therapy system. *Behavior Therapy*, 1971, *2*, 151-169.

Maletzky, B.M. Booster sessions in aversion therapy: The permanency of treatment. *Behavior Therapy*, 1977, *8*, 460-463.

Mann, R.A. The use of contingency contracting to facilitate durability of behavior change: Weight loss maintained. *Addictive Behaviors*, 1976, *1*, 245-249.

Marks, I. and Gelder, M. Transvestism and fetishism: Clinical and psychological changes during faradic aversion. *British Journal of Psychiatry*, 1967, *119*, 711-730.

Marshall, W.L. A combined treatment approach to the reduction of multiple fetish-related behavior. *Journal of Consulting and Clinical Psychology*, 1974, *42*, 613-616.

May, J.G., Jr., Risley, T.R., Twardosz, S., Friedman, P., Bijou, D.W., Wexler, D. Guidelines for the use of behavioral procedures in state programs for retarded persons.

McConaghy, N. Aversive and positive conditioning treatments of homosexuality. *Behavior Research and Therapy*, 1975, *13*, 309-315.

Merbaum, M. The modification of self-destructive behavior by a mother-therapist using aversive stimulation. *Behavior Therapy*, 1973, *4*, 442-447.

Meyer, V. and Crisp, A. Aversion therapy in two cases of obesity. *Behaviour Research and Therapy*, 1964, *2*, 143-147.

Miller, P.M. A behavioral intervention program for chronic public drunkenness offenders. *Archives of General Psychiatry*, 1975, *32*, 915-920.

Mowrer, O.H. and Mowrer, W.M. Enuresis. A method for its study and treatment. *American Journal of Orthopsychiatry*, 1938, *8*, 436-459.

Rachman, S. Aversion therapy: Chemical or electrical? *Behavior Research and Therapy*, 1965, *2*, 289-300.

Ramp, E., Ulrich, R., and Dulany, S. Delayed timeout as a procedure for reducing disruptive classroom behavior: A case study. *Journal of Applied Behavior Analysis*, 1971, *4*, 235-239.

Reisinger, J.J. The treatment of "anxiety-depression" via positive reinforcement and response cost. *Journal of Applied Behavior Analysis*, 1972, *5*, 125-130.

Risley, T.R. The effects and side effects of punishing the autistic behavior of a deviant child. *Journal of Applied Behavior Analysis*, 1968, *1*, 21-34.

Rodriguez, L., and Sandler, J. Unpublished Master's Thesis. University of South Florida, 1978.

Royer, F.L., Flynn, W.F., and Osadca, B.A. Case history: Aversion therapy for fire-setting by a deteriorated schizophrenic. *Behavior Therapy*, 1971, *3*, 229-232.

Sajwaj, T., Libet, J. and Agros, S. Lemon juice therapy: The control of life threatening rumination in a six month old infant. *Journal of Applied Behavior Analysis*, 1974, *7*, 557-566.

Sandler, J. Masochism: An empirical analysis. *Psychological Bulletin*, 1964, *62*, 197-204.

Scholander, T. Treatment of an unusual case of compulsive behavior by aversive stimulation. *Behavior Therapy*, 1972, *3*, 290-293.

Siegel, G.M. Punishment, stuttering, and disfluency, *Journal of Speech and Hearing Research*, 1970, *13*. 677-714.

Soderberg, G.A. Delayed auditory feedback and stuttering. *Journal of Speech and Hearing Disorders*, 1968, *33*, 260-267.

Tate, B.G. Case study: Control of chronic self-injurious behavior by conditioned procedures. *Behavior Therapy*, 1972, *3*, 72-83.

Tate, B.G. and Baroff, G.S. Aversive control of self-injurious behavior in a psychotic boy. *Behavior Therapy*, 1966, *4*, 281-287.

Thorpe, J.G., Schmidt, E., Brown, P.T., and Castell, D. Aversion-relief therapy: A new method for general application. *Behaviour Research and Therapy*, 1964, *2*, 71-82.

Toister, R.P., Coudrau, C.J., Worley, J., and Arthur, P. Faradic therapy of chronic vomiting in infancy: A case study. *Behavior Therapy and Experimental Psychiatry*, 1975, *6*, 55-59.

Tough, J.H., Hawkins, R.P., McArthur, M.M., and Ravenswaay, S.V. Modification of neurotic behavior by punishment: A new use for an old device. *Behavior Therapy*, 1971, *2*, 567-574.

Tyler, V.O., Jr. and Brown, G.D. The use of swift, brief isolation as a group control device for institutionalized delinquents. *Behaviour Research and Therapy*, 1967, *5*, 1-9.

Voegtlin, W.L. Conditioned reflex therapy of chronic alcoholism. Ten years experience with the method. *Rocky Mountain Medical Journal*, 1947, *44*, 807-812.

Vogler, R.E., Lunde, S.E., Johnson, G.R., and Martin, P.L. Electrical aversion conditioning with chronic alcoholics. *Journal of Consulting and Clinical Psychology*, 1970, *34*, 302-307.

Vogler, R.E., Weissbach, T.A., Compton, J.V., and Martin, G.T. Integrated behavior change technique for problem drinkers in the community. *Journal of Consulting and Clinical Psychology*, 1977, *45*, 267-279.

Wahler, R.G. Oppositional children: A quest for parental reinforcement control. *Journal of Applied Behavior Analysis*, 1969, *2*, 159-170.

Weiner, H. Some effects of response cost upon human operant behavior. *Journal of the Experimental Analysis of Behavior*, 1962, *5*, 201-208.

White, G.D., Nielsen, G., and Johnson, S.M. Timeout duration and the suppression of deviant behavior in children. *Journal of Applied Behavior Analysis*, 1972, *5*, 111-120.

Wickramasekra, I. Aversive behavior rehearsal for sexual exhibitionism. *Behavior Therapy*, 1976, *7*, 167-176.

Wilson, G.T., Leaf, R.C., and Nathan, P.E. The aversive control of excessive alcohol consumption by chronic alcoholics in the laboratory setting. *Journal of Applied Behavior Analysis*, 1975, *8*, 13-21.

Wilson, G.T., and Tracey, D.A. An experimental analysis of aversive imagery versus electrical aversive conditioning in the treatment of chronic alcoholics. *Behavior Research and Therapy*, 1976, *14*, 41-50.

Winkler, R.C. Management of chronic psychiatric patients by a token reinforcement system. *Journal of Applied Behavior Analysis*, 1970, *3*, 47-55.

Wright, L. Aversive conditioning of self-induced seizures. *Behavior Therapy*, 1973, *4*, 712-713.

10
Self-Management Methods
Frederick H. Kanfer

The traditional concepts underlying the activities of mental health workers imply an *administrative* model of treatment. This model presumes that clients seek assistance in an earnest effort to change their current problem situations. The helper administers a treatment to which the client submits and which eventuates in improvement in the client's life conditions. This model assigns a caretaking or administrative function to the clinician and a relatively passive, accepting and trusting role to the client. In some conceptual models, for example, those which rely heavily on the modification of the environment as a means for bringing about change (Chapter 7, 9), the client's participation in the helping process is relatively limited. In other approaches that rely heavily on changing cognitive behaviors (Chapter 3, 4) there is a basic presumption that the client is highly motivated to utilize the presented techniques and accepts changes in life-orientation with full cooperation. The view of the client either as a passive recipient, be it of drugs, conditioning treatments, or cognitive reorganizations, or as a person who is eager to change often runs into difficulty because of the paradox of the many clients who seek help on the one hand but resist any external control or guidance toward change, on the other hand. A *participant* model emphasizes the importance of client responsibility in treatment. It represents a shift from the provision of a protective treatment environment toward the offering of rehabilitative experiences in which the client accepts increasing responsibilities for his own behavior, for dealing with the environment and for planning the future. The therapeutic environment is viewed as a transitory support system that prepares the client to handle common social and personal demands more effectively. While treatment methods that emphasize environmental control of behavior rest on the cooperation of another person—a teacher, a helper, a therapist, or a friend—self-management techniques are prescriptive methods that place the burden of engaging in the change process heavily on the client.

In the current literature there is increasing recognition that treatment failures may be due to two important factors. First, the methods may be ineffective. Secondly, the client may fail to comply with the prescribed regimen and the methods may never be given an opportunity to operate. The increasing awareness of the importance of involving the client in the treatment process and abandoning the helper's traditional role as an infallible parenting professional is consistent with the broad social trend toward increasing self-help. Clients nowadays have less confidence in unquestioned professional practices and increased sophistication about the nature and objectives of the helping process. They increasingly demand a participating role in the selection of treatment objectives.

The self-management framework presented in this chapter rests on the following rationale: (1) Many behaviors are not easily accessible for modification by anyone but the client. For example, some intimate and sexual behaviors, some frequently occurring but barely noticeable behaviors, such as timid or mildly aggressive interpersonal behaviors. These often lead to client discomfort even though others may not react to their occurrence. Continuing observation and arrangement of conditions for change might require institutionalization for long periods of time, a highly uneconomical and unrealistic procedure. Therefore participation of the client as a change agent is essential in these cases. (2) Problematic behaviors are often associated closely with self-reactions and with such cognitive activities as thinking, fantasizing, imagining, or planning. These behaviors are essentially inaccessible to direct observation. If a client possesses an adequate behavioral repertoire for acting on the basis of his thoughts, changing the cognitive responses becomes the primary task of the helping process. To monitor and alter these behaviors, the helper must shift major responsibility to the client. (3) Changing behavior is difficult and often unpleasant. Many clients seek assistance, but often they are motivated not so much to change as to alleviate the current discomforts or threats, preferably without altering their behavior or lifestyle. The client's acceptance of a program for change as desirable, feasible and worth working for is a basic motivational requirement. This orientation may constitute the first and most critical target in a self-management program. (4) The utility of a change program lies not only in removing situation-specific problems or particular symptoms. What is learned in therapy should include a set of generalizable skills such as coping responses, assessing situations and behavior outcomes, and developing rules of conduct for common problem situations, which aid the client to avoid or handle future problems more effectively than in the past.

The acceptance of responsibility in treatment requires that the client develop a strong motivation to change. Therefore a critical task of the helper is to motivate the client to seek change actively. In contrast to programs based solely on environmental control or on the helper-client relationship as the exclusive vehicle for change, the early phase of the change process is designed to help the client accept the necessity for change and to develop clear objectives for treatment. Modeling, work assignments, and learning to analyze problems and to work toward their resolution help the client to plan and to engage in more effective cognitive and interpersonal actions. By altering the social and physical environment he can alleviate the difficulty of changing and to ease the maintenance of new behavior patterns. Without establishing incentives for changes and environments in which they can be carried out, treatment effects cannot be expected to last long beyond treatment termination. As new behaviors are carried out by the individual in his daily life and in the absence of the therapist, the helper fades into a role of diminishing guidance. In this sense, the goal of the treatment process is its termination and the helper follows a "principle of least intervention," providing only as much assistance as is needed to enable the client to resume control over his life.

Self-management methods help the clients to acquire new behaviors. The techniques should be viewed as temporary devices. They facilitate the learning process but they do not necessarily become part of the person's everyday repertoire. In learning to use a typewriter, auxiliary charts, mnemonic devices and self-instructions that guide a finger to the correct key are critical in the learning process. But the accomplished typist uses none of these assists. Similarly, such techniques as self-observation, contingent self-rewards, problem solving, or contracts serve the function of facilitating acquisition. As the person settles into a new and satisfying behavior pattern there is decreasing need for their use. However, they are available on future occasions when the client faces difficulties.

The common element in the various forms of self-management methods lies in the therapist's role as an instigator and motivator to help the client start a change program. Sometimes the therapist makes special arrangements to insure that the client's efforts are further supported by the natural environment at home, at school, or at work. Combined with the client's increasing skills to use a variety of techniques in future problem situations, his ability to alter environments can extend the durability of treatment effects beyond the time of treatment (Goldstein and Kanfer, 1979).

The change process is conducted within a negotiation model. The therapist serves as a consultant and expert who negotiates with the client in how to go about change and to what end. The interactions are future oriented in that they focus on the development of general repertoires for dealing with problem situations. They deal with past experiences only as they are needed to help the client recognize inappropriateness of his current behaviors or to facilitate a behavioral analysis by providing information about the conditions under which a maladaptive behavior has developed.

Earlier behavioral clinicians have tended to disregard the client's thoughts and fantasies in planning therapy programs. Indeed, in circumstances where strict control of behaviors is exercised by clearly established rules, as in some institutions, in military organizations, and in cases where the individual is totally dependent on the social or physical environment for survival, arrangements of behavior-environment contingencies can be consistently and thoroughly applied and yield extensive behavior changes. In such environments, the person's reaction to control and his cognitive activities contribute little to the shaping of the behavior. A small child who is totally dependent for satisfaction of his physical needs on the adults in the environment can easily be taught to change his behavior by rearrangement of reinforcement contingencies. Similarly, a person whose social environment consistently reinforces behavior that is executed in a strictly prescribed fashion will adopt the required conduct to avoid trouble and pain and to obtain what positive reinforcement the environment offers.

In our everyday experiences, environmental controls are much less stringent, often contradictory, and frequently resented. Children are often rewarded or punished for the same behavior on different occasions and sometimes even in similar situations by different people. Verbal instructions, adult models in the family, and television screens frequently demonstrate both the punishments and benefits of aggressive behavior. Similarly assertiveness, sexual behaviors, alcohol consumption, smoking, and amoral behaviors are under control of conflicting social and physical consequences. A still larger group of behaviors, often called neurotic, include many interpersonal strategies for controlling other persons or for reducing anxiety or discomfort of conflicting self-reactions. They are often determined by combinations of positive and aversive consequences. It is in the case of these conflicting controls that a person's thinking, fantasies, and other covert reactions exert the greatest influence in modfying the simple input-output relationships, that is, the relationships between the environmental, discriminative, and reinforcing stimuli and the behavior which they aim to regulate.

The framework from which many of the techniques described in this chapter have been derived essentially attempts to combine a Skinnerian approach with research findings from social psychology and cognitive psychology and from current clinical practices. It views self-regulatory behaviors as originating in the person's earlier learning experiences. It is assumed that the social and physical environment ultimately must support self-regulation to maintain its effectiveness. However, skills in managing one's cognitive behaviors and the actions which they control can free the individual, at least temporarily, from immediate control by the current environment. It is also assumed that we can deal with cognitive behaviors in practice, essentially in the same manner as we deal with interpersonal or other publicly observable behaviors. This assumption is a practical necessity, even though our understanding of the underlying cognitive structures and processes is very limited.

The methods described in this chapter provide a general structure for behavioral interview therapy. The procedures can be used in most cases but are supplemented for the individual client with other cognitive methods which are described in Chapters 4 and 11. In addition, specific complaints, such as anxiety, low assertiveness, depression, sexual dysfunction, phobias or others, are attacked with programs or strategies designed to treat these problems. But the general context of the change process is created by combining problem-specific techniques with the present methods. Further, considerations of the interpersonal setting may also invoke the utilization of methods described in Chapters 2, 3 and 11 to provide a maximally facilitating treatment milieu.

A THEORETICAL FRAMEWORK OF SELF-REGULATION

In order to understand the general framework from which various self-management techniques have been derived, it is helpful to consider some of the psychological processes that occur in self-regulation. Social learning theory assumes that much of everyday behavior consists of chains of reactions that have been built up so that a response is cued by completion of the immediately preceding response. For example, typing, driving a car, shaving, preparing breakfast, and many other activities do not consist of discrete acts which require continuous decisions among alternate responses based on the person's judgment of the adequacy of each discrete component. However, when these smooth activities are interrupted, or fail to produce the effects to which the person has become accustomed, the activity will stop and a *self-regulation* process will begin. On the basis of laboratory research and some theorizing, this self-regulation process has been described as a sequence in which three distinct stages can be identified (Kanfer, 1970, 1971). To illustrate these, imagine that a person drives to work. As he turns a corner he finds himself on an unfamiliar street. A behavior disruption occurs. The driver might first pay closer attention to what he is doing. He may ask himself how he happened to get onto this street. This first stage is called the *self-monitoring* or *self-observation* stage and is essentially described as deliberately and carefully attending to one's own behavior. On the basis of past experience with driving to work the person has built up expectations for what should happen when he drives down certain streets and makes a given turn. These might be called *performance criteria* or *standards*—the expectations of what will happen when a well rehearsed behavior is carried out.

The second stage of self-regulation consists of a comparison between the information obtained from self-monitoring and the criteria for the given behavior. This stage has been called the *self-evaluation* stage. It is a discrimination response, a matching which reveals the discrepancy between what one is doing and what one ought to be doing. A close match between performance criteria and information from feedback should result in some satisfaction with oneself, while a large discrepancy would yield dissatisfaction. For example, our driver might note that the corner is familiar but he has turned too soon. He might comment on his foolishness and then correct his behavior.

The third stage in the self-regulation process is motivational. It consists of the administration of *self-reinforcement* contingent upon the degree to which the behavior diverges from the performance standards. Positive self-reinforcement should result in continuation of the interrupted behavior chain. For example, our driver might note that he is not really on a strange street but that only a store sign had been changed. He might then be satisfied that he is on the correct route and continue on his way. However, if his expectations (standards) are not met, he would begin a series of behaviors intended to correct the error. Each time a new response is tried out, the same process is repeated until the standard is approximated, or the person abandons the whole sequence.

The self-regulation model then suggests that persons tend to be alerted when their behavior has unexpected consequences, or when a decision needs to be made about how to proceed. Such interruptions are most common when learning a new activity, finding oneself in a strange situation, or when an environmental reaction has changed. Overall behavioral efficiency is reduced to the extent that any of the three psychological processes that we have described above are carried out inefficiently. For example, if our lost driver were to become panicky because he is late for work he may fail to self-monitor. He may fail to observe where he is and how he got there, trying instead to correct his path by turning at the next street corner without much consideration. If he has not traveled this route very often his performance criteria may be vague, that is, he may not remember where he should have been after the turn and his performance will be erratic. If our lost driver is an individual who has been very critical of himself for the slightest errors in the past, this tendency toward self-criticism (self-punishment) might lead him to become agitated and upset. In clinical situations, numerous methods have been used to increase the effectiveness of behavior at each of the stages of the self-regulation process. Most self-management programs combine techniques that involve standard-setting, self-monitoring, self-evaluation, and self-reinforcement. We will describe these methods as separate elements in the following sections, remembering that the design of an individual program would focus on any of these components, depending on the client's skills and his particular problem.

A sketch of this working model is given in Figure 10.1. It should be noted that this in only a framework that guides our thinking. It has been derived from laboratory research and it has been useful in developing clinical techniques for problems ranging from obesity (Mahoney, 1974) to depression (Fuchs and Rehm, 1977). This does not mean that the model represents the actual and universal presence of these discrete psychological processes. In fact, it is quite likely that the total sequence of criterion setting, self-observation, evaluation, reinforcement, and planning of new actions proceeds rather quickly, often without much thought by the person. Nevertheless, it can help us to organize some of the essential features of the process by which an individual manages his own behavior. The model is similar to others which also stress the importance of the achievement of self-generated criteria as a strong motivation (Bandura, 1977). It is incomplete in that such variables of the causal attribution of outcomes (Heider, 1958; Jones et al., 1971; Harvey, Ickes and Kidd, 1978), the level of emotional arousal, the relevance of social norms (Diener, 1979) and others are suspected to influence the self-regulatory process. However an expansion of the model to account for the role of additional variables must await the availability of a larger number of supporting studies than the few experiments now available.

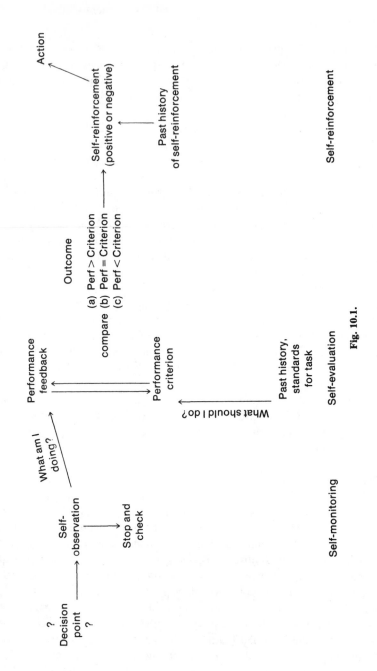

Fig. 10.1.

The model helps us to understand that the task of maintaining one's behavior by reward is much more complex than the learning of operant responses that are selectively reinforced by the environment. In environmentally arranged contingencies, no critical decisions need to be made by the person. For comparison we can alter the example of our driver to one in which his behavior is under external control. Assume that a friend who knows the city very well is sitting next to the driver. As the driver proceeds, the friend confirms correct directions and warns the driver prior to making an incorrect turn. It is the guide who has to plan, decide, and evaluate the driver's actions.

When the question of self-regulation involves behavior that is under strong conflicting consequences, a change process is complicated further by the need to establish acceptable standards. Prior to engaging in self-correcting behavior the individual has to make a commitment. But the commitment to alter a behavior is itself influenced by the variables that lead a person to state such intentions. Various environments provide favorable or unfavorable settings that can determine whether the intentions (the behavior standards) will be achieved. Table 10.1 describes some of the factors that might lead a person to make intention statements. A separate set of factors, however, relates to the question of whether or not the person will initiate and execute a change program. Therefore, when a person comes to ask for help, a major consideration is how to motivate the client to make a decision to change and to initiate the program. Techniques for handling such problems are discussed in later sections of this chapter. Equally important is the reduction of external support for maintaining the problem behavior, at least during the beginning of the program. A drug addict in his old environment or a spouse who is dominated at home may never muster sufficiently strong self-

Table 10.1 Factors That May Influence the Commitment to Execute a Self-Control Program*

Commitment Easier	Commitment Difficult
1. Delayed Program Onset	1. Program begins immediately
2. History of pos. Rf. for promise-making	2. Past failure to keep promises was punished
3. Recent indulgence to satiation	3. Problematic behavior is not perceived to be under client's control—"can't be helped"
4. Guilt, discomfort and fear over action (aversive effects of response) is high	4. Pos. Rf. for problem behavior is high
5. Escape from social disapproval	5. Criteria for change too high
6. Presence of others making promises (modeling and social pressure)	6. Consequences of nonfulfillment are harsh
7. Behavior to be changed is private and cannot be easily checked	7. Behavior is publicly observable
8. Promise is vaguely phrased	8. Support for program planning is not anticipated
9. Promise-making leads to social approval or immediate benefits	

*Note: Expression of commitment does not guarantee execution of the program. Other factors, such as program requirements and reinforcement for execution in its early stages, determine fulfillment of a commitment after it is made.

reinforcers to overcome the environmental rewards for continuing old behaviors. In some instances the reduction of the environmental contingencies alone may suffice to permit the client to solve the problem. If not, self-management techniques can be taught. Their range of effectiveness is greatest when the beneficial effects of the problem behavior are only moderate and the social environment does not actively oppose change (e.g., a dominating spouse who fights the disruption of control which would follow the client's increased assertiveness).

The term self-regulation applies to the general case in which a person directs his own behavior. The behavior may not be very conflictful, as in the learning of a new skill that has previously been observed or in problem solving. (See Chapters 4 and 11 for methods that include training in self-regulation.) When the behavior to be executed or avoided is conflictful, we speak of the redirection as self-control. In clinical problems, it is this special case of self-regulation that is most frequently encountered, and to which self-management methods are most often applied.

In self-management problems the client who seeks help is usually enjoying some aspect of the problem of which he complains. For example, the sexual exhibitionist, the alcoholic, or the shoplifter may protest endlessly about his unhappiness and speak of his earnest desire to change. Indeed, some of the effects of his behavior may be aversive, for example, social rejection, job loss, or police action. At the same time these activities also yield some satisfactions that keep him going. Since the positive consequences are usually immediate, while the aversive consequences may not occur until a later time and may be uncertain, attempts to change such behaviors often require the assistance of a helper. An initial step in treatment may consist of increasing the conflict to motivate the client for change. Discussion of the aversive consequence which the client had previously disregarded, personal encouragement, or realistic confrontation and self-evaluation can shift the client's commitment to change.

Self-Control as a Special Case of Self-Management

In common speech, such terms as self-control, will power, and self-discipline are used interchangeably. Such behavioral dispositions have been considered to be personality traits resulting from the person's biological constitution, or his experience in learning to control his actions and impulses. On the other hand, the behavioral view advocated in this chapter, reserves the term self-control to describe a person's actions in a specific situation, rather than a personality trait. Our definition of self-control requires: (1) that the behavior in question is one that has relatively equal positive and aversive consequences; (2) that prior to the occurrence of the behavior, i.e., earlier in the chain leading up to it, a controlling response is introduced that alters the probability of the response to be controlled; and (3) that although the individual may have been trained in self-control techniques by others, at the time that he performs the controlling response it is initiated by self-generated cues and is not under the direct control of the social or physical environment. Thus, when a person exercises self-control we talk about the fact that, in the absence of immediate external constraint or urging, he engages in the behavior (the controlling response) that originally had a lower probability than that of a more tempting behavior (the controlled response), in such a way that the controlled response is less likely to occur (Kanfer, 1971; Thoresen and Mahoney, 1974).

But this does not mean that self-control is viewed as behavior that unfolds in individual development, independent of environmental influences. On the contrary, its history is related to the person's earlier training and its success is related to the ultimate consequences supplied by the social environment. It is only at the moment of initiating the response that the person is not under direct environmental control. However, the likelihood that a person will begin a self-control program can be influenced by his environment. For example, the decision to start a weight control program can be heavily influenced by: (1) information from a physician that excessive weight is affecting her health; (2) the aftereffects of overeating during a holiday period; (3) inability to fit into most of her dresses; and/or (4) the decision of a friend to diet.

The length of time over which demands for self-control are made is an important consideration in differentiating between two types of self-control which involve different response requirements. In decisional self-control, a person is faced with a choice in which a tempting selection or an escape from an aversive situation is given up in favor of an alternative which has greater ultimate (but usually delayed) utility. Making the decision terminates the behavioral sequence. Rejecting a party invitation in order to study, consenting to work on an overtime shift for increased pay, passing up dessert when the waiter offers it, deciding to board an airplane or a roller coaster which one fears, all are examples of this type of self-control. Once the choice has been made it cannot be reversed. The conflict element which, by definition, is a component of self-control is removed as a determinant of further behavior. The shorter the time available for the decision, the smaller is the influence of fluctuating considerations and variations in the attractiveness of the available reward. Recently trained simple choice responses can quickly terminate the client's agony.

In contrast, resistance to temptation or tolerance of pain over a prolonged interval, during which the conflicting responses can be continually reevaluated, constitute protracted self-control situations. Concentrating on one's studies while a noisy party is in progress in a friend's adjacent apartment, attempting to reduce caloric intake when working in a pastry shop, controlling aggressive behavior while caring for an obstinate, uncooperative child, or continuing to jog or engage in heavy exercise as fatigue increases, are examples of this continuing self-control problem. In these situations the conflict between the two alternatives can continue over an extended time. The desirable response must be executed even though momentary fluctuations in thoughts and emotional or bodily states may increase the temptation to abandon the situation at any moment. Protracted self-control requires a continuing series of decisions to maintain an essentially nonpreferred behavior for the sake of some distant consequence. In comparing the two situations, it becomes obvious that different variables and programs are appropriate for each of them. For example, different programs are necessary to induce a person to make a commitment to avoid alcohol or to turn down invitations to go to a tavern, than to train him to sit at a tavern all evening and refrain from drinking alcoholic beverages. Techniques to master both types of situations are necessary in a complete program. Nevertheless, especially at the beginning, it is simpler to help a person to master decisional self-control situations and to avoid prolonged exposure to temptation. For example, in helping a person withdraw from drug use, strong emphasis is placed on training the client to make decisions that will avoid social, physical, and emotional situations associated with drug intake, rather than to prepare him to tolerate the drug scene and its setting without once again becoming a participant.

To many clients the main obstacle at first is to overcome the attractive aspects of their problem behavior. A sexual exhibitionist, for example, may find himself in a tempting situation with the promise of sexual fulfillment in carrying out the act. Although the prospect of apprehension by the police and the possible consequences of losing his job or going to jail may make him anxious, these possible outcomes are distant and not very certain. It is at this point that training in self-regulation may alter the balance. The client finds himself in a conflictful situation and stops momentarily, wavering between giving in or controlling the behavior. If he is tending toward a course of action that violates the standard that he has previously established for his conduct, it is likely to result in self-criticism, anxiety, or other aversive consequence. As a result it becomes more probable that he will escape from the tempting situation rather than give in. The exhibitionistic client may expose himself if there is little danger of being caught, if the target is attractive, if his previous experiences have all been pleasant and have never been followed by arrest, and if he has not risked grave consequences by previous commitments to his spouse or friends. But he may also call a friend, say a prayer, or take a cold shower if the expectations of dire consequences outweigh the attractions of the approach response.

Our discussion should make it clear that training in self-management requires strong early support from the helper, with the client gradually relying more and more on his newly developed skills. These include skills in (1) self-monitoring; (2) establishment of specific rules of conduct by contracts with oneself or others; (3) seeking support from the environment for fulfillment; (4) self-evaluation; and (5) generating strong reinforcing consequences for engaging in behaviors which achieve the goals of self-control. The concept of self-control implies that an individual can be taught to rearrange powerful contingencies that influence behavior in such a way that he experiences long-range benefits, even though he may have to give up some satisfactions or tolerate some discomforts at first. This approach suggests that self-control is a transitory concept. If an individual fully enjoys an activity, even though it may have long-range aversive consequences, no conflict is created and the question of self-control does not apply. For example, the person who indulged in heavy smoking prior to his knowledge of the aversive consequences of such behavior, or who fully recognizes the dangers but is unwilling to sacrifice his immediate pleasure for a longer life, is not engaging in behavior that falls within the self-control analysis. He is not "failing to exercise self-control." Similarly, the person who had on one occasion engaged in excessive eating but who, over many years, has acquired new eating habits and rarely finds himself torn between dieting and indulging in heavy food, is not exercising self-control when he is eating in moderation. In other words, we speak of self-control only when the person initiates some behavior that attempts, successfully or not, to alter the probability of a problematic act.

The change program itself may be a self-control situation when a client is in conflict between accepting professional help and solving his own problem, or when a treatment program threatens to terminate the pleasurable aspects of the problem behavior. In such cases individuals must be helped to develop self-control techniques to maintain the change program. Direct focus on the client's conflicts about treatment may have to precede efforts toward altering target behaviors. In some cases it is necessary to introduce variables that produce or increase the conflict before treatment can begin. When a person has been referred for treatment by a court or by an agency or another person for a problem which the client does not recognize, discussion of the long-term aversive consequences of the current behavior and increase in the client's concern may be needed for the client's acceptance of the treatment program.

Persons who successfully cope with their difficulties do not seek help. Comparisons of control subjects in experiments in which self-control techniques have been studied and inquiries among persons who have successfully achieved control over conflicting behaviors suggest an overlap between the techniques that have evolved from self-control research and the many methods which people use spontaneously and successfully. Delaying an undesirable act, engaging in competing cognitive or motor behaviors, setting up challenges for oneself, rehearsing the positive consequences of self-control, and using contingent self-praise or self-criticism are widely used methods. But there are differences between those who are successful and those who are unsuccessful in naturally occurring self-control. Perri and Richards (1977) and Perri, Richards, and Schultheis (1977) have found that successful self-controllers differed from their unsuccessful peers in using techniques for longer periods of time, in rating themselves as more committed to personal change, in having higher standards for change at the beginning of their self-management efforts, and in using the methods more frequently and consistently. Further, the authors found that the specific techniques used by successful self-controllers varied according to the particular problem. These data and similar clinical experiences suggest that clients often do have the required skills, or can easily learn them. Most frequently, what is needed is encouragement of deliberate and systematic use of various methods and the development of a positive expectation of their utility.

Individuals who have difficulties in resisting temptation or controlling their behavior in one situation do not necessarily experience similar difficulties in others. From our discussion of self-regulation it should be clear that each situation presents conflicts of differing strengths; varies in the importance of reaching the standards, in the concomitant emotional and biological factors; and differs in what the person is able to do to reach a compromise solution. But skill in self-regulation is neither totally dependent on situations nor is it a personality trait that is ubiquitous. It is presumed that some skills can be acquired. Training should help a client to cope with self-control conflicts in later situations, even though some elements in the situation have changed. This generalization effect has been noted in the clinic but its demonstration in controlled research has been relatively weak. (Richards and Perri, 1977; Turkewitz, O'Leary and Ironsmith, 1975). Recent concern with maintenance of the benefits of behavior change programs is resulting in growing efforts to build into the intervention strategies some preparation for posttreatment maintenance (Goldstein and Kanfer, 1979).

Self-management techniques frequently involve methods of self-control. From what we have said, it should be apparent that the helper's role can be concentrated in three different areas: (1) in helping the individual to establish favorable conditions for carrying out a self-control program and providing initial reinforcement to alter the balance in favor of changing the undesirable behavior (motivation); (2) in helping the individual to acquire specific behavior change techniques that ease the process of change (training); and (3) by reinforcing the client's efforts and successes in carrying out a self-management program (support and maintenance). The importance of the helper's role in the early stages of treatment suggests that the various factors that influence the helper-client relationship (reviewed in Chapters 2 and 3) must also be considered.

The Role of Self-Attribution in Self-Management Methods

In addition to the practical advantages of involving a client in the change program, there are indications from different areas of research that a person's actions are influenced by his beliefs about the causes of the behavior. When a person believes that he has the responsibility for some action; that a successful outcome is due to personal competence; that the behavior is voluntary and not controlled by external threats or rewards; and that he has chosen voluntarily among alternative courses of action; the person tends to learn more easily, to be more highly motivated, and to report more positive feelings than when operating under perceived external pressures. These effects have been noted regardless of the actual truth of the person's belief. For example, Langer (1978) found that people act in chance situations as if they could influence the outcome of a lottery or a chance-determined card game. Liem (1975) found that students given a choice in selecting among different types of classroom sections performed significantly better on exams and reported greater satisfaction with their sections and class leaders in comparison with no-choice subjects. Similarly, residents in a home for the aged who were given greater personal responsibility and choice in their daily routines showed a significant improvement in alertness, active participation and self-rated well-being than control subjects (Langer and Rodin, 1976). The belief that one has a choice also appears related to the perception of increased control over an outcome. For example, choice of the order of taking a number of tests can reduce anxiety (Stotland and Blumenthal, 1964). The opportunities to choose among some components of a total task are many. When children are given the opportunity to choose either self-selected or experimenter-selected reinforcers, they work harder for those which they select themselves. (Brigham and Stoerzinger, 1976; Felixbrod and O'Leary, 1974). In addition, when children could choose between experimenter- or self-selected rewards, they tended to choose the self-selected rewards, even if the same outcomes were obtained and self-selection required more work (Brigham, 1978). Furthermore, when children could choose who controlled the choice of rewards, most chose to select their own consequences. However, when given the opportunity to choose, they worked harder and faster and reacted more positively than when unable to make a choice.

Zuckerman et al. (1978) asked undergraduate students to work in pairs in which only one member of the pair could choose the puzzles which were to be solved and how much time to allot to them. They found that subjects who had control over puzzle selection and timing continued to work on the puzzles significantly longer than subjects who had no choice. A belief that one has control also strongly influences the tolerance of painful stimulation (Averill, 1973; Kanfer and Seidner, 1973; Langer, Janis, Wolfer, 1975).

Kanfer and Grimm (1978) evaluated the effects of perceived freedom of choice on behavior change in a speed-reading task. Subjects who volunteered for the experiment tended to increase in reading speed more than those who were required to participate as part of their college course. Subjects who perceived that they were given a choice in training procedures improved significantly more in reading speed than subjects who believed that they had lost their freedom of choice. These and similar experiments clearly stress the importance of perceived control and shared responsibility in treatment programs. In fact, the availability of extrinsic rewards has often been viewed as disruptive of learning in some situations. Following a review of the literature, Condry (1977) concluded that subjects who worked under extrinsic incentives generally choose easier tasks, are less creative, work harder but produce performance of lower quality and are subsequently less interested in working on the task than nonrewarded subjects working on the same problems. However these findings do not generalize across all conditions. They are more likely to occur when persons are intrinsically interested in the activity. Condry suggests that to develop exploration, self-knowledge and a durable internalized repertoire, ". . . it would be wise to discover how this might be done without the offer of strong extrinsic, task-irrelevant incentives to motivate the individual to engage in the task. . . . It looks as if one can say that what is learned will be better integrated into the individual's schema and more meaningful. Skills learned in this manner appear to be better internalized. Indeed, different skills are utilizing extrinsic as opposed to intrinsic circumstances, different rules are required and followed." (page 473). In the context of the research on forced compliance, Collins and his co-workers (1972, 1976) called attention to the importance of the recognition that the variables associated with learning under external reinforcement may actually be antagonistic to the maintenance or internalization of such skills when extrinsic motivation is no longer present. These data suggest that achieving long-term generalized behavior changes with minimal surveillance might require structuring the change process in ways which encourage clients to accept responsibility for complying with the program (Davidson, 1976). It further suggests that a new behavior pattern can be established initially by external motivation. Pleasing the helper, anticipating immediate and clear social rewards or material benefits, or even obtaining payments from parents and agencies for achieving new skills or nondelinquent behaviors may be useful techniques early in the change process. However, the crucial transition to integrating this behavior into the person's repertoire (internalization) requires that the newly developed skills eventually be maintained and reinforced by the client. Bandura (1977) has suggested that different therapeutic strategies can all be reduced to their operation on the client's self-system. They are effective because all of them alter coping behavior by creating and strengthening expectations of self-efficacy. The clinical implications of attributing change to one's actions have been discussed by Kopel and Arkowitz (1975), who conclude that self-attributed behavior change increases the likelihood of behavior maintenance.

In our society in which autonomy, independence and individuality is strongly emphasized, the client who requires the assistance of the helper to resolve his psychological difficulties is presented with a dilemma. On the one hand, the client seeks the assistance of the helper but on the other hand this requires relinquishing control and complying with the helper's prescriptions and programs. Sufficient evidence has been accumulated in the literature on reactance (Brehm, 1966), and clinical discussions of resistance and counter control phenomena (Davison, 1973) to suggest that a therapist's assumption of control and responsibility for the change program can hamper progress. In fact, in the medical literature compliance with a therapeutic regimen is often remarkably poor even with patients whose survival depends on execution of a doctor-prescribed program (Blackwell, 1976; Davidson, 1976). Taken together, the research findings suggest that an optimal treatment program provides the clients with extensive opportunities to participate in the selection of treatment procedures and to attribute the causes of their behavior change to themselves. Such a course of treatment does not free the helper from responsibility to assist the client and guide him toward proper choices, nor does it relegate the helper to a nondirective role. It speaks for a judicious balance between client and helper participation in such a way that the client never perceives the helper as imposing objectives or strategies. It further emphasizes a continuing need for training the clients to develop motivation toward jointly established objectives and reinforcement for his therapeutic progress.

The acceptance of responsibility in treatment is frequently related to the very problem for which the client seeks help. We have observed at least five patterns which suggest sources of reluctance on the part of the client to assume responsibility. Self-management treatment requires that these sources of reluctance be viewed as prior targets for change before other programs can be begun. These sources are:

1. Clients who have developed life-long habitual dependency patterns are skillful in eliciting care-taking behaviors, maintaining passivity, avoiding decision making, and maneuvering others to take responsibility. They tend to reject the therapist's invitation to participate in their change process. Alterations of these interpersonal patterns in small steps and by gradual increases from a very low level of responsible behavior may represent the focus of treatment during early sessions.

2. Clients who have maintained a fairly consistent and rigid pattern of behavior and who have suffered from the consequences of their psychological difficulties for a long time may be fearful to give up their known, though distressing, state for a new and possibly worse one. These clients are afraid of risks and of the unknown involved in changing. Therapeutic attention must first be focused on reducing the aversiveness of change before a specific program can be undertaken.

3. Clients who have previously learned that their own actions have no strong influence on eventual outcome of events often show both an unwillingness and inability to commit themselves to change or to engage in the therapeutic tasks. Such learned incompetency due to past experiences of helplessness requires involvement in tasks of increasing difficulty that permit clients to alter their self-perception and increase their behavior in controlling their environment.

4. Clients may be genuinely interested in change but lack the skills for initiating a change. Lack in decision making, planning or interpersonal skills may have blocked previous efforts to break out of their rut. For these clients, training and practical exercises in gradually changing their life pattern increases their motivation and skills for changing.

5. When a client presents himself for treatment because he is involved in socially unacceptable behaviors which nevertheless provide him with strong satisfaction, such as addictions or antisocial activities, or when the client is supported by a partner or friend or spouse or an agency for maintaining the current ineffective behavior, a conflict between desiring change and maintaining some element of the status quo may result in reluctance to assume responsibility for change. For such clients clarification of objectives and assistance in helping them to decide on the benefits derived from resolving the conflict may be required before a change process is undertaken.

METHODS FOR THERAPEUTIC CHANGE

Providing the Conditions for Change

Self-management techniques are most easily applied when the client is concerned about his present problem and can anticipate some improvement by its resolution. In the use of self-management techniques it therefore becomes crucial to make change appear possible and desirable. The helper must communicate very early the limitations of his own role to the client. He must convey his expectation that the client will carry out some of the exercises associated with the program, and will take responsibility for initiating and maintaining behavior changes. At the same time the helper assures the client that he will be available to train the client in techniques that make change easier, that he will provide guidance in formulating the change program and treatment goals. Self-management therapy can be structured by giving the client information about the nature of the program but it must also be bolstered by the helper's actions throughout the program. Among these are consistent efforts to facilitate the client's handling of decisions and choices that promote the overall change plan. A helper would not respond to direct inquiry by the client, for example, about the advisability of changing a job or selecting a friend. However, he works with the client so that the elements of a decision are clearly labeled, the outcomes of each alternative are reviewed in terms of their effects on the client and on other people. The choice is then made by the client.

Several methods are available that accomplish the dual purpose of structuring the course of self-management treatment and helping the client to clarify his goals. In this section, three of the most widely used methods will be discussed: contracts, self-monitoring, and task assignments.

Contracts

Legal and social contracts form the basis of our systems of social control. Mutual agreement to work toward a specific goal or to exchange services and goods usually takes the form of some general statement of expectation by each party. In most social contracts the specific consequences of fulfillment or nonfulfillment of the contract by either party are not described. For example, an arrangement to meet a friend can be broken with consequences that are not usually clearly spelled out in advance. On the other hand, a contract to deliver merchandise at a specified time might include provisions for a fixed penalty for nonfulfillment of the contract.

Psychological contracts generally emphasize the positive contingencies for achieving the stated goal. In behavior change programs they are used: (1) to help the client initiate specific actions; (2) to establish clear-cut criteria for achievement; and (3) to provide a mechanism for clarifying the consequences of engaging in the behavior. Contracting provides both the helper and the client with a record of what has been agreed upon and an opportunity to evaluate progress by comparison against the terms of the agreement. It also provides the client with a set of rules that govern the change process, and it gives the client practice in the process of clearly defining goals and instrumental acts to reach them.

Contracts can be unilateral, that is, one party obligates himself toward a change program without expecting specific contributions from the second party, or they can be bilateral. Bilateral contracts, commonly used in marriage counseling, or in families, or between teacher and child, specify the obligations and the mutual reinforcements for each of the parties. Contracts can also be made by an individual with himself, with the helper, with others when the helper serves as a monitor and negotiator, or with a group such as a classroom or a family.

There are seven elements that should be contained in every good behavioral contract. Each of these elements should be spelled out in detail, arrived at by negotiation and accepted fully by the client. Good contracts should have short range goals and should be written. The behaviors required in the contract should be rehearsed prior to commitment by a client, and all efforts should be made to avoid a contract that might be difficult or impossible for the person to attain. The seven elements in the contract provide that:

1. A clear and detailed description of the required instrumental behavior should be stated.
2. Some criterion should be set for the time or frequency limitations which constitute the goal of the contract.
3. The contract should specify the positive reinforcements, contingent upon fulfillment of the criterion.
4. Provisions should be made for some aversive consequence, contingent upon nonfulfillment of the contract within the specified time or with the specified frequency.
5. A bonus clause should indicate the additional positive reinforcements obtainable if the person exceeds the minimal demands of the contract.
6. The contract should specify the means by which the contracted response is observed, measured, recorded; a procedure should be stated for informing the client of his achievements during the duration of the contract.
7. The timing for delivery of reinforcement contingencies should be arranged to follow the response as quickly as possible.

Contracts with Children. When contracts are used with children several additional considerations are important (Homme et al., 1969). The required behavior must be easy to identify. The total task should be broken down into components, and initial contracts should reward small approximations. For example, a contracted target behavior should not be ''keeping the room clean.'' Instead, the first target behavior might be to remove all articles of clothing from the floor and put them in their proper place. A second step might be added later, requiring the child to make his bed. A third contract might require him to organize his play area or his desk in a prearranged way. The contract requirements are gradually increased after each successive target behavior is well established.

The child must be rewarded frequently with small amounts to maintain interest and to communicate the adult's satisfaction. But the rewards should be clearly represented as recognition of accomplishments and not as payment for obedience. The reward must follow the performance immediately after it occurs. Often called grandma's law, this rule simply reflects utilization of the reinforcement principle: The target behavior comes first, the consequence later. The child is never permitted to engage first in a rewarding activity and then required to carry out the target response. The contract must be acceptable to the child and fairly balance the magnitude of reinforcement and the required behavior. The child must always know how much performance is expected and what he can expect as payoff.

The contract must be honest. It is essential that the terms of the contract be carried out by the adult as long as it is in force. In several instances we have observed serious deterioration in slowly built up target behaviors and of the entire change program because the parent failed to fulfill a contract condition. The contract must represent a positive contribution to the child's growth and development and it must be adhered to from day to day. The very essence of the effectiveness of the contract procedure, as of many other self-management techniques, lies in the fact that it becomes a rule for everyday conduct. Neither contract management nor other methods can be reserved for use only on special occasions, on weekends, or in difficult situations.

Contracts with Individual Clients. Contingency contracting is widely used with individual clients. For example, a graduate student came for help because she felt inadequate, had difficulty asserting herself with her roommate, and felt that she was wasting too much time in activities other than her studies. After initial discussion it was decided to focus first on her feelings of inadequacy. To develop a specific objective a behavioral analysis was undertaken. It revealed that the complaint referred mainly to the client's tendency to look back on most social situations and emphasize her failure to have acted decisively or effectively in comparison to others. First a list of positive self-statements was made up to give the client a ready set of self-reinforcers. A contract was then set up in which the client agreed to review her interpersonal activities twice daily, specifically after her lunch hour and before going to bed, and to find at least three positive actions in which she had engaged during a social interchange. After recording these events, she attached positive statements to them and recorded their frequency. The accumulation of 25 contingent positive self-statements was the occasion for her engaging in reading a short story, an activity that she enjoyed very much. The conditions of the contract were gradually increased so that up to ten positive incidents and contingent self-statements per day were required before she could read a short story. After improvement with this problem, behavioral contracts were established that required a minimum of one assertive response, defined as expressing the client's thoughts and attitudes during social interactions. After success in this area, behavioral contracting was extended to rearranging the client's nonproductive but enjoyable activities so that they always followed a period of study or work. Progress in the client's behavior change was followed in interview sessions by considerable encouragement and praise from the helper. The use of contingency contracts in this case was supplemented by relaxation training and practice during periods when the client felt increases in tension. In the process of negotiating and evaluating each of the contracts (which were set up for periods of two to three weeks) the client was taught self-monitoring and goal-setting. She also practiced pinpointing the effects of her own behaviors on others and herself. In 14 weekly sessions, the client's behaviors and her satisfaction with them had sufficiently changed so that treatment was no longer necessary.

Clinical examples of successful behavioral contracting, combined with other self-management techniques, come from the treatment of obesity, excessive smoking, homosexual fantasies, and alcoholism. In each case, the behavioral contracting can be helpful because the client is not faced with the overwhelming task of eliminating the undesirable behavior all at once. For example, one client reported excessive worries about sexual potency. At first the man could not even accept the notion that he would ever be sexually competent. A contract with him and his wife introduced stimulus control that did not attempt to eliminate but only to limit the periods of worry to times when they would not directly interfere with his marital sexual behavior. Sexual courtship behaviors that were specifically unrelated to achievement of orgasm were contracted. Following the general approach proposed by Masters and Johnson (1970) and others, gradual increase in the instrumental behaviors that constituted the early part of the lovemaking chain was practiced. In this case, the behavioral contracts served primarily to reduce the client's fear that he would never be able to change by requiring only small behavior changes at first and by providing a framework within which other self-management techniques could be carried out. Reports of successful contract use are available in cases of drug addiction (Boudin, 1972; Wisocki, 1972), weight control (Tobias, 1972), excessive smoking (Spring et al., 1978), in marital discord (Jacobson, 1977), and other problem behaviors.

Behavioral contracts can be enhanced if the contract is associated with public commitment either to a friend, a spouse, a class, or a group of co-workers. However, caution must be exercised in the use of such public commitments because of the danger that the client might set the criterion for the contracted behavior higher than he can reasonably achieve in order to impress others. Furthermore, the client's difficulties in fulfilling the contract may lead him to avoid a person who knows of the commitment, or to engage in actions that might even endanger the relationship with someone who is a party to the client's unfulfilled contract. This effect is related to the problem of intrinsic motivation and perception of control.

Self-Monitoring

As we indicated in the discussion of the conceptual model of self-management, self-monitoring is an operation that parallels the measurement of behavior in situations where a client is under continuous observation of a therapist or experimenter. Treatment methods which rest primarily on instigating behavior change in the client outside the range of observation of the helper therefore demand some recording of the behavior. And if only the client has access to the behavior, self-monitoring, a refined version of self-reporting, would seem to be the most practical method to assess the client's execution of the self-management program. Our conceptual framework suggests that self-monitoring (SM) however, is not isolated from the person's self-evaluation, nor his tendency to attach contingencies to his behavior. A person who is asked to observe and record his own behavior is helped immediately to become more aware of its occurrence. He also has objective evidence of the change in his monitored behavior over time. Therefore, self-monitoring may be a reactive measure, that is, its very occurrence may alter the behavior which is observed.

In establishing SM as a behavior change procedure, there is an implicit or explicit statement of the criterion for the desirable level of the observed behavior. The client may expect that the SM data will be praised or criticized by the helper, and the client himself may show satisfaction or displeasure as he observes a change or no change in a monitored behavior. Therefore it is critical to separate various functions of SM in self-management practice. SM has often been used only to obtain a record of the frequency of the response prior to the introduction of any treatment procedure. When a client is taught to categorize a target behavior and is then asked to monitor its frequency, the helper may be interested only in assessing the severity of the problem or the conditions under which the target behavior occurs. However, available research literature suggests that the accuracy of self-monitoring, when compared to independent measures of the same behavior, varies widely in different situations (Kazdin, 1974). The schedule on which behavior is monitored, competition from concurrent responses, awareness that SM is independently assessed by an observer, the valence of the target behavior, reinforcement of accurate SM and instructions are among the variables which affect SM accuracy (Nelson, 1977; McFall, 1977). As an assessment instrument therefore, SM may be useful only when independent observations are used to check on the client's reports.

When SM was first used it was intended only to provide a record of baseline behavior. However, it was noted in some instances that the observed behavior changed in a favorable direction. Subsequent research and clinical practice have therefore attempted to utilize SM as a therapeutic technique. Studies with obese patients (Romanczyk, 1974), with smokers motivated to stop (McFall and Hammen, 1971; Lipinski et al., 1975), with school children (Broden, Hail and Mitts, 1971), with study problems (Johnson and White, 1971; Richards, 1975), with agoraphobics (Emmelkamp, 1974), and with retarded adults (Nelson, Lipinski and Black, 1976) have reported reductions in undesirable behaviors. However, other investigators (Mahoney, Moura and Wade, 1973; McNamara, 1972) have failed to reproduce these findings. McFall (1977) has summarized the research evidence as follows: "SM is most likely to produce positive behavioral changes when change-motivated subjects continuously monitor a limited number of discrete, positively valued target behaviors; when performance feedback and goals or standards are made available and are unambiguous; and when the monitoring act is both salient and closely related in time to the target behaviors." (p. 208).

Our current understanding of the effects of SM suggests that under appropriate conditions an effect can be expected at the beginning of treatment, but that it weakens over time. The active elements in producing the effect consist not only of the monitoring activity. Changes in the monitored behavior are enhanced by the implied expectations of progress by the helper and the client's increased self-reinforcement for meeting a therapeutic goal. The client who has been impressed with the absolute necessity of reducing his caloric intake, who has been taught self-management techniques to reduce food consumption, and who may have a contract to engage in reduced eating is likely to respond to self-monitored eating behavior of high caloric foods with more than a simple mark on his monitoring sheet.

Another important feature of SM, often deliberately used by helpers, is that the use of SM may be incompatible with continuation of an undesirable behavior. For example, the author has used SM of aggressive responses and of thoughts of physical violence to interrupt the habitual sequence of behavior which constituted the client's problem. When SM represents a behavior that is incompatible with the target response and strongly reinforced by the therapist and the client, its beneficial influence on changing the undesirable behavior clearly cannot be attributed to SM alone. For example, in a case of the author's, SM of hostile and aggressive thoughts toward a spouse was assigned to a couple with severe marital problems. The monitoring task included making a tape recording of any interactions which threatened to develop into a fight. The couple reported reduced frequency of fighting, and explained laughingly that on several occasions the tape recorder had not been handy. The clients then jointly set up the recorder. By that time, the hostile interpersonal interaction had been interrupted and the couple could no longer remember what they were going to fight about.

A critical feature of SM is the particular behavior selected for monitoring and the time relationship between the behavior and the monitoring. Investigators have reported use of SM for ruminating thoughts, for urges to engage in a problematic behavior, for simple motor behaviors like skin picking or throwing objects, for complex social behaviors such as self-deprecatory statements and many others. SM can also be carried out prior to the occurrence of the undesirable behavior, immediately following it, or at the end of a long interval. Summary recording of the target behavior after several hours or at the end of the day introduces a long delay and weakens any beneficial effects of SM. From all these considerations it is clear that SM is not a sufficiently powerful technique for use as a primary vehicle for lasting behavior change but can be used quite successfully to increase the client's motivation for change. In discussion with the helper, the achievement of a criterion, as represented by a behavioral graph, can serve both as an incentive and later as an occasion for reinforcement by the helper as well as by the client himself. For example, various common self-indulgences, such as buying a luxury item, engaging in a pleasurable activity, or taking a brief rest can be tied directly to the achievement of a change in the target behavior. The monitoring chart can also serve as a visual guide for administration of self-reinforcement.

Rules for Self-Monitoring. In introducing SM to the client the following steps are suggested:

1. Discuss the importance of accurate record keeping with the client and give examples of the utility of SM in the therapeutic program.
2. Together with the client, clearly specify the class of behaviors to be observed and discuss examples to illustrate the limits of this class. Be sure to use frequency counts for behaviors that are easily separable, e.g., smoking a cigarette or making a specific positive self-statement, and use time intervals for behaviors that are continuous. For example, duration of studying is indicated by the time started and stopped. Durations of interpersonal exchanges, or of obsessive ruminations are clocked.
3. Discuss and select an unobtrusive and convenient method for recording, taking care to select a recording instrument that is always available where and when the behavior is likely to occur. For this purpose golf counters, worn like wrist watches, can be used for frequency counts. For low frequency behaviors a client can carry a small supply of pennies in his right pocket and move one to the left when the behavior occurs, transferring the score to a written record at regular intervals (Watson and Tharp, 1977). Similarly, toothpicks, small plastic tokens or other devices can be used. Small note pads, ruled for ease of recording a score, can be conveniently carried in a purse or pocket.
4. Show the client how a set of frequency recordings or time intervals can be graphed for visual inspection.
5. Role play and rehearse the entire sequence of recording with the client. It is also advisable at first either to provide the client with record sheets or to have him purchase the necessary items so that he can rehearse the actual procedure with the instruments at hand.

Self-monitoring should begin with relatively simple response classes and should be confined to the monitoring of only one class of behaviors. As the client becomes more adept, he can be asked to record additional information. A coding system can be developed so that the conditions under which the behavior occurred are also recorded. It is usually necessary to limit these to a few easily distinguishable situations. For example, behavior in the presence of others or when alone can be differentiated by entering the score in two different columns, or by using a second position on a golf counter for tallying one of the two conditions, or by putting items into two different pockets on the same side. In general, clients to whom the mechanics and purpose of the SM procedure has been explained will contribute specific suggestions that are most consistent with their own practices.

Self-monitoring assignments should be reviewed during interviews following the session in which they were assigned. Clients are frequently tempted to bring in long essays or verbal descriptions of the behavior and the circumstances under which critical incidents occur. Such records are not quantifiable and should be discouraged. If the target behavior is very frequent or extends over a long time, it is possible to use a time sampling technique. This method requires that the person make self-observations only during previously specified time intervals. To assure adequate sampling of the behavior, the helper can develop a program, best based on randomization of all the periods during which the behavior occurs, and ask for SM during specified periods only. For persons who interact with others during much of their working day as part of their occupation, the occurrence of particular responses, e.g., aggressive behaviors or subassertive responses, may be sampled by randomly selecting half hour periods during each of a number of days for observation. Care must be taken however that no biases are introduced if the client's activities systematically vary from day to day and his problems are limited to specific situations.

Other variations of SM include the use of the graph for display, either as a reminder to the client or for social recognition and support in a small group. For example, SM data have been displayed by institutionalized clients at their bedside, by family members in an accessible part of the home, or by children in classrooms. Rutner and Bugle (1969) report a case of behavior change with SM in a hallucinating patient who recorded the duration of his hallucinations and posted the graph on the wall. Social reinforcement for progress can certainly add to the effectiveness of this technique.

There are other modifications of SM techniques that require somewhat elaborate equipment. For example, audio- and videotape playback have been used widely as a means by which clients can observe their own behavior. Later, these self-observations serve as a base for attempts to improve the actions. This type of self-observation is generally an integral part of a more complex intervention program. It often involves participation of group members and helpers who initiate a self-correcting process by helping the client to discriminate and pinpoint particular problematic aspects of his interaction behavior. Other helpers then model more desirable behaviors and reinforce the client's approximation to these (see Chapter 5 for discussion of these techniques).

A sophisticated SM technique consists of biofeedback procedures. Clients are helped to recognize variations in physiological activities by means of visual or auditory displays of their heart rate, electrical skin resistance, brain waves or other physiological outputs. These methods are described in detail in Chapter 14.

In summary, SM is a useful component of a total self-management program. It is not sufficiently reliable to serve by itself as an assessment technique, nor has its lasting effect as a behavior change technique been substantiated when it is applied alone, under different conditions, and to different types of behaviors. It can serve as an important program component and motivating device, when combined with contracts, self-evaluation, and self-reinforcement. Its application requires training the client to recognize instances of the target behavior, to record and graph the data and to use the visual data display both as an incentive and as a cue for self-reinforcement contingencies.

Tasks and Assignments

The assignment of particular tasks has long been used as a therapeutic technique (e.g., Herzberg, 1945; Shelton and Ackerman, 1974; Shelton, 1979). However, in a self-management program this feature takes on a central role. The assignment of tasks that are graded in difficulty gives meaning to the helper's structure of self-management methods as procedures that require the client to take responsibility for changing his own behavior. In addition, assignments stress the importance of the gradual change of habitual behaviors outside the helping relationship. The procedure also has the purpose of reducing the client's belief that change is impossible. It provides opportunities for self-observation and clarification of the problems which the client encounters as he engages in new and more desirable behaviors. In addition, the execution of small changes by the client himself should add to his motivation for increased contributions toward the change process on the assumption that self-attribution enhances the process.

Assignments should intensify the involvement in the change process and extend the segments of a client's life in which he becomes alert to opportunities for change. In preparing to execute a task in the daily environment the client should come to perceive the continuity between the treatment sessions and daily life experiences. Working out the details for carrying out a task can also represent a challenge to the client to perceive the environment in a new way, to attempt small behavior changes, or to alter the structure of the physical and social environment. Assigned tasks can also be constructed to give relevance to the therapeutic discussions, to provide additional cues about problematic aspects of the client's daily life, and to offer opportunities for confirmation of the client's ability to tackle his difficulties.

Klinger (1975, 1977) has suggested a motivation theory which can serve as a conceptual base for the integration of task assignments into the self-management change process. Klinger proposes that life experiences and behavior are organized around the pursuit and enjoyment of incentives. When an incentive is salient, it has a pervasive influence on actions, thoughts, and fantasies in that it sensitizes the person to goal-related cues. Klinger describes this as a state of being committed to a goal and calls it a current concern. Such a concern begins with a definite onset, which is a commitment to the attractive goal, and a termination which occurs either at consummation of the objective or disengagement from the incentive. At any time persons have a hierarchy of current concerns. They are committed and involved in pursuing various activities leading to different goals. For example, a person may be committed to pursuing a career, to maintaining an emotional relationship, to engaging in sports or other long-term pursuits. In addition, some current concerns are of short duration. One may be committed to meet a deadline on a report for a case conference that is due at the end of the week. An even shorter current concern may involve eating a meal to reduce one's hunger pains. When one concern is especially dominant in the hierarchy, fantasies, environmental cues, and appropriate instrumental behaviors in the repertoire all tend to combine and increase the likelihood that the goal is obtained. For example, when a strong current concern is to obtain sexual satisfaction, special sensitivity to the behavior of members of the opposite sex, the places where contacts can be established, fantasies about sexual behavior, and other sex-related perceptions and thoughts tend to influence the person's actions until the goal is achieved. Such heightened attention to relevant cues, increased utilization of available skills, and motivating fantasies and thoughts represent resources to be harnessed for increasing a client's motivation to change and to achieve success. During the change process, the treatment objectives ideally represent attractive goals, based on commitment to these objectives. Increasing a current concern can sensitize an individual to search his own repertoire and the environment for ways of achieving the treatment objective and to channel thoughts and fantasies to the same end. For example, when a college student complains of shyness, increased frequency of interpersonal interactions may be a therapeutic objective. Assignments can then help to sensitize him to think about possible opportunities for establishing social contacts to observe others, to obtain information where social activities take place, to imagine and experience how people react to his attempts to make contact, and so on. A task for a client looking for work might be to ask friends for information about jobs, to search newspapers, to imagine himself in the position of other persons at work, and to ask himself while shopping for services or goods what opportunities for work there may be for him. Tasks and assignments can serve to involve the client in the change process by developing specific incentives and maintaining change as a current concern increases.

Homework assignments are presented as tentative efforts toward new behavioral repertoires and to experience new life patterns. They can also be presented in the guise of tryouts for which there are no aversive consequences. It is important that the client participate in planning the particular forms that the assigned behavior takes. Goals should be realistic to minimize the possibilities of failure.

When the client is fearful about some component of a situation, the helper may emphasize a contrived purpose in order to bring about initial emission of the behavior. For example, a client with fears of social interaction may be given a highly specific task that would help him to overcome the initial fear. With an extremely withdrawn client we have used such contrived tasks as going to a drug store for a cup of coffee and specifically recording the number and types of interactions of people sitting at the counter for a 15-minute period. A shy and insecure young woman was asked to attend a social gathering for the specific purpose of obtaining information about the occupational background and current jobs of several (two male and one female) guests. A heavy wine drinker was asked to go to a tavern, order one bottle of beer, and keep a count of the number and approximate age and sex of customers who entered and left the bar. In all these cases, the tasks served several purposes. First, they provided an opportunity for execution of behaviors that had been a problem in the past. At times this helps to dispel the client's expectations that something terrible will occur. Secondly, the client's self-observation and later discussion with the helper can give the client greater efficiency and comfort in his newly acquired role. The client can also be asked to say what he thought his impact was on the behavior of others and to discuss his feelings during the interactions that he witnessed (Kopel and Arkowitz, 1975). These new experiences permit the individual to reevaluate himself and his skills. They also make possible the utilization of problem solving skills acquired in the interview sessions and in his daily life.

In all cases it is important that the assigned behaviors be role played in the presence of the helper and discussed in detail prior to execution.

Learning to role play in itself can be developed as a technique which a client can use in a variety of situations. Essentially, role play in preparation for tasks serves to prepare the client for the situations that he is likely to face. It provides opportunities for the helper to model various behaviors, to clarify the details of the situation and the behavior which is to be executed, and to rehearse and prepare the client in order to reduce surprises and extinguish some of the anxiety that may be associated with the task. The role play includes preparation of a scenario of some interpersonal situation. It can also be a cognitive rehearsal of what the client will later think, fantasize or say to himself. The helper's role initially is to provide guidance and structure both for the role play in the session and for preparing the behavior associated with the assigned task. As the client shows increased competence to develop future scenarios the helper reduces participation, except to maintain encouragement and reinforcement. In addition to serving as a technique for rehearsing and training new skills, role play has also been used to assess existing behavioral skills and it is a common component of some social skills programs. Further discussion of role playing is found in Chapter 6.

In order to help clients to review and evaluate their tasks, self-monitoring and recording in written form is highly desirable. Following our discussion of contracting and self-monitoring, it should be clear that an assignment can become the subject of a small contract. It provides an opportunity to discuss an experience for which both participants have previously planned some guidelines. Evaluation of the assignment often leads directly to the next assignment, whether the client reports progress or discovery of special elements in a situation that has presented difficulties. The helper must be careful to offer encouragement and reinforcement only for those accomplishments that can be attributed to the client's execution of the previously planned behavior and not for successes or failures that have been caused by the behavior of others. When a shy client approaches another person he has accomplished his task. Whether the person accepts or rejects the overture is beyond the client's control and is irrelevant to the achievement of the task objective. As the change program progresses, the client should be encouraged to plan and carry out tasks that contribute to overcoming his problems. Gradually the assignment of tasks can be faded as the change process is completed. During training helpers often complain that in the initial interviews they cannot think of a proper task for the client, but even a first interview offers the opportunity for numerous assignments. Whenever a person is not clear about some aspects of the problem which he describes, whenever he expresses uncertainty about his ability to carry out some behavior, or indicates that he has thought of but never tried a particular behavioral strategy, the helper has themes for possible assignments. The tasks may be relatively small at first, for example, to list desirable outcomes of some relationship, to observe how he responds to other people's anger, to try to respond positively or not to respond to a partner. All these are appropriate task assignments in a first interview.

Self-monitoring and recording of observed events in written form is highly desirable. Finally, the helper's encouragement and reinforcement should be offered not for those accomplishments that depend on the reaction of others, but only for the client's execution of the previously planned behaviors. Client observations and comments are often helpful in preparing the ground for designing later tasks. As the change program progresses, the client should be encouraged to plan his own SM program and carry out tasks that contribute to overcoming his problems.

Modification of the Environment

The client whose problems are suitable for treatment by self-management techniques has probably made repeated previous attempts to alter his behavior. His failure may have been due to lack of environmental support, lack of knowledge of specific behavior change methods, or lack of sufficient self-generated reinforcement for trying to change. The techniques described in the following two sections require only a minimal self-initiated step by the client, namely to trigger a change in the environment in such a way that many subsequent behaviors would naturally follow. For example, once a person steps off the edge of a swimming pool, subsequent events are programmed by the laws of physics and no longer require self-regulation. Similarly, the alcoholic who calls a fellow AA member to accompany him on a walk through the park is programming environmental conditions that will reduce the need for generating self-controlling responses to compete with a quick trip to the liquor store.

The following techniques are summarized under the concept of stimulus control. These procedures set up environmental conditions that either make it impossible or unfavorable for the undesired behavior to occur. Stimulus control methods include such extremes as physical prevention of the undesirable behavior which could include voluntary confinement in an institution, locking oneself in a room, or turning car keys over to a friend. In each case, some undesirable behavior is avoided simply by the fact that the individual has relinquished control over the required behavior to an external controlling agent. Unfortunately, such control is often only temporary in its effectiveness. In addition, it frequently leads to development of avoidance or hostility toward the agent who has been given control. At the other extreme, stimulus control methods include training of self-generated verbal responses without changing the physical environment nor the physical possibility of executing the undesirable behavior. For example, repeated self-instructions that emphasize long-range aversive consequences of the behavior, statements about the positive aspects of tolerating an unpleasant situation or resisting a temptation, self-rewarding statements about one's will power, or similar verbal cues can serve as stimuli that exert powerful control over subsequent action. Self-generated verbal instructions are discussed in detail in Chapter 11.

In the following section we will consider stimulus control techniques that involve manipulations of the physical environment, rearrangement of the social environment, and self-generation of controlling stimuli and controlling responses. They are similar in principle to those discussed in Chapter 11 but somewhat different in method. The techniques to be covered in a later section on covert conditioning overlap considerably with stimulus control methods, since training a person to generate stimuli in fantasy or imagination represents an example of altering controlling stimuli. However, unlike the alteration of external physical stimuli or reprogramming of the social environment, the covert conditioning methods require continued activity by the person in rearranging his own behavior and in reorganizing his habitual ways of thinking.

The introduction of physical controlling stimuli is best accomplished early in the problematic sequence when the elements in the chain leading to the undesirable behavior are relatively weak and many alternate behaviors are competing. Since attempts to alter conflicting behaviors by stimulus control have only transitory effectiveness, in most cases additional self-management techniques are needed to help the individual after external control has temporarily reduced the undesirable behavior.

Stimulus control techniques can be separated according to the function of the technique in: (1) altering the physical environment so that the execution of the undesirable response is impossible; (2) altering the social environment so that the opportunities for target behaviors are heavily controlled by other persons; (3) changing the discriminative stimulus functions so that the target behavior is specifically restricted to particular environments or the presence of distinctive external cues stimuli; or (4) altering the physical or physiological condition of the person so that changes in the target behavior are produced. It should be remembered that, as in all self-control techniques, these methods may reduce the problem behavior, but their effects are substantially increased if a new behavioral repertoire is built up at the same time. This dual approach is especially important when the target behavior can be suppressed or eliminated only through temporary rearrangement of the environment.

Physical Stimulus Control. Numerous clinical reports have described the use of alteration of physical environments to prevent a response. For example, cigarette cases or refrigerators have been equipped with time locks that make access impossible, except at preset intervals. Persons on weight reduction programs have been advised to keep only as much food in the house as can be consumed in a short time, thus eliminating late evening snacking. The ancient use of chastity belts (and other confining garments) represents a use of stimulus control to make sexual contact impossible by altering the physical circumstances. In everyday life most persons use this technique incidentally. Mothers put mittens on small children to reduce thumb sucking, students find isolated areas for study, some persons reject opening charge accounts or carrying charge cards, others play loud music, or flee from houses that hold past memories in order to control undesired behaviors of fantasies.

For most people, the presence of other persons is a strong determinant of behavior. By selecting the right person or environment, the client can relieve himself of much of the burden of generating his own controlling responses. For instance, handing a pack of cigarettes to a friend who has agreed to help you stop smoking makes it more likely that you will quit. With one client who was under indictment for shoplifting, the author established a contract that she would not go to stores except when accompanied by her husband or daughter. Most young adults are familiar with various dating rituals, such as double dating or planning an evening in public places which are designed to control exposure to unwanted sexual advances.

Stimulus Narrowing. A frequent clinical method is to encourage the clients toward gradually decreasing the range of stimulus conditions in which an undesirable behavior occurs, i.e., the behavior is put under S^d control. For example, overweight clients are requested to eat only in the dining room, at a table with a particular colored tablecloth, or in the presence of other family members (Ferster, Nurnberger and Levitt, 1962; Stuart and Davis, 1972). Over a period of time the numerous cues previously associated with eating gradually lose control over the response. Similarly, smoking behavior can be brought under S^d control by restricting smoking to a particular environment. For example, smoking can be gradually eliminated while driving, in the office, in various rooms of the house, or in the presence of certain individuals. Such techniques have been reported by Nolan (1968), and Roberts (1969) who treated excessive smoking by restricting that behavior to a special "smoking chair." Frequently, this technique is combined with the method of making the response execution impossible by keeping cigarette packs or food only in those areas that have been chosen for S^d control Study habits have been considerably improved by setting up specific environments in which no other activities take place (Fox, 1962). In establishing S^d control, the client is asked to leave the study area when daydreaming or engaging in other activities. Sexual relations of married couples have been improved by establishing particular rituals such as candlelight or other mutually shared lovemaking cues in which both partners focus their attention solely on each other. Among the most powerful and convenient S^ds are clocks and watches. Specific time intervals have been employed as cues for engaging in assertive behaviors, smoking, daydreaming, worrying, skin picking, or nail biting. These techniques can be used for two purposes: to reduce the frequency of the behavior by gradually restricting the environment and time during which it occurs, or to increase a response because of its frequent and exclusive association with a particular environment or time interval.

Stimulus control techniques are frequently combined with the method of increasing response cost if the frequency of the target behavior is to be reduced. For example, in addition to requiring that the behavior occur only in a certain place or at a given time, one can gradually increase other demands so that preparation for execution of the behavior becomes more and more cumbersome. Ultimately, the ritual is sufficiently aversive so that the effort outweighs the anticipated positive consequences of the target behavior. For example, in establishing stimulus control over smoking, clients may deliberately place the pack in a distant place, remove matches from the usual location, be required to chew a stick of gum prior to engaging in smoking, put on a "smoking cap," and finally seat themselves in a smoking chair. On several occasions, clients who have been helped to arrange these procedures have reported that the undesirable behavior gradually dropped out, "because it was just too much trouble to go through all that." The establishment of stimulus control requires a slow acquisition period, with small steps of increasing difficulty. Care must be taken that no new elements are added until the prior step is fully mastered.

The use of bodily cues for stimulus control is somewhat more difficult, because such cues are not easily differentiated. However, let us remember that the discriminated function of a set of stimuli is built up because the person has had previous experience in which behaviors emitted in the presence of such S^ds were always followed by either positive or aversive consequences. Thus, characteristic events surrounding or preceding the physiological stimulation may be used to make the S^ds more distinct. The use of antabuse in the control of excessive drinking, and of placebo pills to reduce pains or to increase sexual potency, represent examples of stimulus control procedures, either by actual physiological alteration or by altering only the client's interpretation that bodily changes are occurring. Although satiation or deprivation of an individual have often been considered separately as motivational techniques, these methods can also be used for control of physiological stimuli. For example, low calorie, high bulk foods can reduce cues for eating; for an alcoholic the high intake of nonalcoholic fluids prior to a party may serve to control some of the internal thirst cues that justify drinking.

Techniques of stimulus control are generally used in combination with other methods described in this chapter. For example, if you publicly announce your intention to change, the presence of the persons before whom the commitment is made becomes an Sd affecting the target response. Further, techniques of stimulus control are designed only after a behavioral analysis that reconstructs the chain of events preceding the problem behavior. Some distinct cue for the new (controlling) response is set up early in the chain, when proximity of the target response, high response strength, and the presence of immediate positive reinforcers are not so great that they cannot be overcome. While many of these techniques have been used for centuries, it is their systematic application that permits the client to reorganize his environment in such a way that a problem behavior is most easily altered.

All of the methods mentioned so far have dealt with the reorganization of a person's external environment. Stimulus control techniques have also been developed in which the individual changes the nature of self-generated verbal cues. In contrast to the preceding methods, the control of self-generated stimuli is relatively tenuous, since the individual can easily remove or shut out such cues as verbal instructions, imagined sequences, or thoughts. In altering external controlling stimuli the individual needs only to make one step, the initiation of a chain of events. The subsequent sequence is then determined by the natural environment or by the behavior of others. In the case of self-produced controlling stimuli, the individual must often maintain them despite the presence of temptations in an environment that encourages and supports the problem behaviors. We will be dealing with these self-control methods in a later section of this chapter, and they are also described in Chapter 11.

Changing Self-Generated Behavioral Consequences

In the course of an adult's daily life, only a few of his actions appear to have immediate external consequences. Many others seem to be maintained by the person himself. Despite the accumulation of much research on the conditions that affect the self-reinforcement (Bandura, 1969; Kanfer, 1968, 1977), many issues concerning the processes by which self-reinforcement (SR) operates have not yet been clarified (Bandura, 1976; Goldiamond, 1976). One major issue revolves around the role of external reinforcement in maintaining the target behavior (Jones, Nelson and Kazdin, 1977, Morgan and Bass, 1973) and has led some writers to question the utility of the concept (Catania, 1975, 1976) or its proper usage (Goldiamond, 1976). Indeed, in clinical application the procedures usually combine SR with other components of self-regulation or with distal external reinforcement. The accumulated research in this area, however, suggests both the efficacy of the methods to be described and the heuristic value of conceptualizing them as operations which parallel those carried out in the application of external reinforcement (see Chapter 7 on operant conditioning). Self-reinforcement of operants represents a special type of self-initiating behaviors that permit the individual to maintain or alter his actions with relatively little dependence on the immediate environment. It requires that the person evaluate a previously established contingency and only then deliver a consequence to himself. Skinner (1953) has defined one property of self-rewards by stating that it "presupposes that the individual has it in his power to obtain reinforcement but does not do so until a particular response has been emitted." (pp. 237-238). While this definition emphasizes the contingency of SR on preceding S^ds, it does not provide a complete description of the classes of behavior to be discussed here.

Positive self-reinforcement encompasses two different operations: (1) approaching or consuming a material reinforcer that is freely available in the person's environment. For example, when a person rewards himself for hard work by a cup of coffee or by treating himself to a good meal, he is applying a positive self-administered consequence; or (2) delivery of contingent verbal-symbolic self-reinforcement, such as self-praise for a completed task. In addition, aversive SR may follow a response, delivered in the form of self-criticism, self-punishment, or withholding of positive SR. The self-administered SR procedures involve the administration of external reinforcement by the client himself and to himself. The self-administered positive SRs can be further divided into two groups: (1) self-presentation of a new and commonly unavailable reinforcer that is usually outside the everyday life of the client, such as a luxury item of clothing or attendance at a special event; and (2) the initial denial of some pleasant everyday experience and later administration of it only as a contingent reinforcer for a desired behavior (Thoresen and Mahoney, 1974). For example, making an enjoyable phone call, going to a movie, talking to a friend, or having a cup of coffee may be initially postponed, and carried out only as a reward for accomplishment of a prescribed task. As Thoresen and Mahoney suggest, this requires that the person initially deny himself the experience, introducing a preliminary aversive component in the self-management of behavior. When such easily available reinforcers are contingently administered, then the period of delay and postponement of gratification introduce the conflict elements of a self-control situation, that is, one in which the self-administration of rewards is a behavior to be controlled until a given contingency is met.

Verbal-symbolic SRs consist of such verbal statements as ''I did well,'' ''That was good,'' and other positive self-statements by which the individual communicates his own satisfactions with his achievement. These types of self-reinforcing statements are extremely difficult to examine in the laboratory since they are usually said quietly or only in fragments and are difficult for a client to describe or remember. However, in a change process, deliberate programming of such verbal-symbolic self-rewards can be carried out by first asking the person to say these positive statements aloud, and to make them contingent only later upon a specified event.

A further problem with this last class of SRs is that some events may represent the equivalent of verbal-symbolic SRs in abbreviated form. For example, a self-satisfied smile, a feeling of satisfaction, or even a slight righting of one's posture may represent self-generated reinforcing operations contingent on successful accomplishment of a task. The parallel of external negative reinforcement can also be set up for self-administration. A person can present himself with an aversive stimulus that is removed or terminated only when the self-prescribed escape or avoidance response is carried out. Similarly, a positive event can be contingently removed—a person can plan to stop watching television until he completes preparation for the next day's work. Finally, self-punishment may be carried out by administering a strong aversive consequence following the occurrence of a target behavior. Withholding of a positive SR after previous continued administration, and self-imposed extinction also have been used in self-management programs (see covert extinction). Extinction differs from punishment in that a person stops the pleasant consequence but does nothing else. For example, in an effort to reduce the frequency of ruminations about a lost lover a client may train himself to continue thinking about the person but not fantasize any positive consequence of meeting and interacting with her, or to impose deliberately some unrelated and neutral consequence after the thoughts occur. Figure 10.2 summarizes the possible combinations of these operations, paralleling the various external reinforcement contingencies.

Consequence-Operation

Quality of Consequence	Give	Take Away
Positive	Positive Self-Reinforcement (a) self-administered (b) verbal-symbolic	Covert Extinction self-imposed time-out (temporary)
Aversive	Self-Punishment (a) self-administered (b) verbal-symbolic	Negative Self-Reinforcement (a) self-administered (b) verbal symbolic

Figure 10.2. Some combinations of self-reinforcement

Although training the administration of SR contingencies is more difficult than exposure of a client to external consequences, SR procedures have the advantage that the individual can eventually apply them independently of the helper and that he can also use the same procedures for other problems which may not be related to the central complaint. Laboratory research with children and adults has demonstrated that self-reinforcing operations show the two characteristic properties of reinforcing stimuli—they alter the probability of occurrence of the response that precedes them, and they motivate new learning (Bandura and Perloff, 1967; Kanfer and Duerfeldt, 1967; Montgomery and Parton, 1970). In comparisons with administration of the same reinforcement by another person, positive SR has been shown to be generally equal, if not slightly superior in effectiveness (Johnson and Martin, 1973; Lovitt and Curtiss, 1969). The growing literature on the self-reinforcement concept, most of it carried out with positive SR, has also demonstrated that self-reinforcement is not always independent of the environment (Jones, Nelson and Kazdin, 1977). While SR operations make it possible for a client to be temporarily independent, ultimate positive consequences from the environment, i.e., some success in pursuing behaviors that are self-reinforced and some consistency with the models in the client's environment who demonstrate SR patterns, would seem to be necessary to maintain the newly developed behavior in the long run. Numerous studies have shown that the patterns of self-reinforcement and self-criticisms themselves can be modified by learning. They are probably acquired in childhood by direct training and by observation of contingency relationships and self-reinforcing activities in the social environment (see Bandura, 1969, 1976; Kanfer, 1977; Kanfer and Phillips, 1970, for summaries).

Establishing SR in Individual Adult Programs. As we have suggested, the goal of the helper is to start a behavior change program that is carried out by the client, and to achieve changes that are maintained without continuing social reinforcement. Most such self-management programs incorporate SR as a treatment component. In some cases the deficit in positive self-statements is itself the target behavior. For example, a behavioral analysis may reveal that low rates of positive SR limit the client in achieving his goals. On the other hand, the client may believe that self-praise is undesirable or immodest; he may be excessively self-critical, or show excessively high criteria for achievement so that positive SR rarely occurs.

The following four steps summarize the usual procedures in aiding an individual toward effective use of positive SR.

1. Selection of appropriate reinforcers. Although some questionnaires can aid in the preliminary selection of reinforcers (e.g., Cautela, 1977), it is generally desirable to discuss and negotiate individual reinforcers in interviews with the client. Asking the client about his current practices of self-reward, both symbolic and material, inquiring about luxury items that the client would like to acquire, obtaining verbal statements that would express self-satisfaction, frequently yield suggestions for appropriate SRs. What is often most effective is a rearrangement of behavioral contingencies for self-rewards that the person normally administers noncontingently or only in conjunction with behaviors other than the problem responses. Some novel material SRs can be added as special incentive for a prolonged program. The list of material reinforcers, enjoyable activities and positive self-statements is compiled on the basis of the client's current behaviors. For example, acquisition of inexpensive luxury items that the client has wanted but never obtained might include purchase of a paperback book, a small item of jewelry, clothing accessories, or cosmetics. Among activities, the individual's preference might be a trip to a museum, a rock concert, a weekend vacation, or time spent in hobbies.

Verbal-symbolic reinforcers include positive self-statements that are employed in self-praise, reaffirmation of one's adequacy, self-worth or competence, congratulating oneself on physical appearance, physical strength, social attractiveness, interpersonal skill, or any other appropriate content. It is crucial that the selected reinforcers relate to the client's personal history. They must be acceptable to him as something that he wants, could easily acquire or do, and that would make him feel good. If a complex and long-range program is designed, several reinforcing stimuli should be equated for approximate value so that they can be interchanged. This prevents satiation with a single item or statement. In a long-term program, a series of small reinforcers should also be exchangeable for one large reinforcer at infrequent intervals. A person who has accumulated a predetermined number of symbolic SRs because he has shown improvement in the target response might work toward a larger material reinforcer, such as purchase of a luxury item, contingent upon achievement of a desired goal within a fixed time period. The list of exchangeable reinforcers, therefore, should contain both small items obtained from the person's current activities and larger items that may be just outside the range of daily enjoyments.

2. Specific response-reinforcement contingencies are defined. The client is encouraged to list variations within the target response class and to indicate the precise conditions and methods for delivery of SR. For example, if the person is on a weight control program, a verbal-symbolic reinforcer might be used for such target behaviors as rejecting offers of food, staying within the allotted daily caloric intake, or choosing an alternate low calorie food. In addition, a larger SR, such as buying a new dress or wardrobe accessory, might be made contingent upon achieving a predetermined weight loss within a specified time period. In establishing the response-reinforcement contingency, care must be taken to select a good match. For example, not all SRs are equally appropriate for all responses. It would obviously be foolish to choose the eating of a large meal as an SR for weight loss in an obese client. It has been pointed out (Seligman, 1970) that there are predispositions for some reinforcers to be more effective with particular behaviors. Whenever possible, the SR should be one that is essentially compatible with the target behavior. For example, the obese client might select purchase of a new dress as an SR because such a possession emphasizes the positive aspects of weight loss in terms of physical attractiveness or body size. An appropriate reinforcing stimulus for assertive behavior might be one that enhances the person's feelings of adequacy, self-worth, or physical attractiveness, consistent with the goal of helping the person to develop a sense of equality and personal confidence in relation to others. After the appropriate contingencies are established, specific provisions should be made for the occurrence of both the delivery and recording of SR. On occasion, high frequency of the desirable behavior or involvement in a long-term program may require use of intermittent schedules of reinforcement. For instance, one client who had set small material SRs as his rewards for improving his study habits decided to add both interest value and effectiveness to his SR schedule by setting up an intermittent reinforcement schedule. He accomplished this by using a deck of playing cards. He

assigned SR values only to cards with values above ten. Prior to administering a material SR he would shuffle and cut a deck of cards and reward himself only if a card ten or higher appeared.

3. Practice of procedures. After selecting appropriate reinforcers and establishing reward contingencies, the helper should rehearse with the client several instances of occurrence of the target behavior and the self-reinforcing sequence. In these role playing sessions the helper can improve, simplify and reinforce the client for execution of the behavioral sequence until it is performed smoothly. These role playing sessions are also important because they provide the client with a model and the initial experience in an activity about which he may have doubts or in which he may feel uncomfortable. Of course, the helper's presence, encouragement, and approval not only strengthen the likelihood that the client will carry out the behavior but might also eliminate the common misconception that such simplistic mechanics for self-management require no effort, careful programming, or diligent practice.

4. Checking and revising procedures. The client should bring in records of the target behavior and contingent SRs for discussion with the helper and for necessary adjustments in the procedure. For example, if the target is the general increase in verbal-symbolic SRs, it would be desirable to change responses rather frequently in order to extend the program over a wide range of the client's daily activities. The monitoring sessions also can be used by the helper to model administration of SRs under different conditions. This aids the client to develop a repertoire of appropriate verbal-symbolic stimuli and permits the gradual decrease of small material reinforcers. The ultimate goal of the program is not to eliminate long-range luxury reinforcers completely but to make them sufficiently infrequent, and to increase the demand for achievement to the point where they can be maintained by the client. The real purpose of the program is to help the client to utilize the techniques of self-produced reinforcers as a means of handling psychological difficulties that may arise after contacts with the helper have terminated.

Several studies have reported that the addition of SR improves behavior change programs (Jackson and Van Zoost, 1972; Mahoney, Moura and Wade, 1973; Bellack, Schwartz and Rozensky, 1974). There have been reports of effective use of self-reinforcement to improve study habits, enhance weight reduction, increase dating skills and assertive behavior, raise activity levels in depressed patients, and reduce homosexual fantasies. The SR procedures represent primarily the motivational component of a self-management program; other techniques are also required to provide the mechanical procedures in which SR can be embedded.

Establishment of Self-Reinforcement Programs with Children. Although young children can be taught to establish contingencies for self-reinforcement (Masters and Mokros, 1974; Karoly, 1977), some modifications are required. In most cases an adult first models SR contingencies in detail. Gradually, support and probes are faded as the child shows an increased ability to execute the required behavior sequence alone. Initially, verbal-symbolic SRs are given aloud. For example, a teacher asks a child to repeat a positive self-statement if, after comparing the results of his academic performance with a key, he sees that he has achieved the criterion. Gradually, matching the teacher's performance is neither encouraged nor required, and the teacher fades out of the picture. Both with the individual child and in classroom training, it is often desirable to use token reinforcers initially because of their distinctiveness and because the use of back-up reinforcers for the token avoids boredom and satiation.

Self-Generated Aversive Consequences

There are essentially two different types of self-generated aversive consequences that can be used in the control of behavior—self-punishment and negative self-reinforcement. These two sets of operations differ in that self-punishment is aimed at interrupting or decelerating a response while in negative reinforcement a response is increased and a continuing unpleasant stimulus is escaped or avoided by engaging in an alternate or competing behavior. It has been assumed that the reduction of the unpleasantness or anxiety serves to reinforce the newly learned escape behavior. Verbal-symbolic SRs such as self-criticism or self-deprecating statements, can serve either function. In addition, just as in operant conditioning, an aversive consequence can also consist of programming the removal of a positive stimulus following a response, and it can be used either to decrease the preceding response or to increase a new target behavior. The former is illustrated by leaving a party for self-punishment for having acted foolishly. The negative SR is exemplified by depriving oneself of the company of a lover to enhance studying for an examination. In the second case, the absence of the lover is the unpleasant stimulus escaped by completing one's work.

A somewhat more complex procedure involves levying a fine (removal of money, widely held to be a generalized positive reinforcer) following a response that has been targeted for decrease. For example, in the control of smoking behaviors some clinicians have requested the client donate one dollar to their most disliked political organization after smoking a cigarette. The use of withdrawal of a positive reinforcer has been infrequently reported. In a weight control program, Mahoney, Moura and Wade (1973) found that this procedure was not very effective when used alone. There are, however, some logical advantages to this technique, though there is limited evidence that it works. Since aversive stimuli are not used, the many problems associated with such techniques as self-administered punishment are avoided. At the same time, the practical problems of persuading a person to discontinue a pleasant situation, or to give away or destroy a valuable item, are still not known, this technique has not as yet been sufficiently explored for widespread clinical application.

In self-punishment, a variety of procedures has been used. Self-critical verbal statements, presumably conditioned to earlier aversive consequences, can be systematically attached to the undesired behavior. Unfortunately, self-punishing responses are often common in a client's repertoire and very frequently do not decelerate target behavior. Instead they merely remove the guilt and anxiety accompanying its performance. The author saw a client for whom mild electric shock (administered by a portable battery operated device) was used as a self-punishment. The student, who had complained of sexual rumination during study, was instructed to give himself mild shocks whenever the fantasies occurred. Initially, he reported a decrease in ruminations with this procedure. However, after several days he found their frequency increasing again. In response he increased both the number and intensity of the self-administered shocks. A closer analysis of the procedure indicated that the client had begun to reverse the sequence. He would shock himself briefly after the start of the ruminations. Then, feeling that "he had already paid the price of his bad behavior," he would continue his fantasies and shock himself at intermittent intervals.

Many clients have a long history of childhood experiences in which they discovered that one way to "have your cake and eat it too" is to carry out the undesirable behavior and suffer punishment as well. Helpers who work with parents are familiar with the problem of children who fail to respond to physical punishment. Frequently, the externally administered—and eventually self-generated—punishing response simply serves to alleviate guilt and anxiety associated with the behavior, clearing the way for repetition. Also, unusual individual histories in which punishment served as a positive reinforcer, or as an S^d for affect, lead some clients to use physical self-punishment excessively. For these reasons both verbal-symbolic and physical methods of self-punishment should be used only whenever no alternative is possible. When the physical self-punishment is continuously monitored by a helper, its application may be less problematic. In fact, good results have been reported with this method, using self-administered mild electric shock in variations of aversion therapy (see Chapter 9).

A simple but effective technique has been suggested by Mahoney (1971). A client was instructed to wear a heavy rubber band around his wrist. Upon occurrence of obsessive ruminations that were the target for deceleration, the client snapped the rubber band to produce mild pain. This self-punishment procedure has also been recommended by the author and his students with good results. Self-administered aversive consequences, much like other SRs, may owe part of their effectiveness not so much to their high value as pain producers but because they help to make the undesirable response clearly stand out in the total flow of behavior. They serve as cues for the self-evaluation and self-correction processes that we have described earlier.

Another example of self-administered punishment is the use of an aversive conditioned reinforcer in the thought-stopping technique (Cautela, 1969; Cautela and Wisocki, 1977). The client is asked to think about the ruminations, hallucinations or fantasies that need to be decelerated. When he is well into the behavior he raises his finger and the helper shouts: "Stop!" loudly enough to evoke a startle reaction from the client. After several trials and explanations of the procedure, the client initiates this behavior, first aloud, then imagines himself yelling "Stop!" at the top of his voice. Frequent practice is suggested at first, in addition to actual use of the procedure whenever the problem behavior occurs. This method has been reported to be helpful in eliminating disturbing thoughts.

The utilization of aversive SR in escape paradigms is best illustrated by *covert sensitization*, a procedure that is described in detail in a later section. In essence, the client is trained to imagine an unpleasant event and make its removal contingent upon carrying out the desired behavior. A simpler use of aversive SRs has been made in some weight control programs. The client is instructed to buy a heavy piece of lard or beef fat and to place it in the refrigerator as a continually present aversive stimulus. With successive weight losses the client cuts away pieces of the lard, gradually removing the aversive stimulus.

When a response of excessive frequency is to be modified, *satiation* has been suggested as a behavior change technique. This procedure consists of deliberate repetition of a behavior past the point of desire. For example, an excessive cigarette smoker may be instructed to light and smoke cigarettes continuously until he feels physically ill. Thus, the positive stimulus may lose its reinforcing properties with frequent repetition and acquire an aversive character. After a long and intensive smoking session, lighting a cigarette may actually become a cue for feeling ill or dizzy. The procedure is most frequently used in conjunction with other aversive stimuli, such as confining the person in a small room where the increased smoke level itself becomes noxious, or in conjunction with relief responses (see discussion of the aversion-relief technique in Chapter 9). We have already noted that self-deprivation may constitute a self-imposed aversive consequence. This procedure is illustrated by the withholding of various positive reinforcers when a person feels that he has not behaved appropriately. Giving up an invitation to a dinner, imposing a ban on smoking, on sexual activity, or alcohol intake all may be used as self-imposed aversive consequences.

Covert Conditioning

A widely used technique of behavior modification is Wolpe's systematic desensitization (see Chapter 8). This method of anxiety reduction utilizes self-presented imagery as a substitute for reproducing the actual physical conditions under which a client experiences intense fears. The demonstrated effectiveness of this technique has suggested that behavior changes may be brought about by visual representation of the problem situation while the client is in the helper's office. The major difference between the use of verbal stimuli and visual imagery lies in the fact that the helper has very little control over the self-presented imaginal stimuli. He cannot specify the characteristics of these stimuli and therefore cannot study their direct effects in a clinical setting or in research. Homme (1965) has suggested that covert operants, or coverants, can be treated very much like operant responses, even though the exact nature of these coverants is difficult to ascertain because they are not publicly observable. Based on these trends Cautela (1969) developed a series of covert conditioning procedures. Their clinical use is justified by rather modest empirical data (Mahoney, 1974) and the support of clinical utility (Scott and Rosenstiel, 1975). All of the methods employ client imagery as stimuli, as responses, or as reinforcing events. The various paradigms of covert conditioning parallel those of operant conditioning. We have differentiated these techniques from the use of verbal stimuli because covert processes usually include verbal, symbolic, and imaginal representations that are produced by the client on instruction of the helper. In this section we will illustrate examples of the most widely used techniques, including covert sensitization, covert reinforcement, covert extinction, and covert modeling.

Covert Sensitization. In covert sensitization, the client is asked to imagine a scene that portrays the undesirable behavior and that currently offers some satisfaction to the client. After the positive image is built up to high intensity and vividness, the client is requested to change abruptly into imagining a highly aversive event. Both physical and social aversive stimuli are usually used and modified according to the client's personal history. Then the client is asked to imagine fleeing the problem situations and the aversive events associated with it. After the escape he visualizes relief and reduction of discomfort. Strong positive reinforcement by the helper, and eventually by the client himself, is offered for escaping or avoiding the situation, and verbal statements are used to summarize the implications of the experience. Thus the maladaptive behavior is paired with aversive consequences and escape from the total situation is rewarded by the relief experience. All of these events take place with guidance from the helper.

To illustrate the specific procedure, consider a case in which the target behavior is excessive alcohol consumption. After the helper explains the rationale to the client, positive and aversive consequences are selected that are especially suited for the client. The helper then obtains a description of the usual setting in which the drinking occurs, including many details about the physical setting and the social environment. A preliminary test should be given to be certain that the client has sufficient skills in visualizing critical scenes upon instruction. If the client is deficient in this skill, it can be deliberately built up by practice and training in imagining and describing various events.

An alcoholic client may then be asked to imagine a scene in which he is comfortably seated at a favorite bar. As the helper describes and outlines the scene he asks the client to imagine and visualize all the details of it. When a client appears immersed in the imagery, perhaps imagining that he raises a full glass to his lips, the helper asks him to imagine the aversive event. For instance, it can be suggested that the client gets sick to his stomach and begins to vomit. The helper describes this aversive feature in all its details and asks the client to imagine, visualize, smell, and feel all aspects of it. When the client appears to be experiencing the aversive consequences, the helper then suggests that the client imagine turning away in disgust from the bar and rushing out to get a breath of fresh air. As he does so, a previously established positive event is imagined. For example, as a pretty young woman smiles at him, the client experiences the relief of having escaped from his alcohol habit. Favorable summaries are offered that the client can use as a self-statement, such as "Why do I do silly things like drinking? It only gets me sick." At first, the scenes are worked out together in about ten trials for each scene. Scenes are also varied to encompass different settings and consequences. The client takes alternate turns with the helper in presenting the scene to himself aloud. Some scenes might also involve training in avoidance. For example, the alcoholic might imagine being offered a drink and responding, "No, I won't have any alcohol" and then sensing relief. After practice with the helper the client is instructed to practice the scenes repeatedly between sessions. Some variations of the procedure have been to provide tape recordings of scenes that might be sufficiently general to appeal to several clients and to use in groups whose members share similar target behaviors.

Clinical reports suggest that careful preparation of the client is needed to become proficient in imagining the suggested scenes. The client must be highly motivated and cooperative, and the scenes must be varied sufficiently to provide generality of the effect. Finally, it is important that strong personal reinforcers be used. For instance, if the alcoholic in our example is socially oriented, his vomiting may be portrayed as accidentally soiling an outraged, pretty girl on the bar stool next to him. Similarly, relief stimuli may include social acceptance or approval after he imagines leaving the bar.

Covert sensitization has been found to be clinically useful with numerous problems, including various addictive behaviors that are generally difficult to attack. Most often it is combined with other behavior change methods. Unfortunately, few reports are available in which the procedure was submitted to rigorous scientific analysis. Several methodological problems make evaluation difficult. First, the stimulus events and the behaviors said to constitute the process of covert conditioning, by their very nature, are inaccessible to objective observation and measurement. Secondly, in clinical practice the helper who suggests the scenes modifies their intensity, rate of presentation and duration as he watches the client for signs of the effectiveness of his instruction. As a result, individual administrations vary considerably. Finally, an essential ingredient in covert sensitization is the disruption of the imagined sequence. For instance, the image of sitting comfortably in the bar and consuming large quantities of alcohol is interrupted. In effect, similar results might be obtained by interposing any competing response. Perhaps the interruption of the habitual chain by imagining a more satisfying behavioral sequence rather than an aversive one might accomplish the same results (Foreyt and Hagan, 1973). Nevertheless, this technique has provided a useful clinical tool since it requires no particular stimulus settings, it can be carried out fairly unobtrusively by the client, and it has been reported to be effective in after only a few sessions. It may be most effective when used initially to disrupt a behavior sequence, then combined with other methods to acquire and maintain new activities.

Covert Reinforcement. This method generally parallels the operations carried out in self-reinforcement. The technique differs only in that it involves the self-presentation of an imagined scene rather than a verbal statement. The client is trained to imagine a well practiced scene that is subjectively experienced as happy or pleasant. Cautela suggests further that the helper attach a verbal cue such as the word "reinforcement" to call forth the scene. The imagery is then evoked, as any reinforcing stimulus, contingent on the occurrence of a target response. As in covert sensitization, the imaginal scenes are first practiced with the helper and eventually the client is instructed to deliver the reinforcement to himself.

Covert negative reinforcement consists of practice in imagining an unpleasant situation that can later be used in the place of other aversive reinforcers. In addition to using covert negative reinforcement for deceleration of a target response, Cautela suggests that it may be used as a noxious stimulus for escape conditioning. In this procedure the client first imagines the rehearsed unpleasant scene. Subsequently he imagines the response to be increased. For example, after imagining himself experiencing a very distasteful situation, the client visualizes walking into a room full of people and feeling comfortable, calling up a girl for a date, or engaging in whatever behaviors represent the deficiency in the client's repertoire. Covert negative reinforcement should be used judiciously, since aversive scenes that leave a residual of the unpleasant feeling might actually have the opposite effect, if the behavior to be increased becomes associated with the aversive aftereffects. For instance, a client who selects as an aversive event feeling anxious or vomiting in a situation might not be able to terminate the imagery quickly. If the desirable escape response is one which had previously produced intense anxiety, detrimental effects might follow. Thus this technique must be used with great caution.

Covert Extinction. Parallel to operant extinction procedures, the client is asked to present himself with the target response to be decelerated and to imagine a neutral effect rather than the usual pleasant consequences. For instance, in order to reduce high calorie food intake, the client is asked to imagine himself eating a dish of his favorite ice cream but finding it to be tasteless and having no pleasant effects whatever.

The use of imagery in covert conditioning can be extended to include not only scenes that the person has actually experienced but also imagery about ideal situations, feared situations, or other fantasy constructions. In all of these procedures care must be taken to rehearse the self-presented scenes in great detail in the presence of the helper to ascertain that the necessary elements are indeed self-presented. Despite rehearsal, however, the problem in dealing with imagery techniques remains. Control over the stimuli and responses which the client presents to himself is limited, and corrective interventions by the helper are difficult to carry out.

Covert Modeling. Cautela (1971), Kazdin (1973, 1974, 1975) and others have reported the use of imaginal stimuli as substitutes for live or film models in the reduction of fearful behavior. The procedure combines the covert methods with those of modeling techniques (see Chapter 5). The client practices imagining the aversive scene in detail for a series of trials. Then the client is asked to imagine another person—the model—performing the feared behavior, such as stroking a dog, or entering a crowded room. The helper describes the model as confident, and together with the client sketches the positive characteristics of the model during early constructions of the scene. In a study with subassertive adults, Kazdin (1976) presented subjects with thirty-five scenes. Each scene described a situation in which an assertive response was appropriate and a model who behaved assertively. Kazdin found that covert modeling was effective in increasing assertiveness, as measured by self-reports and behavioral role play. These gains were maintained over a four-month follow-up. Subjects who were asked to describe the imagined scenes aloud and subjects who did not verbalize showed similar improvement. A critical question in the use of covert behaviors is the degree to which a person complies with the helper's request that he imagine or think about an item. Kazdin examined the contents of the verbalizations of his subjects. He found that about half of the subjects elaborated on the scenes and some introduced imagined favorable consequences for the assertive model, though not instructed to do so. These data confirm the importance of evaluating client's use of instructions to imagine, think or self-monitor in order to enhance facilitative elaborations and correct those which may impede progress.

A variation of covert modeling has been described by Susskind (1970) as the idealized self-image technique. The client is asked to imagine some desirable change in his own behavior that is within practical reach. He first describes this behavior, then he actively superimposes his idealized self-image on his current image and observes the gradual enhancement of his self-image. To help in the attainment of the self-idealized image, an incident or experience is recalled which yielded a feeling of accomplishment or success. This feeling is then extended to efforts toward accomplishing the set goal. The client is requested to act, feel, and see himself in his daily routines in ways that are consistent with his idealized self-image. Thus, some imagined changed portion of one's behavior serves as the basis for covert modeling and for intiating behaviors that are congruent with this model. Both the idealized self-image and other covert modeling methods bear some relationship to the use of role play and Kelly's fixed role therapy (1955). A basic assumption is that imagining oneself acting differently and eventually carrying out such behaviors, even if they are first tried out in artificial situations, eventually bring about changes in everyday life. Thus, imagined scenes may serve as standards toward which the client aspires. Eventually they may serve as cues in actual situations.

OTHER SELF-MANAGEMENT PROCEDURES

Anxiety Management

Several techniques have been proposed that differ from systematic desensitization in that the client is not exposed to a specific phobic or anxiety arousing stimulus, either in real life or in imagination. Instead, anxiety is first induced by suggestive instructions or reconstruction of an anxiety arousing scene. After the client shows increased restlessness and tension he is taught to relax. In theory, these approaches (Bornstein and Sipprelle, 1972; Sipprelle, 1967) use anxiety responses as S^ds to which responses that are antagonistic to anxiety are conditioned.

Suinn and Richardson (1971) describe several major steps in anxiety management training. First, the client is told the principles underlying the procedure and their purpose. Deep muscle relaxation training is then introduced. Specific cues for anxiety arousal and for relaxation are identified and rehearsed. Anxiety is induced and quickly followed by imagination of a relaxing and happy scene. Deep breathing serves as a cue for relaxation. After the client is relaxed, anxiety cues are presented and terminated again, a rapid shift to relaxation is introduced. Suinn and Richardson used tape recordings with instructions and appropriate background music or sounds for presenting these sequences. During this process, anxiety cues are labeled for easier discrimination. In essence, these procedures are intended to provide the client with means for terminating anxiety, no matter how produced, in situations where the fear stimulus is not clearly identifiable. In contrast to desensitization methods, which intervene before the occurrence of any anxiety, in anxiety management methods it is the discriminated onset of feeling anxious that leads the client to initiate a self-relaxation sequence. The methods have been found to be successful in reducing the frequency of anxiety attacks in clients. However, once the feeling of anxiety has progressed, the technique does not seem to be effective on that occasion.

Self-Directed Desensitization

Modifications of desensitization procedures (see Chapter 8) include the initial establishment of hierarchies with a helper, followed by self-administered presentation of taped relaxation instructions. Some standard tapes that include hierarchy scenes appropriate for many different clients, have also been prepared for clients with common complaints. In essence, variations of this procedure consist of assigning the client the task of learning relaxation and hierarchy presentations from taped guides. The details of the procedure are generally similar to the contents of the particular technique which is self-directed. As with other self-management procedures however, additional features of the self-directed program include the use of self-monitoring, self-reinforcement and reports to the helper, who must then maintain the client's progress by encouragement and support. The underlying rationale in self-directed desensitization differs from the more common desensitization procedure (in which the client is relatively passive), in that active coping and anxiety reduction are emphasized, rather than the gradual reduction of the fear attached to an object or situation. Numerous variations of the systematic desensitization procedure have been developed by clinicians and researchers. Many of these combine Wolpe's original method with self-management methods by enlarging the role of the client in recognizing and coping with anxiety situations and in using internal cues that signal the beginning of an anxiety episode.

Systematic Rational Restructuring

Goldfried has suggested a procedure that is based on Ellis's rational-emotive therapy (Goldfried and Davison, 1976). After exposure to imagined anxiety provoking situations the client is asked to label the degree of arousal and to use his anxiety state as cue for exploring and describing self-defeating attitudes or expectations about the fear arousing situation. The self-defeating statements are then reevaluated rationally, first with the helper and then by the client himself, and reduction in anxiety is noted after rational reevaluation has taken place. The anxiety provoking situations are arranged hierarchically. Goldfried, Decenteceo, and Weinberg (1974) describe this procedure as one in which the client learns to control his anxiety by modifying the cognitive set with which he approaches potentially upsetting events. In theory, the process is somewhat similar to that in the anxiety management techniques in that the client is taught to utilize internal cues of anxiety as cues for executing newly learned anxiety reducing responses.

Self-Management and Self-Control

In our introduction we have referred to the difference between problems of self-control and problems of self-regulation. Now that the reader is familiar with a variety of techniques for self-management, let us review the applicability of self-management techniques to self-control problems. When we speak of self-control problems we usually emphasize the client's dilemma in embarking upon a behavior change when his current actions give him at least some degree of gratification. It is the building of a controlling response and the conflicting consequences of the current behavior that differentiate self-control problems from those in which self-management is used to rearrange behavioral schedules, to learn how to identify and solve problems, to acquire new skills, or to engage in activities that do not alter the behavioral consequences very much. First, increases in self-control can be obtained by providing a controlling response that eventually replaces the undesirable activity and becomes a habitual response. We have summarized numerous techniques which can be used to achieve this goal, such as stimulus control, strengthening of competing responses, and contingency management. The second feature of the self-control problem is the fact that a problem behavior has conflicting consequences. Self-generated aversive consequences for an undesirable response, increased positive SR, or similar techniques can be used to help the individual alter the balance of these response contingency conflicts. A third feature of self-control concerns the fact that the individual must initiate the new behavioral sequence by himself. Self-instructions, discrimination training and labeling and self-monitoring, among other methods, may be used to accomplish this. Thus we see that self-control may utilize many of the methods described here, but that it is applied to problems that fit the specific definition of the self-control phenomenon. In all self-control programs, many essential elements of self-management are employed. For example, helping the client to set his own goals, to monitor his behavior, to evaluate it, and to reward himself are common features in most programs. Invariably it is the helper's task to provide the intial motivation for behavior change, by interviews, contracts, self-monitoring, and other methods, and to withdraw support gradually as the client becomes more proficient in self-management methods. What differentiates self-control from self-management methods is the nature of the problem to which they are applied, not the methods themselves.

Self-Help Resources

The impetus for self-managed change is not confined to professional helping relationships. Inspirational literature is as old as the written word. More recently, self-help programs by professionals are increasingly invading the list of best sellers. They vary in quality and there is very little research that assesses their influence, effectiveness, or validity (Glasgow and Rosen, 1978). Recent explosions in the number of self-help organizations has resulted in increased interest in books, tapes, films and other instructional devices that are directly available to consumers. Because of the varying quality of these materials, helpers have been reluctant to utilize these resources in professionally supervised behavior change programs. However, when properly selected to meet the client's need, these materials can supplement the self-management methods described in this chapter. Carefully chosen books or programs can be integrated into the change program in the form of assignments. It is a basic requirement that the helper be familiar with their content and that the materials and exercises be discussed in the sessions.

There are three major functions for use of self-help materials in self-management programs: (1) Written self-help books or programs can aid the client as he considers the utility and feasibility of the change program and increases his belief that change is possible. Inspirational literature and illustrations of the accomplishments of persons who previously carried out the program can increase the client's commitment to a change program. (2) Selected self-help materials can extend the range of situations and activities in which new behavioral skills can be explored. Involvement with a self-help manual or book can provide supplementary cues for new behaviors, incentives to take inventory of current repertoires, and examples of situations in which new approaches can be tested out. In this way a book or manual can stimulate a quickened pace of change and a more focused direction of treatment. When a client follows the program or reads the material, he also increases his thinking about the treatment and brings in new ideas and reevaluations for discussion with the helper. (3) Some self-help books and manuals can be used directly as part of the change program to guide the development of specific skills. Clients who need to learn relaxation, anxiety reduction, increased assertiveness or altered sexual responsiveness can utilize available self-help programs directly under supervision of the helper.

In most cases, it is not only a specific class of target behaviors for which improvement can be enhanced. Standardized programs can also guide the client in self-evaluation, goal clarification, problem solving and other psychological processes which are considered essential for satisfactory daily living. Self-help books, programs and self-help organizations represent resources that can supplement interventions beyond the limits of the commonly scheduled one-hour office sessions and create a bridge into the client's daily activities. Similarly, cultural, religious, educational, and recreational programs are not fully employed in most behavior change programs. A client's involvement in a physical training program, a consciousness-raising group, or in an adult education class can represent excellent opportunities for personal growth, for improvement of behavioral repertoires and for testing new skills in different settings. While these resources have been much undervalued, it should be clear that no benefits can be expected to occur simply by the client's participation in such activities. Careful joint planning and clear justification of the relationship of the prescribed activity or exercise to the total objectives of the change process and to the current abilities and limitations of the client are essential in selecting the resources. It is not simply self-management that is sought. Effective and goal directed self-management is the objective of our approach to the behavior change process.

LIMITATIONS AND CAUTIONS

We have suggested that self-management techniques should not be used unless the client accepts the treatment goals as desirable and is motivated toward their achievement. Research evidence for the effectiveness of the programs described in this chapter, although still limited, is generally favorable. The theoretical framework on which self-management techniques rest is still tentative and incomplete. As we have indicated, some investigators have achieved success with procedures that are derived from common theoretical assumptions while others, using slightly different procedures, have not been able to achieve similar results. In part, the difficulty lies in the fact that a self-management program requires the skillful combination of many elements in matching the program to the needs of each individual client, while research usually tests the effects of only one element at a time. Interactions between various components can produce effects that could not have been foreseen from the research evidence on the separate elements.

The combination of individual elements into a program requires a thorough behavioral analysis of the problem before the program is undertaken, as well as a helper-client relationship that can promote the change process. Since targeted behaviors for self-management are often behaviors that are difficult to observe, the helper's reliance on the cooperation of the client is greater than it is in other behavior change methods. It is not infrequent that clients, because of their past history, are unwilling, ashamed, or afraid to describe target behaviors that are of greatest concern to them until they are sure that they can trust the helper. If the circumstances under which the client is referred for help are unfavorable for a trusting relationship, for example, when a client is referred by a court, pressured into treatment by others, or too disturbed to enter interpersonal relationships, self-management methods are not immediately applicable. Under these conditions it is still possible to work toward creating an atmosphere in which prerequisites of self-management are met. However, the appropriate self-management methods can be introduced only after this prior goal is accomplished. Clients with low intellectual skills can be trained in some self-management methods, albeit at a slower pace and with simplified procedures (Guralnick, 1976; Litrownik et al., 1977).

We have stressed at the beginning of the chapter the importance of self-attribution in the self-management program. If a client perceives himself as controlled by the helper, the active cooperation necessary to accomplish the treatment goals may turn into opposition. Research from social psychology (Brehm, 1966) has led to a description of the nature and the effects of reactance, the development of opposition to influence. With increased skill in management of behavior control, more attention has been paid to the conditions under which counter control can and should be exercised (London, 1969). Essentially, self-management techniques are based on the assumption that the helper plays only a temporary and supportive role in guiding the client toward changing his own behavior. It is often tempting for the helper to assume too much of the burden of arranging the environment, or establishing reinforcement contingencies, or influencing criteria and goals without first obtaining the client's cooperation, or at least his agreement. In such a case, a client's opposition to the helper's influence may appear as a failure to carry out the program. It is therefore of prime importance that the helper, at the very beginning of treatment, insure that the target behaviors and techniques are acceptable to the client.

SUMMARY

In this chapter we have presented methods of behavior change based on the assumption that a client can alter his own behavior by the use of certain newly learned skills and by rearrangements of his environment. A brief outline of the theoretical framework of self-regulation was presented, and it was pointed out that even in self-management the client requires initial support and help from his environment. The importance of the client's perception as controlling the behavior change process was discussed. Self-control problems were defined as relating to situations in which the person is enjoying positive consequences of a behavior that ultimately has both positive and aversive consequences. The resolution of such problems was outlined as consisting of the establishment of controlling responses that eventually change the occurrence of the response that needs to be controlled. Such situations may involve the execution of a response, such as smoking or overeating, or the avoidance or withdrawal from a necessary but unpleasant activity, such as working or tolerating mild pain.

Prior to the training of particular self-management techniques the conditions for instigating behavior change must be created. Contracts, role play, self-monitoring, and assignment of tasks aid in motivating the client toward change. Operations parallel to control by external reinforcements have been presented that use positive or aversive self-reinforcement, either of the material or verbal-symbolic type. Similarly, self-produced satiation and deprivation have been described as techniques in the service of behavior change.

One group of change strategies have been classified under the term stimulus control. They may involve rearrangement of the social and physical environment (so that the probability of executing a target behavior is altered) or the use of self-generated behaviors. A special case of rearrangement of self-generated reinforcing consequences has been discussed for imaginal presentation of stimuli and responses, subsumed under the concept of covert conditioning. Several additional methods have been noted that incorporate features of self-regulation.

Most effective self-management programs incorporate the following features, although their particular sequence may be different in each case.

Step 1. A behavioral analysis, including a description of specific problem behaviors, positive and negative reinforcers appropriate for the client's strengths and skills, and the resources in the client's environment that can be enlisted to aid the behavior change process.

Step 2. Observation and self-monitoring of the target behavior.

Step 3. Development of a plan for behavior change. Negotiation of a contract that includes clear specification of the goals to be achieved, the time allowed for the program, and the consequences for achieving it, as well as the methods for producing the behavior change.

Step 4. A brief discussion with the client on the underlying assumptions and rationale of the techniques to be used.

Step 5. Modeling and role play of the desired behaviors.

Step 6. Frequent external verification of progress and of factors that have retarded progress, as well as feedback and reevaluation of the contract.

Step 7. Recording and inspection of qualitative and quantitative data documenting the change. Extension of the desired behavior to many different situations or areas of life.

Step 8. A self-reinforcement program that relies increasingly on the person's self-reactions, is sufficiently varied to avoid satiation, and is effective in changing the target behavior.

Step 9. Execution of new behaviors by the client in his natural environment with discussion and correction of the behavior, as needed.

Step 10. Frequent verbalization of the procedural effects, the means by which they are achieved and situations to which they can be applied in the future.

Step 11. Continuing strong support by the helper for any activity in which the client assumes increasing responsibility for following the program accurately and extending it to other problematic behaviors.

Step 12. Summarizing what has been learned in the change process and preparing the client to transfer the new knowledge and skills to future situations.

REFERENCES

Averill, J.R. Personal control over aversive stimuli and its relationship to stress. *Psychological Bulletin*, 1973, *80*, 286-303.

Bandura, A. *Principles of behavior modification*. New York: Holt, Rinehart and Winston, 1969.

———— Self-reinforcement: Theoretical and methodological considerations. *Behaviorism*, 1976, *4*, 135-155.

———— Self-efficacy: Toward a unifying theory of behavioral change. *Psychological Review*, 1977, *84*, 191-215.

Bandura, A., and Perloff, B. Relative efficacy of self-monitored and externally imposed reinforcement systems. *Journal of Personality and Social Psychology*, 1967, *7*, 111-116.

Bellack, A.S., Schwartz, J., and Rozensky, R.H. The contribution of external control to self-control in a weight reduction program. *Journal of Behavior Therapy and Experimental Psychiatry*, 1974, *5*, 245-249.

Blackwell, B. Treatment adherence. *The British Journal of Psychiatry*, 1976, *129*, 513-531.

Bornstein, P.H., and Sipprelle, C.N. Group treatment of obesity by induced anxiety. *Behaviour Research and Therapy*, 1973, *11*, 339-341.

Boudin, H.M. Contingency contracting as a therapeutic tool in the deceleration of amphetamine use. *Behavior Therapy*, 1972, *3*, 604-608.

Brehm, J.W. *A theory of psychological reactance*. New York: Academic Press, 1966.

Brigham, T.A. Some effects of choice on academic performance. Paper presented at Blacksburg, Virginia, Conference on Choice and Perceived Control, February, 1978.

Brigham, T.A., and Stoerzinger, A. An experimental analysis of children's preference for self-selected rewards. In T.A. Brigham, R. Hawkins, J. Scott and T.F. McLaughlin (Eds.), *Behavior analysis in education: Self-control and reading*. Dubuque, Iowa: Kendall/Hunt Publishing Company, 1976.

Broden, B., Hall, R.V., and Mitts, B. The effect of self-recording on the classroom behavior of two eighth grade students. *Journal of Applied Behavioral Analysis*, 1971, *4*, 191-199.

Catania, A.C. The myth of self-reinforcement. *Behaviorism*, 1975, *3*, 192-199.

————— Self-reinforcement revisited. *Behaviorism*, 1976, *4*, 157-162.

Cautela, J.R. The use of imagery in behavior modification. Paper presented at the Annual Meeting of the Association for the Advancement of Behavior Therapy, Washington, D.C., September 1969.

————— Covert extinction. *Behavior Therapy*, 1971, *2*, 192-200.

————— *Behavior analysis forms for clinical intervention*. Champaign, Illinois: Research Press Company, 1977.

Cautela, J.R., and Wisocki, P.A. The thought stopping procedure: Description, application, and learning theory interpretations. *The Psychological Record*, 1977, *1*, 255-264.

Collins, B.E. Internalization: Towards a micro-social psychology of socialization or enduring behavior control. Unpublished manuscript, University of California at Los Angeles, 1976.

Collins, B.E., and Hoyt, M.F. Personal responsibility-for-consequences: An integration and extension of the "forced compliance" literature. *Journal of Experimental Social Psychology*, 1972, *8*, 558-593.

Condry, J. Enemies of exploration: Self-initiated versus other-initiated learning. *Journal of Personality and Social Psychology*, 1977, *35*, 459-477.

Davidson, P. Therapeutic compliance. *Canadian Psychological Review*, 1976, *17*, 247-259.

Davison, G.C. Counter-control in behavior modification. In L.A. Hamerlynck, L.C. Handy, and E.J. Mash (Eds.), *Behavior change: Methodology, concepts, and practice*. Champaign, Illinois: Research Press Company, 1973.

Diener, E. Deindividuation: The absence of self-awareness and self-regulation in group members. In P. Paulus (Ed.), *The psychology of group influence*. Hillsdale, N.J.: Lawrence Erlbaum Associates, 1979.

Emmelkamp, P.M.G. Self-observation versus flooding in the treatment of agoraphobia. *Behaviour Research and Therapy*, 1974, *12*, 229-237.

Felixbrod, J.J., and O'Leary, K.D. Self-determination of academic standards by children: Toward freedom from external control. *Journal of Educational Psychology*, 1974, *66*, 845-850.

Ferster, C.B., Nurnberger, J.L., and Levitt, E.B. The control of eating. *Journal of Mathetics*, 1962, *1*, 87-109.

Foreyt, J.P., and Hagan, R.L. Covert sensitization: Conditioning or suggestion? *Journal of Abnormal Psychology*, 1973, *82*, 17-23.

Fox, L., Effecting the use of efficient study habits. *Journal of Mathematics*, 1962, *1*, 75-86.

Fuchs, C.Z., and Rehm, L.P. A self-control behavior therapy program for depression. *Journal of Counseling and Clinical Psychology*, 1977, *45*, 206-215.

Glasgow, R.E., and Rosen, G.M. Behavioral bibliotherapy: A review of self-help behavior therapy manuals. *Psychological Bulletin*, 1978, *85*, 1-23.

Goldfried, M.R., and Davison, G.C. *Clinical behavior therapy*. New York: Holt, Rinehart and Winston, 1976.

Goldfried, M.R., Decenteceo, E.T., and Weinberg, L. Systematic rational restructuring as a self-control technique. *Behavior Therapy*, 1974, *5*, 247-254.

Goldiamond, I. Self-reinforcement. *Journal of Applied Behavior Analysis*, 1976, *9*, 509-514.

Goldstein, A.P., and Kanfer, F.H. (Eds.) *Maximizing treatment gains: Transfer enhancement in psychotherapy*. New York: Academic Press, 1979.

Guralnick, M.J. Solving complex discrimination problems: Techniques for the development of problem-solving strategies. *American Journal of Mental Deficiency*, 1976, *81*, 18-25.

Harvey, J.H., Ickes, W.J., and Kidd, R.F. (Eds.) *New directions in attribution research*, Vol. 2. Potomac, Maryland: Lawrence Erlbaum Associates, 1978.

Heider, F. *The psychology of interpersonal relations*. New York: John Wiley and Sons, 1958.

Herzberg, A. *Active psychotherapy*. New York: Grune and Strattton, 1945.

Homme, L.E. Perspectives in psychology—XXIV Control of coverants: The operants of the mind. *Psychological Record*, 1965, *15*, 501-511.

Homme, L., Csanyi, A.P., Gonzales, M.A., and Rechs, J.R. *How to use contingency contracting in the classroom*. Champaign, Ill.: Research Press Company, 1969.

Jackson, B., and Van Zoost, B. Changing study behaviors through reinforcement contingencies. *Journal of Counseling Psychology*, 1972, *19*, 192-195.

Jacobson, N.S. Problem-solving and contingency contracting in the treatment of marital discord. *Journal of Consulting and Clinical Psychology*, 1977, *45*, 92-100.

Johnson, S.M., and Martin, S. Developing self-evaluation as a conditioned reinforcer. In B. Ashem and E.G. Poser (Eds.), *Behavior modification with children*. New York: Pergamon Press, 1973.

Johnson, S.M., and White, G. Self-observation as an agent of behavioral change. *Behavior Therapy*, 1971, *2*, 488-497.

Jones, E.E., Kanouse, D.E., Kelley, H.H., Nisbett, R.E., Valins, S., and Weiner, B. (Eds.) *Attributions: Perceiving the causes of behavior*. Morristown, N.J.: General Learning Press, 1971.

Jones, R.T., Nelson, R.E., and Kazdin, A.E. The role of external variables in self-reinforcement: A review. *Behavior Modification*, 1977, *1*, 147-178.

Kanfer, F.H. Verbal conditioning: A review of its current status. In T.R. Dixon and D.L. Horton (Eds.), *Verbal behavior and general behavior theory*. Englewood Cliffs, N.J.: Prentice-Hall, 1968.

———— Self-regulation: Research, issues and speculations. In C. Neuringer and J.L. Michael (Eds.), *Behavior modification in clinical psychology*. New York: Appleton-Century-Crofts, 1970.

———— The maintenance of behavior by self-generated stimuli and reinforcement. In A. Jacobs and L.B. Sachs (Eds.) *The psychology of private events*. New York: Academic Press, 1971.

———— The many faces of self-control, or behavior modification changes its focus. In R.B. Stuart (Ed.), *Behavioral self-management*. New York: Brunner/Mazel, 1977.

Kanfer, F.H., and Duerfeldt, P.H. Motivational properties of S-R. *Perceptual and Motor Skills*, 1967, *25*, 237-246.

Kanfer, F.H., and Grimm, L.G. Freedom of choice and behavioral change. *Journal of Consulting and Clinical Psychology*, 1978, *46*, 873-878.

Kanfer, F.H., and Phillips, J.S. *Learning foundations of behavior therapy*. New York: Wiley, 1970.

Kanfer, F.H., and Seidner, M.L. Self-control: Factors enhancing tolerance of noxious stimulation. *Journal of Personality and Social Psychology*, 1973, *25*, 381-389.

Karoly, P. Behavioral self-management in children: Concepts, methods, issues, and directions. In M. Hersen, R.M. Eisler, and P.M. Miller (Eds.), *Progress in behavior modification* (Vol. 5). New York: Academic Press, 1977.

Kazdin, A.E. The effect of response cost and aversive stimulation in suppressing punished and nonpunished speech disfluencies. *Behavior Therapy*, 1973, *4*, 73-82.

———— Self-monitoring and behavior change. In M.J. Mahoney and C.E. Thoresen (Eds.), *Self-control: Power to the person*. Monterey, Calif.: Brooks/Cole, 1974.

———— The impact of applied behavior analysis on diverse areas of research. *Journal of Applied Behavior Analysis*, 1975, *8*, 213-229.

———— Assessment of imagery during covert modeling of assertive behavior. *Journal of Behavior Therapy and Experimental Psychiatry*, 1976, *7*, 213-219.

Kelly, G.A. *The psychology of personal constructs*. New York: Norton, 1955.

Klinger, E. Consequences of commitment to and disengagement from incentives. *Psychological Review*, 1975, *82*, 1-25.

—— *Meaning and void.* Minneapolis, Minn.: University of Minnesota Press, 1977.

Kopel, S., and Arkowitz, H. The role of attribution and self-perception in behavior change: Implications for behavior therapy. *Genetic Psychology Monographs,* 1975, *92,* 175-212.

Langer, E.J. Rethinking the role of thought in social interaction. In J.H. Harvey, W.J. Ickes, and R.F. Kidd (Eds.), *New directions in attribution research,* Vol. 2. Potomac, Maryland: Lawrence Erlbaum Associates, 1978.

Langer, E.J., Janis, I.L., Wolfer, J. Reduction of psychological stress in surgical patients. *Journal of Experimental Social Psychology,* 1975, *11,* 155-165.

Langer, E.J., and Rodin, J. The effects of choice and enhanced personal responsibility: A field experiment in an institutional setting. *Journal of Personality and Social Psychology,* 1976, *34,* 191-198.

Liem, G.R. Performance and satisfaction as affected by personal control over salient decisions. *Journal of Personality and Social Psychology,* 1975, *31,* 232-240.

Lipinski, D.P., Black, J.L., Nelson, R.O., and Ciminero, A.R. The influence of motivational variables on the reactivity and reliability of self-recording. *Journal of Consulting and Clinical Psychology,* 1975, *43,* 637-646.

Litrownik, A.J., Franzini, L.R., Geller, S., and Geller, M. Delay of gratification: Decisional self-control and experience with delay intervals. *American Journal of Mental Deficiency,* 1977, *82,* 149-154.

London, P. *Behavior control.* New York: Evanston, and London: Harper and Row, 1969.

Lovitt, T.C., and Curtis, K.A. Academic response rate as a function of teacher and self-imposed contingencies. *Journal of Applied Behavioral Analysis,* 1969, *2,* 49-53.

Mahoney, M.J. The self-management of covert behavior: A case study. *Behavior Therapy,* 1971, *2,* 575-578.

—— *Cognition and behavior modification.* Cambridge, Mass.: Ballinger Publishing Company, 1974.

Mahoney, M.J., and Thoresen, C.E. *Self-control: Power to the person.* Monterey, Calif.: Brooks/Cole, 1974.

Mahoney, M.J., Moura, N.G.M., and Wade, T.C. Relative efficacy of self-reward, self-punishment, and self-monitoring techniques for weight loss. *Journal of Consulting and Clinical Psychology,* 1973, *40,* 404-407.

Masters, J.C., and Mokros, J.R. Self-reinforcer processes in children. In H. Resse (Ed.), *Advances in Child development and behavior,* Vol. 9. New York: Academic Press, 1974.

Masters, W.H., and Johnson, V.E. *Human sexual inadequacy.* Boston: Little, Brown, 1970.

McFall, R.M. Parameters of self-monitoring. In R.B. Stuart (Ed.), *Behavioral self-management: Strategies, techniques and outcomes.* New York: Brunner/Mazel, 1977.

McFall, R.M., and Hammen, C.L. Motivation, structure, and self-monitoring: Role of nonspecific factors in smoking reduction. *Journal of Consulting and Clinical Psychology,* 1971, *37,* 80-86.

McNamara, J.R. The use of self-monitoring techniques to treat nail biting. *Behaviour Research and Therapy,* 1972, *10,* 193-194.

Montgomery, G.T., and Parton, D.A. Reinforcing effect of self-reward. *Journal of Experimental Psychology,* 1970, *84,* 273-276.

Morgan, W.G., and Bass, B.A. Self-control through self-mediated rewards. In R.D. Rubin, J.P. Brady, and J.D. Henderson (Eds.), *Advances in behavior therapy* (Vol. 4). New York: Academic Press, 1973.

Nelson, R.O. Methodological issues in assessment via self-monitoring. In J.D. Cone and R.P. Hawkins (Eds.), *Behavioral assessment: New directions in clinical psychology.* New York: Brunner/Mazel, 1977.

Nelson, R.O., Lipinski, D.P., and Black, J.L. The reactivity of adult retardates' self-monitoring: A comparison among behaviors of different valences, and a comparison with token reinforcement. *Psychological Record*, 1976, *26*, 189-201.

Nolan, J.D. Self-control procedures in the modification of smoking behavior. *Journal of Consulting and Clinical Psychology*, 1968, *32*, 92-93.

Perri, M.G., and Richards, C.S. An investigation of naturally occurring episodes of self-controlled behaviors. *Journal of Counseling Psychology*, 1977, *24*, 178-183.

Perri, M.G., Richards, C.S., and Schultheis, K.R. Behavioral self-control and smoking reduction: A study of self-initiated attempts to reduce smoking. *Behavior Therapy*, 1977, *8*, 360-365.

Richards, C.S. Behavior modification of studying through study skills advice and self-control procedures. *Journal of Counseling Psychology*, 1975, *22*, 431-436.

Richards, C.S., and Perri, M.G. Do self-control treatments last? An evaluation of behavioral problem solving and faded counselor contact as treatment maintenance strategies. Paper presented at Eleventh Annual Meeting of the Association for Advancement of Behavior Therapy, Atlanta, 1977.

Roberts, A.H. Self-control procedures in modification of smoking behavior: Replication. *Psychological Report*, 1969, *24*, 675-676.

Romanczyk, R.G. Self-monitoring in the treatment of obesity: Parameters of reactivity. *Behavior Therapy*, 1974, *5*, 531-540.

Rutner, I.T., and Bugle, C. An experimental procedure for modification of psychotic behavior. *Journal of Consulting and Clinical Psychology*, 1969, *33*, 651-653.

Scott, D.S., and Rosenstiel, A.K. Covert positive reinforcement studies: Review, critique, and guidelines. *Psychotherapy: Theory, Research and Practice*, 1975, *12*, 374-384.

Seligman, M.E.P. On the generality of the laws of learning. *Psychological Review*, 1970, *77*, 406-418.

Shelton, J.L. Instigation therapy: Using therapeutic homework to promote treatment gains. In A.P. Goldstein and F.H. Kanfer (Eds.), *Maximizing treatment gains*. New York: Academic Press, 1979.

Shelton, J.L., and Ackerman, J.M. *Homework in counseling and psychotherapy* (2nd printing). Springfield, Ill.: Charles C. Thomas, 1976.

Sipprelle, C.N. Induced anxiety. *Psychotherapy: Theory, Research and Practice*, 1967, *4*, 36-40.

Skinner, B.F. *Science and human behavior*. New York: Macmillan, 1953.

Spring, F.L., Sipich, J.F., Trimble, R.W., and Goeckner, D.J. Effects of contingency and noncontingency contracts in the context of a self-control-oriented smoking modification program. *Behavior Therapy*, 1978, *9*, 967-968.

Stotland, E., and Blumenthal, A. The reduction of anxiety as a result of the expectation of making a choice. *Canadian Journal of Psychology*, 1964, *18*, 139-145.

Stuart, R.B., and Davis, B. *Slim chance in a fat world: Behavioral control of obesity*. Champaign, Ill.: Research Press Company, 1972.

Suinn, R.M., and Richardson, F. Anxiety management training: A non-specific behavior therapy program for anxiety control. *Behavior Therapy*, 1971, *2*, 498-510.

Susskind, D.J. The idealized self-image (ISI): A new technique in confidence training. *Behavior Therapy*, 1970, *1*, 538-541.

Thoresen, C.E., and Mahoney, M.J. *Behavioral self-control*. New York: Holt, Rinehart and Winston, 1974.

Tobias, L.L. The relative effectiveness of behavioristic bibliotherapy, contingency contracting, and suggestions of self-control in weight reduction. Unpublished Ph.D. dissertation, University of Illinois, Champaign, Ill., 1972.

Turkewitz, H., O'Leary, K.D., and Ironsmith, M. Generalization and maintenance of appropriate behavior through self-control. *Journal of Consulting and Clinical Psychology*, 1975, *43*, 577-583.

Watson, D.L., and Tharp, R.G. *Self-directed behavior: Self-modification for personal adjustment* (2nd ed.). Monterey, Calif.: Brooks/Cole, 1977.

Wisocki, P.A. The successful treatment of a heroin addict by covert conditioning techniques. *Journal of Behavior Therapy and Experimental Psychiatry*, 1972, *4*, 55-61.

Zuckerman, M. Porac, J., Lathin, D., Smith, R., and Deci, E.L. On the importance of self-determination for intrinsically-motivated behavior. *Personality and Social Psychology Bulletin*, 1978, *4*, 443-446.

11
Cognitive Behavior Modification: An Integration of Cognitive and Behavioral Methods

Donald Meichenbaum and
Myles Genest

INTRODUCTION

Interest in the role of cognitive factors in behavior modification has grown immensely in the last six years. A number of books (Beck, et al. 1979; Foreyt and Rathjen, 1978; Ellis and Grieger, 1978; Kendall and Hollon, 1979; Mahoney, 1974; Meichenbaum, 1977) have appeared, as well as two related journals, *Cognitive Therapy and Research,* and the *Journal of Mental Imagery.* In a recent review, Mahoney and Arnkoff (1979) have included under the cognitive-behavioral rubric such techniques as cognitive therapy (Beck, 1970, 1976; Beck et al., 1979); skills training procedures such as stress-inoculation (Meichenbaum, 1977) and anxiety management training (Suinn and Richardson, 1971); problem solving training (D'Zurilla and Goldfried, 1971); and cognitive restructuring procedures such as rational-emotive therapy (Ellis and Greiger, 1978). There are now therapy manuals for the cognitive behavioral treatment of anger, anxiety, depression, pain, drug abuse and other disorders. This work is summarized in four annual newsletters on cognitive behavior modification (see Meichenbaum, 1975-1979), in which the interested reader will find a detailed listing of people, places and references.

This chapter is written from a personal perspective, one with its roots in the development of the approach originally called self-instructional training (Meichenbaum, 1977, Meichenbaum and Goodman, 1971). Since their original presentation, self-instructional methods have been used in treating a wide variety of problems, with varied populations, and they have developed as part of the cognitive-behavioral approach. Beginning with an outline of the self-instructional approach, the chapter will more generally highlight the current status, clinical practice and future directions of cognitive behavior modification (CBM) with both children and adults. Although CBM work with children and adults shares attention with the role of cognition in clinical problems and their treatment, the problems of and therapeutic interventions employed with each group differ sufficiently that it will be worthwhile considering them in turn.

COGNITIVE BEHAVIOR MODIFICATION WITH CHILDREN

The major use of CBM procedures with children has involved the training of self-control skills, especially with hyperactive, impulsive and aggressive children. Other behavioral and academic problems that have been treated by self-instructional procedures include resistance to temptation, delay of gratification, problem solving, reading, and creativity.

Hyperactive, Impulsive Children

A major social problem in schools is the high incidence of hyperactive, impulsive children. According to O'Malley and Eisenberg (1973), for example, five to ten percent of school-aged children are diagnosed as hyperactive. It has been estimated (Grinspoon and Singer, 1973) that 200,000 school children in the United States daily receive some form of medication for treatment of hyperactivity. The second major mode of treatment for these children is environmental control by such means as operant conditioning. One of the initial self-instructional treatment programs was developed to supplement these procedures in order to treat this population of hyperactive, impulsive children.

The impetus for the self-instructional training procedure was the theoretical work of the Soviet psychologists Luria (1961) and Vygotsky (1962). On the basis of his work with children, Luria (1959) proposed three stages by which the initiation and inhibition of voluntary motor behaviors come under verbal control. During the first stage, the speech of others, usually adults, controls and directs a child's behavior. The second stage is characterized by the child's overt speech becoming an effective regulator of his behavior. Finally, the child's covert or inner speech comes to assume a self-governing role. From this hypothetical developmental sequence, a treatment paradigm was developed and successfully used to train impulsive children to talk to themselves as a means of developing self-control (Meichenbaum and Goodman, 1971).

The training regimen included the following procedural steps: 1. An adult model performed a task while talking to himself out loud (cognitive modeling); 2. The child performed the same task under the direction of the model's instructions (overt, external guidance); 3. The child performed the task while instructing himself aloud (overt self-guidance); 4. The child whispered the instructions to himself as he went through the task (faded, overt self-guidance); and finally; 5. The child performed the task while guiding his performance via inaudible or private speech or nonverbal self-direction (covert self-instruction).

Over a number of training sessions the package of self-statements modeled by the experimenter and rehearsed by the child (initially aloud and then covertly) was enlarged by means of response chaining and successive approximation procedures. For example, in a task that required the copying of line patterns, the examiner performed the task while cognitively modeling as follows:

> Okay, what is it I have to do? You want me to copy the picture with the different lines. I have to go slowly and carefully. Okay, draw the line down, down, good; and then to the right, that's it; now down some more and to the left. Good, I'm doing fine so far. Remember, go slowly. Now back up again. No, I was supposed to go down. That's okay. Just erase the line carefully . . . Good. Even if I make an error I can go on slowly and carefully. I have to go down now. Finished. I did it! (Meichenbaum & Goodman, 1971, p. 117)

In this thinking-out-loud phase, the model displayed several performance-relevant skills: (1) problem definition ("What is it I have to do?"); (2) focusing attention and response guidance ("Carefully . . . Draw the line down"); (3) self-reinforcement ("Good, I'm doing fine"); and (4) self-evaluative coping skills and error correcting options ("That's okay . . . Even if I make an error I can go on slowly").

A variety of tasks was employed to train the child to use self-instructions to control his nonverbal behavior. The tasks varied from simple sensorimotor abilities to more complex problem solving abilities. The sensorimotor tasks, (such as copying line patterns and coloring figures within boundaries) provided first the model, then the child, with the opportunity to produce a narrative description of the behavior, both preceding and accompanying performance. Over the course of a training session the child's overt self-statements about a particular task were faded to the covert level. The difficulty of the training tasks was increased over the training sessions, using more cognitively demanding activities. Hence, there was a progression from tasks such as reproducing designs and following sequential instructions, taken from the Stanford-Binet intelligence test, to completing such pictorial series as those in the Primary Mental Abilities test, to solving conceptual tasks such as Raven's Matrices. The experimenter modeled appropriate self-verbalizations for each of these tasks and then had the child follow the fading procedure.

The self-instructional training procedure, relative to placebo and assessment control groups, resulted in significantly improved performance on Porteus Maze, performance IQ on the WISC, and increased cognitive reflectivity on the Matching Familiar Figures Test (MFF). The improved performance was evident in a one-month follow-up. Moreover, it was observed that 60 percent of the self-instructionally trained impulsive children spontaneously were talking to themselves in the posttest and follow-up sessions.

The cognitive behavioral paradigm has now been used successfully to establish inner speech control over the disruptive behavior of hyperactive children (Douglas et al., 1976), aggressive children (Camp et al., 1977), disruptive preschoolers (Bornstein and Quevillon, 1976), cheating behavior of kindergarten and first graders (Monahan and O'Leary, 1971), Porteus maze performance of hyperactive boys (Palkes, Stewart and Freedman, 1972; Palkes, Stewart and Kahana, 1968), and the conceptual tempo of emotionally disturbed boys (Finch et al., 1975), as well as that of normal children (Bender, 1976; Meichenbaum and Goodman, 1971).

The Douglas et al. study nicely illustrates the general treatment approach, as the hyperactive children were initially exposed to a model who verbalized the following cognitive strategies, which the child could in turn rehearse, initially aloud and then covertly. The cognitive strategies included stopping to define a problem and the various steps within it, considering and evaluating several possible solutions before acting on any one, checking one's work throughout and calmly correcting any errors, sticking with a problem through every possible attempt to solve it correctly, and giving oneself a pat on the back for work well done. Verbalizations modeled by the trainer to illustrate these strategies included:

"I must stop and think before I begin." "What plans can I try?" "How would it work out if I did that?" "What shall I try next?" "Have I got it right so far?" "See, I made a mistake there—I'll just erase it." "Now let's see, have I tried everything I can think of?" "I've done a pretty good job!" (Douglas et al., 1976, p. 408)

The cognitive behavioral training was applied across tasks in order to ensure that the children did not just develop task-specific response sets, but instead developed cognitive representations. This latter point needs to be underscored. The process by which socialized (or external) speech develops into egocentric (or internal) speech and then into inner speech requires much consideration. As Vygotsky (1962) noted in *Thought and Language*, this process of internalization and abbreviation should not be viewed merely as a process of faded speech; instead the transformation from interpersonal speech to thought represents qualitative differences in structure. How interpersonal instructions modeled by a therapist, teacher, or parent change into the child's own private speech and thought is a major theoretical and practical question. The answer to this question will have major implications for the potential of cognitive behavioral training with children (see Meichenbaum, 1977; and Toulmin, 1978, for a discussion of these issues).

In fact the concern that self-instructions become internalized is one facet of the central concern with treatment generalization and persistence. The intent (and hope) of cognitive-behavioral methods was that by emphasizing cognitive processes in treatment the likelihood of achieving generalization over time, tasks, and settings would be increased. This generalization, however, was not consistently forthcoming, although some researchers did indeed obtain such generalization.

A number of recent papers (Stokes and Baer, 1977; Meichenbaum and Asarnow, in press) have discussed the generalization issue. An important bridge that may help us better understand the mechanisms required for generalization was forged with the recent developmental research on metacognition.

Metacognition and Treatment Generalization

Metacognitive development refers to the acquisition of knowledge and cognition about cognitive development. To use Ann Brown's phrase, it is "knowing about knowing" or the subject's awareness of his own cognitive machinery and the way this machinery works. Perhaps a quote from Flavell (1976) best captures these executive processes.

> Metacognition refers to one's knowledge concerning one's own cognitive processes and products or anything related to them, e.g., the learning-relevant properties of information or data. For example, I am engaging in metacognition (metamemory, metalearning, metaattention, metalanguage, or whatever) if I notice that I am having more trouble learning A than B; if it strikes me that I should double-check C before accepting it as a fact; if it occurs to me that I had better scrutinize each and every alternative in any multiple-choice type task situation before deciding which is the best one; if I sense that I had better make a note of D because I may forget it. . . . Metacognition refers, among other things, to the active monitoring and consequent regulation and orchestration of these processes in relation to the cognitive objects or data on which they bear, usually in the service of some concrete goal or objective. (1976, p. 232)

Another example captures the metacognitive process: Introspect for a moment about the cognitive and behavioral acts in which you engage to retrieve a bit of information, such as a name, that you have forgotten (i.e., the "tip of the tongue" phenomenon). Consider how you try to retrieve the missing name, the way in which you "massage the associative engrams," and so on. This knowledge of your metamemory processes and how you monitor and control these cognitive processes is what is meant by the term metacognition.

Although the developmental work on metacognition began in the area of memory, it was quickly extended to a variety of areas. These areas include attention (Miller and Bigi, 1978), reading comprehension (Meyers and Paris, 1978; Ryan, in press), self-control (Mischel, Mischel and Hood, 1978), communication (Markman, in press), and other areas. For example, Meyers and Paris found that children could benefit from instruction regarding the means, goals and parameters of proficient reading.

For the purposes of CBM, the metacognitions of interest can be conceptualized as the self-communication one engages in, or the internal dialogue one emits before, during, and after performing a task. Meichenbaum and Asarnow (in press) argued that incorporating and focusing upon such metacognitive skills in CBM training will enhance treatment efficacy and treatment generalization. The teaching of such skills as checking, planning, questioning, self-testing and monitoring of problem-solving should enhance the efficacy of CBM procedures.

A number of training implications that follow from a metacognitive perspective were summarized by Borkowski and Cavanaugh (1979), who described the requirements of generalization instruction:

First, we need to identify several strategies each of which is operative in different learning situations. Second, we need to train children on several strategies, making sure that they know when and how to apply them. Third, we need to train the instructional package so that common elements between training and generalization contexts are evident, and distractors minimal. Fourth, we need to develop child-generated search routines, probably through the use of self-instructional procedures, that encourage the child to analyze a task, scan his or her available strategic repertoire, and match the demands of the task with an appropriate strategy and retrieval plan. Fifth, we need to instruct children in such a way that we utilize whatever skills they possess, in order to bring each child to an awareness of the advantage of executive monitoring and decision-making in solving problems. Finally, we may need to reinforce, in a very explicit way, successful executive functioning in order for it to come under the control of natural environmental contingencies, such as a child's good feelings about solving a difficult problem (p. 54).

We should compare the various CBM training studies that have been conducted against the Borkowski and Cavanaugh checklist. It does not really seem reasonable, for example, to expect that teaching children to self-instruct on the Porteus Maze or some other lab task will transfer to improved classroom performance as assessed by the Conners' Teacher Rating Scale. Instead, the teaching of general self-interrogation strategies or superordinate skills must be central to CBM treatment and the investigator must thoroughly understand both the tasks he uses during training and the ones he uses to test transfer. (See Brown and Campione, 1978, for an articulate statement of the uses involved in maintenance and generalization.)

In short, the field should focus directly on generalization training, or, as Baer, Wolf, and Risley (1968) noted, "Generalization should be programmed rather than expected or lamented." One way to increase the likelihood of such generalization is to have children perform a number of tasks and in each case the child must indicate what the problem is. That is to say, we should train to the point of the child's proficiency at recognizing in both impersonal and interpersonal situations that a problem exists. Once this phase is developed the next phase of training could begin with the child generating response alternatives, and so on. Meichenbaum and Asarnow (in press) discuss how such a metacognitive perspective can be included in a classroom curriculum.

Thus far we have outlined the cognitive-behavioral approach that derives from the self-instructional training model, and have examined the contribution of the metacognition literature to a conceptualization of cognitively mediated change. Now let us turn to an examination of specific methodology and treatment efficacy of CBM with children. In the course of these highlights, the value of particular aspects of the approach and the limitations of CBM will be noted.

Treatment efficacy. The use of CBM with children has been extensively reviewed (Craighead, Craighead-Wilcoxon and Meyers, 1978; Karoly, 1977; Kendall, 1977; Kendall and Finch, in press; Mash and Dalby, 1978; Meichenbaum and Asarnow, in press and Rosenthal, in press). A consistent theme that appears across these several reviews is that, although CBM approaches with children who have self-control problems is encouraging, evidence for the generalization of such treatment effects across settings and over time is equivocal. (Note that a similar set of conclusions could be offered for other behavior management approaches such as operant conditioning (Emery and Margolin, 1977; Coates and Thoresen, in press; and Keeley, Shemberg and Carbonell, 1976.) For example, in the initial Meichenbaum and Goodman (1971) study, improvement was evident on the experimental measures at a four-week follow-up but the treatment effects did not generalize to the classroom. The Palkes, Stewart, and Kahana (1968) study assessed neither generalization nor follow-up, and the Palkes, Stewart, and Freedman (1972) study involved limited training and did not yield improvement at a two-week follow-up. Recent studies, however, by Bornstein and Quevillon (1976) Varni and Henker (in press), and Kendall and Finch (1976, 1978) have obtained generalization of CBM to the classroom.

The results of two CBM studies with children are particularly noteworthy because of their thoroughness. In the Douglas et al. (1976) study the effects of modeling, self-verbalization and self-reinforcement techniques on hyperactive boys was examined. The training period was much more extensive than previous studies, covering three months in which the children were seen for two one-hour sessions per week, for a total of 24 sessions. In addition six sessions were conducted with the child's teacher and 12 with the child's parents. The results indicated that, compared to an assessment control group, the children who received CBM treatment evidenced improvement on a variety of cognitive and motor tasks such as listening, spelling, and oral comprehension tests, but they did not improve on the Connors' Teacher Rating Scale. Once again, evidence for generalization to the classroom as assessed by teacher ratings did not appear, although there was evidence of generalization across academically based cognitive tasks.

In a related study, Camp et al. (1977) employed a think aloud program to teach young aggressive boys to develop answers to four basic questions: "What is my problem?" "What is my plan?" "Am I using my plan?" and "How did I do?" The CBM training yielded significant improvement relative to control groups on a variety of measures, including Porteus Maze, the Matching Familiar Figures test, WISC performance IQ, reading achievement and classroom behavior (teacher ratings).

Two recent studies also have indicated the relative efficacy of CBM procedures with children. Watson and Hall (1978) successfully employed self-control training (relaxation plus Camp et al.'s "think aloud" program) in the treatment of hyperactive fifth and sixth grade boys. Compared to placebo-control training, improvement was evident not only on teacher's ratings (Connors' abbreviated rating scale), but had also generalized to reading comprehension scores. Barkley, Copeland and Sivage (1978) also found that a self-control treatment program that involved self-instruction, self-monitoring, and self-reinforcement was effective in improving hyperactive children's misbehavior and attention to tasks, but the improvement did not extend to achievement scores. Both Watson and Hall, and Barkley, Copeland, and Sivage commented on how readily classroom procedures can be modified to include self-instructional training.

Snyder and White (1977) successfully applied CBM training to institutionalized adolescents. Compared to contingency-awareness and assessment-control groups, the self-instructionally trained adolescents reduced impulsive behaviors, and increased school attendance and self-care responsibilities, all of which were evident at a six-week follow-up. The impulsive behaviors included drug taking, physical aggression toward residents and staff, stealing, and destruction of property. The CBM training focused on problematic self-control situations that the adolescents encountered and highlighted the role of private speech as a contributor to conflicts. The modeling of means-ends problem solving was included in the CBM training regimen.

Dismantling the effects. A brief examination of those studies that have dismantled CBM training with children may help to explain some of the equivocal findings of some of the outcome studies. Recent studies have been conducted to dismantle the complex self-instructional regimen in order to discern the active ingredient(s). Alkus (1976), for example, examined the relative contributions of problem solving vs. coping self-statements vs. reattribution training (Dweck, 1975) in enhancing second graders' academic performance. In classroom training, the problem solving group focused on the definition of the problems and accompanying guiding self-statements. The coping group focused on error-correcting strategies, which included identification of errors and normalizing self-statements of a reinforcing nature. Alkus found that a self-instructional training program that taught children strategies for dealing specifically with errors and concomitant frustration/failure experiences was critical to generalization. The Alkus study is one of several that have attempted to examine the components of self-instructional training (see also Bender, 1976; Bugenthal, Whalen and Henker, 1977; Denney, 1975; Jakibchuk and Smeriglio 1976; Kanfer, Karoly, and Newman, 1975; Meichenbaum and Goodman, 1971).

The study by Bugenthal, Whalen, and Henker deserves special mention because it examined the interaction between the children's motivational style and the particular mode of treatment intervention. Hyperactive boys were individually tutored for two months in a classroom setting: half were instructed in self-instructional training and half received an operant, social reinforcement program. Significant interactive effects were found between the intervention approach and children's attributional style. "Luck" attributors showed greater improvement following the reinforcement method whereas "effort" attributors benefited from self-instructional training. The Bugenthal, Whalen and Henker study highlights the potential value of matching a child's attributional style with attributional assumptions in an intervention package ("different strokes for different folks").

Bugenthal et al. (1978) have conducted a six-month follow-up assessment of the hyperactive children of the 1977 study. In the initial investigation, two tutorial programs were conducted with elementary school-aged boys in a school setting. As noted, one manipulation consisted of contingent social reinforcement whereas the other used self-instructional training. No overall differences in short-term gains were observed between the two treatments, but interactions were observed between a child's medication status, attributions of control, and intervention strategy. The CBM treatment was most effective for children who were not medicated or who had a high sense of personal control. As was evident in the follow-up study, CBM produced significantly stronger long-term benefits in terms of a child's increased perception of personal control over academic outcomes, whereas social reinforcement affected teachers' ratings on the Conners' scale. Bugenthal et al. suggest that the combination of the two treatments would seem to be the best strategy, with the operant procedure administered first, followed by a shift to CBM self-control procedures.

The studies reviewed thus far have illustrated the CBM, self-instructional approach with children, and noted some of the treatment results. Recent investigations in several closely related areas will highlight the breadth of alternatives available and suggest some profitable areas for future studies.

Metacognitive manipulations. A recent study by Kendall and Wilcox (1978) that manipulated the content of the cognitive strategems taught to children illustrates the potential value of teaching metacognitive skills, as compared to concrete, task-specific self-statements. Kendall and Wilcox assessed the relative efficacy of concrete versus conceptual CBM treatment with 12-year-old problem children. The training involved six 40-minute sessions twice a week for three weeks, during which the children were exposed to psychoeducational and interpersonal training. The CBM training included modeling, self-instructional training and response cost procedures. The two treatment groups differed in the nature of the self-instructional training in that a concrete approach focused only on the task at hand whereas a conceptual approach dealt with problem solving in general. The following illustrates the two types of self-instructional style employed.

Concrete self-instructional training.
Problem definition: I'm to find the picture that doesn't match.
Problem approach: This one's a clock, this one's a clock, this is a cup and saucer, and this one is a clock.
Focusing of attention: Look at the pictures.
Self-reinforcement: The cup and saucer are different; (check answer sheet), I got it right. Good job!
Coping statement: Oh, it's not the clock that's different, it's the teacup. I can pick out the correct one next time.
Labeling a response-cost: (performed by the therapist) No, it's not the clock, it's the teacup. You lose one chip for picking the clock.

Conceptual self-instructional training.
Problem definition: My first step is to make sure I know what I'm supposed to do.

Problem approach: Well, I should look at all the possibilities.

Focusing of attention: I should think about only what I'm doing right now.

Self-Reinforcement: (checking the answer sheet) Hey, good job. I'm doing very well.

Coping Statement: Well, if I make a mistake I can remember to think more carefully next time, and then I'll do better.

Labeling a response cost: No, that's not the right answer. You lost one token for not taking your time and getting the correct answer. (Kendall and Wilcox, 1978, p. 13)

The efficacy of the two CBM treatment groups relative to an attention-placebo control group was evident on the performance measure of MFF latency, but not on MFF errors nor on Porteus maze performance. Differences were, however, obtained on teacher ratings (Conners' scale and Kendall-Wilcox-self-control scale), both immediately, and at a one-month period. The treatment effects were stronger for the conceptual labeling group than for the concrete labeling group. Only the CBM group that received conceptual labeling evidenced significant improvement on teacher ratings at follow-up, relative to both the concrete labeling and attention-placebo control groups.

The use of such conceptual labels is consistent with the suggestions from the metacognitive literature (see Meichenbaum and Asarnow 1978). Reminiscent of the suggestion offered by Bugenthal, Whalen, and Henker (1977), one wonders if some combination of concrete and conceptual labeling would prove most effective. Our clinical experience suggests that first giving the child an opportunity to perform a task, then having the child use concrete self-instructions, and finally abstract self-instructions is most useful. For example, consider a study by Zelniker and Oppenheimer (1973), in which they trained impulsive children to improve performance on the MFF by giving training on a DFF (Different Familiar Figures test). The MFF requires the child to find one object that is the same as the standard picture, whereas the DFF requires the child to find one of six figures that is different. The other five alternatives are identical to the standard. Zelniker and Oppenheimer reported that such DFF training transferred to MFF performance. Their study indicates that one can affect the conceptual style of impulsive children by manipulating task characteristics as well as by directly exposing the child to CBM self-instructional training.

Self-instructional training may be most efficacious when administered after the child has acquired elemental skills. Once the subject performs the DFF successfully, the child may be most responsive to self-instructional training, initially of a concrete variety and then of a conceptual type. The literature on self-instructional training with impulsive-hyperactive children suggests that CBM techniques may be less effective in the acquisition of elemental skills, and most useful in inhibiting impulsive responding by subjects who already have skills within their repertoire. These considerations are illustrated in the CBM work on problem solving with children.

Problem-solving training. As in the case of self-instructional training procedures, the problem solving approach to teaching children self-control has received only recent attention and extensive comparative studies with adequate follow-up are few. The problem solving training approach attempts to teach children to become sensitive to interpersonal problems, to develop the ability to generate alternative solutions, to understand means-end relationships and the effects of one's social acts on others. The research by Douglas (1972, 1975) and Spivack, Platt, and Shure (1976) indicate that children with behavior problems require such training.

Among the deficits such children evidence is the tendency to select the first possible solution without developing alternatives or examining consequences, thus failing to conceptualize relevant options. In order to compensate for this deficiency, Spivack and Shure (1974) provided training in two types of social reasoning over some thirty lessons. One focused on the ability to think of alternative solutions to simple conflict situations with peers; the other on the ability to predict likely consequences of a particular solution. The focus of the training, which took the form of a variety of games, was not *what* to think, but rather, *how* to think about interpersonal problems. The initial games dealt with developing specific language and attentive skills, identifying emotions, thinking about how people have different likes and dislikes, and learning to gather information about other people. Final games posed the problem of finding several alternative solutions to interpersonal problems and evaluating cause and effect in human relationships. The training resulted in significant increases in social reasoning abilities. Further, the children showed significant and enduring positive effects in social behaviors with peers, changes which were maintained at a one-year follow-up in kindergarten. A most important aspect of the training program is that positive results were obtained when teachers trained children and when mothers trained their own children. In a personal communication, Spivack described his training as follows:

> Training reduces socially maladaptive behavior by enhancing certain mediating interpersonal cognitive skills of direct relevance to social adjustment. . . . These skills involve the capacity to generate alternative solutions and consequences, and in older individuals the ability to generate means-ends thought.

Recently, a number of programs tailored after Spivack and Shure have been developed to teach children a variety of skills, including self-control. These programs have been conducted by Allen et al. (1976), Elardo (1974), McClure, Chinsky, and Larcen (1978), Meijers (1978), Poitras-Martin and Stone (1977), Russell and Thoresen (1976), and Stone, Hinds and Schmidt (1975). In order to teach such skills, several teaching modes are used, including verbal, behavioral, videotape, cartoon workbook, poster-pictorial and flash-card activities. The pedagogical potential of such training procedures has been illustrated in the recent work on the CBM treatment of academic problems.

CBM treatment of academic problems. Recently there has been increasing research on the possible application of cognitive behavioral procedures to traditional academic concerns, such as reading comprehension, arithmetic, interpersonal problem solving and creativity.

In the same way that the CBM procedures with hyperactive children found impetus in the work of Soviet psychologists, the CBM training approach with academic problems got its start in the work of the American psychologist Gagne. Gagne (1964) uses a task-analysis approach by beginning with a behavioral statement of the instructional objective. Then he investigates the prerequisite behaviors a child must possess in order to perform a desired terminal behavior, thus generating a hierarchy of objectives. Gagne is proposing that an individual's learning of a complex behavior is contingent on his prior acquisition of a succession of simpler behaviors. Thus, the instruction can be based on the cumulative learning process.

The cognitive behavioral training approach follows a similar strategy, except that each step in the hierarchy is translated into self-statements and images or cognitive strategies that can be modeled and rehearsed. Practically, this means that the teacher must be sensitive in performing a task analysis, not only of the behaviors, but also the cognitions, strategies and rules required to perform a task. The teacher can discover the hierarchy of cognitive abilities required by such means as observing his own thinking processes while performing the task or by observing and interviewing children who do poorly or well on the task. The teacher can then translate these cognitive strategies into sets of self-statements that can be modeled and then rehearsed by a student. Moreover, the teacher can cognitively model not only task-relevant, problem solving self-statements, but also coping self-statements. Most teachers very infrequently, if at all, model how they cope with frustrations and failures while performing a particular task (i.e., they are mastery, not coping models). They rarely share with their students the thinking processes and other events that are involved in how they performed the task.

The student is told to perform a task but rarely is shown: (1) how to break the task down into manageable units; (2) how to determine the hierarchy of skills required to perform the task, or (3) how to translate these skills into self-statements and images that can be rehearsed.

One demonstration of the potential of self-instructional procedures with academic problems is a study that attempted to enhance creativity by explicitly modifying what college students say to themselves (Meichenbaum, 1975). Each of three major conceptualizations of creativity represented in the literature was translated into a set of self-statements that could be modeled by the trainer and then practiced by the subjects on meaningful self-selected tasks. Table 11.1 illustrates the variety of self-statements used in training.

The use of such self-statements not only enhanced performance on creativity measures, but engendered a generalized set to handle life situations more creatively. Following training, the clients reported that they had spontaneously applied the creativity training to a variety of personal and academic problems.

Table 11.1   Examples of Self-Statements Used in Creativity Training

Self-statements arising from an attitudinal conceptualization of creativity
Set inducing self-statements
What to do:
    Be creative, be unique.
    Break away from the obvious, the commonplace.
    Think of something no one else will think of.
    Just be free wheeling.
    If you push yourself you can be creative.
    Quantity helps breed quality.
What not to do:
    Get rid of internal blocks.
    Defer judgments.
    Don't worry what others think.
    Not a matter of right or wrong.
    Don't give the first answer you think of.
    No negative self-statements.

Self-statements arising from a mental abilities conceptualization of creativity
Problem analysis—what you say to yourself before you start a problem:
    Size up the problem. What is it you have to do?
    You have to put the elements together differently.
    Use different analogies.
    Do the task as if you were Osborn brainstorming or Gordon doing Synectics training.
    Elaborate on ideas.
    Make the strange familiar and the familiar strange.
Task execution—what you say to yourself while doing a task:
    You're in a rut—okay try something new.
    How can you use this frustration to be more creative?
    Take a rest now. Who knows when the ideas will visit again?
    Go slow—no hurry—no need to press.
    Good, you're getting it.
    This is fun.
    That was a pretty neat answer; wait till you tell the others!

Self-statements arising from a psychoanalytic conceptualization of creativity
    Release controls; let your mind wander.
    Free-associate, let ideas flow.
    Relax—just let it happen.
    Let your ideas play.
    Refer to your experience; just view it differently.
    Let your ego regress.
    Feel like a bystander through whom ideas are just flowing.
    Let one answer lead to another.
    Almost dreamlike; the ideas have a life of their own.

This observation suggests that psychotherapy clients may benefit from such a self-instructional creativity or problem solving regimen. A similar suggestion has been offered by D'Zurilla and Goldfried (1971) in their article on a problem solving approach to psychotherapy.

It should be noted that subjects or clients are not merely given a list of self-statements and told that just saying these things to themselves will make everything better. This strategy reminds one of the exhortative statements made popular by the French psychiatrist Emile Coue, who in the 1920s encouraged everyone to say, "Every day in every way I'm getting better and better." Instead, the present treatment approach is designed to have the client; (1) become aware of the negative thinking styles that impede performance and that lead to emotional upset and inadequate performance; (2) generate, in collaboration with the trainer, a set of incompatible, specific self-statements, rules, strategies, and so on, which the trainee can then employ; and (3) learn specific adaptive, cognitive and behavioral skills.

Clinical Implementation

Elsewhere (Meichenbaum, 1977), has described a host of clinical suggestions for conducting CBM self-instructional training with children. These included (1) using the child's own medium of play to initiate and model self-talk; (2) using tasks that have a high "pull" for the use of sequential cognitive strategies; (3) using peer teaching by having children cognitively model while performing for another child; (4) having the child move through the program at his own rate while building up the package of self-statements to include self-talk of a problem solving variety as well as coping and self-reinforcing elements; (5) guarding against the child's using the self-statements in a mechanical noninvolved fashion; (6) including a therapist who is animated and responsive to the child; (7) learning to use the self-instructional training with low intensity responses; (8) supplementing the training with imagery practice such as the "turtle technique" (Schneider & Robin, 1976); (9) supplementing the self-instructional training with correspondence training (Rogers-Warren and Baer, 1976); (10) supplementing the self-instructional training with operant procedures such as a response cost system (Kendall and Finch, 1976, 1978; Nelson and Birkimer, 1978; Robertson and Keeley, 1974). The following clinical suggestions will illustrate some of the concerns raised in these treatment procedures.

One way to conduct cognitive behavioral training is to use the child's medium of play. The CBM treatment can begin in the midst of ongoing play activities. The therapist can teach the hyperactive, impulsive child the concept of talking to himself and gain the child's attention by using his play activities. For example, while playing with one hyperactive child, the therapist said, "I have to land my airplane: now slowly, carefully, into the hangar.'' The therapist then encouraged the child to have the control tower tell the pilot to go slowly, and so on. In this way the therapist is able to have the child build up a repertoire of self-statements to be used on a variety of tasks. Training begins on a set of tasks (games) in which the child is somewhat proficient and for which he does not have a history of failures and frustrations. The therapist employs tasks that lend themselves to a self-instructional approach and have a high ''pull'' for the use of cognitive strategies. For example, the therapist can have the impulsive child verbally direct another person (e.g., the therapist) to perform a task such as a finger maze while the child sits on his own hands. In this way, the child has to learn to use language in an instrumental fashion in order to direct another person to perform the task. Another technique designed to enhance self-control is to have an older, impulsive child teach a younger child how to do a task. The impulsive child, whose own behavior is actually the target of modification, is employed as a teaching assistant to model self-instructions for the younger child.

In using such CBM procedures, it is important to insure that the child does not use the self-statements in a mechanical, rote, or automatic fashion without the accompanying meaning and inflection. This would approximate the everyday experience of reading aloud or silently when one's mind is elsewhere. One may read a paragraph aloud without recalling the content. What is needed instead is modeling and practice in synthesizing and internalizing the meaning of one's self-statements.

The rate at which the therapist proceeds with the CBM training procedure can be individually tailored to the needs of each child. Some children require many trials of cognitive modeling and overt self-instructional rehearsal whereas others may proceed directly to the state of covert rehearsal after being exposed to a model. For some children the phase of having the child do the task while the therapist instructs the child may foster dependency. In such cases cognitive modeling followed by covert rehearsal may suffice. In some cases it is not necessary to have the child self-instruct aloud. One strength of the training procedure is its flexibility.

The CBM approach also provides some flexibility in how quickly the therapist and the child rehearse comprehensive packages of self-statements. Usually, the CBM training follows the principle of successive approximations. Initially, the therapist models and has the child rehearse simple self-statements such as ''Stop! Think before I answer.'' Gradually the therapist models (and the child rehearses) more complex sets of self-statements.

A key feature of self-instructional training is to view the child as a collaborator in generating and implementing the training package. The trainer can ask the child what advice he might have in doing a task, such as the MFF test, thus trying to tap the child's cognitive repertoire. In our own work we have found that some impulsive children suggest that the other child look at each of the alternatives on the MFF and systematically check each with the standard. But when we monitored the impulsive child's eye movements while doing the MFF he did not follow his own advice. Instead his search strategy while doing the MFF was quite haphazard. Thus, the correct strategy was in his repertoire, but he did not spontaneously employ it in performing the task. The trainer can then indicate that the advice offered seems worthwhile and that he (the trainer) would like to "try on" these suggestions. In this way the child is involved in teaching the trainer. This exchange can then be developed across both impersonal and interpersonal tasks. For example, Goodwin and Mahoney (1975) used a circle game to teach CBM skills to aggressive children. In the game children are placed around a circle and asked to taunt the trainer who is in the middle of the ring. The therapist acts as a cognitive coping model, manifesting behaviors and self-statements by which he can handle the provocations. The children in turn rehearse similar coping skills by following the lead of the therapist.

The CBM training regimen can be supplemented with imagery manipulations, especially in treating young children. One can train the impulsive child to imagine and to subsequently self-instruct. "I will not go faster than a slow turtle, slow turtle." Robin, Schneider, and Dolnick (1976) have used such a turtle imagery procedure in an ingenious way to foster self-control in hyperactive, disruptive school children. The researchers incorporated the turtle image into a story that was read to the class. Following the story, the students imitated the turtle who withdrew into his shell when he felt he was about to lose control. This was followed by relaxation, self-instructional and problem solving exercises to teach self-control and instructions to "do turtle" when losing control. In the study, the teacher spent 15 minutes each day for approximately three weeks in training and achieved reduced aggressive behavior and fewer frustration responses. One could use a variety of different stories and cognitive techniques to teach such self-control behaviors.

The CBM approach to treat impulsivity directly focuses on the child's conscious self-regulatory ability. The same would apply to the treatment of impulsive adolescents and adults. The child's behavior pattern is broken down into smaller, manageable units and in this way the therapist tries to make the subject aware of the chain of events (i.e., environmental situations and behavioral and cognitive reactions) that set off the impulsive and often aggressive behavior. This process is enhanced by performing a diagnostic evaluation of the conditions under which self-control is deficient. By making the client aware of the sequence of events, he can be helped to interrupt them early in the chain and to employ coping procedures.

The CBM approach may be contrasted with other therapy approaches employed with problems of impulsivity. Bergin (1967) indicated: "Impulse control problems are often treated by aversive methods, by analysis of psychodynamics via transference, by modification of self-perceptions and relationships with others, by altering values, etc., but seldom are they dealt with by direct treatment of the self-regulatory defect per se." (p. 116). The present CBM approach focuses on the self-regulation process.

One final note needs to be added to a consideration of CBM with children.

There has been an increasing recognition that child maladjustment and child behavior problems are often accompanied by family conflict and marital discord (e.g., Ferguson and Allen, 1978). A good deal of CBM work is now directed at affecting the parent-child unit (Blechman, Olson, and Hellman 1976, Robin et al., 1977). A CBM problem solving approach with parents is designed to teach parents communication and problem solving skills by having the parents recognize the manner in which their cognitions—hidden agendas, current concerns, expectations, appraisals, attributions, etc.—contribute to marital conflict and, in turn, affect the child. There is increasing recognition that the parents' reactions to the child's misbehavior represents an important target for CBM intervention.

COGNITIVE BEHAVIOR MODIFICATION WITH ADULTS

The focus of our discussion thus far has been on the application of CBM with children. A similar discussion of CBM with adults is more difficult in this limited space because so many different procedures have been subsumed under the CBM heading. The adult populations and problems that have received CBM treatment include clients who have problems with interpersonal anxiety (Goldfried, 1977; Heppner, 1978; Lange and Jakubowski, 1976; Thorpe, 1975), test anxiety (Denney, in press; Wine, in press), anger control (Novaco, in press), pain (Genest and Turk, in press; Turk, in press), depression (Beck et al., in press; Rush et al., 1977; Shaw, 1977; Taylor and Marshall, 1977), addictions (Marlatt and Gordon, in press; Rychtarik and Wollersheim, 1978), sexual dysfunction (Rook and Hammen, 1977), and alcohol abuse (Chaney, O'Leary, and Marlatt 1978; Intagliata, 1978). Also, a number of behavior therapy procedures, such as desensitization, modeling, operant and aversive conditioning, imagery, and behavioral rehearsal, have been altered to highlight the role of cognitive factors (see Meichenbaum, 1977). Thus, a comprehensive review of CBM with adults is beyond the scope of the present chapter. Instead we will provide a descriptive account of the communalities that seem apparent across the respective CBM treatment approaches, and will conclude with a consideration of the emerging theoretical model that is being offered to account for the success of CBM interventions.

It has become obvious that it is impossible to proceed therapeutically along a single dimension, cognitive or behavioral (see Mahoney, 1977; Murray and Jacobson, 1979). Perhaps the unique advantages of both cognitive and behavior therapy procedures could be combined. One could use the behavior therapy procedures of in vivo graded assignments, modeling, behavioral and imagery rehearsal, operant and aversive conditioning, etc., to modify the client's self-statements, images and belief systems. With this in mind, let us consider a model that provides a framework for the many specific treatments that have resulted from the marriage between the technology of behavior therapy and the clinical concerns of cognitive and semantic therapists.

An Overview of CBM with Adults

For descriptive purposes, the CBM therapy process can be viewed as consisting of three phases. These phases do not form a lock-step progression, but can be repeated or returned to as necessary for therapy progress. The first phase is concerned with understanding the nature of the client's presenting problem and formulating an initial treatment plan. In this phase the client and therapist begin to evolve a common view of the presenting problem from which a variety of therapeutic interventions naturally follow. A motivating factor for a number of client to modify his internal dialogue (self-statements and images) and to produce happening and why, to receive assurances that they are not going to "lose their minds," and that something can be done to help them change. It is partly in response to these concerns and also as a way of preparing clients to actively engage in the change procedures that the conceptualization process receives so much attention. During the second phase of CBM training the therapist helps his client to explore, try on, and consolidate the conceptualization of the presenting problem.

Whereas the first two phases of therapy involve preparing the client for change, it is during the third phase of CBM training that the therapist helps the client to modify his internal dialogue (self-statements and images) and to produce new, more adaptive behaviors to be performed in vivo. These behaviors (or personal experiments) will lead to consequences that the client and therapist can then consider in light of the client's prior expectancies and beliefs. This reappraisal can give rise to the production of further new behaviors, and so forth. The third phase of therapy is designed to begin the process of affecting the ongoing reciprocal interactions (Bandura, 1977) between cognition, affect, behavior, and environmental consequences.

The length of time for each of the three phases varies depending on the client's presenting problems, therapist style and skill, goals of therapy, and other factors. In research studies with clients who had common problems, the three phases were successfully completed in eight sessions, whereas some individual therapy has required as many as 40 sessions.

Phase I. Conceptualization of the problem. The role of the conceptualization process in therapy has received insufficient attention from behavior modifiers. The content of therapy prior to a process such as desensitization is rarely discussed. How do we prepare the patient to accept the rationale and the treatment intervention? One way is to try and modify what the client says to himself and his images about his presenting problem or symptom, that is, to modify the perceptions, expectations and attributions. The client usually enters therapy with some conceptualization or definition of his problem. If he is depressed he may complain that he is a victim of his mood changes; if anxious and phobic, external events are viewed as causing his malady. Rarely does the client see the role of his own thinking processes and/or the interpersonal meaning of his behavior as sources of disturbance. One goal of this initial conceptualization phase of therapy is for the therapist and patient to redefine the client's problems in terms that will give the client a sense of control and a feeling of hope, particularly in terms that will lead to specific behavioral interventions. Thus, the therapist tries to understand the client's description and definition of his problem, but does not uncritically accept the client's view of the problem. Instead, the therapist and client attempt to redefine the problem in terms that are acceptable to both of them. It is this reformulation or conceptualization phase that provides the basis for behavior change. There are a variety of ways in which the client and therapist can evolve a common conceptualization. Some therapists are very directive in attempting to convince the client to accept a particular conceptualization by power of their personality, jargon, or position. In some cases such a "hard sell" approach may prove successful.

A preferred way to proceed is to have the client and therapist evolve a common conceptualization, so that the client feels that he is an active participant and contributor. The initial phase of CBM therapy with adults is designed to evolve such a common conceptualization. The manner in which the therapist discusses the presenting problem, the kinds of questions the therapist asks, the type of assessment procedures employed, the content of the therapy rationale, and the kinds of homework assignments given are all used to help evolve a common client-therapist conceptualization.

The initial session of CBM training begins with the therapist exploring the extent and duration of the client's presenting problem. The therapist performs a situational analysis of the client's problem by discussing it not only in a general context, but also in terms of the specific assessment situation in which the client may have participated. Note that CBM therapy can be readily conducted on a group basis (see Genest and Turk, in press; Meichenbaum and Genest, 1978). In group treatment clients can benefit from a group discussion of their faulty thinking styles. Clients can discuss the feelings and thoughts they experienced before, during and after a behavioral assessment situation, or revolving around a prototypic situation. In some cases it may be helpful to have a client close his eyes and "run a movie through his head" of a recent incident involving his problem, reporting the sequence of thoughts, feelings and behaviors. Such an imagery procedure has proved a useful adjunct to the standard interview in eliciting internal dialogue. Another interesting supplement has been the use of videotaping. Clients are asked to perform their maladaptive behaviors (making a speech, handling a phobic object or a pain patient tolerating a laboratory pain) while being videotaped. Immediately after the taping both the client and therapist view the tape while the client tries to reconstruct the thoughts and feelings he was experiencing.

Following a discussion of the client's thinking process in the specific assessment situations, the client explores the range of situations in which he has the same or comparable thoughts, images and feelings. Throughout this first phase, the therapist has to determine the degree to which each client's problem is illustrative of a characteristic thinking style. In one case, a client was obsessive and somewhat phobic about crossing streets. The therapist had to determine to what degree such indecisiveness was a characteristic thinking style evident in a variety of situations. The therapist has to decide whether to focus therapy on making the client aware of and changing such a thinking style, or to focus treatment on the specific presenting problem (i.e., inability to cross streets). The severity and duration of the presenting problem, goals of therapy, and other factors influence this decision.

During this initial phase of therapy the therapist helps the clients to realize the irrational, self-defeating, and self-fulfilling aspects of their thinking style and self-statements and images. We have found that clients often have specific behavioral rituals to cope with stress and anxiety. For example, on an exam day, a high test-anxiety client knew exactly which seat she would sit in, arrived early in order to avoid the fear of being late, and remained isolated in order not to hear what other students were talking about. During the initial sessions, after the clients have offered descriptions of such behavioral patterns, the therapist can wonder aloud about what purpose behavior such as the seating ritual would serve. A plausible answer that the group may produce is that the ritual controlled anxiety and the accompanying negative self-statements and catastrophizing images.

Another way of having the group appreciate the role of negative self-statements is to give a homework assignment to listen to themselves with a "third ear." The purpose of the homework assignment is to strengthen the client's belief that internal dialogue contributes to his problems. Therapists differ in how demanding and structured this homework assignment should be. Some therapists encourage explicit monitoring, recording, and graphing specific behaviors, thoughts, urges, moods, and so on. In part, how one proceeds concerning homework and the other aspects of therapy depends on how one views the role of cognitions.

Note that prior to treatment it is unlikely that the client confronts his thoughts consciously or deliberately when facing problem situations. Rather, as Gold-fried, Decenteceo, and Weinberg (1974) have indicated, because of the habitual nature of one's expectations or beliefs it is likely that such thinking processes become automatic and seemingly involuntary, like most overlearned acts. The client's negative self-statements become a habitual style of thinking, in many ways similar to the automatization of thought that accompanies the mastery of a motor skill such as driving a car or skiing. The therapist can make the client aware of such thought processes and increase the likelihood that the client will in the future notice similar self-statements. The client's faulty cognition may take a pictorial form instead of the verbal form. Beck (1970) reported that a woman with a fear of walking alone found that her spells of anxiety followed images of having a heart attack and being left helpless; a college student discovered that her anxiety at leaving the dormitory was triggered by visual fantasies of being attacked.

In summary, the purpose of the four steps in this initial phase of therapy: (1)

assessment procedures, (2) group discussion, (3) situational analysis, and (4) homework assignment, is to secure information about the client's problems, to lay the groundwork for the therapist and client to evolve a common conceptualization of the presenting problem, and to decide upon the means of therapeutic intervention. Once the client comes to accept the possibility that what he says to himself and imagines influences his behavior, CBM treatment can readily be introduced. This initial phase of therapy highlights the fact that what has traditionally been characterized as nonspecific factors of therapy represent an intimate and key feature of CBM.

Phase II. "Trying on" the conceptualization. The second phase of CBM training with adults is designed to have the clients "try on" and consolidate the conceptualization of their problem. Included in this phase is a discussion of the therapy rationale and therapy plan.

The phase begins with the clients reporting on their homework assignment of monitoring their internal dialogue and automatic thoughts and images. As the clients begin to report these, the therapist can begin to take a more passive role by asking tactfully, "Are you saying that part of your problem is what you are telling yourself? How so?" Such questions should not be used until the clients have explored the content of their cognitions and the self-defeating and self-fulfilling prophecy aspects of this style of thinking. In fact, one can use the client's behavior in the therapy session as a basis to explore cognitions. For example, if the client does not participate in the group, the therapist may ask the client to describe how he is feeling and then to explore the thoughts that are keeping him from participating. In this manner, the clients will work to convince the therapist, each other, and themselves, that a key aspect of their problem is their thinking styles. The clients are beginning to discover that their fears and anxiety are not a property of the external events, but rather that their own thoughts help to elicit and maintain anxiety.

At this point the therapist may introduce the therapy rationale. Throughout the presentation of the rationale, there is a dialogue between therapist and clients. The exact wording, vocabulary level, and format can be adapted to each group. For example, consider the rationale offered in the cognitive behavior modification treatment of test-anxiety (Meichenbaum, 1972; Meichenbaum and Genest, 1977). The therapist says to the group:

"As I listen to you discuss your test anxiety I am struck by some of the similarities in how each of you is feeling and what you are thinking. On the one hand there are reports of quite a bit of tenseness and anxiety in exam situations and in evaluative situations. This seems to take many forms such as stomachs and necks becoming tense, pounding hearts, sweaty palms, heavy breathing, and so on.

the therapist should use the specific reactions offered by group members.

At the same time—and correct me if I am wrong—several of you described how difficult it was for you to focus attention on only the task before you. Somehow, your attention wandered away from what you had to do (such as studying, or taking the exam) to something irrelevant. (Once again the therapist should use reactions offered by group members.) Your thinking, or self-statements and images, seem to get in the way of what you had to do. Your thoughts about catastrophes and how awful the consequences will be because of your not doing well got in the way. (Pause). Have I heard you correctly?''

The therapist may decide to have the group return to the description of their test-anxiety; specifically, to the test assessment situation in which each member participated. What kinds of thoughts and feelings, what self-statements and images did the clients emit in that situation?

The therapy rationale continues:

"In the therapy sessions we are going to work on ways to control how you feel, on ways of controlling your anxiety and tenseness. We will do this by learning how to relax in order to control your arousal and tenseness.

"In addition to learning relaxation skills, we will learn how to control our thinking processes and attention. The control of our thinking, or what we say to ourselves, comes about by first becoming aware of when we are producing negative self-statements, catastrophizing, being task irrelevant, and so forth." (Once again, the therapist and clients should give examples of the negative thinking style.) "The recognition that we are in fact doing this will be a step forward in changing. This recognition will also act as a reminder, a cue, a bell-ringer for us to produce different thoughts and self-instructions, to challenge and dispute our self-statements. In this way we will come to produce task-relevant self-instructions and new, adaptive behaviors. (Pause.) I'm wondering about your reactions to what I have described. Do you have any questions?" (The therapist should determine how the rationale matches the clients' expectations and conceptualization for change.)

Perhaps another example, taken this time from the CBM ''stress-inoculation'' treatment of phobics, will illustrate how the therapist incorporates and shares the theory for change with the client. The training was designed to accomplish three goals: (1) to ''educate'' the phobic clients about the nature of stressful or fearful reactions; (2) to have the clients rehearse various coping behaviors; and (3) to give the client an opportunity to practice his new coping skills in a stressful situation (Meichenbaum, 1977).

The educational phase of the stress-inoculation treatment began with a discussion of the nature of the client's fears. Discussion topics included how he felt and what he thought about when confronted by the phobic objects, and how he was coping with stress in general as well as his phobias in particular. Interestingly, even clients who appear incapacitated can describe coping techniques that they have employed in other stressful areas (e.g., visits to the dentist). The therapist had the group discuss these skills and explore why they were not employed in overcoming the presenting problem.

As part of the therapy rationale, the therapist conceptualized the client's anxiety in terms of Schachter's model of emotional arousal (Schachter, 1966). That is, the therapist stated that the client's fear reaction seemed to involve two major elements: (1) his heightened physiological arousal; and (2) his set of anxiety-producing, avoidant thoughts and self-statements (e.g., disgust evoked by the phobic object, a sense of helplessness, panic thoughts of being overwhelmed by anxiety, a desire to flee). After laying this groundwork, the therapist noted that the client's fear seemed to fit Schachter's theory that an emotional state such as fear is in large part determined by the thoughts the client engages in when he is physically aroused.

It should be noted that the Schachter and Singer (1962) theory of emotion was used for purposes of conceptualization only. Although the theory and the research upon which it is based have been criticized (Lazarus, Averill, and Opton, 1970; Plutchik and Ax, 1967), the theory has an aura of plausibility that clients tend to accept: the logic of the treatment plan is clearer to clients in light of this conceptualization.

In order to prepare the client further for training, the therapist helped the client change his perception of how he behaved in the phobic situation. Instead of viewing his response as a massive panic reaction, the therapist suggested that the client's response seemed to include several phases. In the course of the discussion the following four phases were suggested: (1) preparing for the stressor; (2) confronting or handling a stressor; (3) possibly being overwhelmed by a stressor; and finally, (4) reinforcing oneself for having coped.

The client was encouraged to offer examples of cognitive strategies or self-statements that he could use for coping during each phase. With some support, a package of self-statements similar to that listed in Table 11.2 emerged. The cognitive strategies encouraged clients to: (1) assess the reality of the situation; (2) control negative, self-defeating, anxiety-engendering ideation; (3) acknowledge, use, and possibly relabel the anxiety they were experiencing; (4) "psych" themselves up to perform the task; (5) cope with the intense fear they might experience; and (6) reinforce themselves for having coped. Zane (1978) has recently developed a related CBM approach that he calls "contextual psychotherapy." Note that the cognitive coping reconceptualization provides preparation for the needed in vivo and participant modeling procedures.

Once the client became proficient in the relaxation exercises and the self-instructional techniques, the therapist suggested that the client should test and practice his coping skills by actually employing them under graded, preexposure stressful conditions. One may supplement these in vivo assignments with exposure to laboratory stressors such as receiving an unpredictable electric shock, watching stress-inducing films, or graded imagining of frightening scenes. The more varied and extensive the application training, the greater the likelihood that the client will develop a general learning set, that is, a general way of coping. Coping imagery arranged along a hierarchy of fear producing scenes as well as behavioral rehearsal may also be used in the application phase (see Meichenbaum, 1977).

Table 11.2 Examples of Coping Self-Statements Rehearsed in Stress Inoculation Training

Preparing for a stressor
>What is it you have to do?
>You can develop a plan to deal with it.
>Just think about what you can do about it.
>That's better than getting anxious.
>No negative self-statements: just think rationally.
>Don't worry; worry won't help anything.
>Maybe what you think is anxiety is eagerness to confront the stressor.

Confronting and handling a stressor
>Just "psych" yourself up—you can meet this challenge.
>Reason your fear away.
>One step at a time; you can handle the situation.
>Don't think about fear; just think about what you have to do. Stay relevant.
>This anxiety is what the doctor said you would feel.
>It's a reminder to use your coping exercises.
>This tenseness can be an ally; a cue to cope.
>Relax; you're in control. Take a slow deep breath.
>Ah. good.

Coping with the feeling of being overwhelmed
>When fear comes, just pause.
>Keep the focus on the present; what is it you have to do?
>Label your fear from 0 to 10 and watch it change.
>You should expect your fear to rise.
>Manageable.

Reinforcing self-statements
>It worked; you did it.
>Wait until you tell your therapist (or group) about this.
>It wasn't as bad as you expected.
>You made more out of your fear than it was worth.
>Your damn ideas—that's the problem.
>When you control them, you control your fear.
>It's getting better each time you use the procedures.
>You can be pleased with the progress you're making.
>You did it!

In summary, the stress-inoculation training involved discussing the nature of emotion and stress reactions, rehearsing coping skills, and testing these skills under actual stress conditions. In some sense the emphasis of treatment switches from trying to totally reduce the client's anxiety to training him to function despite his anxiety. If this is achieved, then continued practice would probably lead to further anxiety reduction. This is illustrated by the statements made by a phobic client following CBM treatment. She reported that following treatment she reassured herself by talking to herself. She said:

It (self-instructing) makes me able to be in the situation, not to be comfortable, but to tolerate it . . . I don't talk myself out of being afraid, just out of appearing afraid . . . You immediately react to the thing you're afraid of and then start to reason with yourself. I talk myself out of panic.

Following a series of such successful attempts, she reported that even the feeling of fear dissipated and the amount of anxiety was reduced.

Given the increasing demand on individuals to deal with daily stress, the possibility of using inoculation training for prophylactic purposes is promising. For example, Novaco (1977) has used stress inoculation training on a preventa-tive basis with policemen who are called upon to control anger. The possibility of explicitly teaching persons to cope cognitively by such diverse techniques as information seeking, anticipatory problem solving, imagery and behavioral re-hearsal, task organization, altering attributions and self-labels, shifting attention, or using cognitive reevaluation and relaxation seems to hold much promise (see Meichenbaum and Novaco, 1977). An explicit training program that would teach coping skills and then provide training in handling various stressful situations contrasts sharply with the haphazard way in which most individuals now learn to cope with stress.

Phase III. Modifying cognitions and producing new behaviors. The first two phases of CBM treatment served the purpose of having the therapist understand the client's problems and concerns and of having the client and therapist evolve a common conceptualization. The third phase of CBM treatment is designed to help the client modify his cognitions and to produce new behaviors. How one proceeds at this point varies depending in part on the nature of the presenting problem, the goals of therapy, and the orientation of the CBM therapist.

One way to conceptualize these different modes of intervention is to recognize that a variety of different foci is available. Some CBM therapists such as those who adopt a rational-emotive (RET) approach tend to attack the irrational at-titudes and faulty beliefs of the clients directly. A somewhat different focus and style of CBM intervention for the therapist is to have the client examine the nature of the client's problem solving and coping skills. A variety of behavioral and imagery procedures such as rational restructuring, coping desensitization, as well as a host of other behavior therapy techniques can be employed to teach such cognitive and behavioral skills. A host of behavior therapy procedures can be modified in order to change the client's cognitions and behaviors. For example, the systematic desensitization procedure can be altered, both in its rationale and in how the imagery rehearsal procedures are employed. From a CBM perspective a coping self-control orientation is used in describing the desensitization process and both a cue-controlled relaxation and a coping imagery approach are used. Several studies have indicated that altering the imagery procedure, whereby the client imagines the coping process, enhances the efficacy of the desensitization process (see fourth issue of the CBM newsletter, Meichenbaum, 1979 for a summary of these studies and Meichenbaum, 1977 for clinical examples of these procedures).

Similarly, modeling procedures can be altered to include a coping CBM orientation. CBM modeling approaches deliberately emphasize a model's verbalizations of the problem solving steps, coping attitudes, and other self-instructions and images needed to help the client learn how to develop techniques to generate strategies and response alternatives, and not just what is an appropriate response. Bruch (1978) has summarized data for the efficacy of cognitive modeling that indicates that when the model's verbalizations of cognitive processes accompanies behavioral examples it is more effective than just exemplar modeling alone.

Another focus of intervention for CBM therapists has been on behavior itself. Beck et al. (in press), when working with depressed patients, attempt to have the client engage in graded homework task assignments. In this way the CBM therapist can help the client collect data that is incompatible with his prior expectations of what he thinks the outcomes would actually be. In turn, the CBM therapist has the client come to recognize the range of situations in which he has similar expectations, appraisals, and attributions and to recognize and change the faulty aspects of his thinking (e.g., magnification, arbitrary inferences, overgeneralization, dichotomous reasoning and the like). The use of such graded in vivo exposure and behavioral exercises represents a central feature of all CBM work. For example, rational-emotive therapists regularly have clients engage in ''shame exercises,'' whereby the client can receive feedback that will cause them to question and dispute their belief systems.

The point, as noted above, is that to characterize a therapy as being either cognitive or behavioral is just too simplistic. The CBM therapist is as concerned with using environmental consequences, as is the behavior therapist, but for the CBM therapist such consequences represent informational feedback trials that will provide the client with an opportunity to question, reappraise and gain distance from his cognitions and maladaptive behavior. The CBM treatment approach can intervene at various points, namely, at the point of cognitive structures (beliefs, meaning systems), cognitive processes (automatic thoughts and images, problem solving coping skills), behavioral acts, and environmental consequences. The CBM approach can also intervene by influencing the content of the client's thoughts and the client's style of thinking. Wherever the initial focus of intervention may be, if durable and generalizable change is to occur, then several different foci will be involved. For example, although one may begin CBM therapy with behavioral acts, this will then have reverberating results affecting the environmental consequences and how they are appraised. This reappraisal will affect the preceding and accompanying internal dialogue that will, in turn, affect behavior. Such changes will in turn lead to new consequences that will result in the client to further reevaluate his thinking style and beliefs. Similarly, if one intervenes at the point of cognitions, it is important that this results in the client generating and implementing new behaviors or conducting in vivo personal experiments.

A FINAL WORD

Rathjen, Rathjen and Hiniker (1978) have summarized well over twenty different CBM procedures designed to effect the "reciprocal determinism" cycle or the interaction between cognition, affect, behavior, and environmental consequences. In fact, the list of CBM intervention procedures is becoming as long as a classic list of behavior therapy procedures once was (Ullmann and Krasner, 1965). If progress is to be made, however, the CBM approach must not develop a preoccupation with techniques per se, but must instead struggle with developing a testable theory of behavior change. Some recent attempts toward such theory development have been offered by Bandura (1977), Meichenbaum (1975, 1977), Meichenbaum and Butler (in press) and Mischel (1973). It is hoped that continued research will mature into a cognitive social-learning theory that will explain behavior change and that will have implications for how best to intervene.

REFERENCES

Alkus, S. Self-regulation and children's task performance: A comparison of self-instruction, coping and attribution approaches. Unpublished doctoral dissertation, University of California, Los Angeles, 1976.

Allen, G., Chinsky, J., Larcen, S., Lochman, J., and Selinger, W. *Community psychology and the schools: A behaviorally oriented multi-level preventive approach.* Hillsdale, N.J.: Lawrence Erlbaum Associates, 1976.

Baer, D., Wolf, M., and Risley, T. Some current dimensions of applied behavior analysis. *Journal of Applied Behavior Analysis,* 1968, *1,* 91-97.

Bandura, A. Self-efficacy: Toward a unifying theory of behavioral change. *Psychological Review,* 1977, *84,* 191-215.

———. The self-system in reciprocal determinism. *American Psychologist,* 1978, *33,* 344-358.

Barkley, R., Copeland, A., and Sivage, C. A self-control classroom for hyperactive and impulsive children. Unpublished manuscript, Milwaukee Children's Hospital, 1978.

Beck, A. Cognitive therapy: Nature and relation to behavior therapy, *Behavior Therapy,* 1970, *1,* 184-200.

———. *Cognitive therapy and emotional disorders.* New York: International Universities Press, 1976.

Beck, A., Rush, J., Shaw, B., and Emery, G. *Cognitive therapy of depression.* New York: Guilford Press, 1979.

Bender, N. Self-verbalization versus tutor verbalization in modifying impulsivity. *Journal of Educational Psychology*, 1976, *68*, 347-354.

————. Verbal mediation as an instructional technique with young trainable mentally retarded children. *Journal of Special Education*, 1977, *11*, 449-455.

Bergin, A. A self-regulation technique for impulse control disorders. *Psychotherapy: Theory, Research, and Practice*. 1967, *6*, 113-118.

Blechman, E., Olson, D., and Hellman, I. Stimulus control over family problem-solving behavior: The family contract game. *Behavior Therapy*, 1976, *7*, 686-692.

Borkowski, J., and Cavanaugh, J. Maintenance and generalization of skills and strategies by the retarded. In N. Ellis (Ed.), *Handbook of mental deficiency: Psychological theory and research*. Second Edition. Hillsdale, N.J.: Lawrence Erlbaum, 1978.

Bornstein, P., and Quevillon, R. The effects of a self-instructional package on overactive preschool boys. *Journal of Applied Behavior Analysis*, 1976, *9*, 176-188.

Bower, G. Contacts of cognitive psychology with social learning theory. *Cognitive Therapy and Research*, 1978, *2*, 123-146.

Brewer, W. There is no convincing evidence for operant or classical conditioning in adult humans. In W. Weimer and D. Palermo (Eds.), *Cognition and the symbolic processes*. Hillsdale, N.J.: Erlbaum Associates, 1974.

Brown, A., and Campione, J. Permissible inference from the outcome of training studies in cognitive development research. *Quarterly Newsletter of the Institute for Comparative Human Development*, 1978, *2*, 46-53.

Brown, A., Campione, J., and Murphy, M. Maintenance and generalization of trained metamnemonie awareness of educable retarded children. *Journal of Experimental Child Psychology*, 1977, *24*, 191-211.

Bruch, M. Type of cognitive modeling, imitation of modeled tactics, and modification of test anxiety. *Cognitive Therapy and Research*, 1978, *2*, 147-164.

Bugenthal, D.B., Collins, S., Collins, L., and Chaney, L. Attributional and behavioral changes following two behavior management interventions with hyperactive boys: A follow-up study. *Child Development*, 1978, *49*, 247-250.

Bugenthal, D., Whalen, C., and Henker, B. Causal attributions of hyperactive children and motivational assumptions of two behavior-change approaches: Evidence for an interactionist position. *Child Development*, 1977, *48*, 874-884.

Camp, B., Blom, G., Hebert, F., and Van Doorninck, W. "Think aloud": A program for developing self-control in young aggressive boys. *Journal of Abnormal Child Psychology*, 1977, *8*, 157-169.

Chaney, E., O'Leary, M., and Marlatt, G. Skill training with alcoholics. *Journal of Consulting and Clinical Psychology*, 1978, *46*, 1092-1104.

Coates, T., and Thoresen, C. Self-control and educational practice or do we really need self-control? In D. Berliner (Ed.), *Review of Research in Education*, Itasac, Illinois: Praeger, in press.

Cowen, E. Baby steps toward primary prevention. *American Journal of Community Psychology*, 1977, *5*, 1-22.

Craighead, E., Craighead-Wilcoxon, L., and Meyers, A. New directions in behavior modification with children. In M. Hessen, R. Eisler, and P. Miller (Eds.), *Progress in behavior modification*. (Vol. 6) New York: Academic Press, 1978.

Denney, D. The effects of exemplary and cognitive models and self-rehearsal on children's interrogative strategies. *Journal of Experimental Child Psychology*, 1975, *19*, 476-488.

————. Self-control approaches to the treatment of test anxiety. In I. Sarason (Ed.), *Test anxiety: Theory research and application*. New York: Lawrence Erlbaum, in press.

DiGiuseppe, R., Miller, N., and Trexler, L. A review of rational-emotive psychotherapy: Outcome studies. *The Counseling Psychologist*, 1977, *7*, 64-72.

Douglas, V. Stop, look and listen: The problem of sustained attention and impulse control in hyperactive and normal children. *Canadian Journal of Behavioral Science*, 1972, *4*, 259-281.

Douglas, V. Are drugs enough?—to treat or to train the hyperactive child. *International Journal of Mental Health*, 1975, *5*, 199-212.

Douglas, V., Parry, P., Martin, P., and Garson, C. Assessment of a cognitive training program for hyperactive children. *Journal of Abnormal Child Psychology*, 1976, *4*, 389-410.

Dweck, C. The role of expectations and attributions in the alleviation of learned helplessness. *Journal of Personality and Social Psychology*, 1975, *31*, 674-685.

D'Zurilla, T., and Goldfried, M. Problem-solving and behavior modification. *Journal of Abnormal Psychology*, 1971, *78*, 107-126.

Elardo, P. Project AWARE: A school program to facilitate social development of children. Paper presented at the Fourth Annual Blumberg Symposium, Chapel Hill, North Carolina, 1974.

Ellis, A., and Grieger, R. *Handbook of rational-emotive therapy*. New York: Springer, 1978.

Emery, R., and Marholin, D. An applied behavior analysis of delinquency: The irrelevancy of relevant behavior. *American Psychologist*, 1977, *32*, 860-873.

Finch, A., Wilkinson, M., Nelson, W., and Montgomery, L. Modification of an impulsive cognitive tempo in emotionally disturbed boys. *Journal of Abnormal Child Psychology*, 1975, *3*, 49-52.

Flavell, J. Metacognitive aspects of problem-solving. In L. Resnick (Ed.), *The nature of intelligence*. Hillsdale, N.J.: Lawrence Erlbaum, 1976.

Foreyt, J., and Rathjen, D. *Cognitive behavior therapy: Research and application*. New York: Plenum Press, 1978.

Frank, J. *Persuasion and healing*. Baltimore: Johns Hopkins Press, 1961.

Furgeson, L.R., and Allen, D. Congruence of parental perception, marital satisfaction, and child adjustment. *Journal of Consulting and Clinical Psychology*, 1978, *46*, 345-346.

Gagne, R. Problem solving. In A. Melton (Ed.), *Categories of human learning*. New York: Academic Press, 1964.

Genest, M., and Turk, D. A proposed model for group therapy with pain patients. In D. Upper and S. Ross (Eds.), *Behavioral group therapy: An annual review*. Champaign, Illinois: Research Press, in press.

Glass, C., Gottman, J., and Schmurack, S. Response acquisition and cognitive self-statement modification approaches to dating skills training. *Journal of Counseling Psychology*, 1976, *23*, 520-526.

Goldfried, M. The use of relaxation and cognitive relabeling as coping skills. In R. Stuart (Ed.), *Behavioral self-management: Strategies, techniques and outcomes*. New York: Brunner/Mazel, 1977.

Goldfried, M. Anxiety reduction through cognitive-behavioral intervention. In P. Kendall and S. Hollon (Eds.), *Cognitive-behavioral interventions: Theory, research and procedures*. New York: Academic Press, in press.

Goldfried, M., Decenteceo, E., and Weinberg, L. Systematic rational restructuring as a self-control technique. *Behavior Therapy*, 1974, *5*, 247-254.

Goodwin, S., and Mahoney, M. Modification of aggression via modeling: An experimental probe. *Journal of Behavior Therapy and Experimental Psychiatry*, 1975, *6*, 200-202.

Gottman, J., and Markman, H. Experimental designs in psychotherapy & research. In S. Garfield and A. Bergin (Eds.), *Handbook of psychotherapy and behavior change*. Second edition. New York, John Wiley, 1979.

Grinspoon, L., and Singer, S. Amphetamines in the treatment of hyperactive children. *Harvard Educational Review*, 1973, *43*, 515-565.

Heppner, P. A review of problem-solving literature and its relationship to the counseling process. *Journal of Counseling Psychology*, 1978, *25*, 366-375.

Intagliata, J. Increasing the interpersonal problem-solving skills of an alcoholic population. *Journal of Consulting and Clinical Psychology*, 1978, *46*, 489-498.

Jakibchuk, Z., and Smeriglio, V. The influence of symbolic modeling on the social behavior of preschool children with low levels of social responsiveness. *Child Development*, 1976, *47*, 838-841.

Kanfer, F., Karoly, P., and Newman, A. Redirection of children's fear of the dark by competence related and situational threat related verbal cues. *Journal of Consulting and Clinical Psychology*, 1975, *43*, 257-258.

Karoly, P. Behavioral self-management in children: Concepts, methods, issues and directions. In M. Hersen, R. Eisler, and P. Miller (Eds.), *Progress in behavior modification*, Vol. 5. New York: Academic Press, 1977.

Keeley, S., Shemberg, K., and Carbonell, J. Operant clinical intervention: Behavior management or beyond? Where are the data? *Behavior Therapy*, 1976, *7*, 292-305.

Kendall, P. On the efficacious use of verbal self-instructional procedures with children. *Cognitive Therapy and Research*, 1977, *1*, 331-341.

———. Developing self-control in children: A manual of cognitive-behavioral strategies. Unpublished manuscript, University of Minnesota, 1979.

Kendall, P., and Finch, A. A cognitive-behavioral treatment for impulse control: A case study. *Journal of Consulting and Clinical Psychology*, 1976, *44*, 852-859.

———. A cognitive-behavioral treatment for impulsivity: A group comparison study. *Journal of Consulting and Clinical Psychology*, 1978, *46*, 110-118.

Kendall, P., and Hollon, S. (Eds.), *Cognitive-behavioral interventions: Theory, research and procedures*. New York: Academic Press, 1979.

Kendall, P., and Wilcox, L. A cognitive-behavioral treatment for impulsivity: Concrete versus conceptual labeling with nonself-controlled problem children. Unpublished manuscript, University of Minnesota, 1978.

Kieslar, D. Some myths of psychotherapy research and the search for a paradigm. *Psychological Bulletin*, 1966, *65*, 110-136.

Klinger, E. *Meaning and void: Inner experience and the incentives in people's lives*. Minneapolis: University of Minnesota Press, 1977.

Kovacs, M., and Beck, A. Maladaptive cognitive structures in depression. *American Journal of Psychiatry*, 1978, *135*, 525-530.

Kuhn, T. *The structure of scientific revolutions*. Chicago: University of Chicago Press, 1962.

Lange, A., and Jakubowski, P. *Responsible assertive behavior: Cognitive-behavioral procedures for trainees*. Champaign, Illinois: Research Press, 1976.

Lazarus, R., Averill, J., and Opton, E. Towards a cognitive theory of emotion. In M. Arnold (Ed.), *Feeling and emotion*. New York: Academic Press, 1970.

Luria, A. The directive function of speech in development. *Word*, 1959, *15*, 341-352.

———. *The role of speech in the regulation of normal and abnormal behaviors*. New York: Liveright, 1961.

Mahoney, M. *Cognition and behavior modification*. Cambridge, Mass.: Ballinger, 1974.

———. Reflections on the cognitive-learning trend in psychotherapy. *American Psychologist*, 1977, *32*, 5-13.

Mahoney, M., and Arnkoff, D. Cognitive and self-control therapies. In S. Garfield and A. Bergin (Eds.), *Handbook of psychotherapy and behavior change*. Second edition. New York: John Wiley, 1979.

Markman, E. Realizing that you don't understand: A preliminary investigation. *Child Development*, in press.

Marlatt, G., and Gordon, J. Determinants of relapse: Implications for the maintenance of behavior change. In P. Davidson (Ed.), *Behavior of medicine: Changing health lifestyles,*. New York: Brunner/Mazel, in press.

Mash, E., and Dalby, J. Behavioral interventions for hyperactivity. In R. Trites (Ed.), *Hyperactivity in children: Etiology, measurement and treatment implications*. Baltimore, Md.: University Park Press, 1978.

McClure, L., Chinsky, J., and Larcen, S. Enhancing social problem-solving performance in an elementary school setting. *Journal of Educational Psychology*, 1978, *70*, 504-513.

Meichenbaum, D. Cognitive modifications of test anxious college students. *Journal of Consulting and Clinical Psychology*, 1972, *39*, 370-382.

———. Enhancing creativity by modifying what subjects say to themselves. *American Educational Research Journal*, 1975, *12*, 129-145.

———. Toward a cognitive theory of self-control. In G. Schwartz and D. Shapiro (Eds.), *Consciousness and self regulation*. Vol. 1. New York: Plenum Press, 1976.

———. *Cognitive-behavior modification: An integrative approach*. New York: Plenum Press, 1977.

———. Cognitive behavior modification newsletter. Volumes 1, 2, 3, and 4. Unpublished manuscripts, University of Waterloo, 1975-1979.

———. Teaching children self-control. In B. Lahey and A. Kazdin (Eds.), *Advances in child clinical psychology*. Vol. 2. New York: Plenum Press, 1978.

Meichenbaum, D., and Asarnow, J. Cognitive-behavior modification and metacognitive development: Implications for the classroom. In P. Kendall and S. Hollon (Eds.), *Cognitive behavioral interventions: Theory research and procedures*. New York: Academic Press, in press.

Meichenbaum, D., and Butler, L. Toward a conceptual model for the treatment of test anxiety: Implications for research and treatment. In I. Sarason (Ed.), *Test anxiety: Theory, research and applications*. New York: Lawrence Erlbaum, in press.

Meichenbaum, D., and Genest, M. Treatment of anxiety. In G. Harris (Ed.), *The group treatment of human problems: A social learning approach*. New York: Grune and Stratton, 1977.

Meichenbaum, D., and Goodman, J. Training impulsive children to talk to themselves: A means of developing self-control. *Journal of Abnormal Psychology*, 1971, *77*, 115-126.

Meichenbaum, D., and Novaco, R. Stress inoculation: A preventative approach. In C. Spielberger and I. Sarason (Eds.), *Stress and anxiety*, Vol. 5. New York: Halstead Press, 1977.

Meijers, J. *Problem-solving therapy with socially anxious children*. Amsterdam, The Netherlands: Alblasserdam-Kanters, B.V., 1978.

Meyers, M., and Paris, S. Children's metacognitive knowledge about reading. *Journal of Educational psychology*, 1978, *70*, 680-690.

Miller, P., and Bigi, L. Children's understanding of attention, or You know I can't hear you when the water's running. Unpublished manuscript, University of Michigan, 1976.

Mischel, W. Toward a cognitive social learning reconceptualization of personality. *Psychological Review*, 1973, *80*, 252-283.

Mischel, W., Mischel, H., and Hood, S. The development of knowledge of effective ideation to delay gratification. Unpublished manuscript, Stanford University, 1978.

Monahan, J., and O'Leary, D. Effects of self-instruction on rule-breaking behavior. *Psychological Reports*, 1971, *29*, 1059-1066.

Murray, H. *Explorations in personality*. New York: Oxford Press, 1938.

Murray, E., and Jacobson, L. Cognition and learning in traditional and behavioral therapy. In S. Garfield and A. Bergin (Eds.), *Handbook of psychotherapy and behavior change*. Second Edition. New York: John Wiley, 1979.

Nelson, W., and Birkimer, J. Role of self-instruction and self-reinforcement in the modification of impulsivity. *Journal of Consulting and Clinical Psychology*, 1978, *46*, 183.

Novaco, R. *Anger control: The development and evaluation of an experimental treatment*. Lexington, Mass.: Lexington Books, 1975.

————. A stress inoculation approach to anger management in the training of law enforcement officers. *American Journal of Community Psychology*, 1977, *5*, 327-346.

————. The cognitive regulation of anger and stress. In P. Kendall and S. Hollon (Eds.), *Cognitive-behavioral interventions: Theory research and procedures*. New York: Academic Press, in press.

O'Malley, J., and Eisenberg, L. The hyperkinetic syndrome. *Seminars in Psychiatry*, 1973, *5*, 95-103.

Palkes, H., Stewart, M., and Freedman, J. Improvement in maze performance on hyperactive boys as a function of verbal training procedures. *Journal of Special Education*, 1972, *5*, 237-342.

Palkes, H., Stewart, M., and Kahana, B. Porteus maze performance after training in self-directed verbal commands. *Child Development*, 1968, *39*, 817-826.

Plutchik, R., and Ax, A. A critique of "Determinant of emotional states" by Schachter and Singer (1962). *Psychophysiology*, 1967, *4*, 79-82.

Poitras-Martin, D., and Stone, G. Psychological education: A skill-oriented approach. *Journal of Counseling Psychology*, 1977, *24*, 153-157.

Rathjen, D., Rathjen, E., and Hiniker, A. A cognitive analysis of social performance. In J. Foreyt and D. Rathjen (Eds.), *Cognitive behavior therapy: Research and application*. New York: Plenum Press, 1978.

Robertson, D., and Keeley, S. Evaluation of a mediational training program for impulsive children by a multiple case study design. Paper presented at American Psychological Association, 1974.

Robin, A., Kent, R., O'Leary, D., Foster, S., and Prinz, R. An approach to teaching parents and adolescents problem solving communication skills: A preliminary report, *Behavior Therapy*, 1971, *8*, 639-643.

Robin, A., Schneider, M., and Dolnick, M. The turtle technique: An extended case study of self-control in the classroom. *Psychology in the Schools*. 1976, *13*, 449-453.

Rogers-Warren, A., and Baer, D. Correspondence between saying and doing: Teaching children to share and praise. *Journal of Applied Behavior Analysis*, 1976, *9*, 335-354.

Rook, K., and Hammen, C. A cognitive perspective on the experience of sexual arousal. *Journal of Social Issues*, 1977, *33*, 7-29.

Rosenthal, T. Applying a cognitive behavioral view to clinical and social problems. In G. Whitehurst and B. Zimmerman (Eds.), *The functions of language and cognition*. New York: Academic Press, in press.

Rush, A., Beck, A., Kovacs, M., and Hollon, S. Comparative efficacy of cognitive therapy and pharmacotherapy in the treatment of depressed outpatients. *Cognitive Therapy and Research*, 1977, *1*, 17-38.

Russell, M., and Thoresen, C. Teaching decision-making skills to children. In J. Krumboltz & C. Thoresen (Eds.), *Counseling methods*. New York: Holt Rinehart and Winston, 1976.

Rychtarik, R., and Wollersheim, J. The role of cognitive mediators in alcohol addiction with some implications for treatment. *Journal Supplement Abstract Service*, Manuscript number 1763, 1978.

Schachter, S. The interaction of cognitive and physiological determinants of emotional state. In C. Spielberger (Ed.), *Anxiety and behavior*. New York: Academic Press, 1966.

Schachter, S., and Singer, J. Cognitive social and physiological determinants of emotional state. *Psychological Review*, 1962, *69*, 379-399.

Schneider, M., and Robin, A. The turtle technique: A method for the self-control of impulsive behavior. In J. Krumboltz and C. Thoresen (Eds.), *Counseling methods*. New York: Holt, Rinehart and Winston, 1976.

Shaw, B. Comparison of cognitive therapy and behavior therapy in the treatment of depression. *Journal of Consulting and Clinical Psychology*, 1977, *45*, 543-551.

Shure, M., and Spivack, G. *Problem solving techniques in childrearing.* San Francisco: Jossey-Bass, 1978.

Snyder, J., and White, M. The use of cognitive self-instruction in the treatment of behaviorally disturbed adolescents. Unpublished manuscript, Wichita State University, 1977.

Spivack, G., Platt, J., and Shure, M. *The problem solving approach to adjustment.* San Francisco, Jossey Bass, 1976.

Spivack, G., and Shure, M. *Social adjustment of young children: A cognitive approach to solving real-life problems.* San Francisco: Jossey Boss, 1974.

Stokes, T., and Baer, D. An implicit technology of generalization. *Journal of Applied Behavior Analysis,* 1977, *10,* 349-367.

Stone, G., Hinds, W., and Schmidt, G. Teaching mental health behaviors to elementary school children. *Professional Psychology,* 1975, *6,* 34-40.

Suinn, R., and Richardson, F. Anxiety management training: A nonspecific behavior therapy program for anxiety control. *Behavior Therapy,* 1971, *2,* 498-510.

Taylor, F., and Marshall, W. Experimental analysis of a cognitive-behavioral therapy for depression. *Cognitive Therapy and Research,* 1977, *1,* 59-72.

Thorpe, G. Desensitization, behavioral rehearsal, self-instructional training and placebo effects on assertive-refusal behavior. *European Journal of Behavioral Analysis and Modification,* 1975, *1,* 30-44.

Toulmin, S. The Mozart of psychology. *New York Review of Books,* 1978, *25,* 50-56.

Turk, D. Coping with pain. A review of cognitive control techniques. In M. Feuerstein, L. Sachs and I. Turkat (Eds.), *Psychological approaches to pain control;* in press.

Ullmann, L., and Krasner, L. *Case studies in behavior modification.* New York: Holt, Rinehart and Winston, 1965.

Varni, J., and Henker, B. A self-regulation approach to the treatment of the hyperactive child. *Behavior Therapy,* in press.

Vygotsky, L. *Thought and Language.* New York: Wiley, 1962.

Watson, D., and Hall, D. Self-control of hyperactivity. Unpublished manuscript, LaMesa School District, 1977.

Whalen, C., and Henker B. Psychostimulants and children: A review and analysis. *Psychological Bulletin,* 1976, *83,* 1113-1130.

Wine, J. Cognitive attentional theory of test anxiety. In I. Sarason (Ed.), *Test anxiety: Theory, research and application.* New York: Lawrence Erlbaum, in press.

Zane, M. Contextual analysis and treatment of phobic behavior as it changes. *American Journal of Psychotherapy,* 1978, *32,* 338-356.

Zelniker, T., and Oppenheimer, L. Modification of information processing of impulsive children. *Child Development,* 1973, *44,* 445-450.

12
Expectations, Hypnosis, and Suggestion in Behavior Change
William C. Coe†

THE ROLE OF EXPECTATION IN THERAPEUTIC CHANGE

The task in this chapter is twofold: clarifying the role that expectation plays in enhancing positive change, and demonstrating the use of hypnotic and suggestive techniques to help people change. These topics are only related through the general effects which expectations have on all therapies. The effectiveness of hypnotic or suggestive therapies rests no more on expectancy effects than do any other forms of therapy. While they offer examples of the use of expectancy in psychotherapy, other approaches could as easily be used for the same purpose.

The importance of a person's expectations to the outcome of treatment has long been recognized. Similarities among healers from many persuasions, including witchdoctors and psychotherapists, have been pointed out, and the importance of expectations may overshadow effects of the treatments they claim to administer. Drugs and other therapies appear at times to be no more effective than the patient's faith in the treatment. These curative effects are often called placebo effects or side effects, which is meant to point out that they are not specific to the treatment effects or purposely created. They exist nevertheless, sometimes to a remarkable degree, and should therefore be considered in administering helping procedures.

†I am indebted to Harrison Madden for his thoughtful comments on the manuscript. His suggestions about induction, therapeutic strategies and meditation were especially helpful.

Three Principles Related to Healers and Healing

Torrey (1972) suggests that a patient's faith and motivation for improvement are determined by several factors: (1) the degree to which the therapist's ability to name the disease and its cause agrees with the views of the patient; (2) the degree to which the therapeutic techniques employed are considered by the patient to be of value in helping him; and (3) the degree to which the therapist's personal qualities match the patient's expectations of what a therapist should be like.

Each principle encompasses strong cultural and subcultural value components, both for the therapist and for the patient. Therapists need to be aware of the effects these factors may have, adjusting their approach in order to maximize their therapeutic potential. For example, when therapists find themselves trying to persuade a client to accept the therapist's personal views about therapy, (with which the client disagrees) it may be best to refer the client to another therapist whose views are more congruent with the client's beliefs and values.

Naming the Problem and Its Cause. Naming the disease entity may in and of itself be effective in alleviating many of the client's problems. Being able to assign a label and point out a cause indicates to the client that there is someone who understands what is happening to him. Labeling also implies that something can be done to alleviate the suffering. However, when the healer's label does not agree with the client's view of "mental illness" (or psychological maladjustment), further therapeutic contact is less likely to be helpful. If, for example, the client views psychological problems as being related to unconscious repression of traumatic childhood experiences, the label of a therapist who shares these views is much more likely to be perceived as competent, and thereby enhance the client's faith. For a therapist of a different persuasion to be effective, he must at least begin by working from the client's viewpoint, and/or spend a considerable amount of time reeducating the patient to the therapist's particular views.

Another example is that of very religious persons who attribute their suffering to punishment for their sins. Such persons might profit more by seeing a priest for confession and atonement than they would by seeing a psychotherapist who views their problems in behavioral and environmental terms. Such persons may view a behavior therapist as one who does not understand the "workings of God."

Congruence of beliefs and therapeutic techniques. Therapists' treatment procedures logically follow from their views of causation. The behavioral therapist employs techniques for learning and unlearning habits, the psychoanalyst uses techniques for discovering unconscious conflicts, and so on. Likewise, depending upon their beliefs of why they are suffering, clients have expectations about the kinds of techniques that will benefit them. The client's cultural or subcultural milieu are often important in this respect.

Illustrative is the problem found in Anglo clinics trying to help Mexican-

Americans. Therapists who do not recognize the importance of Mexican-American social norms will have difficulty as helpers. For example, if a Mexican-American couple comes for marital problems, it is important to recognize the accepted roles of men and women within their subculture. Teaching the woman to enjoy sexual intercourse and/or to become more dominant in her relationship with her husband, will most likely serve no useful function in maintaining their marriage. The Mexican woman generally expects and is expected to be submissive and not to enjoy sexual intercourse. A dominant wife threatens the male's masculine identity, and a woman who enjoys sex is suspected of being promiscuous (Torrey, 1972). It is unlikely that this couple would return for therapy with such a "naive, degenerate" therapist. The *curandero* of their subculture, the priest of the church, would probably be of more help. He would be more likely to share the couple's views and expectations and better able to implement steps toward change.

Personal qualities of the therapist. Everyone has his own view of how a psychologist or psychiatrist should look and behave. Views vary a great deal from, "They're all crazy!" to "They're all wise, knowledgeable and helpful." In general, people who contact therapists do so on the assumption that they are authorities who hold competencies that will be of help. This expectation in itself may enhance resolving their problems. The therapist's office may also have an effect. Diplomas, certificates of membership in prestigious professional organizations, licenses, and other emblems establishing the therapist as a legitimate healer in American culture, enhance the client's expectancies of being helped. The location of the office may also be a factor. Clients who hold common middle class values may be quite impressed by a "plush" office, as it indicates financial success and, by association, professional success. Clients who are less conformist may have an opposite reaction, categorizing the therapist as "straight" and as someone who is unable to understand their views.

Some recent experimental evidence supports these notions. Bloom, Weigel and Trautt (1977) examined the effects of office decor (traditional versus humanistic) and therapist sex on the therapist's credibility. They found that male therapists in traditionally decorated offices were perceived as more credible than their counterparts in humanistic offices, but female therapists were perceived as more credible in the humanistic setting than they were in the traditional setting.

The dress and grooming of the therapist may have similar effects. Long hair, styled hair, mod clothing or business suits, among other characteristics, will tend initially to label the therapist for the client, and these early impressions may help or hinder therapy. Clearly, the physical surroundings and the therapist's appearance can have important effects. Alert therapists will recognize these effects and work to arrange (or rearrange) them in their favor.

Therapist qualities of warmth, genuineness, and understanding have been emphasized by Lazarus (1971) among others. As a general rule, these qualities seem desirable regardless of the therapist's theoretical orientation. People differ, however, about the degree of activity they expect of therapists, how directive or passive they should be, and the relative amount of time they should spend talking during the session. For example, a businessman who expects to unload his tensions through cathartic sessions would probably expect and desire traditional, listening therapists as opposed to therapists who are quite active in their sessions. It is up to individual therapists to be alert to their clients' expectations and to employ them advantageously.

Recently, Beutler, Pollack and Jobe (1978) found that the acceptance or rejection of values in the client-therapist relationship were related to process variables and therapeutic outcome. Their major finding was a strong positive relationship ($r = .76$, $p < .01$) between global improvement and the degree to which clients adopted their therapist's values. They also found, however, that clients' or therapists' acceptance of each others' values need not be complete. "Apparently, the therapists' attitude toward the patients' values has its greatest impact on the patients' feeling of growth, and patients' attitude toward the therapists' values seem more strongly related to the development of trust and attraction . . ." (p. 199).

Perhaps one of the most important variables is the therapist's belief that a client can be helped. A study by Lerner and Fiske (1973) showed that the therapist's belief that he could help a client was a better predictor of outcome than such client attributes as socioeconomic level, which has been claimed to predict outcome in the past. It seems quite likely that therapists subtly communicate their optimism or pessimism to their clients, and thereby affect their clients' expectations of a positive or negative outcome.

Finally, and related to the therapist's expectations for his client's success, is the plausibility of the therapist's techniques to the client. That is, if clients can be convinced that a particular procedure will alleviate their suffering, the probability of success is substantially raised. For example, McReynolds, et al. (1973) found that systematic desensitization, a behavioral technique for treating phobias, was no more effective than other techniques presented in an equally convincing way. The degree to which techniques are convincing to clients is influenced by all of the variables we have discussed so far and illustrates their importance in therapy.

Techniques for Enhancing Expectation Effects

All of the variables described above may be important in enhancing client expectations of being helped. Torrey (1972) discusses three suggestive techniques that are widely utilized in our culture for enhancing expectations: direct suggestion, symbolism, and magical formulas.

Direct suggestion may be intentionally or unintentionally employed by physicians and psychotherapists in the course of their contact with their clients. As examples, while writing a prescription for a drug, physicians may say, "Take this and you will feel better." In so doing, they give a direct suggestion that the drug is effective, thereby raising the client's expectations for success. Or, as behavior therapists outline programs for change, they may add something like, "This program will help you accomplish your goals," or "You will find this program easy to follow and effective in . . ." Again, a direct suggestion to expect success is given. The antithesis of these positive suggestions would be something like: "Well, we might as well try such and such, what have we got to lose?" At best, the client hopes whatever it is will work, even though the therapist seems doubtful.

As Americans become more familiar with Eastern cultures and religions, the use of symbolism is gaining importance. Symbolism exists in the form of rituals which are believed to bring about certain desired end states, such as relaxation, symptom removal or contact with God. Hypnosis and relaxation training are the most popular forms of symbolism employed in American psychotherapy and will be covered more extensively in later portions of this chapter. Meditation approaches also include symbolic rituals, which are becoming more widely accepted. Humanistic and psychoanalytic procedures include rituals as well.

Symbolic rituals may be of tremendous importance in enhancing the effectiveness of therapy for some people. The performance of the hypnotic induction ritual, for example, is a signal that something profound and of great importance might occur. Rituals not only enhance the client's expectations but therapists are often equally as convinced of their effectiveness, further enhancing the effect for the client. Rituals are only effective, however, insofar as they jibe with other expectations and beliefs of clients. When they are counter to their beliefs, they can have a detracting effect.

Magical formulas exist in our society mainly in the form of psychoactive, prescription drugs. For example, there are over-worked housewives who will attest to the effectiveness of tranquilizers prescribed by her family physician, even when they are really sugar pills (placebos). They help her through the drudgery of housework and to be more patient with her children. Mental health propaganda has convinced her that her stress is caused by a "nervous condition," and her physician has confirmed her diagnosis. Her physician has also prescribed an acceptable cure in our culture, a pill, accompanied with the statement, "Almost without exception, these conditions are helped by taking one of these tablets each morning." This effect, of course, is not limited to housewives. Many persons in our culture accept the prescription of medications as solutions to problems.

In another culture, physicians might find magic formulas effective in a different way. A member of a "primitive" society may profit more by wearing the physician's prescription in a sack around his neck, in the manner of his society's rituals for healing, than by ingesting it. Their expectations about illness and treatment are quite different from those of Americans. They believe that evil spirits cause illness and that "medicine" serves to drive them away. Therefore, why not keep it near at all times and even save it for a friend or relative who may become afflicted later?

In sum, suggestion may be a major consideration for enhancing the effectiveness of many therapies. Suggestions may be of considerable benefit, providing they are congruent with clients' views of the world, and their expectations for therapy. Frank (1961 and 1972) also presents evidence for the importance of expectancy variables in both medical and psychological therapies. His work has shown that any treatment which reduces anxiety and arouses hope, can effect a cure.

Applying Expectation and Social Influence in Therapy

Placebo Therapy. Fish (1973) has examined the application of expectancies in therapy, specifically, the use of placebos. Therapy is viewed as occurring in three major stages: pre-therapy, therapy, and post-therapy. The last stage, post-therapy, deals less directly with expectancy, but the pre-therapy and therapy stages necessitate the consideration of these variables for successful implementation.

Considerations during the pre-therapy (the placebo formulation stage) include the qualities of the therapist, and the client's problems, expectations and world view. Knowledge of these factors is essential in drawing up a therapeutic contract which takes advantage of placebo principles.

In the therapy stage, the strategies devised in the pre-therapy stage are implemented. It is communicated to clients that a cure will result if they do certain things, and the healing ritual begins. Once positive changes occur, the therapist can refer to them as proof of the treatment's effectiveness, creating further expectancies which enhance the client's response to treatment.

The post-therapy stage consists of steps designed to maintain the cure. Self-reliance is emphasized as are changes in the client's environment.

Social Influence Therapy. Gillis (1979, Gillis and Berren, 1975) sees his approach as a new school of psychotherapy. His ideas are based on previous studies of the therapeutic process (e.g., Fish, 1973; Frank, 1973; Goldstein, 1975; Strong and Matross, 1973), but he has systematized the social psychological views of these studies and emphasizes this view in the therapist-client interaction. The central aspect of his position is that the important events in psychotherapy are the result of therapists gaining a position of power in the relationship with their clients and then using their power to convince clients that they should adopt a new way of seeing themselves and their situations. Establishing this position of influence, and the concomitant belief by the client that therapy will be of benefit, are the critical elements of effective therapy. Specific therapeutic techniques which are applied (insight, reflection of feelings, positive reinforcement, etc.) are important only insofar as they provide a vehicle for establishing influence and delivering the healing message.

Gillis believes that all psychotherapies have a common basis in the nature of the relationship between the partners. He cites several aspects of current research in psychotherapy to support this notion: (1) psychotherapies from various theoretical persuasions appear to be almost equally effective; (2) nonprofessional approaches (e.g., A.A., Synanon) seem as effective as professional; (3) persons with minimal training in orthodox procedures appear equally as effective as their highly trained counterparts; and (4) evidence for the effectiveness of "extraordinary techniques" (e.g., nude encounters, primal scream) all point to the likelihood that the effectiveness of psychotherapy has little to do with theoretical systems or specific techniques. Further, the evidence for placebo and expectation effects in medicine and psychology provide evidence for the importance of interpersonal influence processes. As a result, the essential goal of psychotherapy is a change in clients' perspectives in the ways that they regard their situations.

To bring about the above goal, therapeutic strategies can be derived from the literature on influence and power in relationships. These strategies may then be employed directly in order to enhance the influencing capacity of the therapist, which leads to positive therapeutic outcomes.

Gillis postulates three stages of therapy. Each is outlined below along with examples of therapeutic gambits used in each.

Stage 1—Enhancing expectations of benefits: The first task is having the client take the therapist seriously and to come to believe that therapy can be beneficial. Three separate tactical operations are suggested to accomplish this goal.

One method may be to increase the clients' commitment to therapy by increasing the severity of "initiation rites." If clients must invest energy in order to enter therapy, they will value it more. The point is to present preliminary events which the client experiences so that he feels he has given some time and effort to becoming a part of therapy. For example, clients may be required to undergo time-consuming psychological tests; they may have to sign up on waiting lists for an appointment, or they may initially be given an appointment hour which is not convenient. The point is not to create undue stress or capriciously withhold assistance in cases where clients are obviously in need of help, nor are such tactics recommended for persons who are initially unmotivated to commit themselves to therapy—they may use them as an excuse not to come back. But such techniques may be effective for clients.

Second, it is important for clients to believe that therapy is helpful. One group of clients may be asked to help by talking highly of their own therapy experience to other clients in the waiting room. An older client's participation in this way also helps to increase his own beliefs in the benefits of therapy.

Third, it is important that the prestige of the therapist be enhanced in the clients' view. To this end, the clinic secretary may remark how fortunate a client is that he was assigned to Dr. X because many clients seem to prefer Dr. X. Another tactic is to have colleagues interrupt therapy sessions on the pretense that they need Dr. X's advice on important matters.

Gillis cautions, however, that expectations of positive results from therapy may backfire when clients expect too much. Should this be the case, countermeasures are suggested. For instance, clients are assured that "things often get worse before they get better,'' or that therapy is painful but the pain often precedes the benefits to come.

The therapist must also maintain the client's esteem. Interpretations which are always correct to some extent (''no miss'') can be useful to this end. For example, ''Underneath that anger there's an awful lot of hurt,'' or ''Your problem seems not so much a personal failing as it is an unrealistically high standard you hold for yourself.'' Other such comments can be constructed from contemporary concerns, like the need for better communications, the need to express feelings directly, etc. The point is that popular ways of viewing difficulties are likely to be believed by the client, and when the therapist points them out, it should reflect positively on the client's perception of the therapist as wise.

Other credibility-maintaining statements can come from remarks which suggest that the therapist holds special knowledge about unconscious processes. For example, remarks on nonverbal communications can enhance the therapist's power—''You seem calm as you say that, but the tightness in your body tells me that it must mean more to you.'' Comments on unconscious feelings can also be helpful. For example, ''I believe that unconsciously there is more anger there than you can admit at this point,'' or ''While you say it doesn't bother you much, there must be some unconscious resentment.''

Stage 2—Establishing a position of power: Overlapping with the first stage, this stage uses other tactics to enhance and solidify the power of the therapist in the relationship. Two broad categories are recognized: command power and friendship power.

Command power is the power derived from being an expert, someone who can directly control the relationship in a superior-subordinate sense. Some examples of procedures for establishing command power are: (1) the use of powerful arguments; (2) the use of physical force; and (3) the use of esoteric interpretations. Therapists may also employ confusion tactics. These tactics leave clients bewildered and unable to control the interaction. For example, the therapist may request the client to practice symptoms. Many other tactics are suggested by Gillis.

Friendship power results in an allegiance of the client to the therapist. The therapist gains the position of being able to make demands on the client because of the attractiveness of the relationship. ''Baring the throat'' amounts to the therapist admitting to the client that he is failing in his efforts to help the client. The result is that the client tries to be more helpful. However, a therapist must be quite sure of himself and have sufficient experience to employ such a move at the appropriate time. These sorts of approaches require caution to prevent their backfiring.

Ingratiation tactics, which are techniques meant to make oneself more attractive to others, may also be used. Some are: expressing liking for the other; flattering the other, stressing similarities between one another, announcing your best attributes in a noncompetitive way. As Gillis states, there are innumerable ways of making oneself more likable and attractive. They are ''limited only by the ingenuity of the therapist.''

Stage 3—Using the power to implement change: During this stage the healing rituals are invoked. The main task for the clinician is to choose one which makes sense to the client in that it will help. Gillis considers several factors of critical importance at this stage: (1) Clients should be given evidence that they are improving. This can be done by graphs, as behaviorists tend to do, or in more subtle ways as other therapists do; (2) Clients should be inspired to act as if they have a desirable attribute by suggesting that they in fact do have it. One technique is the "hidden agenda." The therapist takes whatever the client is doing as an example of the kind of response toward which they have been working. The client is complimented on his progress; (3) "Repetition" of noted changes in the desired direction can also be effective. Gillis cites an example of a marital therapist who continued to inform a couple that the husband was becoming more forceful and the wife less dominant in their relationship, even when there was little objective evidence that that was the case. The couple increasingly came to take on the roles attributed to each of them.

The way in which the problem is defined makes the task of demonstrating improvement easier. It is probably best to leave the definition of the problem vague enough so that the therapist is relatively free to demonstrate progress at will. For example, the problem may be defined as "poor communication," or "existential dilemma." Some goals are also relatively easy to achieve, such as "expressing anger." Defining the problem as one like these makes it more flexible to tactical employment. When a client has difficulty in defining the problem it may be especially useful for the therapist to define it for the client, and in such a way that they can then proceed to solve it.

A final change maneuver is "simply telling the patient to act, think or feel differently." The probability of the client following directions is greatly increased if the power of the therapist has been established in the relationship.

Gillis recognizes that his approach has not been adequately evaluated from a scientific viewpoint although evidence from his work and that of his colleagues suggests that the techniques have short-term, positive effects (Berren and Gillis, 1976; Childress and Gillis, 1977; Friedenberg and Gillis, 1977; Gillis, 1974; Venzor, Gillis, and Beal, 1976). Nevertheless he feels justified in pursuing his school of thought as long as data is being gathered to evaluate its effectiveness. Other therapies have been employed for years with no more evidence for their effectiveness—though this is not sufficient justification in itself to start a new system of therapy.

Gillis also notes that the clients for whom influence therapy should be maximally useful are those who have been described as demoralized. Clients with nonspecific concerns regarding therapeutic goals make good candidates for influence maneuvers. Gillis recommends social influence therapy for clients who are anxious and depressed, who are losing hope, and feel they don't measure up to their own or others' expectations.

Finally, Gillis addresses the ethical issues which may be involved in the admitted manipulation of clients. Of course, for some therapists techniques which are designed to influence clients without their awareness will seem repugnant. Gillis recognizes this, but he places the ethical emphasis on assisting clients in reaching their presumed goals. His ethical concern lies with therapists who continue using "tactics of questionable effectiveness or who fail to submit their methods to empirical verification." In turn, he pledges to continue to evaluate his own tactics.

HYPNOSIS AND HYPNOTIC TECHNIQUES

Hypnosis has characteristically been associated with the mystical, the strange, the unusual and the dramatic. The mass media and popular literature nearly always report hynpotic experiences as the ultimate of wonderment—the dramatic cure, the multiple personality, or the powerful influence of the hypnotist. From the mesmerizer of the 18th century to the stage hypnotist of the present, the lay public has been exposed to hypnosis as a phenomenon of power and influence. The more conservative views of hypnosis, although present since its beginnings, have been given scant attention. In recent times hypnosis is being viewed increasingly as a legitimate therapeutic tool in medicine, dentistry, and psychotherapy. Less dramatic expectations are replacing the overstated ones, but an aura of mystery and sensationalism remains. Unfortunately, the image of hypnosis as mysterious has caused some practitioners to avoid its use, and persons who might benefit from it shy away. This same aura, on the other hand, opens its practice to otherwise unqualified persons who take advantage of people looking for the instant cure.

What is Hypnosis?

The usual hypnotic procedure is to begin by administering an "induction"— instructions which are designed to lead subjects from their usual ways of viewing the world (the "waking state") into a less critical, more receptive mode of functioning (the "trance state"). Clients are often requested to gaze at an object while the hypnotist repeats a variety of suggestions, including those leading to relaxation, heightened awareness of sensations, and tiring of the eyes. After their eyes close, the hypnotic state is deepened with further suggestions, usually of going deeper and deeper into hypnosis and becoming less and less aware of events other than the hypnotist's voice. In response to the hypnotist's requests, a good subject, may perform seemingly striking behaviors, like suggested changes in bodily sensations or selective forgetting.

Induction procedures and hypnotic suggestions are similar whether they are employed in group hypnosis, individual hypnosis, or self-hypnosis, the main difference lies in the number of people participating, and the presence or absence of a hypnotist.

Describing the usual operations in hypnosis is not, of course, a satisfactory scientific explanation of the nature of hypnosis. However, such an explanation has not yet been offered. While many questions remain, most of the earlier notions about a trance state, the excessive power of the hypnotist, and so on, are being replaced by less exaggerated, and more naturalistic explanations based on psychological and social psychological concepts (see, for example, Barber, Spanos and Chaves, 1974; Coe, 1978; Coe and Sarbin, 1977; Hilgard, 1977; Orne, 1977; Sarbin and Coe, 1972).

The uses of hypnosis and autosuggestion have been expanded and refined, but in many instances they are still quite similar to those employed a hundred years ago. It often seems that independent investigators have simply rediscovered the usefulness of self suggestions, or interactive suggestions, only to relabel them so they fit within a preferred theoretical framework.

Historical Background†

It is impossible to date exactly the first appearance of hypnotic or hypnotic-like techniques. Eastern cultures have long recognized the usefulness of meditative procedures and self-suggestion, but the acceptance of hypnosis into Western practice began less than two hundred years ago when a Viennese physician, Franz Antoine Mesmer (1734-1815) attempted to bring hypnotic phenomena under scientific study. His techniques came to be known as "mesmerism," a term still used to describe persons in trance-like states.

Employing the tenets of astrology, Mesmer believed that some principle must permeate the universe, a force that could be identified with electricity or magnetism. His thinking led him to experiment with the effects that magnets might have on his patients. He tried different methods—passing magnets over them, stroking their bodies, and so on. He obtained some cures, probably for afflictions which later came to be considered hysterical. To his surprise, however, he found that the magnet was not necessary. Simply making passes with his hands or stroking his patients, produced similar effects. Mesmer believed that he had discovered a source of universal force, that in some way he was able to redistribute his patients' bodily fluids in a curative way. He called this process "animal magnetism," postulating an animal fluid, a life force similar to magnetism, which he was able to redistribute thus bringing about a cure. His was the first theory to attribute clients' responses to the powers of the hypnotist.

Mesmer gained a great deal of notoriety in Paris and eventually scientific commissions were appointed to examine his claims. Their findings did not support his theory and he eventually fell into disrepute, but his followers continued to teach and practice the art of animal magnetism for many years throughout Europe and America.

†For a detailed history of hypnosis see Hilgard (1965) or Sarbin and Coe (1972).

James Eisdale, a British surgeon working in India, began using mesmerism for anesthetic purposes in the mid 1800's (chemical anesthetics had not yet been discovered). He reported over 100 operations where patients were apparently free from pain and the death rate from surgical shock was greatly reduced. About the same time, Ward, a physician in England, reported the amputation of a leg under mesmerism with no apparent pain. However, there was much furor over his report, with claims of deception marking its objective examination. Considering the pressing need, it would seem that mesmerism might have been admitted as a valid medical tool, and it might have been, but for the discovery of nitrous oxide (laughing gas), ether, and chloroform at about the same time. The anesthetic effects of these agents could be explained on a physiological basis and were thus more acceptable to the medical profession.

Mesmerism's acceptance came with a new theoretical explanation and a change of name. James Braid (1795-1860), a Scottish physician, became interested in mesmeric phenomena about the same time that Eisdale was performing his work. Braid was impressed by the fact that hypnotized subjects were unable to open their eyes, that a paralysis of the eye muscles had apparently taken place. He reasoned that a change in the nervous system had occurred because of the fatigue and paralysis of the nervous centers controlling the eyes. Thus he reinterpreted mesmeric behavior into more acceptable neurophysiological terms, naming the phenomena "nervous sleep" or "neurohypnotism"; later abbreviated to "hypnotism."

Hypnotism had finally been admitted to the arena of scientific controversy and study. The primary disputes from then on centered about its nature rather than whether or not it occurred. Since that time many respected scientists—Charcot, Bernheim, Janet, Freud, Binet, Wundt, Hull—studied hypnotic phenomena, and the various helping professions have slowly added it to their armementarium of therapeutic tools.

Considerations for Enhancing Expectancy Effects

Almost everyone has some ideas about hypnosis and the behaviors that occur in the hypnotic setting—the more their expectations are in agreement with the hypnotist's, the more likely it is that they will be good hypnotic subjects. It behooves hypnotists to clarify what they expect. However, if a person is unwilling to cooperate he cannot be hypnotized; the potential hypnotic subject must be motivated to enter the relationship. The closer the subject's expectations for his own conduct match the requests by the hypnotist, the more likely it is that he will be responsive. Coupled with motivational factors are certain abilities which appear to be required in hypnosis, that is, concentration and absorbed imagining. It is also clear, however, that a number of individuals will simply comply with the hypnotist's instructions and not experience their conduct as unusual.

The conditions of the environment and the characteristics of the hypnotist can make a difference in the level of responsiveness as well. Usually, both the setting

and the hypnotist's appearance are designed to encourage the subject's cooperation. Style of dress, age, general professional manner, and office decour all add
to the perception that the hypnotist is a competent, trustworthy person. Before
the hypnotic induction has begun, these factors have entered into the relationship
and have the potential for modifying the subject's response.

The wording of most inductions is aimed at increasing the subject's motivation
by providing cues which indicate what is expected of them. Initial suggestions
are usually quite easy to follow and usually center around body relaxation,
closing of the eyes, heaviness of the body. Suggestions gradually progress toward behaviors which require higher levels of imaginal ability and concentration
and are more difficult to perform.

The termination of hypnosis again usually provides clear instructions that
subjects can expect a shift in roles back to those of experimental subject or
nonhypnotized client. In fact, subjects who respond well may be trained to enter
hypnosis upon a brief signal which eliminates the need to repeat time-consuming
induction procedures in later sessions.

Induction of Hypnosis

The study of hypnosis has been greatly facilitated by the development of standard
measuring instruments which operationally define hypnosis. The items on these
scales have typically been associated with hypnotic behavior since Mesmer's
time.

The most commonly used scales today, the Stanford Hypnotic Susceptibility
Scales, Form A and B and Form C (SHSS) (Weitzenhoffer and Hilgard, 1959
and 1962) are work samples of hypnosis. Subjects are hypnotized and their
responses to typical hypnotic suggestions are recorded. Their total score (range
of 0-12) indicates the degree to which they have responded to hypnotic procedures. Administration requires approximately 45 minutes, with the hypnotist
reading the instructions verbatim. Because these scales are very structured, they
are especially useful for novice hypnotists who are still unsure of themselves with
induction procedures.

Administration of the scales, as with nearly all hypnotic approaches, begins
with a general discussion of hypnosis. It is an open-ended exchange in which an
attempt is made to reduce any fears or hesitancies subjects might have about
hypnosis. The purpose is to put them at ease, establish rapport, and enlist their
cooperation. A waking suggestion is then administered. Subjects are told that
hypnosis is primarily the response to suggestion and that the waking suggestion is
an example of what hypnosis will be like. "Postural sway" is the first item on
the SHSS, A and B. The hypnotist stands behind the subject and says that in a
moment he is going to be asked to think of falling backwards. The hypnotist
continues to suggest swaying and falling until the subject falls backward or until
the standard instructions have been completed.

After the waking suggestion, subjects are seated in a comfortable chair. A spot on the wall, slightly above eye level, serves as a point of concentration. Subjects are asked to concentrate on the spot while the hypnotist reads a standard induction procedure which consists of instructions to elicit further cooperation, increasing suggestions of heaviness, drowsiness, and relaxation, and finally suggestions of eye heaviness and lid closure. The hypnotist then gives suggestions to deepen the trance—counting backwards from 20 to one with the suggestion that with each count the subject will go deeper and deeper into a pleasant state of hypnosis. Ten hypnotic suggestions (items) are then administered. For example, "Your eyes are tightly shut, glued together, you cannot open them—try!" For clinical purposes, therapists may not want their clients to fail. The expectations of cooperative subjects may be increased when they respond positively to suggestions.

The SHSS, Form C includes more cognitive items which may be useful in clinical practice, for example, age regression, hypnotic dream, and positive and negative hallucinations. Again, the structure of this scale may be reassuring to the neophyte hypnotist. The scale also includes a section on autohypnosis, another induction technique, presented in some detail. It should be especially helpful where teaching relaxation is considered an important part of therapy.

Milton H. Erickson has been one of the major proponents of the use of hypnosis in psychotherapy and has made many contributions in the form of unique induction and therapeutic techniques. It is helpful to examine one of his induction techniques because it points out the wide variety of ways that influence communications may be phrased during hypnotic transactions. Erickson (1964; Erickson, Rossi and Rossi, 1976; Haley, 1967) describes a confusion technique which he reports to be effective for a variety of purposes. He claims it to be very helpful with resistant subjects who try to analyze what is happening during induction and therefore do not concentrate and respond well. A flow of words which is very difficult to understand and to follow is presented in a serious, intent manner. Erickson uses plays on words, changes in verb tenses, and irrelevancies that are meaningful out of context, but in the context of the verbal flow they are confusing and distracting. The point of the technique is described as follows: "Thus the subject is led almost to begin a response, is frustrated in this by then being presented with the next idea, and the whole process is repeated with a continued development of a state of inhibition, leading to confusion and the growing need to receive a clear-cut comprehensible communication to which he *can make* a ready and full response." (p. 183)

The following illustration of inducing hypnosis for the purpose of age regression shows how well Erickson incorporates irrelevant material, verb tenses, and so on to create confusion in subjects until they are ready to accept any clear path of understanding, and consequently, the hypnotist's suggestions.

I am so very glad you volunteered to be a subject. You probably enjoyed eating today. Most people do though sometimes they skip a meal. You probably ate breakfast this morning, maybe you will want tomorrow something you had today, you have eaten it before, perhaps on Friday like today. Maybe you will next week. Whether last week, this week, or next week, makes no difference. Thursday always comes before Friday. This was true last week, will be true next week and is so this week. Before Friday is Thursday and before June is May, but first there is 'whan that Aprille with its shoures soote,' and March followed the snows of February but who really remembers the 6th of February. And January 1st is the beginning of the New Year of 1963 and *all that it will bring*. But December brought Christmas. But Thanksgiving preceded Christmas and all that shopping to get done and what a good dinner. (p. 188)

These communications are then continued, introducing more factual material from the patient's history and progressively moving him backwards in time. (In the above example the quote from Chaucer about April was personally relevant to the patient. It carried associations with a definite date in his history.) Although most of Erikson's work is based on clinical report, his examples are usually convincing and offer new ideas for more stringent testing.

A technique called "pacing" (Bandler and Grinder, 1975) may be useful as a transition to other induction techniques. The point is for the hypnotist to provide overt and/or covert feedback on any part of the client's ongoing experience. Examples of overt pacing would be verbal comments like these: "As you sit there in the chair, listening to my voice, with your feet resting on the floor . . ." Covert pacing includes feedback which does not appear to be consciously intended by the hypnotist. As examples, mirroring the client's posture or hand placements, assuming his verbal tone and speed, breathing in rhythm with the client. Pacing is believed to produce the feeling in clients that the hypnotist is "with" them, "understands" them and that they are in "good hands."

There are many ways of inducing hypnosis and it is not clear that one is more effective than another. It is probably a good idea for therapists to be familiar with several techniques. Weitzenhoffer (1957) and Kroger (1977) offer numerous methods.

There is also evidence that the usual inductions of hypnosis are not necessary to bring about increased responsiveness to suggestions. T.X. Barber and his colleagues (1965; 1969; 1978; Barber, Spanos and Chaves, 1974) have shown that instructions to imagine and instructions which motivate subjects (task-motivating instructions) result in increased responsiveness to many of the usual kinds of hypnotic suggestions. These sorts of instructions, as opposed to calling the procedure "hypnosis," may be potentially useful when subjects appear to have negative attitudes towards hypnosis.

Barber and Wilson (1977) and Wilson and Barber (1978) have recently developed a nonauthoritarian technique, responses to which they measure with their Creative Imagination Scale. Their technique is to use "think-with" instructions which are meant to demonstrate how subjects can use their imaginations creatively to experience certain events and to create positive attitudes and expectations that they will be able to do so. They introduce "think-with" instructions by giving examples of what to do: "Think of the scene and become involved in it."—and what not to do—"Do not take the negative attitude that you cannot do it.'' Positive attitudes toward being able to imagine creatively along with such examples precede the actual administration of the scale. (Verbatim instructions are presented in Barber and Wilson, 1977, p. 46). If Barber's findings are stable, ''think-with'' instructions may be more effective than techniques which have been historically employed to induce hypnosis.

Increasing Responsiveness to Hypnosis

A question related to induction procedures has to do with increasing a person's responsiveness to hypnotic (or nonhypnotic) suggestions. It was believed earlier that hypnotic responsiveness was a rather stable trait of the person (Hilgard, 1965). Repeated administrations of hypnosis resulted in shorter induction times but little or no increase in responsiveness to suggestions. Also, in support of a stable trait explanation, longitudinal study over a period of years showed high positive correlations for hypnotic responsiveness.

Various techniques have been tested more recently which suggest that responsiveness can be increased, especially in moderately low and moderately susceptible subjects (Diamond, 1974; 1977a; 1977b). Studies which have demonstrated increases in responsiveness have employed specific procedures other than the usual hypnotic induction. Diamond (1977a) outlines what appear to him to be the three core components of these procedures:

1. *Optimal learning factors:* Included here are procedures which (a) increase subjects' motivations to experience hypnosis, (b) increase attention to the hypnotist and the training procedures, (c) employ successive approximations to the desired response (shaping), (d) provide practice of newly learned responses, (e) offer reinforcement for successful experiences, and (f) provide feedback on the appropriateness of subjects' responses.

2. *Attitudinal and set:* These procedures include methods which increase subjects' motivations and positive acceptance of hypnosis before the actual experience begins. They include relaxation, reduction of fears, attitudes or expectations which interfere, building of interpersonal trust, and demonstrations of receptive perception.

3. *Cognitive strategy:* Diamond believes this factor to be the most important of the three. Procedures are aimed at teaching subjects optimal ways to respond internally to hypnotic instructions in order to experience them. Included are (a) suspending reality concerns, (b) controlling imaginations in accord with the aims of the suggestions, and (c) focusing thought and attention on the suggestions.

As far as therapy is concerned, it is not at all clear that high levels of hypnotic responsiveness are necessary for most purposes. Nor is it clear that hypnotic imagery is more useful than nonhypnotic imagery. It is possible that the expectations which clients hold for hypnosis are the most important aspects for therapeutic outcome. Nevertheless, the procedures outlined above should offer helpful guidelines for clinicians who wish to increase hypnotic responsiveness in their clients.

Evaluative Uses (Diagnosis)

Hypnosis has been employed as a diagnostic tool by therapists of psychodynamic orientations.

One use is to explore the basis for physical complaints which cannot be attributed to organic pathology. The patient may be hypnotized after which it is suggested that his symptoms will disappear. If the symptoms in fact, disappear, the difficulty is believed to be functional (nonorganic). Dramatic results have been observed in some cases. A patient whose arm is paralyzed, for instance, may have complete freedom of movement following hypnotic suggestions to that effect. There is a problem however with this symptom-removal technique. It is possible that hypnotically induced analgesia could mask the actual pain from a physical disorder. For example, suggesting that a patient who complains of back pain will no longer feel the pain and be able to stand upright, may accomplish this task during the hypnotic session. However, the possibility of a physical cause for the complaint of pain cannot be eliminated on this basis alone.

Another psychodynamic diagnostic method seeks to use hypnosis as a vehicle for uncovering psychological conflicts which are believed to underlie physical disorders. Rosen (1953) applied hypnosis in this manner to patients whose physical difficulties had not responded to medical diagnosis and treatment. He often does not inform patients that they are to be hypnotized, but explains that he is going to demonstrate a method that will help them to relax. They are told to focus on the bodily region of their discomfort, that their attention may wander but it will return. The patient's reactions are used to help induce hypnosis. The clinician times his speech to the client's breathing and comments on behaviors that occur spontaneously—(flushing, tremulousness, foot tapping, and so on), sometimes before the patient has become aware of them. Remarks on these naturally occurring phenomena are made in such a way as to lead the patient to believe that they follow a physiological pattern which is to be expected. Then, the patient is told that other phenomena, which the hypnotist describes in minute detail, will occur. However, these phenomena are impossible on a physiological or anatomical basis, for example, the patient's hand is numb (glove anesthesia). When these phenomena occur they must therefore be in response to the hypnotist's suggestions and indicate that the patient is being led into hypnosis. The therapist then proceeds in various ways to try and uncover the psychological reasons behind the difficulty.

Fantasy evoking methods are often used to uncover psychological dynamics. One technique is to suggest that the patient is seated in a theater whereupon the master of ceremonies appears in front of the curtain. It is suggested in detail that the master of ceremonies is experiencing the same symptoms as those of the patient. It is then suggested that the curtain is opening and a shocked look crosses the face of the master of ceremonies—a look of surprise, because on the stage, he sees the cause of the symptoms. The therapist then waits for signs of emotional responses before asking for a description of the scene. The scene may have personal relevance to the patient's difficulties and thereby help to direct further psychotherapeutic efforts.

Therapeutic Uses

Suggestive Approach. It would seem that the most direct therapeutic use of hypnosis is to suggest that patients' symptoms would disappear after they awake. This posthypnotic suggestion technique is an old approach and typical of Freud's early work with hypnosis. Numerous reports have indicated that symptoms can be effectively eliminated in this way. However, there is still a good deal of controversy about simply removing symptoms because many psychoanalytically oriented therapists believe that the symptom may be replaced by one which is more debilitating, or its loss may bring on a severe underlying psychological disorder and worsen the patient's condition. As a consequence, an alternative technique has been developed by therapists who are concerned about the possibility of symptom substitution.

Rather than suggesting that the patient will be symptom free, a less debilitating symptom can be suggested in its place. That is, the hypnotist gives the patient a substitute symptom to serve the function of the original one. A salesman with a facial tic might be treated by suggesting that the tic would move to a less obvious part of his body, such as his toe or finger and thereby interfere less in his occupation.

Karlin and McKeon (1976) have nevertheless recommended the symptom removal approach through hypnosis within the broader framework of Lazarus's (1976) behaviorally-oriented multimodal therapy. They reason that if a client's pressing complaints can be dealt with effectively early in therapy, then other less pressing, but perhaps more important aspects of the client's problems can be approached.

Direct suggestion for symptom removal or symptom substitution sometimes appears to produce dramatic cures although they are much rarer than the popular literature would lead one to believe. However, a word of caution is in order in regard to the hypnotic relief of pain. Hypnotically relieving pain might serve to mask the painful concomitant of a real physical disorder which then goes untreated.

Hypnosis and Insight Psychotherapy. Hypnosis may be used as an adjunctive technique to speed the progress of traditional psychotherapy. The general hypothesis of these approaches is that hypnosis facilitates the awareness of unconscious material. How it is combined with therapy will depend upon the therapist's overall strategy and therapeutic techniques.

Wolberg (1948) uses hypnosis in conjunction with psychoanalysis, a technique he terms "hypnoanalysis." (See also Gill and Brenman, 1959). Because it is believed that unconscious material may be more readily obtained with hypnosis, Wolberg regards hypnosis as a useful tool in breaking through therapeutic resistance and speeding insight.

In Wolberg's use of hypnosis, the patient is trained to enter deep hypnosis upon a signal from the analyst. (Although this may take a number of sessions, Wolberg believes it is a necessary step because later in treatment the patient may build up resistances and refuse to be hypnotized. Hypnosis is called upon when resistances are encountered and the therapist wishes to pass through them quickly.) After the signal for hypnosis is given, one of many techniques to uncover the unconscious material is applied. Training in these techniques is also accomplished before the formal analysis begins. Some of these are described below:

1. Hypnotic Dream

   In this procedure the patient's fantasies are used to provide meaning to a particular class of stimuli. For instance, if a patient seems to block during free association around material associated with his mother, he would be hypnotized and the analyst would suggest a dream which reflects the significance of the material. The content of the dream is interpreted in the same way as are other dreams.

2. Automatic Writing

   The client is given a paper and pencil after being hypnotized, with the suggestion that he write the important elements associated with some analytic material. The client is presumably unaware of what he is writing—the written response occurs as if the hand were dissociated from conscious thoughts. The resulting message is then submitted to psychoanalytic interpretations.

3. Age-Regression and Revivification

   The hypnotist suggests that the subject is becoming younger and younger, returning to a specific time in his life. A reliving of the experiences at that time is suggested and the content is again used for the psychoanalytic session.

Jacob Conn (1968) uses hypnosis in dynamic psychotherapy in a way he terms "hypnosynthesis." The basic premise is that patients will use hypnosis to synthesize and bring together disparate aspects of their lives which then result in more harmonious functioning. Conn does not emphasize the past nor does he direct his patients toward recalling forgotten memories. He supports the importance of the patients' preconceived ideas about psychotherapy and his picture of the ideal therapist. Thus, Conn sees patients as active participants in their own recovery. Therapy is aimed at helping them liberate the natural strengths they have in resolving their own difficulties.

Hypnosis for Conn is a permissive procedure. He does not seek to induce deep levels of hypnosis; rather he allows patients to determine their own level on the basis of their needs. Patients are not challenged while in trance, nor is it necessary that they act out their conflicts with extreme emotionality. Conn believes that patients who do so are trying to please the doctor because they believe that that is the way they will improve. He finds that patients can speak quietly about even very traumatic events if instructed accordingly.

Hypnosis in Behavior Therapy. Behavior therapists most often employ hypnosis for enhancing relaxation and/or imagery. Wolpe (1969) recommends that behavior therapists learn the techniques for inducing hypnosis. Weitzenhoffer (1972) points out that hypnotherapists have employed methods for some time which are quite similar to techniques now called behavior therapy, the main difference being that the uses of learning principles has been largely unrecognized by hypnotherapists, or not applied systematically when they were.

Kroger and Fezler (1976) described a method they call "imagery conditioning." Positing that all persons are capable of hypnotic involvement, they combined techniques from behavior therapy and psychodynamically oriented hypnotherapies. Clients are trained to respond hypnotically and self-hypnotically to standard images which may then be employed later to reverse unwanted conditioned responses (symptoms). For example, the first series of images are aimed at having the client recall the five basic senses while hypnotized. The therapist presents scenes which stimulate recall, like walking along the beach, feeling the cold, wet, firm-packed sand, the warmth of the sun, the taste of salt in the air, etc. Later in therapy the ability to recall warmth may be related to sexual scenes which are aimed at counterconditioning the feelings associated with unsuccessful sexual interactions. The authors present many problem areas (e.g., sexual problems, alcoholism, phobias, depression, asthma) along with specific imagery conditioning approaches.

In Wolpe's technique of *systematic desensitization* (see Chapter 8) clients who experience phobias are: (1) trained to relax deeply; (2) develop a list of scenes in ascending order based on the degree to which they arouse fear; and (3) imagine these scenes in the same order while remaining relaxed. The goal is to desensitize the client's fear to the actual situations. Relaxation techniques which utilize hypnosis may be used similarly. The hypnotic techniques may be more successful than nonhypnotic techniques for some clients. However, there is no way at present to predict with certainty which clients will respond more favorably. It is also possible that the induction of hypnosis will enhance the imaginative capacity of some clients. Imagined scenes should therefore be more similar to actual settings, thereby increasing the generalization of learning to real-life circumstances.

Cautela's (1967) covert sensitization technique (see Chapter 10) is also quite similar to methods which have been, and are being, employed by hypnotherapists (Weitzenhoffer, 1972). Cautela (1975) has more recently recognized the similarity of his technique to those of hypnotherapists but states that it remains to be demonstrated whether hypnosis adds anything positive or not.

Weitzenhoffer (1972) presents a number of other hypnotherapy approaches which may be interpreted as using a learning theory paradigm. He also points out that hypnosis may add to therapy by increasing client motivation and helping to establish a strong relationship between the client and the therapist.

Whether the induction of hypnosis will enhance the effectiveness of behavioral techniques has not been definitely established. Lazarus (1973) offers some evidence that clients who request hypnosis show more positive gains if hypnosis is used than they do if it is not used. Coe, St. Jean, and Burger (in press) also showed that the expectation of hypnosis may enhance the vividness and control of visual imaging. It would seem, then, that the choice of calling a therapeutic approach hypnotic or nonhypnotic, for example, self-hypnosis versus relaxation training, should be made on the basis of the client's expectations and attitudes toward hypnosis. Exactly the same procedures can be employed whether or not the word hypnosis is mentioned. Although some suggestions were offered earlier about the expectations and attitudes of people who seem to be more accepting of hypnosis, we know of no foolproof way of deciding whether or not a particular client's expectancies will be enhanced by the term hypnosis. At this point, it remains for the clinician to reach that decision. Nevertheless, it behooves therapists to be aware that simply calling their techniques "hypnotic" may enhance therapeutic progress for some persons.

Spanos and Barber (1976) compared hypnosis with systematic desensitization (Wolpe, 1958), implosion therapy (Stampfl and Levis, 1967, 1968), and Cautela's (1967, 1970, 1971) covert sensitization, reinforcement and extinction procedures. Each of these behavioral techniques employ subjects' imaginings as the primary vehicle in creating behavioral change. Their review of studies from hypnosis and these behavioral areas led them to conclude that relaxation instructions may not be nearly as important as previously thought insofar as they: (1) lead to actual physical relaxation and; (2) are important in determining positive outcomes of therapy or increased hypnotic responsiveness.

Variables which were found in both hypnosis and the behavioral techniques which were also related to increased hypnotic responsiveness and positive therapeutic outcomes, were:

1. Motivation: It is important that subjects (clients) wish to be hypnotized or helped. The therapist (hypnotist) can increase motivation with instructions aimed at obtaining involvement and interest.

2. Attitudes and Expectancies: It is important that subjects hold positive attitudes and expectations toward hypnosis or therapeutic techniques. Therapists engender positive attitudes and expectancies by explaining their techniques and expounding on their effectiveness.

3. The Wording of Suggestions: Hypnotic suggestions and therapeutic sugges-

tions characteristically provide specific information about the overt behavior and the cognitive activity expected of the subject. The suggestions provide a cognitive strategy, for example, imagining a series of fearful scenes on a hierarchy, from which it is implied that behavioral change will occur.

4. Involved Imagery: Subjects are more responsive to hypnosis and therapy when they report being involved in their imaginative tasks. Vividness of imagery by itself is not as important, as is the involvement in the imagery. Further, it seems that when imaginings are of the sort that "if things were so . . . then . . ." the desired behavioral change would occur, they are more effective, whether or not they are the specific imaginings suggested by the therapist.

Spanos and Barber are cautious in that they realize that there are many more variables involved which have not been adequately studied. Also, any one of the above variables by itself represents only part of the overall picture and the interactive characteristics of these and other variables require investigation.

In sum, it appears that hypnotic procedures and cognitive behavioral techniques have a good deal in common and that in some cases hypnosis may enhance the effectiveness of the behavioral techniques. The similarities between the two also suggest an interesting area for collaborative research which might delineate more clearly the interactive effects between external circumstances, cognitive activity and behavior.

Controlling Pain. One of the oldest uses of hypnotic techniques has been for the control of pain. Works by Hilgard and Hilgard (1975), Kroger (1977) and Kroger and Fezler (1976) all contain rather thorough reviews of the topic. Pain associated with cancer, obstetrics, surgery, migrane and dentistry has been eliminated or significantly reduced in some cases in each of these areas. Our discussion will be limited to the various hypnotic approaches that have been employed and to the question of how susceptible to hypnosis clients need be to benefit.

Most investigators agree that for optimal outcome the particular technique or techniques which are used should be tailored to the individual client's needs and past experiences. Knowing which techniques may be most useful is determined through interview and/or trial and error. The following are commonly used:

1. Direct Suggestion: In this approach direct suggestions are given for anesthesia (no feeling) or analgesia (no pain) usually by having clients recall previous times when they had actually experienced the phenomenon. Imagery is often utilized. For example: "Novocaine is now being injected into your hand (leg, mouth, etc. depending on site of pain), it is starting to become numb and insensitive, etc." Sometimes it is helpful to transfer suggested anesthesia from one part of the body to another. If a person suffers from back pain, anesthesia of the hand may be induced first and

demonstrated by pinching or pricking. The person is then told that he is capable of anesthesia in other areas, whereupon transfer toward the critical area is suggested.

2. Altering the Experience: There are times when pain cannot be eliminated but the experience of it may be altered so that it becomes more tolerable. In a person suffering diffuse pain it might be suggested that the pain becomes more concentrated in a limited area, like the hand. Erickson (1967) displaced intractable abdominal pain of a terminal cancer patient to an equal pain in the left hand. The patient, although he favored his hand and had less use of it, was subsequently capable of participating in positive interactions with his family during the final months of his life than he had been with his abdominal pain.

   The sensation of pain may also be changed to a less distracting one. For example, it may be possible for the client to reinterpret the sensation as a "tingling" rather than a pain. When the problem is one of intermittent pain, posthypnotic amnesia for the pain may be suggested, thereby reducing the anticipatory dread and anxiousness of another episode. Barber (Note 2) reported a case in which intermittent pain was reinterpreted as a welcome event because when it occurred, it was to be viewed as a signal that it would soon be gone.

3. Redirecting Attention: There are several ways to focus attention to other concerns so that the pain is less noticeable or ignored. One technique is simply to deny that the painful part of the body exists. "Your arm is no longer there, your sleeve is empty and just hanging, there is no sensation at all." Similarly, an "out-of-the-body" experience may be suggested. It is as if the person is not in his body and therefore cannot receive its sensations. Age regression has also been used. The person is regressed to a previous time of his life where he was not experiencing pain and therefore he does not experience the pain of the present. Another similar technique is to have the client become imaginatively involved in some pleasant or interesting experience, like watching a favorite TV program or lying on the beach by the ocean. Redirecting attention is most useful when pain is of a limited duration, as in surgery or dental procedures, or when patients must remain inactive and can spend much time in their imagined situations.

4. Focusing on Pain as New: Barber, Spanos and Chaves (1974) recommend another technique. Instead of trying to ignore the pain, clients are asked to focus on the sensation as something new and different, something they should try to describe and learn all about. What color is it? Is it thin? Broad? Heavy? Light? Does it change? and so on.

   Regardless of the specific hypnotic or self-hypnotic suggestions that are employed, other aspects related to pain are incorporated in therapy. Relaxation is nearly always a part, the function of pain as a biological warning system is discussed, the meaning of pain to the client is examined and the relationship of the therapist and client is considered important. People who suffer from chronic pain are especially likely to have other problems that must be worked with in addition to the reduction of the pain.

Investigators differ on whether persons must be highly susceptible (as measured by standard susceptibility scales) in order to benefit from hypnotic analgesia. Hilgard and Hilgard (1975) after reviewing the clinical literature and laboratory pain studies conclude that there is a positive relationship between susceptibility level and responsiveness to analgesic suggestions. If so, the number of persons who could benefit would be limited. However, Barber (1977), Note 1, Note 2 and Schafer and Hernandez (1978) do not agree. The latter investigators believe that "most motivated patients can achieve sufficient levels of hypnosis to alleviate pain." (p. 143). They offer an approach which is meant to optimize the therapeutic context for the client to respond to hypnotic procedures.

Barber, (1977) who reported a 99 percent success rate in dental patients believes that the reason some people have not responded to hypnosis in other studies is because of the way suggestions were given. In his study he used a procedure he called "rapid induction analgesia" (RIA) which in most cases took less than 11 minutes. The procedure is administered immediately before the patient sees the dentist; a posthypnotic cue (touching the shoulder) is given for rapid reentry into hypnosis once they are in the dentist's chair. The wording of the suggestions is indirect and permissive, which Barber believes avoids arousing resistances in the patient. Barber (Note 2) compares a direct and indirect suggestion for relaxation. The direct suggestion:

"You are going to relax now . . . You are becoming more and more relaxed with each breath you take . . . You are now feeling more relaxed . . . Feel that relaxation spreading throughout your body."

Now any of these sentences can be responded to with a negation: "No, I am not/cannot relax now. I am not becoming more and more relaxed," etc.

An example of an indirect suggestion, communicating the same idea:

"I wonder, as you continue sitting quietly right there . . . I wonder if you can enjoy feeling more and more relaxed with each comfortable breath you take. You might notice the relaxation more than the enjoyment . . . or you may begin experiencing the enjoyment even more than the relaxation; I don't know, but I can wonder."

No matter whether the subject is trying to resist, or trying to succeed, there is no logical way to reject those suggestions. The suggestions don't say anything directly about the subject or the subject's experience or the subject's behavior. They directly comment upon the hypnotist. The subject can become more and more interested in what the hypnotist is saying, since there is no jeopardy in doing so." (pp. 3-4)

While the issue of who can be helped with pain control by hypnosis remains to be resolved, reports like Barber's deserve serious attention. The benefits of hypnotic analgesia for those who experience it are several. The reduction in pain medications reduces the problem of addiction and other unwanted side effects; the risks of harm from chemical anesthesia in surgery, especially to older persons and others for whom it is contraindicated are reduced; the potential negative effects of anesthetics on infants during childbirth is minimized; and drastic, surgical measures for pain reduction may be avoided.

SELF-HYPNOTIC TECHNIQUES

Self-hypnosis, variously called autohypnosis or autosuggestion, is a technique in which clients learn to give suggestions to themselves. A therapist-hypnotist usually performs the initial training, although in some cases phonograph records and literature may be the only source of instruction. In fact, Ruch (1975) and Johnson and Weight (1976) found that subjects who were not initially instructed by a hypnotist had more positive outcomes in the long run.

In nearly all of these approaches, clients are expected to practice in order to increase their responsiveness to suggestions. Explicit, or at least implicit, is the message that the hypnotist will only be necessary for a short time, perhaps two or three sessions, and that the main burden for therapy rests with the client.

After an initial interview, most self-hypnotic approaches begin with relaxation training. Relaxation training generally starts with the induction of hypnosis, either through standard techniques or progressive relaxation. At some point subjects are usually shown that they can relax all the muscles of their body by focusing on one small group at a time. While thinking of specific muscles, suggestions are given that they will relax, they will become limp and heavy, let go, allow tension to flow out, and so on. Other methods of teaching relaxation are presented in Wolpe (1969, p. 100) and Lazarus (1971, p. 273). It is a good idea for therapists to be familiar with several techniques because clients may vary as to which suits them best. With practice, clients learn to concentrate on their bodies and to bring about relaxation with self-suggestions. Many people appear to be able to accomplish rather complete relaxation in a relatively short time, or at least they learn to relax much more than they had before.

Teaching Relaxation and Absorbed Concentration

A technique which the author has found helpful in introducing clients to the use of imagination and concentration will be described in detail.

The technique is presented as one which will help to reduce general tension and to apply self-suggestions in the most effective way. The technique begins with a demonstration that shows clients that they can be successful in taking suggestions, in giving them to themselves, and in bringing about positive changes.

Clients are told that what they are about to learn is best viewed as a skill, and as with other skills, they can become more adept at it with practice. Expectations of an instant cure or dramatic effects are played down. Rather, clients are encouraged to employ certain natural abilities, not normally used by people, in a systematic way.

In the use of this technique, with the client either sitting across from you or beside you, begin by telling him that you wish to explain the most effective way to use suggestions. You can say:

"There are several things I would like to explain about taking suggestions, or giving them to yourself, so that they will be most effective. To begin with, there are a couple of things you should try and avoid. The first is trying to work too hard at the task. It is an easy-feeling sort of task, not one requiring what we ordinarily think of as hard concentration, or hard work. If you take the attitude that you must work hard, you will find that thoughts about working, instead of the suggestions you wish to use, will become the dominant thoughts. A second common problem is that when suggestions begin to have their effects, especially when you are first learning, it may seem a bit unusual, or interesting. The tendency is to try and analyze what is going on—to figure it out—but when you do, the suggestions are broken up, and their effects cease. If you will think of your mind as a river that flows along at a steady pace, allowing your thoughts to progress at the same pace, over and over again—easy, not forced, just flowing along at a nice, easy pace—your suggestions will become the dominant thing of interest, and will have their greatest effects. The whole thing is really a rather easy, relaxed technique. If you should become distracted, that's all right, just go back to your thoughts, letting them flow through, over and over, so that they become the only thing of importance for that time. Don't worry about distractions. They are likely to occur, especially when you are first learning. Simply recognize that you have been distracted and redirect your attention back to the slow, easy flow of suggestion you were giving."

At this point, any questions the client might have should be answered by reiterating what you have said already.

The next step is to introduce a suggestive task to which almost everyone will respond. By so doing, the chances are maximized for clients to be successful in their first experience with suggestions.

The First Experience. The suggestion I use is called the Chevrul Pendulum. A thread, or light string, approximately the length from your elbow to your fingertips, with a moderately heavy bob of some sort attached, like a small key, is the only equipment needed. The client rests his elbow on the desk (or chair arm) and holds the loose end of the thread between the thumb and forefinger with the wrist bent at approximately a right angle. The bob then hangs straight down and away from the arm, an inch or so above the surface. It is suggested that the client focus on the bob and think of it doing different things, such as making circles, swinging back and forth in predetermined directions, and so on. The following is a verbatim demonstration of its administration:

I want you to hold this little bob just the way I do. (Demonstrate the proper way to hold the thread.) That's it, just hold it so you can sit there comfortably and relax. Now I want you to take the attitude just for a moment or so, that that little bob is the only thing of importance to you. That's it, just focus your gaze on it, and begin trying to discover all you can about it. (It is helpful if the bob has designs, colors, or other irregularities on it.) That's it, look at it carefully, trace all around its outline, notice any geometric shapes that may be on it, like circles—squares—perhaps you can even find rectangles if you look carefully. Just try to learn everything you can about that little bob, think of it as a new and different experience, something unique, something you would like to know everything about. Notice its colors—notice how this varies from spot to spot, and how it changes—as you become more interested in the bob, you notice that in fact it becomes more the center of your attention. Your vision narrows, things in the side of your vision tend to grey out, to become less important. The bob in fact becomes the center of your attention—now watch it very closely, because in a moment it is going to begin doing something—it will begin moving back and forth, back and forth, back and forth.

At this point the bob may be naturally moving in one direction or another. It is helpful and encouraging to the subject to increase the natural movement that is occurring. Continue with the same suggestions, trying to time your suggestion to the tempo of the movement of the bob.

Back and forth, back and forth, more and more, farther each time, back and forth, back and forth, freer and freer, freer and freer, back and forth, back and forth, etc. (Once the movement is well established you are ready to change to a new movement.) Now the bob will change its direction—it's going to begin making a round, round circle. Round and round, round and round, round and round. There, it's beginning to go now, round and round—rounder and rounder, rounder and rounder. You can imagine a circle below it, and it's tracing right around that circle, rounder and rounder, rounder and rounder, etc.

Subjects vary a good deal as to their magnitude of response. However, even a very small response in the suggested direction can be quite a convincing experience. By this time you have demonstrated that your client is able to take suggestions. The next step is to show them that they can give suggestions to themselves. A few persons seem to be unable to respond to this task, but it is usually apparent that they are breaking their train of thought, often indicated by jerky movements of the bob. If this happens, it is good to stop and ask what they are doing, what they are thinking. Usually, they are committing one of the errors you have already cautioned about. A brief discussion of the problem before returning to the task may be enough. If the difficulty is still not overcome, you can start the bob in the direction suggested, letting clients follow the swing with their thoughts in order to grasp the tempo. As their thoughts fall into the rhythm of the bob, suggestions for change of direction are usually effective, and they will have learned something about taking suggestions.

Now I want you to think of the bob going back and forth again—right toward you and toward me." When the direction of the bob has changed into a stable movement, ask them to think of a circle again. After a circle is created, suggest that they think of the bob slowing down and coming to a stop. When it is almost stopped, take it from them and proceed as follows:

"What was that like for you?" The usual response is one of amazement or surprise, indicating that it has been a new and unusual experience. If they do not voluntarily say that it seemed as if their thoughts were moving the bob, ask directly if they had that impression. Most people feel that their thoughts were controlling the bob at least a little, although clients vary on the degree to which they report being aware of their fingers moving.

Go on to explain, ''There is nothing really so unusual about this. You did not notice your fingers moving for two reasons. First, your attention was very focused on the bob, therefore, you did not notice the small movements in your fingers. Had you focused on your fingers, you would have noticed the movements. Focusing on the suggestions rather than your fingers is an example of being able to take suggestions well. Your attention becomes focused upon the suggestions and then other things are less likely to be noticed. Secondly, the small movements in your fingers were exaggerated by the length of the string, such that the movement of the bob would seem quite large compared to the very small muscle movement necessary to create it. The movement of the bob demonstrates how your thoughts can affect your muscles or other organs of your body. Your nervous system sends a message to the proper places in the body, in this case the muscles of your hand and fingers, and the appropriate actions result. At any rate, you have had a chance to see how you can take suggestions, and the effects they might have. You have also seen that you can give yourself suggestions with the same results. Now I would like you to move to that comfortable chair and we will continue teaching you how to relax completely, and to place yourself in a state where suggestions will have their maximum effects for you.''

At this point the client moves to a comfortable chair (if not already in one). A recliner or couch which completely supports the client's body is most appropriate for this part of the training. Once seated, explain that it is always important to practice relaxing in a position where all of the muscles are able to ''let go.'' The muscles should not have to support any part of the body so that the setting is maximized for the complete release of all muscular tension. Caution against crossing legs or resting hands on the stomach, a normal practice for many people when they sit or lie down, because the weight of one part of the body on another makes some muscle tension necessary in order to support the part on top.

Once the person is comfortably settled, begin by demonstrating a suggestion that is easy to follow, explaining that you start with an easy suggestion because response to it tends to increase the responsiveness to further suggestions. At this point, I often refer back to the way that they became more adept at following suggestions to the bob once they had started.

An easy suggestion is to ask them to look at a spot between their eyes—at hairline level. This forces them to roll their eyes up and back so that strain is created. Touching the spot on their forehead with your finger, telling them to remember it. Then explain that they are to try and see the spot as an X and to focus on it. Before going on, be certain that they demonstrate by rolling their eyes up into the proper position. Explain that by looking at the spot, the natural strain created in their eyes becomes an easy thing to focus on. Their eyes will become tired, their eyelids will become heavy, and soon they will feel like closing. Caution them not to fight the suggestion but to let their eyes close as the suggestions have their effects and they await your further instructions. Move back to your chair, ask the client to focus on the spot, and proceed as follows:

I want you to look right at that spot, keep your attention right on the spot—notice the strain in your eyes, how it seems to grow and grow—straining more and more, the strain in your eyes is becoming greater and greater, more and more strain, more and more strain, your eyes become tireder and tireder, tireder and tireder. (If you notice that the client's eyes are beginning to blink slightly, suggestions of blinking can be included also.) Your eyes are blinking, becoming heavier and heavier—eyes tired, tired from straining, straining more and more, greater and greater strain—eyelids becoming heavier now, heavier and heavier, heavier and heavier, wanting to close, feeling heavier and heavier, etc.

Most people will close their eyes within a few minutes. If you notice that they are looking away, or blinking excessively as if to reduce the strain, caution that they should not fight the response. "Let it occur, let the heaviness creep in, let your eyelids close slowly as the heaviness takes over." If it is taking some time for their eyes to respond, you may want to suggest that as you count their eyes will become heavier and more and more strained. Then you can simply begin counting, continuing to suggest strain and heaviness between counts. As long as they continue to focus on the spot and create strain, you should be able to outlast even the most unsuggestible clients by continuing to count. A few clients seem not to respond well to this suggestion. They constantly look away, blink a good deal, and tend to stop their eyes from closing naturally. I often stop the procedure with these people and tell them that responding to this suggestion is not really necessary for our purposes. Simply have them close their eyes and go on with the rest of the training.

As the client's eyes close, you continue, Fine, now leave your eyes closed and let your eyes roll forward. Feel the strain going out of your eyes, and as you feel the strain going out of your eyes, think of the strain going out of your entire body—your body just letting go, dropping into the chair, going limp, limp, heavy and relaxed. As your eyes close and roll forward, and you feel the strain going out of your eyes, that is a cue for the strain to begin going out of your entire body. Think of the strain as flowing right out of your body—from your eyes, throughout your body, right out of your toes. Your body loosening, dropping into the chair—relaxing.

Now I want you to think only of your right foot. Turn all your attention to your right foot. Think of nothing but your right foot—your right foot is the only thing that is important. As you turn your attention to your right foot, you become more aware of it than you were a moment ago. You may notice small changes in sensation—perhaps a slight tingling—or a change in temperature—you become more aware of your right foot than you were before. Notice the shoe on your foot, feel its pressure around your toes—on the ball of your foot—on your arch—on your heel—over the top. As you become very aware of your right foot, think of it going limp—limp and loose. Your right foot, relaxing, letting go, dropping down, loosening, letting go, relaxing. Feel your toes spread slightly as the muscles let go, loosen and drop, letting all the weight of your foot into the chair, the chair supporting your foot entirely—your foot becoming heavy, heavy and limp, limp and relaxed. Your right foot just letting go, letting go completely—looser and looser, more and more relaxed. With each thought of relaxation, the muscles let go just a little bit more, just a little bit more. The tension flows out of the muscles as they loosen, loosen and let go. Now think of the muscles in your lower right leg loosening, dropping, going limper and limper, more and more relaxed, more and more relaxed. The muscle on top letting down, dropping down right on through the calf muscle, letting go, hanging, hanging loosely and limply—relaxed.

The same sorts of suggestions are given for various muscle groups as you progress through the client's body. My usual order is as follows: right foot, lower right leg, upper muscles of the right leg, then the entire right leg and foot.

Now I want you to imagine your entire right leg and foot. Think of it as being separated off from the rest of your body—as if it is off by itself, completely relaxed, limp and loose, all the muscles hanging, letting go, loosening and letting go—your entire right leg and foot relaxing, more and more relaxed with each thought. The chair doing all the work, your leg and foot letting go, letting go.

The point of starting with smaller muscle units like the foot, lower leg and upper leg, and then incorporating the entire leg and foot, is to show the type of progress they can expect. That is, at the beginning they will only focus on small muscle groups where success is more likely. As they become more adept at relaxing, they should be able to relax increasingly larger groups of muscles at the same time. The eventual goal is for them to be able to sit down, close their eyes, and relax their entire body in a matter of seconds.

The order proceeds: left foot; lower left leg; upper left leg; entire left leg and left foot; both legs and both feet; right hand; right forearm, upper right arm; right shoulder; entire right shoulder, arm and hand; left hand; left forearm; upper left arm; left shoulder; entire left shoulder, arm and hand; area across both shoulders; both shoulders, arms, and hands; chest; breathing, stomach; hips; lower back, middle back; upper back; entire body from shoulders to the feet; neck; jaw; lips; nose; right cheek; left cheek; eyelids; eyebrows; forehead; entire face; scalp and ears; entire head and neck; entire body. It is helpful if the therapist simultaneously experiences these muscles loosening. Your own feelings can act as a guide in saying the proper words, such as "dropping," and "letting go."

The neck and shoulder muscles are often sources of tension. The following suggestions seem to be helpful.

"Now think of the area right across your shoulders, right across your shoulders, from shoulder to shoulder, and letting those muscles drop, drop right down and back into the chair. Let your arms and hands just hang from your shoulders. Let your shoulders just drop into the chair— loose, looser, letting go, dropping down, relaxing—shoulders dropping and relaxing—now think of your chest. Think of your chest relaxing, dropping down, loosening, letting go. As you notice your chest, you notice that your body can breathe by itself. Your body will simply take care of itself, and you can let all of your muscles relax. Imagine yourself standing off watching your body take care of itself, breathing by itself. As you let your muscles relax, letting all your muscles go, your body just takes care of itself. Think to yourself, 'my body breathes itself, my body breathes itself,' and you notice that your body will just take care of itself. Your muscles can loosen and relax, you can let go all the tension in your body, and your body simply takes care of itself."

The following suggestions are useful for the neck region. "Now let your neck relax, loosen, let go. Let your head move slightly, slightly from side to side as you feel the muscles in your neck letting go and loosening. Let the chair do all the work in holding your head up. Let your head rest on the chair and let your neck muscles loosen and relax, loosen and relax, letting go completely, letting go completely."

The face is important also. You can suggest that the jaw is going slack, "slack and limp, loose, slack and relaxed." If clients are responding well, their mouths will open slightly. Some people are hesitant to let their mouths open. It may take some encouragement for them to let their jaw go limp and to let their lips part. It is helpful to suggest this specifically, even thinking of their tongue lying on the bottom of their mouth, loosening and relaxing.

The next step is to show the client how to deepen concentration to thoughts. The basic technique is to have them imagine going downward, having everything "come in" around them so that their thoughts and your words become the center of importance. There are a number of ways to suggest deepening—going down an elevator or a stairway, or floating down on a cloud. Presenting a rather neutral suggestion may be best. For example, "you are floating down." Some clients are afraid of elevators, stairways or other things; it is difficult to predict what might be negative for a particular person. I usually suggest something like the following:

> "Now that you have relaxed your entire body, part by part, I want you to imagine that you are just moving out of your body, standing off, as if watching your body just relaxing in the chair, taking care of itself, breathing easily and relaxing. With each breath your body loosens a little bit more, becomes more and more relaxed, and you begin to float downward—downward, deeper and deeper. With each breath you are moving down, down—deeper and deeper—more and more attention to your thoughts and to my words. Your body is taking care of itself. Your muscles are completely relaxed. All the tension is flowing out and you are able to attend more and more to your thoughts. Attending more and more to your thoughts and my voice so that suggestions you give to yourself, or that I give to you, will have maximum effects. Down, deeper and deeper, deeper and deeper, more and more relaxed, more and more concentrated on your thoughts. I am now going to count from one to ten and with each count you will go deeper and deeper, your thoughts will become more and more the center of your attention so that what you suggest for yourself will have its maximal effect."

After reaching ten, suggest that they will be able to practice on their own and have no difficulty in arousing themselves whenever they wish.

The session may be completed in the following way. "Now you are deeply relaxed, paying complete attention to your thoughts and my voice, you will be able to do this for yourself with practice, and your thoughts will have maximum effect. In a moment I am going to count from ten to one. When I reach one, I want you to open your eyes and arouse yourself. You will feel refreshed from having relaxed so well. With each count, however, I want you to suggest to yourself that by practicing this technique you will be able to overcome your difficulties more readily, more sensibly, and through your own control. I am now going to count from ten to one and with each count suggest to yourself that by practicing this technique you will gain control over your difficulties and resolve them more readily. Ready now, ten-nine-eight-seven-six-five-four-three-two-one."

Most clients arouse rather slowly. They will usually look at you, smile stretch, or in other ways show that they have been relaxed. Once in a while a person falls asleep. It is usually easy to tell during the procedure, but if you are not certain, and they have not opened their eyes, simply say in a loud voice, "Wake up!" I have never had great difficulty in arousing a person.

Once aroused, ask what the experience was like. Were there any difficulties at particular points? Or in relaxing particular muscles? Are there any questions? Discuss ways that should help overcome any difficulties which may have been experienced. Reiterate the technique, including the purpose of starting with small groups of muscles and progressively moving to larger ones until, in a very short time, they should be able to easily imagine their entire body relaxing and their concentration deepening. The technique should be practiced twice a day if possible. Tell clients to contact you should they run into any problems before seeing you the next time.

Once a person has learned to relax and to focus on thoughts, the groundwork has been laid for the application of many procedures which involve imagining. There is the initial benefit of relaxation itself, and the client will soon be ready to participate in other techniques.

Relaxation on a Signal

Relaxation training in itself may prove beneficial for clients who suffer from chronic tension states and associated psychophysiological disorders (migraine headaches, ulcers, asthma, insomnia, etc.). Training may take the form described above, until the client is able to attain deep relaxation in a relatively short period of time. Or training may take the form of a more direct hypnotic procedure.

One approach is to induce hypnosis with suggestions of deep relaxation. A posthypnotic suggestion is given that when awakened and the hypnotist says "relax," the client will again experience relaxation. That is, the client is trained to become hypnotized on a signal, and the hypnotic state is defined as one of deep relaxation. After the client is responding reliably to the hypnotist's signal, it is suggested that he can relax and go into the same state. The final step is to suggest that it is only necessary to think "relax," and relaxation will follow.

Whatever method is used, the final objective is for persons to respond to their own mental signal. Thinking "relax" will automatically begin to relax the body. Tense individuals may derive a great deal of benefit from this approach. When they notice the first signs of tenseness, they can think "relax," and prevent the buildup of more tension. In the process, the physiological responses associated with tension states are reduced, thereby reducing the irritating effects on the body. For example, early signs of an impending migraine headache, or the tensing of the bronchial tubes in an asthmatic, may serve as cues to begin relaxing. A busy executive with stomach problems can think "relax" during a hectic part of his schedule. The crippling, physiological side effects of emotional arousal should therefore decrease.

The same procedure may be used to ease and facilitate childbirth. Relaxation is almost always an integral part of a natural birth program although other aspects of childbirth are usually incorporated as well. Suggestions that pain is completely normal, and that its occurrence during childbirth is not especially important, tend to reduce negative, anxiety-arousing expectations. Training usually includes teaching the movements associated with labor and what to expect during birth. By the time the client is ready to deliver, she will have developed the ability to relax, know when to expand energy bearing down, and not fear what happens. She becomes a partner in the delivery, with practical skills and a positive attitude.

Self-Hypnosis and Self-Control

The two previous sections on self-hypnosis can be viewed as utilizing many of the same concepts and techniques as do the behaviorally-oriented, self-control approaches described in Chapter 10 and 11. Black (Note 3), in his review of self-hypnotic and self-control procedures, pointed out many similarities between them. However, he has also correctly pointed out that self-hypnotic techniques have not been as systematic and structured as have self-control techniques.

It would be redundant to reiterate all of the self-control procedures which were described in other chapters, but it is worth noting that the bodies of knowledge from self-hypnosis and self-control are being brought together. Black and Thoresen (1978) offer a model for self-hypnosis from a "cognitive social-learning perspective." It is of interest because, unlike stated theorires of hypnosis, they emphasize the reciprocal interactions of the person, the environment and the behavior in understanding self-hypnosis. Their position is much in keeping with that of Sarbin and Coe (1972), Coe and Sarbin (1977) and Coe (1978) who postulate a contextualist view of hypnosis as opposed to the mechanistic/formist views of trance theories (Gill and Brenman, 1959; Hilgard, 1977). Diamond (1978) (Note 5) has offered a "cognitive skills model" of hypnosis which emphasizes its potential in training for increased self-control. Combining his work with that of Katz (in press) and Katz and Crawford (1978) (Note 6) he notes three advantages for clinical application: (1) persons previously dismissed as "unsusceptible" by trance models may be trained to be more responsive; (2) clients are more likely to perceive themselves in their own control and thereby maintain and generalize therapeutic effects; and (3) clients are likely to increase their feelings of self-esteem because of their effective use of hypnotic skills.

It will be useful to outline the major characteristics of self-control procedures noted by Black (Note 3) in order that therapists who wish to emphasize this aspect of self-hypnosis may do so more effectively. They are: (1) the use of verbal and imaginal procedures which mediate all inputs and outputs of the person; (2) being aware of one's actions and environmental contingencies through the use of systematic observation of one's own behavior; (3) restructuring the environment in order to increase or decrease the probability of certain cues and responses occurring; (4) creating commitment through self-messages to enhance motivation, expectations and attribution of the problem source; and (5) evaluation of the consequences of interventions, the setting of goals, and behavioral programming related to goals.

OTHER SUGGESTIVE TECHNIQUES

Autogenic Training

Shultz and Luthe (1959) developed a method of therapy which makes major use of autosuggestion. Their approach is to teach control of bodily and imaginal functions through autosuggestion. The therapist maintains rather close control throughout training (which may take a considerable amount of time) and carefully watches his clients' progress, helping them to overcome any difficulties they may encounter.

Therapy starts with simple suggestions that one's left arm will relax. Gradually, more limbs and muscle groups are incorporated. When satisfactory control is gained over the muscles, suggestions for controlling various organ systems are added, for example, the client is instructed to think repeatedly, "my body breathes itself," "my body breathes itself," etc. The point is that repeated suggestions on specific functions leads to their control. As clients gain control over musculature and internal functioning, they move toward the production of suggested fantasy, such as controlling colors, sounds, and so on. Once the skills of concentrated fantasy are learned, they may be used to focus on problems in living and the resolution of psychological conflicts.

Meditation

There has been increasing interest in various meditative techniques for therapeutic purposes (e.g., Cauthen and Prymak, 1977; Davidson, Goleman and Schwartz, 1976; Goleman, 1976a, 1976b; 1977; Goleman and Schwartz, 1976). One of the most widely publicized is transcendental meditation (TM) (Maharishi, 1972).

It is beyond the scope of this chapter to detail the numerous variations in meditation. The basic task in most meditative approaches is to sit quietly and maintain concentration on a particular thought. According to Goleman (1976a), meditators become more relaxed as they practice and at the same time they become more alert by learning to control their concentration. He claims, and studies support him, that as a result, meditators are better able to deal with stressful situations. Meditators appear to become more aroused when threat is imminent, but they recover more quickly after the stressful situation has passed. Because they do not remain mobilized for stress following the incident, they are less likely to experience the "threat-arousal-threat spiral," therefore they are capable of perceiving threat more accurately in the future and responding with arousal only when it is necessary. While meditative techniques may have value for stress related difficulties, the empirical results are not always in agreement (Brown, 1977; Cauthen and Prymak, 1977; Pagano, 1976; Parker, Gilbert, and Thoreson, 1978). The following material will illustrate the relationship of suggestive techniques to meditation.

Meditation is an important part of some Yogas. See Eliade (1970) for a more comprehensive treatment of Yoga and its practice. Many Yogas are primarily religious in nature with the purpose of progressing toward a "union" and a focus on devotion. These are not covered here. One type of Yoga, which Barth (1974) has termed "nova yoga," or the yoga of the imagination, employs techniques which are similar to those used in self-hypnosis.

The following is an example of meditation instructions (Devi, 1963). The subject uses a candle as a fixation point.

> "Now keep your eyes steady upon the flame and don't let them wander. Start breathing rhythmically. Next close your eyes, and try to retain the impression of the flame. You can visualize it clearly, hold the picture, but if the light eludes you, open your eyes for another look at the light. Close them again and see if you are able to envision the flame this time. Repeat this until you are able to capture and hold the impression.
>
> If you are still unsuccessful, try the same procedure again the following day, and continue trying until you have succeeded. Do not hurry or force anything—do not try too intensively. Not only will such an approach not expedite matters but it may even retard everything. Remember that it is most important to remain inwardly relaxed and motionless."

The subject is instructed further to contemplate the light and to ponder its characteristics—its shape, color and so on. The light is to be thought of as something of "goodness" and "divinity," and meditation upon those ideas should follow. Progression moves to imagining the light within oneself, contemplating its goodness which disperses "the darkness of ignorance, of loneliness, of fear, hatred, lust, jealousy, greed, anger, envy." The purpose is to reach an inner harmony, a peace with one self through the use of positive self-suggestions. Exercises to relieve tension are also taught, and healthful, well-rounded diets are recommended.

Psychocybernetics

Psychocybernetics, as formulated by Maltz (1960), is a popular "do-it-yourself" technique employing self-suggestion. Maltz's system is based on the importance of a person's self-image, and its effects on attitudes, motives and behavior. He believes that self-image holds a position of primary importance in guiding and directing a person's life. The purpose of his method is to help people develop realistic, positive self-images.

According to Maltz, self-image is developed and changed through experiences. Experiences come from direct interaction with the environment or through imagination, both being effective modifiers of how people view themselves. It is the effect of imaginative experiences that in part justify the use of self-suggestive techniques in psychocybernetics.

Maltz cites many case examples and supports his ideas with medical reports, scientific findings and quotes from great men and the Bible. His personal conviction is also notable throughout his book, raising the expectancies and hopes of his readers through exercises and formulas for successful living. For example, the first exercise is to reread at least three times per week, for the first three weeks, a chapter that tells how the brain works as an automatic servo-mechanism in finding answers, and how people have an instinct for success which, through creative imagination, can become actual. The next exercise is to use the imagination for thirty minutes each day, making the images as vivid and detailed as possible (imagining a motion picture screen may be helpful) because imaginings are actually practice experiences that can affect self image and, as such, they will have more impact the closer they approach actual experiences. The task is for people to imagine themselves behaving successfully. A shy person, for example, imagines that he is very outgoing and successful in a group situation.

Maltz offers constructive ideas about such things as happiness, success, failure, etc. For example, in presenting the "success-type" personality the word "success" is used as a memory aide for its essential ingredients, each letter a mnemonic for a positive quality:

S-ence of direction
U-nderstanding
C-ourage
C-harity
E-steem
S-elf-confidence
S-elf-acceptance

The entire program is aimed at shaking people from the belief that they are helpless victims of their world by demonstrating they are capable of controlling and choosing their own destiny.

CONCLUSIONS ON THERAPEUTIC APPROACHES

Evaluation of Therapeutic Effectiveness

Evaluating the effectiveness of hypnosis is no less difficult than evaluating the effectiveness of any kind of psychotherapy. The same research problems are present. Among others is the difficulty of defining and measuring improvement and deciding what constitutes adequate control groups. See Bergin and Garfield (1971) for a more detailed discussion of these issues.

Using the results from published case studies, Barrios (1970) pointed out that psychoanalysis results in a 38 percent recovery rate after an average of 600 sessions, Wolpean behavior therapy a 72 percent recovery rate after an average of 22 sessions, and hypnotherapy a 93 percent recovery rate after an average of six sessions. We cannot, of course, simply accept these figures as valid comparisons among the three therapies, but they should at least alert us to the positive potential of including hypnotic techniques among other therapeutic skills.

The specific techniques employed in the outcome reports were not what many professionals usually expect of hypnosis, that is, direct symptom removal or uncovering. "The current trend is to use hypnosis to remove the negative attitudes, fears, maladaptive behavior patterns, and negative self-images underlying the symptoms. Uncovering and direct symptom removal are still used to a certain extent, but usually in conjunction with this new main function." Barrios indicated that "light" hypnosis is probably sufficient in these reconditioning approaches. Therefore, there is little limitation of application because of the client's degree of susceptibility.

Barrios also notes that the range of clients and their concomitant disorders, who have benefited from hypnotherapy is extensive. Diagnostic categories included psychophysiological disorders, neurotic disorders, personality disorders, and some psychotic disorders. In keeping with the concept of expectancy, Barrios views the hypnotic induction as an effective method for establishing confidence and belief in the therapist. In turn, a strong personal relationship should develop where the therapist's words will be more effective in bringing about constructive change.

Two more recent studies suggest that hypnotic and/or suggestive techniques have positive therapeutic effects in psychophysiological problems.

Barber (1978) reviewed the effects of hypnosis and suggestion on psychosomatic phenomena concluding that they affect cutaneous and glandular functioning, probably through local alterations in blood flow which is mediated by suggestions incorporated into ongoing cognitive activity. Friedman and Taub (1977) evaluated the effects of hypnosis alone, biofeedback alone, hypnosis and biofeedback combined, and no treatment on essential hypertension. They found significant improvement at the six-month follow-up study for the hypnosis alone and biofeedback alone but not for the combination treatment or the no treatment conditions.

Similarities Across Techniques

In looking back over the uses of hypnosis, autohypnosis and other suggestive techniques, several communalities can be observed: (1) the use of verbal and nonverbal cues to enhance positive expectations and client motivation; (2) the use of relaxation and imagery for attaining therapeutic goals, and with the exception of the psychodynamic approaches; (3) an emphasis on self-control.

Positive expectations and motivations are incorporated in all, either formally or by implication. The examination of expectation and placebo therapies in the first part of this chapter also indicates the importance that persons from diverse persuasions place on these variables. It would appear that therapists from all schools should include the task of increasing motivations and positive expectations in their therapeutic work.

The use of imagery is less consistent but quite prevalent, and if one can assume that thoughts, attitudes, etc. contain associated imagery, then nearly all therapeutic approaches could be said to involve imagery work. It is premature, however, to conclude, on the basis of current data, that imagery functions to increase motivation, expectation and attitude, or contains specific value of its own. Nevertheless, therapists should recognize the potential for positive changes through imagery techniques.

The emphasis on self-control is less obvious across the techniques although its presence is clearly emphasized in some. The behavioral literature most clearly recommends it, as do the techniques presented earlier in this chapter for increasing hypnotic susceptibility. However, clients who expect psychologists to heal them are not motivated for self-control, nor are they ready to accept the idea that their difficulties, which they may view as shameful or degrading, are of their own doing. Such persons must be moved slowly in the direction of taking responsibility for handling their problems. Clients must view self-control approaches as personally acceptable and potentially effective if they are to be effective at all.

OTHER CONSIDERATIONS

The "Power" of Hypnosis

People inevitably ask, "Can hypnosis cure me of smoking? Of obesity? Of bad habits? Of uncontrollable fantasies?" The question presumes an extraordinary power that has been attributed to hypnosis through the mass media. Stage hypnotists encourage the public to believe that hypnosis is a strange and powerful influencing technique—that people can be made to surpass their normal capacities or to change in ways that are so dramatic as to be unbelievable. Newspaper reports of medical hypnosis emphasize the dramatic while at the same time ignoring less dramatic clinical results and experimental investigations. The historical origins of hypnosis as a magical influencing power, plus the indiscriminate reporting of spectacular individual cases, has led many people to regard hypnosis as either a cure-all or something to be feared and avoided.

Obviously, if hypnosis were as effective in changing behavior as these claims imply, prisons, mental hospitals and welfare agencies would be empty. If a hypnotist could whisk away a craving for alcohol, the debilitating effects of psychosomatic illness, or the performance of antisocial behavior simply by suggesting it, personal adjustment would certainly be simple. Unfortunately, such is not the case. Hypnosis is not a cure-all, the hypnotist has no mysterious powers, and most of the dramatic reports can be accounted for by variables other than the induction of hypnosis. However, a brief exploration of some of the powers attributed to hypnosis is relevant within the context of this discussion.

Antisocial Conduct. One commonly asked question is, "Can people be made to do something against their will while under the influence of hypnosis?" There is no sense denying that unethical hypnotists at one time or another have induced their subjects into immoral actions, such as public exhibitionism, sexual intercourse and theft. However, it is just as likely that other unethical "helpers" (friends, teachers, bartenders, drug pushers, among others) have taken advantage of persons in the same way. The difference is in how one chooses to explain the behavior—whether it is attributed to a hypnotic trance or to more readily understandable variables.

Two arguments are generally submitted to support the notion that subjects will commit acts against their will, or perform feats of strength and ability beyond their capacity under hypnosis. The first is usually presented in some modified form of the hypothesis: "If subjects are hypnotized deeply enough, they can be induced to perform acts against their will." Such a statement can never be proved or disproved without an accompanying quantitative definition of the depth of the trance. If subjects perform an antisocial act (apparently against their will), it could be said that they were hypnotized enough. If subjects do not perform the antisocial act, then they must not have been hypnotized enough. Such reasoning can only serve the purpose of supporting an already established belief—it can never be submitted to a crucial test.

The second argument is usually stated something like this: "Hypnotized persons will perform acts which are apparently against their will if they have an unconscious desire to do so." Again, such a statement is only useful to support a belief; it cannot be tested empirically. If subjects perform an act which appears to be against their will, then they had an unconscious desire to do so. If they refuse, then they must not have had the desire.

Orne (1962) reviewed the evidence relating to hypnosis and antisocial conduct. One group of studies approached the question on the assumption that simply giving suggestions for an act which would be criminal (when, in fact, in the experimental setting it is not) was sufficient to state that subjects perceived the act as criminal. For example, subjects who were given a rubber knife with the suggestion that it was a real knife, were told to stab one of the experimenters. If they complied, the assumption was that they did so with the belief that they would actually stab the person. What must be determined is whether or not the subjects perceived the act as criminal. It is possible that subjects understood that they were expected to comply but knew very well that they were not really going to hurt anyone. When such situations are made real, such as asking a girl to undress in public, subjects almost always refuse.

Other studies have been conducted but they all suffer from being unable to separate the understanding that subjects are participating in an experiment as compared to real-life experiences.

A study by Coe, Kobyashi, and Howard (1973) attempted to overcome many of the weaknesses of earlier experimental designs. The antisocial request was to help a graduate student hypnotist sell heroin off-campus. While the results were not definitive, the important factor which determined whether or not subjects sold heroin was their own belief about drugs. Hypnosis apparently had no facilitating effect in and of itself; subjects were willing to sell the drug if they did not believe drugs were bad, and vice versa.

Criminal Cases. The criminal literature on hypnosis and antisocial conduct are of two main types: sexual offenses committed against subjects by hypnotists, and the commission of acts by subjects which led to the hypnotist's material gain. Individual cases will not be detailed except to note that the explanation offered by protesting individuals was that hypnosis was the reason they performed the criminal acts.

In regard to sexual misconduct, especially in a psychotherapeutic setting, a number of other possible explanations may be offered. First, the sexual relationship may simply have been a fantasy on the part of the patient. Second, it is probably more common than is widely known that therapists and patients become sexually involved in therapy, with or without the use of hypnosis. Because of these two factors it is impossible to evaluate the significance of hypnosis over and above the other emotional and interpersonal factors in operation.

In the cases where persons claimed that they were forced to perform antisocial acts for the benefit of the hypnotist (there are only a few such cases) there has been a long-term relationship between subject and hypnotist. The influence of the relationship could just as easily account for the subject's behavior.

It would be misleading to say that the evidence clearly indicates that hypnosis cannot be employed for unethical or illegal purposes. The question has not yet been evaluated satisfactorily. However, the more sophisticated the designs in controlling variables, such as the personal relationship, the expectations that the request is part of an experiment, and the subjects' moral stance toward the act, the less likely does it appear that hypnosis plays a crucial part in the commission of antisocial acts. (See also Coe, 1977).

Exceptional Abilities. Another question people often ask regarding hypnosis is whether it can induce superhuman capacities. A common demonstration of super strength is often performed by stage hypnotists. The hypnotist suggests that a subject's body will become completely rigid and then suspend the subject between two chairs, with the neck on the edge of one chair and the heels on the edge of the other. By itself, the suspension seems impossible, but the hypnotist may test the audience's credulity further by standing on the subject's stomach or chest. The power of this demonstration fades however when it is known that any man of robust physique can duplicate the same event without hypnotic suggestion—and that most people can suspend themselves in this manner for a short time without undue discomfort.

Other demonstrations seem to support the ability of hypnotic subjects to become blind or deaf at the suggestion of the hypnotist. These studies will not be detailed except to point out that Barber's experiments with highly motivated control subjects who were not hypnotized, resulted in similar unusual behaviors (Barber, 1969).

Increases in memory, learning and physical endurance are other feats which have been attributed to the powers of hypnosis. However, when adequate controls are utilized, these demonstrations are not very startling. For example, studies attempting to increase learning capacity have been variable, although none have shown very significant increases because of hypnosis. In fact, in some studies, hypnosis has been shown to reduce the speed of learning.

Is Hypnosis Dangerous? Probably the greatest danger with hypnosis are subjects' beliefs that it is dangerous, and/or similar beliefs held by hypnotists. Certainly, in the hands of competent professionals the use of hypnosis is much less dangerous than the administration of drugs or many other medical procedures. On the other hand, untrained individuals who attempt to deal with emotional difficulties and problems of living, whether they employ hypnosis or other therapeutic tools, may inadvertently create unnecessary stress for the individual.

Because of public and professional prejudices against hypnosis its greatest danger is probably to the hypnotist, not the subject. Even though there is no definitive evidence that hypnosis is harmful, it may be used as an explanation for unfortunate complications.

The aftereffects (sequelae) to experimental hypnosis have been studied by Coe and Ryken, 1979; Faw, Sellers, and Wilcox, 1968; Hilgard, 1974; and Hilgard, Hilgard, and Newman, 1961. The general findings indicate that when nonhypnotized comparison groups are included, subjects who have been hypnotized do not demonstrate more negative aftereffects and, in fact, may derive more positive effects, than their nonhypnotized subjects.

Qualifications for Hypnotic Techniques and Training

It has been stated throughout the chapter that hypnosis may be employed by psychotherapists of varying persuasions as well as professionals from other areas (especially medicine and dentistry). Hypnosis is best employed as an auxilliary procedure with other therapeutic tools, it is not a method of therapy in itself. The general qualifications for someone who uses hypnosis, therefore, should be the same as those required in whatever discipline it is to be employed— psychotherapy for example.

The use of hypnosis has been legitimized by medicine and psychology for only a little over 15 years. The American Psychological Association has a separate division for persons interested in hypnosis, and the medical, dental and psychological professions have board qualifications for practitioners of hypnosis. Some states have enacted laws controlling its use.

A professional desirous of employing hypnosis in conjunction with his practice must learn hypnotic techniques. Rosen et al. (1962) have discussed views of training for hypnosis in medicine, and Moss, Logan, and Lynch (1962) have discussed the same topic for psychology. In general, there appears to be a conservative view toward who is qualified to employ hypnosis and what is considered proper training in hypnotic techniques. The induction of hypnosis is quite simple to learn. A tape recorded induction, for example, can produce results very similar to that of an experienced hypnotist. While there are many ways to induce hypnosis (Haley, 1967; Kroger, 1977; Weitzenhoffer, 1953), all seem to be about equally effective. It is therefore not difficult for otherwise untrained persons to induce deep hypnosis in susceptible persons, even though they may not know what to do after the person is hypnotized. It is not too surprising then that things might get out of hand with an untrained person.

Formal courses that teach hypnosis are rare in American universities, although some are offered. Workshops and courses are sponsored several times a year by the two main hypnosis societies in the United States. Information may be obtained by writing to the Society for Clinical and Experimental Hypnosis, 140 West End Ave., New York, New York 10023, or the American Society of Clinical Hypnosis, 800 Washington Ave. S.E., Minneapolis, Minnesota 55414. The workshops range from the beginner's level to specialized and advanced uses of hypnosis.

Coe (1965) has recommended a way to teach oneself hypnotic techniques for experimental purposes. It requires background reading, a qualified person on call, actual experience administering waking suggestions and a standard hypnotic scale. While its purpose is to qualify persons to carry out research, it is also a reasonable way for clinicians to begin their early training.

CONCLUSIONS AND SUMMARY

Two topics were presented in this chapter. One centered on the enhancing effects of expectancies in psychotherapy; the other on the uses of suggestive techniques in helping people change.

Expectancy is related to all forms of psychotherapy, not just the suggestive therapies, and should be taken into account by all therapists. While expectancy alone cannot account for therapeutic outcome, it probably plays an important part in all techniques. Whenever clients seek out professionals they expect certain things. How these expectations are met and dealt with will have an impact on the outcome of the relationship.

Various uses of hypnosis were also presented. These techniques have been employed in many ways and for many kinds of difficulties. "Depth" therapists claim that hypnosis speeds the progress of therapy in its use as a tool for uncovering unconscious material. Hypnosis may also be employed as a psychodiagnostic technique in discovering underlying, dynamic causes of difficulties or conflicts. Hypnosis is used in behavior therapy to bring about relaxation and to enhance imaginative ability. While derived from different theoretical backgrounds, many hypnotherapeutic techniques appear to be quite similar to those employed by behavior therapists.

Evidence was also presented which suggests that hypnotic approaches may be quite effective as a therapeutic tool and should be considered part of every therapist's armamentarium.

Several approaches to self-suggestions were also discussed, all of which emphasize the use of clients' imaginal abilities and the power of their own thoughts. Self-hypnosis, autogenic training, yoga and meditation, and psychocybernetics served as examples.

The chapter concluded with topics of interest related to hypnosis, namely, the "powers" of hypnosis, and the training and qualifications for employing hypnosis.

REFERENCES

Bandler, R. and Grinder, J. *Patterns of the hypnotic techniques of Milton H. Erickson, Vol. I.* Cupertino, Ca.: Meta Publications, 1975.

Barber, J. Rapid induction analgesia: A clinical report. *American Journal of Clinical Hypnosis,* 1977, *19* (3), 138-147.

———. Measuring "hypnotic-like" suggestibility with and without "hypnotic induction"; psychometric properties, norms and variables influencing response to the Barber Suggestibility Scale (BSS). *Psychological Reports,* 1965, *16,* 809-844.

———. Maximizing the effectiveness of hypnosis in the treatment of chronic pain. Paper presented to the Second World Congress, International Association for the Study of Pain, Montreal, Aug. 28, 1978.

———. Maximizing the effectiveness of hypnosis through indirect suggestion. Paper presented at the American Psychological Association meetings, Toronto, Aug. 31, 1978.

Barber, T.X. *Hypnosis: A scientific approach.* Princeton, New Jersey: Nostrand, 1969.

Barber, T.X., Spanos, N.P., and Chaves, J.F. *Hypnosis, imagination and human potentialities.* Elmsford, N.Y.: Pergamon, 1974.

Barber, T.X. "Hypnosis," suggestions and psychosomatic phenomena: A new look from the standpoint of recent experimental studies. In J.L. Fosshage and P. Olsen (Eds.) *Healing: implications for psychotherapy.* N.Y.: Behavioral Publications, 1978.

Barber, T.X., and Wilson, S.C. Hypnosis, suggestions, and altered states of consciousness: Experimental evaluation of the new cognitive-behavioral theory and the traditional trance-state theory of "hypnosis." *Annals of the N.Y. Academy of Science,* 1977, *296,* 34-74.

Barrios, A. Hypnotherapy: A reappraisal. *Psychotherapy: Theory, Research and Practice,* 1970, *7,* 2-7.

Barth, G.F. *Nova Yoga: The yoga of imagination.* N.Y.: Mason and Lipscomb, 1974.

Bergin, A.E., and Garfield, S.L. (eds.) *Handbook of psychotherapy and behavior change,* New York: John Wiley and Sons, 1971.

Berren, M.R., and Gillis, G.S. The use of "failure models": An application of social comparison theory to changing maladaptive attitudes. *Journal of Contemporary Psychology,* 1976, *8* (1), 47-51.

Beutler, L.E., Pollack, S., and Jobe, A. "Acceptance," values, and therapeutic change. *Journal of Consulting and Clinical Psychology*, 1978, *46*, (1), 198-199.

Black, D.R. Review of self-hypnotic and self-control procedures. Unpublished manuscript, Stanford Univ., Counseling Psychology, Stanford, CA., 1978.

Black, D.R., and Thoresen, C.E. Self-hypnosis: A cognitive social learning perspective. Paper presented at the American Psychological Association meeting, Toronto, Aug. 1978.

Bloom, L.J., Weigel, R.G., and Trautt, G.M. "Therapeugenic" factors in psychotherapy: Effects of office decor and subject-therapist sex pairing on the perception of credibility. *Journal of Consulting and Clinical Psychology*, 1977, *45*, 867-873.

Brown, D.P. A model for the levels of concentrative meditation. *International Journal of Clinical and Experimental Hypnosis*, 1977, *24* (4), 236-273.

Carrington, P. *Freedom in meditation*. Garden City, N.Y.: Avehn Press, 1977.

Cautela, J.R. Covert sensitization. *Psychological Reports*, 1967, *20*, 459-468.

―――. Covert reinforcement. *Behavior Therapy*, 1970, 1, 33-50.

―――. Covert extinction. *Behavior Therapy*, 1971, *2*, 192-200.

―――. The use of covert conditioning in hypnotherapy. *International Journal of Clinical and Experimental Hypnosis*, 1975, *23*, (1), 15-27.

Cauthen, N.R. and Prymak, C.A. Meditation versus relaxation: An examination of the physiological effects of relaxation training and of different levels of experience with Transcendental Meditation. *Journal of Consulting and Clinical Psychology*, 1977, *45*, 496-497.

Childress, R., and Gillis, J.S. A study of pretherapy role induction as an influence process. *Journal of Clinical Psychology*, 1977, *33* (2), 540-544.

Coe, W.C. A procedure for teaching oneself hypnotic techniques for experimental purposes. *International Journal of Clinical and Experimental Hypnosis*, 1965, *13*, 144-148.

―――. The problem of relevance versus ethics in researching hypnosis and antisocial conduct. *Annals of the N.Y. Academy of Sciences*, 1977, *296*, 90-104.

―――. The credibility of posthypnotic amnesia: A contextualist's view. *International Journal of Clinical and Experimental Hypnosis*, 1978, *26*, 218-245.

Coe, W.C., Kobyashi, K., and Howard, M.L. Experimental and ethical problems in evaluating the influence of hypnosis in antisocial conduct, *Journal of Abnormal Psychology*, 1973, *82*, 476-482.

Coe, W.C. and Ryken, K. Hypnosis and risks to human subjects. *American Psychologists*, in press, 1979.

Coe, W.C., and Sarbin, T.R. Hypnosis from standpoint of a contextualist. *Annals N.Y. Academy of Sciences*, 1977, *296*, 2-13.

Coe, W.C., St. Jean, R.L., and Burger, G.M. Hypnosis and the enhancement of visual imagery. *International Journal of Clinical and Experimental Hypnosis*, in press.

Conn, J.H. Hypnosynthesis: Psychobiologic principles in the practice of dynamic psychotherapy utilizing hypnotic procedures. *International Journal of Clinical and Experimental Hypnosis*. 1968, *16*, 1-25.

Davidson, R.J., Goleman, D.J., and Schwartz, G.E. Attentional and effective concomitants of meditation: A cross-sectional study. *Journal of Abnormal Psychology*, 1976, *85*, 235-238.

Devi, Indra. *Renew your life through yoga*. New York: Prentice Hall, 1963.

Diamond, M.J. Modification of hypnotizability: A review. *Psychological Bulletin*, 1974, *81*, 180-193.

―――. Issues and methods for modifying responsivity to hypnosis. *Annals of the N.Y. Academy of Sciences*, 1977a, *296*, 119-128.

————. Hypnotizability is modifiable: An alternative approach. *International Journal of Clinical and Experimental Hypnosis*, 1977b, *25* 147-166.

————. Clinical hypnosis: Toward a cognitive-based skill approach. Paper presented at the American Psychological Association meeting, Toronto, Aug. 1978.

Eliade, Mircea. *Yoga: Immortality and freedom*, 2nd Ed., (W.R. Trask, Trans.). N.Y.: Bollingen, 1970.

Erickson, M.H. The confusion technique in hypnosis. *American Journal of Clinical Hypnosis*, 1964, *6*, 183-207.

Erickson, M.H. An introduction to the study and application of hypnosis for pain control. In Lasner, J. (Ed.), *Hypnosis and psychosomatic medicine*. N.Y.: Springer-Verlag, 1967.

Erikson, M.H., Rossi, E.L., and Rossi, S.H. *Hypnotic realities: The induction of clinical hypnosis and the indirect forms of suggestion*. N.Y.: Irvington Publications, 1976.

Faw, V., Sellers, D.J., and Wilcox, W.W. Psychopathological effects of hypnosis. *International Journal of Clinical and Experimental Hypnosis*, 1968, *16*, 26-37.

Fish, J.M. *Placebo therapy*. San Francisco: Jossey-Bass, 1973.

Frank, J.D. *Persuasion and healing*. Baltimore, Md.: Johns Hopkins Press, 1961 and 1973.

Friedenberg, W.P., and Gillis, J.S. An experimental study of the effectiveness of attitude change techniques for enhancing self-esteem. *Journal of Clinical Psychology*, 1977, *33* (4), 1120-1124.

Friedman, H. and Taub, H.A. The use of hypnosis and biofeedback procedures for essential hypertension. *International Journal of Clinical and Experimental Hypnosis*, 1977, *25* (4), 335-347.

Gill, M.M., and Brenman, M. *Hypnosis and related states: Psychoanalytic studies in regression*. New York: International Universities Press, 1959.

Gillis, J.S. Social influence in psychotherapy: A description of the process and some tactical implications. *Pilgrimage Press Monographs, Counseling and Psychotherapy Series, Vol. 1*, #1, 1979.

————. Therapist as manipulator. *Psychology Today*, 1974, Dec., 90-95.

Gillis, J.S., and Berren, M.R. (Eds.) *Social influence in psychotherapy: Readings and commentary*. Chicago: Nelson Hall, 1975.

Goleman, D.J. Meditation helps break the stress spiral. *Psychology Today*, 1976a, *9* (9), 82.

————. Meditation and consciousness: An Asian approach to mental health. *American Journal of Psychotherapy*, 1976b, *30* (1), 41-54.

————. *Varieties of the meditative experience*. N.Y.: E.P. Dutton & Co., 1977.

Goleman, D.J. and Schwartz, G.E. Meditation as an intervention in stress reactivity. *Journal of Consulting and Clinical Psychology*, 1976, *44*, 456-466.

Gordon, J.E. (Ed.) *Handbook of clinical and experimental hypnosis*. New York: MacMillan Co., 1967.

Haley, Jay (Ed.) *Advanced techniques of hypnosis and therapy: Selected papers of Milton H. Erickson, M.D.* New York: Grune and Stratton, 1967.

Hilgard, E.R. *Hypnotic susceptibility*. New York: Harcourt, Brace, and World, 1965.

————. The problem of divided consciousness: A neodissociation interpretation. *Annals N.Y. Academy of Science*, 1977, *296*, 48-59.

Hilgard, E.R. and Hilgard, J.R. *Hypnosis in the relief of pain*. Los Altos, Ca.: Wm. Kaufmann, 1975.

Hilgard, J.R. Sequelae to hypnosis. *International Journal of Clinical and Experimental Hypnosis*, 1974, *22*, 281-298.

Hilgard, J.R., Hilgard, E.R., and Newman, M.R. Sequelae to hypnotic induction with special reference to earlier chemical anesthesia, *Journal of Nervous and Mental Diseases*, 1961, *133*, 461-478.

Johnson, L.S., and Weight, D.G. Self-hypnosis versus heterohypnosis: Experimental and behavioral comparisons. *Journal of Abnormal Psychology*, 1976, *85*, 523-526.

Karlin, R.A. and McKeon, P. The use of hypnosis in multimodal therapy. In Lazarus, A.A. *Multimodal behavior therapy*. N.Y.: Springer, 1976.

Katz, N.W. Hypnotic inductions as training in cognitive self-control. *Cognitive therapy and research*, in press.

Katz, N.W., and Crawford, V.L. A little trance and a little skill: Interaction between models of hypnosis and type of hypnotic induction. Paper presented at the Society for Experimental and Clinical Hypnosis, Chapel Hill, N.C., Oct. 1978.

Kroger, W.S. *Clinical and experimental hypnosis, 2nd edition*. Philadelphia: J.B. Lippencott, 1977.

Kroger, W.S. and Fezler, W.D. *Hypnosis and behavior modification: Imagery conditioning*. Philadelphia: J.B. Lippencott, 1976.

Lazarus, A.A. *Behavior therapy and beyond*. New York: McGraw-Hill, 1971.

————. "Hypnosis" as a facilitator in behavior therapy. *International Journal of Clinical and Experimental Hypnosis*, 1973, *21*, 25-31.

————. *Multimodal behavior therapy: BASIC ID*. N.Y.: Springer, 1976.

Lerner, Barbara and Fiske, D.W. Client attributes and the eye of the beholder. *Journal of Consulting and Clinical Psychology*, 1973, *40*, 272-277.

Maharishi, Mahesh Yogi. *The science of living and the art of being*. N.Y.: Signet Books, 1972.

Maltz, M. *Psychocybernetics*. Englewood Cliffs, New Jersey: Prentice-Hall, 1960.

McReynolds, W.T., Barnes, A.R., Brooks, S., and Rehagen, N.J. The role of attention-placebo influences in the efficacy of systematic desensitization. *Journal of Consulting and Clinical Psychology*, 1973, *41*, 86-92.

Moss, C.S. *Hypnosis in perspective*. New York: MacMillan, 1965.

Moss, C.S., Logan, J.C., and Lynch, D. Present status of psychological research and training in hypnosis: A developing professional problem. *American Psychologist*, 1962, *17*, 542-549.

Orne, M.T. The nature of hypnosis: Artifact and essence. *Journal of Abnormal and Social Psychology*, 1959, *58*, 277-299.

————. The construct of hypnosis: Implications of the definition for research and practice. *Annals N.Y. Academy of Sciences*, 1977, *296*, 14-33.

Pagano, R.R., Rose, R.M., Stivers, R.M., and Warrenburg, S. Sleep during Transcendental Meditation. In T.X. Barber, et al. (Eds.) *Biofeedback and self-control: 1975-76*. Chicago: Aldine, 1976.

Parker, J.C., Gilbert, G.S., and Thoreson, R.W. Reduction of autonomic arousal in alcoholics. *Journal of Consulting and Clinical Psychology*, 1978, *46* (5), 879-886.

Rosen, H. *Hypnotherapy in clinical psychiatry*. New York: Julian Press, 1953.

Rosen, H., Kaufman, M.R., Lebensohn, Z., and West, L.J. Training in medical hypnosis. *Journal of American Medical Association*, 1962, *180*, 693-698.

Ruch, J.C. Self-hypnosis: The result of heterohypnosis or vice-versa. *International Journal of Clinical and Experimental Hypnosis*, 1975, *23*, 282-304.

Sarbin, T.R., and Coe, W.C. *Hypnosis: A social psychological analysis of influence communication*. New York: Holt, Rinehart, and Winston, 1972.

Schafer, D.W. and Hernandez, A. Hypnosis, pain and the context of therapy. *International Journal of Clinical and Experimental Hypnosis*, 1978, *26* (3), 143-153.

Shapiro, D.H. and Zifferblatt, S.M. Zen meditation and behavioral self-control: Similarities, differences and clinical applications. *American Psychologist*, 1976, *31*, 519-532.

Shultz, J.H. and Luthe, W. *Autogenic training*. New York: Grune and Stratton, 1959.

Spanos, N.P. and Barber, T.X. Behavior modification and hypnosis. In M. Hersen, et al. (Eds.) *Progress in behavior modification, Vol. 3.* N.Y.: Academic Press, 1976, 1-44.

Stampfl, T.G. and Levis, D.J. Essentials of implosive therapy: A learning-theory-based psychodynamic therapy. *Journal of Abnormal Psychology,* 1967, *72,* 496-503.

————. Implosive therapy: A behavioral therapy? *Behavior Research and Therapy,* 1968, *6,* 31-36.

Strong, S.R., and Matross, R. Change process in counseling and psychotherapy. *Journal of Counseling Psychology,* 1973, *20,* 25-37.

Torrey, E.F. *The mind game: Witchdoctors and psychiatrists.* New York: Emerson Hall, 1972.

Venzor, E., Gillis, J.S., and Beal, D.G. Preference for counselor response styles. *Journal of Counseling Psychology,* 1976, *23* (6), 538-542.

Weitzenhoffer, A.M. *General techniques of hypnotism.* New York: Grune and Stratton, 1957.

Weitzenhoffer, A.M. and Hilgard, E.R. *Stanford Hypnotic Susceptibility Scale, Forms A and B.* Palo Alto, California: Consulting Psychologists Press, 1959.

————. *Stanford Hypnotic Susceptibility Scale, Form C.* Palo Alto, California: Consulting Psychologist's Press, 1962.

Wilson, S.C., and Barber, T.X. The creative imagination scale as a measure of hypnotic responsiveness: Applications to experimental and clinical hypnosis. *American Journal of Clinical Hypnosis,* 1978, *20* (4), 235-249.

Wolberg, L.R. *Medical hypnosis, Volume I and II.* New York: Grune and Stratton, 1948.

Wolpe, J. *Psychotherapy by reciprocal inhibition.* Stanford, Ca.: Stanford University Press, 1958.

————. *The practice of behavior therapy.* New York: Pergamon, 1969.

13
Group Methods
Morton A. Lieberman

INTRODUCTION

In today's urban (and even not so urban) America, almost any bulletin board contains testimony that groups are "in" as a medium of choice for changing people. It has been estimated that upward of five million Americans have at one time or another participated in some type of group activity aimed at personal growth or change in *encounter groups*. A few million others are members of self-help groups; tens of thousands have been patients in some form of *group psychotherapy*. What sorts of groups, what sorts of members, what sorts of problems, and what sorts of people assume the function of helping others to change? These four questions require somewhat lengthy answers to convey some sense of the current scene, because the range of applications, methods, participants, and agents of change has increased geometrically over the last two decades.

Who Comes to Groups and Why Do They Come?

The most reasonable answer is, nearly every kind of person with almost every conceivable psychological or social complaint. The goals of group clients vary all the way from reducing juvenile delinquency in others to reducing weight in themselves. Some among the clientele of current-day healing groups bring problems once taken almost exclusively to mental health professionals—severe personal or interpersonal concerns. Others face no immediate serious stress, but seek the group in hope that it will provide them with clues to personal enrichment—that participation in a shared effort at growth will help them actualize unused but available personal potential. Another sizable part of the clientele are those who see themselves as limited not by general aspects of their own personalities or personal situations, but by specific problems that impinge on them because of their relationship to a social order which they feel suppresses them because of sex, sexual mores, race, age, and so on. Finally, groups can be found which contain members who claim no motive for belonging other than to widen their experience, to share, to enjoy, or to learn to enjoy communion with others.

When one turns to the question of *what sorts of groups* make up the current scene, the divergence seen is equal to that of the type of clients and their goals. The litany of labels—Gestalt, transactional analysis, confrontation therapy, marathon, encounter, sensory awareness, T-Groups, self-help groups, consciousness-raising groups, all in addition to the more traditional forms of group psychotherapy—does not aid in clarifying what sorts of things are thought by each school to be the essential ingredients of change or cure. Some group leaders on the current scene believe passionately in the healing qualities of group-generated love; others believe just as passionately in the curative powers of hate, seeing the basic stuff of change as stemming from the experience of primary rage. Some depend solely on talk therapy; others use music, lights, and the clench of human bodies. And many groups have no appointed or formal leaders.

Can the Current Use of Groups Be Described by Who It Is Who Leads Them?

Can the sense of confusion be reduced by organizing the array of forms and techniques according to the background, education, or professional discipline of those who purvey group people-changing services? No. For those who have made themselves available to lead such groups may have been prepared by long years of training in prestigious professional institutions, by participation in two-week institutes, or purely by personal commitment. Nor would a sense of order stem from examining the location of such activities. Many personal change-oriented groups are to be found in traditional help-giving institutions, such as mental hospitals, schools, or social agencies; some meet in the offices of mental health practitioners in private practice. Many are found in growth centers, a new institution specifically formed for conducting such groups. Church basements, dormitories, and living rooms have also become the scene of people-changing groups.

The diversity of goals, clientele, form of activity, leadership, and setting of people-changing activities in groups may suggest why attempts to evaluate the consequences or effects of all these activities have yielded equal diversity. These effects range from ably-documented findings suggesting major behavioral attitudinal and personality changes—the reconstruction of individuals—to equally well-documented examples of the severe debilitation of individuals stemming from their participation in change-oriented groups.

This chapter aims to apprise the reader, both descriptively and analytically, of the current use of groups in all their diversity, and to establish some reasonable signposts which may help to organize the vast array of activities now characteristic of healing groups. What are the historical as well as current forces that have shaped the practices so abundant in our society? Why do therapists, leaders, or organizations place people in groups for healing purposes? What theories underlie group-based healing? What assumptions underlie each of these theories with respect to who are appropriate clients; what definitions of illness or pathology are implicit or explicit in various theoretical perspectives; what events do diverse theoretical perspectives imply as necessary for growth, development, or positive change? What is seen as the role or task of the leader or therapist? And finally, how do these divergent theories assess the role of the group in the curative process? The last half of this chapter will focus on a general theory of group-based healing which starts with an examination of the *unique properties of the group* for helping people in psychological distress as the base from which to discuss answers to questions of what the leader or central person must do in order to accomplish the task or goal of the group. Particular emphasis is placed on how to read or diagnose groups in order to make appropriate, helpful interventions. Finally, the critical events that must transpire in order for people to use the group as a meaningful personal learning environment are examined.

Why Use Groups?

The use of groups for systematically helping individuals in distress is of relatively recent origin in modern mental health practice. It is perhaps helpful to recall, however, that small groups have always served as important healing agents; from the beginning of recorded history, group forces have been used to inspire hope, increase morale, offer strong emotional support, induce serenity and confidence, or counteract many psychic and bodily ills. Religious healers have always relied heavily on group forces, but when healing passed from the priestly to the medical profession, the deliberate use of group forces fell into a decline concomitant with the increasing sanctity of the doctor-patient relationship.

The strangeness experienced by many seekers of psychiatric help when confronted with the help-giving conditions of groups is the resultant of a complex process affecting both those who seek the help as well as those who give it. The development of psychiatry as an entrenched part of modern medicine was, in part, predicated on the idea that "scientific medicine" must at all costs distinguish itself from healing which stemmed from nonscientific traditions. Modern Western psychiatry was even more plagued than other branches of medicine with the need to become "scientific." In its beginnings, the medical treatment of psychological problems required, for its legitimization as a branch of medical science, a clear differentiation between its methods and those that preceded it in folk societies, where highly developed group-based techniques were used for curing psychological illness within the framework of the family, the group of similar sufferers, the village, or the religious community. This association of "pre-scientific" therapies with group forms perhaps influenced psychiatry away from utilization of group techniques.

Until the recent advent of the *new group therapies*, it has been expected in Western culture that personal help be given by *one* person—it may be the corner bartender, a personal friend, or a professional, such as lawyer, doctor, or clergyman, but what is important is that it is expected that the context in which it is rendered will be private, intimate, and exclusive. Even in such congregate bodies as the family or the church, it is generally assumed that personal help will be offered and received in a private, two-person relationship, not through the congregate as a whole. The genesis of modern psychiatry within the general Western cultural context in the first half of the twentieth century did not, in other words, contain conditions suitable for the flourishing growth of group-based healing technologies.

In the early 1900s, Joseph Pratt (1907), a Boston internist, organized classes for tubercular patients—"The class meeting is a pleasant social hour for members . . . made up as a membership of widely different races and different sexes, they have a common bond in a common disease. A fine spirit of camaraderie has developed. They never discuss their symptoms and are almost invariably in good spirits. . . ." (1907). Pratt's therapy had many similarities to current-day inspirational group psychotherapy; he hoped to overcome the pessimism of the patients, to discourage neurotic secondary gains from illness, and to encourage self-confidence.

Isolated individuals in the early 1900s reported similar sets of experiences to those of Pratt. In Europe, for example, Alfred Adler established guidance centers that used group concepts in treating working-class patients. An early and important influence in the development of group psychotherapy was the use of the healing group by Jacob L. Moreno, who is best known for his development of psychodrama (1953). The analogies between Moreno's approach to the healing groups and those described in anthropological literature is impressive. The patient is provided the opportunity to express himself freely through drama, trying the role of himself or others he feels are significantly related to his present problems. The patient often enacts scenes from his past, while other persons (whom Moreno called alter egos) articulate feelings, moods, responses, and so on which may not be evident to the patient himself (a kind of Greek chorus orchestrated by the therapist). In England, the work of Trigant L. Burrow was an important, but unfortunately unrecognized, influence in the area of the use of groups. Burrow, a psychoanalyst, became dissatisfied with the emphasis psychoanalysis placed on the individual, an emphasis that he felt excluded examination of social forces. In the early twenties, Burrow initiated the use of the group context for the analysis of behavioral disorders in relationship to social forces and coined the term "group analysis" to describe the treatment setting (1927).

Thus, the techniques characteristic of current group treatment practices were clearly evident in the first quarter of the century. The inspirational character of Pratt's groups has many modern counterparts in the self-help movement, such as Alcoholics Anonymous, Recovery Inc., and Weight Watchers. The employment of the expressive part of the person through dramatization as part of the curative process forms a major component of many current group methodologies. Finally, the use of the group social context for psychoanalytically-oriented analysis is still very visible as a major direction in current practice. By and large, however, the efforts of the early proponents of group methods were isolated; their predominantly pragmatic concerns did not lead them or others to explore the conceptual grounds underlying the use of groups for therapeutic benefit.

By the time the reader has reached this chapter and has noted that out of all the preceding chapters only one discusses the use of groups for change (therapeutics), it would seem to be reasonable to question, why place clients in groups? It should perhaps be noted that at different times and in different cultures the forces might be just the opposite, and it would seem "abnormal" or unusual to have one healer and one patient. The examples of healing cults in folk societies amply express that in many societies the ordinary or the usual way of healing may be within a social or multi-person context. It does seem sensible to ask, nevertheless, how it is that patients began to be placed in groups for treatment in this culture. Although there is no single answer to this question, there are several important factors which have helped to accelerate the use of groups for healing purposes.

The current use of group psychotherapy did not develop in full force until the 1940s. Although, as the history of the forces impinging upon group therapy indicates, there were clear-cut signs of a movement to the use of groups for healing functions prior to that time, these were small and isolated attempts without much reverberation within psychiatric circles. Foremost among the reasons is the simple pragmatics or economics of the situation. In time of short supply of psychiatric personnel, such as during World War II, and increased need for service, the "reasonableness" of treating patients in groups came to the fore. This "discovery" has been made over and over again in various segments of the healing professions—the spread of group forms was much influenced by the social pragmatics of picking professionals to treat larger numbers of people, and, to some extent, shaped by the economics of fee structures—forces that cannot be ignored in explaining the development and spread of groups for healing functions.

A second major impact directing the professional to the use of groups developed out of the changing nature of theory with regard to both the nature of man and the genesis of his psychological ills. An increasing emphasis on an interpersonal view of man and the suggestion that psychological disturbance might be intrinsically related to problems of relationships among people—a social rather than intrapsychic phenomenon—made the jump from a dyad (a two-person interaction) to multi-person treatment situations an easy transition.

The practice of the healing professions is littered in its history with examples of serendipity—the chance discovery that groups seem to be potent constructive forces in the healing of psychological illness. This is a theme that cannot be omitted when examining the question of why therapists place patients in groups. Psychotherapists are a restless lot, and the practice of healing is never stabilized. Inner doubt, feelings of failure, discouragement, and frank therapeutic despair are the common lot of the mental health professional. The search for new techniques, modalities, or procedures is unending, a theme that may explain in part the current popularity of group practice.

Finally, the personal needs and gratification of the healer, a topic fraught with apprehension, concern, and frequent avoidance, is also present as one of the factors that move therapists to place patients in groups rather than dyads. The excitement, stimulation, the need for novelty, are a few of the "reasons" that have directed therapists toward the use of groups. For many practitioners, the sanctity and the privacy and the ability to concentrate totally on one other human being, and the opportunity that such an intimate relationship offers for exchange, is a prime attraction of the individual psychotherapeutic relationship. There are others, however, who need different arenas, for whom an audience, a chance to observe rather than hear about behavior, an opportunity to wield a different form of influence, are more attractive.

An Illustration of the New and Not So New

Before proceeding to examine the various systems of people-changing that occur in groups, it may be useful to have some image of group psychotherapy, both as it has commonly been practiced within traditional mental health settings and in some of the "newer therapies." The initial session of a traditional therapy group, for example, would be something like this:

About nine people file into a room slowly, tentatively. Each has seen only one other person in the room: the therapist, a week earlier in a diagnostic interview. Some appear reluctant, some enthusiastic, but all have come to this first meeting with at least the willingness to go along with the therapist's belief that the group could be useful to them. They sit in a circle, quiet and expectant. Their posture seems anxious. What will go on here? What can go on here? What will the therapist do? Several in the group have had previous psychotherapy. One woman begins the interaction by describing the disappointments she has experienced in previous treatments. A note of desperation and near panic is discernible in the responses of others to her wail of self-negation and helplessness. Sympathetic offerings of similar tales of woe are heard from various people in the room. From time to time the therapist comments, pointing out the fearful expectations of the various group members.

Underneath the stories and histories offered by various members, the therapist "hears" the patients asking each other a set of questions only hinted at in what they are saying. And underneath the questions about others in the room lie still another set all having to do with the person himself. Why did you come? What are your hopes? What forms does your "illness" take? Do you feel that this may do me any good at all? Are you as sick as I? Am I as sick as you? How strange, perhaps even insane, is the arrangement whereby I come to a group of neurotics to get better. Above all what is the "doctor" over there planning to do for me? I don't like people—why must I be here? Who are these others and what have I to do with them?

Thus, group therapy begins. The patients begin an experience in treatment which they may understandably feel violates expectations they bring from their experience in other doctor-patient relationships. Often group therapy patients cannot see what good it will do an unhappy neurotic person to share his problems with other neurotic sufferers. Is it enough to reassure him, as some therapists indeed believe, that "a problem shared is a problem helped," or to provide a context founded on the assumption that misery not only loves but is relieved by company? What of the therapist? Will he, by virtue of some rare professional training and intuitive attributes, be able to understand, diagnose, and change the troublesome personality problems of a lifetime? And, at that, of a roomful of people simultaneously? He—the therapist—obviously expects something useful to come from the interactions of these people, but how does he see the members to be of use to each other when he remains silent and passive so long? What does he expect will happen?

At the other end of the group treatment continuum, we can imagine another group of people temporarily migrating to a growth center. Their arrival is noisier, more buoyant, more playful; they are in vacation garb, their talk is more free and more reminiscent of the first evening of summer camp than the still, anxious scene of the group therapy session. They are likely to have a speaking knowledge of Maslow, Rogers, Berne, and Perls, and of the latest people-changing procedures. They express their desire for change freely and seem eager to get to know one another. They seem hardly able to await the morning's beginning; if some appear a bit anxious, others are enthusiastic about the drama that will unfold. All know in general what they can expect to happen but seem restless to generate the specific emotions and events which will form the content of their shared experience.

What will the leader, whom they have never met, be like? What will he do or expect of them? In the back of their minds are the accumulation of images based on what they have heard from friends and the popular press—images which are mixed with desires to become changed people. Will it work for me? What about the others? Will they really get to know me? Can I trust them? Will they help me?

They do not have long to wait: the leader begins with an explosion of his inner feelings. He may be sleepy this morning, he may not have wanted to come, he may look around and find the group full of "unattractive people" and "tell it like it is" without pausing. On the other hand, he may express his total positive regard for all and quickly exhibit a readiness to accept any behavior expressed. He may then launch into a set of instructions, perhaps suggesting, "all of you look so 'up tight' that we ought to loosen up and begin by playing a childhood game.

The images evoked by these two settings are intended to suggest that the group-based people-changing business in our society today has diverse assumptions, allegiances, and expectations, to such an extent that it might appear sheer folly to consider them under the same rubric.

COMPARISONS AMONG CURRENT-DAY HEALING GROUPS

A scanning of the field of group-based activities whose central task is the psychological and behavioral alteration of individuals and the relief of human misery would suggest that the range of such activities might be grouped under four major types which are distinguished from one another mainly by whom they see as appropriate clientele and what they regard as the major function(s) of the group. At one end of the continuum would be those activities that formally fall within the purview of societally sanctioned, professionally-led groups—*group psychotherapy*. Group therapy explicitly employs a *medical* model. Its avowed public goal is "cure," or the production of mental health, and sees as its relevant population those who define themselves as seeking release from psychological misery. The group members are generally called "patients," who are thought by the therapist (and probably themselves) to be psychologically "ill" and to exhibit "sick" behavior. An important implication of this emphasis is that some individuals would be considered as appropriate candidates for the method and others (the "psychologically healthy") would not.

At the opposite end of the professional continuum are a variety of *self-help movements*—Alcoholics Anonymous, Synanon, Recovery Inc., and so forth, up to perhaps as many as 216 separate organizations. By intention these groups are not professionally led. As lay movements, however, they share with group psychotherapy some restrictive notions of appropriate clientele. The definition of appropriate clientele is usually much narrower than in group psychotherapy, but there are clear-cut inclusion-exclusion principles. One must be an alcoholic, an abuser of drugs, a child abuser, a parent of a child who has a particular disease, and so forth. The range for any particular self-help movement's attention is limited to individuals who have a common symptom, problem, or life predicament.

A third set of healing groups occurs under the rubric of the *Human Potential Movement,* including such variously labeled activities as sensitivity training, encounter groups, and so on. Although there are many instances where such groups are led by nonprofessionals, they usually do involve professionals, whether legitimized by traditional psychological and psychiatric training or by newer short-term training institutions. A major distinction between the previously-mentioned activities and encounter or growth groups is that the latter view themselves as having universal applicability. Unlike group therapy which implies psychological illness and patient status, or self-help programs which are directed at a common problem of members, the encounter movement considers its activities relevant to all who want to grow, change, and develop.

Finally, we come to *consciousness-raising groups,* which share with the self-help groups the insistence on nonprofessional orientation and peer control, but unlike the self-help groups have broad criteria for inclusion. Although they do not take in everyone, as does the Human Potential Movement, consciousness-raising groups are formed on the basis of such certain *general* demographic similarities as sex, race, ethnicity, age, or sexual behavior. The tie that binds is not a common psychological syndrome but a general social characteristic of a large sub-group of people; the membership criteria, in other words, permit wide latitude regarding personal particularities.

STRUCTURAL AND TECHNICAL DIFFERENCES AMONG GROUPS

Perhaps the most important technological change reflected in the newer forms of healing groups as compared to more traditional psychotherapeutic groups is reflected in techniques for *lessening the psychological distance* between the leader and the participants. A variety of methods serves this function: the transparency of the therapist (he reveals his own personality), the use of informal setting, the trend of leaders to assume the stance of participant, the diminution of the importance of expertise of the leader, his presentation of self more nearly as a peer and, finally, the use of physical contact—touching—are all innovations which seem calculated to reduce the psychological distance between the changer and the changing.

Few guides exist to assess the importance of such a change from the traditional patient-therapist relationship. Perhaps all that can be said for sure is that such changes reflect current changes in social mores, which have increasingly moved away from emphasis on the priestly status of healing professionals and other experts. The new forms, having developed more recently, could be said to be more sensitive than the old to current cultural expectations.

A second major distinction between therapy and encounter groups, on the one hand, and most self-help and consciousness-raising groups, on the other, relates to their conception of the function of the group as a mechanism for personal change. Both psychotherapy and encounter groups of almost all theoretical persuasions share, as a fundamental assumption, a view of the group as a *social microcosm,* a small complete social world, reflecting in miniature all of the dimensions of real social environments. It is this aspect of the group—that is, its reflection of the interpersonal issues that confront individuals in the larger society—that is most highly prized as the group property which induces individual change. Varying types of encounter and psychotherapeutic schools of thought of course differ over which transactions are most important—those between patient and therapist or those *among* patients. They also differ regarding which emotional states are most conducive to positive change. But underneath all the activities that fall into these two types lies the assumption that cure or change is based on the exploration and reworking of relationships in groups.

Self-help groups and consciousness-raising groups develop a rather different stance to the issue of the group as a social microcosm. The interaction among members as a vehicle for change appears to be somewhat de-emphasized. The group is a supportive environment for developing new behavior not primarily within the group, but outside. The group becomes a vehicle for cognitive restructuring, but analysis of the transactions among members is not the basic tool of change.

Another characteristic that contrasts these four systems is the degree to which they stress *differentiation* versus nondifferentiation among their members. Being "neurotic," having psychological difficulty, or being a patient, are vague and relatively unbound identifications, compared to being a member of a racial minority group or a woman in a consciousness-raising group. Being interested in growth and development is obviously a more vague, indistinct basis for forming an identity with a communal effort than being an alcoholic or a child abuser. It is easier for consciousness-raising groups and self-help groups to stress identity with a common core problem than it is in psychotherapy and other groups. Although it is typical for a psychotherapeutic group to go through a period of time in which similarities are stressed, this is usually an early developmental phase and represents an attempt of the group to achieve some form of cohesiveness. It is not the raison d'*être* of the group, as it may be for a consciousness-raising or self-help group. In fact, there is some evidence that encounter group participants who remain committed to a sense of similarity are less likely to experience positive change. The potency of both self-help groups and consciousness-raising groups, on the other hand, appears to stem from their continued insistence on the possession of a common problem; their members believe themselves to derive support from their identification with a common core issue.

An obvious distinction among the various systems of group-based healing rests in their *attribution system*—the interpretive theories explicitly and implicitly communicated regarding the source of human misery and how one resolves it; for example, the degree to which the systems emphasize internal versus external sources of the problem. Psychoanalytically-oriented psychotherapeutic groups attribute the source of psychological difficulty to the personal past. Women's consciousness-raising groups emphasize an external locus of the problem: an impersonal, sexist society. In our attempt to understand what processes may be psychotherapeutic, I believe we have paid too little attention to the effect of varying attribution systems on change. In comparing several theories of personal change employed in encounter groups (Gestalt, transactional analysis, Rogerian, and so forth) it was found that it made little difference which theory was "taught," as long as some cognitive structure was taken away from the group to explain one's problems and how to resolve them. Whether this observation would fit the larger differences in attribution systems one can assume between, for example, psychotherapeutic groups and women's consciousness-raising groups, is a major unknown.

APPROACHES TO HEALING

The student interested in learning how to lead healing groups faces a far more complex task than he would have had less than ten years ago. Theories, techniques, client systems, and goals have expanded to an extent which enormously complicates the process of learning how to conduct such groups. Which theory to choose, how to sort among techniques, how to apply appropriate methods to particular clients, may appear to the beginner to require the wisdom of Solomon.

It would be foolhardy to assume that the reader has arrived at this chapter *tabula rasa* regarding theories of changing people. It is more likely that most readers have been exposed to ideas about their personal change that represent some amalgam of behaviorism, humanistic psychology, and probably also dynamic theories of personality and therapeutic technique. It may, therefore, be useful to review briefly ideas stemming from these three orientations and examine their influence on group-based healing activities. In so doing, it is crucial to recognize that nearly every theory or set of ideas about changing people in groups has been derived from theoretical systems related to dyadic models of therapy.

Behavioral Models

Behavioral models, perhaps best expressed in social learning theory terms, advance various mechanisms as essential for change induction—arousal enhancement and reduction, modeling, cognitive restructuring, and so forth. The specific mechanisms and their operations are delineated in several chapters of this book, so that the reader need not be treated to yet another review of behavioral approaches. Behavioral approaches, however well they may serve in dyadic contexts, involve some serious theoretical as well as technical problems when they are applied to groups. By choosing to place several individuals into a group setting for change induction, we construct a social system that has a number of important properties that do not characterize dyads. These unique properties of the group fundamentally alter the relationship between the central person (leader, therapist) and members in ways which mere technical adaptations on his part will not overcome.

Those who have attempted to use a behavioral orientation in groups assume implicitly that the leader is in precise control of the situation—that he has the power to change, to desensitize, to model, and so forth, all the behavior that is desired. This implicit assumption limits the utility of behavioral approaches in the group context. Power and influence are considerably more diffused in a multi-person relationship than they are in a dyad. The sources of power and the ability to wield it become complex issues where more than two are gathered together. The nature of the reward-punishment system in groups may differ from dyads in some important aspects: for example, the ultimate punishment in a dyad is withdrawal of love; in a group, it is exclusion, a punishment more under the control of the group than of the leader. Thus, the precision that so attracts people-changers to behavioral therapies is probably considerably reduced in a group context, where influence is a function of how the social system takes place. Another example is the dilemma inherent in behavioral theories in talking about the role of the others in the group. Statements like, "The members will reinforce, will model, will vicariously learn," are commonplace in this approach. It is as if the theoreticians assume that the group members will do just the right thing at the right time so that they will be facilitative, and that producing these responses in the collectivity is open to strategies in accordance with social learning theory.

Most social psychologists would agree that which behaviors become reinforced in groups can perhaps be best explained in terms of group norms—those shared but unexpressed agreements among members about what is appropriate and inappropriate behavior. Again, there is an implicit assumption among behavioral technicians that group norms will be harmonious with the intention of the central person. Recent studies, however, indicate that group norms are not necessarily or primarily a function of leader behavior or leader desires. Thus, approaching change induction in groups with a behavioral orientation presents some tricky theoretical and technical issues which tend, as yet, not to be addressed in the behavioral literature. As with most other theories of change derived from examination of dyadic experience, the failure of behavioral approaches to take account of the most salient feature of groups, namely that they represent a complex social system not only with unique properties for change, but also with unique problems, reduces the power of change strategies that have demonstrated success in the dyadic context.

Humanistic Approaches

There are a number of ideas and ways of looking at people-changing that have their roots in the humanistic-existential perspective. As in both the dynamic and behavioral perspectives, there are differences among various positions which can be broadly classified under this rubric. They all, however, share a common view of the nature of man, the source of his plight, and what is required for him to grow or change. The elements of this perspective are what most distinguish the humanistic orientation from behavioral as well as dynamic views. Emphasis is placed on the human being as a developing person and the goal is actualization of latent potential. The most widely known humanistic system is that developed by Carl Rogers (1970), originally for group therapy and later applied to encounter groups. The core set of ideas in Rogers's thinking relate to how the therapist or leader can be a facilitative human being. Rogerians regard three general conditions as crucial in a relationship between facilitator (therapist-leader) and client(s): (1) the acceptance (unconditional positive regard) of the client or the group; (2) the empathetic understanding of another human being; and (3) genuineness as a way of communicating to others, which necessitates trusting one's own feelings. These three conditions have been amply portrayed in an impressive series of research studies begun in the fifties by Rogers and his students. Truax and his colleagues (1967) have reasonably established that these three basic conditions of relationship between therapists and clients in dyadic relationship are facilitative and lead to positive outcome. Of interest here is that few new concepts have been developed within the humanistic framework to take account of the social forces introduced when change induction takes place in the group. It is apparently assumed that the leader, facilitator, or therapist can establish these three conditions with each individual in the group and copy the situation he institutes in a dyad. Yet, what is of importance here is that Truax and Carkhuff indicate that in their own studies the same three therapist-induced conditions which were shown to be robust in their positive influence in individual therapy were nowhere near as powerful in the group situation. As practiced from the Rogerian perspective, the group is used for support, for a sense of communion, and for a source of feedback. The theoretical system, however, contains no means of analyzing group forces or of relating therapist interventions to the dynamics of the group as a social system. The approach of such leaders to the group is reminiscent in many ways of the "great man" view of history. Implicit in the emphasis on the establishment of basic trust and acceptance and empathy is the assumption that the leader will be able to be facilitative to the group by the force of his own person and, perhaps, set an example as well as directly aid people in changing.

Although it uses the group quite differently, the Gestalt approach also embraces a fundamentally positive view of the nature of man and his psychosocial needs. As compared to Rogerian-oriented leaders, Gestalt leaders are much more active, make far more use of techniques of confrontation, and generally involve their members in many more structured exercises or games. Nevertheless, in much the same way as Rogerian practitioners, they make minimal use of group forces beyond communion and support. Thus, these approaches clearly differ in their techniques and in their assumptions about conditions which induce change; they share, however, the underlying perspective that human problems arise more from the social experience of a man than from negative inner forces. They also are alike in their tendency to make limited use of the whole group as a source of change-induction.

Dynamic Approaches to Person-Changing

As with the behavioral and humanistic-existential approaches, there are many theoretical and technological contributions that can be broadly classified as fundamentally dynamic orientations. Their historical roots are psychoanalytic, so that what most distinguishes this set of approaches from those already discussed is their view that the source of human misery is intrapsychic—inner conflicts which an individual has carried over a lifetime. Therapy involves the cognitive mastery, both generically and currently, of these conflicts. Two major processes are involved in therapeutics—the interpretation of resistance and the analysis of transference. Resistance is viewed as stemming from the fundamental ambivalence of the person and is felt necessary to defend against discovering aspects of himself that he fears will be painful. Ambivalence is also expressed in that change is desired yet also resisted. Transference in a classical sense, of course, refers to the set of feelings about current people that have their roots in significant early relationships. These core ideas have been translated into group therapy *in toto*, so that the classic set of operations of dynamically-oriented group therapists are the interpretation of resistance and the analysis of transference. They view the group as a major source of stimulation of the lifelong conflicts and issues confronting the members. From this perspective, the fundamental contribution of the group to the treatment process is that it permits the patient to better understand and observe the nature of his neurotic operations. The content of transference is handled by viewing the group as a place where multiple transference distortions can take place, although by and large the focus is still on the person of the therapist. In practice, groups conducted within a psychoanalytic framework appear to take on the special coloration of the tradition; for example, in such groups it is common to observe the interpretive role traditionally played by the analyst in the dyad being taken over by members of the group.

Other dynamic theorists have made much more considerable use of the group. Because Alfred Adler and his students conceived of man's main problems as fundamentally social, Adlerian group psychotherapists attribute greater potency to the group, not only because it reveals or highlights members' conflicts and maladjustments but also because it offers corrective influences. The *social* nature of psychopathology, the conception that psychological illness is a product of interaction with others, also underlay the work of Harry Stack Sullivan (1953). Sullivan saw most of therapy as having to do with acquainting the patient with the various processes and techniques which are his maneuvers for minimizing or avoiding anxiety responses derived from early social interactions. The group as social microcosm, then, offers for the Sullivanian group therapist the basic stuff of analysis, the important interactional components.

It is important to recognize that these three general orientations to person change—behavioral, humanistic-existential, and dynamic—all have been derived from theory and experience generated in dyadic therapeutic relationships. By and large, as these orientations have been increasingly adopted for use in group therapeutic contexts, there has been extensive innovation in techniques for applying them. There has been virtually no examination, however, of whether crucial differences between group and dyadic change contexts may not make theoretical reexamination and development a requisite for effective selection of techniques.

THE UNIQUE POWERS OF THE GROUP*

What then are the special properties of groups, as opposed to dyads, which are not to be overlooked when groups are used as the medium for personal change? Five capacities of groups are particularly important in their influence on the therapeutic experience of the client: (1) the capacity of the group to develop *cohesiveness* or sense of belonging; (2) the capacity of the group to *control* (reward and punish) behavior; (3) the capacity to define *reality* for the individual; (4) the capacity to induce and release powerful feelings *(emotional contagion);* and (5) the capacity to provide a contrast for *social comparison* and *feedback.* What are the implications of these properties for the induction of productive, psychotherapeutic experiences in the group context?

The Capacity of Groups to Develop Cohesiveness

This capacity reflects the phenomenal experience of communion or belongingness which is most often operationally defined as the attractiveness of the group to its participants. Roughly, cohesiveness plays the same role in group therapy as the positive transference relationship between the doctor and patient in dyadic therapy. In recent years, there has been a marshaling of evidence on studies of individual psychotherapy that point to the importance of the transference relationship between the therapist and patient. Researchers such as Truax and Carkhuff (1967) have presented findings which support the thesis that qualities of this relationship, such as high levels of accurate empathy, nonpossessive warmth and genuineness, or patients who are liked or consider themselves liked by the therapist, are more likely to improve in psychotherapy. The group context does not as readily offer the opportunity to establish such relationships between each member and a single leader. The group property of cohesiveness, however, plays the same role, for it is this sense of belongingness that motivates the members to stay in the group and to work with it, and that eases the pain associated with

---

*The section on the unique powers of the group is a summary of material presented in a paper: Lieberman, M. A., Lakin, M., and Whitaker, D. S. The group as a unique context for therapy. *Psychotherapy: Theory, research and practice.* Vol. 5, No. 1. Winter, 1968.

therapeutic exploration. Cohesive groups are those which offer a member almost unconditional acceptance no matter what his history and behavior have been outside of the group. They offer support for risk-taking; they provide the psychological "glue" that permits the members to reveal themselves; as a social microcosm they provide a setting for public esteem and consequently for one's own esteem.

The Capacity of the Group to Control Behavior

Closely associated with and dependent on the level of cohesiveness is the group's capacity to control behavior and to provide a system of rewards and punishments. As microcosms of a larger society, groups develop their own cultures and depend on special rules and standards which they establish as they extend their lives. How much one talks, what one talks about, what one doesn't talk about, even the way one talks about certain things, are aspects of how members behave over which the group wields influence. Such control over individual behavior is a central property of a group, including a therapy or growth group. The group member is almost inevitably confronted with pressure from others to change his behaviors or his views. The need to be in step, to abide by the rules, is a powerful factor inducing conformity in the group. Disregard for the rules means the potentiality of punishment. The ultimate punishment available to the group is the power of exclusion—either psychological or physical. In dyadic therapy, the patient does not fear exclusion if he does not go along with the therapist, but loss of the therapist's respect or love. Note then that we are dealing with two very different psychological experiences leading to similar behavior—conformity. A strong force additionally pulling members toward conformity is the group's most prized reward—its *power to offer the authenticating affirmation of one's peers.* The experience of "consensual validation" (approval by members who have become important) appears to be the most salient and gratifying experience in group therapy, more powerful than the affirmation of the therapist. The power of groups to exact conformity also frequently induces fear in people, and there is much evidence not only that groups have a very real capacity to induce conformity, but also that members fear punishment for departure from the group's "rules." It is important to note, however, that the norms that are developed which determine what characteristics of behavior are open to group influence, are never generated by a single person in the group, but are shared agreements. It is the person's belief that he has some power to influence the development of norms and standards in a group that reduces, to some extent, the fears and other negative feelings stemming from the capacity of groups to induce conformity.

The Capacity of the Group to Define Reality for Its Members

In dyadic psychotherapy, one of the major roles of the therapist is to contribute meaning to the patient's behavior—to provide *labels* for his thoughts, his feelings and fantasies, and his transactions with others, both current and past. Most schools of verbal psychotherapy view *understanding* by the client as a prime effect to be sought through psychotherapy; developing understanding (insight) is of course not simply a matter of the therapist labeling or lending meaning, which produces this sought-after state, but a goal to which a variety of therapist interventions are directed.

An important group property is the influence the group exerts on how each person should view himself, the group as a whole, and others in the group; thus in a group situation it is not only the leader who has a salient role in providing insight and understanding, or attributing meaning; the social system, the collection of participants, also adds to that meaning collectively. The group's capacity to define reality is dramatically illustrated by an incident in a group therapy course given by the author in which psychiatric residents observed two classmates working as therapists with an ongoing group. The observers watched from a darkened observation room and discussed the proceedings afterward with the two therapists. Before the eighth session began, the window blinds were removed for cleaning, so that the patients could see the observers through the one-way mirror. The two student therapists felt that since all the patients knew they were being observed there was no need to call off the observation. As the patients arrived one by one, each looked particularly closely at the large observation mirror and then took his seat. The meeting began with members talking about how difficult it is to communicate with people, ''particularly when you couldn't see them—in telephone conversations, etc.'' They referred to the observers (which they had not done in previous sessions) with statements like, ''It's uncomfortable. I don't like being observed because it's one-sided. The observers can see the patients but the patients cannot see the observers.'' The meeting went on in this vein for about a half hour and then shifted to other topics. After the session, when the two therapists joined the other residents to discuss the session, the observers asked the therapists why they had not intervened and brought some sense of ''reality'' to the group by pointing out that the observers could be seen for the first time. They answered that the light had shifted and the observers couldn't really be seen. Their belief was so strong that several of us had to accompany them into the therapy room to demonstrate that obviously the group could see the observers—perhaps not every facial gesture, but clearly their outlines at least.

This illustrates an instance of a group's capacity to define its own, special reality. The two therapists, who had entered the session knowing the observers could be seen, and the patients, who collectively upheld as ''reality'' the illusion that the observers could not be seen, had *consensually* redefined reality to meet their own needs.

The Capacity to Induce and Reduce Powerful Feelings

Historically, emotional contagion was the first phenomenon to interest investigators of groups. LeBon (1960) and Freud (1940) pointed out that powerful, primitive affects can be released in groups. Individuals may get carried away, experience feelings which they later believe are uncharacteristic of themselves and act on feelings without displaying their typical controls. This potential of groups can have either positive or negative effects on therapy. An individual may experience previously frightening feelings, with a new acceptance rather than his old sense of terror; he experiences, in other words, the corrective emotional experience of finding that the feelings are not overwhelming or that the feared consequences do not occur. Negative affect may occur when an individual is overwhelmed by affect and must defend himself against a group by literal or psychological withdrawal, or by the invocation of undesirable psychological defenses. The potential to stimulate emotionality, although, again, not peculiar to therapeutic groups, is an important quality of groups which bears directly on the sorts of personal learning or changes which take place in group people-changing contexts.

The Capacity of the Group to Provide a Context for Social Comparison

This fifth characteristic of groups is also an important influence in the therapeutic contexts. Group therapy patients frequently compare their attitudes toward their parents, husbands, wives, children; their feelings about things that are happening in the group; what makes them sad, happy, guilty, and angry; the ways that each typically deals with and expresses anger, affection, and so on. Such comparisons occur naturally and facilitate revision of the patient's identity by suggesting to him new possibilities for feeling, perceiving, and behaving. The availability in a group to examine a number of perspectives because different individuals present new vantage points is an important property inherent in the group situation. It occurs perhaps most powerfully in the therapeutic context because we have placed individuals in a social system which expects, often demands, that they talk about their behavior. Social comparisons occur as a natural outgrowth of these demands.

These group properties create conditions that engage the group member in a number of activities and concerns which differ from those of the patient in dyadic treatment. In comparison with the latter, the group member gets little practice in reflecting about himself and his interactions with others, in associating about his own feelings, in analyzing dreams, in linking present and past experiences, or penetrating covert meanings; he is too busy actively interacting and finding a viable place for himself in the group. He gets greater practice, however, than the patient in dyadic treatment, in expressing his feelings to peers, in noting the consequences of such expressions, in attempting to understand and empathize with others, in hearing from others about his impact on them, and in comparing himself with others.

Do these differing balances in experience lead to differences in outcome? It is commonly assumed that the group member should end up getting help of much the same order as he would have obtained in a dyadic relationship. It is perhaps helpful to test this assumption against, first, the end-state of the person at the close of the change process (symptoms, conflicts, defenses, interpersonal patterns, and the like); and second, the meta-learning achieved (learning how to approach problems, how to confront and resolve conflicts, and how to cope with anxiety).

Three aspects of the individual's end-state are relevant: (1) the symptoms or presenting complaint; (2) the revision of maladaptive patterns, the relinquishment of neurotic defenses, or the resolution of neurotic conflict; and (3) the unsought, positive side-effects. Symptom relief, for example, may be achieved at different rates. The placebo effect, (see Chapter Twelve for detailed discussion), critical in many instances of rapid symptom relief, seems to us unique to the dyad. Particular behavior changes or conflict resolutions may be accomplished better by one or the other of the two settings depending on the nature of the problem, the composition (if a group), and so on. For example, a therapy group whose composition encouraged a patient to maintain an established neurotic pattern might be less effective than individual therapy. On the other hand, a group which led a patient to experience positively a previously-feared emotion through emotional contagion, might be more effective than individual therapy.

Finally, the two treatment contexts may be conducive to different secondary benefits. For example, difficulty in giving to others may be only peripherally related to the person's presenting complaint or core conflicts but, nevertheless, an issue. Since giving to others is often a focal concern in a group, many opportunities appear for each member to note the nature of his anxieties about giving and to try out new forms of giving behavior. Thus, changes in "giving" behavior may occur sooner, or more directly, than in individual therapy.

The two contexts may also call attention to different aspects of humanness. In group contexts, members are likely to be struck by the common needs for basic kinship, for sharing with others, of persons who on the surface appear quite different. They may be impressed both by the difficulties in communicating meaningfully to others, and by the profound rewards experienced when such communication proves possible. The dyad, in contrast, does not directly facilitate such experiences.

The differences for meta-learning may be even greater than the differences in end-state outcomes. In any form of treatment the person often adopts a style of approaching problems which reflects the emphases of the treatment orientation to which he has been exposed. It is not unusual for a patient to emerge from psychoanalysis with an increased tendency to pay attention to his dreams, to deduce emotional meaning from forgetting, to search out unrecognized feelings when he notes inconsistencies in his behavior. A person who has undergone group treatment may be more likely to seek out feedback from others, to make social comparisons, to test out behavior interpersonally. An appreciation of the intensive positive and negative forces inherent in the face-to-face social microcosm that is the group treatment context is perhaps the single most helpful guide in developing a realistic picture of both the problems and potentials inherent in using groups for personal change.

Although some theorists such as Bion (1961) and Ezriel (1950) have in fact initiated their explorations of group therapeutic processes on the premise that groups have unique properties, most examples of this orientation predate recent developments in the group people-changing enterprise. They are based solely on observations of traditional settings, and have not as yet been extended to account for the changed conceptions of clients and functions which the new forms represent. These social systems-oriented theorists have attempted to take both group properties and individual dynamics into account in developing a unified theory of group therapy. Of interest is the role that the therapist is seen to play under such conditions. The English school has used the word ''conductor'' to explain the function of the therapist in the group; perhaps a more descriptive, if less human, concept which has also been applied is that the group therapist or leader acts as a social engineer whose most important function is to help the social system (the group) to develop norms and other systems properties which will permit effective psychotherapy to take place. Perhaps a useful way of describing systems-oriented conceptions of group psychotherapy is to distinguish between what have been called therapeutic conditions and therapeutic mechanisms. The former implies the *context* for change or learning—in a dyad it is the characteristics of the relationship, in the group it is the characteristics of the social system. In both situations the role of the therapist is considered to be to enhance the positive aspects of the condition so that change can occur. This is not the same as saying that the therapeutic relationship is in itself therapeutic. It *is* to say that certain events that facilitate growth must happen to the person in treatment, events that we have labeled therapeutic mechanisms.

LEADERSHIP FUNCTIONS IN THE GROUP SETTING

It is but a small step from a consideration of the unique properties of groups that are relevant to therapeutics to the issue of how therapists or leaders must behave in such a context to maximize the group potentials for participants in the group. Essential to the process of effective therapeutics is the ability of the therapist to gauge the feeling-states and progress of his client. Effective group therapy can take place only in a setting in which the leader or therapist has access to sufficient feedback about the state of his clients to diagnose their needs and adjust his behavior accordingly. The group therapist in essence has two clients—the social system he has helped to create that forms the context for therapeutics or change, and each individual in that system. Without feedback, it is impossible for a therapist or leader to diagnose individual and group needs to an extent where he can be helpful. One needs to know when to intervene, in what way, what needs to be done when the group is working well and when it is not, when it is being useful and when it is not.

A moment's reflection will probably suffice to indicate that such a requirement places considerable demand on the central person. What does he listen to in order to "read" the group and derive relevant feedback to gauge his interventions? Does he rely on his feelings—if he is bored, then perhaps everyone in the group is bored, and he must do something about it. If he is angry, perhaps all are angry. Such a course is obviously fraught with danger, for one of man's unfortunate traits is his great capacity for projection, a capacity that seems to be magnified when facing a group. It is difficult to disentangle one's own feelings from those of the others around him, and more often than not, trusting one's own feelings in a group situation may simply mean ascribing one's feelings to a collectivity that does not share them. On the other hand, the therapist may be able to distinguish between what it is he feels and what the others feel, yet decide that the most relevant source of feedback is the level of enthusiasm, aliveness, or vibrancy that the group is expressing. The assumption here is that when people are expressing or experiencing intense positive feelings, the group is on target; conversely, when these feelings are at low ebb, the group is in trouble and needs new inputs. Level of enthusiasm as expressed by group members, however, is a poor gauge of how well the group is serving its participants in their quest for change. Group members may be highly enthusiastic about their experience; yet the group may be a poor learning environment, inducing very little positive change.

Another cue the therapist might wish to attend to is the participant's indications that he is doing okay—that he is perceived by them as competent, helpful, and so forth. Again, unfortunately, members' perceptions of competence, expertise, and so forth, have not proven to be useful to gauge how helpful the group actually turns out to be. Leaders can, for example, substantially increase members' impressions of their expertise or competence simply by involving them in a large number of structured exercises or games. These activities prove to be interesting to participants, but not to be highly useful learning experiences.

What diagnostic tools, then, can therapists or group leaders use to "read" the group and determine when and how to intervene? Descriptions follow of two approaches which take account of the social forces that have powerful effects in group-based people-changing contexts. Each of them looks at somewhat different aspects of the group social system and derives from somewhat different theoretical perspectives. The first (Focal Conflict Model) offers a diagnostic tool to help translate the conversations, themes, and so on that make up the activities of the group into an orderly explanation of the real, but far more covert, concerns of the groups. The second concept is an approach to understanding what particular groups consider important, as indicated by agreements shared among participants regarding appropriate and inappropriate behavior, thoughts, and feelings in the group. Group norms are the rules or guidelines which may be observed to operate in any social system but which participants are often unaware of until someone expresses them. These two conceptual frameworks are not definitive, for there are many perspectives for systematically examining social systems, they have been chosen because of their importance in relation to groups designed to achieve personal change. There are other well-researched models that describe problem solving, role-assumption, and other characteristics of groups that may be more useful for diagnosing work groups than therapeutic groups.

A FOCAL CONFLICT MODEL*

In any therapy group in which the therapist does not control the content or the procedure, a session is likely to take the following form. As the patients gather, there is a period of unofficial talk—perhaps about some event from the preceding session, perhaps about an experience that someone has had since the last meeting, or perhaps about some neutral outside happening. Several conversations may go on at once, with the patients talking in pairs or threes; one or two may be silent. The conversation may be general. The atmosphere might suggest depression, tension, distance, or casual friendliness. Then at some signal—perhaps the closing of a door, the arrival of the therapist, or simply the clock indicating that the starting time has arrived—the session "begins."

After a pause or a longer silence, an initial comment is made. It may reflect some personal concern, some reaction to the previous session, or some reference to the current situation. The speaker may direct his comment to the therapist, to another patient, or to the entire group. The initial comment is followed by another which may or may not appear related to the first. If it seems related, it may be a response to the topic just introduced, or it may be stimulated by the emotion of the original statement and have little to do with the content. It may be a response to some relationship established earlier in the group's history. Comment follows comment, and a conversation develops. There is some coherence to this conversation, so that the group can be described as talking "about" something. Occasionally the conversation may become disjointed. There may be abrupt shifts in logic, lapses into silence, and illogical elements. The mood may shift, and the rhythm and pace of the discussion may vary. Some patients may talk a great deal, others very little. From time to time, the therapist may enter the discussion, directing his remarks to one person or to the group in general. He may comment about the mood of the group, the character of the interaction, or a problem of a patient.

Some comments get "lost" in the group, as if no one hears them; others are built upon and form the predominant topics and themes. The patients may express such emotions as anger, delight, suspicion, nervousness, or superiority. Some feelings and attitudes are expressed in words; others come through in nonverbal behavior. Certain patterns may emerge in terms of who dominates, who is silent, who talks to whom, and who expresses what feelings. After about an hour of complex interaction, the therapist will signal that the time is up, and the group will disperse. It will meet a few days later for another session.

---

*Material on the focal conflict model is abridged from Whitaker, D.S. and Lieberman, M.A. *Psychotherapy through the group process.* New York: Aldine-Atherton, 1964, Chapter 1.

What has happened? We assume that the diversity observed during a group-therapy session is apparent rather than real and that the many different elements of the session "hang together" in relation to some underlying issue. For example, the first session of an inpatient group was marked by long tense silences, brief staccato periods in which the patients compared notes about physical ills but seemed careful to avoid references to psychological worries, and an animated period in which the patients discussed the architecture of the hospital and wondered whether it was well designed and built on solid ground. On the surface these elements are diverse and unrelated, but they gain a certain coherence if one assumes that they all refer to some shared underlying uneasiness about having been placed in a group, and a shared concern about the competence and strength of the therapist. As another example, a group of patients which had been meeting for some time was told that the sessions were to be interrupted for the therapist's vacation. They warmly wished him a good time, ignored him for the rest of the session, and turned to an older member for information about college admission procedures and policies about "dumping" students after the end of the first year. Again, these elements gain coherence if one assumes that they all refer to shared underlying feelings about the impending separation from the therapist.

In this view, the observable elements of the session constitute the manifest material. These elements include not only content, but also nonverbal behaviors, mood, pace, sequence, and participation pattern. Thus, an animated period in which everyone joins the discussion is an element of the session, as is a period of desultory conversation or a period of sober but ritualistic "work" on one patient's problems. A seating pattern in which the chairs on either side of the therapist are left vacant is an element of the session, as is a seating pattern in which male and female patients take chairs on opposite sides of the room. Nonverbal behaviors—looking only at the floor when speaking, directing oneself exclusively to the therapist, or directly engaging one another—are also important elements.

We assume that a subsurface level exists in all groups, but is hardest to detect in groups in which the manifest content is itself relatively coherent and internally consistent. When a group is talking about something, one might assume that this is all that is happening. In the brief illustrations just presented, one group was talking about architecture, and the other about college policies. Yet, even when the group situation consists of a conversation which is coherent in itself, we assume that another level of meaning also exists, for, even in such a group, breaks and shifts occur in the topic under discussion. There are reversals and nonverbal accompaniments, suggesting that to assume that only a conversation is going on is to miss an important aspect of the situation. In therapy groups, covert levels are most apparent in groups of sicker patients, where there is less capacity to maintain coherence on an overt, public level. However, even in nontherapeutic groups, one can observe the same phenomenon.

The covert meaning of the manifest material is not likely to be within the patients' awareness. From the patients' point of view, the conversation *is* about architecture or college admission policies. But an observer is in a position to grasp the underlying issue. Once he ''sees'' the core issue, aspects of the session which might on the surface appear diverse, contradictory, or meaningless, gain coherence and meaning.

This view assumes that the successive manifest elements of the session are linked associatively, and that they refer to feelings experienced in the here-and-now situation. Whatever is said in the group is seen as being elicited not only by the strictly internal concerns of the individual, but by the interpersonal situation in which he finds himself. Of all the personal issues, worries, impulses, and concerns which a patient *might* express during a group session, what he actually expresses is elicited by the character of the situation. Moreover, a comment is likely to include a number of elements and is responded to selectively by others. An individual may make a comment which includes a half-dozen elements. As the others listen to an individual's highly personal contribution, they will respond to certain aspects and ignore others. The aspects which are picked up and built upon are in some way relevant to the other patients and gradually become an emerging shared concern. As this suggests, the group-relevant aspect of an individual's comment is defined by the manner in which the other patients react to it. To cite an example, in an inpatient group a patient told a story about a man who had been misunderstood when he used the word ''intimate.'' It was known that this was a personal concern of this patient, who was always apologizing for his sexual thoughts. However, the comments by other patients elaborated on the ''misunderstood'' aspect of his comment and ignored the ''intimate'' aspect. We therefore assume that being misunderstood was the shared concern and that the issue of intimacy was not a common concern.

We assume that the content of the session, no matter how seemingly remote, refers to here-and-now relationships and feelings in the group. The patients who worry about the competence of the architect and the strength of the building are really worrying about the competence and strength of the therapist. The patients who complain about college administrators who ''dump'' their students after the first year are really expressing resentment toward the therapist. The same is true for elements of the session other than the manifest content. Nonverbal behavior, such as a seating arrangement in which male and female patients sit on opposite sides of the room, might reflect concern about heterosexual contact in the group. A participation pattern in which one patient is allowed to dominate might mean that the others are using him to protect themselves from having to participate.

We view the covert, shared aspects of the group in terms of forces and counterforces, particularly those involving the shared impulses, wishes, hopes, and fears of the patients. For example, in a session presented in detail later, there emerged scattered clues that many of the patients in the group wished to be unique and to have special close relationships with the therapist. At the same time, there was awareness that the other patients would not permit this and then, more strongly, fear that the therapist would punish them or retaliate in some way. As the session went on, the patients seemed to search for things that they had in common, finally agreeing that they were all alike in some surface traits. Such a session can be understood in light of the force of the wish to have a uniquely gratifying relationship with the therapist, and the counterforce of the fear of retaliation. The wish and the fear constitute opposing forces; the fear prevents the wish from being expressed directly or perhaps even recognized. The wish cannot be pursued actively or thoroughly satisfied. At the same time, the wish cannot quite be given up and keeps the fear in the foreground. This situation creates tension in the group. The patients are beset with strong, conflicting feelings and impulses which are, at best, only dimly perceived. Strong impulses are exerting pressure, yet the patients can neither express nor recognize them. Under such circumstances, the patients attempt to find some way of dealing with their conflicting wishes and fears. In the above illustration, the search for things in common and the final agreement that everyone is alike can be seen as an attempt to allay their fears. It is as if the patients were saying, ''Don't punish me; I didn't ask the therapist for anything special.'' Of course, such a solution cannot really be satisfying, since it involves renouncing the wish. It might temporarily reduce anxiety, however.

In attempting to describe the covert, shared aspects of the group's life, we have adopted a theoretical language which utilizes the key terms ''group focal conflict,'' ''disturbing motive,'' ''reactive motive,'' and ''solution.'' The events of a group therapy session are conceptualized in terms of a slowly emerging, shared covert conflict consisting of two elements—a disturbing motive (a wish) and a reactive motive (a fear). These two elements constitute the group focal conflict. The term ''group focal conflict'' summarizes the key features of this view of groups, indicating that the disturbing and reactive motives conflict, pervade the group as a whole, and are core issues engaging the energies of the patients. Concomitant with the group focal conflict, one sees various attempts to find a solution. A group solution represents a compromise between the opposing forces; it is primarily directed to alleviating reactive fears but also attempts to maximize gratification of the disturbing motive.

No two group sessions are exactly alike in the group focal conflict which emerges. Even when similar feelings are involved, they are expressed in unique imagery. The solution may also vary in the manner in which it copes with the patients' fears and in the extent to which it satisfies and expresses the disturbing motive.

The impulses and fears involved in a group focal conflict exist outside the awareness of the patients. Although an outside observer can perceive and link the covert references to a shared concern, the individual who is in the focal conflict does not have this perspective. Under some circumstances, the patients may become aware or may be helped to become aware of these feelings. Ordinarily, however, and especially during the period in which the focal conflict is emerging, the patients are not in a position to recognize the character of the disturbing or reactive motives. A solution differs in character from either a disturbing or a reactive motive. It is usually expressed in more direct terms and is more readily observed. The patients may be aware of the content of the solution, although they are not likely to perceive its relevance to the underlying focal conflict.

Solutions may be successful or unsuccessful; in order to be successful, a solution must be unanimously accepted and must alleviate anxiety. Unanimity is necessary, for if one patient fails to accept such a solution as "all be alike," it cannot be effective. If one patient opposes asking the therapist to rule against a deviant patient, he is interfering with the solution. But unanimous acceptance does not imply that everyone must indicate overt willingness to abide by the solution. Most typically, acceptance is implicit, and some patients indicate through silent acquiescence that they will not interfere. Solutions also vary in the manner in which they deal with the associated conflict. Some solutions concentrate on the reactive fears; it is as if patients are so concerned about their fears that they adopt a solution which copes with their fears at the expense of satisfying the associated wish. For example, the solution "all be alike" was established in response to this focal conflict: "wish to be unique and singled out by the therapists for special gratification" versus "fear of retaliation." This solution dealt exclusively with the fear. It reduced the fear of retaliation by renouncing the wish for a uniquely gratifying relationship with the therapist. Other solutions alleviate reactive fears and still allow some gratification or expression of the disturbing motive. The solution in which the patients banded together to express angry compliance was of this type—it relieved fears of abandonment by making it impossible for anyone to be singled out for abandonment and rejection and, at the same time, allowed the disguised expression of resentment toward the therapists. In this case, the solution allowed for the disguised rather than direct expression of the disturbing motive. In other instances, one sees solutions which reduce fears and simultaneously permit the direct expression of the disturbing impulse.

The detailed illustration to be presented now should not be regarded as typical, except insofar as it demonstrates how the manifest material of a session refers to covert concerns and how a single group session may be summarized in focal-conflict terms.

The session to be described is the first of a reorganized inpatient group which included eight male patients, three female patients, and two female therapists. Only one patient was regarded as psychotic, two were alcoholics, and the rest were suffering from acute anxiety which had reached incapacitating proportions. Five of the patients had previously been in group therapy with Dr. T. The other six, as well as the other therapist, Dr. E., were participating in the group for the first time.

Dr. T. made a general statement about the purposes of the group. She commented that the group presented an opportunity for the patients to talk about whatever was important to them—events in the hospital, personal problems, or things that happened in the group. She introduced Dr. E. and announced the meeting schedule.

Such an opening offers little structure, yet communicates to the patients that they are expected to attend and to take responsibility for determining the content of the sessions.

> Carl said that he would drop a bombshell into the group by asking Dr. E. how her hair could look like she combed it with an egg-beater and yet look so good.

When Carl uses the term "bombshell," he is calling attention to the daring and perhaps potentially dangerous quality of his comment. His comment has both an aggressive and a sexual flavor. It focuses the attention of the group immediately on the new therapist.

> There was a brief silence. Tim said, "That was a left-handed compliment," and there was general laughter in the group. Carl said that his wife was too fussy about her hair, and Tim made some comment about his wife's hair. Margaret defended Carl's wife by saying that he should either compliment her or coax her into changing her hair style.

Apparently Carl was right, and his comment was really a bombshell, because the group seemed momentarily stunned into silence. Tim's comment seemed to provide tension release for the group by making explicit both the hostile and complimentary aspects of Carl's bombshell. Carl then felt impelled to take back the hostile elements of his comment by comparing Dr. E. to his wife, to Dr. E.'s benefit. With Margaret's attack on Carl there is a suggestion of a battle drawn on sexual lines.

To this point in the session, several potential focuses have appeared, but it is difficult to see which way the group will move. There has been a direct approach to one of the therapists which seems to have both sexual and hostile elements to it, but in any case emphasizes the femaleness of the therapist. It certainly brought Carl to the forefront of the group and focused attention on him. There followed a retreat toward a discussion about outside persons and a hint of contention within the group. But so far, an underlying trend is not apparent.

> Dr. T. suggested that there might be some feeling in the group because there were women patients present for the first time. The group did not respond to this comment but continued talking in a general way about hair styles.

This was a premature intervention—a guess at a focus which seems to have missed the point. Underlying this intervention was some assumption that the heterosexual problem being introduced had to do with feelings among peers. In a sense, the comment asks the patients to focus on their feelings for one another. The patients are not prepared to do this and continue their discussion of hair styles, which could be seen as a displaced and symbolic expression of sexual interests.

A trend toward focusing on sexual interests and impulses seems to be emerging, but neither the target nor the implications for the group are clear.

> Melvin, who had been silent up to this time, commented that he wanted a medal for being in a therapy group for the third time. Carl said that this was the fourth time he had been in a group, and Melvin said that he would have to back down.

On the face of it, this is an abrupt shift in content and focus. Although in a different area, this comment, too, has a bombshell quality. Melvin seems to be wanting to gain some kind of recognition or attention, either from the therapists or from the patients, by pointing out that he is special. He points to the difference between himself and all the others and perhaps, secondarily, reminds the group that there are both old and new members present. Carl immediately attacks Melvin's claim to specialness and superiority. He is competitive and effectively gains the upper hand by implying that, if anyone is special and deserving of recognition, it is he and not Melvin.

> Jean commented that she was an alcoholic and therefore had different problems from all the other patients. Carl said, "We're all addicted," but Tim argued that this was not true. A discussion followed in which the patients tried to arrive at a definition of "addiction." Carl suggested that Tim might be addicted to sleep. Carl said that his wife thinks he is an alcoholic.

Jean makes her own claim to distinction. Like Melvin, she is immediately countered by Carl, who, this time, rather than suggest that he himself is superior, suggests that everyone in the group is the same and that Jean, therefore, has no claim to being special. It is interesting that it is always Carl who insists that everyone is alike and no one is special. Others in the group are not ready to agree with him.

At this point in the session, one might hypothesize that an issue is developing as to whether people are unique or the same. Two patients, Melvin and Jean, have made distinct bids to be singled out. Carl's first comment—the bombshell—might also be regarded in this light. By that comment, Carl was clearly lifting himself out of the mass of patients and making himself conspicuous; in particular, he was bringing himself to the attention of one of the therapists. From a focal-conflict point of view, a disturbing motive may be emerging which involves a wish to be unique and to receive a special attention. The object of the wish is not clear. For Carl, it is the therapist; for Melvin, it is probably the therapist (a medal from whom?); for Jean, it is less clear. The reactive motive—the force which keeps the wish from fruition—it not clear. All we can see is that one of the members, Carl, will not allow anyone to satisfy this wish. Whenever anyone makes a bid for uniqueness, Carl interferes. It is uncertain how the rest of the group feels about this issue. Perhaps they don't care; perhaps they care very much but are letting Carl fight their battle for them. In terms of focal-conflict theory, Carl is also suggesting a solution—"let's all be alike"; it is as if he is saying, "Let's not let anyone win this competition." But there is no evidence yet that anyone else supports this view.

> Tim and Melvin (both old members) began to talk about Dr. Y. (a psychiatrist who had been permitted to sit in as an observer of several previous sessions). They referred to an argument the group had had at that time about the cost of psychiatric treatment.

If one paid attention only to the content of this portion of the meeting, it might appear that these two patients are wondering whether the feelings stirred up in the group may be too much to handle. Perhaps they are indirectly questioning whether the group sessions will be worthwhile. However, the interactive characteristics of this episode suggest another line of thought.

Both Tim and Melvin were old members. By discussing a topic which was meaningless to the new people in the group, they excluded the new members from the conversation and brought sharply into focus the difference between the old and the new. Entirely apart from the content of their conversation, this behavior might be regarded as an interesting variation on the theme of claiming uniqueness. Before, each member has made a personal bid for attention or uniqueness. Now, two members collaborate in their attempt to establish a special place for themselves in the group. This behavior may be seen as a solution to the developing focal conflict. One might conceptualize such a focal conflict in the following manner:

disturbing motive	reactive motive
wish to be unique and singled out for special gratification from the therapists	interference by other patients

The behavior of Tim and Melvin partly involves giving up the wish to be unique, but still attempts to reserve a special place in the group for themselves as old members. The reactive motive does not involve feelings of fear or guilt, or the like, but simply indicates that, thus far, any bids for uniqueness have been blocked by another patient.

> Two of the new patients, Sam and Margaret, began to ask Dr. E. questions. Sam asked whether tranquilizing drugs would help him. Dr. E. asked whether they had helped him in the past. Margaret asked whether tranquilizers were sedatives. Dr. E. responded with medical information. At this point, both Tim and Melvin reacted with exaggerated pleasure. Tim said, "For the benefit of new personnel, doctors do not answer questions in this group, so this is really something."

Here, Sam and Margaret interrupted the conversation between Tim and Melvin. In effect, they did not permit reminiscences about special experiences. At the same time, they made their own bid for attention. These two new patients were seeking attention from the new therapist in the group. When it looked as if they were succeeding, Tim and Melvin interfered. Although they were ostensibly telling Sam and Margaret that they were getting something special, they were also implicitly telling both the patients and the new therapist that an old standard was being violated. Thus they are not only interfering with Sam and Margaret's bid to gain special notice from the therapist, they are also re-emphasizing the differences between the old and new members. Here one sees a repetition of what has occurred earlier: a bid for a therapist's attention is blocked by other patients. Such repetition strengthens the hypothesis that a disturbing motive which involves a wish to receive something special from the therapists is operating. It also strengthens the assumption that the other patients will not allow anyone to be singled out in this way.

This interpretation re-emphasizes the interactive characteristics of the group.

Turning to the content, one might wonder why the patients focus on tranquilizers rather than on something else. It is not clear whether this focus carries a symbolic implication, whether it expresses some wish to have things calmed down in the group, or whether it merely grows out of some private assumption that this is what doctors are for.

> Melvin referred to a discussion the group had had a number of meetings previously about automobiles. He then told Carl that this meeting would be a good opportunity to sell chances (again referring to something that had happened in a previous session). There was some talk among Carl, Tim, and Melvin about the cost of the chances and about Ford, Mercury, and Lincoln cars (all these were topics which had been discussed in previous sessions).

This conversation involves strengthening ties among old members and excluding the new members. Earlier it was suggested that in the group a solution was developing which would reserve a special place for the old members. It is as if the old members were saying, "Perhaps we cannot be unique and receive special attention as individuals, but at least let us band together to exclude these new-comers." The car conversation suggests that this solution is gaining adherents and being put into practice.

> Dr. T. suggested that the group was asking Dr. E. a lot of questions in order to find out what sort of person the new doctor was. The group responded with laughter. Dr. T. then suggested that the group was concerned about the new members versus the old members and pointed out that some of the conversations introduced by old members could not possibly be understood by new members.

The first portion of this comment appears irrelevant to the shared concerns which seem to be developing in this group. The reference to curiosity about Dr. E. does, however, touch on the wish, which several patients have revealed, to get close to Dr. E. and obtain special help from her. More clearly, however, the second portion of the therapist's comment directly confronts the old members with the alliance they are establishing and makes one aspect of the developing focal-conflict pattern—the solution—explicit.

> Tim said he really wanted an answer to the question he was about to ask and asked Dr. E. about a shot he had had which produced anesthesia in his arm. Dr. E. did not answer this question directly. The group began to discuss spinal taps. They expressed considerable apprehension about this procedure and wanted to know why it was used. The gist of the conversation was that spinal taps were about the most painful and horrible treatment that one could undergo.

Again, this constitutes an abrupt shift in topic. It might seem that the patients have not heard Dr. T.'s intervention or at least are not responding to it. But interactive characteristics show the patients turning away from Dr. T. and toward Dr. E. In terms of content, the discussion about injections and spinal taps may be a symbolic expression of the patients' feeling that doctors are potentially danger-ous and capable of inflicting great pain in the guise of aid. It seems reasonable to suppose, then, that the patients actually are reacting to Dr. T.'s intervention. This intervention had blocked a developing solution by communicating disapproval. Perhaps it has elicited some covert angry reaction which the patients now express by turning to Dr. E. The content also suggests that the patients perceive Dr. T.'s intervention as a punitive one. Perhaps they are indicating indirectly and symbolically that the therapist's previous comment was as punitive as actually performing a spinal tap. Perhaps—although this is more speculative—they feel that their angry reaction deserves punishment. It is not clear which aspect of the therapist's comment they are responding to—whether it is the exposure of their solution to exclude the new members or whether it is the exposure of their curiosity about Dr. E. In any case, the reaction is a strong one, as is demonstrated by the primitive quality of the symbolism—spinal taps and anesthesia.

From a focal-conflict point of view, the therapist's intervention has led to a shift in the reactive motive. Previously the wish was held in check by an awareness that other patients would block any bid for uniqueness; now it is held in check by a fear that the therapist will punish the patients. It is as if the therapist will disapprove of not only the wish to be special, but even of the modified solution—a special place in the group for the old members.

It is interesting to note, parenthetically, that in this instance Dr. E. did not respond directly to the patients' questions. She appears to be responding to the earlier suggestion that to answer questions is to violate a custom of the group.

The group began to talk about the value of their meetings.

> Alan said that he might learn to get along with this group, but added, "What good will it do me with friends and relatives?" Jean said, "I am a stranger, and yet you talk to me." Carl said, "This is because we've been through the same thing." Jean talked about Alcoholics Anonymous and said that the value of the group was that "you think you are alone, but you're not." Carl said that he would feel free to talk about anything in this group.

This portion of the session displays a drop in morale and then a recovery. The first part, in which the group is devalued, may express veiled anger toward the therapist; it may also suggest the patients' sense of despair when confronted with difficult issues and feelings. Then, rather abruptly, there is a shift in mood. The patients become more friendly to one another. For the first time, they begin to break down the barriers between the old and new members. (Jean, a new member, tells Carl, an old member, "I am a stranger, and yet you talk to me," and Carl responds, "This is because we've been through the same thing.") There is a new emphasis on the value of peers and the possibility of closeness among them.

From the point of view of the group's focal conflict, this shift suggests a renunciation of the wish to be unique (the disturbing motive), as well as the adoption of a new solution. The patients' friendly overtures may indicate that they will no longer insist on being unique, nor will the old members insist on being a special subgroup. It seems reasonable to suppose that the shift in the reactive motive—from the threat of active interference by other patients to the fear of punishment by the therapist—has led to this change. With such intense, primitive fears involved in the reactive motive, it seems that the only solution is to renounce the wish.

> Dr. T. responded to Carl's comment by saying that an important issue in the group would be what people felt that they could talk about and what they felt they could not talk about. Alan said that the group might be a place where he could learn to understand himself. Tim said he did not know what his problems were, but he did know his symptoms. He described them as eating, sleeping, and indefinitely postponing any attempt to do his job. Jean said she felt the same way and described a drinking pattern in which she drank alone until she was stuporous, ate nothing, and sipped straight whisky for weeks at a time. There was some conversation between Jean and Tim, identifying common problems.

The therapist's comment seems to be an attempt to slow down the headlong rush into complete trust and suggest to the group that it is appropriate to move more slowly. The interaction between Tim and Jean is a combination of the previous friendliness but has now shifted to sharing the content of problems. In part, the patients seem to be turning to one another for support; in part, they may be mollifying the therapist by doing what they assume the therapist wants them to do. In either case, this portion of the session may be seen as a solution which focuses largely on the reactive motive. It is an attempt to deal with fears about the therapist's displeasure.

> Melvin brought up the subject of hypnotism. He said that he trusted his individual therapist, Dr. J., and would let him do anything, even hypnotize him. Jean said that Dr. J. had tried to hypnotize her once and that it had not worked. Ella said the same thing. Several patients asked Melvin about hypnotism, expressing a good deal of skepticism. Sam asked whether the pills he took produced the same effect as hypnosis. Alan suggested that sleeping was really like being hypnotized. Dr. T. asked, "You mean that everyone has been hypnotized?" Alan described blackout spells he had had. Jean and William were asking him questions about his spells as the session ended.

GROUP NORMS

As a shared idea of appropriate behavior in a particular social system, norms not only influence participants, but are perceived by each member as being accepted by most others in the system. Behavior which violates such ideas of what is the "right way" to behave is ordinarily treated as deviant, and is sanctioned by some means or another to reduce its occurrence, and thus to return the system to its prior equilibrium. Ordinarily, sanctions do not need to be exerted frequently or vigorously; rather, the anticipation of sanctions is often as effective in controlling deviant behavior as is actual application.

Norms and associated sanctions provide a certain amount of stability and predictability in social life; members of the social system know what to expect of

each other. Although group members seldom discuss the norms which characterize the group, the group norms nevertheless serve as a simple substitute for
interpersonal pressures and *ad hoc* influence tactics; they are, in effect, an
unwritten social contract which can be invoked when troublesome behavior
arises. Norms can be seen to be a crucial aspect of the culture of people-changing
groups. The success of such groups depends, in large respect, on the creation of a
tiny society which is separated from and marked off from the surrounding culture. In most day-to-day contacts it is widely accepted as a violated norm if one
openly objects to the appearance or behavior of other persons, or reveals his own
feelings about issues culturally-defined as private or too personal. Such behavior
is usually defined as "rude," "sick," or "weird," and occurs rarely even
among intimates. People-changing groups, however, generally create norms
which may be counter to those of the larger culture; talking about interpersonal or
inner feelings is generally viewed as a decisively good idea, and avoidance of
such behavior is ordinarily defined as bad. Similarly, people-changing groups
often support norms which encourage closer relationships than are typical of
ordinary social transactions. It is difficult to conceive of a personal change
group, regardless of type, which does not develop norms that are distinctive from
and often opposite to the normative culture of the larger society. For whatever
one's view of appropriate mechanisms for personal change, most change systems
are predicated on the assumption that, to be successful, they must present differences compared to the participants' ordinary life; otherwise one would need to
ask why positive changes are not made, at least for the people who come into
such groups, in their ordinary life situation.

The group leader or therapist who has chosen to work with his clients in a
group situation must ask himself how he can develop group norms which are
conducive to treatment or change. It is not a matter of introducing norms into the
group situation, for all groups develop norms. It is as unthinkable to imagine a
social system without norms which define appropriate and inappropriate behavior
as it is to imagine an earth without gravity, for in a normless society, no one
would know what to do or what to expect of others. The issue for the group
leader is one of using whatever influence he has to develop norms which will
facilitate the therapeutic goals of the group. Before he can do so, however, he
must be able to "read" the group correctly; he must know what the norms are as
the members perceive them. He must also be cognizant that although certain
norms may be discernible in most personal-change groups, they may take on
special colorations depending on the particularities of composition and so forth of
each group as a social entity. It is imperative, therefore, that the leader develop
methods or strategies for understanding the specific norms in the system he is
working in. Most germane to change induction are the norms that relate to the
boundaries of the system, the criteria for group membership, what can and
cannot be talked about, what emotional expressions are legitimate and illegitimate. It is these areas of regulation that directly affect the therapeutics of any
change-directed group.

How to Determine Group Norms

Although the concept of norms may be foreign to most people, almost everyone engages in adjustive behavior or accommodations based on some assessment of what norms are at work in the contexts in which they find themselves. Most people, upon entering a new group or a new culture, automatically engage in search behavior directed toward determining what is appropriate and inappropriate behavior in this situation. Most of us usually scan the scene in a new situation; we observe what others appear to be doing, and how it differs from what we are accustomed to. We probably seek, although implicitly, to determine regularity of behavior in the new group or new culture. We probably note that certain things get talked about and others do not, that certain attitudes or emotions are "okay" to express and others are not; we may note that people seem to take turns and that at the end of a specified period of time almost all the members of the group have talked about equally. We are, in a word, studying the norms of the group. We are attempting to find out what is expected of us; what is appropriate and what is prohibited behavior.

One approach to "diagnosing" the norms of a group or any social system is to look, more consciously than we would in everyday life, for regularities of behavior, both behaviors that are present as well as those that are absent. Such a process of observation, akin to the familiar methods of anthropologists, allow norms to be discerned. Over time, in a group, other types of observations will produce information about the normative characteristics of that particular social system. We will note over some period of time that certain members appear to become the focus of the group's attention. We may note at such times that there is considerable intensity involved in focusing on particular members. More often than not, it seems as if most of the group members are ganging up on a particular member and trying to change or alter his behavior. As events progress a little further, the group may become even more intense; what were at first relatively benign attempts to get a particular member to change his behavior now become a more charged group effort, with anger predominating. If all these efforts of the group do not succeed in getting the member to alter his ways (which they usually do not), the group begins to "withdraw" its attention from this member to the point where he almost becomes a nonperson in the group—ignored, isolated, as if he were not there.

What has happened? More likely than not, the member in question violated a basic group norm. He may have taken a point of view that was considered offensive in this particular group, or he may have expressed an intense positive or negative feeling for another member of the group, or done any one of a number of other things that this group considered inappropriate. Group norms are most easily discerned when they are violated by a member. When a group works hard on the member to get him to alter his attitudes or behavior, then gets aggressive toward him and, finally, abandons him, it is a safe bet that the group is out to protect a norm it considers vital. Observation of repeated incidents of the sort just described is likely to reveal the group's norms in their rawest form. Without being aware of it, these sorts of cues are quite similar to those most people use in everyday life to determine "what goes on" or what doesn't in a particular setting; frequently it is what they conclude from such observations that helps them decide whether or not the group is one to which they want to belong.

There is still another way to discern group norms that can be analogized to what people often do when they enter an unfamiliar setting—a new college, a new social group, a new job, a foreign country, or whatever. If they want to "fit in," they ask a friend or acquaintance such things as, "what to wear," "what's the usual tip around here," and so forth. In so doing they are in actuality asking the other person's help in determining what the norms of the new situation are. They are applying the anthropologist's time-honored method of using an informant to discover the unwritten and generally unarticulated social regulations that govern the culture under investigation. In much the same way, a group leader or therapist can determine norms he may be unaware are influencing a group by asking each participant, through administration of a simple questionnaire, what array of behaviors the group would find acceptable or unacceptable. Although all three methods just described may be used, the last is the simplest and most quickly enables the leader or therapist to ascertain the norms of the groups he works with.

A concrete example of this approach, in comparing the normative structures of women's consciousness raising groups, encounter groups and psychotherapy groups, was the use of a questionnaire in which participants were asked the appropriateness—inappropriateness of a variety of behaviors. These behavioral items refer to underlying normative characteristics of such groups. A factor analysis of the questionnaires provided four normative dimensions—self disclosure (talking about personal problems and inadequacies); affective relationships (expressing feelings about other members in the group); membership criteria (absences and minimal participation in discussions), and boundaries (member-member relationships as well as relationships with members to outsiders).

Table 13-1 shows the four normative dimensions as well as the particular behavioral items, comparing consciousness raising groups, encounter and psychotherapy groups. The table shows the average proportion of members who stated that such behavior was appropriate in their group.

A comparison of the norms in these three systems suggests that consciousness raising groups differ from both other systems in respect to self-disclosure and boundaries. Looking at the specific items suggests that consciousness raising groups are likely to prohibit disclosure of particular information about each other both in regard to positive and negative feelings. These are behaviors highly encouraged in encounter and psychotherapy groups and suggests as previously discussed, that the social microcosm aspects, the exchange of feelings about one another is not a central characteristic of such groups compared to encounter and psychotherapy.

A similar theme is found in those normative items classified under boundaries, for consciousness raising groups do not support behavior that is critical of one another or differentiating among members. In contrast, the normative structure in most psychotherapy and encounter groups, despite their ideological differences, reveal considerable similarity.

THERAPEUTICS AND THE ROLE OF THE LEADER

Up to this point, we have talked about how groups have come to be used as a medium for personal change. Still, we have skirted the main question—what is it that occurs in such settings that is essential to changing people. The fundamental assumption underlying all theories of changing people through groups is that as time passes the group, as a social microcosm, will increasingly generate in each

Table 13.1   Normative Comparisons

	Consciousness Raising (36 Groups)	Encounter (17 Groups)	Therapy (16 Groups)	—
Self Disclosure				
Disclosure to Outsiders	6%	32%	13%	
Shout	34%	68%	61%	
Say Who Like	32%	79%	75%	
Sexual Attraction	19%	33%	17%	
Affective Relationships				
Cry	89%	66%	82%	
Hug	90%	74%	68%	
Plead	72%	64%	72%	
Discuss Dreams	84%	74%	55%	
Do Not Interrupt	13%	24%	34%	
Boundaries				
Dislike	19%	47%	57%	
Like	32%	79%	75%	
Tell Group Off	38%	42%	42%	
Behavior Wrong	17%	48%	42%	
Do Not Joke	58%	34%	38%	
Do Not Bring Friends	21%	10%	0%	
Membership Criteria				
No Intention of Changing	22%	17%	.08%	
Say Nothing	37%	14%	31%	

member those feelings, thoughts, or behaviors that are at heart troublesome to him. Whether one begins with a psychoanalytic assumption that dynamic conflicts are at issue, or looks at interpersonal relationships as the source of personal problems, or takes a strictly behavioral position, fundamentally each position views—as the initial step in change—the elicitation, directly or indirectly, of the issues that are troublesome to the participant. The display, internally or overtly, of these troublesome issues in a context that is in some important ways different from ordinary life constitutes the first step in the therapeutic process.

In a most general way, the next step in this sequence of change is that the behavior, thought, or feeling must be experienced by the person in a way that is different from his previous history. The person has to "learn" that what he had feared or expected if he behaved, thought, or felt in a particular way will not necessarily occur, that a calamity will not befall him, that getting close to people, depending on them, fighting with them, or whatever, does not always bring dire consequences; that there are more ways of achieving sought-after goals or fulfilling needs than he had previously thought, and so forth. What has to happen in a group for members to reap such benefits is what the business of change induction in groups is all about. It is most important for the reader to recognize that the current state of knowledge about people-changing is primitive; no formula has been advanced that will suffice for every case. The evidence that can be brought to bear all leads to the conclusion that people-changing is complex. Whether in groups or dyads, no single method or set of techniques has been shown to change all, but few have been tried that will not change someone. It is this observation that some are changed by almost any kind of system people have thought about, and not everyone is changed by any system ever developed, that creates the complexity (as well perhaps as the excitement) of developing more sophisticated theories about the essential ingredients of individual change.

Some people are helped by seeing others go through an experience; the elicitation of their own related problems is indirect rather than direct. They experience new learnings through watching others try out feared behavior rather than by doing so themselves. Some learn through an internal cognitive response—a new recognition that the conflict they previously felt between their wants and fears is not as certain as they had once thought. Still others may observe that some group members are able to meet their needs by using behaviors that never occurred to them and are encouraged by these "good examples" to try the same. Some are unburdened to discover that no one is shocked by their deep hidden secrets which have always made them feel ashamed or guilty. Still others experiment with new behaviors in a situation that may be the first to appear safe and supportive to them and are thereby encouraged to change.

What, then, is the therapist's or leader's role in facilitating change for group members? How will he insure that the group setting will elicit the troublesome thoughts, feelings, and behaviors that people bring? How can he help the members experience new thoughts, feelings, and behaviors in ways that release them from the fears with which they previously associated them?

An examination of the variety of theoretical positions about people-changing in groups would reveal a large number of terms or concepts to describe things therapists or leaders do: interpreting resistance, confronting, reflecting, supporting, developing role playing scenes, acting as the observing ego, precipitating crises for the group by not acting in accord with ordinary patient expectations, reinforcing, modeling, making contracts, setting up ground rules, protecting, expressing acceptance, communicating genuineness and positive regard, analyzing transference, teaching, being a whole person, disclosing personal feelings, expressing feelings, interpreting group dynamics, interpreting individual dynamics, challenging, being provocative, and so forth. The descriptive and conceptual labels used to describe the work of a therapist are indeed broad and far-ranging. It is possible, however, to bring some order to the vast array of descriptive titles of leader behavior and function.

Sensitivity group leaders see their role as helping members understand themselves and others through understanding the group process. Such leaders characteristically focus on the group as a whole, and on the members' transactions with each other. They attempt to explain what the group as a whole is doing, focusing on such issues as group maintenance, cohesiveness, power and work distribution, sub-grouping, scapegoating, and so on.

Gestalt therapy leaders stress the wholeness of the individual. Change is viewed as a sub-intellectual process which is mediated by helping the individual get in touch with the primitive wisdom of the body. There is little use of the group or, for that matter, the other group members. In the classical practice of this methodology, there is an empty chair, "the hot seat," next to the leader, to which the members come one by one to "work" with the leader. In Gestalt groups, much emphasis is placed on heightened emotionality, or understanding what the body is telling one by its posture or by its numerous autonomic and musculoskeletal messages. The leader often helps members to resolve inner conflicts by holding dialogues between the disparate parts of the psyche. The participation of the other members is minimal; often their primary function is simply to verify what the leader says by their presence, like the all-seeing Greek chorus.

Transactional analysis leaders work with each of the group members in turn. The term transactional analysis refers to the transactions among ego states (parent, child, and adult) within one individual, rather than transactions among individuals. Establishing learning contracts (the setting of specific goals) is a typical characteristic of this approach. Formal teaching of the analytic model is stressed, so that patients in the group can apply this conceptual system to themselves and to the behaviors of others.

Basic encounter group leaders emphasize the experiencing and deepening of interpersonal relationships and the liberating of somatic restrictions. They believe that by breaking free of social and muscular inhibitions, people can learn to experience their own bodies and other people in a different and fuller sense. The group leader's focus is on both the individual and the interpersonal relationships within the group. The basic encounter leader often suggests exercises for members to perform to help shuck constricting inhibitions. The emphasis is on doing and experiencing; the cause or meaning of the persisting restrictions is of minor consequence.

Client-centered group therapy is an adaptation of Rogerian individual psychotherapy. Most of the leader's attention is centered on interpersonal or intrapersonal dynamics; he rarely focuses on the group as a whole. He is to behave as a model of personal development, establishing the conditions of genuineness, unconditional positive regard, and empathy, that are received in Rogerian therapy as the basic ingredients of the therapeutic relationship.

Attack therapy emphasizes the expression of anger; each member in turn is systematically attacked and explored by the others in the belief that if one is attacked long enough in his weak areas he will strengthen them. This procedure is called "the game" in Synanon byecause, once the group meeting is over, the atmosphere changes quickly to one of warm support. The Synanon form of attack therapy differs from other models having a similar emphasis in that the Synanon groups are composed of both experienced and inexperienced members, so that much of the work of the system is done not by the leader but by several "experienced game players." In other forms of attack therapy, the leader is almost exclusively the confronting agent.

Psychodramatic approaches to group-based change induction are adaptations of ideas developed by Jacob L. Moreno, the founder of psychodramatic therapy. The basic format is the construction of role-playing or psychodramatic exercises, directed toward providing a means for participants to act out heretofore blocked behaviors or feared emotional relationships in a "safer" setting. The technology involves the assumption that a person can learn from direct experience (if he plays a role in the exercise) or vicariously (if he observes the psychodrama).

As discussed earlier, psychoanalytically-oriented group therapy focuses on the inner dynamics, especially the early history, of the individual as they are expressed in the group. Such groups tend to be less emotionally charged, more rationally based, with heavier focus on intellectual mastery of inter- and intrapersonal forces operating in the group. The therapist acts as an observing ego, interpreting resistance and analyzing defenses of individuals as they are played out in the group social microcosm.

Through studying 16 leaders (Lieberman, Yalom, and Miles, 1973) representing these eight theoretical orientations as they actually worked in groups, using observers' ratings as well as members' perceptions of their behavior, four fundamental functions were isolated that described most of the behavior of all these leaders: emotional stimulation, support, meaning-attribution, and executive functions. All leaders, no matter what their theoretical orientation, employ some behavior in these four areas, although they differ widely with regard to the amount and the particular emphasis on any one—some leaders are primarily emotionally stimulating, others spend the majority of their time involved in executive functions, and so forth. Other leaders combine support with meaning attribution, others emphasize stimulation and support, and so on.

Emotional Stimulation

All personal change groups emphasize the emotional involvement of the participants. At its most elemental level, the stimulation function of the leader is
response-demand behavior. The leader uses some tactic or strategy to engage
participants and elicit emotional responses. The tactics involved in exercising
this function are varied and range from the leader revealing his own feelings
(leader transparency) to challenging, confronting, participating as a group
member rather than the leader, exhorting, drawing attention to self, demonstrating or modeling on the leader's part by risk-taking, expressing anger, warmth,
and love, and so forth. Other strategies leaders use to stimulate emotions among
the members may involve role-playing scenes, simulated games, or various
structured exercises, arrangements the leader suggests to involve the members in
activities such as "trust walks," "break-in," and the like.

Each of these leader tactics varies with regard to the intensity of the demand
for response. Leader strategies also vary in the degree to which they involve
direct relationship to a particular participant as opposed to the generation of more
elaborate structures involving many participants for invoking emotional responses. Some leaders employ relatively low levels of stimulating behavior,
using invitations, elicitations, and questions; others evoke high-intensity responses through challenging, confrontation, and personal revelation. What is
important is that all leaders, no matter what their theoretical persuasion, act as if
one fundamental function of their role is to elicit emotional responsiveness in the
participants.

The historical change with regard to this form of behavior is of interest. A
fundamental difference between personal challenge groups that stem from traditional psychotherapeutic orientations and the so-called newer therapies is the
degree to which each type emphasizes emotional stimulation. Classical forms of
group therapy stem from a tradition that suggests that just placing participants in
small face-to-face groups for personal change creates high levels of excitement
and stimulation, so that the major function of the therapist is seen to be to manage
this potent climate. In traditional forms of group therapy it is also assumed that
change takes a long time, a perspective that probably minimizes the importance
of emotional stimulation. The new change systems generally view change as
possible in relatively brief periods of time, and perhaps emphasize intensity of
stimulation as a means of speeding up the process. Despite these differences,
however, it is important to recognize that all forms of therapy perceive emotional
involvement and responsiveness as central to the change process and all provide
techniques for seeing to it that participants come forth with such responses.

Support-Caring Function

Any group designed to effect personal change is bound to create anxiety or
tension in its members. Personal change groups are fraught with potential for
anxiety-induction—no one is sure what may happen next, exceedingly personal

topics often get discussed, and interactions among members may evoke highly emotional events. Finally, although members may deeply desire to change, they may feel apprehensive about giving up old ways of behaving for new ones. Thus, a basic function of every leader of a people-changing group is to teach the group to manage the anxiety inherent in the change process. Although all leaders exhibit behaviors directed toward supporting and caring for group participants, the variation in both the amount and kind is great. Some theories of group-based people-changing, for example those growing out of Rogerian tradition, are in good part characterized by an emphasis on the establishment of supportive relationships to members with whom the leader works. Genuineness, positive regard, empathy, are the terms of this framework, and such leaders emit greater amounts of such behavior.

Therapists influenced by the English Tavistock school of group analysis consider a relatively high degree of anxiety a necessary condition for change, and other differences among various theoretical positions with regard to the support-caring function can be seen in whether leaders institute supportive processes directly or indirectly. Some leaders offer warmth, caring, support, affection, praise, and encouragement through their own activities. Other leaders perceive provision of an accepting setting and manage the tensions that the change-producing situation induces as a basic function. Such leaders are more likely to operate indirectly, attempting to create situations in which the group members themselves offer the greatest source of support. Direct observations of leaders suggest, however, that no matter what their school of orientation or theoretical position, all are involved to some extent in providing direct support, affection, friendship, encouragement, praise, and support to others.

Meaning Attribution

The unknown or unrecognized has always been fearful to men. Since time immemorial, the basic function of healers in society has been to aid man to conquer fear by making the unknown knowable or at least less threatening. Leaders of people-changing groups are no different. A fundamental function they perform is to create meaning. They label feelings and events that participants may undergo without full awareness. They attribute meaning to experiences occurring in the group or to a particular member with the intention of rendering a higher level of understanding of what lies beneath the experience. Whether they embrace the more traditional therapeutic concepts such as insight or speak in terms of the newer, more experience-based, people-changing movements, all leaders perform this function. How they do it and what particular meanings or labels they ascribe to experience differ widely. The methods of transmission also vary considerably. Some leaders use modeling as their primary means of giving cognitive structure to salient emotional experiences; other leaders make use of more formal educational methods traditionally employed to upgrade conceptual internalization. Some directly teach general systems of how to understand behavior, others label experiences as they occur so that participants will view them with a new perspective. Some teach how to change by providing exercises intended to leave participants with new views about themselves and their relationships to others—ideas which they can apply to achieve more effective behavior patterns away from the group. Other leaders focus the attention of participants more on the processes they believe underlie the achievement of change, introducing concepts which may range from classic Freudian to more socially-oriented Lewinian to those deriving from more contemporary biopsychic frameworks. The methods and the labels vary; what is important is that all leaders of people-changing groups provide members with some means of translating feelings and behavior into *ideas*.

Executive Function

Theories and theorists differ widely about how to use the social properties of the group for therapeutic benefit. Some theories ignore consideration of group-level phenomena; the leader's relationship with individual members is presented as the sole source of change; other theories acknowledge that one is obviously constructing a social system when working with groups, yet provide no concepts about the social system nor techniques using the social system as a therapeutic force. A smaller number of theories and theorists see the major work of the therapist or group leader to be centered around developing a viable and therapeutically productive social system. Nevertheless, all leaders of personal change groups direct some of their attention to the management of the group as a social system.

Anything the leader does that has to do with the workings of the group as a social system are aspects of the leader's executive function. Some leaders are laissez-faire with respect to this function; they do very little to alter how the group is functioning. Other leaders rely little on the usual forms of executive function as a therapeutic means for confronting the group with its need to develop its own resources. Such leaders do not totally abrogate the executive function but rather spend much of their efforts on helping the group to reflect on the meaning of the absence of ordinary executive functions to them as a group as well as to each individual in it.

It is helpful to examine the leader's executive functions with regard both to direct and indirect interventions. Direct interventions are those behaviors the leader carries on during the course of the group which are directed toward how the social system is functioning. Indirect interventions are things leaders do when they organize groups which are intended to enhance the therapeutic qualities of the group. Direct interventions include such leader acts as suggesting or setting rules (which may range from simple rules regarding the time and place of the group's meeting to strictures about the relationships among members outside of the treatment or group situation), discussing the group's goals with the members, suggesting that the group has spent enough time on a particular topic, stopping or blocking, for example stopping the group from "scapegoating" one member, or getting the group to reflect what it is doing. Behaviors directed toward aiding the group to make a decision or suggesting various procedures that the group can follow are other forms of the executive function.

The most powerful indirect executive functions of the leader or therapist involve the selection of persons to be in the group, the "preparation of the person" before he enters the group, and the composition—the array of individuals who make up the group. The principles and controversies that govern these three considerations are beyond the scope of the current chapter. Suffice it to say here, with regard to selection, a considerable body of clinical observations would suggest (although empirical evidence is inconsistent) that some types of individuals can work better in a group situation than in a dyad, and vice versa. With regard to preparation, clinical observation and empirical research both strongly indicate that the expectational sets of individuals entering groups can be altered by various procedures prior to the beginning of the group, and that the nature of the expectational sets and the view the person has of what to look for in the group and what to expect can make a difference in the functioning of the group, particularly in its initial stages. Finally, composing the group membership in some ordered way has also been clinically and empirically demonstrated to be a powerful strategy for affecting the productivity of a change group.

EXPERIENCES THAT MAKE FOR CHANGE

The overall process of change through group methods can be thought of in terms of two central and interdependent aspects of the group experience. The group characteristics already discussed prescribe the conditions which define the context in which the sought-for changes are to take place. The other important aspect of the group change-induction system is the "package" of events or change mechanisms, such as self-disclosure, getting and giving feedback, or expressing strong emotions, which are expected to effect alterations in members' feelings, thoughts, or behavior. If one imagines how frightening such experiences can be under certain conditions, the interdependence of these two aspects of people-changing groups can be readily recognized. Many leaders and participants in group change programs assume that self-disclosure, for example, is unconditionally therapeutic. Yet it is a safe bet that certain members will not engage in such behavior unless they feel a certain degree of confidence in the group. The group conditions, in other words, must be such that members need not feel chronically anxious and can afford to drop their usual defensive maneuvers at least in relation to some of the events which take place in the group.

A number of the types of events usually witnessed in people-changing groups have been often regarded as inherently productive of positive change. Some change mechanisms will be quite familiar to anyone acquainted with dyadic helping relationships; others can only take place in a multi-person situation. None of these events has been shown to be necessarily successful with all people, nor under all conditions. They represent a distillation of what is generally regarded in the people-changing groups as important.

Expressivity

Emotional expression is an important element of the change process in most theories of group change. In some theoretical systems the expression of positive feelings is stressed; in others, the expression of negative feelings, especially hostility and anger. Expression of feelings about important life events is sometimes viewed as crucial. Theories differ considerably both with regard to the kind of emotional expressions considered important and to the importance placed on this change mechanism. Freud initially considered catharsis an important mechanism of change; he saw stifled emotions as a major impediment to mental health and a major source of symptoms. Later Freud and psychoanalytic theorists who followed him considerably de-emphasized the cathartic dimension in the change process. In sharp contrast, in some of the "new therapies" (Gestalt, various encounter techniques, and certain self-help groups such as Synanon) considerable emphasis is placed on emotional expression as a central element of change. The assumption is that unless the person is freed to express both negative and positive feelings toward others directly and openly, the road to change will be blocked. A number of distinctions can be made with regard to the function of expressivity in particular orientations. Intense feelings may be considered important only when they are cathartic (get out previously blocked feelings), or only when they are expressed towards others in the "here and now" group, or only when they involve re-living critical events from the person's life outside the group. Theoretical systems also differ with regard to whether emotional expression is received as an end in itself or simply a necessary step in a more complex change process involving other elements, such as cognitive mastery. Gestalt therapists, for example, see the expression of intense affect as an end in itself, and frequently encourage emotional expression toward current figures in the group. In contrast, women's consciousness-raising groups may emphasize emotional expression, particularly of an angry variety, much more in a cathartic fashion, directing such emotional expression toward society, rather than the members of the group itself. On the other hand, self-help movements like Alcoholics Anonymous do not view emotional expression as central to changing people. In general, the more traditional group psychotherapists place less emphasis on emotional expression (although they do not ignore it) as compared to leaders of the new orientations, which have highlighted expressivity as a mechanism of change. Clients in many group-based change systems report the ability to express both angry and positive feelings in the group as important in their view of the experience. It is of interest that frequently other people's intense emotional expressions are viewed by participants in groups as being more important to them, a phenomenon that will be discussed under a different mechanism (spectator therapy).

Self-Disclosure

Self-disclosure is the explicit communication of information that a group participant believes other members would be unlikely to acquire unless he told it to them, and which he considers so highly private that he would exercise great caution regarding whom he told it to. Although the experience of self-disclosure in individual psychotherapy has been discussed by several theorists, it is important to recognize that disclosure to a single paid professional is quite different in meaning from disclosure to a group of peers. It feels less dramatic and is less anxiety-laden to reveal private information to a single professional than to a group. Group participants imply that it is easier to reveal themselves in a one-to-one relationship than in a group; yet they indicate more exhilaration over such acts in a multi-person situation. Some theorists, such as Jourard (1964) and Mowrer (1964), see self-disclosure as the primary therapeutic mechanism, the *sine qua non* of growth. Group change systems in which guilt is perceived as a primary issue confronting people also stress self-disclosure as a curative mechanism. For example, revelation plays an important role in many of the self-help movements, particularly Alcoholics Anonymous. In general, the newer therapies place more emphasis on self-disclosure than the more traditional theories of group therapy. As with emotional expression, self-disclosure can be considerd a primary mechanism in terms of its effect on the person who discloses, as well as a secondary mechanism in the sense that frequently the self-disclosure of other people appears to be a salient therapeutic experience for certain individuals.

The particular content of self-disclosure—what sort of information gets disclosed—probably depends on the values of the particular change system. In some groups, events associated with guilt or shame appear to be stressed; in others, revelations are more geared to the person's feelings, thoughts, and fantasies about other group members. What is important, however, is that generally the content makes little difference when compared to the sense that persons who self-disclose have engaged in a risky and essentially social act; self-disclosure appears to be useful only when the initiator's intention of sharing of deeply personal material is understood, appreciated, and correctly interpreted by the group collectivity. In other words, the power of self-disclosure is *not* that what is said has been said for the first time. (This is rare; in one study participants indicated that only 14 percent of all self-disclosures were first-time disclosures.) It is the sense of well-being and confidence in other human beings and the feeling of acceptance that seem to be the active ingredients in making self-disclosure an important mechanism of change. Finally, it is worth noting that self-disclosures may be seen as cathartic events, much like the expression of intense emotions. It is the sense of relieving oneself in the social context that characterizes some self-disclosures, while others appear to be valuable to the participant when the act of self-disclosing leads to some cognitive mastery, some sense that the person achieves an understanding of the meaning and implications of what he has disclosed. As with most change mechanisms that are seen as generally productive, the context is overriding. In a context where it is not appreciated or accepted, self-disclosure is negatively rewarded; when it is accepted and appreciated by the other group members, it is more likely to have therapeutic benefit. There is some evidence that when self-disclosure occurs prior to the building of a cohesive group, it is less beneficial than when it occurs after some sense of trust and sharing has developed.

Feedback

Of all the learning mechanisms associated with personal change and development through groups, feedback—the receipt of information about how one is perceived by peers—is unique to the group situation. Theories wherein psychopathology is viewed as social in origin tend to emphasize feedback as a curative mechanism more than theories that emphasize intrapsychic determinants of pathology. It appears, however, that some form of feedback is seen as important in almost all theories of group-induced change. It appears also that feedback responds to a very basic human need, the need to find out where we stand, how we are seen by others. Group members perceive feedback to be one of the most salient experiences in their participation in groups. Generally, the closer (in time) feedback is given on a specific behavior, the more effective it is. The form in which it is transmitted also seems to be an important factor in determining its utility. Feedback appears to be helpful to the degree that it is concrete, that is, easily understood by the person because it is related to a particular event and given within a relatively unthreatening context.

Leader strategies vary widely with regard to feedback. Some leaders stress feedback as a central mechanism; they engage in a considerable amount of active teaching about the nature of feedback, frequently model feedback behavior, and use other strategies to encourage its occurrence. Other leaders appear less active in encouraging or teaching about feedback, but generally seem to support it when it occurs. As with the expression of emotions, there probably are differences with regard to the content and valence of feedback among different systems—some seem to generate more negative or critical responses; others, more positive-supportive observations.

The Experience of Intense Emotions

All theories of therapy deeply involve the emotional life of the person. The experience of strong affects is closely related to the expressive mechanism already discussed, but does not necessarily require that the person engage in the direct expression of feelings; in this view, it is sufficient to experience strong positive or negative emotions whether or not they are expressed. The concept of the "corrective emotional experience" articulated by Alexander (1946) describes the function of the experience of intense emotions. The basic principle of treatment advanced by Alexander is to expose the patient, under more favorable circumstances, to emotional situations which he could not handle in the past. For Alexander, corrective emotional experience involves the experience of strong affect accompanied by reality-testing. The change group offers innumerable stimuli to generate intense emotions in members. The events of the group life activate issues in the individual's core problem areas—competition, intimacy, dependency, and so forth. It is likely that during the course of any healing group, affective issues will come up among members that are related to the person's problem area. Other characteristics of the group, for example the frequent contagion of affects in which individuals are "carried away" by the emotional expression of others, may unleash feelings certain members have been previously unable or unwilling to experience. Among different theories of people-changing in groups somewhat different aspects of emotional experience are emphasized. Psychoanalytically-oriented group psychotherapists are prone to emphasize and select out strong emotional experiences that recapitulate characteristics of earlier experiences; those who emphasize the interpersonal aspects of groups are more likely to stimulate intense experiences revolving around interpersonal relationships in the group without seeking directly to relate them to the re-living of past events. The newer therapies are, in good part, based on the diagnosis that much of the plight of modern man stems from the mutilation of the ability to experience intense emotions. Hence, their technology has been built to design devices which increase sensory awareness through the stimulation of physical feelings and emotion-provoking experiences. Many of the structured exercises which are practiced repeatedly in the newer therapies and which are used to induce mediation, inner fantasy, heightened interpersonal responsiveness, and so on, are partly aimed at revitalizing what are considered atrophied pathways to intense feelings about one's inner life, one's body, and one's relationship to others. Again, in some theories curative forces are assigned to negatively-toned emotions (anger, rage, and so forth), while others are more directed toward inducing positive emotions, especially love.

The Experience of Communion

The unique attribute of the group to provide its members with a feeling of oneness with others, a sense of belonging to a collectivity, has become increasingly emphasized in recent years, perhaps in response to the view that contemporary society lacks the ability to provide for such needs. Communion appears to be one of the driving, if unverbalized, needs of participants in personal change groups. The achievement of a sense of communion can be seen as a primary therapeutic mechanism insofar as individuals who first experience it through groups learn that it is possible to feel toward others in a way they had not previously experienced. In many theories the experience of communion is seen as an important step and is emphasized more as a condition which can lead to increasing trust and openness and, in turn, to facilitating change processes. Phenomenologically, many participants in groups emphasize communion as a primary aspect of their learning. Women's consciousness-raising groups, for example, particularly emphasize communion as a core element of the change process because they ascribe modern women's problems in part to alienation from other women. In general, while more traditional psychotherapists perceive the experience of communion as an important by-product of the group, they do not emphasize it as having primary therapeutic value. Groups that are usually outside the professional tradition, such as many self-help and consciousness-raising groups, are more likely to place primary emphasis on the experience of communion as a mechanism of personal change.

Altruism

Although participants do not enter change-induction groups to be helpful to others, a common experience unique to the group is that individuals can be genuinely facilitative for others. The low self-esteem and poor conceptions of self so characteristic of neurotic patients often prevent them from feeling they can be genuinely helpful to other human beings. Yet, they frequently do feel helpful to others in the group to an extent that appears critical and, in this sense, a primary therapeutic mechanism.

Spectatorism

It is not uncommon in a psychotherapeutic group or in other change-inducing groups to note that a few people have been quiet and inactive throughout the history of the group. Yet, such individuals may clearly express a sense of having benefited from the group and have been shown to have achieved gains on empirical measures of outcome. Apparently, such people can learn something useful just by being in a situation where others are having critical and significant emotional experiences. The most likely explanation of this process is that such situations clarify issues which are critical to the spectator. The work of Bandura (1969) on imitative learning may have relevance to understanding the nature of spectatorism (see Chapter 5 on modeling). Personality characteristics are also relevant to understanding this mechanism of change, for it appears that not all participants in a group are equally able to identify with others and make use of their experiences. When one asks group participants at the end of a meeting what were the most important events, more often than not they select strong emotional experiences or meaningful self-disclosures of others as being personally most significant for them. Although it is not fully understood as a mechanism of change, spectator-derived gains occur very frequently in groups. It is reasonable to assume that the spectator employs some cognitive processes to make use of what others are experiencing in connection with his own problematic areas.

Many self-help groups capitalize on this phenomenon; for example in Alcoholics Anonymous the formal process of telling others "how it is with me" appears to provide some opportunity for identification for nonactive participants, as well as serving other functions.

Discovering Similarity

The relief that group participants so frequently experience when they discover that their problem is not unique appears to be one of the more positive subjective experiences offered to individuals through groups. Many of the self-help and consciousness-raising groups are purposely organized around maximizing the experience of similarity as a basic mechanism of support and alleviation of problems. Other group change-induction systems differ considerably in the degree to which a sense of similarity among participants is viewed as curative. Nevertheless, in most newly-formed groups the discovery of similarity seems important to the participants regardless of how much the leader makes of it through particular interventions. The process by which this experience is change-inducing is rather opaque. Phenomenologically, it seems to be an important experience for the person and appears to offer relief from a negative image of self. As with many mechanisms of change, it is difficult to isolate its specific contribution to outcome or change.

Experimentation

A unique property of a group situation is the setting it offers participants to experiment with new forms of behavior under low risk. All formal systems of group psychotherapy and many of the newer group therapies are maximally constructed to encourage participants to try out new behaviors. Experimentation tends to be viewed as an important mechanism of change to the degree that a theoretical position views the group as a social microcosm. Experimentation seems to be less stressed in most self-help and consciousness-raising groups. Some group change-induction systems have developed formal procedures for encouraging experimentation—role playing is a prime example. Many proscriptive interventions of leaders—suggestions for trying out new ways of relating, and so forth—are aimed at inducing change through experimentation. The assumption is that having done something once under the protection of the group, the person may be more fortified to do it in the outside world. It is clear that this mechanism is highly dependent on group conditions. The ability of individuals to experiment implies that the group offers a sense of safety and lower threat than the real world. It also requires some specification of the person's problem and of alternative ways of behaving. Often, participants get ready to adopt a new stance in the outside world through a long chain of events, perhaps beginning with discovering through watching others that there are alternative ways to achieve a desired goal; this discovery may lead to thinking over, then trying out alternative behavior in the group and, finally, in the external situation. For this complex chain of events to occur, many properties of the group must be conducive. The group norms, for example, must support decisions to experiment.

Modeling

The concept of modeling has been well described and discussed in other chapters (see Chapters 5 and 6). That it does occur in groups is not questioned; little is known, however, about the conditions under which modeling is enhanced, or to what degree modeling implies what the participants do or only what the leader does. There is some evidence that modeling may work as a prime mechanism for maintaining change. In following up individuals who made positive gains in encounter groups, it was found that modeling, an internalization of how particular participants or leaders would have handled the situation, proved to be an important element in the change-maintenance process. Thus, although modeling is clearly an important mechanism, it is a poorly understood mechanism in the group situation. There is little knowledge available about the conditions under which it occurs, what characteristics of leaders encourage modeling, and how one determines what behavior is to be modeled and what is not.

The Inculcation of Hope

Group situations often generate events that inspire hope in participants. Frank (1961) has more than adequately described the importance of hope as a factor in change. Simply put, hope is a feeling that one can change and that the group (or the individual) can be responsible for such change. Group situations offer many stimuli to increase hope; for example, seeing other members in the group successfully grapple with problems or seeing others who have changed as the result of their participation in the group. The leader or therapist is probably less important in inculcating hope in the group than in the dyadic situation. The evidence of what is happening to others which is before the eyes of most group participants is probably more powerful than the hope-inducing behavior generated by leaders. Some group therapeutic systems employ hope as a central change-induction mechanism. This is particularly characteristic of self-help and consciousness-raising groups. The type of "game group" practiced by Synanon, in which new and experienced members are mixed, provides a classic example of seeing others who have been in the same boat, who have shared the same misery, and have conquered it. Opportunities to hear testimonials of those who have conquered their problems as offered in Alcoholics Anonymous and the positive belief systems presented by many self-help movements, clearly are intended to inculcate hope.

Cognitive Factors

For many of the therapeutic mechanisms that have been reviewed, there is an implicit suggestion that some cognitive aspects are involved. Yet, there has been much confusion and considerable debate concerning the role of cognitive factors in the group curative process. Traditional psychotherapeutic systems growing out of dynamic psychiatry have clearly emphasized the role of cognitive factors, usually expressed in terms of insight into the neurotic processes at work. The more modern group therapies have generally placed less emphasis on cognitive factors in learning. Some theories stress cognitive mastery, but view it as understanding or discovering previously unknown or unacceptable parts of the self which need not relate to historical events in a person's life. Some systems of treatment overtly train their participants to use a particular cognitive model. For example, in transactional analysis groups, leaders frequently use traditional educational modes for teaching participants the framework for analyzing experience. Other systems rely on more incidental or less formal educational processes, which are usually generated by the leader pointing out or interpreting events as they occur. Some systems of change see cognitive mastery as being generated both directly when a person is involved in some experience in the group, as well as indirectly by seeing others have experiences and partaking and identifying with their experiences for cognitive mastery. Most systems of psychotherapy and many self-help groups stress cognitive mastery with regard to personal life history, and understanding is sought in that arena. Groups such as women's consciousness-raising provide cognitive mastery not so much for understanding personal life histories but rather for understanding oneself in the light of societal models. In general, there have been a wide variety of devices for inculcating cognitive mastery, and an even wider range of frameworks through which to understand experience.

Although cognitive learning has been de-emphasized in some of the newer therapies, recent evidence (Lieberman, Yalom, and Miles, 1973) suggests that the most effective mechanisms for learning in encounter groups involve some elements of cognitive mastery. For example, it was found that the degree of frequency of self-disclosure in and of itself was not salient in explaining who experienced positive outcomes, but that self-disclosure which involved some sort of cognitive mastery or understanding of the self-disclosure was highly related to positive outcome. In general, the cognitive mastery of experience was established as a positive force. Experiences in and of themselves seem to be less important than when they were mediated through cognitive factors. The degree to which the particular kind or nature of cognitive mastery is important is a major unanswered question. To what degree is the proposition advanced by psychoanalytic theoreticians about genetic cognitive mastery valid, compared to cognitive mastery of current interpersonal operations? Does it make a difference whether the person understands himself and his experiences with a psychoanalytic framework or a framework stemming from interactional systems or even a sociocultural system? It may be that any consistent system which the person finds useful for understanding experience is a crucial element, and the particular content of the system is less relevant.

STUDIES OF OUTCOME

This review of group methods would not be complete without some acknowledgement of the state of the art and current knowledge about the effectiveness of change induction groups. This final section, then, examines the entire published report during 1973-74 of group psychotherapy, experiential groups, consciousness raising activities, and self-help groups. The 47 published articles and dissertations addressed either the simple question: Does it work? or the more complex question: Which works better?

Does it work and how well? Of the studies shown in Table 13.2 , 17 were concerned with ostensibly normative college populations, another eight with adult "normals," and the remaining 22 with individuals seeking various forms of help at mental health agencies. Of these 22, nine involved the neurotic problems of college-aged and adult populations, and only two involved psychotic populations. Ten focused on various forms of deviant behavior—primarily alcoholism and drug abuse—but did include other forms of abuse (such as overeating). An occasional study reported on the use of groups for other problems such as community relationships (police/delinquents).

Some General Trends in Design of Outcome Studies

Two-thirds of the studies surveyed used some form of control with the majority providing active alternative treatment or simulation of treatment rather than "inert" or "nonactive" control groups. Many of the controls chosen were based on sophisticated research strategies and creative design, using active or alternate treatment methods and often involving true random assignment. In contrast, some of the inert control groups were primitively chosen and represented no more than a nodding afterthought to research design.

The range of measures was broad, as were the populations and conditions of treatment. Some studies relied totally on one self-report scale; others used a multimethod approach. None met the more stringent requirements for excellence in design. The most popular measure of outcome was the POI; 20 percent of the studies used this instrument. However, this turned out to be problematic. Recall that a majority of the studies surveyed are those of the encounter group/sensitivity training variety, in which values of self-development, openness, honesty, etc. are intrinsic to the method itself. The POI closely matches the value systems portrayed in such groups; consequently, it is difficult to distinguish this measure from the overt values of the change-induction system itself. Other frequently used measurement devices were testimony reports, standard personality inventories such as the MMPI or the CPI, measures of state or trait anxiety, symptomatology, and various standard and commonly accepted indices of self-acceptance and self-ideal congruity. A few studies used peer measures of change; surprisingly few used leader judgments of change. Only one used third-party measurement. Other favorites included the FIRO, the Hill Interaction Matrix, and the Rotter. Some studies relied on situation type tests—frequently little more than standard replication of the change induction system itself, such as self-disclosing behavior to a stranger, as an index of how well this particular behavior was learned. Eight of the 47 studies used one form or another of behavioral index ranging from measures of attendance to assessments of alcohol consumption or weight loss.

Table 13.2, which contains brief summaries of outcome studies, is divided into two main parts: Part 1 surveys outcome studies in which the investigators contrast treatment conditions with inert control groups (or no control at all); Part 2 scans those studies which emphasize comparative treatment modalities.

Simple Outcome Studies. Of the 31 studies reported in Part 1, 14 are directed toward college students. All but two of the 14 reported positive results—lower anxiety, increased internal locus of control, increased social interaction, increased self-esteem, value changes, and decreased discrepancy between self and ideal. The two studies of college samples showing negative results—Kaye's (1973) on academic failures and Lunceford's (1973) on black female undergraduates—involved populations that ordinarily may have had values incongruous with sensitivity training/encounter groups. Although less numerous, studies reporting the effects of encounter or sensitivity training on adults echo similar themes. Educated middle class adults who participate in sensitivity training groups show the same pattern of positive results as do college students. When studies using similar group settings were directed at populations probably not value-congruent with the particular group, such as that by Fromme, Jones and Davis (1974) on a conservative population (fundamentalist background), they showed converse results—in this instance, an increase in emotional disturbance. Although having different goals and using different measures, the study reported by Kroeker, Forsyth and Haase (1974) on attitude shifts for ghetto dwelling adolescents and police demonstrates the limitations of such groups for particular populations. Studies of addict populations are inconsistent. Some reported positive results, while others—and again, this seems to relate to populations that may be more value incongruent with the particular group—found negative results.

The positive results from most reported studies on the effects of groups cannot be explained away on the basis of inadequate controls. Nevertheless, these 31 studies do not measurably increase our knowledge about change-induction groups. Too many rely upon change measures that offer little more than attitude-change evidence. More important, the particular change conditions are usually unspecified. They range, with similar outcomes, from peer-controlled groups with sets of tasks to accomplish, to groups led by sophisticated leaders. In addition, the fact that such groups work best with "volunteer subjects," i.e. people who seek such settings, ordinarily with positive expectations of change, leads one to question the robustness of these findings. The fact that individuals less likely to be changed are also those whose values are less congruent with the particular set espoused by such groups casts doubt on the meaningfulness of the findings. Further, the range of human behaviors considered appropriate for assessing outcome is relatively narrow in most studies.

Comparative Treatment Studies. Part 2 of Table 13.2 reports on studies that involved some form of comparative treatment. They range from relatively informal designs in which specific directions were given to leaders on their leadership role in regard to highly distinct leadership conditions—such as group versus individual context, token versus nontoken environment, peer-controlled versus leader-led groups—to indirect learning conditions, such as groups of students observing other groups of students as they experience intensive face-to-face groups. As a rule this set of research reports was more tightly designed than the first set, though the outcome criteria were for the most part similar.

Four major types of research are apparent: (1) comparative treatments—various forms of groups treatment, usually sharing theoretical underpinnings but emphasizing variations in technique, content focus, or mode of communication (see Part 2A of table 13.2); (2) some variant of comparison of groups—again groups within the same theoretical tradition but distinguished on the basis of leader-led or peer-controlled groups (see Part 2B of table 13.2 and its discussion in the section on boundaries); (3) research reports comparing types of treatment, individual treatment, and group treatment, or comparing different forms of groups, behavioral and "talk" therapy (see Part 2C of table 13.2); and (4) studies which report on alterations of time arrangements, usually time-extended versus time-concentrated situations (see Part 2D of table 13.2).

Comparative techniques. Overall, studies of structured techniques or learning devices produced results favoring the particular technique which interested the investigator. Ten studies examined comparative treatments in which one of the treatments emphasized greater structure or specific technical interventions. Six of these produced results affirming the investigators' hypotheses that groups using each particular technical "advantage" examined—video feedback, nonverbal emphasis, induced anxiety, structured groups, assertiveness training versus talk, etc.—derived greater benefit than comparable groups not using these techniques. Several studies of this genre produced negative results, that is, no differences were found between particular treatment conditions. Included here were the failure to find the effectiveness of token reinforcement for physically ill patients, the failure to find distinctions between affect-oriented and cognitively oriented T-groups, the ambiguous results reported on obese women in regard to group therapy versus a self-maintained manual for controlling eating. (In this last example, some differences were found with regard to eating habits and attitudes, but not with regard to weight loss.)

Two studies were of particular interest. Both contained unusual "placebo" groups and both produced results which suggest that nonspecific therapeutic factors may be responsible for the major effects reported in many of the outcome studies reviewed in Part 1. McCardel and Murray (1974) utilized an on-site control group. Subjects had expected to participate in change-induction groups, but instead they were exposed only to recreational activities and relatively non-intense interactive events. Nevertheless, this condition produced high changes comparable to the other treatment conditions—structured and unstructured sensitivity training. McLeish and Park (1973) studied various group treatment forms as well as two conditions for groups of observers. Increases in empathy, the only positive finding for the treatment conditions, occurred just as strongly among the observers.

The core question—to what degree do the comparative treatments transcend nonspecific treatment conditions—remains open. On balance, the studies reported favor specific directed interventions over less directed interventions (structure versus unstructure). But the possibility of the enthusiasm and bias of the experimenter affecting the results cannot be ignored. Furthermore, the fact that the structured formats appear more effective may be less a result of the particular intervention system than of the influence of structure on the purveyor. Most of the groups were conducted by relatively inexperienced leaders trained in particular methods. It is quite likely that "knowing what to do," a powerful anxiety reducer, may have been the more significant active ingredient than the particular form of intervention itself. Without increased knowledge of the particular mechanisms of change, that chain of events between the input and output variables, it is difficult to make generalizations from these studies. Finally, it is difficult to evaluate two sets of conflicting results, i.e. that (1) structured intervention techniques are better, or (2) peer-controlled groups are as good as or occasionally better than leader-led groups. This is especially true when the leaders use many of the specific intervention systems tested in the research reports just described.

Comparative Treatments. Studies which compared treatment modalities generally reported no differences. The question may again be one of general or nonspecific treatment conditions. However, it is also likely that the indices used to measure outcome are relatively insensitive to the potentialities of different treatment contexts such as group and individual psychotherapy.

Time arrangements. Several studies on time alterations show evidence indicating greater effectiveness of time-intensive groups. Although the findings point in this direction, the conceptual underpinnings of time arrangements in therapy are so indeterminate that, without some knowledge about the underlying mechanism, it is difficult to build from the results.

To extract the fundamentals from the range in studies directed toward answering the question: Does the group change induction work? is, to say the least, a difficult task. Few researchers question the fact that individuals who participate in such settings are likely to benefit. More specific agreement, however, about what benefits, for whom, and under what conditions, are beyond our grasp, as the reader can plainly appreciate through the sample of studies presented.

It is important that researchers utilize the newly-developed assessment procedures to measure the effectiveness of various change-inducing groups. Statistical procedures that address problems of measurement error; sophisticated frameworks that take into account various prospectives of assessment—the clients, other interested parties such as the therapists and significant others; and societal prospective on functioning are currently available to increase the specificity and meaningfulness of outcome research. The movement as represented by current studies toward comparative analyses across change systems, as well as large-scale samples, promises to bring some order to a field that currently shows major symptoms of disarray and lack of meaningful progress.

Table 13.2. Studies of outcome.

PART 1 Outcome of Treatment versus Inert Control Group or No Control

Author	Sample	Method	Finding
Arbes & Hubbell (1973)	16 male, 14 female self-referred undergraduates	Random assignment to one of two experimental groups. 2½ hr/7 wk or a control group. FIRO-B, Concept Specific Anxiety and Interpersonal Relationship Rating Scale pre-post	Ss improved on almost all scales of Concept Specific Anxiety Scale & Interpersonal Relationship Scale. FIRO-B (expressed affects) subscale used
Barrett-Lennard et al. (1973-74)	62 mental health professionals	2 wk encounter group workshop. Open-ended Qs 6 mo after participation. Change ratings (77% rates agreement)	Change in level of self-regard, interpersonal behavior, and attitudes for majority of Ss
Battle & Zwier (1973)	8 male chronic hospital elopers	21 weekly therapy sessions	Group effective in reducing absences
Brown (1973)	54 chronically mentally ill patients under medication	Assigned to 3 groups: 1. using tokens to reinforce comments and reports about community adjustment; 2. nontoken group stressing support for community adjustment; 3. medication supervision only	Observed no differences between treatment conditions
Cooper (1974)	30 members of helping profession	1 wk sensitivity group. Neuroticism scale of EPI and a behavior change Q by participants, friends, and family members	Increase in neuroticism on EPI, not "confirmed" by family and friends 2 wk later

Table 13.2 (Continued)

Author	Sample	Method	Finding
Deleppo (1973)	Drug addicts in self-help treatment and methadone maintenance	Comparison between the effects of peer-directed psychotherapy and methadone on MMPI scores	Self-help group scored significantly lower on Depression and Psychopathic Scales
Diamond (1974)	Phase I: 39 grad students; Phase II: 44 equivalent Ss	Investigated effects of encounter group on locus of control (Rotter). Phase I: 3 groups led by supervised grad students and 1 no-treatment control group; Phase II: 4 encounter groups	Increases in internal locus of control
Dies & Sadowsky (1974)	Women in dormitory living on 3 separate floors; women on 2 other floors were control group	Experimental Ss provided with group experience. Semantic differential ratings of atmosphere and self-reported number of acquaintances	Improvement in semantic differential ratings and increase in number of acquaintances
Felton & Davidson (1973)	61 high school low achievers	57 session, 3/wk and nontreatment control. Rotter I-E pre-post	Increase in internality
Foulds (1973)	14 undergraduates who had signed up for encounter group	Six 4-hr sessions/wk. Ss rated themselves and others on 29 semantic differential scales pre-post. 14 control undergrads from waiting list	Increases in positive rating of self and others
Fromme et al. (1974)	A "conservative population" of 91 county extension agents	One wk T-group. CPI and TSCS pre-post	10 of 18 CPI scales showed Ss becoming more cautious, inhibited, defensive, disorganized, and emotionally upset. TSCS less conclusive. 2 scales (Personality Interpretation and Ethical Self-Concept Scale) showed decline and 3 improved (physical self-concepts)
Gilligan (1974)	50 T-group volunteers, college students	24 hr in a weekend, compared to a nontreatment group of 55 student volunteers. POI pre-post and 6 wk followup	Post-test, Ss impoved on 6 of 12 scales. 6 wk, Inner Direction, Self-Regard and Acceptance of Aggression significant

Table 13.2 (Continued)

Author	Sample	Method	Finding
Herz et al. (1974)	144 aftercare patients	Randomly assigned to group or individual therapy with first year psychiatric residents. Therapist rating after 1 yr on PAS and HSR, patient self-report	No differences. Therapists preferred groups. Group patients more enthusiastic
Kaye (1973)	27 academically unsuccessful undergrads	In 2 T-groups for 18 sessions/10 days. Control groups: (*a*) balloted out of T-group participation; (*b*) refused the invitation; (*c*) academically successful students. HIM-B, FIRO-B, and LIC pre-post and 8 mo later	HIM-B initially increased on post-test but decreased 8 mo later. No other changes
Kilmann (1974)	9 university students	10 hr marathon group on state and trait anxiety pre-post	Anxiety state showed decline; anxiety trait was unchanged
Kilmann & Auerbach (1974)	84 institutionalized female narcotic drug addicts	Randomly assigned to (*a*) a marathon (23 hr) directive group following defined and planned exercises; (*b*) nondirective marathon group where therapist relinquished responsibility	Ss in nondirective therapy declined in anxiety trait; directive therapy Ss showed increase, controls stayed same
Kleeman (1974)	Undergrads from 25 colleges; 188 participants and 140 control non-participants, of whom 141 of former and 89 of latter were involved in original experiment and replication; follow-up involved 97 Ss and 89 controls	Wrightman's Philosophy of Human Nature Scale and a self-report of self-determining and motivating behavior pre-post. Ss participated for 29-40 hr during an academic term	Positive changes on Philosophy of Human Nature Scales
Klingberg (1973)	48 male seminary students	POI, Frankl's Purpose in Life Test, and Broen's Religious Attitude Inventory given pre-post in professionally and self-directed (leaderless) T-groups	No consistent differences

Table 13.2 (Continued

Author	Sample	Method	Finding
LaCalle (1973)	Mexican American and non- Mexican American drug addicts on methadone	Assigned to four groups. 1. Mexican Americans on methadone only; 2. on methadone with group therapy; 3. non- Mexican Americans on methadone only; 4. non-Mexican Americans on methadone with group therapy. A behavioral Q and CPI	Methadone treatment Ss improved in observable behavior; no improvement in the methadone plus group therapy Ss
Lunceford (1973)	Black female undergrads	Weekend encounter group; non- participant control group. TSCS pre-post	Only one significant subscale difference: Ss increased in category of personal self
Margulies (1973)	40 middle management employees	One T-group and one control group. POI given pre-post	Positive changes in self-actualization
Martin & Fischer (1974)	38 Ss aged 17-45	One weekend (30 hr) encounter group. Ss named 38 persons like selves for control group. Adjective Checklist given pre-post	4 of 13 Adjective Checklist Scales improved; 1 self-concept and 3 social skills
McIntire (1973)	17 randomly assigned Ss aged 22 to late 50s	Met 5 hr/wk for 6 wk. POI given pre-post and a year later	2 days after, Inner Directed and Self-Acceptance POI scales increased. Still significant at year
Posthuma & Posthuma (1973)	73 Unitarian Church members	Ss met in encounter group for one 12-hr session followed by 10 weekly 2-hr sessions; Placebo control group met for 10 content oriented, 3-hr sessions; nontreatment control group. Self-reports on behavioral Change Index used to assess casualties post- and at 6 months	Negative indices undifferentiated among three groups by 6-mo followup
Reddy (1973)	36 YMCA administrators	Met in three 10-day residential sensitivity groups. POI given pre-post and at one year. Multiple Affect Adjective Checklist given daily to measure anxiety. No control group	All three groups reported changes. Variance on 9 of 12 POI subscales. Correlations of pre-post to post-followup negative, suggesting ''late bloomers.'' Anxiety scores positively related to POI scores in one group over followup year

Table 13.2 (Continued)

Author	Sample	Method	Finding
Redfering (1973)	18 female delinquents who had participated in previous study	Received group counseling during year following previous study in which Ss had given significantly more positive connotative meanings to concepts of father, mother, self, and peers. One year followup tested these effects	Positive effects were still present on all concepts except those of peers as measured by the Semantic Differential Technique
Romano & Quary (1974)	68 undergrads, former encounter group participants	Responded to followup Q on harmful effects of their group experience (25% of original group did not respond)	67 reported that they had not been harmed by the groups
Vicino et al. (1973)	96 undergraduate volunteers	Ss took set of self-administered exercises. Outcome measures by "Who am I," peer-ratings, and Bills, Rokeach & Marlowe Crowne personality inventories. Eight experimental and 4 control (delayed treatment) groups	Reduction in discrepency between self and ideal. Other indices not different. Despite positive change, member satisfaction with groups was low
Walton (1973)	25 undergraduates	Met in two encounter groups, 14 1-hr sessions. Control group of 9 undergrads enrolled in seminar on counseling concepts and procedures for increasing self-actualization. POI and 16 PF, pre-post	Gains on Inner Direction and Spontaneity scales of POI and Adventuresome and Creative Personality prediction scales of the 16 PF. Controls increase on POI Nature of Man
White (1974)	85 undergrads; control group of 75 undergrads	Met in human potential lab for 2½ hr/wk. POI pre-post. Control group of 75 undergrads matched for sex and age	Ss increased on Self-Actualizing, Reactiv Spontaneity, and N e of Man subscales

PART 2 Comparative Treatment
    A. Specific techniques

Archer & Kagan (1973)	Undergraduates in T-groups	Compared Ss led by undergraduate paraprofessionals using videotape feedbacks with limited structure encounter group model and non-treatment control. Empathy test, POI, and peer relationship ratings	Participants in interpersonal process recall video feedback groups score higher than unstructured encounter and control group

Table 13.2 (Continued)

Author	Sample	Method	Finding
Bolan (1973)	College student volunteers	"Experimental" group and "standard" encounter group. Compared differences resulting from two approaches to encounter groups; experimental group used nonverbal and verbal activities. POI and FIRO-B.	Experimental Ss showed more gain on Time Competence, Inner Directed, and Self-Acceptance scales-POI
Bornstein & Sipprelle (1973)	40 obese male and female volunteers	Four groups: 1. nontreatment control group; 2. therapy, relaxation group; 3. therapy; 4. induced anxiety therapy. Weight loss assessed post-test, 3 mo and 6 mo later	No significant differences post-test. Significant differences in weight loss favored induced anxiety group compared to others at 3 and 6 mo followup
Dye (1974)	56 associate degree nursing freshmen	Five groups: 1. encounter-tape group; 2. affect- oriented T-group; 3. cognitively oriented group using verbal and nonverbal interactions; 4. placebo group maintaining journal of critical life events: 5. nontreatment group. TSCS, Manifest Anxiety Scale, State Trait Anxiety Inventory, and Affect Adjective Checklist, HIM-B pre-post, and 1 month post-test	No significant differences between the groups were found
Hagen (1974)	54 obese female undergraduates	Three conditions: 1. group therapy; 2. use of written manual (biblio therapy); 3. group therapy and biblio-therapy combined. Weight loss was outcome measure	All treatment groups showed more weight loss than controls. Ss reported group treatments significantly more helpful than manual only. Changes in eating habits but not in physical activity were different across groups
Hand et al. (1974)	25 adult patients with agoraphobia	Each patient received 12 hr exposure (flooding) in vivo for 3 days, 4 hr/day. 3 groups structured to increase social cohesion during exposure; other 3 unstructured to expose members to minimal group influence. Behavioral tests and phobic anxiety measured	Structured groups improved more than unstructured groups 3 and 6 mo later

Table 13.2 (Continued)

Author	Sample	Method	Finding
McCardel & Murray (1974)	47 Ss recruited from campus ad	Three weekend groups whose methods varied from highly structured, exercise- oriented techniques to nonstructured. At-home and on-site controls, the latter led to believe that they were also in encounter group but given only recreational activities. POI, Marlow- Crowne Scale, Rokeach Dogmatism Scale, and peer rankings given pre-post and at 10 wk	Significant differences on 7 of 12 POI scales. On-site control group and 3 encounter groups did not differ on any measure. Followup confirmed these findings
McLeish & Park (1973)	94 teacher trainees	Two types of human relations training: self-analytic treatment (SAT) or direct communications treatment (DCT) for two types of observer groups: Bales O group and clinical (nontrained) O group. 15 sessions. Park Matheson Human Relations Videotape Test, Park Matheson Group Process Analysis Test, Cambridge Survey of Education Opinions, and Rokeach Dogmatism Tests given pre-post	No changes found on personality and attitude measures, but DCT participants and Os were higher on measures of empathetic understanding
Rimm et al. (1974)	13 male college students responding to newspaper ad to join T-group for help in controlling anger	Ss randomly assigned to assertive training group or placebo group. Controls talked about anger. Lawrence Assertive Inventory, Rotter I-E, ratings of Ss responses to situations	No treatment effects on Rotter or Lawrence Inventory. Ss showed improvement on rated responses to situations

PART 2 Comparative Treatment
      B. Peer versus leader

Author	Sample	Method	Finding
Conyne (1974)	48 Ss enrolled in counselor education course	3 facilitator-directed sensitivity training group experiences and 3 self-directed experiences on development of intrapersonal perceptions of congruency and disclosure. Congruency assessed by group semantic differential and disclosure assessed by Johari window	No differences between treatments found. All groups increased in self-congruency and self-disclosure. 4 mo followup showed self-disclosure scores stable, but not self-congruency scores

Table 13.2 (Continued)

Author	Sample	Method	Finding
Hunt et al. (1973)	40 university students in counseling center	Professionally led group met 2 hr/wk for 8 wk; 1 encounter- tape group met for 3 hr/wk for 5 wk; another had an active member; third had an active member and met for a weekend. 5 controls were on waiting list at counseling center. Miskimins Self, Goal, Other Discrepancy Scale given pre-post	Only Ss in encounter tape group with no active member decreased their discrepancy between present and desired self-concept
Kroeker et al. (1974)	60 inner city youths (15-21 yr) and 48 Rochester policemen	Human relations program. Ss randomly assigned to 1 of 3 workshops or 1 of 3 control groups. Youths attended on average of 4.5 workshops, policemen 3.5. Alienation Index Inventory and a TAT of police-black youth potential conflict situations	Pretesting effects far out-weighed experimental effects. No significant differences between Ss and controls

PART 2 Comparative Treatments
        C. Comparative Modes

Author	Sample	Method	Finding
Miller et al. (1973)	30 male alcoholics	Compared 3 types of treatment: electrical aversion conditioning; group therapy (confrontational psychotherapy); control conditioning. All Ss given instructions designed to produce high expectancy for therapeutic success. Pre-post measures of alcohol consumption and attitudes toward alcohol obtained using an analog ''taste test'' assessment	No differences found among groups
Newcomer & Morrison (1974)	Institutionalized retarded children	3 groups: individual play therapy; group therapy; or nontreatment control group Denver Developmental Screening Test given pretest and after 3 10-session blocks of therapy	Non treatment group did not change while scores for individual and group therapy groups increased across sessions. No differences between group and individual therapy

Table 13.2 (Continued)

Author	Sample	Method	Finding

PART 2 Comparative Treatments
   D. Time

| King et al. (1973) | 57 undergraduates | Studied changes in self-acceptance measured before and after participation in a marathon or a prolonged encounter group. Six groups: 3 met 24 hr each (marathon); 3 prolonged encounter groups met 3 or 4 hr/wk for 14 weeks; also control group and nontreatment control Lesser Self-Acceptance and Smith Social Approval scales pre-post | Both treatment conditions increased self-acceptance, but marathon group members were significantly lower than others in self-acceptance both pre- and post-test. Self-acceptance scores not associated with need for social approval |
| Ross et al. (1974) | 12 female narcotic addicts | Compared treatment of 6 Ss in a 17-hr marathon and 6 in group therapy in daily 2-hr sessions for 2 weeks. Lexington Personality Inventory | Both treatments reduced scores on neurotic triad of MMPI. Marathon also showed more change toward internal control |

[1]The following abbreviations are used throughout text and in Table 13.3 of this article.

CPI	California Psychological Inventory
EPI	Eysenck Personality Inventory
FIRO	Fundamental Interpersonal Relations Orientation
HIM	Hill Interaction Matrix
HSR	Meninger Health Sickness Rating
LIC	Leary Interpersonal Checklist
PAS	Problem Appraisal Scale
16PF	Cattell Sixteen Factor Personality Test
POI	Personal Orientation Inventory
Rotter I-E	Rotter Internal-External Scale
TAT	Thematic Apperception Test
TSCS	Tennessee Self-Concept Scale

REFERENCES

Alexander, F., and French, T.M. *Psychoanalytic therapy*. New York: Ronald Press, 1946.

Arbes, B.H., and Hubbel, R.N. Packaged impact: A structured communications skills workshop. *Journal of Counseling Psychology*, 1973, *20*, 332-37.

Archer, J., and Kagan, N. Teaching interpersonal relationship skills on campus: A pyramid approach. *Journal of Counseling Psychology*, 1973, *20*, 535-40.

Bandura, A. *Principles of behavior modification*. New York: Holt, Rinehart and Winston, 1969.

Barrett-Lennard, G.T., Kwasnik, T.P., and Wilkinson, G.R. Some effects of participation in encounter group workshops: An analysis of written follow-up reports. *Interpersonal Development*, 1973-4, *4*, 35-41.

Battel, E., and Zwier, M. Efficacy of small group process with intractable neuropsychiatric patients. *Newsletter for Research in Mental Health and Behavioral Science*, 1973, *15*, 15-17.

Bion, W.R. *Experiences in groups*. London: Tavistock Press, 1961.

Bolan, S.L., *A study exploring two different approaches to encounter groups: The combination of verbal encounter and designed nonverbal activity versus emphasis upon verbal activity only*. Ph.D thesis. 1973. *Dissertation Abstracts*, Ann Arbor, Mich: Univ. M-films No. 73-14390.

Bornstein, P.H., and Sipprelle, C.N. Group treatment of obesity by induced anxiety. *Behavior Research and Therapy*, 1973, *11*, 339-41.

Brown, T.R. Evaluation of a group centered aftercare system. NIMH Grant MH-21975 Rep., 1973.

Burrow, T. The group method of analysis. *Psychoanalytic Review*, 1927, *14*, 268-280.

Conyne, R.K. Effects of facilitator-directed and self-directed group experiences. *Counselor Education and Supervision*, 1974, *13*, 184-89.

Cooper, C.L. Psychological disturbance following T-groups: Relationship between the Eysenck Personality Inventory and family/friends perceptions. *British Journal of Social Work*, 1974, *4*, 39-49.

Deleppo, J.D. *Assessment of personality changes of drug addicts under two types of treatment modalities*. EdD thesis. *Dissertation Abstracts*, 1973, Ann Arbor, Mich: Univ. M-Films No. 73-23545.

Diamond, M.J. From Skinner to Satori? Toward a social learning analysis of encounter group behavior change. *Journal of Applied Behavioral Science*, 1974, *10*, 133-48.

Dies, R.R., and Sadowsky, R. A brief encounter group experience and social relationships in a dormitory. *Journal of Counseling Psychology*, 1974, *21*, 112-25.

Dye, C.A. Self-concept, anxiety, and group participation as affected by human relations training. *Nursing Research*, 1974, *13*, 184-89.

Ezriel, H. A psychoanalytic approach to group treatment. *British Journal of Medical Psychology*, 1950, *23*, 59-74.

Felton, G.S., and Davidson, H.R. Group counseling can work in the classroom. *Academic Therapy*, 1973, *8*, 461-68.

Foulds, M.L. Effects of a personal growth on ratings of self and others. *Small Group Behavior*, 1973, *4*, 508-12.

Frank, J. *Persuasion and healing*, Baltimore: Johns Hopkins Press, 1961.

Freud, S. *Group psychotherapy and the analysis of the ego*. New York: Boni and Liveright, 1940.

Fromme, D.K., Jones, W.H., and Davis, J.O. Experimental group training with conservative populations: A potential for negative effects. *Journal of Clinical Psychology*, 1974, *30*, 290-296.

Gilligan, J.F., Sensitivity training and self-actualization, *Psychological Reports*, 1974, *34*, 319-25.

Hagen, R.L., Group therapy versus bibliotherapy in weight reduction. *Behavior Therapy*, 1974, *5*, 222-34.

Hand, L., Lamontagne, Y., and Marks, I.M. Group exposure (flooding) in vivo for agoraphobics. *British Journal of Psychiatry*, 1974, *124*, 588-602.

Herz, M.I., Spitzer, R.L., Gibbon, M., Greenspan, K., and Reibel, S. Individual versus group aftercare treatment. *American Journal of Psychiatry*, 1974, *131*, 808-12.

Hurst, J.C., Delworth, U., and Garriott, R. Encountertapes: Evaluation of a leaderless group procedure. *Small Group Behavior*, 1973, *4*, 476-85.

Jourard, S.M. *The transparent self: Self-disclosure and well-being.* Princeton, N.J.: Van Nostrand, 1964.

Kaye, J.D. Group interaction and interpersonal learning. *Small Group Behavior*, 1973, *4*, 424-48.

Kilmann, P.R. Anxiety reactions to marathon group therapy. *Journal of Clinical Psychology*, 1974, *30*, 267-68.

Kilmann, P.R., and Auerbach, S.M. Effects of marathon group therapy on trait and state anxiety. *Journal of Consulting and Clinical Psychology*, 1974, *42*, 607-12.

King, M., Payne, D.C., and McIntire, W.G. The impact of marathon and prolonged sensitivity training on self-acceptance. *Small Group Behavior*, 1973, *4*, 414-23.

Kleeman, J.L. The Kendall College Human Potential Seminar model: Research. *Journal of College Student Personnel*, 1974, *15*, 89-95.

Klingberg, H.E. An evaluation of sensitivity training effects on self-actualization, purpose in life, and religious attitudes of theological students. *Journal of Psychology and Theology*, 1973, *1*, 31-39.

Kroeker, L.L., Forsyth, D.R., Haase, R.F. Evaluation of a police-youth human relations program. *Professional Psychology*, 1974, *5*, 140-54.

LaCalle, J.J. *Group psychotherapy with Mexican-American drug addicts.* Ph.D. thesis, 1973, *Dissertation Abstracts*, Ann Arbor, Mich: Univ. M-Films No. 73-22675.

LeBon, G. *The crowd: A study of the popular mind.* New York: Viking, 1960.

Lieberman, M.A., Yalom, I., and Miles, M. *Encounter groups: First facts.* New York: Basic Books, 1973.

Lunceford, R.D. *Self-concept change of black college females as a result of a weekend black experience encounter workshop.* Ph.D. Thesis, 1973, *Dissertation Abstracts*, Ann Arbor, Mich.: Univ. M-Films No. 73-22678.

Margulies, N. The effects of an organization sensitivity training program on a measure of self-actualization. *Student Personnel Psychology*, 1973, *5*, 67-74.

Martin, R.D., and Fischer, D.G. Encounter group experience and personality change. *Psychology Reports*, 1974, *35*, 91.

McCardel, J., Murray, E.J. Non-specific factors in weekend encounter groups. *Journal of Consulting and Clinical Psychology*, 1974, *42*, 337-45.

McIntire, W.G. The impact of T-group experience on level of self-actualization. *Small Group Behavior*, 1973, *4*, 459-65.

McLeish, J., and Park, J. Outcomes associated with direct and vicarious experience in training groups: III. Intended learning outcomes. *British Journal of Social and Clinical Psychology*, 1973, *12*, 359-73.

Miller, P.M., Hersen, M., Eisler, R.M., and Hemphill, D.P. Electrical aversion therapy with alcoholics: An analogue study. *Behavior Research and Therapy*, 1973, *11*, 491-97.

Moreno, J.L. *Who shall survive?* New York: Beacon House, 1953.

Mowrer, O.H. *The new group therapy.* Princeton, N.J.: Van Nostrand, 1964.

Newcomer, B.L., Morrison, T.L. Play therapy with institutionalized mentally retarded children. *American Journal of Mental Deficiency*, 1974, *78*, 727-33.

Posthuma, A.B., Posthuma, B.W. Some observations on encounter group casualties. *Journal of Applied Behavioral Science*, 1973, *9*, 595-608.

Pratt, J.H. The class method of treating consumption in the homes of the poor. *Journal of the American Medical Association*, 1907, *49*, 755-579.

Reddy, W.B. The impact of sensitivity training on self-actualization: A one-year follow-up. *Small Group Behavior*, 1973, *4*, 407-13.

Redfering, D.L. Durability of effects of group counseling with institutionalized delinquent females. *Journal of Abnormal Psychology*, 1973, *82*, 85-86.

Rimm, D.C., Hill, G.A., Brown, N.N., and Stuart, J.E. Group-assertive training in treatment of expression of inappropriate anger. *Psychological Reports*, 1974, *34*, 791-98.

Rogers, C.R. *Encounter groups*. New York: Harper and Row, 1970.

Romano, J.L., Quary, A.T. Follow-up of community college C-group participants. *Journal of College Student Personnel*, 1974, *15*, 278-83.

Ross, W.F., McReynolds, W.T., Berzins, J.I. Effectiveness of marathon group psychotherapy with hospitalized female narcotics addicts. *Psychological Reports*, 1974, *34*, 611-16.

Sullivan, H.S. *The interpersonal theory of psychiatry*. New York: Norton, 1953.

Truax, C.B. and Carkhuff, R.R. *Towards effective counseling and psychotherapy: Training and practice*. Chicago, Ill.: Aldine, 1967.

Vicino, F., Crusall, J., Bass, B., Deci, E., and Landi, D. The impact of process: Self-administered exercises for personal and interpersonal development. *Journal of Applied Behavioral Science*, 1973, *9*, 737-56.

Walton, D.R. Effects of personal growth groups on self-actualization and creative psychotherapy. *Group Process*, 1973, *14*, 490-94.

White, J. The human potential laboratory in the community college. *Journal of College Student Personnel*, 1974, *15*, 96-100.

14
Biofeedback
Edward S. Katkin and Steve Goldband

Biofeedback refers to any technique that uses instrumentation to provide a person with immediate and continuing signals concerning bodily functions of which that person is not normally conscious. Usually, biofeedback connotes external feedback from visceral organs such as the heart or blood vessels, but it also refers to feedback from any physiological function, including central nervous system activity (brain waves) and peripheral striate muscular activity which may not be providing normal feedback (after a stroke, for instance). Miller (1975) has pointed out that learning to control visceral responses may be likened to learning to shoot a basketball. Whereas the muscles used to shoot baskets provide the learner with immediate and usable feedback, the smooth muscles, glands, and blood vessels that are the typical target organs of biofeedback researchers do not provide readily usable feedback. With electronic interfaces, usable feedback can be obtained which the learner can employ in modifying previously uncontrollable functions, according to the same principles used to increase the field goal percentage of a basketball player.

Brief History

Biofeedback represents a specific form of treatment; in practice it may be seen to resemble in important ways the variety of therapeutic techniques gathered under the rubric of behavior modification. Just as the origins of behavior therapy may be linked rather directly to learning theory and the experimental analysis of behavior, biofeedback may be seen to derive from the scientific fields of psychophysiology, learning theory, and the experimental analysis of behavior, having emerged rather directly from basic research on the instrumental conditioning of autonomically mediated behavior (Crider, Schwartz, and Schnidman, 1969; Katkin and Murray, 1968; Katkin, Murray, and Lachman, 1969).

Instrumental Control of Autonomic Responses

Traditionally, learning theorists had assumed that "for autonomically mediated behavior, the evidence points unequivocally to the conclusion that such responses can be modified by classical, but not instrumental, training methods." (Kimble, 1961, p. 100). Explanations for the apparent inability to condition autonomic nervous system (ANS) responses instrumentally usually were founded upon the observation that the ANS did not interact directly with the external milieu, thus it was assumed to be incapable of functioning instrumentally. It was also thought that the ANS was solely a motor system, and lacking an afferent function, it was incapable of learning by reinforcement principles (Smith, 1954).

Yet, despite this testimony, a number of empirical investigations carried out both in the United States and the Soviet Union suggested that autonomically mediated responses *could* be shaped by instrumental conditioning (Kimmel, 1967). The key to these early studies was the introduction of appropriate technology which allowed the autonomic responses to interact directly with the environment. With the use of electronic devices and logic circuitry it was possible to create conditions in which changes in skin resistance, heart rate, or blood flow could be detected, differentially reinforced, and conditioned. Early reports from the laboratories of Kimmel (Kimmel and Kimmel, 1963; Kimmel and Hill, 1960; Kimmel and Sternthal, 1967); Shapiro (Birk et al., 1966; Crider, Shapiro, and Tursky, 1966; Shapiro, Crider, and Tursky, 1964); and Miller (DiCara and Miller, 1968; Miller, 1969; Miller and DiCara, 1967) all signaled the end of a scientific era in which the distinction between motor learning and autonomic learning was considered fundamental.

The new findings were not accepted without controversy, however, of which the most intense focused on the so-called "mediation" issue. Katkin and Murray (1968) argued that there were no unequivocal data on the instrumental conditioning of ANS responses that could be shown to be independent of skeletal or cognitive mediators, and they suggested further that it was probably impossible to design experiments to obtain such data. Although Miller and his colleagues had successfully demonstrated instrumental conditioning in the curarized rat, a finding which seemed to rule out the possibility that such responses were skeletally mediated, recent reports (Dworkin and Miller, 1977; Miller and Dworkin, 1974) indicate that the findings on curarized rats continually have resisted replication. This failure to replicate has been discussed in terms of certain undesired peripheral autonomic and central nervous system effects of curare and of difficulties in maintaining a stable animal preparation with artificial respiration (Hahn, 1974; Roberts, 1974). Moreover, curare does not affect the central nervous system linkage between cardiovascular or other autonomically mediated behaviors and somatomotor behaviors (Black, 1974). That is, central somatomotor activity may initiate peripheral autonomic and skeletal motor activity, but the latter cannot be observed because the muscles are paralyzed. With respect to this central linkage, therefore, the use of curare cannot provide a critical experimental test of the role of central somatomotor processes in learned visceral control (Obrist, et al.).

While investigators such as Miller attempted to develop strategies to demonstrate the instrumental conditionability of ANS responses independent of potential mediators, other investigators argued that the mediation issue was totally irrelevant to the issue of using reinforcement to modify autonomic responses (Crider, Schwartz, and Shnidman, 1969). Black (1974) pointed out that a distinction must be drawn between the *conditioning* of ANS responses (a theoretical concept) and the *controlling* of ANS responses (a technological problem); and Katkin and Murray (1968), while arguing strongly that instrumental ANS conditioning could not be demonstrated, suggested that the technology that had emerged from the controversial research was already on its way to making a clinical, applied contribution: "For those . . . whose primary goal is to gain control over ANS function, and for whom theoretical problems concerning possible mediators and underlying phenomena are less important, it may be unnecessary to demonstrate the pure phenomenon of instrumental conditioning." (p. 66). Later, Katkin (1971) suggested a strategy for clinicians that would exploit possible mediators rather than trying to eliminate them:

> for those who want to control autonomic activity for clinical or therapeutic reasons an alternative procedure would be first to determine accurately the relationship between certain voluntary skeletal actions and their associated autonomic response patterns, and then to reinforce the voluntary responses. Similarly, . . . relationships between cognitive activity and autonomic responses can be determined, and subjects may then be reinforced for certain specified thoughts. (p. 23)

Out of this milieu there emerged a pragmatic approach to the problem of instrumental control of autonomic functions which was based upon the skills acquisition model (Lang, 1974) implied by Miller's analogy of learning to throw a basketball through a hoop.

With the theoretical debates behind them, and rapidly developing technology ahead of them, both the research community and the clinical community adopted the skills acquisition model and have tried to apply it as broadly as possible to the treatment of psychiatric and psychosomatic disorders.

AREAS OF APPLICATION

Biofeedback applications during the past decade have been addressed primarily to the treatment of specific disorders. Among these have been somatic disorders such as headaches, high blood pressure, and migraine, as well as common psychological disorders such as anxiety and tension. In addition, attention has been directed recently toward the prevention of disorders presumed to be stress related. For example, some clinicians have focused their efforts on the training of specific biobehavioral responses that might be used to prevent the onset of such symptoms as tension headache or high blood pressure.

Treatment of Specific Syndromes

Anxiety and general tension. There are two fundamental approaches to the treatment of anxiety and tension with biofeedback. One of these involves feedback-assisted deep relaxation training via electromyographic (EMG) feedback applied to any one or combination of a number of muscle groups.

A second biofeedback technique for anxiety reduction and tension reduction is discrete brainwave (EEG) feedback, usually involving alpha wave and/or theta wave feedback (Glueck and Stroebel, 1975). Although this type of biofeedback was quite popular in the early development of the field, it has yielded to other forms of feedback partly because of the methodological complications inherent in its use and partly because of some controversies about its actual clinical effectiveness (Kamiya, 1968; Plotkin, 1976; Plotkin and Cohen, 1976; Travis, Kondo, and Knott, 1975; Valle and Levine, 1975).

Tension headache. One of the most pervasive symptoms of our time, tension headache frequently has been considered to be a symptomatic expression of general psychological tension or distress. Although there have been a few attempts to alleviate tension headache with vascular feedback, the most successful approaches have utilized EMG biofeedback, especially for frontal muscle relaxation (Budzynski et al., 1973). Biofeedback for tension headache is now considered relatively standard treatment in many headache treatment centers and pain clinics.

Migraine. The symptoms of migraine are considerably different from those of tension headache. Migraine is a vascular disorder caused by a cycle of excessive cerebral vasoconstriction followed by rebound vasodilatation. The cause of vascular changes is still unknown, but the resultant symptoms are easily recognized. During the early vasoconstrictive phase, the patient may report any of a variety of visual disturbances including scintillating scotoma, hemianopia, and, for many, a distinctive pattern of radiating gridlike visual illusions. As the cerebral vasculature shifts from a constricted to a dilated stage the visual disturbance clears up and is followed by extreme pain on one side of the head, often over the eye, but frequently radiating throughout the entire side of the head. In some cases the pain is bilateral, and in many cases the head pain is associated with nausea. The general treatment for such attacks is the administration of vasoconstrictive drugs to prevent the pain associated with the vasodilatative phase. However, if the drugs are administered after the dilatation has begun they are usually ineffective; therefore, the patient must receive the drugs during the early constrictive phase of the episode. In addition, there are a variety of potential negative side effects associated with the use of vasoconstrictors, so that many physicians tend to prescribe such low-level doses as to be ineffective in relieving the symptoms. For these reasons, a nonpharmacological treatment of migraine is desirable.

Biofeedback as a method for the treatment of migraine has been popular since the early reports from the Menninger Clinic (Sargent, Green, and Walters, 1972, 1973), suggesting remarkable success with this problem. The general strategy originally designed was to train patients to decrease vasodilatation in the head and to simultaneously increase vasodilatation at the hands, thereby training the patients to create an integrated shift of blood volume from central to peripheral sites. Later, it was suggested that training for increased vasodilatation at the hands was sufficient to result in therapeutic effectiveness (Turin and Johnson, 1976); the most common technique for achieving this is to train patients to warm their hands, using skin temperature biofeedback. The correlation between blood volume and skin temperature is quite high, and the technical ease with which temperature feedback may be carried out makes it the technique of choice.

Essential hypertension. Another vascular disorder for which psychological stress is presumed to be an etiological factor is essential hypertension, or excessively high blood pressure for which there is no apparent physiological cause. Biofeedback for blood pressure presents a particular challenge for instrumentation, and simple, commercially available clinical instruments are still not available. Thus blood pressure biofeedback is primarily a basic research area. The primary problem that blood pressure biofeedback presents is that it is difficult to obtain continuous measures of blood pressure in order to present the patient with the ongoing feedback. Typical cuff measurements require the inflation and deflation of a pressure cuff, and can be carried out no more than once or twice per minute. A number of technological developments based on logic modules or computer control have been devised to overcome this problem (Tursky, Shapiro and Schwartz, 1972), but none of these is economically feasible for widespread use. Recently, Steptoe, Smulyan, and Gribbin (1976) have demonstrated that the time interval between the ventricular contraction of the heart (detected as the R-wave of an electrocardiogram) and the arrival of the pulse wave at the radial artery (wrist) is inversely correlated with mean arterial blood pressure. The researchers presented evidence to demonstrate that biofeedback of the velocity of the pulse wave may be used effectively for training patients to reduce blood pressure. Although more basic research on this technique is required, there have already been some commercially designed instruments for pulse wave velocity feedback that may be useful for clinical biofeedback for blood pressure reduction.

Cardiac rate disorders. Some of the earliest basic research on instrumental autonomic conditioning involved the modification of heart rate. The rate at which the heart beats is simple to measure: simple rate measures can be obtained from electrocardiogram (EKG) connections to the wrists and/or ankles. For this reason, and because of its ease of quantification, heart rate feedback has long been a mainstay of the biofeedback research establishment. Typically, however, the clinician has not adopted heart rate biofeedback techniques for the purpose of raising or lowering heart rate in and of itself (although there is much interest in applications to such disorders as tachycardia—an abnormally fast heart rate). Rather, the strategies more commonly employed have been to use cardiac rate feedback to treat specific disorders of cardiac function such as cardiac arrhythmias and cardiac neurosis.

Specific muscular dysfunctions. EMG biofeedback for specific muscular disorders has become quite common in the general field of rehabilitation medicine. Three treatment strategies may be discerned: (1) detecting and feeding back neuromuscular potentials in currently nonfunctional muscles, in such conditions as hemiplegia, nerve injury, and reversible physiological block; (2) inhibiting undesired motor activity in conditions such as spasmodic torticollis and various kinds of spasticity; and (3) coordinating and controlling a series of muscle actions, in conditions such as fecal incontinence.

Localized pain reactions. In addition to EMG feedback for headache, and temperature and vascular feedback utilized for migraine, there have been a number of attempts to use biofeedback for the alleviation of other forms of localized pain reactions (see Turk, Meichenbaum, and Berman, 1979).[1] Among the types of treatment tried are alpha brain wave feedback (Melzack, 1975) and EMG feedback of jaw muscle activity for the alleviation of tempero-mandibular joint (TMJ) pain, a severe complication of excessive muscle tension in the tempero-mandibular joint, associated with bruxism of the teeth.

Sexual dysfunction. Although not a major application of biofeedback, there have been some research reports which describe the application of blood volume biofeedback for the control of penile tumescence in impotent men. This technique requires the placement of a strain gauge around the penis and the feedback of information concerning penile diameter (Csillag, 1976; Rosen, Shapiro, and Schwartz, 1975). There have also been attempts to use biofeedback and specific forms of reinforcement to alter a patient's sexual preference (Barlow et al., 1975).

Seizure disorders. Although still in early research stages, there have been reports that brain wave biofeedback of cortical frequencies between 14-16 Hz (called the sensorimotor rhythm, or SMR) can contribute to the reduction in frequency of epileptic seizures. Although it is not likely that clinical practitioners will find this application to be a primary treatment for such disorders, it holds the promise of becoming a useful adjunct to more traditional pharmacological treatments of seizures (Sterman, McDonald, and Stone, 1974; Kaplan, 1975; Lubar and Bahler, 1976).

Prevention of Stress Related Disorders

Although the bulk of current work in biofeedback has been addressed to the treatment of the specific syndromes described above, there has also been increasing interest in the possibility of using biofeedback for preventive intervention. The general strategy represented in this work is to train people to gain a greater degree of voluntary control over their involuntary reactions to a variety of stimuli which might be specific stress elicitors. An example of such an approach might be to use biofeedback to train phobic subjects to develop a high degree of voluntary control over their elicited autonomic responses. Thus, they can learn to impose autonomic self-control when confronted with a phobic stimulus object that might otherwise elicit a large and undesirable autonomic response. Other possibilities for such training could be its use by business executives who respond to normal daily stressors with elevated blood pressure to help them sustain moderate levels of blood pressure in the face of stress. Recent reports from Shapiro's laboratory (Sirota, Schwartz, and Shapiro, 1974, 1976) indicate that voluntary control of human heart rate can reduce one's autonomic and phenomenological response to aversive stimulation. Furthermore, Shapiro and his colleagues (Victor, Mainardi, and Shapiro, in press) have demonstrated that biofeedback training may have some utility in helping people to alleviate pain when presented with the cold pressor.

It is also likely that biofeedback techniques will be a useful adjunct in a variety of stress management programs that rely on relaxation training. Benson (1975) has described a wide variety of beneficial therapeutic results attributable to regular deep relaxation training using biofeedback as an adjunct in such training. Harris et al. (1976) have demonstrated that regularly sustained, slow, deep breathing serves to modulate autonomic responses to both the anticipation of a painful electric shock and the actual delivery of that shock. These findings suggest that biofeedback training for the maintenance of steady respiration may serve to prevent or modulate stress responses to specific external stimuli. Thus, although the use of biofeedback as a tool for preventive stress management training has not been developed as extensively as it has for the treatment of specific symptoms, there is a growing body of literature to suggest that it may be an equally important area of application.

Classification of Areas of Biofeedback Application

Biofeedback therapy involves the measurement, quantification, and feedback of responses that represent the final common paths of at least three different segments of the nervous system. Brain wave feedback involves direct assessment of central nervous system cortical activity; heart rate, blood pressure, and peripheral vascular and skin temperature feedback involve the assessment and quantification of responses mediated by the autonomic nervous system; and EMG biofeedback represents assessment and quantification of responses mediated by the peripheral somatic nervous system. Normally an individual possesses little or no ability to discriminate accurately the occurrence of either central cortical responses or peripheral autonomic responses; however, it is quite common for most people to discriminate responses mediated by the peripheral somatic nervous system. As we noted at the beginning of this chapter, the muscles used to shoot baskets, or to move food from our plates to our mouths, provide us with immediate and usable feedback; but the smooth muscles, glands, and blood vessels that are often target organs of biofeedback do not provide us with readily usable feedback. It may prove useful to classify biofeedback treatments on the basis of the extent to which a patient is able to discriminate the target response without external feedback.

In the event that a patient has a relatively accurate, reliable, and consistent ability to discriminate a response, it is unlikely that biofeedback therapy will provide him with any useful additional information; rather, the primary purpose of biofeedback is to use instrumentation to augment a patient's ability to discriminate and therefore control otherwise nondiscriminable responses. Such responses fall into one of three categories:

1. Normally nondiscriminable responses such as brain wave activity, peripheral vascular responses, cardiac rate responses, electrodermal responses, and other responses mediated by the autonomic nervous system;
2. Usually discriminable responses over which the patient functionally has lost control. Examples are chronic muscle tension in the head and neck area leading to tension headache, chronic tension of muscles in the jaw area leading to TMJ pain, and/or a variety of general bodily symptoms which are direct sequelae of unrelieved muscle tension. Although the muscle groups in question are those which under ordinary circumstances are generally subject to voluntary discrimination and control, it is often the case that the patient with symptoms is unable to use his normal abilities to bring these muscles under control. Specific biofeedback treatment here is useful to augment and facilitate the acquisition of such control;
3. Usually discriminable responses over which the patient has lost control because of organic lesion. Examples of such loss are hemiplegia and other paralyses subsequent to strokes and/or spinal injuries.

The clinician who plans to carry out a program of biofeedback treatment for symptom removal needs to take into account the specific nature of the response in question. Furthermore, he must carefully assess the relationship between the symptoms to be treated and the underlying physiological response. In the following section, we will address ourselves to the issue of specific techniques for carrying out biofeedback with emphasis on the importance of careful assessment and the role of perceptual discrimination of target responses as an important component of treatment outcome.

PROCEDURE

The Importance of Careful Assessment of Symptoms

Perhaps the most important phase of treatment planning for biofeedback is the careful assessment of the nature of the problem to be treated. At the simplest level this requires a determination of the modality of treatment to be applied. Will EMG, skin temperature, or peripheral vascular feedback be the treatment of choice? These decisions cannot be based exclusively on the patient's report of symptomatology, but must also be based on careful analyses of the underlying process leading to the symptoms. For example, if a patient complains of headache it is important to take a careful history and do a thorough diagnostic evaluation to determine whether the headache is attributable to gross muscle tension or whether it is a specific vascular headache such as migraine or a histamine headache. It is particularly important when dealing with pain symptomatology that a careful analysis of the underlying source of the pain be carried out before attempting any specific treatment modality.

A case study taken from the files of our clinic might be instructive to illustrate this point. Mrs. X, a 54-year-old woman, contacted our clinic requesting biofeedback help for migraine headaches with which she had been suffering for over 30 years. She described a typical story of migraine, including unilateral pain, associated with visceral distress, visual aura preceding onset of the headache and some relief from vasoconstrictive drugs. Furthermore, the client told us that her headache began during her young adulthood and followed a regular pattern for more than 30 years. At about the time of menopause a number of stressful events occurred simultaneously. Her father died of cancer and her husband was stricken with a progressively deteriorative cancer which necessitated a series of major surgeries over the next few years. Although still living, her husband was in very poor health and she was experiencing enormous psychological stress. During these years she reported that the intensity of her migraines decreased and underwent what she believed was a minor qualitative change, but their frequency had increased to the point where she was totally debilitated and unable to function. Given the increased responsibilities placed upon her by her husband's illness, the debilitating migraine was particularly maladaptive and she felt increasingly unable to cope with the demands placed upon her. She had been to a series of physicians who had prescribed varying vasoconstrictive drugs, pain killers, tranquilizers, and perhaps even placebos, none of which alleviated her continuing migraine distress.

Mrs. X is an experienced migraine sufferer who is fairly familiar with most of the treatments available and had read more than the average layman might concerning biofeedback treatment. When she came to the clinic she asked for hand warming and/or head cooling therapy because she was familiar with the research literature which indicated that temperature feedback was the indicated form of therapy for migraine. During the diagnostic interviewing, however, it became apparent that although Mrs. X had undoubtedly suffered from migraine most of her adult life, the headaches she was describing at the current time did not conform to the standard description of migraine. Furthermore, Mrs. X indicated, as mentioned above, that the frequency had increased and the quality of headache had changed somewhat in the past few years, coincident with her menopause. Knowing that female migraine sufferers frequently become symptom free after menopause and being aware also that there was a radical increase in life stress coincident with her menopause, it began to appear that the client had developed a pattern of chronic muscle tension headache which she was accustomed by habit to describing as migraine. The change in quality and intensity that she described could be explained as the development of a different source for the headache discomfort, i.e., a shift from vascular headache to muscular headache; the increase in frequency could be attributed to the fact that her life stress had elicited from her an almost continuing state of chronic elevated muscle tension. Consequently, the clinical team decided that immediate relief might be obtained more directly from biofeedback for muscle tension around the head than from hand warming or head cooling.

At this point the clinicians were faced with a ''patient management'' credibility problem. Upon presenting information to the client it became necessary to tell her we did not perceive migraine to be the major problem. This is a difficult bit of information to communicate to someone who has admittedly suffered from migraine for many years; consequently a treatment decision was made to provide the patient with both biofeedback for hand warming and biofeedback for frontal area muscle tension reduction. To the extent that the effective therapeutic agent in skin temperature feedback for migraine is really the induction of relaxation, the addition of this skin temperature feedback could only be seen as an adjunct to our presumed main goal—tension reduction. But what if we were wrong in our diagnosis and Mrs. X was in fact suffering from an unusual variation of a true migraine disorder? In that case skin temperature feedback might be a more appropriate treatment and we included it.

The point of this case study is that even in situations with a seemingly clear diagnostic label, it is important to recognize that there might be several factors which could lead to a misdiagnosis and a potentially inappropriate form of treatment. One cannot always assume that the syndrome to be treated can be understood through past history. Assessment of current functioning of a client and careful attention to the specific description of the syndrome pattern is fundamentally important.

In treating complex phenomena such as cardiac arrhythmias there are similarly important diagnostic questions which must be addressed. Weiss and Engel (1971) have noted that the mechanisms of cardiac control are quite complex, involving at least two underlying physiological processes. The implications of this are clear; if a patient produces, for instance, premature ventricular contractions only through a sympathetically mediated route, and biofeedback of heart rate leads to learned control of that heart rate via parasympathetic vagal control, then it is unlikely that the biofeedback would have any facilitative effect on reducing the symptoms. Shapiro and Surwit (1976) have noted that precise knowledge of the underlying mechanism of a symptom may have clear implications for treatment choice. As they have pointed out, if a cardiac symptom is exacerbated by increased sympathetic tone, then the object of treatment might be to reduce sympathetic tone, and cardiac feedback may not be the most efficient means to that end. In other words, the appropriate selection of a biofeedback treatment modality is integrally related to a proper understanding of the relationship of the underlying psychophysiological process to the clinical symptom.

Casual diagnosis of the specific cause of a patient's symptoms may not necessarily lead to an obvious choice of location for biofeedback treatment. For instance, a patient who suffers from tension headaches may or may not derive maximum therapeutic benefit from EMG feedback to muscles of the head. It is possible that biofeedback for muscle tension reduction in the head muscles will be an effective treatment, but it is also possible that for certain patients biofeedback treatment for general muscle relaxation in the arms, or in the trunk might be equally effective or in some cases more effective.

The clinician must be prepared to make individual judgments based upon the mode of tension expression for the individual patient, and to revise those judgments as treatment progresses. For instance, more careful assessment of the source of the symptoms might require that before treatment begins, a series of baseline muscle potential recordings be taken from various sites that might be possible contributors to the pain. The frontal area, as well as the neck and masseter (jaw) areas might be examined. The clinician can note which of these muscle groups appears to be manifesting the most tension, and by testing with relaxation instructions, he can observe the degree to which the patient has differential voluntary control over their relaxation. Next, it is essential to monitor the frequency and intensity of reported symptoms, preferably by having the patient keep a detailed log. If you are getting excellent results in the biofeedback, but no reduction of symptomatology, then there is good reason to assume that the particular physiological function that is being controlled is not a contributor to the symptom. Like the behavioral psychologist searching for the effective reinforcer, the biofeedback therapist is in a constant search for the clinically relevant physiological function.

The neatness of the treatment package presented by biofeedback instrumentation may easily lull the clinician into a false sense of security about his treatment choice. It is essential that accurate behavioral assessment be employed in decision making about biofeedback therapy for there is always the risk that the client may be presenting symptomatology for which there are alternative, more effective somatic treatments or alternative, less obvious but equally important avenues of psychotherapeutic intervention that might be indicated. It is important for the clinician to assess the background of the patient's problems and to be certain that the particular form of treatment to be employed represents a rational choice. What we are particularly concerned about is the seductive but nevertheless ever present danger that the clinician may become overly technique-oriented when faced with the glittering and interesting electronic instruments normally employed in the biofeedback procedures.

Finally the clinician must assess the particular purpose of the biofeedback treatment. Is he going to employ a strategy which will lead to permanent change in physiological response levels or is he going to employ a strategy which is directed toward teaching the patient to modify responses to specific situations?

Psychophysiological Indexes and Methods of Measurement

An integral part of any biofeedback application is the detection and feedback of a biological response. An understanding of the basic principles of psychophysiology is therefore invaluable for the safe and effective use of biofeedback instrumentation. In this section, we will present material on safety in the use of instrumentation, followed by a brief discussion of the rationale and techniques behind measurement of EKG, EMG, blood pressure, temperature, and other clinically useful biological functions.

Safety. The physical safety of both client and therapist should always be an overriding concern in the use of biofeedback instrumentation (Pope, 1978). The greatest potential hazard from instrumentation is, of course, electric shock; any time an electrode is attached to a client, the possibility exists of a current flow through the client's body. Current flow is usually considered to be the index of danger in electric shock. It is a direct function of voltage, and an inverse function of resistance in the circuit. A dangerous level of current flow can arise from improperly designed equipment, a failure in equipment, or an operator error. Since virtually all biofeedback involving electrical measurement involves surface (rather than internal) electrodes, the resistance of the client's skin provides some natural protection against shock from small voltages. For example, with a contact resistance of 2500 ohm/cm^2 for two electrodes of one square centimeter each, a rather large potential of 50 volts is required to produce a potentially dangerous 10 milliamps of current flow.

From the standpoint of the clinician, electrical safety is largely a matter of purchasing proper instruments, using them according to instructions, and employing common sense. The Executive Board of the Biofeedback Society of America, and the National Association of Biofeedback Instrument manufacturers have adopted the Safe Current Limits Standard for medical apparatus of the Association for the Advancement of Medical Instrumentation. This standard guards against design problems that might lead to shock hazard. The purchase only of devices carrying a notation that they abide by the standard is a first step toward safety. In addition, the manufacturer's directions for connecting the case of line powered equipment to a proper earth ground should be strictly followed to prevent dangerous ground loop hazards. If connectors are modified between the electrodes and the apparatus, they should be designed so that it is impossible to accidentally connect the client to a source of current. Finally, it is good practice to arrange the therapy room so that the client cannot accidentally touch any conductive object connected to ground, such as appliances, water pipes, and telephones.

Electrodes. For those biological measures which detect electrical activity, it is necessary to attach electrodes to the subject. These measures include EKG, EMG, and EEG. The electrodes usually employed are either stainless steel or composed of a hybrid material such as silver/silver chloride. In addition, an electrolyte, or conductive gel, is usually placed between the electrode and the skin to improve contact conductance and reduce measurement artifacts. Finally, the electrode is attached to the subject either by an adhesive disk or "collar," tape, or an elastic band of some type.

The site for electrode attachment is sometimes prepared by washing with mild soap, rubbing with acetone, or light abrasion with sandpaper, to remove dead skin, skin oils, and other material which could interfere with a good contact. Site preparation is most critical in EEG and EMG work and less critical in the use of EKG.

Electrocardiography. Measurement of heart rate is usually accomplished by the attachment of electrodes in such a way as to detect the electrical activity of the beating heart, or electrocardiogram (EKG). The EKG is characterized by a complex waveform, a part of which is a sharp voltage spike, called the R wave, which corresponds to contraction of the left ventricle. In biofeedback for heart rate, this spike is usually detected by a circuit which is sensitive to a given voltage level, called a Schmitt trigger. If the interval between spikes is measured in seconds, the heart rate can be readily computed in beats per minute as Rate=60/inter-beat interval. It is this rate which is commonly displayed on feedback devices.

For the purpose of biofeedback of heart rate, two measurement electrodes and one reference (ground) electrode are commonly used. The two signal electrodes may be placed at any two sites which straddle the heart; a convenient placement is on the client's left ankle and right forearm. The ground electrode is often placed on the client's right ankle.

Electromyography. The detection of muscle activity is usually accomplished by measurement of electrical activity, called electromyography, or EMG. When a single muscle fiber contracts, an electrical potential—the muscle action potential (MAP)—is produced. Although the measurement of single fiber MAPs has been important in certain basic research, clinical biofeedback is ordinarily addressed to the relaxation or tension of whole groups of such cells. If surface electrodes are used to measure EMG, as is usually the case, the MAPs from many cells beneath the electrode sites are detected. Most biofeedback instruments use some technique for integrating or averaging these MAPs to produce an output which reflects the overall level of muscle contraction beneath the electrodes.

Particularly in EMG biofeedback, the clinician must be aware of the correspondence between the conceptually important measurement and the measurement provided by a given technique at a given site. For example, it is often reported that feedback of the frontalis muscle (a muscle in the forehead) is given to augment relaxation, using electrodes on the temples. Such a placement, however, will provide feedback of numerous muscles in addition to the frontalis. Nevertheless, if one is using feedback to teach general relaxation, it is probably just as well to give information about a variety of muscles simultaneously. On the other hand, relaxation of one muscle group does not necessarily spread to relaxation of other groups. Thus it may be useful to provide EMG feedback from several sites to maximize a general relaxation effect.

Blood volume assessment. In a variety of clinical biofeedback applications, the biological response of interest is the volume of blood flow at a peripheral site. This volume is primarily determined by the state of constriction or dilation of peripheral blood vessels. There are at least three techniques available which assess blood flow—plethysmography, temperature sensing, and mechanical tranduction.

The use of plethysmography in the measurement of blood flow is based on the fact that phasic changes in the reflectance of, or permeability to light of tissue result primarily from changes in blood flow. A transmission plethysmograph is a device with a light source and a photocell which are placed on opposite sides of the tissue of interest (for example, the ear lobe). The amount of light transmitted to the photocell from the light source is proportional to the blood flow in the tissue. Similarly, a reflectance plethysmograph provides a source of light and a photo-detector, but they are mounted side by side. The device is attached in proximity to the skin, and the amount of light reflected from the skin is used as an index of blood flow.

A plethysmograph can ordinarily provide only change information, not a measurement of absolute level, and so can be used only for training changes within a session. This makes its use in longer term treatment somewhat problematic, since the client and therapist have no objective means of tracking the client's progress across sessions. On the other hand, plethysmograph measurement is very simple, inexpensive, and comfortable.

A second technique for measuring blood flow is by the use of temperature sensing. When blood courses through vessels, it warms the surrounding tissues and the heat is simultaneously dissipated to the cooler environment. Thus the more blood that flows through tissue, the higher the temperature at which the tissue will be. An electronic component called a thermistor has the property of having its electrical resistance reduced in proportion to elevations of its temperature. If a small current is passed through a thermistor placed against tissue, the amount of current flow is an index of the temperature of the tissue. Furthermore, the measurement system can be calibrated so that it yields absolute units (degrees) which can be compared from session to session.

Finally, mechanical transducers can be used to measure blood flow. A piezoelectric crystal produces a small voltage which is proportional to mechanical strain in the crystal. If the crystal is mounted so that movement of a sensor causes it to bend, the sensor can be mounted over an artery, and the blood flow through the artery can be indexed by the changing voltage of the crystal. Such devices are probably more useful for measurement of fast-changing (phasic) blood flow, such as pulse pressure, than slower changing (tonic) flow, such as peripheral dilation. They cannot easily provide absolute indices of change, but they are fast-responding and can be used at some sites (the temporal artery for example) where other techniques are more prone to artifacts. Crystal transducers have been the primary means of measuring the pulse wave in pulse wave velocity measurement, and have been used in place of temperature sensors in experimental work with migraine headache.

Blood pressure. Although the reduction of blood pressure in hypertensive individuals has been one of the greatest hopes of the biofeedback movement, as yet technical and theoretical barriers have prevented widespread clinical use of feedback for blood pressure. The measurement of blood pressure is based on the fact that a sound is produced by the turbulence of a partially occluded artery. This sound, called a Korotkoff or K-sound can be detected by a human or electronic sensor when an occluding cuff is inflated to a pressure between the diastolic (resting) and systolic (peak) pressure of an artery. Measurement is obtained by inflating the cuff to a pressure greater than systolic pressure and deflating it slowly until the first sound is heard. The pressure at this point is systolic blood pressure. The cuff is further deflated until the last sound is heard. This pressure is diastolic blood pressure.

The standard technique can be automated so that the inflation, listening for K sounds, and deflation are all electronically controlled. But even with automation, the time for a measurement is typically about 30 seconds. Thus feedback could only be given infrequently. Tursky, Shapiro, and Schwartz (1972) devised a cuff which remains constantly inflated at the subject's systolic blood pressure on a previous trial. The presence or absence of K sounds on each beat is then fed back to the subject as feedback for either increasing or decreasing BP. Refinements of this system have made it possible to provide feedback of a more continuous nature by the use of a computer which controls the cuff to track the subject's pressure. However, the complexity and expense of this system have meant that it is still an experimental tool.

An alternative technique which holds some promise for blood pressure feedback is called pulse wave velocity (PWV) feedback. This technique is based on the observation that the velocity of blood pumped by the heart in its travel to a peripheral site is proportional to its pressure. Thus, if a device senses the heart beat (R-wave), followed by the pulse, say, at the wrist, and computes the time between them, it can feed back this indirect measure of blood pressure to the client.

Although studies have found the PWV is highly correlated to systolic BP under certain conditions (Obrist et al., 1978; Steptoe, Smulyan, and Gribbin 1976) widespread clinical adoption of PWV as an index of blood pressure awaits more research with clinical populations under controlled conditions. It is important to note, though, that PWV holds the promise of a noninvasive, relatively inexpensive measure that can provide beat by beat information in an absolute, analog form.

Electroencephalography. The electroencephalogram measures electrical activity of the cerebral cortex. Electrodes placed on or just below the skin of the scalp provide very low amplitude signals. These signals are usually amplified and filtered so that waves of only certain frequencies will pass through. Some feedback device is then activated by the presence or absence of waves at the critical frequencies.

Researchers have defined the presence of signals in at least four frequency bands in the human EEG: (1) delta waves of 1-3 Hz in deep sleep; (2) theta waves of 4-7 Hz in early sleep stages; (3) alpha waves of 8-13 Hz in relaxed wakefulness; and (4) beta waves of 14-30 Hz during mental activity.

Early biofeedback was focused on the alpha state, based largely on optimistic reports that subjects producing high alpha density felt peaceful and meditative. Later work, however, called into question these early hopes, finding that alpha was not always experienced pleasurably (Walsh, 1974), and that production of alpha may be primarily associated with visual rather than attentional phenomena (Plotkin, 1976). Recently alpha feedback has been used in attempts to moderate chronic pain (Melzack and Perry, 1975). However, no clear-cut successes have been reported to date.

Another component of the EEG is the sensorimotor rhythm (SMR), a 14-16 Hz wave recorded over the sensorimotor cortex. Sterman and his colleagues (Sterman, 1977) have pioneered work which teaches epileptic patients to increase SMR density in an effort to reduce the incidence of seizures. Lubar and Bahler (1976) and Seifert and Lubar (1975) have also had success in the reduction of seizures with SMR feedback, although it is unclear whether the gains will prove to be enduring.

Strain gauge measurement. Some bodily functions of interest are most readily measured not by their electrical activity but by detection of mechanical movement. In this category are respiration, the operation of sphincters, and penile tumescence. In such situations an apparatus is arranged so that the response changes the pressure in, or mechanically stretches a transducer. This change is converted into a varying voltage which is amplified and fed back. Engel, Nikoomanesh, and Schuster (1974) have reported successful treatment of fecal incontinence, for example, through the use of feedback from the internal and external rectal sphincters. There is also the possibility (Price[2]; Barlow et al., 1975) that sexual arousal in impotent men can be increased with the help of feedback for the erectile response. There has also been some work in training reduced response in treatment of patients with sexual deviations. The evidence so far seems to indicate that it is easier to reduce response than increase it with feedback.

Miscellany. Although space does not permit elaboration, several other biofeedback techniques have been used which deserve mention. The Galvanic Skin Response is a measure of palmar sweat gland activity related to emotional arousal. While a broad research base exists for GSR, little has been done with it clinically as yet.

The pH of the stomach is related to ulcer formation. Through the use of rather cumbersome techniques, some work has been done to train ulcer patients to reduce stomach pH (Welgan, 1974; Whitehead, Renault and Goldiamond, 1975).

Feedback for airway resistance has been used to treat asthma (Levenson 1974; Levenson et al., 1974;[3] Vachon and Rich, 1976).

Finally the accomodation of the visual system to objects at varying distances has been fed back in attempts to improve visual acuity in myopic patients (Epstein, Hannay and Looney 1975).[4]

BIOFEEDBACK AS SELF-MANAGEMENT: PROCEDURAL ISSUES

Having decided that a client's symptoms are amenable to biofeedback treatment, and having decided also upon the specific form of treatment being employed, the clinician must face a number of serious procedural issues concerning the administration and ultimate evaluation of therapeutic success. Among these issues are: (1) the establishment of an appropriate baseline against which to compare the treatment effect; (2) appropriate criteria for reinforcement of the patient's responses; (3) decisions about the modality of feedback; and (4) the creation of conditions for appropriate assessment of therapeutic outcome. None of these issues is unique to biofeedback; all of them are commonly discussed in the literature on self-management and self-control. The goal of effective biofeedback therapy is to enable the patient to control or modify his physiological responses without continuous feedback of those responses. Thus, if the patient is to be freed from bioelectric connections, he must acquire the skills necessary for self-management of the targeted autonomic responses. No less important, the patient must also acquire the motivation to use these self-management skills, and the ability to discriminate situations which might elicit undesirable physiological responses.

One characteristic that distinguishes biofeedback from other forms of self-management however, is that the necessary skills needed may not be readily available to the client before treatment. Therefore emphasis must be placed on the *acquisition* of specific skills. This is not necessarily true in all forms of self-management training. For instance, if an obese patient wants to learn to control his eating habit, he must learn to identify situations which provoke excessive eating. In addition, he must learn specific responses which may alter his motivation to eat. However, it is not likely that the therapist will be required to teach an obese person the specific motor skills needed to keep his mouth closed to prevent the entry of food. In biofeedback therapy, however, the client must not only learn to identify provocative situations and be motivated to alter his responses; he also must learn to recognize what those responses are. The therapist must pay special attention to helping the patient discover his baseline of responding in order to identify changes in it.

Baseline Measurement

The therapist should be alerted to the fact that the introduction of biofeedback techniques themselves may elicit elevated levels of responding, thus an arbitrarily high baseline may be observed in the first few sessions. It is important, therefore, that the therapist obtain multiple resting baseline levels of the physiological response in order to be certain of reasonable reliability and in order to feel confident that the initial level from which treatment will begin represents a valid assessment of the subject's true baseline. In addition, the therapist will often discover that elevated levels of muscle tension, for instance, can be reduced substantially by simple verbal instructions for either general or specific muscle relaxation. It is important to remember that the primary purpose for biofeedback is to provide help in learning to control functions over which normal control is absent. Thus, baseline measures should be assessed *after* the patient has already achieved as much control as he can without biofeedback. A case study might illustrate this point more clearly.

Mr. S was referred to our biofeedback clinic from a distinguished cardiac clinic in the midwest. Mr. S is a 28-year-old factory worker who suffered an apparent heart attack while at work and was rushed to the emergency room of his local hospital, in a state of semiconsciousness, complaining of a crushing pain in the chest, and radiating pain and numbness down through his left arm. He was taken to an intensive care unit where, in a matter of hours, he showed a complete recovery. Cardiological examination in the local hospital could find no evidence of cardiac disease and neurological exam revealed no problems. Mr. S showed repeated episodes of the "heart attack" over the next few weeks and was referred to a cardiac care center where, over the course of a week, he was examined carefully and had extensive neurological and cardiological exams. The results of those exams as well as psychiatric evaluations suggested that his pain and numbness was being caused by excess tension and he was told to contact our biofeedback clinic. It should be noted that before we received this client, we obtained a complete medical record from the cardiac center to be sure that we were not dealing with a subtle neurological or cardiological problem. After studying the records and interviewing Mr. S for a few hours, we were convinced that we were dealing with a rather complicated psychiatric disorder which expressed itself through unusually high levels of body tension which may have resulted in the experience of pain. We proposed to the client, who was extremely resistive to psychotherapy and who, in many ways, was typical of "insightless" patients, that we would use biofeedback to teach him muscle relaxation and that we were optimistic that when he learned to gain total control of his striate musculature and relax it at will, that he might lose his symptomatology. Before beginning the treatment, we took some baseline measures of electromyographic voltage levels of the frontal area of Mr. S's head. Much to our surprise, we found that during a ten-minute rest period, with Mr. S in a reclining chair, his eyes closed in a darkened room, and having received instructions designed to induce deep relaxation, Mr. S manifested a mean muscle tension level of 50 mv. (The typical patient in a similar situation can be expected to show levels between 1 and 3 mv.) In order to communicate more clearly the enormous level of tension this figure represented, note that a number of workers in our clinic tried to tighten up their jaw, head, and neck muscles sufficiently to generate 50 mv. over a ten-minute period. Not one clinician was successful in doing so and all reported that after 2-3 minutes of such tension, they experienced intense pain. Yet Mr. S reported to us that he found the experience of reclining in the chair with his eyes closed and listening to the relaxation instructions quite pleasant and that he felt he was as relaxed as he had ever been in that situation. He did not seem to be aware that he was generating an enormous amount of muscle tension. Close scrutiny of Mr. S during these relaxation periods indicated that his jaw muscles were clenched tightly and the visible signs of muscle tension in the face were obvious.

Before proceeding with any biofeedback treatment the clinician simply indicated to Mr. S what had been observed and told him that he might consider paying special attention to the muscles in his jaw—unclenching his teeth, allowing his chin to droop slightly, and just letting the tension flow out of his jaw muscles. He was then asked to sit back again for ten more minutes, concentrating on keeping the jaw unclenched. During the next 10-minute rest period, the mean microvoltage level recorded from Mr. S was below 5 mv.—only one-tenth of the previous amplitude. Astonishingly Mr. S reported that he could not feel the difference between the two conditions. Yet when he was presented with the record obtained from the EMG machine, he was impressed that there was in fact a serious change in the level of his muscle tension. It was explained to him that the clinician considered the new level as a starting point and that the biofeedback machine would now be used to give him more refined feedback to enable him to reduce the voltage discriminately below that level of 5 mv.

The point of this case study is obvious. Had the clinician begun the biofeedback before he had administered to Mr. S the simple instructions about relaxing his jaw muscles, he might have discovered what appeared to be a magnificent treatment effect (as indeed it would have been, but the real treatment and the real value of the biofeedback begins at the point where the patient cannot normally gain control without biofeedback. In this case study, as you can see, significant treatment effects were obtained by the use of simple instructions based on simple but intelligent observations. Biofeedback becomes useful after that point, not before.

As treatment progresses, the therapist will note that he can structure the format so that he can evaluate therapeutic progress by comparing the patient's initially determined baseline response level to his baseline level in any given session. In addition to using initially determined baseline and session to session baselines, the therapist may want to measure trial by trial baselines *within* a given session. For instance, the biofeedback program may be structured so that the patient receives alternate "time in" and "time out" sessions in which feedback is available and then not available. The patient's level of physiological responsivity can be assessed continuously, and within a given feedback session, physiological responses during time in-time out can be evaluated with time out periods functioning as trial by trial baseline measures. In this manner the therapist can evaluate not only the long term progress of the patient but the short-term rate of progress within a given session. The evaluation of therapeutic progress can be based either upon sequential changes in the time out periods or on the basis of changes in the degree of discrimination between time in and time out periods. The subject who is successfully acquiring self-management skills may continue to show self-control during the time out periods, whereas the patient who is learning to respond well to feedback but is not learning effective self-management may show large discrepancies between response levels during the time in and time out periods. These individual assessments may be particularly useful in indicating to the therapist whether his ultimate goals of teaching the patient self-control outside the clinical situation are being obtained. Thus, the careful assessment of baselines throughout the therapeutic procedure allows the therapist to evaluate not only the patient's ability to use biofeedback effectively but more importantly the patient's ability to self-control his physiological responses in the absence of contingent biofeedback.

Baseline variability. Crucial decisions about the administration of treatment depend upon knowledge of the individual subject's variability around his own baseline. In order for the therapist to provide the subject with veridical feedback about his own improvement, judgments must be made about whether the subject's change in response level exceeds that which might have been expected by his normal variability around that level. The assessment of baseline variability, therefore, is an essential component in determing the criteria for reinforcement in the treatment program.

Criteria for Reinforcement

If the therapeutic goal in biofeedback is, for instance, the reduction of a hypertensive patient's systolic blood pressure from 180mm Hg to 120mm Hg, it is important not only to provide the subject with continuous biofeedback of his blood pressure level, but to give him some veridical information concerning the times at which his blood pressure has been reduced by a significant amount. Although it is not necessary for the clinician to calculate standard deviations of blood pressure level for any given session, it is important that he be able to discriminate the difference between a patient whose blood pressure normally varies 20mm Hg/min. around his baseline as compared to a patient whose blood pressure varies only 5mm Hg/min. around his baseline. There are great differences from patient to patient and the therapist must be sensitive to establishing criteria for reinforcement that are consistent with an individual patient's own variability.

Although laboratory research on biofeedback has often used monetary incentives for facilitating self-control of physiological responses, in clinical practice a patient's own knowledge of successful self-control constitutes the primary reinforcement. Typically in a biofeedback treatment situation the subject will receive continuous feedback about his physiological response. Consequently, he receives a constantly changing array reflecting the variability of his baseline. How is the subject to know when the changes that he perceives represent random variation rather than significant therapeutic progress? It is the therapist's responsibility to establish criteria for reinforcement which provide the subject with the information necessary to evaluate when his own responses are therapeutically meaningful. At the simplest level the therapist can provide the patient with a verbal statement of what his goal for the session will be. This verbal statement will be based upon the therapist's knowledge of the patient's expected variability so that, for instance, if a subject has a baseline heart rate of 100 bpm. and an expected range between 90 and 110 bpm., the therapist can indicate to the patient that his goal for the session is to keep his heart beating at, say, a level somewhere in the low 90's. Consequently if a subject sees a decrease in heart rate level from 110 to 105, he will not misinterpret this as therapeutic progress, whereas a change in heart rate level of similar magnitude but from 100 to 95 can be interpreted as progress because of the verbal instructions from the therapist. Thus the goal is to reinforce the subject for changes from his mean baseline level, not to reinforce responses that are simply in the appropriate direction. Of course, the therapist must reassess the baseline on a regular basis, and the reinforcement criterion must be updated as the baseline changes. In the early stages of training the subject will be reinforced for small responses that are below the mean but still within his normal range of variability. As training progresses, the criteria for reinforcement can become more stringent, with reinforcement defined as changes that exceed the normal range of variability.

The reader will note that the rules that govern the therapist's criterion setting for reinforcement are identical in principle with the rules for the shaping of any operant response. Similarly, the therapist must be sensitive to all of the principles that underlie operant response shaping and must be prepared to modify his criteria in accordance with the individual behavioral record of the subject. As the patient begins to develop increasingly greater approximations to the desired physiological response level, the criteria for reinforcement can be made increasingly stringent. It is likely that as the therapy progresses, the degree to which the reinforcement criterion becomes more stringent will represent, in and of itself, another source for evaluating therapeutic progress.

The criteria which are employed for reinforcement have implications not only for the acquisition of self-control, but for the enhancement or debilitation of motivation for success. If the therapist sets initial reinforcement criteria that are too stringent for the subject to comply with, it might result in a variety of counter-productive negative self statements that might lead the subject to adopt a pessimistic attitude and withdraw prematurely from continuing treatment. If, on the other hand, the therapist should apply reinforcement criteria which are too lenient, the patient may be disappointed to discover that although he is apparently doing well, he is enjoying little or no symptom reduction; this also can lead to negative consequences with respect to motivation for continuing therapy. It is difficult, if not impossible, to advise a biofeedback therapist about the specific establishment of reinforcement criteria for any given patient, but it is never impossible to recommend sensitivity in making initial determinations. One arbitrary rule of thumb is that at the beginning of the treatment program a criterion for reinforcement be established so that a subject on average receives reinforcing feedback about half the time for any given session. This brings us back again to the importance of discriminating between a session baseline and a treatment program baseline. Whereas the patient may be receiving reinforcement approximately half the time in any given session, this is based upon his baseline for *that* session. With respect to his *initial pretreatment baseline*, the patient may be functioning at a far more effective level, and he should be apprised of that fact as he makes such progress. Thus, reinforcement criteria are probably best based upon session by session baselines and not based upon initial pretreatment baseline assessment. If reinforcement were based on initial pretreatment baseline assessment, it is likely that as therapy progressed the criteria for reinforcement would become far too lenient.

Sensory Modality of Feedback

Most of the commercially available biofeedback equipment allows the patient to obtain his biofeedback in either an auditory or a visual mode, or both. Although at first glance the distinction between a visual or an auditory analogue of the physiological response may seem to be trivial, the therapist may discover that there are important reasons to choose either one or the other type of feedback depending upon both the inherent nature of the response being modified and the patient's individual preferences. A striking example of a case in which auditory feedback would be much preferred over visual feedback may be found in the use of an alpha feedback machine to increase a subject's ability to maintain a high level of alpha density and/or amplitude. It is well known that ocular activity can create artifactual contamination of alpha wave recordings and lead to inaccurate and misleading interpretations of the EEG record; Plotkin (1976) has demonstrated that alpha feedback in general may be explained more by ocular activity than brainwave activity. While the ultimate interpretation of alpha wave biofeedback still awaits more intensive research, it is obvious that it would be preferable to use analogue auditory feedback of the alpha signal rather than visual feedback so that eye movement can be controlled adequately.

On the other hand, if the therapist using EMG feedback wants to establish a goal level toward which the patient should strive, it is generally easier to provide the patient with a visual rather than an auditory representation of that goal level. Different manufacturers have provided a variety of formats for visual feedback, including light bars, light circles, video screens with various monochromatic as well as polychromatic displays. Less exotic and less expensive visual displays include pointer needles on a voltmeter, or digitized readings on a digital voltmeter to provide subjects with continuous feedback about the voltage level of their response. Auditory feedback is generally designed so that the subject hears a continuous tone whose pitch varies proportionately with the level of his response. Alternately, volume can be varied, but most therapists have chosen to manipulate the pitch of an auditory signal rather than the volume of such a signal for providing feedback.

Whether the therapist ultimately decides to use visual or auditory feedback depends of course upon the availability of equipment, but ideally it should depend on more than that. Some initial discussion with the client about differences in comfort with the modalities should be taken into consideration. There is little evidence at the present time to suggest that one modality or the other will necessarily be more effective, but there is reason to believe that auditory feedback with eyes closed may facilitate a general state of reduced arousal or relaxation as compared to visual feedback. Thus, if the primary purpose of the biofeedback training is to facilitate general relaxation, it is likely that an eyes-closed auditory feedback modality will be preferable to an eyes-open visual feedback modality. Yet it should be noted that some of the more elaborate visual displays commercially available are similar to modern video computer games and are engaging and interesting; they may enhance the subject's motivation for participating in the biofeedback therapy and may be more attractive to some patients than the relatively monotonous eyes-closed auditory feedback modality. Once again, there are no empirical data to guide the therapist in making an intelligent choice and final decisions will rest upon a variety of individual factors.

Parametric research studies could easily be carried out to investigate the relative effectiveness of one modality versus another for a variety of syndromes but to date there has been very little attention to these issues in the systematic research literature and very little variation exists in techniques for presenting feedback. Almost all of the available biofeedback equipment employs either visual or auditory feedback and there has been very little exploration of the use of other sensory modalities as effective feedback vehicles. For instance, it is quite possible that one could provide subjects with tactile sensations proportional to their physiological response. Such a technique would have obvious advantages for providing biofeedback to people with visual or hearing impairments, but these are not the only reasons for inquiring into the efficacy.

It is important to note that there is little scientific evidence to guide the therapist in his choice of sensory modality, but he should keep in mind that the ultimate effectiveness of the treatment depends upon the subject's knowledge of the results. Thus it is likely that clients who feel more comfortable interpreting visual feedback should receive it, whereas clients who feel more comfortable with auditory feedback should be so treated. Some investigators have suggested that combined auditory and visual feedback doubles the reinforcement but there is little empirical evidence to support this notion. If the client feels comfortable there is no reason not to give both visual and auditory feedback simultaneously.

Assessment of Outcome

After all the procedural issues concerning baseline assessment, reinforcement criterion, and feedback modality have been ironed out, the therapist comes to the bottom line—evaluating the success or failure of the treatment. In evaluating therapeutic outcome an important distinction must be made. There are some syndromes in which the physiological responses constitute the malady itself. An example would be biofeedback treatment for essential hypertension. In this disorder, sometimes referred to as "the silent killer," the definition of the disorder *is* the elevated blood pressure. Most patients do not have subjective awareness of their elevated blood pressure, and if they report symptoms of distress they are more likely to be secondary phenomena rather than primary. Consequently, successful outcome of a biofeedback treatment program for high blood pressure can be readily defined by changes in blood pressure level. Other syndromes, such as migraine headache are defined by subjective report of pain and associated symptoms. Biofeedback for migraine is not directed to the symptoms but is directed to the presumed underlying mechanisms (i.e., vascular control). It is possible in treating someone for migraine with, say, skin temperature biofeedback, that one can teach the person to achieve excellent control of the skin temperature but fail to have any impact on the frequency and intensity of the migraine episodes. Thus the biofeedback may be seen to be a great success for training physiological self-control but a complete failure for alleviating the syndrome in question.

In addition to making a clear distinction between the success of self-control vs. the success of symptom reduction the biofeedback therapist must also be aware of the distinction between success in the clinic and success outside the clinic. This problem was alluded to in the discussion of baseline assessments and the importance of time in and time out periods for evaluating the degree of generalized self-control.

Placebo Effects

Biofeedback, as much as any other form of psychological treatment, and perhaps more so, is potentially susceptible to nonspecific placebo effects. Although the practicing clinician may find it unimportant to distinguish whether his client has improved because of an active treatment effect or a nonspecific effect, the ability to differentiate one from the other has important implications for the eventual refinement of techniques and generalizability to other patients. Consequently, while relatively unimportant for the individual client, it remains extremely important for the therapist to have some insight into the relative contribution of specific and nonspecific factors in the treatment process. There are also certain unique considerations that distinguish biofeedback from other forms of behavior modification.

Strictly speaking, the concept of placebo refers to the use of a pharmacologically inactive agent which is administered to a patient for a variety of reasons, including the failure to identify a diagnosable disorder. Often, but not always, the placebo administration results in symptom reduction. It must be understood that the positive therapeutic results of placebo administration should be relatively random. That is, it is expected that a placebo will show neither disease specificity, nor interpatient reliability. In either of these events the agent would lose its definition as a placebo, and be reclassified as an active treatment, even if its mechanism were not well understood. It is not the case that a treatment is classified as a placebo because its mechanism is not understood; rather, it is classified as a placebo precisely when its mechanism is well understood, and there is no pharmacologically valid reason for it to succeed.

In the area of psychotherapy, the term placebo has been borrowed from medicine and employed frequently. In the psychotherapeutic sense, therefore, a placebo should refer to a type of treatment that is known to have no valid specific treatment effect but which superficially appears to the patient to be an active form of psychotherapy. In other words, placebo psychotherapy should look like therapy, should sound like therapy, and *should cause the patient to expect that he is receiving therapy*. Nevertheless, the treatment should be understood to have no valid theoretical mechanism by which it could actually *be* therapy.

Among the many reasons for the rapid development of the field of behavior modification in the past two decades has been the greater precision with which outcome studies of its effectiveness could be designed. Many forms of behavior modification, and especially biofeedback, specify precise theoretical mechanisms, supposedly independent of therapist characteristics, which are expected to produce operationally defined symptom reduction. Within the context of this greater definitional precision, a variety of placebo possibilities present themselves.

Controlled research on placebo effects in behavior modification techniques has usually focused on the issue of patient expectancy for success. The general strategy has been to define a placebo therapy that is presented to the patient with instructions that lead the patient to expect success as much as he would with the actual treatment. Careful steps are usually taken to equate time and effort of the therapist and to create conditions that are similar to the actual therapy. Finally, care is usually taken to insure that there are no experimenter bias or demand characteristics associated with the outcome evaluation.

As careful as these procedures have been, it is not clear that they have been entirely effective. Kazdin and Wilcoxon (1976) have suggested that the procedures of the treatments themselves, rather than any characteristics of the therapist or demands of the evaluation, may generate different expectancies for success because of differential credibility. Lick and Bootzin (1975) have focused on the mechanisms by which expectancy effects may work in systematic desensitization. Assuming that there is no magical or mystical manner by which expectancy leads to therapeutic success, Lick and Bootzin stated that to "the extent to which placebo manipulations work they must operate by mechanisms different from those traditionally proffered to explain the efficacy of (systematic desensitization)." (p. 926). They then suggested the following possible mechanisms. First, expecting to be cured of fear, the patient may test the expectancy by exposing himself to the feared object, thus leading to some increment in extinction of the fear. Second, expectancy changes may encourage greater attention to cues that represent improvement, leading to greater *report* of gain. Third, since the expectancy of improvement would be cognitively dissonant with knowledge that one still has symptoms, the dissonance may create heightened drive to continue testing reality as described above, further facilitating the actual desensitization process. Lick and Bootzin have speculated that any or all of these mechanisms might lead to changes in a patient's self-report of therapeutic gain as well as a change in overt behavior indicative of such gain.

Even if a placebo therapy for biofeedback should lead to differential expectancy, it is unlikely that the mechanisms postulated by Lick and Bootzin would be applicable. First, self-reports of symptom reduction are rarely the primary criteria for success in biofeedback; quantitative changes in psychophysiological response activity are. Second, if the effect of the placebo is to cause the subject to voluntarily test the therapeutic hypothesis, it is less likely to be carried out in the visceral arena. A patient can approach a feared object in a runway more readily than he can reduce his blood pressure just to test an hypothesis.

Biofeedback for tension headaches, migraine headaches, or other forms of *subjective distress* is theoretically presumed to work via specific measurable alterations of muscle tension, vasoconstriction, skin temperature, etc. While a placebo treatment may significantly alter the patient's subjective report of symptom reduction, it is not likely that it would similarly result in altered physiological patterns. To be sure, it is still possible that proper placebo control research on biofeedback may be contaminated. Nevertheless, our thesis is that biofeedback therapy, by its very nature, is a better candidate for careful evaluation with placebo control than other forms of behavior modification, and the results of placebo studies of biofeedback should be relatively easy to interpret. With that in mind, the following section will review the current research literature on the clinical effectiveness of biofeedback therapy along a number of dimensions, specifically analyzing the degree to which treatment effectiveness has been demonstrated to be greater than that attributable to a placebo.

SYNOPSIS OF RESEARCH LITERATURE ON THERAPEUTIC EFFECTIVENESS

Striate Musculature

Clinically, there have been three main foci of interest in skeletal muscular biofeedback: (1) rehabilitation of patients who have lost normal muscular control; (2) headache treatment; and (3) anxiety reduction and relaxation enhancement.

Rehabilitation. Successful use of muscle potential feedback in rehabilitation medicine has been reported by several investigators who have used three general treatment strategies:

1. Detecting and feeding back neuromuscular potentials in currently non-functional muscles, in conditions such as hemiplegia, nerve injury, and reversible physiological block:
2. Inhibiting undesired motor activity and increasing voluntary control of desired movement, in conditions such as spasmodic torticollis and various kinds of spasticity; or
3. Coordinating and controlling a series of muscle actions, in conditions such as chronic fecal incontinence.

Several researchers (Andrews, 1964; Brudny et al., 1974; Johnson and Garton, 1973; Marinacci and Horande, 1960) have reported case studies of successful individual treatment of hemiplegic patients by use of feedback from needle or skin EMG electrodes placed in or over the affected muscles. Booker, Rubow, and Coleman (1969) also reported a case study in which they successfully trained a patient afflicted with paralysis of one side of the face to control the facial muscles by teaching him to match a signal from the unaffected side.

In a series of studies Brudny, Grynbaum and Korein (1974), Brudny et al.

(1974), and Cleeland (1973) have reported successful treatments of spasmodic torticollis, a disease of uncertain etiology in which the finely tuned movement and postural control of the head and neck are disturbed. Using a combination of both conventional physical therapy and biofeedback, Swaan, van Wieringen and Fokkema (1974) reported improvement in seven patients who had undesirable muscle contractions of the knee caused by hemiplegia or poliomyelitis. In a somewhat related application, Jacobs and Felton (1969) were successful in training ten patients with neck injuries to relax rigid neck muscles. Finally, Engel, Nikoomaresh, and Schuster (1974) taught six patients with chronic fecal incontinence to control the functioning and synchronization of external and internal anal sphincters, producing relief of clinical symptoms that was maintained for five years.

The use of electromyogram feedback for muscular rehabilitation is impressive in that many of the patients treated were from a chronically disabled population in which traditional rehabilitation efforts had been partially or completely unsuccessful. Yet the successful reports all take the form of case studies, and there are *no* placebo controlled experimental evaluations of the specific efficacy of biofeedback.

Treatment of tension headache. Although muscular feedback has met with little success in the treatment of migraine (Sargent, Green, and Walters 1973; Wickramasekera, 1973b), electromyographic feedback from the frontal muscles of the forehead has been reported to be effective in relieving tension headache. Budzynski and his associates (Budzynski and Stoyva, 1973; Budzynski, Stoyva, and Adler, 1970), Wickramasekera (1972, 1973a), and Raskin, Johnson, and Rondestvedt (1973) have reported successful cases of treatment of chronic tension headache. A report by Epstein, Hersen, and Hemphill (1974) also detailed the treatment of a headache patient who responded well to muscle tension biofeedback but who had difficulty sustaining low headache levels without continuous feedback. In addition, Budzynski, et al. (1973) reported the results of a controlled experiment in which a group of subjects receiving EMG biofeedback showed greater headache reduction than a control group who received pseudofeedback.

Thus, good results have been reported for treatment of tension headaches both in case reports (Budzynski, Stoyva, and Adler, 1970) and in one controlled study (Budzynski et al., 1973). However, the particular role of biofeedback has not been clarified by the case studies, as the successful technique usually included both laboratory feedback training and home relaxation practice. Even in Budzynski et al.'s (1973) controlled outcome study, the authors emphasized that they considered daily practice outside of the laboratory setting "critical." In addition, it is highly likely that the attention-placebo control used in this study was quite ineffective, for two thirds of the subjects in Budzynski et al.'s control group dropped out of the study complaining that "the training was having no effect on their headaches." (p. 290). Further research is clearly needed to investigate the specific versus the interactive effects of muscle tension biofeedback and relaxation in the treatment of headaches.

Anxiety reduction and relaxation enhancement. Muscle tension feedback has been used, with mixed results, in a number of uncontrolled attempts to reduce anxiety and/or enhance relaxation. Raskin, Johnson, and Rondestvedt (1973), for example, reported little success of frontalis muscle feedback treatment of ten chronically anxious patients, although accompanying symptoms of tension headache and insomnia showed some improvement. In an uncontrolled study, Budzynski (1973) achieved success with six out of eleven sleep-onset insomnia patients with a treatment combination of muscle tension feedback and theta EEG feedback. Budzynski and Stoyva (1973) asserted that systematic desensitization is more successful when aided by muscle tension feedback, although they provided no empirical data to support their assertion.

In one controlled study, Davis et al. (1973) used frontalis muscle feedback combined with relaxation in treatment of severe and nonsevere asthmatic children. In the nonsevere patients, relaxation training with biofeedback resulted in a greater reduction of asthma symptoms than relaxation training alone or a control procedure in which patients were told to "relax." None of the experimental procedures were effective with the severely asthmatic children.

Thus, although there is considerable face validity for the effective treatment of skeletal muscular disorders with electromyographic feedback, as well as a considerable number of clinical case reports to support its use, there are no adequately controlled experiments to document the specific effectiveness of such treatment. Similarly, there appears to be no conclusive evidence that muscle tension biofeedback treatment is effective in reducing anxiety. As with studies of tension headache treatment, those reporting positive results used other procedures, such as EEG theta feedback, relaxation, or systematic desensitization, combined with muscle tension feedback. Therefore, the specific role of muscle tension feedback in the alleviation of anxiety remains unclear.

Heart Rate

There has been a great deal of experimental work aimed at controlling the human heart rate, much of it done with normal subjects. A typical experimental design for this research consists of subjects attempting to raise or lower their heart rate with a variety of different kinds of feedback reinforcement—lights, oscilloscope patterns, slides of landscapes, or pictures of nudes. These studies have typically shown that normal subjects can raise and lower their heart rates to some extent and can decrease heart rate variability, but there are some limitations on how the results of these studies may be interpreted. It is difficult to assess whether the small decreases in rate obtained were the results of the feedback process itself, or could be accounted for by general relaxation, or even whether the reduction could have been more efficiently obtained by other methods. Studies of physiological changes associated with transcendental meditation (Wallace, 1970; Wallace and Benson, 1972) and progressive relaxation (Paul, 1969), for instance, have found heart rate decreases that equal and sometimes exceed changes obtained in biofeedback experimentation.

Typically the clinician has not adopted cardiac rate biofeedback techniques for the purpose of raising or lowering heart rate in and of itself. Rather, the strategies more commonly employed have been to use cardiac rate feedback to treat a specific type of cardiac dysfunction, such as cardiac arrhythmias.

Cardiac Arrhythmias

Engel and his associates (Engle and Melmon, 1968; Weiss and Engel, 1970, 1971), were the first to report work involving a clinical cardiac population. Their series of case reports dealt with the treatment of eight patients suffering from premature ventricular contractions (PVCs). Weiss and Engel (1971) reported that five of these eight patients showed a decrease in PVCs after biofeedback treatment; follow-ups showed that four patients had maintained a low PVC frequency. Unlike the studies with normal subjects mentioned earlier, Weiss and Engel devoted a great many sessions to treatment and did extended follow-up (up to 21 months). A later report from the same laboratory (Engel and Bleecker, 1974) presented the case history of another patient who had successfully decreased the number of PVCs with the help of biofeedback. The same report also documented the successful treatment of three tachycardia patients. In yet another case study, Bleecker and Engel (1973) reported on the biofeedback treatment of a patient with Wolff-Parkinson-White syndrome, a heart conduction defect. The patient eventually learned to maintain normal conduction without feedback.

In addition to these reports from Engel and his colleagues, case report evidence of successful work with cardiac patients is accumulating from other laboratories. Scott et al. (1973) reported successful treatment of two tachycardia patients, and Miller (1974) has noted that "Pickering . . . has replicated learned specific voluntary control (of premature ventricular contractions) of two patients he is training. It seems unlikely that such specific voluntary control could be a nonspecific placebo effect." (p. 685). Miller's optimism notwithstanding it is fair to say that these case studies reported by Engel and Pickering have not employed controls for nonspecific effects, nor have they employed some of the single case study design elements discussed by Hersen and Barlow (1976). While it is difficult to disagree with the dramatic results obtained by Engel and his colleagues, it is also clear that almost half of the subjects treated for arrhythmias did not show success. No clear explanation of this important subject-specific treatment effect is apparent.

Blood Pressure Control

Shapiro and his colleagues, while reporting a series of successful attempts to train normotensives to control their blood pressure, have obtained inconsistent results with hypertensives (see Shapiro, Mainardi, and Surwit, 1977; Shapiro and Surwit, 1976). In the first published study on the clinical treatment of essential hypertension with biofeedback, Benson et al. (1971) taught five out of seven hypertensive patients to lower their systolic blood pressure 16 to 35 mm Hg.

Similar attempts to train patients to lower their diastolic pressure, however, were not as successful. Schwartz and Shapiro (1973) found that only one of seven patients was able to learn to reduce diastolic pressure. To confound the meaning of the above data even further, Elder et al. (1973) found opposite results; they reported that they had more success in training hypertensives to reduce diastolic pressure than systolic pressure.

Miller (1975) has reported one relatively successful case of treatment of a partially paralyzed hypertensive woman who achieved good control of her blood pressure in the laboratory but had to be restored to antihypertensive drugs after some personal emotional stresses. According to Miller, this patient was able to regain control a few years later; among his other subjects, most fared considerably worse. Attempts to achieve similar success on 27 patients in his laboratory produced "considerably poorer, not really promising, results." (p. 244).

None of the reported clinical studies has presented evidence that the magnitude of blood pressure decrease obtained by biofeedback is greater than could be obtained by simple methods of suggestion, relaxation, or merely adapting to the training situation. Grenfell, Briggs, and Holland (1963) have detailed the enormous power of placebo and expectancy effects in the pharmacological treatment of hypertension; there is little reason to believe that biofeedback treatment is less vulnerable. Patel (1973) reported, for instance, that she was able to obtain significant blood pressure reductions among hypertensive patients in her clinical practice by providing them with skin resistance feedback and training them to modify their skin resistance level. Since skin resistance is generally regarded as a reasonably useful index of overall autonomic arousal level, it is likely that Patel was helping to train her patients to relax. In a later study, Patel (1975) reported that with a combination of yoga exercises and biofeedback, patients were able to lower theier systolic and diastolic pressures both during rest and in response to everyday emotional stresses. Along similar lines, Datey et al. (1969) reported the successful use of yoga in the treatment of renal and essential hypertension. The results of these studies indicate that it is possible, and perhaps likely, that a combination of treatment modes such as relaxation training, biofeedback, and hypnosis may provide a potential nonmedical treatment for essential hypertension. They do not attest to the relative value of biofeedback per se in the treatment process.

Kristt and Engel (1975), on the other hand, have reported results with five patients that provide somewhat stronger evidence for a specific biofeedback treatment effect. Their patients, all of whom suffered hypertension for at least ten years, were given training in alternately raising and lowering systolic blood pressure. They were then asked to monitor their systolic blood pressure at home and report the results to the experimenters. Kristt and Engel reported that their patients were able to reduce systolic pressure significantly at home using the techniques they had learned in the laboratory, and that the blood pressure reductions were independent of changes in heart rate, alpha activity, breathing rate, and triceps brachii muscle tension. These findings, in contrast to earlier ones, are less likely to be explained as a by-product of general relaxation. Nevertheless, the Kristt and Engel study does not constitute controlled experimental evidence. The components which led to its successful outcome remain to be analyzed.

Migraine Headaches

Behavioral approaches to migraine treatment have focused on either relaxation training as a form of preventive therapy for the initial vasoconstrictions (which are sympathetic arousal phenomena), or alternately, on biofeedback treatment for the specific migraine vascular responses. Common sense would suggest that biofeedback for blood flow to the head would be a reasonable starting point for migraine treatment, and indeed early research on the phenomenon began there. Although plethysmographic recording allows direct measurement of blood flow, many investigators have chosen to use the simpler, equally valid measure of skin temperature as an index of blood volume. The majority of commercially available biofeedback instruments for migraine treatment operate on the temperature principle.

In 1972, Sargent, Green, and Walters reported great success in treating migraine patients by teaching them to warm their hands relative to their heads. Since that early report there have been many more reports of clinical cases indicating that hand warming alone is sufficient to relieve migraine, but until recently, there were no experiments to evaluate this claim. However, Blanchard, et al. (in press) have reported that a carefully controlled comparison reveals that progressive relaxation leads to the same reduction in migraine frequency and intensity as hand warming biofeedback. In addition, Kewman and Roberts (1979)[5] have just obtained data to indicate that hand cooling had the same therapeutic effect as hand warming. Thus, on the basis of the available evidence it must be concluded that the use of biofeedback for the treatment of migraine may be beneficial to patients, but not because of any specific power of biofeedback. Rather, it appears that in the treatment of migraine, biofeedback is a rather powerful placebo.

Electrical Activity of the Brain

One of the most widely investigated and widely publicized applications of biofeedback involves control of the electrical rhythms of the brain. Much public attention has been focused on the specific application of biofeedback to the control of alpha rhythm. Outside of the laboratory this research was often seen as ushering in a new era of mind-body unity, and many centers sprang up around the country (usually near campuses) promising that the feats of Eastern Zen and yoga masters—who had practiced and studied for decades—might soon be possible for anyone with a feedback machine and a few days' training.

Several years and many research articles later, reports of alpha biofeedback are much more cautious. Researchers have found that it is difficult for subjects to increase alpha above the levels spontaneously produced under normal relaxed conditions (Paskewitz and Orne, 1973). After conducting a series of alpha feedback studies, Lynch, Paskewitz, and Orne (1974), for instance, concluded that: "The data do suggest that alpha densities observed in the feedback situation have less to do with feedback per se or a learning process than with the experimental situation and Ss' own natural alpha densities." (p. 399). Other experimenters have reported that instructional set (Walsh, 1974) and subject expectations (Valle and Levine, 1975) can have a profound influence on subjective reports of the feedback experience.

Plotkin (1976), and Plotkin and Cohen (1976) have recently reported carefully controlled experiments on the effects of different control strategies for occipital alpha production, in which they have been unable to find any evidence for a relationship between the strength of alpha and the occurrence of the "alpha experience." Plotkin and Cohen concluded that "the 'alpha experience' *as a whole* is not directly or intrinsically associated with enhanced occipital alpha strength." (p. 17). Plotkin's unusually careful experiments suggested that the primary attribute of the alpha experience is reduced oculomotor activity, or "not looking." (Mulholland, 1968, 1972).

While many lay centers have been experimenting with alpha feedback for "growth experiences," a number of investigators in research laboratories have also been attempting to evaluate the potential effectiveness of brain wave feedback for the alleviation of disorders such as epilepsy.

Epilepsy. The earliest mention of brain wave feedback as a treatment of epilepsy was made by Miller (1969) who claimed there was "some success" in training epileptic patients to suppress abnormal paroxysmal spikes in their EEG. Lang (1970) also reported that Forster and his associates had successfully treated a patient who had developed photic seizures. But the most comprehensive program of research on the treatment of epilepsy by brain wave feedback has been in Sterman's laboratory.

Sterman and his associates (Sterman, 1973; 1977a, 1977b; Sterman and Friar, 1972; Sterman, Macdonald, and Stone, 1974) have trained epileptics to increase the amount of "sensorimotor rhythm" (SMR), defined as a rhythm of 12-14 Hz recorded above the central part of the cortex. Training in SMR as a treatment for epilepsy was suggested initially by the finding that SMR-trained cats were resistant to seizures. Over a period of 3-18 months, Sterman and his associates used SMR feedback in patients with whom chemotherapy had failed to control seizure activity. Although seizure activity during the biofeedback training period was markedly reduced in these patients, within a few weeks after the cessation of biofeedback training there was a sharp increase in symptoms, suggesting either that the treatment must be considerably longer to be effective or that biofeedback offers a treatment that can only temporarily control, but not cure, seizure activity in epileptics.

In a similar attempt to control seizures with SMR training, Kaplan (1975) found that she could achieve some success (two out of three patients) when employing feedback of brain wave activity in the 6-12 Hz range, rather than the SMR range reported by Sterman. Kaplan has suggested that Sterman's and her own results may have been caused by the *nonspecific relaxation* induced by the EEG feedback, and that it may therefore be premature to assume that the outcome was attributable to a specific effect of SMR feedback. Sterman (1977a) has noted that Kaplan's failure to obtain positive results, as well as Kuhlman and Allison's (1977) findings that feedback in the alpha range seemed to be associated with reduced seizure frequency, suggest that there are unresolved technological problems involved in the appropriate detection and reinforcement of specific brain wave frequencies.

In general, all forms of EEG biofeedback have produced few positive clinical results. Sterman's work with epileptics represents an exception, in that his case reports are dramatically suggestive of important benefits for seriously impaired epileptic patients. Although Sterman and his associates have only reported on a small group of epileptics who have been treated to date, their chronicity of symptoms and their failure to respond to chemotherapy, offer strong support for at least the transitory effectiveness of EEG training treatment. Nevertheless, there are no carefully controlled experiments to support Sterman's case reports, and Kaplan's (1975) suggestion concerning the nonspecific relaxation associated with such training should lead the reader to be cautious in drawing any conclusions about its clinical effectiveness.

CONCLUSIONS AND CAUTIONS

Shapiro and Surwit (1976) in their review of the biofeedback literature arrived at the gloomy conclusion that "there is *not one* well controlled scientific study of the effectiveness of biofeedback and operant conditioning in treating a particular physiological disorder." (p. 113). Unfortunately, our update provides little reason to revise that conclusion. On the other hand, Katkin, Fitzgerald, and Shapiro (1978) have pointed out that although there have not been well controlled experimental demonstrations of the efficacy of biofeedback therapy, the dramatic results reported with neuromuscular reeducation and with amelioration of seizure disorders were "suggestive" of active treatment effects. Rogers and Kimball (1977)[6] however, have adhered to stricter criteria. Discussing the neuromuscular biofeedback research, they have concluded that while "most of these studies showed fantastic results, several sources of internal invalidity . . . may well account for these effects. These studies are . . . inadequate in their control for the operation of even the most weak confounding variable . . ." (p. 43).

Whether one wishes to focus on the "fantastic" outcomes of the clinical case studies or on the inadequacy of the experimental controls employed to evaluate them, the inescapable facts are not only that no well controlled scientific studies demonstrating the effectiveness of biofeedback therapy exist, but that there are remarkably few *attempts* to demonstrate such effectiveness. Researchers too frequently have omitted appropriate controls from their experiments. Even single-patient case reports rarely include appropriate baseline controls or other single-case control observations which might enhance the credibility of their conclusions (Hersen and Barlow, 1976).

It is clear that much of the current interest in the clinical application of biofeedback has focused on the treatment of physiological symptoms of medical or psychosomatic disorders; problems of a more traditional psychological or psychiatric nature have not received as much attention from clinical biofeedback research, an omission which is ironic, since the early excitement about biofeedback was generated by investigators who saw new ways of approaching traditional philosophical and psychological issues about the nature of consciousness and transcendent experiences. While there are still many investigators concerned with these issues, the bulk of therapeutic research on biofeedback has been addressed to cardiovascular problems, central nervous system disease, and rehabilitation medicine. Biofeedback has become a central focus of the discipline that Birk (1973) has called "behavioral medicine" more than it has for behavioral psychology. Indeed the more successful and more significant contributions to date have been in areas of behavioral medicine—muscular rehabilitation, epilepsy control, headache treatment, and cardiac dysfunction. Applications to more traditional psychological areas such as altered states of consciousness, anxiety reduction, and relaxation enhancement have yielded less promising results. Yet whatever promise biofeedback holds for the evolving discipline of behavioral medicine, it will be lost unless there is tighter experimentation and more systematic attempts to isolate the active treatment effects from the placebo effects (see Katkin and Goldband, in press).

We would like to make a final comment concerning the enormous attention that biofeedback has received within the professional community. Despite the clear lack of experimental evidence to support assertions of its effectiveness as therapy (Melzack, 1975; Miller, 1974; Schwartz, 1973; Shapiro and Surwit, 1976), increasing numbers of clinicians are incorporating biofeedback into their practice. Workshops to train clinical biofeedback practitioners are heavily attended, and many cassette-tape trained biofeedback practitioners are gainfully employed from one end of the continent to another. It is not uncommon to see secondary sources describe Miller's and Shapiro's remarkable success in treating essential hypertension, even as these authors take great pains to publish clear statements of caution about the actual effectiveness of their treatments. The pattern of enthusiasm is similar in some ways to the enthusiasm shown about the introduction of projective testing, various forms and varieties of psychotherapy, and, within modern medicine, the flirtations with vitamin treatments for cancer and cholesterol reduction for the prevention of heart disease. There is a powerful desire among health and health-related professionals to be able to provide treatment. It is incumbent upon the serious professional to temper that desire with an appreciation for the value of hard evidence and the need for caution and patience. Biofeedback may provide future generations with important new weapons against disease. The current state of evidence neither supports nor denies that hope.

APPENDIX: AIDS TO PRACTICE

By this time the reader may feel that he would like to try some biofeedback applications in clinical practice and he may come to the sudden realization that, after having surveyed the literature on various technical issues such as baseline setting and criterion setting and having fully addressed the questions of the appropriateness of the technique and its potential effectiveness, he is still not able to actually implement the procedures. This chapter was not intended to provide a detailed, step by step "how to" program. However, the reader should be alerted to the availability of textual material as well as an audio cassette library that is available and useful for developing specific treatment skills.

As a first step, the practitioner must obtain some specialized biofeedback equipment; there are a number of manufacturers competing for his business. In almost all cases, the manufacturers of biofeedback equipment provide instruction manuals with descriptions of procedures concerning the use of the equipment and including such details as preferred ways of presenting relaxation instructions and techniques for using the equipment for the assessment of baseline and criterion. The novice will find that the technical manuals supplied by the manufacturers will, in most cases, be sufficient to start him on his practice. In addition, there are a number of other sources to which the practitioner may turn. One very useful text is *Clinical biofeedback: A procedural manual* by Kenneth R. Gaarder and Penelope S. Montgomery. This book, published in 1977 by the Williams and Wilkins Company, supplies detailed information for the practitioner. In addition to this book, there are a wide variety of cassette tapes available providing information on details for treatment of specific disorders, and also providing overviews and theoretical explanations of the rationale underlying biofeedback treatment. There are no fewer than 50 different cassette tapes on the market today, most of them containing information presented by leaders in the field. These tapes are widely advertised in the professional journals, and they are also available for purchase through the manufacturers of biofeedback equipment. The new practitioner who feels insecure will discover that the manufacturers manuals, Gaarder and Montgomery's text, and a variety of cassette tapes will provide reassurance and guidance to enable clinical work to begin with minimal difficulty. Finally, it has been our observation from training graduate students in the technique that the most effective training procedure is to try it yourself—there is no more effective way to become familiar with the procedures and to understand the experience of using biofeedback. The most obvious choice of feedback for such self-training would be muscle potential feedback for relaxation.

NOTES

[1]Turk, D.C., Meichenbaum, D.H., & Berman, W.H. *The application of biofeedback for the regulation of pain: A critical review.* Manuscript submitted for publication, 1979.

[2]Price, K.R. *Feedback effects on penile tumescence.* Paper presented to Eastern Psychological Association., 1973.

[3]Levenson, R.W., Manuck, S.B., Strupp, H.H., Blackwood, G.L., & Snell, J.D. *A biofeedback technique for bronchial asthma.* Paper presented to the Biofeedback Research Society, 1974.

[4]Epstein, L.H., Hannay, H.J., & Looney, R. *Fading and reinforcement in the modification of visual acuity.* Paper presented to the Association for the Advancement of Behavior Therapy, 1975.

[5]Kewman, D.G., & Roberts, A.H. *Skin temperature biofeedback and migraine headaches: A double-blind study.* Manuscript submitted for publication, 1979.

[6]Rogers, T., & Kimball, W.H. *Nonspecific factors in biofeedback therapy.* Paper presented to Society for Psychophysiological Research, 1977.

REFERENCES

Andrews, J.M. Neuromuscular re-education of hemiplegic with aid of electromyograph. *Archives of Physical Medicine and Rehabilitation*, 1964, *45*, 530-532.

Barlow, D.H., Agras, W.S., Abel, G.C., Blanchard, E.B., and Young, L.D. Biofeedback and reinforcement to increase heterosexual arousal in homosexuals. *Behaviour Research and Therapy*, 1975, *13*, 45-50.

Benson, H. *The relaxation response.* New York: William Morrow, 1975.

Benson, H., Shapiro, D., Tursky, B., and Schwartz, G.E. Decreased systolic blood pressure through operant conditioning techniques in patients with essential hypertension. *Science*, 1971, *173*, 740-742.

Birk, L. (Ed.). *Biofeedback: Behavioral medicine.* New York: Grune & Stratton, 1973.

Birk, L., Crider, A., Shapiro, D., and Tursky, B. Operant electrodernal conditioning under partial curarization. *Journal of Comparative and Physiological Psychology*, 1966, *62*, 165-166.

Black, A.H. Operant autonomic conditioning: The analysis of response mechanisms. In P.A. Obrist, A.H. Black, J. Brener, and L.V. DiCara (Eds.) *Cardiovascular psychophysiology*. Chicago: Aldine, 1974.

Blanchard, E.B., Theobald, D.E., Williamson, D.A., Silver, B.V., and Brown, D.A. A controlled evaluation of temperature biofeedback in the treatment of migraine headaches. *Archives of General Psychiatry*, in press.

Bleecker, E.R., and Engel, B.T. Learned control of cardiac rate and cardiac conduction in the Wolff-Parkinson-White syndrome. *New England Journal of Medicine*, 1973, *288*, 560-562.

Booker, H.E., Rubow, R.T., and Coleman, P.J. Simplified feedback in neuromuscular retraining: An automated approach using EMG signals. *Archives of Physical Medicine and Rehabilitation*, 1969, *50*, 621-625.

Brudny, J., Grynbaum, B.B., and Korein, J. Spasmodic torticollis: Treatment by feedback display of the EMG. *Archives of Physical Medicine and Rehabilitation*, 1974, *55*, 403-408.

Brudny, J., Korein, J., Levidow, L., Grynbaum, B.B., Lieberman, A., and Friedmann, L.W. Sensory feedback therapy as a modality of treatment in central nervous system disorders of voluntary movement. *Neurology*, 1974, *24*, 925-932.

Budzynski, T.H. Biofeedback procedures in the clinic. *Seminars in Psychiatry*, 1973, *5*, 537-547.

Budzynski, T., and Stoyva, J. Biofeedback techniques in behavior therapy. In D. Shapiro, T.X. Barber, L.V. DiCara, J. Kamiya, N.E. Miller, and J. Stoyva (Eds.), *Biofeedback and self-control 1972: An Aldine Annual on the regulation of bodily processes and consciousness*. Chicago: Aldine, 1973.

Budzynsky, T., Stoyva, J., and Adler, C. Feedback-induced muscle relaxation: Application to tension headache. *Journal of Behavior Therapy and Experimental Psychiatry*, 1970, *1*, 205-211.

Budzynski, T.H., Stoyva, J.M., Adler, C.S., and Mullaney, D.J. EMG biofeedback and tension headache: A controlled outcome study. *Psychosomatic Medicine*, 1973, *35*, 484-496.

Cleeland, C.S. Behavior techniques in the modification of spasmodic torticollis. *Neurology*, 1973, *23*, 1241-1247.

Crider, A., Schwartz, G.E., and Shnidman, S. On the criteria for instrumental autonomic conditioning: A reply to Katkin and Murray. *Psychological Bulletin*, 1969, *71*, 455-461.

Crider, A., Shapiro, D., and Tursky, B. Reinforcement of spontaneous electrodermal activity. *Journal of Comparative and Physiological Psychology*. 1966, *61*, 20-27.

Csillag, E.R. Modification of penile erectile response. *Journal of Behavior Therapy and Experimental Psychiatry*, 1976, *7*, 27-29.

Datey, K.K., Deshmukh, S.N., Dalvi, C.P., and Vinekar, S.L. "Shavasan": A yogic exercise in the management of hypertension. *Angiology*, 1969, *20*, 325-333.

Davis, M.H., Saunders, D.B., Creer, T.L., and Chai, H. Relaxation training facilitated by biofeedback apparatus as a supplemental treatment in bronchial asthma. *Journal of Psychosomatic Research*, 1973, *17*, 121-128.

DiCara, L.V., and Miller, N.E. Changes in heart rate instrumentally learned by curarized rats as avoidance responses. *Journal of Comparative and Physiological Psychology*, 1968, *65*, 8-12.

Dworkin, B.R., and Miller, N.E. Visceral learning in the curarized rat. In G.E. Schwartz and J. Beatty (Eds.) *Biofeedback: Theory and research*. New York: Academic Press, 1977.

Elder, S.T., Ruiz, Z.R., Deabler, H.L., and Dillenkoffer, R.L. Instrumental conditioning of diastolic blood pressure in essential hypertensive patients. *Journal of Applied Behavior Analysis*, 1973, *6*, 377-382.

Engel, B.T., and Bleecker, E.R. Application of operant conditioning techniques to the control of the cardiac arrhythmias. In P.A. Obrist, A.H. Black, J. Brener, and L.V. DiCara (Eds.), *Cardiovascular psychophysiology*. Chicago: Aldine, 1974.

Engel, B.T., and Melmon, L. Operant conditioning of heart rate in patients with cardiac arrhythmias. *Conditional Reflex*, 1968, *3*, 130.

Engel, B.T., Nikoomanesh, P., and Schuster, M.M. Operant conditioning of rectosphincteric responses in the treatment of fecal incontinence. *New England Journal of Medicine*, 1974, *290*, 646-649.

Epstein, L.H., Hersen, M., and Hemphill, P. Music feedback in the treatment of tension headache: An experimental case study. *Journal of Behavior Therapy and Experimental Psychiatry*, 1974, *5*, 59-63.

Glueck, B.C., and Stroebel, C.F. Biofeedback and meditation in the treatment of psychiatric illnesses. *Comprehensive Psychiatry*, 1975, *16*, 303-321.

Grenfell, R.F., Briggs, A.H., and Holland, W.C. Antihypertensive drugs evaluated in a controlled double-blind study. *Southern Medical Journal*, 1963, *56*, 1410-1416.

Hahn, W.W. The learning of autonomic responses by curarized animals. In P.A. Obrist, A.H. Black, J. Brener, and L.V. DiCara (Eds.), *Cardiovascular psychophysiology*, Chicago: Aldine, 1974.

Harris, V.A., Katkin, E.S., Lick, J.R. and Habberfield, T. Paced respiration as a technique for the modification of autonomic response to stress. *Psychophysiology*, 1976, *13*, 386-391.

Hersen, M., and Barlow, D.M. *Single case experimental designs*. New York: Pergamon, 1976.

Jacobs, A., and Felton, G.S. Visual feedback of myoelectric output to facilitate muscle relaxation in normal persons and patients with neck injuries. *Archives of Physical Medicine and Rehabilitation*, 1969, *50*, 34-39.

Johnson, H.E., and Garton, W.H. Muscle re-education in hemiplegia by use of electromyographic device. *Archives of Physical Medicine and Rehabilitation*, 1973, *54*, 320-323.

Kamiya, J. Conscious control of brain waves. *Psychology Today*, 1968, *1*, 57-60.

Kaplan, B.J. Biofeedback in epileptics: Equivocal relationship of reinforced EEG frequency to seizure reduction. *Epilepsia*, 1975, *16*, 477-485.

Katkin, E.S. *Instrumental autonomic conditioning*. New York: General Learning Press, 1971.

Katkin, E.S., Fitzgerald, C.R., and Shapiro, D. Clinical applications of biofeedback: Current status and future prospects. In H. Pick, H. Leibowitz, J. Singer, A. Steinschneider, and H. Stevenson (Eds.), *Psychology: From research to practice*. New York: Plenum 1978.

Katkin, E.S., and Goldband, S. The placebo effect and biofeedback. In R. Gatchel and K. Price (Eds.), *Clinical applications of biofeedback: Appraisal and status*. New York: Pergamon, in press.

Katkin, E.S., and Murray, E.N. Instrumental conditioning of autonomically mediated behavior: Theoretical and methodological issues. *Psychological Bulletin*, 1968, *70*, 52-68.

Katkin, E.S., Murray, E.N., and Lachman, R. Concerning instrumental autonomic conditioning: A rejoinder. *Psychological Bulletin*, 1969, *71*, 462-466.

Kazdin, A.E., and Wilcoxon, L.A. Systematic desensitization and nonspecific treatment effects: A methodological evaluation. *Psychological Bulletin*. 1976, *83*, 729-758

Kimble, G.A. *Hilgard and Marquis' conditioning and learning* (2nd ed.). New York: Appleton-Century, 1961.

Kimmel, E., and Kimmel, H.D. A replication of operant conditioning of the GSR. *Journal of Experimental Psychology*, 1963, *65*, 212-213.

Kimmel, H.D. Instrumental conditioning of autonomically mediated behavior. *Psychological Bulletin*, 1967, *67*, 337-345.

Kimmel, H.D., and Hill, F.A. Operant conditioning of the GSR. *Psychological Reports*, 1960, *7*, 555-562.

Kimmel, H.D., and Sternthal, H.S. Replication of GSR avoidance conditioning with concomitant EMG measurement and subjects matched in responsivity and conditionability. *Journal of Experimental Psychology*, 1967, *74*, 144-146.

Kristt, D.A., and Engel, B.T. Learned control of blood pressure in patients with high blood pressure. *Circulation*, 1975, *51*, 370-378.

Kuhlman, W.N., and Allison, T. EEG feedback training in the treatment of epilepsy: Some questions and some answers. *Pavlovian Journal of Biological Science*, 1977, *12*, 112-122.

Lang, P.J. Autonomic control or learning to play the internal organs. *Psychology Today*, 1970, *4*, 37-41.

———— Learned control of human heart rate in a computer directed environment. In P.A. Obrist, A.H. Black, J. Brener, and L.V. DiCara (Eds.), *Cardiovascular psychophysiology*. Chicago: Aldine, 1974.

Levenson, R.W. Automated system for direct measurement and feedback of total respiratory resistance by the forced oscillation technique. *Psychophysiology*, 1974, *11*, 86-90.

Lick, J., and Bootzin, R. Expectancy factors in the treatment of fear: Methodological and theoretical issues. *Psychological Bulletin*, 1975, *82*, 917-931.

Lubar, J.F., and Bahler, W.W. Behavioral management of epileptic seizures following EEG biofeedback training of the sensorimotor rhythm. *Biofeedback and Self-Regulation* 1976, *1*, 77-104.

Lynch, J.J., Paskewitz, D.A., and Orne, M.T. Some factors in the feedback control of human alpha rhythm. *Psychosomatic Medicine*, 1974, *36*, 399-410.

Marinacci, A.A., and Horande, M. Electromyogram in neuromuscular re-education. *Bulletin of Los Angeles Neurological Society*, 1960, *25*, 57-71.

Melzack, R. The promise of biofeedback: Don't hold the party yet. *Psychology Today*, 1975, *9*, 18-22, 80-81.

Melzack, R., and Perry, C. Self-regulation of pain: The use of alpha feedback and hypnotic training for the control of chronic pain. *Experimental Neurology*, 1975, *46*, 452-469.

Miller, N.E. Learning of visceral and glandular responses. *Science*, 1969, *163*, 434-445.

―――― Biofeedback: Evaluation of a new technique, *New England Journal of Medicine*, 1974, *290*, 684-685.

―――― Clinical applications of biofeedback: Voluntary control of heart rate, rhythm, blood pressure. In H.I. Russek (Ed.), *New horizons in cardiovascular practice*. Baltimore, Md.: University Park Press, 1975.

Miller, N.E., and DiCara, L. Instrumental learning of heart rate changes in curarized rats: Shaping and specificity to discriminative stimulus. *Journal of Comparative and Physiological Psychology*, 1967, *63*, 12-19.

Miller, N.E., and Dworkin, B.R. Visceral learning: Recent difficulties with curarized rats and significant problems for human research. In P.A. Obrist, A.H. Black, J. Brener, and L.V. DiCara (Eds.), *Cardiovascular psychophysiology*. Chicago: Aldine, 1974.

Mulholland, T. Feedback electroencephalography. *Activitas Nervosa Superior*, 1968, *10*, 410-438.

―――― Occipital alpha revisited. *Psychological Bulletin*, 1972, *74*, 176-182.

Obrist, P.A., Howard, J.L., Lawler, J.E., Galosy, R.A., Meyers, K.A., and Gaebelein, C.J. The cardiac-somatic interaction. In P.A. Obrist, A.H. Black, J. Brener, and L.V. DiCara (Eds.), *Cardiovascular psychophysiology*. Chicago: Aldine, 1974.

Obrist, P.A., Light, K.C., McCubbin, J.A., Hutcheson, J.S., and Hoffer, J.L. Pulse transit time: Relationship to blood pressure. *Behavior Research Methods & Instrumentation*, 1978, *10*, 623-626.

Paskewitz, D.A., and Orne, M.T. Visual effects on alpha feedback training. *Science*, 1973, *181*, 360-363.

Patel, C.H. Yoga and biofeedback in the management of hypertension. *Lancet*, 1973, *7837*, 1053-1055.

―――― 12-Month follow-up of yoga and biofeedback in the management of hypertension. *Lancet*, 1975, *7898*, 62-64.

Paul, G.L. Physiological effects of relaxation training and hypnotic suggestion. *Journal of Abnormal Psychology*, 1969, *74*, 425-437.

Plotkin, W.B. On the self-regulation of the occipital alpha rhythm: Control strategies, states of consciousness, and the role of physiological feedback. *Journal of Experimental Psychology: General*, 1976, *105*, 66-99.

Plotkin, W.B., and Cohen, R. Occipital alpha and the attributes of the "alpha experience." *Psychophysiology*, 1976, *13*, 16-21.

Pope, A.T. Electrical safety in the use of biofeedback instruments. *Behavior Research Methods & Instrumentation*, 1978, *10*, 627-631.

Raskin, M., Johnson, G., and Rondestvedt, J.W. Chronic anxiety treated by feedback-induced muscle relaxation. *Archives of General Psychiatry*, 1973, *28*, 263-267.

Roberts, L.E. Comparative psychophysiology of the electrodermal and cardiac control systems. In P.A. Obrist, A.H. Black, J. Brener, and L.V. DiCara (Eds.) *Cardiovascular psychophysiology*. Chicago: Aldine, 1974.

Rosen, R.C., Shapiro, D., and Schwartz, G.E. Voluntary control of penile tumescence. *Psychosomatic Medicine*, 1975, *37*, 479-483.

Sargent, J.D., Green, E.E., and Walters, E.D. The use of autogenic feedback training in a pilot study of migraine and tension headaches. *Headache*, 1972, *12*, 120-125.

Sargent, J.D., Green, E.E., and Walters, E.D. Preliminary report on the use of autogenic feedback training in the treatment of migraine and tension headaches. *Psychosomatic Medicine*, 1973, *35*, 129-135.

Schwartz, G.E. Biofeedback as therapy: Some theoretical and practical issues. *American Psychologist*, 1973, *28*, 666-673.

Schwartz, G.E., and Shapiro, D. Biofeedback and essential hypertension: Current findings and theoretical concerns. *Seminars in Psychiatry*, 1973, *5*, 493-503.

Scott, R.W., Blanchard, E.B., Edmunson, E.D., and Young, L.D. A shaping procedure for heart rate control in chronic tachycardia. *Perceptual and Motor Skills*, 1973, *37*, 327-338.

Seifert, A.R., and Lubar, J.F. Reduction of epileptic seizures through EEG biofeedback training. *Biological Psychology*, 1975, *3*, 157-184.

Shapiro, D. Operant-feedback control of human blood pressure: Some clinical issues. In P.A. Obrist, A.H. Black, J. Brener, and L.V. DiCara (Eds.), *Cardiovascular psychophysiology*. Chicago: Aldine, 1974.

Shapiro, D., Crider, A.B., and Tursky, B. Differentiation of an autonomic response through operant reinforcement. *Psychonomic Science*, 1964, *1*, 147-148.

Shapiro, D., Mainardi, J.A., and Surwit, R.S. Biofeedback and self-regulation in essential hypertension. In G.E. Schwartz and J. Beatty (Eds.), *Biofeedback: Theory and research*. New York: Academic Press, 1977.

Shapiro, D., and Surwit, R.S. Learned control of physiological function and disease. In H. Leitenberg (Ed.), *Handbook of behavior modification and behavior therapy*. Englewood Cliffs, N.J.: Prentice-Hall, 1976.

Sirota, A.D., Schwartz, G.E., and Shapiro, D. Voluntary control of human heart rate: Effect on reaction to aversive stimulation. *Journal of Abnormal Psychology*, 1974, *83*, 261-267.

Sirota, A.D., Schwartz, G.E., and Shapiro, D. Voluntary control of human heart rate: Effect on reaction to aversive stimulation: A replication and extension. *Journal of Abnormal Psychology*, 1976, *85*, 473-477.

Smith, K. Conditioning as an artifact. *Psychological Review*, 1954, *61*, 217-225.

Snyder, C., and Noble, M.E. Operant conditioning of vasoconstriction. *Journal of Experimental Psychology*, 1968, *77*, 263-268.

Steptoe, A., Smulyan, H., and Gribbin, B. Pulse wave velocity and blood pressure change: Calibration and applications. *Psychophysiology*, 1976, *13*, 488-493.

Sterman, M.B. Neurophysiologic and clinical studies of sensorimotor EEG biofeedback training: Some effects on epilepsy. *Seminars in Psychiatry*, 1973, *5*, 507-525.

———Clinical implications of EEG biofeedback training: A critical appraisal. In G.E. Schwartz and J. Beatty (Eds.), *Biofeedback: Theory and research*. New York: Academic Press, 1977a.

——— Effects of sensorimotor EEG feedback training on sleep and clinical manifestations of epilepsy. In J. Beatty and H. Legewie (Eds.), *Biofeedback and behavior*. New York: Plenum Press, 1977b.

Sterman, M.B., and Friar, L. Suppression of seizures in an epileptic following sensorimotor EEG feedback training. *EEG and Clinical Neurophysiology*, 1972, *33*, 89-95.

Sterman, M.B., Macdonald, L.R., and Stone, R.K. Biofeedback training of the sensori-motor electroencephalogram rhythm in man: Effects on epilepsy. *Epilepsia*, 1974, *15*, 395-416.

Swaan, D., van Wieringen, P.C.W., and Fokkema, S.D. Auditory electromyographic feedback therapy to inhibit undesired motor activity. *Archives of Physical Medicine and Rehabilitation*, 1974, *55*, 251-254.

Travis, T.A., Kondo, C.Y., and Knott, J.R. Alpha enhancement research: A review. *Biological Psychiatry*, 1975, *10*, 69-89.

Turin, A., and Johnson, W.G. Biofeedback therapy for migraine headaches. *Archives of General Psychiatry*, 1976, *33*, 517-519.

Tursky, B., Shapiro, D., and Schwartz, G.E. Automated constant cuff-pressure system for measuring average systolic and diastolic blood pressure in man. *IEEE Transactions on Biomedical Engineering*, 1972, *19*, 271-275.

Vachon, L., and Rich, E.S. Visceral learning in asthma. *Psychosomatic Medicine*, 1976, *38*, 122-130.

Valle, R.S., and Levine, J.M. Expectations effects in alpha wave control. *Psychophysiology*, 1975, *12*, 306-310.

Victor, R., Mainardi, J.A., and Shapiro, D. Effect of biofeedback and voluntary control procedures on heart rate and perception of pain during the cold pressor test. *Psychosomatic Medicine*, in press.

Wallace, R.K. Physiological effects of transcendental meditation. *Science*, 1970, *167*, 1751-1754.

Wallace, R.K., and Benson, H. The physiology of meditation. *Scientific American*, 1972, *226*, 85-90.

Walsh, D.H. Interactive effects of alpha feedback and instructional set on subjective state. *Psychophysiology*, 1974, *11*, 428-435.

Weiss, T., and Engel, B.T. Voluntary control of premature ventricular contractions in patients. *American Journal of Cardiology*, 1971, *26*, 666. (Abstract)

————— Operant conditioning of heart rate in patients with premature ventricular contractions. *Psychosomatic Medicine*, 1971, *33*, 301-321.

Welgan, P.R. Learned control of gastric acid secretions in ulcer patients. *Psychosomatic Medicine*, 1974, *36*, 411-419.

Whitehead, W.E., Renault, P.E., and Goldiamond, I. Modification of human gastric acid secretion with operant-conditioning procedures. *Journal of Applied Behavior Analysis*, 1975, *8*, 147-156.

Wickramasekera, I. Electromyographic feedback training and tension headache: Preliminary observations. *American Journal of Clinical Hypnosis*, 1972, *15*, 83-85.

————— Effects of EMG feedback training on hypnotic susceptibility: More preliminary observations. *Journal of Abnormal Psychology*, 1973a, *82*, 74-77.

————— Temperature feedback for the control of migraine. *Journal of Behavior Therapy and Experimental Psychiatry*, 1973b, *4*, 343-345.

Author Index

Subject Index

ABOUT THE EDITORS AND CONTRIBUTORS

Frederick H. Kanfer (Ph.D., Indiana University) is professor of psychology at the University of Illinois. His primary interest is in developing the necessary conceptualizations and methods to provide a broad behavioral framework for application to personal and social problems.

He was awarded a Diplomate in Clinical Psychology from the American Board of Examiners in Professional Psychology. He is a Fellow of the American Psychological Association and has held office in the Division of Clinical Psychology and in the Association for the Advancement of Behavior Therapy.

Dr. Kanfer has taught at Washington University, St. Louis; at Purdue University; in the Department of Psychiatry at the University of Oregon Medical School; and at the University of Cincinnati. (He is currently Professor of Psychology at the University of Illinois.) He was a Fulbright Scholar to Europe and has been visiting professor and consultant to various agencies dealing with psychological problems, both in the United States and in Europe. In addition, he has served on editorial boards of several psychological journals and has published over 100 articles. He is co-author of *Learning Foundations of Behavior Therapy* and co-editor of *Maximizing Treatment Gains*. His experimental work is primarily in the area of self-regulation, self-control and altruism.

Arnold P. Goldstein (Ph.D., Pennsylvania State University) is professor of psychology at Syracuse University. His primary interest is in behavior modification, skill training, and interpersonal relationships. He is a Fellow of the American Psychological Association and a member of the Association for the Advancement of Behavior Therapy and the Society for Psychotherapy Research.

Dr. Goldstein has taught at the University of Pittsburgh Medical School and served as a research psychologist at the VA outpatient research laboratory in Washington, D.C. He was a Visiting Professor at the Free University of Amsterdam, Holland, in 1970, and at the University of Hawaii in the summer of 1972. He has published over forty articles and is author, co-author, or editor of *Therapist-Patient Expectancies in Psychotherapy; Psychotherapy and the Psychology of Behavior Change; The Investigation of Psychotherapy; Psychotherapeutic Attraction; The Lonely Teacher; Structured Learning Therapy; Changing Supervisor Behavior; Skill Training for Community Living; Prescriptive Psychotherapies; Prescriptions for Child Mental Health and Education; Police Crisis Intervention; Hostage; Police and the Elderly;* and *Maximizing Treatment Gains.*

Curtis D. Booraem
Fairview State Hospital

W.C. Coe
Psychology Department
California State University
Fresno, California

John V. Flowers
Program in Social Ecology
California State University
Irvine, California

M. Judith Furukawa
Psychology Department
University of Washington
Seattle, Washington

Myles Genest
Psychology Department
University of Waterloo
Waterloo, Ontario

Steve Goldband
Department of Psychology
State University of New York
Buffalo, New York

Anita P. Goldfried
East Setauket, New York

Marvin R. Goldfried
Psychology Department
State University of New York
Stony Brook, New York

Arnold P. Goldstein
Psychology Department
Syracuse University
Syracuse, New York

David W. Johnson
Psychological Foundations
University of Minnesota
Minneapolis, Minnesota

Frederick H. Kanfer
Psychology Department
University of Illinois
Champaign, Illinois

Paul Karoly
Psychology Department
University of Cincinnati
Cincinnati, Ohio

Edward S. Katkin
Department of Psychology
State University of New York
Buffalo, New York

Morton A. Lieberman
Department of Behavioral Sciences
(Human Development)
and Department of
Psychiatry
University of Chicago
Chicago, Illinois

Donald Meichenbaum
Psychology Department
University of Waterloo
Waterloo, Ontario

Richard J. Morris
Psychology Department
University of Arizona
Tucson, Arizona

Martha Perry
Psychology Department
University of Washington
Seattle, Washington

Jack Sandler
Psychology Department
University of South Florida
Tampa, Florida